Technological Change
and Regional Development in Europe

90 0664792 5

Contributions to Economics

http://www.springer.de/cgi-bin/search_book.pl?series=1262

Sven-Morten Mentzel
Real Exchange Rate Movements
1998. ISBN 3-7908-1081-9

Lei Delsen/Eelke de Jong (Eds.)
The German and Dutch Economies
1998. ISBN 3-7908-1064-9

Mark Weder
Business Cycle Models with Indeterminacy
1998. ISBN 3-7908-1078-9

Tor Rødseth (Ed.)
Models for Multispecies Management
1998. ISBN 3-7908-1001-0

Michael Carlberg
Intertemporal Macroeconomics
1998. ISBN 3-7908-1096-7

Sabine Spangenberg
The Institutionalised Transformation of the East German Economy
1998. ISBN 3-7908-1103-3

Hagen Bobzin
Indivisibilities
1998. ISBN 3-7908-1123-8

Helmut Wagner (Ed.)
Current Issues in Monetary Economics
1998. ISBN 3-7908-1127-0

Peter Michaelis/Frank Stähler (Eds.)
Recent Policy Issues in Environmental and Resource Economics
1998. ISBN 3-7908-1137-8

Jessica de Wolff
The Political Economy of Fiscal Decisions
1998. ISBN 3-7908-1130-0

Georg Bol/Gholamreza Nakhaeizadeh/Karl-Heinz Vollmer (Eds.)
Risk Measurements, Econometrics and Neural Networks
1998. ISBN 3-7908-1152-1

Joachim Winter
Investment and Exit Decisions at the Plant Level
1998. ISBN 3-7908-1154-8

Bernd Meyer
Intertemporal Asset Pricing
1999. ISBN 3-7908-1159-9

Uwe Walz
Dynamics of Regional Integration
1999. ISBN 3-7908-1185-8

Michael Carlberg
European Monetary Union
1999. ISBN 3-7908-1191-2

Giovanni Galizzi/Luciano Venturini (Eds.)
Vertical Relationships and Coordination in the Food System
1999. ISBN 3-7908-1192-0

Gustav A. Horn/Wolfgang Scheremet/Rudolf Zwiener
Wages and the Euro
1999. ISBN 3-7908-1199-8

Dirk Willer
The Development of Equity Capital Markets in Transition Economies
1999. ISBN 3-7908-1198-X

Karl Matthias Weber
Innovation Diffusion and Political Control of Energy Technologies
1999. ISBN 3-7908-1205-6

Heike Link et al.
The Costs of Road Infrastructure and Congestion in Europe
1999. ISBN 3-7908-1201-3

Simon Duindam
Military Conscription
1999. ISBN 3-7908-1203-X

Bruno Jeitziner
Political Economy of the Swiss National Bank
1999. ISBN 3-7908-1209-9

Irene Ring et al. (Eds.)
Regional Sustainability
1999. ISBN 3-7908-1233-1

Katharina Müller/Andreas Ryll/Hans-Jürgen Wagener (Eds.)
Transformation of Social Security: Pensions in Central-Eastern Europe
1999. ISBN 3-7908-1210-2

continued on page 422

Ludwig Schätzl · Javier Revilla Diez
(Editors)

Technological Change and Regional Development in Europe

With 88 Figures and 81 Tables

Physica-Verlag
A Springer-Verlag Company

Series Editors
Werner A. Müller
Martina Bihn

Editors
Professor Dr. Ludwig Schätzl
Priv.-Doz. Dr. Javier Revilla Diez
University of Hannover
Department of Economic Geography
Schneiderberg 50
30167 Hannover
Germany
schaetzl@wigeo.uni-hannover.de
diez@wigeo.uni-hannover.de

ISSN 1431-1933
ISBN 3-7908-1460-1 Physica-Verlag Heidelberg New York

Cataloging-in-Publication Data applied for
Die Deutsche Bibliothek – CIP-Einheitsaufnahme
Technological change and regional development in Europe: with 81 tables / Ludwig Schätzl; Javier Revilla Diez (ed.). – Heidelberg; New York: Physica-Verl., 2002
(Contributions to economics)
ISBN 3-7908-1460-1

Physica-Verlag Heidelberg New York
a member of BertelsmannSpringer Science+Business Media GmbH

Printed in Germany

Softcover Design: Erich Kirchner, Heidelberg

SPIN 10859647 88/2202-5 4 3 2 1 0 – Printed on acid-free and non-aging paper

Preface

This book presents the findings of the extensive research programme funded by the Deutsche Forschungsgemeinschaft (German Research Council) and entitled 'Technological Change and Regional Development in Europe'. The goal of this programme was to carry out research by means of empirical surveys into the relationship between technological change and regional development. Over a period of six years, a total of 50 research projects have been undertaken in three phases, each lasting two years. This research programme has succeeded in actively involving leading German regional scientists from many universities as well as non-university research institutions. In addition, numerous research projects were carried out in close co-operation with internationally renowned partners.

We should like to express our gratitude for the support provided by the Deutsche Forschungsgemeinschaft. Without their financial backing of the research programme, it would not have been possible to undertake such an ambitious project. Thanks also go to the contributors of this volume for their willingness to participate in our joint project. We wish in addition to acknowledge the contribution of Prof. Dr. Philip Cooke whose refereeing of the chapters has enhanced the quality of the work presented here. Finally, our thanks go to Angela Spence for her expert editorial assistance, linguistic editing and the preparation of the Index, and also Franco Vaio for taking care of the technical aspects and production of the final copy. Their combined efforts have been crucial for successfully bringing together contributions from so many different authors in a single volume.

July, 2001

Prof. Dr. Ludwig Schätzl
PD Dr. Javier Revilla Diez
Department of Economic Geography,
University of Hannover

Contents

Part B: The Network Paradigm and Regional Development

Part C: Sectoral Studies

1 Technological Change and Regional Development in Europe: An Introduction

Ludwig Schätzl and Javier Revilla Diez
Department of Economic Geography, University of Hannover

1.1 Context

The current debate about knowledge-based economic development has been directing the interest of numerous scientific disciplines to the questions of how and where knowledge arises. The structural change triggered by globalisation is increasing the competitive pressure on firms, which have to put innovative products on the market at ever decreasing intervals. Increasing interaction between the different actors is required by the complexity of innovation processes. Successful development of new products, processes and organisational solutions is thus the result not solely of innovative decisions within an isolated firm, but depends on the whole business environment. Innovation is no longer understood as a straightforward linear sequence leading from basic research to production, as suggested by previous models of innovation. It is now recognised that innovation processes are far more complex. Within innovation economics, the chain-linked innovation model has become commonly accepted. In this model, each phase of the innovation process is linked to all the other phases, with a continuous exchange taking place between researchers, producers and customers. The concentration on core competences, which the need for flexible specialisation has made even more essential, is forcing firms to enter into innovation co-operation agreements with other actors, such as customers, suppliers, producer service firms, competitors and research institutions.

The recent findings of innovation research with regard to the origin and diffusion of new knowledge are leading to a revaluation of the relevant spatial level. Despite catch phrases such as the 'global village' or 'global competition', technological developments take place in concrete locations. Firms choose locations which offer them the most favourable framework conditions not only for production or marketing, but also for innovation activities. The availability of renowned research institutions, qualified human capital, suitable infrastructure, providers of risk capital and high-value 'soft' location advantages, as well as suitable co-operation partners, is proving to be of decisive importance.

Against this background, the Deutsche Forschungsgemeinschaft approved the research programme 'Technological Change and Regional Development in Europe' in October 1991. The goal of this programme was to carry out research into the relationship between technological change and regional development by means of empirical surveys. Over a period of six years, a total of 50 research projects have been undertaken in three phases, each lasting two years. This extensive research programme has succeeded in actively including leading German regional scientists from universities and non-university research institutions, including the German Institute of Urban Affairs (Difu), the Fraunhofer Institute for Systems and Innovation Research (ISI), and the Kiel Institute of World Economics and Centre for European Economic Research (ZEW). The broad spectrum of fields involved underlines the high degree of interdisciplinarity. Those participating in this project come from the fields of Economics, Business Management, Economic Geography, Political and Social Sciences. In addition, numerous research projects were carried out in close co-operation with internationally renowned partners.

The empirical basic research had both a theory and policy orientation. The surveys were crucial for the examination of complex hypotheses concerning the regional implications of technological change. At the same time, they also served as an important basis for decisions concerning technological, economic and regional policy. The sectoral surveys involved the manufacturing and the business service sectors. In addition, a detailed analysis was made of the role of research institutions in the innovation processes of firms. The geographical focus of the empirical surveys lay in the core regions of Europe. In addition to surveys carried out in Germany (both West Germany and the former Democratic Republic), France, Great Britain and the Netherlands, research projects were also carried out in regions at the periphery of the EU, such as Wales, Stockholm and Barcelona, as well as in Eastern Europe (e.g. Slovenia). The research programme was thus successful in including regions at different levels of development and with different institutional framework conditions.

1.2 The Structure of the Book

The objective of this book is to provide a greater understanding of the crucial relationships between technological change and regional development. The studies gathered represent some of the scientific outcome of the above mentioned research programme. Before being approved for publishing, they were refereed by Prof. Dr. Philip Cooke and subsequently revised. The book is divided into three main parts.

Part A, *Innovation and Regional Development*, contains seven chapters which deal principally with the connection between innovation capacity and regional dynamics. The first chapter by **Ernst Giese** provides new insights into the spatial structure of invention activities in Germany. For this purpose, the domestic patent applications registered by the German Patent Office between 1992 and 1994 were analysed. A total of 100,000 patent applications were assessed. The author shows that invention activities in Germany are strongly influenced by agglomeration economies and affected by firm size and sectoral effects.

On the basis of Romer's endogenous growth model, **Eckhardt Bode** demonstrates that a high density of manufacturing R&D accelerates regional per capita income growth. Interestingly, he shows that R&D productivity and growth are found to be fostered by intensive interdisciplinary – rather than technology-specific – knowledge spillovers among researchers, as well as by spillovers from nearby universities. In addition, he argues that growth determinants other than R&D, such as urbanisation economies, have to be incorporated into regional growth analysis.

Franz-Josef Bade, Annekatrin Niebuhr and **Matthias Schönert** focus their analysis on the question of whether the economic disparities between urban agglomerations and peripheral areas is likely to converge or diverge. By using time series for several indicators, including human capital development, the authors conclude that the central tendencies of spatial structural change in Germany – (relative) gains of urban fringe and peripheral areas, and (relative) losses in the agglomerations and their cores – are extremely stable. The stability of spatial structural change suggests that the deconcentration process will continue in the near future.

The connection between technology adaptation and productivity, and the regional economic effects in East and West Germany are then examined by **Michael Fritsch** and **Jörn Mallok**. By using data for 104 match paired East and West German industrial establishments, they demonstrate that there are considerable differences with respect to their productivity performance as well as the quality of their physical capital stock. East German establishments adopted computerised machinery later than their West German counterparts, and tend not to use it as 'intelligently'. Not only the quality of the equipment, but also the way in which it is used has a significant impact on productivity performance.

The three following chapters deal with firm start-ups and their importance for regional economic development. **Oliver Burgel**, **Andreas Fier**, **Georg Licht** and **Gordon Murray** analyse the effect of internationalization on the growth of high-tech start-ups. Based on a survey for British and German high-tech start-ups, they confirm that rapid expansion into foreign markets, the technological sophistication of products, and experience on the part of entrepreneurs leads to higher sales. In order to increase economic success, the authors suggest that high-tech founders should be internationally orientated from the early development stages of their entrepreneurial activities.

In their analysis of the survival of firms, **Johannes Hampe** and **Martin Steininger** investigate differences between industries in the life duration of new firms and the significance of the regional location for the probability of survival. They reveal that many more enterprises are founded in the service sector than in manufacturing, but also that many more of these start-ups 'die young'. It is shown that the probable life duration in agglomeration areas is overall greater than in rural areas. The survey also provides empirical evidence that sectors with a greater proportion of co-operating firms have a higher growth rate. Other positive factors are a large number of employees at the time of foundation and the fact that a firm has the legal form of limited company.

Christine Tamásy then evaluates the regional economic impact of innovation centres in Germany. On the basis of a survey of 108 German innovation centres, the author shows clearly that this popular instrument of local technology policy fulfils its political expectations only in part. Although most innovation centres achieve their main goal, namely the promotion of new firms by enhancing their chances of survival and success, their contribution to the initiation of start-ups has been negligible. The regional economic effects (creation of new jobs and intensification of technology transfer) have also been minimal.

The second section of the book, Part B, *The Network Paradigm and Regional Development,* brings together eight chapters whose focal point is the examination of innovation activities of businesses and research institutions and their effects on the regional economy. On the basis of current approaches of innovation research, which take into account the systemic and evolutionary character of innovation processes, these studies reveal that intensive co-operation with intra-regional and interregional co-operation partners have a positive effect on the success of innovation and, ultimately, on the entire development of firms and regional development.

The relationship between innovation networks and regional development is analysed by **Rolf Sternberg**. Based on the results of comprehensive surveys in eleven European regions, undertaken as part of the European Regional Innovation Survey (ERIS), he makes it clear that highly linked firms are more successful in terms of innovation output and employment than firms without innovation linkages. With respect to the spatial range of such linkages, it is shown that intensive intra-regional as well as interregional linkages foster firm growth.

By introducing the concept of Metropolitan Innovation Systems, **Javier Revilla Diez** provides insights in the next chapter into innovative activity and innovation networking in the metropolitan regions of Barcelona, Stockholm and Vienna. Despite certain similarities between these regions, the innovative capacity of their innovation systems differ markedly. Across all the regions, however, it is shown that vertical co-operation relationships predominate in the external co-operation networks of manufacturing firms. The spatial proximity of co-operation partners is also important, but at the same time the innovation actors also have co-operation partners outside the region, confirming the gateway function of the metropolitan innovation systems.

Knut Koschatzky and **Andrea Zenker** provide empirical evidence that the size of a firm significantly affects its innovative behaviour and pattern of co-operation, and that there are differences between manufacturing firms and business-related service firms. Small manufacturing and service firms mainly behave similarly and tend to be more regionally oriented in their knowledge acquisition than large firms. In particular, small firms in intermediate and rural areas depend strongly upon knowledge sources available at the regional level, and therefore suffer a disadvantage compared with larger firms which make more frequent use of knowledge and information sources from outside the region.

The role of research institutes in regional innovation systems and the nature of their co-operation with various public research establishments (universities, Fachhochschulen and non-university research institutions) in three German regions (Baden, Hannover and Saxony) are explored by **Michael Fritsch** and **Christian Schwirten.** They show that collaboration is widespread and not limited to regional partners. Such inter-research co-operation is driven by several motives

– the gaining of ideas for research work being the most important. In the case of EU-funded research consortia, financial motives are particularly important, which raises questions about the effectiveness of EU funding policy.

Jörg Maier and **Frank Obermaier** examine the influence of innovative milieus on the innovative capability and competitiveness of regions. Their analysis focuses on the importance of the embeddedness of firms within their regional environment. A number of key factors are defined, and four case-study regions in Bavaria are assessed with respect to their creative milieu. The authors derive a series of important policy implications from the innovative milieu approach relating to the development of local strategies.

Jürgen Oßenbrügge and **Christian Zellner** make an effort to determine whether or not the biotech industry in the region of Munich represents a regional innovation system. The authors find that the spatial concentration of biotech firms does not necessarily mean that a dense network of input and output relations exists within a cluster. They demonstrate that knowledge and technology transfer often occurs on an international scale. However, the exchange of tacit knowledge is facilitated by spatial proximity, stressing the importance of untraded interdependencies and relational assets in a region.

The two following chapters discuss the effects of organisational innovations in firms. **Simone Strambach** examines the effects of the socio-economic contexts characterising the German and British innovation systems on the processes of interaction and learning regarding organisational innovation. Since the 1990s there has been a rapid succession of different organisational models and principles concerning production processes, but many organisational innovations have also gone far beyond production, influencing the way the internal and external know-how resources are used and integrated, thus affecting the firm's organisational learning capacity.

Boris Braun and **Reinhold Grotz** compare environmental management systems (EMS) in British and German manufacturing firms in order to assess their influence on the diffusion of environmental know-how. More specifically, the study analyses the role of different stakeholders and the effects of network integration as well as the economic, ecological and technological outcomes of EMS in firms which have implemented the European Eco-Management and Audit Scheme (EMAS). The authors demonstrate that the diffusion of environmental know-how is effectively supported by inter-firm networking. Agglomeration and urbanisation effects seem to be of less importance.

The final section, Part C, *Sectoral Studies*, provides a number of examples of innovation processes in selected sectors. An effort has been made to adopt a broad approach, not considering only the so-called high-tech branches. The innovation activities of many sectors which until now have received little attention in existing studies have also been taken into account.

Michael Plattner has chosen a sectoral concept to discuss the relevance of human capital and knowledge transfer for spatial clustering. In relation to processes of concentration, the geographical level of different kinds of relationships between firms have been analysed. On the basis of the evolution of new sectoral clusters in the East German semiconductor industry, it is shown that the vertical, horizontal, and informational interactions develop specific spatial patterns of influence over innovation.

In the following chapter **Rainer Voß, Martina Brandt, Ulla Große** and **Frank Hartmann** have examined eight case studies of innovation projects in two fields of environmental biotechnology (biological land reclamation and biogas production) in the Berlin-Brandenburg and Saxony regions. The investigation has focused not only on the innovative behaviour of the firms themselves, but also the influence of the behaviour of milieu protagonists on the entrepreneurial innovation process.

The locational impacts of new information and communication technologies used for retailing in Germany are analysed by **Sven Henschel**. Research undertaken in Greater Hannover and Leipzig shows the different positions in the life cycles of store types, and different location networks of food retailing as a result of the system transformation in the new German states. Market areas with high degrees of competition or high selling space capacities have a greater share of scanner installations. Due to this, supposedly weak locations can achieve higher quality, which will have an enduring influence on the location pattern of food retailing.

Hans-Dieter Haas and **Sven Siebert** provide an analysis of the packaging industry. During the 1990s, the sector underwent profound changes in its regulatory framework. The authors have made an extensive empirical study of the industry, including packaging manufacturers and users of packaged-ware. They find a strong relationship between the general political conditions dominating structures and the spatial behaviour of influential actors in the packaging market during times of considerable upheaval.

Barbara Lenz provides insights into the changing organisation of production in the European horticultural sector as well as the influence of technology. She deals with the question of how different types of enterprise contribute to the production of flowers and pot plants, and tries to deduce rules for the structure of a flower production chain. As a result, a logical order of businesses in the pelargonium production chain can be shown and explained, including the role of technologies in and between firms in the horticultural sector.

As in the previous papers, **Thorsten Hülsmann, Jürgen Pohl** and **Norbert Rehle** explore processes of innovation, but this time in the more low tech industry of costume jewellery production. They analyse in particular the institutional setting of norms, routines and conventions, hence assessing the regionally based cultural dimension of innovation processes. In contrast to the majority of industrial districts of the Italian type, the regional production systems of costume jewellery production in Europe have not yet become comprehensively global.

PART A Innovation and Regional Development

2 The Spatial Pattern of Invention Activities in West Germany 1992-1994

Ernst Giese
Department of Geography, Justus-Liebig-University of Giessen

2.1 Introduction

This chapter presents the results of a research project undertaken in collaboration with the Division of Statistics of the German Patent Office (Dr. Siegfried Greif and Dieter Schmiedl). The purpose was to investigate regional innovation potential in Germany with the help of patent indicators. Our project therefore had two main aims: firstly, to identify where successful research and invention activities in technical and scientific fields are taking place in Germany. Secondly, to clarify the causes which can be held responsible for the spatial distribution of invention activities. As the geographical distribution of invention performance is already well documented in the "German Atlas of Patents" (Greif 1998), we have focused on the analysis of the spatial pattern of invention activities.

The starting point for this research project was the idea that the patent system represents a useful instrument for the analysis of invention activities, and that patent data can be taken as an indicator for recording and assessing research and invention activities. Patent applications provide a rich source of information on the nature and regional origins of both the applicant and inventor according to place of residence and, thus, indirectly the location of the research institute. However, care has to be exercised in using patent data since:

- not every invention becomes the subject of a patent application,
- applications for patents are not only made to protect inventions, but also for strategic economic reasons, for example to secure and expand markets, for advertising purposes and for reasons of prestige,
- not every application leads to the issue of a patent,
- not every invention subject to a patent application becomes a marketable product or process.

The number of patent applications therefore does not provide an exact indication of the number of inventions in a region, but an approximation. The validity of patent data has already been thoroughly discussed elsewhere (see Giese and von Stoutz 1998). But despite the constraints that have to be taken into account, it nevertheless remains more informative and suitable than most other quantitative benchmarks for the assessment of research and invention activities in a given region.

The fact that companies, under current conditions, usually seek legal protection for technical innovations of importance with respect to their place in the market makes patents particularly suitable as a tool for indicating any potential, or lack of potential, for technical innovation. The number of employees engaged in research and development (R&D) presents a less valid and less reliable variable because, in contrast to patent applications, this is an input parameter of the R&D process rather than an output parameter. High R&D expenditures are not necessarily proportional to the 'yield' of innovation.

The aim of our research project was to acquire information on the spatial distribution of patent activity in Germany and invention activities based on this information. Since the goal of economic progress is not invention itself but the marketable product, we needed lastly to obtain information on the economic performance and development potential of different regions of Germany.

In order to acquire information on the spatial distribution of patent activity in Germany, and hence on invention activities, we analysed all domestic patent applications[1] registered by the German Patent Office between 1992 and 1994. The domestic patent applications submitted directly to the German Patent Office, as well as those made by German applicants to the European Patent Office requesting protection in Germany, were taken into account. Patent applications for one and the same invention, registered at both the German Patent Office and the European Patent Office were counted as one application. A total of 100,000 patent applications were assessed.

The quantitative analysis is based on a simple black box model, in which the number of employees engaged in R&D in manufacturing industry is entered as the input parameter and the number of patent applications as output parameter (see Fig. 2.1). An exhaustive company-based analysis of invention activities which followed the whole process of invention (from the abstract idea of a product to its eventual manufacture) was carried out in a study by von Stoutz (1999) in which he investigated the research, development and invention activities of industrial companies in the Central-Hessian region.

Our analysis of the spatial distribution of patent applications has been confined to former West Germany for the following reasons:

- a comparison of conditions in East Germany with those in West Germany appeared to be somewhat premature so soon after reunification. In addition, only 4.5 percent of patent applications were submitted in East Germany in 1992 (Deutsches Patentamt Jahresbericht 1994),
- the spatial units are not comparable. Whereas the former West Germany is divided into 327 counties (Stadt- and Landkreise), East Germany, which covers roughly one third of the area of West Germany, has 220 counties,

[1] Information regarding patent applications is usually disclosed 18 months after registration.

- no comparable data are available for further analysis. For example, no data are available regarding the numbers of people employed in R&D.

Patent applications have long been used to measure the development of national economies, but only a few detailed and reliable *regional* analyses of inventive activity of individual national economies have been carried out (see, for example, Acs *et al.* 1992, 1994; Greif 1992; Feldman 1994; Feldman and Florida 1994; Audretsch and Feldman 1994; Breschi 1994).

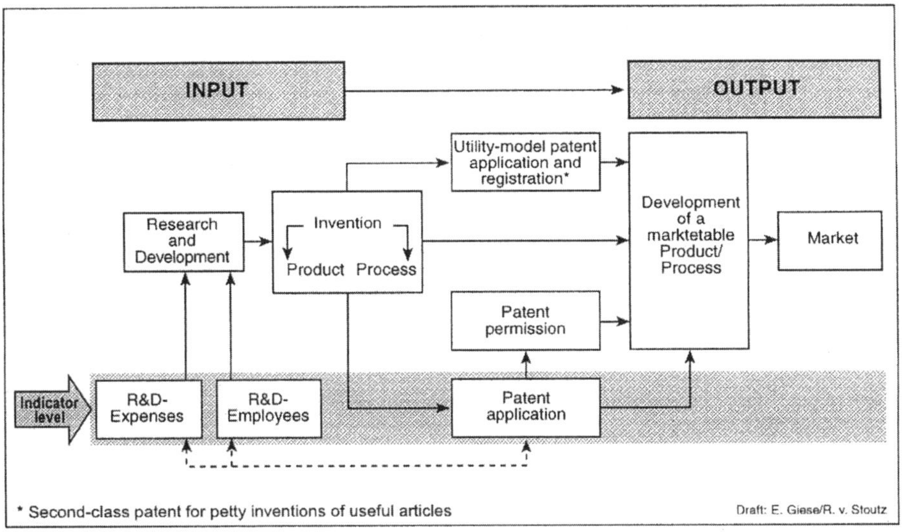

Fig. 2.1 Position of patent applications in the economy's developmental process

2.2 Methodological Problems of Coverage and Data Processing

The German Patent Office registers patent applications according to the location of the applicant, but the place of registration need not correspond with the location of the invention or the location of the research institute. This applies especially to major businesses and businesses with multiple subsidiaries, whose location of patent registration is usually separate from the location of the invention. Since about 70 percent of patent registrations come from companies with more than 1,000 employees – in the chemical industry this figure is 90 percent – one can assume that the spatial distribution of patent applications does not correspond to the location of the actual invention.

In order to analyse the spatial aspect, it was therefore necessary to obtain some indication of the location of the research institute or the invention. This was possible since the home address of the inventor is also given on the application form. From this one can indirectly infer the location of the research institute. However, tracing back patent registrations to the location of the research institute is not only extremely time-consuming – practically all of the 100,000 patent applications would have to be individually assigned – but also presupposes the availability of expert knowledge. Fortunately, this task was undertaken by Siegfried Greif, head of the Statistics Division of the German Patent Office, and his assistants.

The usefulness of assigning patent applications to the location of the invention becomes evident when one compares Figs. 2.2 and 2.3. It can be seen that the distribution of patent applications in the chemical industry according to the location of the applicant differs considerably from the distribution according to the location of the inventor.

The problem becomes more evident when we consider the spatial distribution of patent applications of a large company such as the Robert Bosch Corporation which has its company headquarters in Stuttgart (see Table 2.1). The legal residence of the inventors (location of the research institute) of the patents of this corporation registered in 1992 by its head office spread across 84 counties. Of these patent applications, 66 percent can be traced back to the counties surrounding Stuttgart (the Stuttgart labour market region), 22 percent to the rest of Baden-Württemberg, and the remaining 12 percent across the rest of Germany.

Table 2.1 Patent applications submitted to German Patent Office in 1992 by Robert Bosch Corporation Headquarters in Stuttgart

Location of Inventor (Research Institute)	
Ludwigsburg	37.1 %
Stuttgart	13.9 %
Esslingen	5.6 %
Böblingen	5.4 %
Rems-Murr	4.1 %
Calw	0.2 %
Total (Labour Market Region of Stuttgart)	66.3 %
Reutlingen	4.2 %
Heilbronn	3.3 %
Rastatt	2.8 %
Enzkreis	2.7 %
Rest of Baden-Württemberg	21.9 %
Rest of Germany	11.8 %

Source: German Patent Office

As already mentioned in the introduction, the smaller the geographical unit of reference chosen, the greater the risk of misinterpretation. One of the causes of this variation is that companies often submit their patent applications in bulk (see Giese and von Stoutz 1998). In smaller areas, the patent applications frequently derive from a single company. In the Marburg-Biedenkopf county, for example, the number of patent applications was heavily influenced by the patenting behaviour of the former Behringwerke company. In surveys dealing with patent applications in smaller geographical areas therefore considerable short-term fluctuations may emerge (see Fig. 2.4 for a graphic representation). In order to avoid the risk of misinterpretation, data from three consecutive years were taken – 1992, 1993, 1994 – and a mean value calculated for each.

Instead of counties, labour market regions have often been used as the spatial unit of reference for regional analysis (see Eckey *et al.* 1990; Höher 1997). These have an advantage over counties and districts because they are functional units of reference, in that the workplace and the place of residence usually coincide. Thus, using the labour market region as a basis, it is no surprise that there is less difference between the number of patent applications by location of applicant and location of inventor. The spatial distribution is similar. If one compares the two distributions, the correlation coefficient increases from $r = 0.7327$ to $r = 0.9714$. If one applies the number of patent applications per 10,000 employees in manufacturing industry, the correlation coefficient increases from $r = 0.4264$ to $r = 0.8204$. It is thus advisable that the analysis of spatial distribution of patent applications be carried out on the basis of the labour market region.

2.3 Spatial Distribution of Patent Applications in West Germany

Fig. 2.5 represents the spatial distribution of domestic patent applications according to the legal residence of the inventor on the basis of counties. It reveals that patent activities are widely spread across the country and are concentrated only in a few core regions. These are predominately urban agglomerations, which are the source of over 60 percent of the domestic patent applications registered at the German Patent Office.

The three most important urban agglomerations in terms of patent applications are the regions of Stuttgart and Munich, and the Rhine-Main region. These are followed by the Cologne-Bonn, Rhine-Neckar, Düsseldorf and the Ruhr urban agglomerations in order. Of all patent applications, 45 percent according to the location of the inventor and 54 percent according to the location of the applicant are found in these regions. We can therefore deduce that research and invention activity is strongly concentrated spatially. Gini coefficients and Lorenz curves calculated for patent applications and R&D employment confirm these results (see Fig. 2.6). The strong spatial clustering of research and invention activity suggests that these are integrated into spatially referenced systems in which close contact and the spatial proximity of the participating actors, and thus their rapid access to new knowledge, has an important influence on invention activities as well as on the degree of success achieved by such innovations.

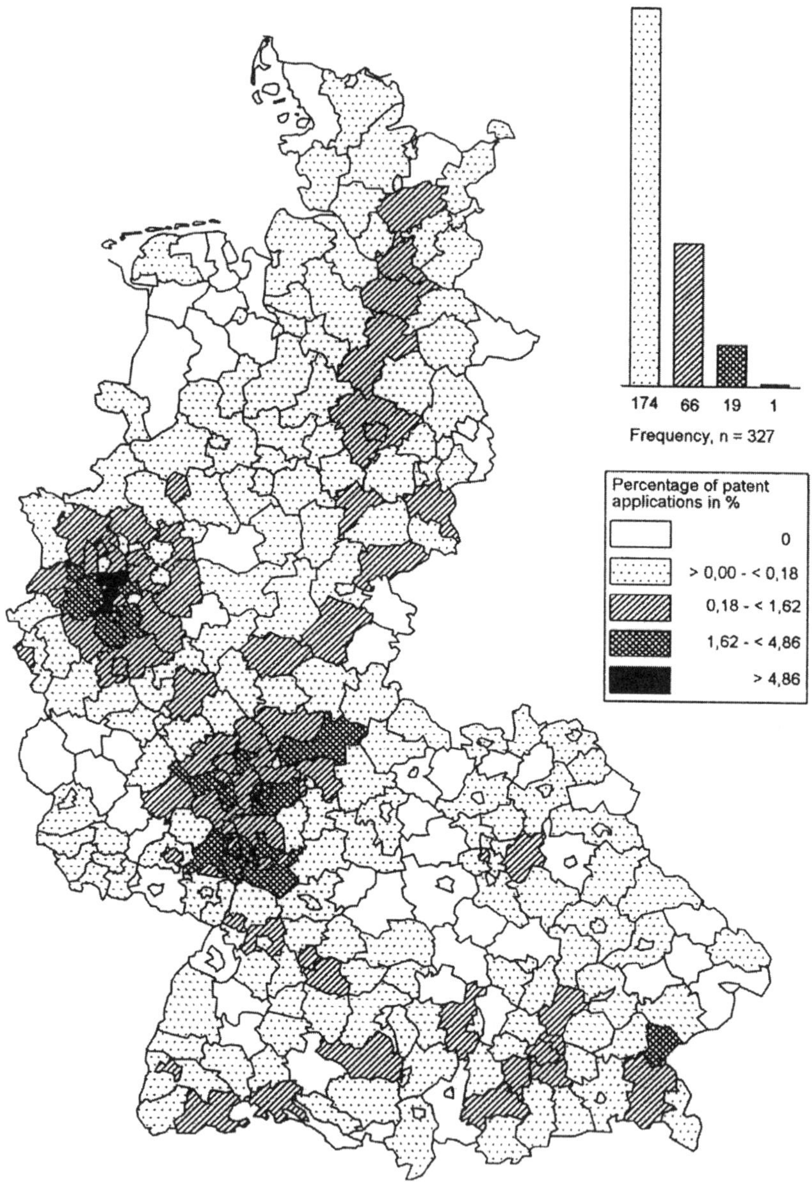

Fig. 2.2 Domestic patent applications by chemical industry in West Germany to German Patent Office in 1992, by location of inventor (research institute)

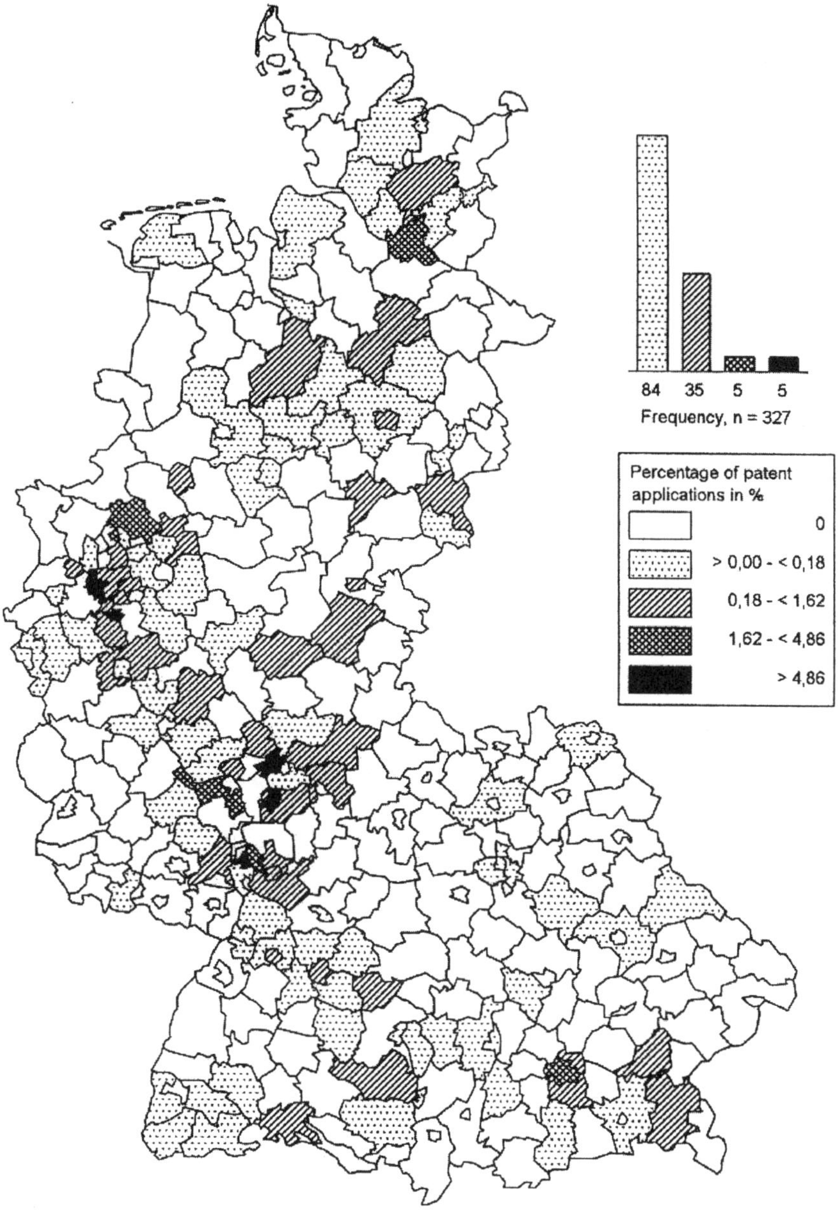

Fig. 2.3 Domestic patent applications by chemical industry in West Germany to German Patent Office in 1992, by location of applicant

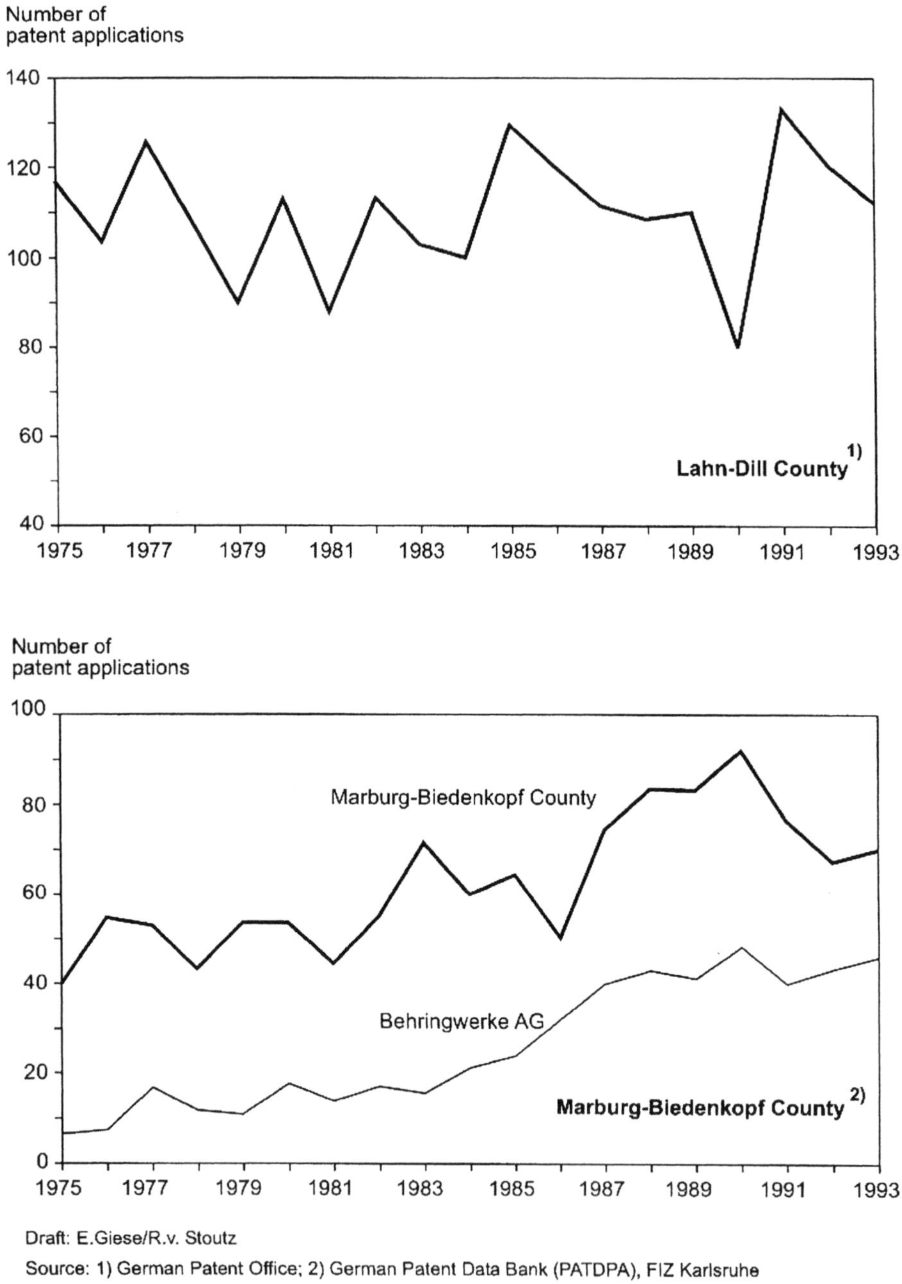

Fig. 2.4 Total domestic patent applications submitted to German Patent Office 1975-1993 in counties of Lahn-Dill and Marburg-Biedenkopf

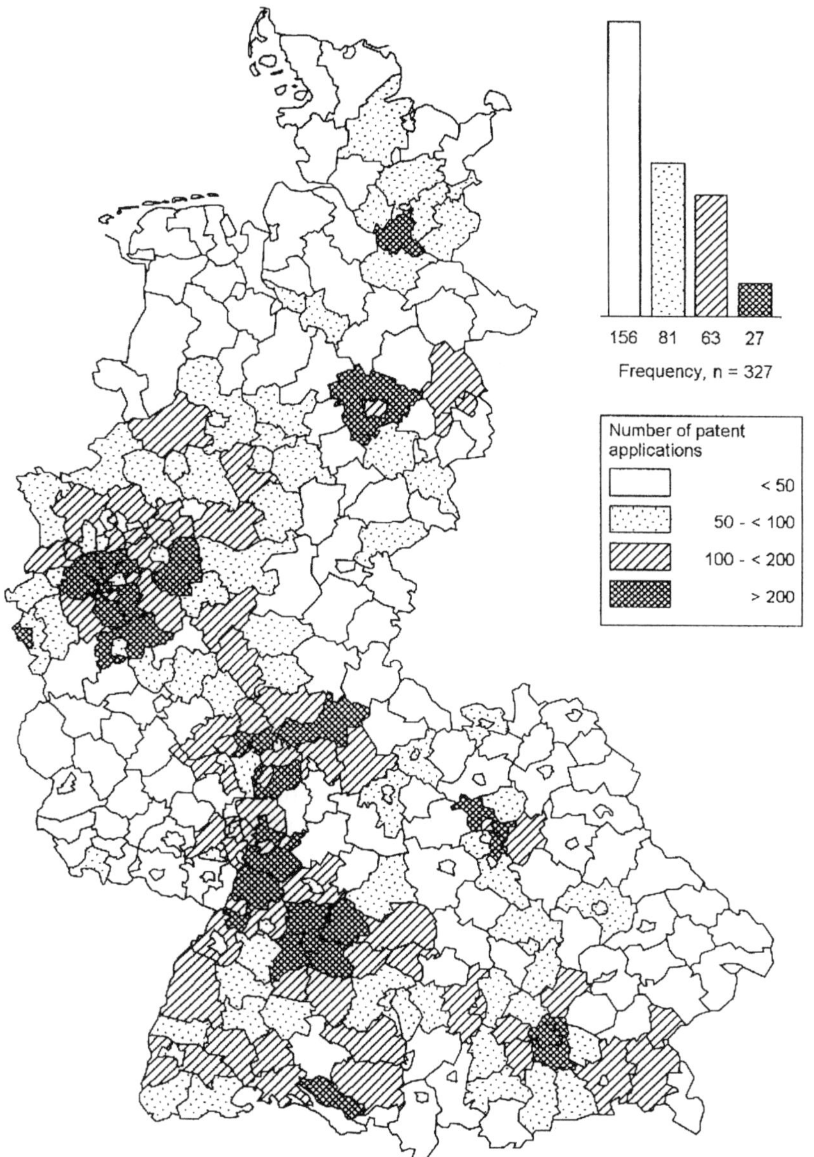

Fig. 2.5 Number of domestic patent applications submitted to German Patent Office according to location of inventor (research institute): averages for 1992, 1993, and 1994 for Western Germany

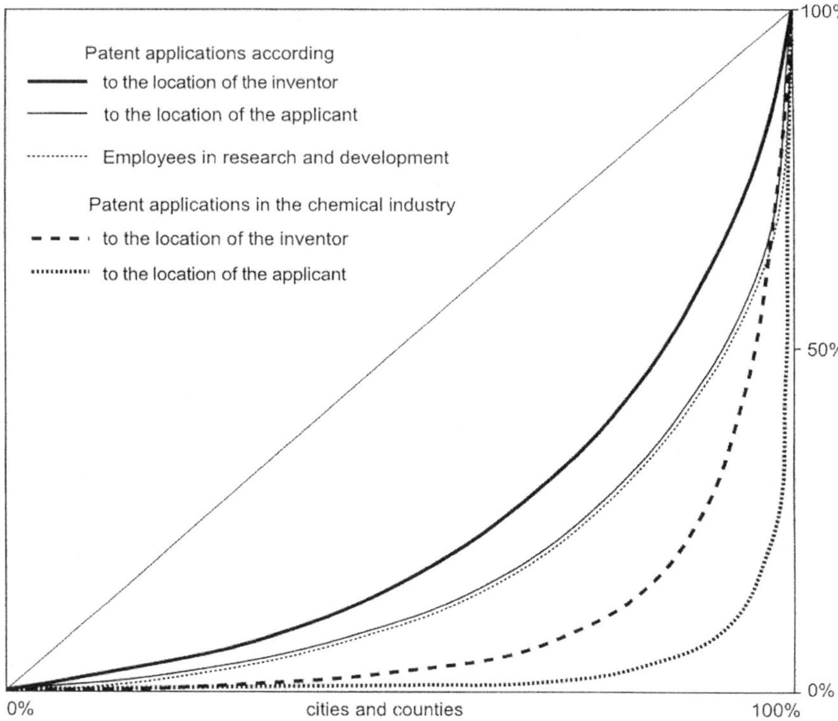

Own compilations; data source "Deutsches Patentamt"

Fig. 2.6 Lorenz curves of domestic patent applications submitted to German Patent Office in 1992 and R&D employment in 1991 in West Germany

Fig. 2.6 shows that the spatial concentration of research and invention activity varies according to the branch of industry or technical sector. Hence spatial reference systems may be of varying importance to different processes of innovation. In other words, a specific infrastructure may be necessary for the development of technology in a given technical branch. Breschi (1994) has already concluded for instance that in the chemical-pharmaceutical and the electric-electronic industries the spatial concentration of patenting activity is much stronger than in traditional branches of industry (e.g. mechanical engineering).

In the study conducted by von Stoutz (1999) on research and invention activities in Central-Hessian companies, one of the aspects investigated was whether there were any intra-regional co-operation and network connections between companies or with other participants in the R&D field (e.g. research institutes owned by universities). The study revealed that 35 percent of companies applying for patents co-operate with universities or technical colleges, and 20 percent network with other companies within the same region involved in the field of research. This suggests that there may be internal networks of companies within regions, but to a much lesser extent than thought initially. These networks, for the most part, affect partners located outside the Central-Hessian region.

A more differentiated examination of the spatial distribution of patent applications is possible by representing patent applications on the basis of labour market regions (see Table 2.2). It can be seen that not only are large labour market regions such as Stuttgart, Munich, Frankfurt, active in research and invention, but also smaller labour market regions such as Karlsruhe, Münster, Tübingen, Augsburg, Wuppertal/Solingen/Remscheid, Braunschweig, Mainz, Hagen, Aachen, Krefeld, Ulm, Würzburg, etc. Almost all of these labour market regions have universities, technical colleges, and research institutes, and are characterised by the predominance of small and medium-sized industrial companies (SMEs) which are, in contrast to major industries, less likely to have their own R&D department, and are thus more dependent on research institutes. The proximity of universities, coupled with easy access to the knowledge acquired at these universities, seems to be an important source and prerequisite for the invention activities of SMEs. This diagnosis is supported by a study conducted by Link and Rees (1990) who, on the basis of their research in the United States, have come to the conclusion that small companies benefit more from the R&D expenditures of universities than do large companies.

Table 2.2 Number of domestic patent applications submitted to German Patent Office (averages 1992, 1993, 1994) and number of R&D employees in manufacturing industry (1991) in West Germany according to labour market regions

Rank	Labour market region (n = 158)	No. patent applications according to location of: Inventor		Applicant		R&D employees[2)]	
			%		%		%
1	Stuttgart	2589	9.2	3334	10.4	30144	10.6
2	München	2092	7.4	3581	11.1	24389	8.6
3	Frankfurt	1788	6.3	2708	8.4	21736	7.7
4	Mannh./Heidel./Ludw.	1553	5.5	1894	5.9	15388	5.4
5	Köln/Bonn	1272	4.5	1721	5.4	14059	5.0
6	Nürnberg	1145	4.1	662	2.1	13270	4.7
7	Düsseldorf	866	3.1	1199	3.7	8668	3.1
8	Essen/Bochum	839	3.0	722	2.2	8050	2.8
9	Hamburg	728	2.6	942	2.9	10423	3.7
10	Hannover	501	1.8	599	1.9	5559	2.0
11	Karlsruhe	412	1.5	345	1.1	5063	1.8

(Continues)

Table 2.2 (Continued)

12	Wuppert./Sol./Remsch.	407	1.4	591	1.8	3253	1.1
13	Münster	355	1.3	399	1.2	2722	1.0
14	Tübingen/Reutlingen	299	1.1	198	0.6	2342	0.8
15	Augsburg	298	1.1	222	0.7	3255	1.1
16	Dortmund	291	1.0	315	1.0	3092	1.1
17	Hagen	289	1.0	338	1.1	2037	0.7
18	Aachen	287	1.0	201	0.6	2008	0.7
19	Braunschweig/Salzgitter	280	1.0	148	0.5	2428	0.9
20	Mainz	278	1.0	233	0.7	1473	0.5
21	Krefeld	266	0.9	156	0.5	3215	1.1
22	Ulm	265	0.9	216	0.7	3043	1.1
23	Würzburg	258	0.9	265	0.8	1782	0.6
24	Wolfsburg	257	0.9	400	1.2	3753	1.3
25	Pforzheim	256	0.9	215	0.7	1635	0.6
26	Heilbronn	256	0.9	232	0.7	1681	0.6
27	Duisburg	250	0.9	239	0.7	4928	1.7
28	Saarbrücken	246	0.9	220	0.7	2615	0.9
29	Freiburg	241	0.9	213	0.7	1739	0.6
30	Bremen	236	0.8	257	0.8	6439	2.3
31	Siegen	221	0.8	221	0.7	1850	0.7
32	Wiesbaden	221	0.8	284	0.9	1520	0.5
33	Friedrichshafen	220	0.8	255	0.8	3874	1.4
34	Aschaffenburg	217	0.8	128	0.4	1116	0.4
35	Ingolstadt	216	0.8	199	0.6	1515	0.5
	West Germany*	28259	100	32135	100	283669	100
	Germany**	30957		34825			

Source: [1] Greif 1998, [2] Employment Statistics of Federal Labour Office; Prof. F.-J. Bade (University of Dortmund).
* Without Berlin.
** 3868 patent applications in Germany could not be classified to any location of inventor.

2.4 Differing Spatial Productivity in Research

A graphic representation of the absolute number of patent applications illustrates, above all, a size effect. It should not be surprising that in regions where reputed research institutes are highly concentrated, the number of discoveries and inventions is also high. Comparing the number of patent applications (according to the location of the inventor) with the number of R&D employees[1] on the basis of labour market regions, we find a high correlation coefficient ($r = 0.9871$; $R^2 = 0.9744$). The number of patent applications increases linearly in labour market regions with the increase in the number of R&D employees in manufacturing industry (see Fig. 2.7).

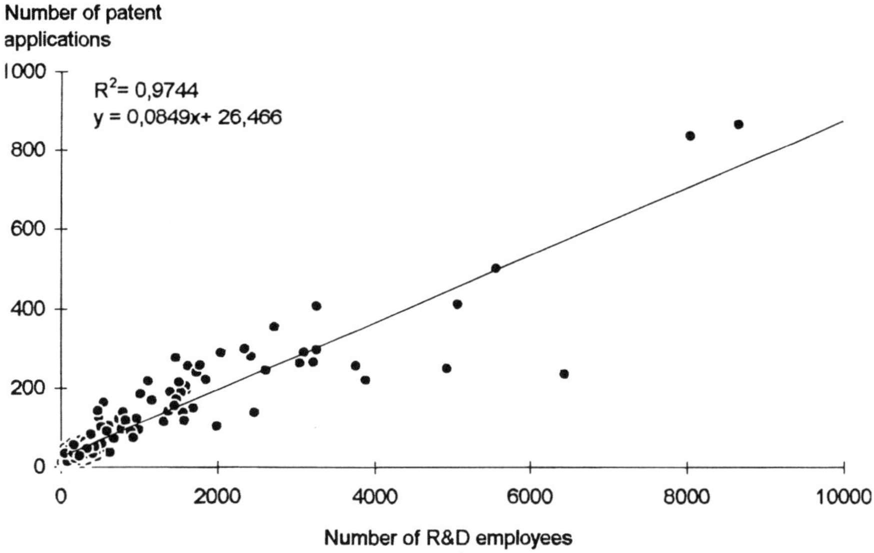

Fig. 2.7 Relationship of number of patent applications (yearly averages 1992, 1993, 1994) on number of R&D employees in manufacturing industry (1991) based on labour market regions

Several different methods can be employed to eliminate the size effect. One is to calculate the residuals of the regression of patent applications on the number of R&D employees. The difference between the actual number of patent applications in the respective labour market regions and the regression of the expected number (independently of the available number of R&D employees) is thus determined.

Another method which eliminates the size effect derives from the shift analysis approach. This method assumes that a quantitatively compatible input (number of employees) in all areas of West Germany would result in a similar output (number of patent applications), i.e. an equal distribution of patents. It is then possible to

[1] The number of R&D employees (which includes engineers, chemists, and scientists) was obtained from employment statistics of the Federal Labour Office. An alternative data source for employment statistics is the R&D Statistics of the SV-Scientific Statistics, Ltd. of the Union for German Science Foundation. These data were not used for various reasons (for further information see Koschatzky 1997; Specht 1999).

calculate a fictitious value of patent applications for each region in West Germany, which specifies how many patent applications should be made in individual regions according to the number of R&D employees.

$$\textit{Fictitious value of patent applications} =$$

$$= \frac{\textit{No. of patent applications in West Germany}}{\textit{No. of R\&D employees in West Germany}} \times \textit{No. of R \& D employees in the region}$$

This fictitious value was compared to the actual number of patent applications in the region (differential model of the shift analysis approach). The difference is known as the Total Net Shift (TNS). Fig. 2.8 shows the result of this calculation. The chart indicates in which labour market regions there are particularly large numbers of patent applications compared to the R&D personnel, in other words, where the research yield is exceptionally large. If the residuals of the regression were illustrated accordingly, they would show a very similar distribution pattern, notwithstanding a few exceptions. Regions with high positive TNS and residual values appear to be concentrated in southern Germany, predominately in Baden-Württemberg and Bavaria. The northern federal states Schleswig-Holstein, Lower Saxony, Hamburg and Bremen, as well as Rhineland-Palatinate and Saarland do not appear at all.

This indicates that the two core regions of high research productivity are Stuttgart and Munich. Stuttgart is surrounded by a ring of labour market regions with high positive values (Pforzheim, Heilbronn, Schwäbisch-Gmünd, Göppingen, Tübingen, and Reutlingen). Similarly, Munich is also surrounded by labour market regions with high research productivity, reaching from Landsberg to Weilheim and Bad Tölz, and from Rosenheim to Altötting. Two other market regions – Garmisch-Partenkirchen and Traunstein – are partly included in this ring. The metropolitan regions of Munich and Stuttgart are therefore not only the areas with the highest number of patent applications but also the highest research productivity.

What is remarkable in this case is that according to the relativised values of patent applications, the large labour market regions are no longer dominant, but almost without exception the small and medium-sized market regions such as Mainz, Rosenheim, Aschaffenburg, Bad Tölz, Aachen, Hagen, Münster, Wuppertal/ Solingen, Würzburg, Wiesbaden, Freiburg, Tübingen, etc. The larger labour market regions in fact draw attention on account of their high negative TNS values. This observation leads to the assumption that over a certain order of magnitude, research productivity in labour market regions begins to diminish. If the TNS values on the basis of labour market regions is correlated to the number of R&D employees as well as the percentage of R&D employees in manufacturing industry, in both cases the correlation coefficient is negative. This value is, however, so small that no conclusions can be drawn.

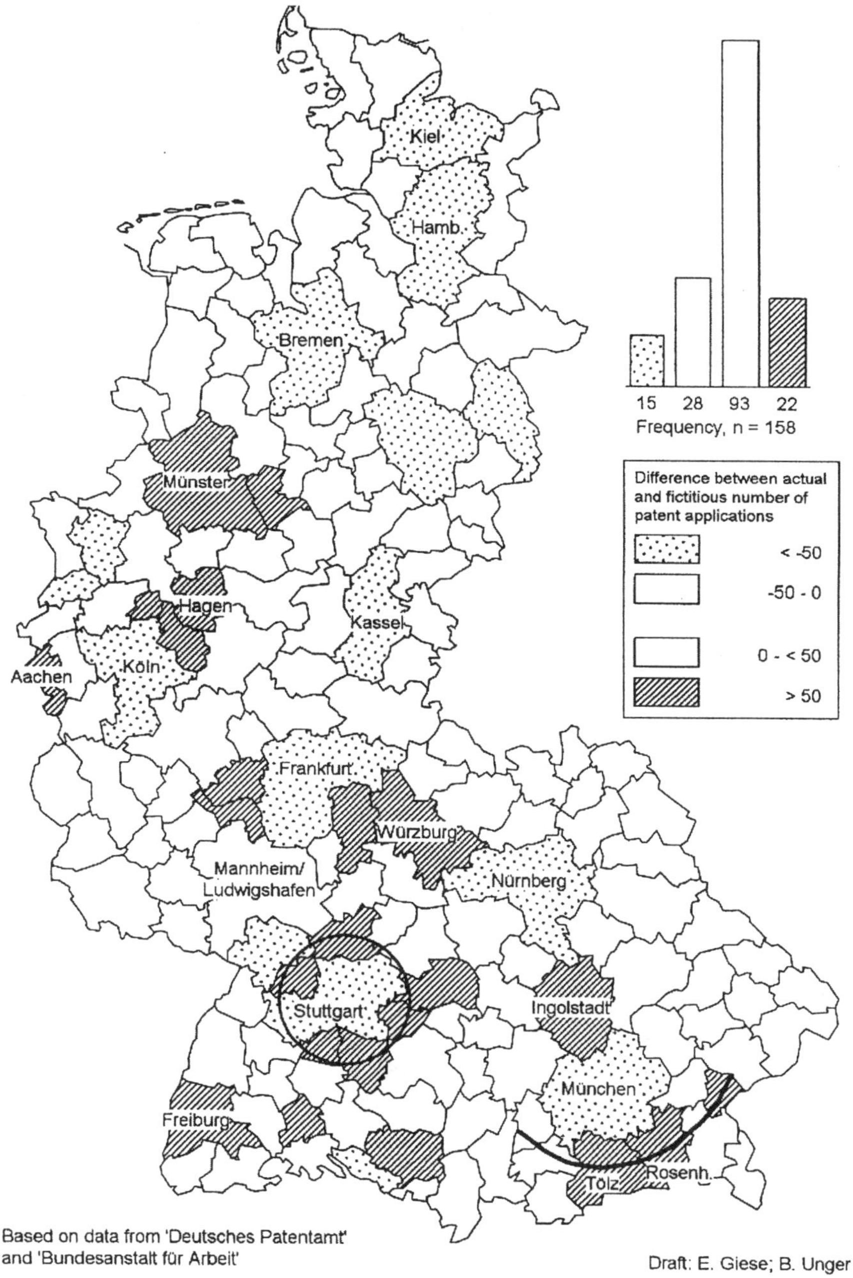

Fig. 2.8 Total Net Shift of patent applications (yearly averages 1992, 1993, 1994) applied to R&D employees in manufacturing industry (1991) in West Germany based on labour market regions

2.5 Causes of Variation in Spatial Distribution of Patent Applications

It has already been indicated in the introduction that the spatial distribution of patent applications corresponds to the spatial distribution of R&D employees. The dependence of the number of inventions in a given region on the number of R&D personnel was verified by a high correlation coefficient (r = 0.9871). It has been pointed out that this dependence can be ascribed to a simple size effect. In the following section we attempt to establish to what extent the dependence of patent applications on the number of R&D employees is the consequence of size effect. For this purpose, both reference variables have been relativised, each being divided by the number of employees in manufacturing industry.

If we correlate the relativised values as above (see Fig. 2.9), the result is a much lower correlation coefficient (r = 0.5516, R^2 = 0.3043). This indicates that there are other factors which can better explain the spatial distribution of patent application for technical inventions in West Germany than the spatial distribution of R&D staff.

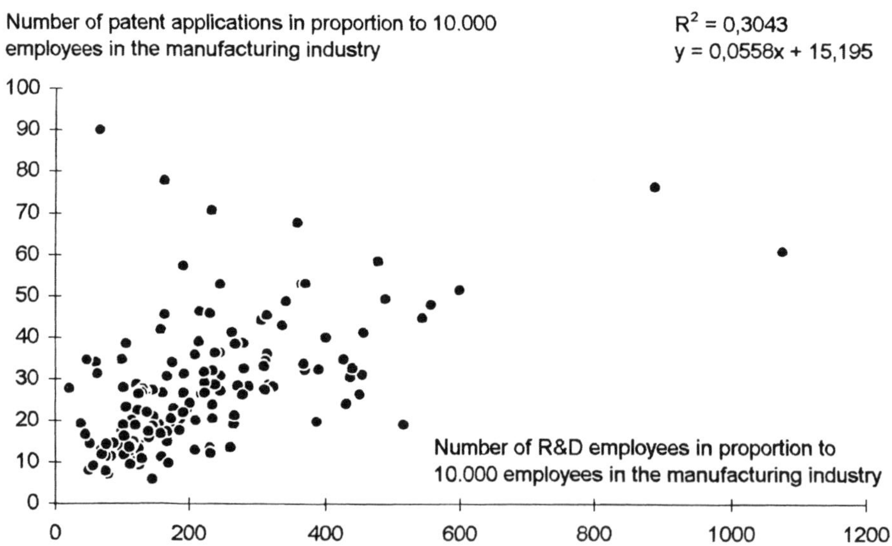

Fig. 2.9 Relationship of number of patent applications (yearly averages 1992, 1993, 1994) on number of R&D employees (1991) for every 10,000 employees in manufacturing industry in West Germany based on labour market regions

The significance of the spatial distribution of patent applications can only really be grasped when the distribution is analysed according to economic branches and the size of companies. Distinct differences become visible if one breaks down the number of patent applications according to the size classifications of companies. It can be claimed that the number of patent applications increase roughly with the size of the respective companies (see Licht and Zoz 1996; Giese and von Stoutz 1998). Because of their size advantage, larger companies seem to be more innovative than smaller companies (Schumpeter's hypothesis; see Giese and Nipper 1984; Scherer 1991; Acs and Audretsch 1991; Cohen and Klepper 1996; Audretsch and Vivarelli 1996; Bertscheck and Entorf 1996; Giese and von Stoutz 1998). Around 70 percent of domestic patent applications are made by companies whose workforces exceed 1,000 employees. In the chemical industry, this figure is as much as 90 percent. In fact, 64 percent of patent applications alone were carried out by companies in the chemical industry, whose workforce exceeds 10,000 employees (see Giese and von Stoutz 1998). Thus, the spatial distribution of patent applications is determined by the location of large companies (see Figs. 2.2 and 2.3).

However this statement requires qualification with respect to the evaluation of the invention performance of companies in a given region, since the patenting activities of SMEs differ considerably from those of large companies. This can be seen, among other things, from the fact compared with their number and economic significance (turn-over, gross value added, number of employees) that SMEs register considerably fewer patents than large companies. In manufacturing industry in the Federal Republic of Germany, 46 percent of the gross product and 58 percent of the turnover is produced by SMEs employing under 1,000 people. However, companies of this size make only 30 percent of the patent applications. The reasons for the varying patent activities have been discussed in Giese and von Stoutz 1998. It has been concluded that the spatial distribution pattern of patent applications with respect to both the location of the applicant and the location of the inventor, is determined by the location of the large-scale industry.

The number of patent applications not only varies with the size of the company, but also with the branch of industry and the technical branch to which the company belongs. Thus, companies in the chemical industry or in electronics tend to apply for patents more often than companies in mechanical engineering or vehicles construction. Likewise, technical branches such as gauging/inspection, vehicle construction, mechanical components, medicine, and basic electrical components, have registered more patents, than branches of machine tools/ metalworking, plastic manufacturing, and fuel-powered engines. Achieving an adequate understanding of the spatial distribution pattern of patent applications depends to a large degree on the kind (economic and technical branch) and size of the company located in a given region. This means that a detailed analysis of the spatial pattern of inventive activity needs to deal separately with both the industrial or technical branch and the size classification of company.

Acknowledgement

I should like to thank Prof. Dr. F.J. Bade of the University of Dortmund for his help in providing and processing data material concerning R&D employees.

References

Acs, Z.J., Audretsch, D.B. (1991) R&D, Firm Size and Innovative Activity. In: Acs, Z.J. Audretsch, D.B. (eds.) Innovation and Technological Change. University of Michigan, 39-59

Acs, Z.J., Audretsch, D.B., Feldman, M.P. (1992) Real Effects of Academic Research: Comment. American Economic Review 82, 363-367

Acs, Z.J., Audretsch, D.B., Feldman, M.P. (1994) R&D Spillovers and Recipient Firm Size. Review of Economics and Statistics 76, 336-340

Audretsch, D.B., Feldman, M.P. (1994) R&D Spillovers and the Geography of Innovation and Production. Discussion Paper FS IV 94-2. Wissenschaftszentrum Berlin

Audretsch, D.B., Vivarelli, M. (1996) Firm Size and R&D Spillovers. Small Business Economics 8, 249-258

Bertscheck, I., Entorf, H. (1996) On Non-Parametric Estimation of the Schumpeterian Link between Innovation and Firms Size. Empirical Economics 21, 401-426

Breschi, S. (1994) Spatial Patterns of Innovation: Evidence from Patent Data. CESPRI, Bocconi University, Milan

Cohen, W.M., Klepper, S. (1996) A Reprise of Size and R&D. The Economic Journal 437, 925-951

Eckey, H.F., Horn, W., Klemmer, P. (1990) Abgrenzung regionaler Diagnoseeinheiten zum Zwecke der regionalen Wirtschaftspolitik. Universitätsverlag Brockmeyer, Beiträge zur Struktur- und Konjunkturforschung, Band 29, Bochum

Feldman, M.P. (1994) The Geography of Innovation. Kluwer Academic Publishers, Boston

Feldman, M.P., Florida, R. (1994) The Geographic Sources of Innovation: Technological Infrastructure and Product Innovation in the United States. Annals of the Association of American Geographers 84, 210-229

Giese, E., Nipper, J. (1984) Die Bedeutung von Innovation und Diffusion neuer Technologien für die Regionalpolitik. Erdkunde 38, 202-215

Giese, E., von Stoutz, R. (1998) Indikatorfunktion von Patentanmeldungen für regionalanalytische Zwecke in der Bundesrepublik Deutschland. Raumforschung und Raumordnung 56, 414-420

Greif, S. (1992) Die räumliche Struktur der Erfindungstätigkeit. Grundlagen für einen Patentatlas der Bundesrepublik Deutschland. Studien zur Wirtschaftsgeographie. Justus-Liebig-Universität Gießen, Gießen

Greif, S. (1998) Patentatlas Deutschland. Die räumliche Struktur der Erfindungstätigkeit. Deutsches Patentamt, München

Höher, M. (1997) Erfassung und Bewertung regionaler Arbeitsmärkte in Hessen unter besonderer Berücksichtigung qualitativer Merkmale. Schriften des Zentrums für regionale Entwicklungsforschung der Justus-Liebig-Universität Gießen 71, Münster, Hamburg

Koschatzky, K. (1997) Regionale Innovationsindikatorik, dargestellt am Beispiel der Raumordnungsregionen Neckar-Alb und Schwarzwald-Baar-Heuburg. Raumforschung und Raumordnung 55, 48-58

Licht, G., Zoz, K. (1996) Patents and R&D. An Econometric Investigation Using Applications for German, Europe and US Patents by German Companies. ZEW, Discussion Paper 96 – 19, Mannheim

Link, A.-N., Rees, J. (1990) Firm Size, University Based Research, and Returns to R&D. In: Acs, Z.J., Audretsch, D.B. (eds.) Innovation and Technological Change. University of Michigan, Ann Arbor, 60-70

Scherer, F.M. (1991) Changing Perspectives on the Firm Size Problem. In: Acs, Z.J., Audretsch, D.B. (eds.) Innovation and Technological Change. University of Michigan, Ann Arbor, 24–38

Specht, J. (1999) Industrielle Forschung und Entwicklung: Standortstrategien und Standortvernetzungen. Am Beispiel der Regionen Rhein-Main, Bodensee und Dresden. Reihe Wirtschaftsgeographie, Bd. 14, Münster

SV-Wissenschaftsstatistik GmbH (1996) Forschung und Entwicklung in der Wirtschaft 1993-1995. Arbeitsschrift 1996, Essen

Von Stoutz, R. (1999) Forschungs-, Entwicklungs- und Erfindungstätigkeit mittelhessischer Industrieunternehmen unter besonderer Berücksichtigung regionalspezifischer Einflüsse. Europäische Hochschulschriften, Reihe 4, Geographie 19, Frankfurt

3 R&D, Localised Knowledge Spillovers and Endogenous Regional Growth: Evidence from Germany

Eckhardt Bode
The Kiel Institute of World Economics, Kiel

3.1 Introduction

In the past decade, various models have been developed which aim at explaining long-term economic growth endogenously. In particular, knowledge-based models of endogenous growth following Romer (1990) or Aghion and Howitt (1992) assume that private, profit-oriented researchers both produce and benefit from intertemporal knowledge spillovers that improve their productivity over time and as technical progress is made. It is hypothesised that, in equilibrium, there is a positive linear relationship between income growth and the number of researchers in an economy.

For regional economists, endogenous growth theory has been of particular interest because it helps overcome the long-lasting divide between neoclassical theory and polarisation approaches (e.g. Myrdal 1957; Hirschman 1958; Kaldor 1970). Several interesting, though not new questions have received a more stringent theoretical foundation: Are knowledge spillovers – at least to some extent – localised in the sense that the spatial diffusion of new knowledge does not occur instantaneously, but is subject to some kind of transport costs? Does income – due to localised knowledge spillovers – grow faster in centres of knowledge creation than in peripheral regions?

Although the process of knowledge diffusion cannot be observed directly, a large number of empirical studies have provided evidence on the existence, extent and economic effects of both 'spaceless' and localised knowledge spillovers. Reviewing the literature, Griliches concludes that "... R&D spillovers are present, their magnitude may be quite large, and social rates of return remain significantly above private rates" (Griliches 1992, p.43). More recent studies that explicitly refer to endogenous (regional) growth models tend to confirm this view. Cheshire and Carbonaro (1996), for example, have identified a significantly positive impact of R&D density and knowledge spillovers on income growth in European metropolitan areas (Functional Urban Regions). However, their indicator of R&D density – the number of research labs of 'Fortune 500' firms per million inhabitants – is somewhat crude. Moreover, their estimated elasticity of R&D output with respect to the number of research labs is no less than 4, indicating implausibly high economies of scale in R&D.

In West Germany, it is far from obvious that R&D employment has had a positive impact on regional income growth in the past two decades. Regions with a high density of industrial researchers in 1976 have not – on average – grown any faster than regions with a low density (Fig. 3.1). The same holds for absolute numbers of researchers and for different regional aggregates. Thus, either standard idea-based endogenous growth theory contributes little to the explanation of regional growth in Germany, or the effect of R&D on regional income growth is concealed by other forces fostering or hampering growth.

In the present paper we will argue that the latter holds. It will be shown that, first, regional differences in the intensity of knowledge spillovers, and thus in R&D productivity, have to be taken into account to identify the impact of R&D on regional growth, and second, that there are – at least in the medium-term of about two decades – economic forces other than R&D determining income growth.

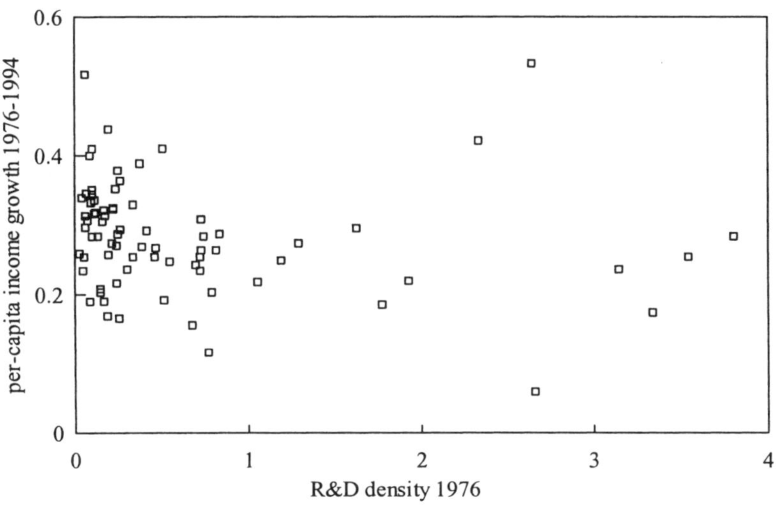

Source: See Appendix.

Fig. 3.1 Density of R&D employment and per capita income growth in 75 West German regions 1976-1994

The paper is organised as follows. First, the impact of R&D on regional income growth, as hypothesised by standard models of endogenous growth, will be estimated (Section 3.2). Although the poor correlation between R&D employment and growth is obvious from Fig. 3.1, it is informative to make a thorough analysis of regression results and test statistics in order to understand better why the model fails to fit the data. In Section 3.3, an extended growth model will be outlined and tested and, finally, Section 3.4 summarises and draws some conclusions.

3.2 Basic Growth Model

Description of the Model

As a theoretical basis we use the idea-based growth model developed by Paul Romer in his pioneering article 'Endogenous Technological Change' written in 1990. Since the model has been frequently discussed in the literature, we confine ourselves to a very brief description of some of its central features in the regional context. Each regional economy within a country is assumed to consist of three sectors: an innovative R&D sector, a local intermediate goods industry, and a final consumer good industry. In each region, the R&D sector develops $\dot{N}_r$ new blueprints per unit of time (EMBED) according to:

$$\dot{N}_r = \delta Q_r H_{Nr} \tag{3.1}$$

using human-capital intensive labour (H_{Nr}) and region-specific, publicly available knowledge (Q_r) as inputs. The productivity term δ is assumed to be identical across regions. Each innovation creates new knowledge which is assumed to be only partially excludable. The excludable part of knowledge, which is embodied in the blueprint and protected by a patent, is sold competitively to an intermediate goods sector, where it allows production of one variety of a capital good (at constant marginal costs) to be used as input in the final consumption good sector.

The non-excludable part of knowledge spills over to all other researchers in region r. Assuming each innovation creates the same amount of non-excludable knowledge, the region-specific knowledge stock accumulates over (discrete) time in direct proportion to the number of blueprints:

$$Q_{rt} = N_{rt} = \sum_{\tau=-\infty}^{t} \dot{N}_{r\tau} \tag{3.2}$$

In equilibrium, with labour being in fixed supply, the periodical growth rate of real (per-capita) income ($\hat{y}_r$) is determined by the rate of technical progress ($\hat{N}_r$), which, in turn, depends on the number of highly-qualified workers engaged in R&D:[1]

[1] Provided the supply of human-capital intensive labour is not too small, there is a positive number of researchers in the R&D sector developing new blueprints. If the supply of human-capital intensive labour is small, it is absorbed completely by the consumption goods industry. In this case, no R&D is undertaken. See Romer (1990, p. 91) for details.

$$\hat{y}_r = \hat{N}_r = \delta H_{Nr} \tag{3.3}$$

For present purposes, we assume deviations of the actual growth rate from this equilibrium to be either constant across all regions r (C) or random and normally distributed with zero mean and constant variance across regions, that is:

$$\hat{y}_r = C + \delta H_{Nr} + e_r , \qquad e_r \sim \mathrm{N}(0, \sigma^2_e). \tag{3.4}$$

Data and Method

The data set used to test (3.4) comprises 75 West German regions[1], which have been defined following economic criteria (commuting patterns). Those which may be characterised as agglomerations (29 regions), comprise at least one core city with hinterlands. The remaining 46 regions, referred to as peripheral regions, have as far as possible been organised following economic criteria.[2] The period of analysis, 1976-1994, which was restricted by the availability of a consistent data set, is defined as one period. The dependent variable, the growth rate of per capita income, is defined as $\hat{y}_r = \ln y_{r,1994} - \ln y_{r,1976}$.[3] The explanatory variable (H_{Nr}) is approximated by the number of engineers, natural scientists, and mathematicians with academic education employed in manufacturing per square kilometre, denoted *RDDENS*. The standardisation controls for differences in geographical size of regions which may distort the regression results. Employment data have been taken from the public social security insurance statistics which cover about 80 percent of all persons employed. Although this data source covers self-employed persons only if they participate voluntarily in the German public social-security insurance system, it is the most detailed and reliable statistic available at regional level in Germany. Researchers at universities and other public institutions are excluded, as well as those employed in service industries.

To analyse the properties of regression residuals and parameters, several statistical tests of the assumptions of regression theory, namely homoscedasticity, parameter stability, and the absence of spatial autocorrelation and of spatial lag dependence, have been made. Autocorrelation among neighbouring regions has

---

1 Since data on East Germany are not available for the years before 1991, to cover a sufficiently long time period, we have had to restrict the analysis to West German regions. Berlin, which was an island within the former GDR for most of the period under consideration, has been excluded from the analysis.

2 The striking advantage of this concept of regional disaggregation vis-à-vis the concept of planning regions (*Raumordnungsregionen*) developed by the *Bundesanstalt für Landeskunde und Raumordnung* (now *Bundesamt für Bauwesen und Raumordnung*, BBR) is that regions have been defined irrespective of borders of the *Bundesländer*. See Bode (1998) for details.

3 See the Appendix for a more detailed description of the variables used throughout this chapter.

been tested for using Moran's I tests, and several tests based on the Lagrange-Multiplier (LM) principle which are offered by the software package SPACESTAT (see Anselin 1988, 1995; Anselin and Florax 1995 for methodological details). Seven different spatial weight matrices have been specified for each test. Tests for homoscedasticity and parameter stability are based on the usual F-statistics (referred to as FH and FS) which compare sums of squared residuals of subsamples of regions.

Three possible sources of heteroscedasticity and parameter instability have been tested for by appropriate definitions of subsamples: (i) the 29 agglomerations are compared to the 46 peripheral regions to identify differences resulting from the density of population and economic activity (subsequently referred to by A⇔P), (ii) 40 northern German regions are compared to 35 regions in the south to identify differences resulting from the German north-south divide in economic activity and prosperity (see Soltwedel 1986) (N⇔S), and (iii) 33 'poor' regions with per-capita income below the national average in 1976 are compared to 42 'rich' regions to identify differences resulting from per-capita income levels (P⇔R).

Regression Results

Estimating (3.4) by OLS produces highly unreliable estimates because the basic assumptions of the OLS method are violated (Table 3.1). First, the test statistics indicate highly significant spatial autocorrelation and lag dependence among neighbouring regions.[1] Second, F-tests indicate heteroscedasticity between agglomerations and peripheral regions (A⇔P), which is also highly significant ($p<0.01$). The residual variance of agglomerations (adjusted for degrees of freedom) is nearly twice that of peripheral regions. Third, the tests indicate significant parameter instability between northern and southern German regions (N⇔S). Obviously, the regression model (3.4) is misspecified. Neither are the residuals i.i.d. nor are the parameters C and δ constant across regions.

There may be several reasons for the misspecification. Autocorrelation and spatial lag dependence indicate that there are significant economic ties between neighbouring regions, possibly because of interregional knowledge spillovers, or, more generally, because of spillovers of growth impulses. Parameter instability indicates that the intensity of localised knowledge spillovers differs between regions and that income growth is driven by factors other than R&D, such as agglomeration economies and diseconomies, which have not been incorporated into the theory.

---

[1] Table 3.1 reports only the test which produces the lowest prob-value, i.e. indicating autocorrelation with the highest probability. 'Prob' is the probability of erroneously rejecting the H_0 of no autocorrelation. As a rule of thumb, a prob-value lower than 5% indicates that there is a significant influence (e.g. autocorrelation).

Table 3.1 Test of the basic growth model[a]

Variable	Estimate		Prob
C	0.29		0.00
RDDENS	-0.02		0.14
R^2(adj.)		0.02	
SSR		0.48	
F	2.20		0.14
Spatial autocorrelation (lowest prob.)[b]	5.80		0.00
Spatial lag dependence (lowest prob.)[b]	26.25		0.00
Homoscedasticity (FH)[c]		A⇔P	
Parameter stability (FS)[c]		N⇔S	

[a] Cross-section OLS regression, 75 West German regions. Dependent variable: growth rate of real per capita income 1976-1994.
[b] Lowest error probability of several test statistics (Moran's I, LM-tests) assuming different spatial weights matrices.
[c] Entries refer only to tests that reject the H_0 of homoscedasticity, or parameter stability, respectively, at the 5% level.
Source: own calculations.

3.3 Extended Growth Model

Since the currently available theoretical literature on (regional) economic growth has paid little attention to analysing the growth effects of factors other than R&D, such as diseconomies of agglomeration, or to opening the 'black box of innovation' (Aghion and Tirole 1994), we have to use information provided by the recent empirical literature on growth determinants, and the intensity of localised knowledge spillovers. In the next section we will make use of this information by assuming that growth theory explains only part of the whole story of regional economic growth, and by modifying the basic growth model to allow for systematic regional differences in R&D productivity. The resulting empirical model is tested again using the same regional disaggregation and time horizon as before.

Outline of the Model

Sources of regional differences in R&D productivity: The most simple theoretical approach to allow for regional differences in R&D productivity within the basic growth model is to assume the region-specific public knowledge to accumulate not on a one-to-one basis with the number of innovations, but on a $(1+\psi_r)$-to-one basis. Equation (3.2), the 'production function' of the local public good, then reads:

$$Q_{rt} = \left(1+\psi_r\right)N_{rt} = \left(1+\psi_r\right)\sum_{\tau=-\infty}^{t}\dot{N}_{r\tau}, \qquad r = 1, ..., R, \tag{3.5}$$

yielding the region-specific innovation rate:

$$\hat{N}_r = \delta_r H_{Nr} = \delta(1+\psi_r)H_{Nr} \tag{3.6}$$

where $(1+\psi_r) \geq 0$ is the region-specific parameter of the intensity of localised knowledge spillovers. It determines the level rather than the growth rate of the knowledge stock. $-1 \leq \psi_r < 0$ indicates positive but incomplete knowledge diffusion, at $\psi_r = 0$ the model is identical with the basic model, and $\psi_r > 0$ may result from knowledge spillovers from external sources like universities in addition to spillovers among industrial researchers. This simple modification allows for some more flexibility while Romer's (1990) crucial assumption of constant returns to scale with respect to publicly available knowledge and the properties of steady-state equilibrium remain unchanged.

One source of regional differences in R&D productivity, suggested by empirical investigations by Bröcker (1989), Glaeser *et al.* (1992), Henderson *et al.* (1995), Bode (1998), Büttner (1999), and Kelly and Hageman (1999), is sectoral or technological specialisation.[1] They have found evidence in favour of inter-industry knowledge spillovers generally fostering regional growth more than spillovers within industries. Following these authors, we assume a measure of sectoral concentration of R&D employment in manufacturing industry (*RDCONC*) to be an element of ψ_r. A second source of regional differences in R&D productivity may be spillovers from universities. Basic research at universities may produce new knowledge that adds to the publicly available knowledge stock in their neighborhood. These spillovers are described statistically by the number of scientific posts at universities and *Fachhochschulen* (*URES*).[2]

Other growth determinants: To allow for additional growth determinants other than R&D, we assume the constant term and the residual in equation (3.4) to be a function of additional explanatory variables **X** and an i.i.d. error term ε, i.e.

$$C_r + e_r = \beta \mathbf{X}_r + \varepsilon_r, \qquad \varepsilon_r \sim \mathrm{N}(0, \sigma^2_\varepsilon) \tag{3.7}$$

Since a stringent and comprehensive theoretical assessment of growth determinants is lacking, it is hard to identify the main factors, other than R&D,

---

[1] For a theoretical analysis of tax-financed government research within a Romer-type model see Park (1998). Empirical evidence on the positive impact of public on private research have been provided, among others, by Herden (1992), Reinhard and Schmalholz (1996), Jaffe (1989), Audretsch and Stephan (1996), Anselin *et al.* (1997), and Bode (1998).

[2] In addition, regional differences in R&D productivity may result from productivity differences between industries and technologies which translate, via regionally varying specialisation patterns, into differences in aggregate regional productivities. However, since data sufficiently disaggregated by sector or technology are not available for German regions, this source of productivity differences cannot be accounted for in the present investigation.

driving income growth. To solve this problem we have specified a large number of potential indicators based on a wide variety of available statistical information. Applying appropriate selection routines, we then have selected those variables that appeared to have a statistically significant impact on growth. These variables are: population density (*POPDENS*) and its log (ln*POPDENS*), the share of manufacturing industries in overall regional employment (*MANSH*), the degree of specialisation of the region's manufacturing industries on the production of goods (*PRODSH*), the growth rate of overall regional employment (*EMPGR*), and the share of scientific personnel at universities in total regional workforce (*UNIV*).[1] Of course, such a selection procedure does not allow clear-cut conclusions to be drawn about the economic forces behind the explanatory variables. Based on plausibility, however, the results may give some indication of what kinds of economic forces are at work.

Because of the lack of a consistent and comprehensive theoretical base, it is of utmost importance to carefully analyse the properties of the regression residuals and parameters. In particular, the sources of spatial dependence (autocorrelation and/or lag dependence) have had to be explored. Since the test statistics do not, per se, allow clear-cut decisions about the true nature of underlying spatial dependences, some test regressions have been necessary.[2] These regressions, which are not reported here in detail, have suggested that the spatial inferences result from spatial lag dependence but not from spatial autocorrelation.[3] Thus, a spatially lagged endogenous variable has had to be introduced which, in general, is the weighted average of per capita income growth rates of neighbouring regions, that is:

$$lagged\ dependent_r = \mathbf{W}\hat{\mathbf{y}}_r \tag{3.8}$$

With respect to the spatial weight matrix $\mathbf{W}$ defining the spatial structure and intensity of interdependences we have tested various specifications. Although several different matrices have been successful in removing both autocorrelation and lag dependence, the best fit obtains with a matrix $\mathbf{W}_y$ that takes into consideration income growth rates of all regions belonging to the same *Bundesland* (or the same *Bundesländer*) as the respective region, weighted by their relative real per-capita income in 1976. In other words, the lagged dependent

---

[1] A more detailed description of the variables is given in the Appendix to this chapter.

[2] In fact, the tests may indicate spatial autocorrelation although spatial lag dependence prevails, and vice versa.

[3] To test, first, whether interregional knowledge spillovers from universities, and from manufacturing researchers are responsible for spatial autocorrelation in the basic model we have specified potential variables like those used by Bode (2001). They have removed neither spatial autocorrelation nor spatial lag dependence. Second, a spatial error model has removed autocorrelation but not spatial lag dependence, according to the respective test statistics. Moreover, the common-factor hypothesis (see Anselin 1988) has been rejected suggesting that the spatial error model is misspecified. Details are available from the author upon request.

variable producing the best fit is virtually the growth rate of the *Bundesland* the region belongs to, excluding the respective region itself.

Summing up, the empirical specification to test the extended growth model has been obtained by substituting into (3.4) the determinants of $\delta_r = \delta\,(1+\psi_r)$, and of C_r+e_r, and by assuming a linear functional form:

$$\begin{aligned}\hat{y}_r &= C + \delta\, RDDENS_r \\ &+\delta\alpha_1\, RDCONC_r \cdot RDDENS_r + \delta\alpha_2\, URES_r \cdot RDDENS_r \\ &+\beta_1\, POPDENS_r + \beta_2 \ln(POPDENS_r) + \beta_3\, MANSH_r \\ &+\beta_4\, PRODSH_r + \beta_5\, EMPGR_r + \beta_6\, UNIV_r \\ &+ \beta_7\, lagged\ dependent_r + \varepsilon_r,\end{aligned} \tag{3.9}$$

where $\varepsilon_r \sim N(0, \sigma^2_\varepsilon)$, and $r=1, ..., 75$.[1]

Regression Results

The regression results for the extended model (3.9) shown in Table 3.2 reveal that heteroscedasticity and parameter instability have been removed by the modification.[2] The probabilities of erroneously rejecting the hypotheses of homoscedasticity and parameter stability are far above the critical 5 percent level. The same holds for spatial autocorrelation.

With respect to the parameter estimates R&D employment (*RDDENS*) now shows a highly significant positive impact on income growth, as is hypothesised by the growth model. The error probability (prob-value) is below 0.1 per cent. The point estimate of 0.28 indicates that, over the 18-year period, a region with two researchers per km² has *ceteris paribus* grown some 28 percent, or about 1.4 percentage points annually, faster than a region with only one researcher per km². However, the impact of R&D on growth appears to depend heavily on the intensity of localised knowledge spillovers. First, the estimated negative parameter of *RDCONC* which is also significantly different from zero both individually and jointly with the parameter of *RDDENS*, indicates that knowledge spillovers seem to be much less intense in regions which are specialised in only a few technologies, or industries, than in regions with a diversified R&D landscape.

---

1 Equation (3.9) has to be estimated by Maximum Likelihood instead of OLS because OLS produces inconsistent estimates in the presence of a lagged dependent variable (Anselin 1988, p. 55 f.).

2 It has, however, been necessary to neutralise an obvious outlier, Fulda, by a dummy *DUM(FD)*. In spite of various attempts we did not succeed to explain this region's income growth to a similar extent than those of other regions.

Table 3.2 Tests of the extended growth model[a]

Variable	Parameter	Estimate	Prob
C		−1.42	0.000
RDDENS	δ	0.28	0.000
RDCONC[b]	$\delta\alpha_1$	−0.27	0.000
URES[b]	$\delta\alpha_2$	2.6E−3	0.000
POPDENS	β_1	−1.0E−3	0.000
ln(*POPDENS*)	β_2	0.18	0.000
MANSH	β_3	−0.35	0.000
PRODSH	β_4	1.29	0.000
EMPGR	β_5	0.34	0.000
UNIV	β_6	19.19	0.012
Lagged dependent ($\mathbf{W}_y$)	β_7	0.31	0.005
DUM(*FD*)	β_8	0.29	0.000
ln L		103.09	
pseudo R^2		0.68	
SSR[c]		0.28	
Spatial autocorrelation (LM; lowest prob.)		1.00	0.317
Homoscedasticity (Breusch-Pagan)		5.79	0.833
Parameter stability (LR-test; lowest prob.)		14.59	0.148

[a] Cross-section Maximum Likelihood regressions, 75 West German regions. Dependent variable: growth rate of real per capita income 1976-1994.
[b] Multiplied by *RDDENS*. [c] Sum of Squared Residuals.
Source: own calculations.

The parameter α_1, which is estimated to be almost −1 (−0.27/0.28), indicates that intra-industry spillovers play only a minor role.[1] Second, the estimated growth effects of (intra-regional) university spillovers are significantly positive, indicating that, ceteris paribus, academic research at universities does contribute to the regional knowledge accumulation.

As far as additional growth determinants are concerned, both population density (*POPDENS*) and its log (ln*POPDENS*) appear to have a significant impact on income growth, but with different signs. The most plausible economic force explaining this relationship is urbanisation economies and diseconomies.[2]

---

[1] Although this result is intuitively plausible if we take into account that major technological innovations in the past decades, e.g. in biotechnology or microelectronics, have been achieved by combining different technologies, it does, of course, not preclude positive externalities resulting from the location of single industries, with respect to technologies. However, the Silicon Valleys or Route 128s seem to have been the exception rather than the rule in Germany.

[2] Although many authors suggest urbanisation economies and diseconomies to be indicated statistically by absolute population (e.g. Glaeser 1998) population density is a more

Simulations reveal that the combined growth effect of both variables takes the usual inversely U-shaped functional form. It is estimated to be positive over the whole range of actually observed regional population densities (60-1,000 inhabitants per km²), i.e. that urbanisation economies dominate the respective diseconomies.

The next two variables for which significant growth effects have been estimated are *MANSH*, the share of manufacturing industries in total regional workforce, and *PRODSH*, the share of (blue-collar) production workers within manufacturing. While the negative parameter of *MANSH* indicates that high specialisation on manufacturing industries seems to deter growth,[1] the positive parameter of *PRODSH* indicates that specialisation by these industries on the manufacturing of goods (instead of in-house services) seems to dilute the negative sectoral effect. One possible explanation may be that a region's growth performance does not simply depend on the progress it made in the course of structural change at the sectoral level, i.e. from manufacturing to service industries. It also depends on the progress the industries made in organisational change, i.e. through outsourcing out service provision, thereby concentrating on core competences in manufacturing of goods.

The growth rate of regional employment (*EMPGR*), which controls for variations of factor inputs during the period under consideration, and (iv) the share of scientific personnel at universities in the total regional workforce (*UNIV*), which may be attributed to local multiplier effects of universities resulting from the demand by universities, their personnel, and their students for local goods and services, also seem to have a positive impact on regional income growth. Finally, the significantly positive parameter of the lagged dependent variable, which is the growth rate of per-capita income in the *Bundesland* the region belongs to, may suggest that, firstly, there are substantial growth spillovers between neighbouring regions, and, secondly, that *Bundesland*-specific economic policies may affect income growth in the regions.

3.4 Summary and Conclusions

Empirical evidence based on a cross-section of 75 West German regions in the period 1976-1994 indicates that there is a positive impact of R&D on regional income growth, as has been hypothesised by Romer-type models of endogenous

---

appropriate indicator where agglomerations are compared to peripheral regions. No one would expect a geographically big, but sparsely settled peripheral region to exhibit the same extent of urbanisation economies as a densely settled city region just because both have the same number of inhabitants.

[1] Of course, there are significant differences in growth performance between different industries depending, inter alia, on income elasticities of their products, or the speed of technical progress. This heterogeneity, however, is hard to account for to a sufficient extent at the aggregate level. The employment share of mature industries (agriculture, mining, steel, textiles, shipbuilding), e.g., did not show an unambiguously significant impact on income growth.

growth, where growth is driven mainly by knowledge creation and spillovers. However, regional differences in the sources and intensities of knowledge spillovers have to be controlled for. Our results suggest that geographical proximity to universities enhances productivity of R&D in manufacturing industries, and that inter-industry spillovers are more intensive and more productivity-enhancing than intra-industry spillovers. The exchange and combination of knowledge about different technologies appears, in general, to be more fruitful than the exchange of knowledge about similar technologies. Moreover, additional determinants of regional growth other than R&D have to be controlled for. Urbanisation economies, for example, have been found to significantly affect regional growth, at least in the medium-term of about two decades.

Given the state-of-the-art in growth-theoretic modelling, however, the results of an empirical investigation like the present one have to be taken as preliminary. There are still some 'black boxes' left in the underlying theoretical model. An empirical assessment of the effects of knowledge spillovers on R&D productivity and regional income growth must necessarily to some extent be *ad hoc* since theory has not yet provided a consistent and comprehensive analysis of the determinants and intensities of knowledge spillovers. The multiplicity of factors other than R&D driving regional growth cannot be assessed convincingly unless theory provides at least some ideas on plausible interrelationships between the different determinants and income growth. Hopefully, future theoretical research on regional growth will extend endogenous growth models to strengthen the theoretical back-bone of future empirical work on the determinants of innovation and growth.

Acknowledgements

The author wishes to thank Franz-Josef Bade, Frank Bickenbach, Gerd Hansen, Lars Kumkar, Horst Siebert, and Rüdiger Soltwedel for their helpful comments. Financial support from the Deutsche Forschungsgesellschaft is also gratefully acknowledged.

Appendix

A.1 Definitions of variables

$\hat{y}_r$ growth rate of regional per capita income (real gross value added per inhabitant), calculated as $\hat{y}_r = \ln y_{r,1994} - \ln y_{r,1976}$. Source: public statistics held by the *Bundesländer*.

$RDDENS_r$ R&D density, indicated by the number of engineers, natural scientists, and mathematicians with academic education employed in manufacturing industries per square kilometre. Source: public social security insurance statistics.

$RDCONC_r$ sectoral concentration of R&D employment, calculated as the share of researchers in the two manufacturing industries (out of 33) in the region's total R&D employment in manufacturing that had the highest absolute numbers of researchers in 1976. Source: public social security insurance statistics.

$URES_r$ spillovers from universities, approximated by the absolute number of scientific posts at universities and *Fachhochschulen* (divided by 1,000) in 1976. Source: *Wissenschaftsrat.*

$POPDENS_r$ population density, indicated by the number of inhabitants per square kilometre in 1976. Source: public statistics held by the *Bundesländer*.

$MANSH_r$ specialisation on manufacturing industries, approximated by the share of manufacturing industries in the region's total employment in 1976. Source: public social security insurance statistic.

$PRODSH_r$ specialisation in manufacturing production, approximated by the share of blue-collar workers in production, stock-holding and distribution in total manufacturing employment in 1976. Source: public social security insurance statistics.

$EMPGR_r$ growth rate of total regional employment 1976-1994. Source: public social security insurance statistics.

$UNIV_r$ multiplicator effects of universities, approximated by the share of scientific posts at universities and *Fachhochschulen* in total regional employment. Source: *Wissenschaftsrat.*

A.2 Descriptive statistics

Table A.1 Descriptive statistics

Variable	Mean	StdDev	Minimum	Maximum
$\hat{y}$	0.33	0.11	0.06	0.70
RDDENS	0.65	0.89	0.03	3.81
RDCONC[a]	0.57	0.14	0.31	0.98
URES[a]	2.63	6.89	0	41.08
POPDENS	238.87	187.07	73.54	1015.70
ln(*POPDENS*)	5.27	0.61	4.30	6.92
MANSH	0.43	0.10	0.22	0.63
PRODSH	0.72	0.05	0.57	0.80
EMPGR	0.19	0.12	-0.12	0.46
UNIV	8.9E-4	1.1E-3	0.00	4.2E-3

[a] Multiplied by *RDDENS*.
Source: own calculations.

Table A.2 Pearson correlation coefficients[a]

	RDDENS	*RDCONC*	*URES*	*POPDENS*	ln(*POPDENS*)	*MANSH*	*PRODSH*	*EMPGR*	*UNIV*
RDDENS	1	0.20	0.57	0.84	0.81	0.08	-0.75	-0.40	0.28
	0	0.09	0.00	0.00	0.00	0.50	0.00	0.00	0.02
RDCONC		1	0.03	-0.05	0.01	0.16	-0.16	0.04	0.09
		0	0.78	0.70	0.90	0.17	0.17	0.72	0.44
URES			1	0.48	0.50	-0.21	-0.64	-0.18	0.41
			0	0.00	0.00	0.07	0.00	0.12	0.00
POPDENS				1	0.93	-0.03	-0.60	-0.54	0.30
				0	0.00	0.80	0.00	0.00	0.01
ln(*POPDENS*)					1	-0.01	-0.69	-0.60	0.40
					0	0.96	0.00	0.00	0.00
MANSH						1	0.19	-0.11	-0.23
						0	0.10	0.35	0.04
PRODSH							1	0.36	-0.42
							0	0.00	0.00
EMPGR								1	-0.11
								0	0.34
UNIV									1
									0

[a] Prob-values below the correlation coefficients.
Source: own calculations.

References

Aghion, P., Howitt, P. (1992) A Model of Growth Through Creative Destruction. Econometrica 60(2), 323-351

Aghion, P., Tirole, J. (1994) Opening the Black Box of Innovation. European. Economic Review 38(3), 701-710

Anselin, L. (1988) Spatial Econometrics: Methods and Models. Kluwer, Dordrecht

Anselin, L. (1995) SpaceStat V. 1.80 User's Guide

Anselin, L., Florax, R.J. (eds.) (1995) New Directions in Spatial Econometrics. Springer, Berlin

Anselin, L., Varga, A., Acs, Z. (1997) Local Geographic Spillovers Between University Research and High Technology Innovations. Journal of Urban Economics 42(3), 422-448

Audretsch, D.B., Stephan, P.E. (1996) Company-Scientist Locational Links: The Case of Biotechnology. American Economic Review 86(3), 641-652

Bode, E. (1998) Lokale Wissensdiffusion und regionale Divergenz in Deutschland. Kieler Studien 293. Mohr, Tübingen

Bode, E. (2001) Is Regional Innovative Activity Path-dependent? An Empirical Analysis for Germany. Kiel Working Paper 1058. Kiel Institute of World Economy

Bröcker, J. (1989) Determinanten des regionalen Wachstums im sekundären und tertiären Sektor der Bundesrepublik Deutschland 1970–1982. Florentz, Munich

Büttner, T. (1999) Agglomeration, Growth, and Adjustment. ZEW Economic Studies, Heidelberg

Cheshire, P.C., Carbonaro, G. (1996) Urban Economic Growth in Europe: Testing Theory and Policy Prescriptions. Urban Studies 33(7), 1111-1128

Glaeser, E.L. (1998) Are Cities Dying? Journal of Economic Perspectives 12(2) 139-160

Glaeser, E.L., Kallal, H.D., Sheinkman J.A., Shleifer, A. (1992) Growth in Cities. Journal of Political Economy 100(6), 1126-1152

Griliches, Z. (1992) The Search for R&D Spillovers. Scandinavian Journal of Economics 94 (Suppl.), 29-47

Henderson, J.V., Kuncoro, A., Turner, M. (1995) Industrial Development in Cities. Journal of Political Economy 103(5), 1067-1090

Herden, R. (1992) Technologieorientierte Außenbeziehungen im betrieblichen Innovationsmanagement. Physica Verlag, Heidelberg

Hirschman, A.O. (1958) The Strategy of Economic Development. Yale University Press, New Haven Conn.

Jaffe, A.B. (1989) Real Effects of Academic Research. American Economic Review 79(5), 957-970

Kaldor, N. (1970) The Case for Regional Policy. Scottish Journal of Political Economy 17, 337-348

Kelly, M., Hageman, A. (1999) Marshallian Externalities in Innovation. Journal of Economic Growth 4(1), 39-54

Myrdal, G. (1957) Economic Theory and Underdeveloped Regions. Duckworth, London

Park, W.G. (1998) A Theoretical Model of Government Research and Growth. Journal of Economic Behaviour and Organization 34(1), 69-85

Reinhard, M., Schmalholz, H. (1996) Technologietransfer in Deutschland: Stand und Reformbedarf. Duncker & Humblodt, Berlin

Romer, P.M. (1990). Endogenous Technological Change. Journal of Political Economy 98(5), 71-102

Soltwedel, R. (1986) Süd-Nord-Gefälle – Signal für politischen Handlungsbedarf? In: von Voss, R., Friedrich, K. (eds.), Das Süd-Nord-Gefälle. Bonn Aktuell, Stuttgart

4 Spatial Structural Change: Evidence and Prospects

Franz-Josef Bade[1], Annekatrin Niebuhr[2] and Matthias Schönert[3]
[1] Faculty of Spatial Planning, Dept. of Economics, University of Dortmund
[2] HWWA Hamburg Institute of International Economics
[3] BAW Bremen Institute for Economic Research

4.1 Introduction

According to the results of one current report on European regional prospects (ERECO 1997), convergence cannot be expected in Europe. This conclusion is significant for two reasons. Firstly, it belongs to a growing number of recent studies (see Irmen and Blach 1997; Klemmer 1996; Stahl 1997) which give a somewhat pessimistic assessment concerning the further development of regional disparities, after a period of predominantly optimistic appraisals (e.g. Seitz 1995). The special issue of the journal Regional Studies ('Regional Futures' 1997, Vol. 31.5) can also be classed with these rather critical opinions of the prospects of convergence. In their introductory survey the editors point out that a (further) reduction of regional differences in economic performance is unlikely to occur (Asheim and Dunford 1997). The analysis of Fagerberg and Vespagen (1996), Fagerberg *et al.* (1997) provides corresponding evidence. They conclude that regional disparities – after a decrease in the 1970s – have recently stopped declining.

Secondly, the change in expectations has accompanied a change of focus. Whereas earlier studies were mainly concerned with regional differences in employment growth, recent investigations focus on regional convergence of per capita income. However, the indicators do not necessarily lead to the same inference: the ratio income per capita is influenced by changes in both numerator and denominator. Therefore, "the same statistical rate of productivity growth can in fact be the outcome of very different processes" (Camagni and Cappellin 1984, p. 154).

Although the ambivalent interpretation of per capita income is quite well-known in development theory (e.g. Nohlen and Nuscheler 1992), its critical importance has rarely been acknowledged in the recent debate on regional convergence. One of the few exceptions is the study of Blanchard and Katz (1992). They show that dynamic regions in the US with an above average growth of employment and income only achieve corresponding increases of per capita income with a certain time lag. If income and employment evolve in the same direction, the ensuing variation of income per capita must inevitably be smaller than the change of income overall. In contrast, the change of income per capita will exceed the overall change of income, if denominator and numerator of the ratio move in opposite directions. Consequently, analysing solely per capita income tends to underestimate the success of dynamic regions, whereas it overestimates the economic growth of declining regions if decreases of employment are greater than those of income (see Cuadrado-Roura *et al.* 1997 for corresponding evidence for Europe).

A further limitation of previous studies concerns the reliability of conclusions about future convergence or divergence tendencies. Most convergence studies are based on cross-sectional analysis including only a few points in time (e.g. Sala-i-Martin 1996; Seitz 1995). Frequently the long-term growth path of a region is entirely determined by the comparison of two observations.[1] The dynamic phenomenon of economic growth is condensed to an average rate of change that implies a constant slope of each region's time trend. Consequently, neither the direction of change nor its stability can be thoroughly investigated (Quah 1993). Thus, Carlino and Mills, in contrast to the above-mentioned scepticism about regional disparities, conclude that "cross-sectional studies generally offer evidence in support of convergence, whereas time-series studies find the opposite to be true" (Carlino and Mills 1996, p. 598).

The intention of the following analysis is to remedy these deficiencies and derive precise conclusions on the stability of spatial structural change in general and on the development of agglomerations and rural areas in particular. The present study differs from previous analyses in several respects and uses an alternative approach to provide evidence on regional disparities and their prospective development.

First, instead of investigating convergence of per capita income, we analyse employment and income separately. Our belief is that in order to achieve reliable results a detailed analysis of both indicators seems to be more appropriate. To take adequately into account the dynamics of regional growth paths, the analysis is based on time-series for these indicators from 1976 to 1996. However, due to this long period, the data is limited to West Germany.

Second, in order to provide a comprehensive assessment of the future development of regional disparities, a forward-looking indicator has been included as well. We use human capital as an indicator for regional growth prospects, because the regional stock of human capital is commonly considered as a central precondition for successful development – particularly with regard to rapid technological change.

The rest of the paper is organised as follows. Section 4.2 provides a brief survey of empirical evidence on regional disparities. Deficiencies of previous findings and reasons for the still controversial debate on regional disparities are discussed. In Section 4.3, the central tendencies of spatial structural change in West Germany

---

[1] Rare exceptions are the studies of Carlino and Mills (1996), Canova and Marcet (1995) or Tondl (1997).

are examined. We propose a distinct methodology in order to remedy existing shortcomings. Applied methods, data sets and the regional system are described. We firstly focus on the quantitative aspects of spatial structural change, determining the main trends in regional income and employment growth and discussing their stability. By comparing the spatial growth tendencies of both variables, conclusions with respect to regional development of income per capita are derived. We then consider the regional growth process from a forward-looking perspective. Regional development of human capital is analysed with the purpose of providing a broader basis for an evaluation of future growth paths. Finally, in Section 4.4, we give a summary of the results derived and discuss the implications for the further development of regional disparities in West Germany.

4.2 Spatial Structural Change – Empirical Evidence

Most studies investigating the spatial distribution of economic activity in Germany are restricted to employment data. Although they differ widely in the methods and database used, they generally come to the same conclusion, that rural-peripheral regions are favoured by the long-term changes in spatial structure (e.g. Bade 1987; Peschel and Bröcker 1990). As in other industrialised countries (Keeble 1986; Frey 1993; Molle 1997), the urban agglomerations in Germany achieved far less economic success than would be expected on account of the repeatedly quoted agglomeration economies, as anticipated in the concerns cited above.[1]

Spatial deconcentration of economic activity takes place on two levels, analogous to the different scale of the processes referred to as suburbanisation and disurbanisation.[2] *Suburbanisation* involves small-scale changes inside agglomerations, i.e. when the urban fringe clearly develops more favourably than the centre of the agglomeration (e.g. Gatzweiler and Schliebe 1982; Bucher and Kocks 1987; Bade 1987, 1991; Seitz 1996). The densely populated agglomeration cores tend to attain the lowest employment growth of all spatial categories. Suburbanisation is not restricted to the large agglomerations. These small-scale shifts of economic weight can be observed for other cities in Germany too. However, in these areas the intra-regional differences in growth rates are weaker (Irmen and Blach 1994).

Disurbanisation of economic activity has been observed since the 1960s. This large-scale process of deconcentration is characterised by a negative correlation between a region's degree of density and growth (see Uebe 1967; Hoppen 1979; Nieth 1980; Peschel 1983). The unfavourable development of urban agglomerations as a whole results in their having a declining share of national economic activity – despite the high growth rates of the urban fringe. All studies

---

1 For a discussion of the relative advantages of agglomerations in the course of structural change see e.g. Gaebe (1987, 199-205) or Bade (1997, 248-249).

2 To distinguish the processes of spatial deconcentration several terms such as 'counterurbanisation' (Berry 1964) are employed. A survey of the various definitions is provided by Gaebe (1987) or Irmen and Blach (1994).

provide evidence of a slow, but nevertheless definite decrease in spatial concentration. However, disurbanisation cannot (alone) be explained by suburbanisation and the spatial expansion of agglomerations. Firstly, the distance between some of the particularly dynamic regions and the agglomerations is too large. Secondly, the regions located in the direct neighbourhood of agglomerations often achieve only modest growth rates (Bade 1987, 1991).

Despite these undeniably positive findings for rural regions, their growth prospects are now, as ever, the subject of a controversial discussion. This is to some extent due to the theoretically based supposition that in recent years general economic conditions have changed to the detriment of rural regions, e.g. as a consequence of establishing the common market, the opening up of East European countries and the progressive international division of labour (see e.g. Klemmer 1996; Stahl 1997; Irmen and Blach 1997).

Moreover this uncertainty about the further development of regional disparities has empirical causes. It is in part due to neglect in using forward-looking variables like human capital, though in some studies the spatial structure of this indicator is analysed. In these studies human capital is usually measured by the educational level of employees or R&D employment. Summarising the results of previous studies, the spatial structure of human capital is characterised by a significant centre-periphery differential. With the increasing agglomeration of a region, the share of highly skilled labour or R&D employees in total employment rises. Compared with agglomerated regions, rural areas are poorly endowed with human capital (Recker and Schütte 1982, Müller 1984; Bade 1987; Pliquett 1988; Legler 1994; Gehrke and Legler 1998; ZEW *et al.* 2000).

Far more uncertain are the findings concerning the *development* of these disparities. Uncertainty exists in two respects. First, the conclusions drawn are not unambiguous – some authors expect a deepening of disparities (e.g. Böltken *et al.* 1988; Beise *et al.* 1999), others suppose that the spatial concentration of human capital will decline (e.g. Franck 1995; Bade 1997). Second, the uncertainty is once more caused by the restricted empirical basis. The majority of studies are limited to just a few observations for the cross-sectional data set.[1] The consequences for the reliability of conclusions – especially with regard to regional growth prospects – have already been mentioned above.

The intention of the present paper is to remedy the uncertainty about regional growth prospects by providing comprehensive evidence on the central tendencies of spatial structural change in Germany. Furthermore, human capital as a forward-looking indicator is analysed in order to supply additional information on the future development of regional disparities.

---

[1] The analysis of human capital on a regional level is usually limited to one or two observations.

4.3 Central Tendencies in Spatial Structural Change

Data and Regional System

The basis of the empirical study is a combination of three data sources, and has allowed a comprehensive time-series analysis of regional development in West Germany between 1976 and 1996. To investigate the quantitative aspects of spatial development all available data sources were used, including:

- Official estimates of regional employment from the *Arbeitskreis "Erwerbstätigenrechnung des Bundes und der Länder"* for 1980 and 1987-1994.
- Regional data on gross value added from the national accounts of the German *Länder* for 1980, 1990 and 1992.
- Regional employment covered by the social insurance system (about 80% of all employment) and the regional sum of wages and salaries from German employment statistics, annual data for 1976 until 1996.

Time-series for entire regional employment and gross value added were generated by calculating the observations missing from official data, using the corresponding annual information from the employment statistic (see Bade and Niebuhr 1999 for a detailed description of the estimation method).

The analysis of regional human capital is based on data from the German employment statistic. In addition to the availability of annual data, the employment statistic possesses the advantage that the data set is differentiated for level of education as well as for the occupation of the employees (see Bade and Schönert 1997). So the employment statistic allows consistent time-series analysis of both forward-looking variables – highly skilled labour and R&D employment – from 1976 to 1996.

Special emphasis has been given to large-scale changes in spatial structure. Therefore the following description focuses on the development of spatial categories. The findings presented are restricted to the comparison of the corresponding growth paths, although we are aware of the fact that individual development in these spatial categories is not homogenous. But the conclusions derived below are not affected by this limitation. Detailed results for selected regions are provided in Bade and Schönert (1997), Bade and Niebuhr (1999), Niebuhr (1999) and Schönert (2000). The analysis of central tendencies in regional development is based on a division into four spatial categories according to the criteria location and density. The starting points of this regional system are the large urban agglomerations in West Germany[1], partitioned into agglomeration centre and urban fringe. By means of this subdivision, shifts in economic weight

[1] Due to the long-term character of the study, the analysis is restricted to West Germany. For East Germany, in view of the transformation process, the required data sets are not available, nor could a time-series analysis provide reasonable conclusions.

between core and fringe of agglomerations can be recorded. The area outside the agglomerations comprises the peripheral regions, which are characterised by an unfavourable location and an extremely low population density. The remaining regions outside the agglomerations are designated as low density regions.

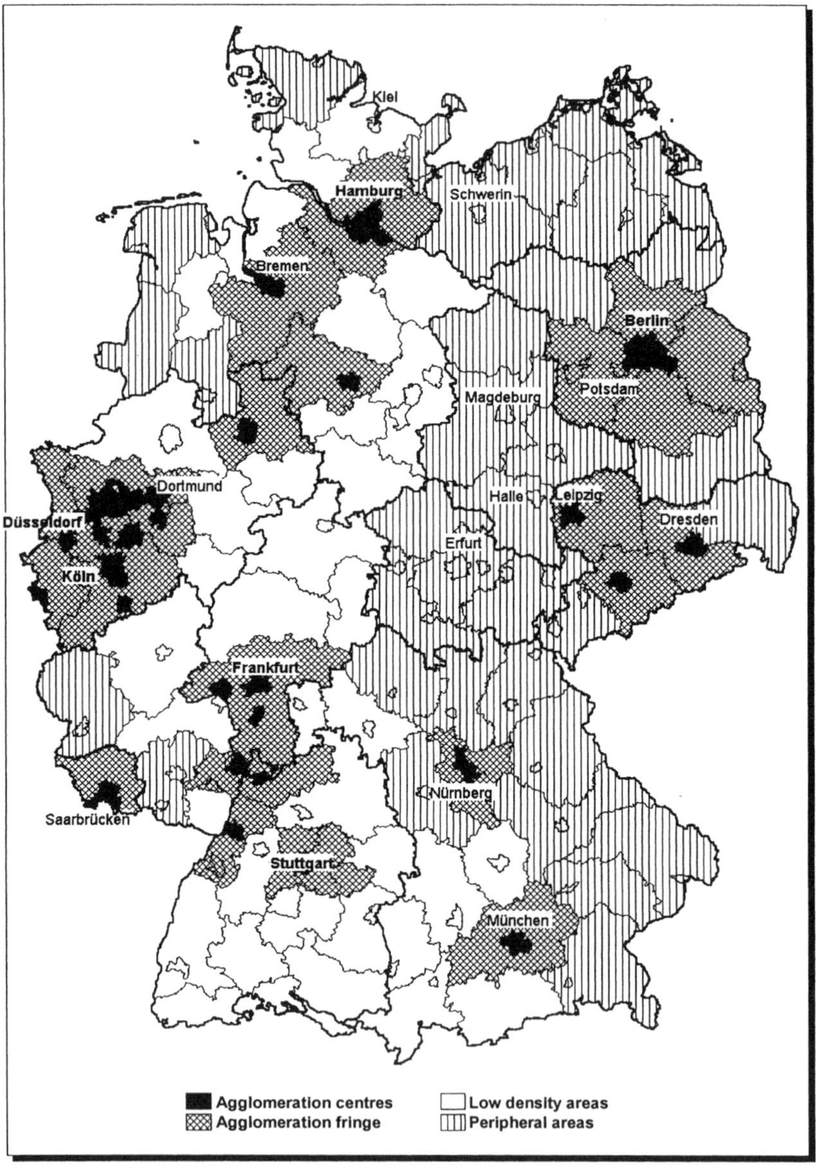

Fig. 4.1 Spatial categories

The data set permits a time-series study of regional development based on several indicators. Thus the analysis offers a comprehensive insight into the past and future dynamics of spatial structural change. We concentrate on the relative development of spatial categories, i.e. on regional growth paths in relation to the national average. Hence, general effects like cyclical fluctuations are excluded. They affect the whole economy and all regions in roughly the same manner. However, in this study, spatial particularities are the focus of interest. Development relative to the national average coincides with the change of regional share in the entire (national) amount of the indicator considered.

The Quantitative Perspective – Employment and Income

Fig. 4.2 provides a first insight into the development and stability of spatial structural change in West Germany. In order to provide an impression of the long-term tendencies, employment data from earlier *Arbeitsstättenzählungen* have been utilised. Employment growth since 1961 is characterised by obvious differences between spatial categories. Both the urban fringe and peripheral regions have achieved an employment increase of roughly 30 percent since the early 1960s. When the structural change of employment is considered, the agglomeration centres are unambiguously on the losing side. In these core areas the number of employed persons declined by 20 percent.

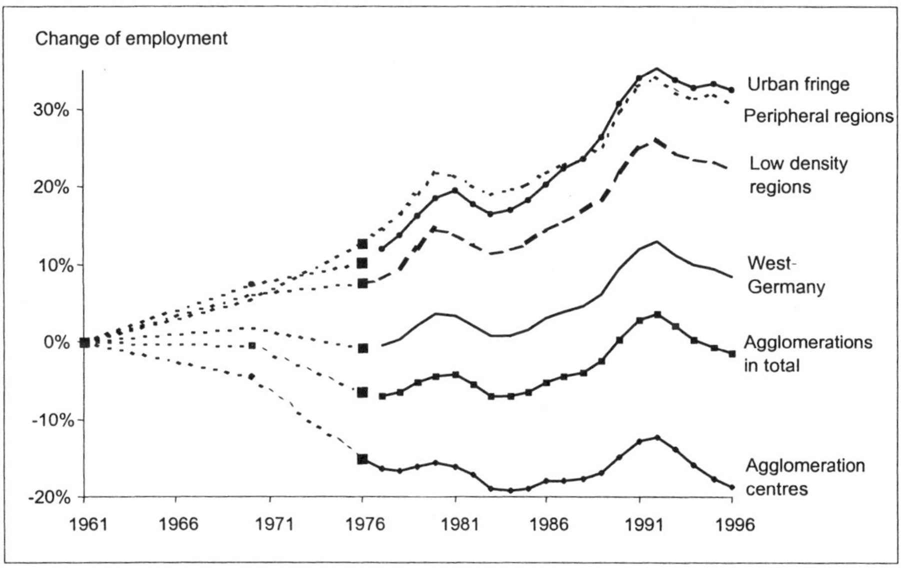

Source: Arbeitsstättenzählung, Arbeitskreis Erwerbstätigenrechnung der Länder, employment statistics, own calculations.

Fig. 4.2 Employment growth of spatial categories since 1961

However, for the agglomerations *as a whole,* employment growth is balanced: gains in the urban fringe compensate for losses in the cores. But the nature of the development indicates that this result is due at least in part to the economic upturn since the mid 1980s. The effects of the upswing (as well as the impact of recessions for example after 1982 or 1993) are apparent in the growth paths of all spatial categories. In the following, we accentuate the regional particularities of development by excluding these national effects. For that purpose, development of spatial categories relative to average (national) employment growth is analysed (see Fig. 4.3). In contrast to the period considered for the description of absolute growth trends (since 1961), the analysis of relative growth paths is restricted to the period between 1976 and 1996 due to the availability of annual data.

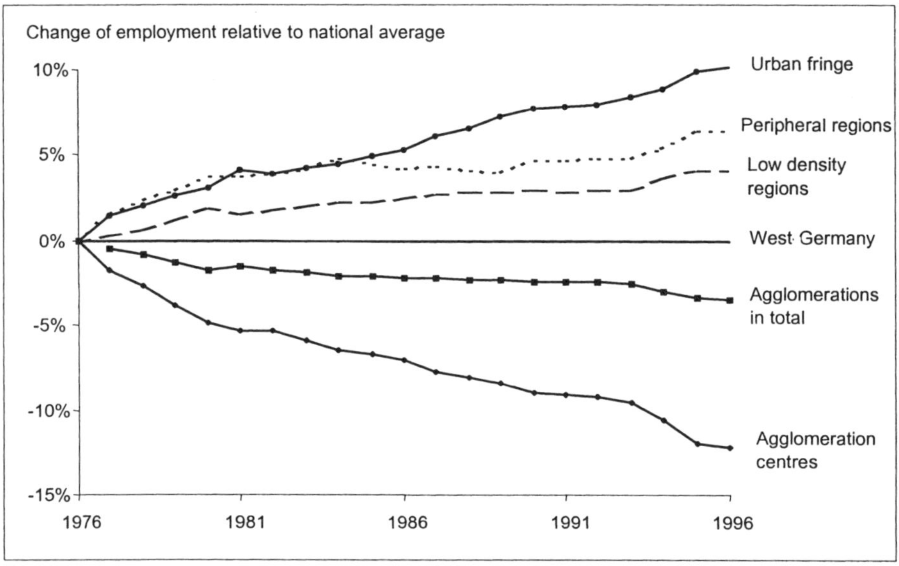

Source: Arbeitsstättenzählung, Arbeitskreis Erwerbstätigenrechnung der Länder, employment statistic, own calculations.

Fig. 4.3 Relative employment growth paths of spatial categories since 1976

The relative development of spatial categories since 1976 is characterised by instantly recognisable trends. Due to below average employment growth, the share of agglomeration centres in national employment declined by roughly 12 percent. In contrast to this, particularly the urban fringe (+10 percent) and the peripheral regions (+6 percent) increased their corresponding shares. As a result of the unfavourable development in the agglomeration centres, the economic weight of agglomerations in total decreased too (–3 percent), despite the dynamic growth process in the urban fringe. Even without a detailed statistical analysis[1], it is obvious that the spatial deconcentration at both scales, i.e. suburbanisation and disurbanisation, can be assessed as long-term trends. In this respect the results of earlier studies are clearly confirmed. However, at the same time we can see that the intensity and direction of spatial structural change are not totally regular. For example, the relative growth paths of peripheral regions and agglomerations at first very clearly diverge. However, by the mid 1980s, the dynamic of the peripheral regions weakens, whereas the agglomerations achieve average employment growth until the early 1990s. Subsequently the relative growth paths of both spatial categories start to diverge again.

Variations of this kind can be observed for the relative growth paths of other spatial categories as well. These changes raise the question whether we can consider the central tendencies of spatial structural change under these circumstances as stable, or whether the deviations constitute (statistically detectable) structural instabilities. Elsewhere we have carried out a detailed statistical analysis (see Bade and Niebuhr 1999). Here we confine ourselves to the corresponding findings. The following results are based on a stability analysis of an assumed linear trend of the relative growth path (estimated by OLS or GLS) and tests of structural change (F-test and CHOW test). More or less pronounced deviations from the estimated linear trend are identified for all spatial categories. But the F-test and CHOW test reject the hypothesis of structural change for each relative growth path examined. Therefore, we can conclude that no general alteration of the direction of spatial structural change has occurred. The relative growth paths of spatial categories are stable, it is merely the intensity of spatial growth discrepancies that fluctuates over time.

We complete our analysis of the quantitative aspects of spatial structural change with a brief study of regional income growth (see Fig. 4.4). The relative development of income for spatial categories exhibits the same main tendencies as regional employment growth. On the one hand there are income gains, particularly of the urban fringe and peripheral regions, on the other, there are losses in the agglomerations and their centres. Moreover, for most spatial categories the changes in economic weight – measured by their share of national employment or income – are of the same magnitude. The share of agglomeration centres in national production declined by roughly 11 percent (employment: −12 percent), while the urban fringe realised an increase of about 11 percent (employment: +10 percent). As for employment the income share of agglomerations in total declined by 3 percent.

Only for the peripheral regions is there a rather pronounced deviation from the relative growth path of employment. Whereas for employment the respective share rose by approximately 6 percent, the relative gain in income of peripheral regions (nearly +10 percent) is clearly higher. This difference between the development of income and employment growth of peripheral regions – from a

[1] "But what is wrong with visual examination of time-series data? Don't we see one part of the truth with the naked eye, another part through the microscope?" (Brems 1977, p. 84).

relative perspective – is largely due to the greater income growth in the 1990s. The relative growth paths started to deviate in 1988, although for both indicators gains of peripheral regions increased in this period. This result coincides with the observation that income per capita of peripheral regions did not converge to the national average before 1988. In total – for the whole period between 1976 and 1996 – peripheral regions could only achieve a modest decrease in the gap in per capita income. Measured as a percentage of the national average, income per capita of peripheral regions increased from 81.4 percent to 83.7 percent. Caused by the parallel (relative) growth of income and employment, the relation of income per capita to the corresponding national average remained almost unchanged. This applies particularly to the other spatial categories.

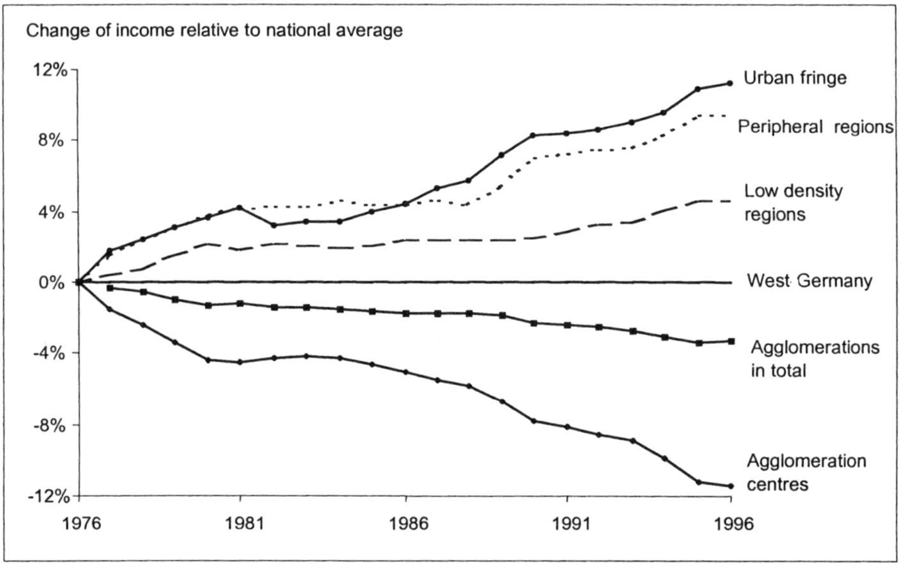

Source: National accounts of German Länder, employment statistics, own calculations.

Fig. 4.4 Relative income growth paths of spatial categories since 1976

These findings confirm the results of Blanchard and Katz (1992) cited in the introduction – if income and employment evolve in the same direction, the variation of income per capita is comparatively small. In contrast, if income and employment evolve in opposite directions, the change of income per capita exceeds the change in overall income. Economic development in the urban fringe and agglomeration centres provides evidence for both cases. Growth of employment and income is far above average in the urban fringe, nevertheless, the increase of income per capita (+157 percent) does not deviate from the development in the agglomeration centres. But in the agglomeration centres, growth of overall income is below average and employment even declined (–4 percent) between 1976 and 1996.

In summary, it can be stated that from a quantitative perspective, deconcentration as a central tendency of spatial structural change proves to be rather stable. For the regional development of both indicators, a decline of concentration in large agglomerations in West Germany is characteristic. On the whole, no fundamental change of direction has taken place. Insofar as there are deviations from the development trends, they indicate further spatial deconcentration to the detriment of agglomerations. Thus, so far the results confirm the findings of convergence studies that suggest (relative) β-convergence for regions in West Germany (see Seitz 1995; Schalk and Untiedt 1996). But at the same time, the almost unchanged relations of income per capita relative to the national average point to a rather modest convergence of absolute levels.

Regional Growth Prospects – Human Capital

Technological change is commonly viewed as a major factor in the future development of regional disparities. A central assumption in this context is that regional competitiveness in industrialised countries is based on the ability to transform knowledge into innovation. Hence, the capability of a region to cope with technological change is a decisive determinant of its growth prospects (e.g. Tödtling 1990; Freeman 1994). Undisputedly, the human capital of a region is one of the most important locational conditions for coping with the effects of rapid technological change.[1] For instance, growth theory emphasises the role of technological progress for economic growth and also its close relation to the education and abilities of the workforce (e.g. Kuznets 1961; Denison 1961; Griliches 1996). Therefore, human capital – measured by the educational level of the workforce or R&D employment – supplies important information about regional development prospects in a setting of rapid technological change.

The continuing trend of rising human capital is a conspicuous feature of structural change in industrialised countries (e.g. Buttler and Tessaring 1993). This development is reflected by employment data, e.g. the enormous increase in the number of employees with an academic degree. Between 1976 and 1996 the growth of highly qualified employees in West Germany amounted to roughly 150 percent, whereas the number of employees without vocational training decreased by 34 percent. These changes of qualification structure generally characterise the development of all regions. Nevertheless, the results of previous studies point to a significant *centre-periphery differential*. Far more uncertain are the findings concerning the *development* of these disparities.

At the level of spatial categories, significant growth differences can be observed between 1976 and 1996 (see Fig. 4.5). Due to continuous below average growth in highly skilled employment, the relative development of agglomeration centres is characterised by a stable decline in the corresponding share of the national stock of human capital (in total about –11 percent). As a result of these (relative) losses,

[1] For an analysis of regional specialisation and concentration of R&D intensive industry sectors in Germany see e.g. Sternberg (1996).

even as a total, the agglomerations only registered a modest increase in the number of employees with academic education, and a decreasing share (–4 percent). On the other hand, the relative growth paths of peripheral regions (+20 percent) and the urban fringe (+18 percent) reveal an extremely favourable development, clearly above the national average. On the whole, the relative growth paths of spatial categories prove to be very stable. Irrespective of the economy-wide conditions, the growth of peripheral regions on average has exceeded national development by about 1 percent per year. In contrast to this, growth of the agglomeration centres is annually more than 0.5 percent below average growth in West Germany.

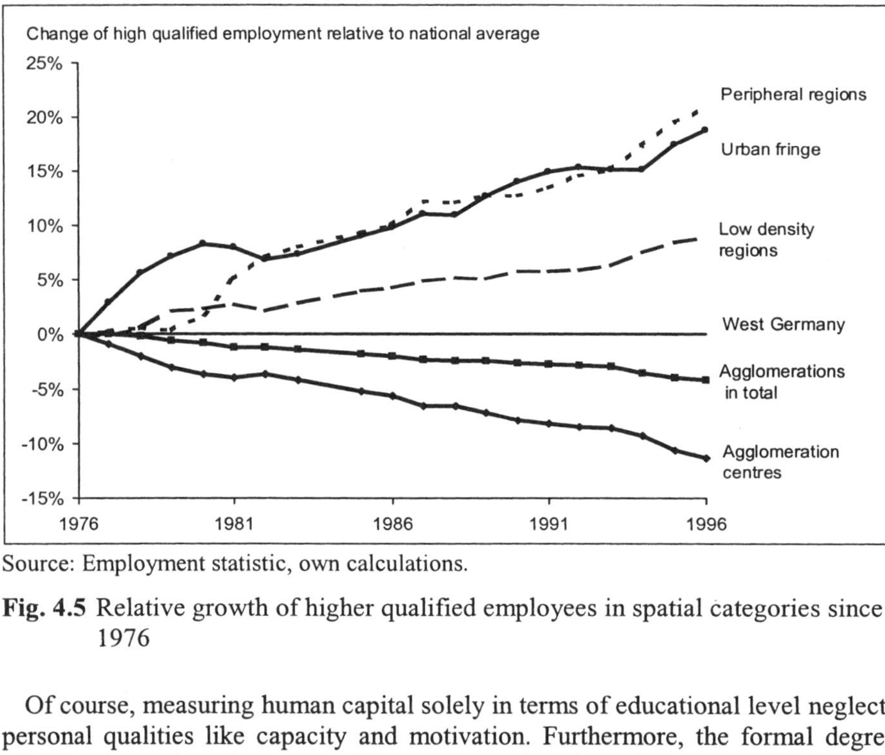

Source: Employment statistic, own calculations.

Fig. 4.5 Relative growth of higher qualified employees in spatial categories since 1976

Of course, measuring human capital solely in terms of educational level neglects personal qualities like capacity and motivation. Furthermore, the formal degree qualifications of employees provide no information about the characteristics of the corresponding workplace. The frequently cited example of taxi drivers with academic degrees demonstrates that education only contributes to an increase in human capital if the acquired skills are actually used in the production process. Considering the functional characteristics of a work place remedies this deficit, because the function measures the real occupation of an employee. In this context, research and development (R&D) is a widespread indicator. The importance of R&D is based on the technical ability of enterprises to innovate, which results in the development of innovative products and processes. The innovative potential of the staff is in fact no guarantee of the economic success of an enterprise, but it is –

particularly with regard to technological change – an important precondition for successful development.

The expansion of R&D employment is – like the increasingly qualified workforce – a common and clear trend of structural change. Between 1976 and 1996 the number of employees in R&D in West Germany increased by roughly 74 percent all over the country. The development of spatial categories exhibits a pattern that closely resembles the general spatial tendencies of human capital measured by academic degrees. Over the entire period, the agglomeration centres and the agglomerations as a whole constantly attained below average growth of R&D employment, while all other spatial categories achieved growth rates above the national average (see Fig. 4.6). Slight deviations from the spatial growth paths of human capital can be observed for the regions outside the agglomerated areas. For R&D employment, the favourable development outside the large agglomerations occurs with a time lag, particularly for peripheral regions. Whereas above average growth of highly skilled employment is noticeable from the beginning of the observation period, significant (relative) gains in R&D employment do not become evident until the 1980s. However, taken over the entire period, this is of minor importance: the peripheral regions achieved an almost identical increase of share in the national amount for both R&D employment and highly skilled labour (+18 percent and +21 percent respectively).

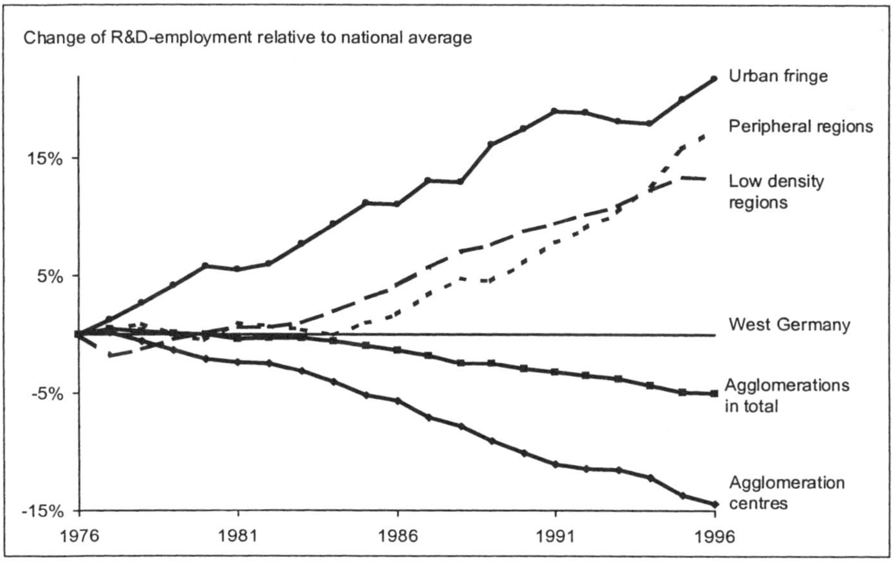

Source: Employment statistic, own calculations

Fig. 4.6 Relative R&D employment growth paths of spatial categories since 1976

It can be stated that the spatial development of human capital indicators is characterised by significant similarities. The agglomeration centres are definitely the losers from spatial structural change. Over the whole period analysed, their growth in terms of these indicators is below the national average. The impressive increases of the urban fringe cannot compensate for the unfavourable development of agglomeration centres. As a consequence, the share of agglomerations in total human capital declined continuously. In summary, the central tendencies of spatial structural change – the (relative) gains of the urban fringe and peripheral areas, and (relative) losses of agglomerations and their centres – prove to be very stable for human capital on the level of spatial categories. The stability of spatial structural change suggests that the deconcentration process of human capital, which is one of the most important regional conditions for coping with technological change, will continue in the near future.

4.4 Conclusions

The empirical results of the present paper reveal that the long-term process of spatial deconcentration has not come to an end. Despite fundamental changes in general economic conditions – like the establishing of the common market or the opening up of East European countries – the relative growth paths of spatial categories are extremely stable. The deviations from development trends rather indicate further spatial deconcentration to the disadvantage of agglomerations. The concerns that economic conditions had changed to the detriment of rural-peripheral regions and caused an extension of regional disparities have not proven to be justified so far.

Furthermore, spatial deconcentration also applies to essential factors of regional growth prospects, like highly skilled labour or R&D. As for the quantitative indicators, above average growth of these crucial functions is not restricted to the urban fringe. Regions that are characterised by a disadvantageous peripheral location also achieve favourable development. So both past development from a quantitative perspective and spatial structural change of human capital point to a sustained decline of regional disparities in West Germany.

Irrespective of the definitely positive findings for peripheral regions, we ought to be cautious for several reasons. First, there are exceptions to the rule, i.e. some peripheral regions deviate from the above-average development observed for the corresponding spatial category. Therefore, the process of deconcentration that characterises regional growth *on average* should first of all be considered as an encouraging sign. In contrast to the traditional prejudices concerning the backwardness and poor growth prospects of peripheral regions, deconcentration proves that rural areas are able to attain the prerequisites essential in a setting of rapid structural and technological changes.

Second, the below average development of the agglomeration centres frequently implies an absolute increase of the variable analysed, especially when qualitative indicators like income per capita or human capital are considered. Apart from periods of severe recession, the total amount of these variables increases in the agglomeration centres. Only employment differs from the other indicators in this respect. Whereas in the long term overall employment tends to decline in the agglomeration centres, the number of highly qualified employees and the quantity of jobs in sophisticated service functions will probably increase further – even though below average.

Finally, it has to be considered, that with regard to the share of high quality jobs in total employment, there still exist significant disparities between agglomerated and rural areas. Although at first glance it seems paradoxical, these differences seem more likely to widen than to weaken in the future. This development is an inevitable consequence of the continuing growth of these activities in large urban agglomerations. Even a below average growth rate in the agglomeration core will cause increasing differences in the share of high quality jobs in total employment (measured in percentage points). Due to the general increases in income, the same coherence applies to regional differences in per capita income despite the detectable β-convergence. Studies of regional disparities usually analyse convergence from a relative perspective. Such an analysis applied on generally growing economies is continuously confronted with a possible (apparent) contradiction: that relative convergence might coincide with divergence of absolute levels. So, the issue of convergence or divergence frequently also remains a matter of interpretation (Bröcker 1998).

References

Asheim, B., Dunford, M. (1997) Regional Futures. Regional Studies 31, 445-455

Bade, F.-J. (1987) Regionale Beschäftigungsentwicklung und produktionsorientierte Dienstleistungen. Deutsches Institut für Wirtschaftsforschung Sonderheft 143, Duncker & Humblot, Berlin

Bade, F.-J. (1991) Regionale Beschäftigungsprognose 1995. Mitteilungen aus der Arbeitsmarkt- und Berufsforschung 24, 25-44

Bade, F.-J. (1997) Zu den wirtschaftlichen Chancen und Risiken der ländlichen Räume. Raumforschung und Raumordnung 4/5, 247-259

Bade, F.-J., Niebuhr, A. (1999) Zur Stabilität des räumlichen Strukturwandels. Jahrbuch für Regionalwissenschaft 19, 131-156

Bade, F.-J., Schönert, M. (1997) Regionale Unterschiede und Entwicklungstendenzen in der Qualität der Arbeitsplätze. Geographische Zeitschrift 85, 67-80

Beise, M., Gehrke, B., Legler, H. (1999) Attraktivität Deutschlands und seiner Regionen für Forschungs- und Entwicklungsaktivitäten. Informationen zur Raumentwicklung 1, 31-44

Berry, B.J.L. (1964) Cities as Systems Within Systems of Cities. Papers of the Regional Science Association 13, 147-163

Blanchard, O.J., Katz, L.F. (1992) Regional Evolution. Brookings Papers on Economic Activity 2, 1-75

Böltken, F., Irmen, E., Runge, L. (1988) Ausgewählte aktuelle Trends in der räumlichen Entwicklung. Informationen zur Raumentwicklung 11/12, 711-729

Brems, H. (1977) Reality and Neoclassical Theory: On Eichner and Kregel. Journal of Economic Literature 15, 72-83

Bröcker, J. (1998) Konvergenz in Europa und die Europäische Währungsunion. In: Fischer, B., Straubhaar, T. (eds.) Ökonomische Konvergenz in Theorie und Praxis,

Veröffentlichungen des HWWA-Instituts für Wirtschaftsforschung – Hamburg 41, 105-135

Bucher, H., Kocks, M. (1987) Die Suburbanisierung in der ersten Hälfte der 80er Jahre. Informationen zur Raumentwicklung 11/12, 689-707

Buttler, F., Tessaring, M. (1993) Humankapital als Standortfaktor. Argumente zur Bildungsdiskussion aus arbeitsmarktpolitischer Sicht. Mitteilungen aus der Arbeitsmarkt- und Berufsforschung 4, 467-476

Camagni, R.P., Cappelin, R. (1984) Structural Changes and Productivity Growth in the European Regions. Regional Research in an International Perspective, München, 153-200

Canova, F., Marcet, A. (1995) The Poor Stay Poor: Non-Convergence across Countries and Regions. CEPR Discussion Paper 1265, London

Carlino, G.A., Mills, L. (1996) Testing Neoclassical Cconvergence in Rregional Incomes and Earnings. Regional Science and Urban Economics 26, 565-590

Cuadrado-Roura, J.R., Mancha, T., Garrido, R. (1997) Regional Productivity Patterns in Europe. Does the Core-Periphery Dilemma Exist? Paper presented at the 1997 Congress of the European Regional Science Association, Rome

Denison, E.F. (1961) The Sources of Economic Growth in The United States. Committee for Economic Development, New York

ERECO European Economic Reseach and Advisory Consortium (1997) European Regional Prospects - Analysis and Forecasts to 2001, München

Fagerberg, J., Verspagen, B. (1996) Heading for Divergence? Regional Growth in Europe Reconsidered. Journal of Common Market Studies 34, 431-466

Fagerberg, J., Verspagen B., Caniëls, M. (1997) Technology, Growth and Unemployment across European Regions. Regional Studies 31, 457-466

Franck, M. (1995) Neue Konturen regionaler Arbeitsmarktdisparitäten am Ende des Wiedervereinigungsbooms? Raumforschung und Raumordnung 4, 53, 260-270

Freeman, C. (1994) The Eeconomics of Technical Change. Cambridge Journal of Economics 18, 463-514

Frey, W.H. (1993) The New Urban Revival in the United States. Urban Studies 30, 741-774

Gaebe, W. (1987) Verdichtungsräume. Strukturen und Prozesse in weltweiten Vergleichen. Teubner, Stuttgart

Gatzweiler, H.-P., Schliebe, K. (1982) Suburbanisierung von Bevölkerung und Arbeitsplätzen - Stillstand? Informationen zur Raumentwicklung 11/12, 883-913

Gehrke, B., Legler, H. (1998) Regional Concentration of Innovative Potential in Western Germany. DIW-Vierteljahreshefte zur Wirtschaftsforschung 2, 99-112

Griliches, Z. (1996) The Discovery of the Residual: A Historical Note. Journal of Economic Literature 33(9) 1324-1330

Hoppen, H.-D. (1979) Industrieller Strukturwandel, Duncker & Humblot, Berlin.

Irmen, E., Blach, A. (1994) Räumlicher Strukturwandel - Konzentration, Dekonzentration und Dispersion. Informationen zur Raumentwicklung 7/8, 445-464

Irmen, E., Blach, A. (1997) Typen ländlicher Entwicklung in Deutschland und Europa. Informationen zur Raumentwicklung 11/12, 713-728

Keeble, D. (1986) The Changing Spatial Structure of Economic Activity and Metropolitan Decline in the United Kingdom. In: Ewers, H.-J., Goddard, J.B., Matzerath, H. (eds.) The Future of the Metropolis. de Gruyter, Berlin, 171-199

Klemmer, P. (1996) Entwicklungsrisiken ländlicher Räume. In: Jenkis, H.W. (ed.) Raumordnung und Raumordnungspolitik. R. Oldenbourg, München, 450-480

Kuznets, S. (1961) Capital in the American Economy. Studies in Capital Formation and Financing 9, University Press, Princeton

Legler, H. (1994) Regionale Verteilung industrieller Forschungskapazitäten in Westdeutschland. ZEW Wirtschaftsanalysen, Quartalshefte des Zentrums für Europäische Wirtschaftsforschung, Mannheim, 415-434

Molle, W. (1997) The Regional Economic Structure of the European Union: An Analysis of Long-Term Developments. Zeitschrift für Wirtschafts- und Sozialwissenschaften 117, 13-32

Müller, J. (1984) Regionale Qualifikationsstrukturen im Süd-Nord-Vergleich. Niedersächsisches Institut für Wirtschaftsforschung (ed.) Süd-Nord-Gefälle in der Bundesrepublik? Thesen und Beobachtungen, Hannover, 131-151

Niebuhr, A. (1999) Räumliche Wachstumsstrukturen. Theoretische Erklärungsansätze und empirische Befunde für die Bundesrepublik Deutschland. Schriften des Instituts für Regionalforschung der Universität Kiel 16, V. Florentz, München

Nieth, E. (1980) Industriestruktur und regionale Entwicklung. Duncker & Humblot, Berlin

Nohlen, D., Nuscheler, F. (1992) Was heißt Entwicklung? In: Nohlen, D., Nuscheler, F. (eds.) Handbuch der Dritten Welt: Grundprobleme, Theorien, Strategien, Dietz. J. H./LibriF, Bonn, 55-75

Peschel, K. (1983) Der strukturelle Wandel der Industrie in den Regionen der Bundesrepublik 1960 bis 1976. In: Müller, J.H. (eds.) Determinanten der räumlichen Entwicklung. Schriften des Vereins für Socialpolitik, Neue Folge 131, Duncker & Humblot, Berlin, 125-172

Peschel, K., Bröcker, J. (1990) Hypothesen und Fakten zur regionalen Entwicklung der Beschäftigung in der Bundesrepublik Deutschland 1970-1987. Allgemeines Statistisches Archiv 74, 71-97

Pliquett, B. (1988) Regionale Unterschiede des Einsatzes qualifizierter Arbeitskräfte in den Industriesektoren der Bundesrepublik Deutschland. Universität Münster, Hochschulschrift, Münster

Quah, D. (1993): Empirical Cross-section Dynamics in Economic Growth. European Economic Review 37, 426-434

Recker, E., Schütte, G. (1982) Räumliche Verteilung von qualifizierten Arbeitskräften und regionale Innovationstätigkeit. Informationen zur Raumentwicklung 6/7, 543-560

Sala-i-Martin, X. (1996) Regional Cohesion: Evidence and Theories of Regional Growth and Convergence. European Economic Review 40, 1325-1352

Schalk, H.J., Untiedt, G. (1996) Technologie im neoklassischen Wachstumsmodell: Effekte auf Wachstum und Konvergenz. Jahrbücher für Nationalökonomie und Statistik 215/5, 562-585

Schönert, M. (2000) Das personelle Innovationspotenzial. Empirische Ergebnisse zur Entwicklung regionaler Disparitäten in der Bundesrepublik Deutschland. BAW Institut für Wirtschaftsforschung, Regionalwirtschaftliche Studien, 18, Bremen

Seitz, H. (1995) Konvergenz: Theoretische Aspekte und empirische Befunde für westdeutsche Regionen. Konjunkturpolitik 41, 168-198

Seitz, H. (1996): Die Suburbanisierung der Beschäftigung: Eine empirische Untersuchung für Westdeutschland. Jahrbücher für Nationalökonomie und Statistik 215, 69-91

Stahl, K. (1997) Divergenz und Konvergenz der regionalen Wirtschaftsentwicklung aus der Sicht der Raumwirtschaftstheorie. Zeitschrift für Wirtschafts- und Sozialwissenschaften 117, 53-72

Sternberg, R. (1996) Regionale Spezialisierung und räumliche Konzentration FuE-intensiver Wirtschaftszweige in den Kreisen Westdeutschlands – Indizien für Industriedistrikte? Berichte zur deutschen Landeskunde 1, 133-155

Tödtling, F. (1990) Räumliche Differenzierung betrieblicher Innovation. Erklärungsansätze und empirische Befunde für österreichische Regionen. Ed. Sigma, Berlin

Tondl, G. (1997) The Changing Pattern of Regional Convergence in Europe. Paper presented at the 1997 Congress of the European Regional Science Association, Rome

Uebe, W. (1967) Industriestruktur und Standort. Regionale Wachstumsunterschiede der Industriebeschäftigung in der BRD 1950- 1962. Kohlhammer, Stuttgart.

ZEW – Zentrum für Europäische Wirtschaftsforschung, *et al.* (2000) Zur technologischen Leistungsfähigkeit Deutschlands – Zusammenfassender Endbericht (Gutachten im Auftrag des Bundesministeriums für Bildung und Forschung).

5 Machinery and Productivity: A Comparison of East and West German Manufacturing Plants

Michael Fritsch[1] and Jörn Mallok[2]
[1] Faculty of Economics and Business Administration, Bergakademie Freiberg
[2] Mechanik Center Erlangen GmbH

5.1 Technology and Economic Performance: Basic Hypotheses

A central question in economics, as well as in other social sciences, concerns the impact of technology on economic performance. The answer to this question has enormous implications for policies that try to stimulate competitiveness and economic development. For example, if modern machinery does not more or less automatically lead to better economic performance, then a policy that mainly involves subsidies for investment in physical capital may not resolve the 'real' problem and may, therefore, turn out to be rather ineffective. However, there have been only a few systematic microeconomic empirical analyses of this issue, most of them carried out fairly recently.[1] One striking result of this research is the high degree of heterogeneity revealed with regard to the effects of technology on the performance of firms, as well as the variety and complexity of factors responsible for the range of possible outcomes. Obviously, the relationship between technology and economic performance is not deterministic. There usually exists a considerable degree of freedom with respect to the choice, implementation and usage of technology. And the way in which the technology is implemented is of crucial importance for the impact of that technology.

If a wide range of alternatives exists for implementing and using a specific technology, then the question arises as to what might characterise a 'good' or a 'bad' usage of that technology with regard to economic performance for the respective microeconomic unit (firm, establishment). In this chapter we report the results of a research project which has attempted to assess the impact of production technology on the productivity of East and West German manufacturing establishments. In particular, we have tried to identify factors that may characterise an 'intelligent' use of technology that leads to improved

[1] See Hitchens *et al.* (1990, 1993) Hitchens *et al.* (1995), Finegold and Wagner (1999). The previous work of one of the authors in this field is summarised in Ewers *et al.* (1990a, 1999b).

performance.[1] We expected that the substantial productivity and capital stock differences between East and West German establishments would provide a relatively good opportunity to identify the relationship between technology and productivity.

The remainder of this contribution is organised as follows. Section 5.2 gives an overview of productivity differences in our sample of matched East and West German manufacturing establishments, based on a brief description of the data base. Section 5.3 then concentrates on the ways in which the quality and use of equipment might contribute to an explanation of these productivity differences. Finally, we give some brief information on the relative importance of other factors that may influence the productivity performance of our sample (Section 5.4) and then draw some policy conclusions (Section 5.5).

5.2 The Data Base and Measurement Issues

The analysis is based on interviews with 104 small and medium-sized single plant manufacturing firms.[2] These establishments were selected according to the 'matched-pair' approach: for each of the 52 East German establishments in the sample, there is a West German establishment of similar size (number of employees) with a comparable product programme, manufactured using similar production methods.[3] Thirty of these matched pairs were specialised in mechanical engineering, the other pairs were selected from wood-working and wood-processing (eight pairs), the clothing industry (four pairs) and from the food and beverage industry (ten pairs).

Generally, the establishments were rather small. Nearly 40 percent had less than 50 employees and 29 percent had less than 20 employees. About 17 percent of the establishments had more than hundred employees; none had more than 250. Geographically, the East German establishments were located in a number of regions spread over the entire former GDR (German Democratic Republic) with varying degrees of population density. The West German counterparts were situated in regions of similar population density. We use gross value added per workhour as the measure of productivity. Therefore, productivity is always taken to mean labour productivity. The gross value added was calculated as turnover

---

[1] For a more detailed analysis of the causes of productivity differences see Fritsch and Mallok (1998) and Mallok (1996).

[2] The terms 'establishment' and 'firm' are used here synonymously. The interviews were conducted in spring and summer of 1993. The main reason for concentrating exclusively on single plant firms was to ensure that the differences found could be clearly assigned to a certain location.

[3] For the 'matched-pair' approach see Hitchens *et al.* (1990, in particular pp. 107-109) and bibliographic references given there. The main advantage of the matched-pair approach is that it assures that the differences found are not caused by differences with regard to the match-criteria in the subsamples.

minus expenses for raw materials and final goods.[1] We have not attempted to determine net value added, as this would have required a survey of the consumption of capital, i.e. of depreciation. Since depreciation, as documented in the ledgers, is generally determined by tax-laws and might only approximately reflect the actual depletion of capital stock within a specific period, we have abstained from attempting to assess the net value added. Furthermore, due to the measurement problems involved, particularly as regards an East-West German comparison, no evaluation of capital volume was carried out.

Table 5.1 presents the median values of gross value added per workhour for both East and West German establishments. Labour productivity in East German manufacturing establishments reached on average 44.1 percent of their West German counterparts. Comparisons of individual pairs of matched establishments showed that the West German establishments were more productive in 87.7 percent of all cases. The relatively low value for labour productivity in East German establishments corresponds to a much lower rate of utilisation of machinery and personnel. On average, the personnel utilisation rate in West German companies was about 90 percent of normal full capacity, whereas the East German rate was much lower at 63 percent. Table 5.1 also shows the gross value added per workhour in East and West German establishments as determined by a utilisation rate of 100 percent.[2] Even though the median values of productivity for the East German sample are considerably higher than those achieved with actual utilisation, the East German enterprises only reached 67 percent of the West German levels. Even after excluding the influence of various personnel utilisation levels, a considerable difference in productivity between East and West remains.

Table 5.1 Gross value added per workhour in East and West German manufacturing establishments, 1992

	East German Firms*	West German Firms*	East-West Ratio (%)	Matched pair comparison**
Actual value	22.4	50.8	44.2	87.8 (49)
With full utilisation of personnel	36.3	57.6	67.3	77.6 (49)

* Median values (DM).

** Percentage of West German matched establishments with superior productivity performance; number of matched establishment pairs in brackets.

[1] The gross value added is hereby defined too expansively as further cost categories such as expenditures for services, insurance premium, bank-account fees etc. would have to be subtracted as well. Since these data could only be ascertained at considerable cost and difficulty, in this study they were omitted.

[2] Data on the rate of personnel utilisation obtained from the interviews made it possible to estimate productivity with 'normal full utilisation of personnel.'

5.3 The Impact of Machinery on Productivity

In analysing the relationship between machinery and productivity, we will first describe the quality of the physical capital stock, and then turn to the technological skills of the personnel. After this we consider the implementation and use of the machinery and finally provide a multivariate analyses of the impact of machinery on productivity.

Quality of the Physical Capital Stock

It has become well known that capital stock in the former socialist countries of Eastern Europe was, on average, less technologically advanced than in the industrialised economies of the West. The main reasons for this were the overall deficiencies of an economic regime which led to a chronic shortage of the hard currency necessary to import modern equipment from the West, as well as the embargo of Western governments on high-tech equipment exports to the East.[1] In addition, the maintenance and upkeep of the physical capital stock tended to be deficient causing relatively frequent malfunctioning and long machine idle times.

In our assessment of the physical capital stock in the firms interviewed, we made a basic distinction between computerised and conventional (i.e. non-computerised) equipment. Fig. 5.1 shows the adoption rates of computerised equipment in production in East and West German establishments in different years. In 1980, 9.6 percent of the West German establishment used computerised equipment in production, while only 1 percent of the East German establishments did. In 1989, we found an adoption rate of 9.6 percent in the East German firms compared to 38.5 percent in the West German firms. By 1992, the East German establishments had increased their adoption rate to 42.3 percent, but still lagged behind the West German firms which then had an adoption rate of about 56 percent. Not only did the East German establishments adopt computer numerically controlled (CNC) machines relatively late, but the share of computerised equipment in production was lower in the East (15.7 percent compared to 25.1 percent for the West German adopters).[2] However, as a result of the late adoption of CNC machines by the East German firms, their stock of computerised equipment is of a relatively recent vintage, which may be considered a future competitive advantage.

---

[1] There were also some CNC machines produced in the GDR as well as in some other former communist-block countries (like Czechoslovakia and Russia), but these were only small quantities and often available only for firms producing goods for export to Western countries. With regard to the quality of their mechanical components, these CNC machines of domestic production were comparable to Western products, but the electronic devices were of very low quality, technologically far behind and subject to frequent breakdowns.

[2] Figures are based on counts of the main aggregates in production with the machines weighted with the number of workplaces.

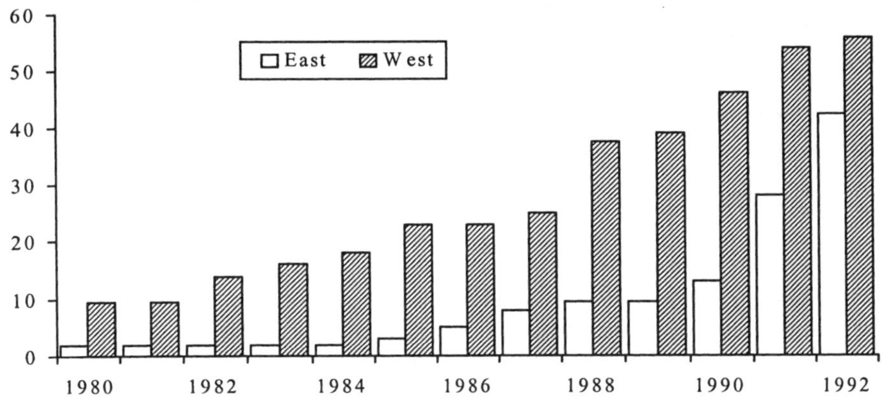

Fig. 5.1 Percentage of East and West German establishments using CNC machines in production 1980-1992

With respect to the composition of their older CNC machinery, East German establishments have a further disadvantage which relates to the socialist procurement system. Under the old regime, firms had to apply in most cases to a central agency for approval of the import of computerised machinery (like CNC machines) from the West. Such requests were frequently turned down by the bureaucrats, but when a request was approved, the bureaucrats themselves selected the supplier that *they* believed to be favourable and often altered the specification of that equipment.[1] Therefore, even if East German establishments possessed more than one computerised machine, the configuration tended not to be optimal. A firm's stock of CNC machines was therefore frequently rather heterogeneous, i.e. from different suppliers with different programming systems, etc. This not only led to relatively high learning costs in acquiring the knowledge needed for using the machines, it was also an impediment for linking them by means of information technology. Moreover, due to shortages of hard currency and the restrictions on travel abroad, the East German firms did not receive the same amount of training as their Western counterparts. Moreover, repair and replacement parts for this machinery (after the expiry of the warranty period) had to be home-made due to the shortage of hard currency.[2]

With regard to the age structure and composition of the conventional, non-computerised equipment, we found no significant differences between East and

[1] In many cases the agency seemed to have simply collected the applications and then ordered a relatively large number (in order to get a discount) of relatively cheap machines.

[2] In West Germany the workers normally receive at least one week's training (generally from the suppliers) when a new CNC machine is implemented. In most cases no such training was provided by the socialist procurement agencies in East Germany.

West German firms. However, due to a relatively low level of maintenance under the socialist system, part of the conventional machinery was in a relatively bad shape so that the average machine idle times with respect to this equipment in the year 1992 were higher (4.3% of total machine run time) than in the West (3%).

It has been quite frequently hypothesised that the physical capital stock of the East German establishments would have to be completely replaced in order to become competitive (so-called 'junkyard hypothesis' see Sinn and Sinn 1992). Our evidence suggests that this view is far too extreme. No doubt there are a considerable number of establishments or production lines where practically complete replacement is unavoidable in order to be able to survive under the new market conditions (mainly to attain high enough product quality), but in nearly all the East German firms we visited, a considerable part of the machinery was still well suited for production purposes, sometimes with minor adjustments and additions (see Mallok 1996 for details).

Technological Skills

The skill of personnel using computerised equipment like CNC machines has frequently been identified as a crucial determinant of the productivity of such equipment (Hitchens, Wagner and Birnie 1990, 1993). With regard to handling conventional machinery, we found only minor differences between the East and the West German establishments. In East Germany, virtually every worker on the shop floor was skilled (a *Facharbeiter*) and had passed a two year apprenticeship. In the West German establishments there was a considerable number of unskilled workers on the shop floor. However, those that had passed an apprenticeship were trained for about one year longer than their East German counterparts and it can be assumed that this longer training period resulted in a higher level of skills. Moreover, according to the common method of work organisation under the socialist regime, the East German workers tended to be specialised in a relatively narrow range of activities and normally had only limited opportunities to gain experience in a variety of different fields.[1] By contrast, their Western counterparts had wider opportunities.

Stimulated by frequent shortages of certain inputs like the non-availability of replacement parts under the socialist system, the East German workers developed somewhat higher improvisation talents. Such 'flexible' tacit skills could partly compensate for lacking experience with modern computerised equipment that was a result of relatively late adoption and low diffusion of these kinds of machinery. Evidently, the implementation of the computerised machinery was on average far less advanced compared to the West. This also constituted a severe obstacle for East German workers to accumulate knowledge on the usage of this technology. As a result, the CNC-programming skills of the East German workers were clearly

[1] This statement is based on the judgement of the interviewer and the management of the enterprises visited. For a detailed analysis of East-West differences in skills see Mallok (1996), Hitchens *et al.* (1993) and Hitchens *et al.* (1995).

far behind the abilities of their West German counterparts (for a detailed analysis see Mallok, 1996).

Use of the Machinery

While there were no significant differences between the East and West German firms with regard to the use of conventional machinery, we found that the East German firms were less advanced in their use of computerised equipment. This might have been due to the shorter learning period caused by relatively late adoption. Several indicators in our data illustrate this delay of the East German firms with respect to the use of computerised equipment. A further major aspect is the degree of integration of computerised machines into their technological environment. If, for example, CNC machines are combined with automatic conveyer systems, production can be run fully automated for a certain period of time. About 21 percent of the West German CNC adopters, but only 13.5 percent of the East German adopters had implemented such fully automated production processes. Another important issue with respect to the integration of the computerised equipment is the linkages of these machines by means of information technology (IT), like DNC, CIM or CAD/CAM[1] applications. Clearly, the West German users of computer aided technology were much more advanced in this respect.

The degree of advancement in the use of the physical capital stock may also be characterised by the ability to exploit the potential of the technical opportunities a machine provides. The share of technical opportunities actually used also gives an indication of the quality of the decision to buy the machine – if a firm invests in a machine that provides significantly more than is needed, this might reflect the choice of an inappropriate technology. In the interviews, an estimate of the degree to which the firms use the potential of their conventional and their computerised machinery was made.[2] With respect to conventional machinery, we found that both the East and the West German firms used on average about 94 percent of the technological possibilities provided. However, the East German firms were clearly lacking in the use of their computerised equipment, employing only 68 percent of the potential compared to an average of 85 percent in the West German subsample (there was considerable heterogeneity within both subsamples).

The share of direct, on-site CNC programming may be regarded as another indicator for advanced usage of computerised equipment in production as well as a reflection of the respective skills of the workforce. In general, we found that the share of adopters practising on-site CNC programming was about the same in both

---

[1] DNC: Direct Numerically Controlled; CIM: Computer Integrated Manufacturing; CAD: Computer Aided Design; CAM: Computer Aided Manufacturing.

[2] This assessment concentrated on key parts of the machinery and was made in a discussion with the interview partner. Such a procedure can of course lead to bias due to subjective judgements involved. However, if there should be such a bias, it should not differ much between the establishments because all interviews were conducted by the same person (who is a trained engineer).

subsamples, however, the West German adopters were doing a somewhat larger fraction of their total CNC programming on-site.

The cost advantage of manufacturing on a CNC machine compared to a conventional machine depends mainly on the complexity of the parts to be produced and on batch size. As a general rule of thumb, manufacturing by means of CNC machines is disadvantageous for small batches of simple parts. Such use is an indication for non-optimal application of the equipment. On average the West German CNC adopters manufactured only 5 percent of their simple-parts-in-small-batches output on computerised machinery compared to 20 percent for the East German adopters. This appears to clearly indicate deficiencies in the use of CNC machinery by a considerable number of East German firms.

The average reject rate for production in the East German firms (4.3 percent compared to an average of 3.0 percent in the West German subsample) could be seen as a consequence of the lower quality of physical capital stock as well as the lower expertise in the operation of the machinery. However, this interpretation is at least questionable: our interviews revealed that the higher reject rate of the East German firms may be attributed to their attempts to increase utilisation capacity by accepting orders for tasks in which they were relatively inexperienced.

Bivariate Analyses

Table 5.2 shows the correlation coefficients for the relationship between indicators reflecting the quality and the use of the physical capital stock on the one hand and productivity on the other. All coefficients have the expected sign. According to the values of the respective correlation coefficients, the utilisation of technological opportunities and the share of on-site CNC-programming show the strongest relationship with productivity. The percentage of machine idle time and the dummy variable for the implementation of fully automated production processes have only a relatively weak impact on economic performance. The time since first CNC adoption, the share of CNC machines related to overall machinery in production and the degree of IT integration[1] are of medium importance in this respect.

There are a number of remarkable correlations between the time since first CNC adoption and other technology indicators (Table 5.3).[2] Not surprisingly, the earlier the respective establishment started to use computerised equipment in production, the higher the proportion of CNC machines. This is because firms that adopted early tended to subsequently buy additional CNC machines. In those establishments that adopted early, also the implementation of automated production processes, the utilisation of technological opportunities, the degree of IT integration and direct CNC programming tended to be more advanced. Only

---

[1] The indicator for IT integration gives the number of interfaces between a given set of functional areas of the firms (e.g. construction, quality control, manufacturing, stockkeeping) linked by means of information technology.

[2] All correlations reported in Table 5.2 are restricted to establishment that had already adopted CNC machinery.

the ratio of machine idle to total machine run time does not show any systematic variation with respect to the time since first adoption. The positive correlations between time since first adoption and indicators that reflect the implementation of the technology suggest that acquiring the knowledge necessary for advanced usage of computerised equipment needs time.

Table 5.2 Correlation coefficients between technology indicators and productivity*

Indicator	Correlation coefficients
Time since first CNC adoption (years, all establishments)	0.22[b]
Time since first CNC adoption (years, adopters only)	0.42[a]
Share of CNC machines as % of all machinery in production	0.20[c]
Fully automated production processes implemented (%)	0.15
Machine idle times as % of total machine run time	-0.10
Utilisation of technological opportunities (%)	0.27[a]
Degree of IT integration	0.23[b]
Reject rate (%)	-0.12
Share of on-site CNC programming (%)**	0.29[c]

* Spearman rank-correlation coefficients. [a] Statistically significant at the 1% level. [b] Statistically significant at the 5% level. [c] Statistically significant at the 10% level.
** Related to overall CNC-programming time (CNC-adopters only).

Table 5.3 Correlation coefficients between time since first CNC adoption and other technology indicators (CNC adopters only)*

Indicator	Correlation coefficients
Share of CNC machines as % of all machinery in production	0.41[a] (52)
Fully automated production processes implemented (yes=1/no=0)	0.36[a] (47)
CNC machine idle time as % of total machine run time	-0.01 (17)
Utilisation of technological opportunities of CNC equipment (%)	0.36[b] (39)
Degree of IT integration	0.43[a] (51)
Share of on-site CNC-programming (%)	0.38[b] (42)

* Spearman rank-correlation coefficients; number of cases in brackets.
[a] Statistically significant at the 1% level. [b] Statistically significant at the 5% level.

Multivariate Regression Analysis

Some regression analyses were carried out in order to assess the relative importance of machinery in generating high productivity. The share of CNC machines related to overall machinery was used to measure the quality of the physical capital stock. The indicators for the utilisation of the technological opportunities of equipment and for the degree of IT integration represent the usage of the machinery.[1] The utilisation rate of personnel was included to account for the impact of overstaffing on productivity. Three dummy variables account for an industry specific effect, with the mechanical engineering industry being the control group.

Four alternative models were tested (the results are shown in Table 5.4). All the variables mentioned above are contained in Model I. It reveals the strong impact of the personnel utilisation rate, whereas the share of CNC machines and the usage of the capital stock seem to be of about equal importance. In order to account for the specific problems of the East German establishments, a dummy variable for the location was included in Model II (East Germany = 1; West Germany = 0). This proved to be highly significant, with a beta coefficient (that can be interpreted as measures for the relative importance of the variables) at least twice as large as the coefficient for any other variable. Due to the inclusion of this dummy variable, the share of explained variance (R^{2adj}) as well as the F-value rise considerably. Because the dummy variable for location accounts for systematic differences between the East and the West German establishments the coefficients for the utilisation rate of personnel and for the share of CNC machines now have considerably lower values. Moreover, the impact of the utilisation of technological opportunities is lower due to the introduction of the dummy variable for location. While the share of CNC machines is no longer statistically significant, the two indicators for the usage of the machinery prove to be relevant for productivity performance.

There was some degree of correlation between the share of CNC machines and the two indicators for the usage of machinery in the data. In order to test for the impact of multi-collinearity, Model III omitted the measure for the quality of the physical capital stock, and Model IV contained this measure, but not the variables for the usage of the equipment (see Table 5.4). In Model III (which does not contain the variable for the quality of the capital stock) the indicators for the usage of the machinery proof to be significant while in Model IV (in which these variables are omitted) the CNC-share shows no significant impact. This clearly indicates the relatively high importance of the usage of machinery for productivity performance in relation to the quality of the physical capital stock as such.

[1] The share of on-site CNC programming was not used because of missing values for establishments that had not already adopted computerised equipment in production.

Table 5.4 Regressions to explain productivity differences*

Variable	I	II	III	IV
		Model		
Dummy for location in East Germany	-	-0.47[a] (5.31)	-0.49[a] (5.78)	-0.50[a] (5.59)
Utilisation of personnel (%)	0.40[a] (4.58)	0.22[a] (2.51)	0.20[b] (2.37)	0.25[a] (2.90)
Share of CNC machines (%)	0.18[c] (1.94)	0.05 (0.58)	-	0.09 (1.09)
Utilisation of technological opportunities (%)	0.26[a] (2.88)	0.18[b] (2.21)	0.17[b] (2.11)	-
Degree of IT integration	0.18[c] (1.92)	0.17[b] (2.17)	0.17[b] (2.29)	-
Dummy for wood-working and wood-processing industry	0.01 (0.12)	-0.01 (0.17)	-0.02 (0.29)	-0.02 (0.23)
Dummy for clothing industry	-0.11 (1.21)	-0.13 (1.75)	-0.14 (1.95)	-0.13 (1.66)
Dummy for food and beverages industry	-0.10 (1.21)	-0.03 (1.10)	-0.07 (0.85)	-0.03 (0.42)
R^{2adj}	0.32	0.48	0.48	0.45
F value	7.52	12.25	14.26	14.53
Number of cases	99	99	101	100

* OLS estimates. The first row shows the beta coefficient, t-values in parentheses.
[a] Statistically significant at the 1% level. [b] Statistically significant at the 5% level. All equations are statistically significant at the 1% level. Control group for the industry dummies was the mechanical engineering industry.

5.4 Further Determinants of East-West Differences in Productivity Performance

What factors other than the physical capital stock and its use caused productivity differences in our sample, particularly between the East and West German establishments? A major reason for the low degree of capacity utilisation in the

East German firms was the shortage of demand due to the lack of competitiveness of their products. Most of the East German establishments experienced serious problems in the conversion to competitive goods and services. This transformation constituted a key obstacle. Nearly all the East German firms were unfamiliar with establishing market relationships with suppliers and customers. Moreover, they had difficulties in achieving comparable terms and conditions in their supplier and customer relationships in relation to their West German competitors. The East German firms frequently had to pay higher prices for inputs, received less revenue for their goods and services and had to compete on lower profit margins.

Another major reason for the productivity shortfall of many of the East German firms was the existence of severe deficiencies in the field of internal work organisation. Obviously, cost efficiency and customer-orientation tend to be tacit skills that are often hard to convey to workers trained in a socialist system. Further disadvantages of East German establishments were caused by the relatively bad condition of the region's infrastructure, particularly in the field of transport and telecommunications.[1]

5.5 Conclusions

The results of our analysis suggest that the impact of a firm's physical capital stock on its productivity performance is often overestimated. Other factors seem to have a larger influence. According to our findings, the way machinery is used is at least as important for a firm's productivity as the quality of the machinery. Therefore, policies that aim to improve what might be called the 'technological standard' of firms should not merely concentrate on investment in modern equipment. To provide help for firms choosing adequate machinery and making better use of their existing physical capital stock may have an even bigger effect on their performance than measures such as subsidies on investment in physical capital that primarily try to stimulate the adoption of modern technology.

With respect to East Germany and other post-socialist countries of Eastern Europe our analysis showed that there is no need for a complete replacement of the old capital stock in order for the firms to be competitive. There is no doubt that in many firms some new machinery should be introduced. However, the crucial problem is to decide which parts of the physical capital stock should be retrofitted or substituted by which kind of new equipment. Advice concerning this decision may have a much larger impact on economic performance than any type of financial assistance.

[1] For a more detailed analysis of the causes for East-West German productivity differences see Fritsch and Mallok (1998) and Mallok (1996).

References

Ewers, H.-J., Becker, C., Fritsch, M. (1990a) The Nature of Employment Effects of New Technology. In: Matzner, E., Wagner, M. (eds.) The Employment Impact of New Technology - The Case of West Germany. Avebury, Aldershot, 23-41

Ewers, H.-J., Becker, C., Fritsch M. (1990b) The Effects of the Use of Computer-Aided Technology in Industrial Enterprises – It's the Context that Counts, in: Ronald Schettkat and Michael Wagner (eds.), Technological Change and Employment – Innovation in the German Economy. de Gruyter, Berlin/New York, 25-63

Finegold, D., Wagner, K. (1999) Transforming the German Metalworking Industry: Moves Towards Numerical Flexibility. Work Study 48(3), 81-87

Fritsch, M., Mallok, J. (1998) Surviving the Transition: The Process of Adaptation of Small and Medium-sized Firms in East Germany. In: Brezinski, H., Franck, E., Fitsch, M. (eds.) The Microeconomics of Transition and Growth. Elgar, Cheltenham, 163-184

Hitchens, D.M.W.N., Birnie, J.E., Hamar, J., Wagner, K., Zemplinerová, A. (1995) Competitiveness of Industry in the Czech Republic and Hungary. Avebury, Aldershot

Hitchens, D.M.W.N., Wagner, K., Birnie, J.E. (1990) Closing the Productivity Gap: A Comparison of Northern Ireland, The Republic of Ireland, Britain and West Germany. Avebury, Aldershot

Hitchens, D.M.W.N., Wagner, K., Birnie, J.E. (1993) East German Productivity and the Transition to the Market Economy. Avebury, Aldershot

Mallok, J. (1996), Engpässe in ostdeutschen Fabriken ("Bottlenecks in East German plants"). Edition Sigma, Berlin

Sinn, G., Sinn, H.-W. (1992) Jumpstart: The Economic Reunification of Germany. MIT Press, Cambridge, MA

6 The Effect of Internationalisation on the Rate of Growth of High-Tech Start-Ups: Evidence for the UK and Germany

Oliver Burgel[1], Andreas Fier[2], Georg Licht[2] and Gordon Murray[1]
[1] London Business School, UK
[2] Centre for European Economic Research, Mannheim, Germany

6.1 Introduction

Much attention in empirical research on entrepreneurship has been devoted to the growth and survival of young enterprises. Economic policy-makers too are increasingly attempting to improve the climate for the genesis and growth of new businesses. Arguably, this is due to a widespread belief of the large potential for job creation by successful, new businesses. More recently, the rapid internationalisation of high-tech start-ups has generated increasing attention. It is argued that a global markets presence is essential for a high-tech firm's long term success, including its ability to reap acceptable profits from innovation. Case study evidence suggests that early internationalisation contributes to success in high-tech markets. The step from home to foreign markets is often associated with increased growth prospects. 70 percent of UK firms (and 60 percent of German firms) in our sample of high-tech start-ups consider the potential of foreign markets for long-term company growth as their main motive for international business activities. Exploitation of the potential of foreign markets appears especially important for young firms acting in technological niches with typically short product life cycles. They often have to recover considerable initial R&D expenses and investments in human/capital assets in relatively short periods of time. Invariably, international business activities are more costly and time consuming for a small firm than the alternative of exclusively serving a local or national home market. A perverse result of rapid internationalisation is that it may initially actually retard firm growth. Therefore, the growth-enhancing effects of international business activities may be seen as ambiguous – at least in the short run.

In this study we examine these issues in more detail. By looking at high-tech start-ups in two European countries we are able to shed light on the importance of firm-specific factors, 'regional' endowments and the effects of rapid sales internationalisation on the performance of start-ups in the early stages of their life cycle. Depending on the specific characteristics of the firms, their founders and their products, we have shown in previous work that early international expansion is an important feature of many high-tech start-ups (e.g. Bürgel *et al.* 1998).

This chapter is structured as follows. The next section briefly summarises the existing research on international sales, innovation and performance at the firm level. The data and theoretical foundations for our empirical model are then described. After that, we present the empirical results concerning the growth of high-tech start-ups with and without international sales in their early years. Finally, we summarise the main result and draw our conclusions.

6.2 Review of the Recent Literature

In the field of industrial economics, several authors have looked at the export probabilities of plants, and the relation of international sales to firm performance. Roberts and Tybout (1997) stress that the sunk cost of market entry is important in explaining the export decision. Employing a dynamic discrete-choice model, they show that sunk entry costs and past export experience are important determinants of current export status. Using US data, Bernard and Jensen (1999) show that 'above average quality' firms become exporters. However, the direction of causality is important and being an exporter does not affect the 'quality' of a firm. Bernard and Jensen also show that the export status has a positive impact on the growth of firms. Similar results are presented by Bernard and Wagner (1997) for Germany. However, the evidence presented in Clerides *et al.* (1998) is not consistent with the 'learning-by-exporting' hypothesis. It indicates that the superior performance of exporters is accounted for by a self-selection process of the better firms. In addition, Wakelin (1998) shows that past innovations positively effect the export probability of large UK firms. For German service firms, Ebling and Janz (1998) demonstrate that it is more likely that innovation results in exports than vice versa.

However, these empirical results have been obtained using data from well established, medium and large sized firms. Small start-up companies in high-technology market may exhibit substantially different characteristics. There is however some literature dealing more specifically with the performance and internationalisation of young high-technology firms. McDougall and Oviatt (1996) show that increased international exposure only enhances firm performance when international market entry is accompanied by a change in the firm's strategy. Bloodgood *et al.* (1996) looked at high-tech ventures two years after their IPO. They found that internationalisation was positively related to the absolute level of sales but not to sales growth. Lindqvist (1991), McDougall *et al.* (1994), Bell (1995), as well as Reuber and Fischer (1997) point towards the effects of specific technological advantages and the international work experience of the founders on the likelihood of international sales in the early stages of firm's life cycle. Only McDougall and Oviatt (1996) and Bloodgood *et al.* (1995) specifically examine the performance of internationalising start-ups. Yet, their findings remain somewhat inconclusive. We know of no study which has investigated this issue with non-US data generated using a random sample of firms.

6.3 Theoretical Framework

Our basic approach is to employ the standard empirical growth models well-known from the literature on firm growth (see surveys by Sutton 1998 and Caves 1998) and to augment these models by employing specific variables relevant to international sales. We not only look at the average growth rate of the firm, but also examine more closely whether or not internationalisation increased the number of fast growing firms (often called 'gazelles'). It is these 'fast track' firms (Storey 1994) which are the most important enterprises when looking at the macro-economic impact of start-ups. The standard econometric growth model can be written as:

$$\ln\left(\frac{A_{t+1}}{A_t}\right) = \sum_{i=0}^{n} \beta_i \cdot \ln(\mu_i) + (\theta - 1) \cdot \ln(A_t) + \varepsilon \qquad (6.1)$$

where A represent a performance measure (sales, employment) and t and t+1 indicate time periods. μ can be thought of as a measure for, or a proxy of, a particular factor effecting the average growth rate of the i-th group of firms (e.g. a certain industry). β indicates whether these features are associated with above or below average growth rates. Davis *et al.* (1996) argue that firm growth is largely driven by idiosyncratic features (e.g. management strategies) and that standard economic variables (like industry, size, foreign competition) explain firm growth rather imperfectly. Our data allow us to uncover some of those idiosyncrasies, for example the human capital endowment of the firm or peculiar product and owner characteristics.

Gibrat's Law proposes that θ–1 is 0 and ε is a normally distributed, random effect. This law simply says that firm size depends on a series of random shocks, and the size distribution within a homogenous group of firms is log normal. However, existing evidence (see Caves 1998) stresses that Gibrat's Law does not hold for firms which are both young and small. Here increased size negatively impacts on growth. So, we should expect that θ will be smaller than 1 in order for the rate of growth to decrease with firm size. In addition, the literature points unequivocally to a negative effect of firm maturity on growth: simply put - older firms grow less quickly. As both size and age dependency are fairly well established in the economic literature (see Sutton 1998), we viewed a replication of these common results as corroborating the model specification chosen. In addition, we hypothesise that additional factors affect the average growth rate and should be included as part of the vector μ equation (6.1). In line with empirical findings from the international entrepreneurship literature (Bloodgood *et al.* 1996; McDougall *et al.* 1994; Lindqvist 1991; Reuber and Fischer 1997), we expect a positive impact on young firm growth from early internationalisation, greater human capital of the founders, higher technological sophistication of the product, and a low degree of diversification. Most importantly, international sales are expected to foster firm growth.

Data Collection and Sampling

One important aim of this study was to analyse the internationalisation of start-ups with a relatively large sample of firms utilising a comparable basis of selection in both Germany and the UK. Arguably, results are more reliable when data from firms with different national backgrounds are employed. Given the existing differences in the trade patterns, technological infrastructures and national educational systems, combining data from both countries offered the opportunity to 'filter out' the influence of these factors on a high-tech firm's behaviour towards international markets.

The Questionnaire: Our data were generated through a mail survey and employed a four page questionnaire which was identical in both countries. The questionnaire included variables to measure 'transaction costs' during the sales process and proxies for situation in which high transaction might occur, e.g. complex installations. In addition, information on the international experience of the founder(s) was requested. We also asked respondents several general questions about the characteristics of their firm, including details of the goods and services produced as well as the resources devoted to product and process development. Finally, the respondents were asked to rank different motivations for international activities, and to determine the scale of costs and other constraints which they had experienced during this process.

Definition of High-tech Start-ups or New Technology Based Firms (NTBFs): For the purpose of this study, a high-tech start-up is defined as being a legally independent company which is no older than ten years and operates in a high-technology sector(s) (see Appendix). We use the list of high technology sectors established by Butchart (1987) to determine the relevant sectors in manufacturing. In addition, we have included start-ups from selected service industries which where found to be R&D intensive in a recent German study (Licht *et al.* 1997). One arguable weakness of our study is that we neglect high-start ups in low-tech industries. Rather than targeting low technology sectors searching for occasional high technology start-ups, our approach resulted in an increased likelihood of obtaining responses from technology-intensive firms in our mail survey.

Data Sources and Sampling Frame: We use sampling frames generated from similar data sources in both countries. Sampling was based on firms operating in the industries defined above, which had at least three employees in 1997 and had been founded between 1987 and 1996. To identify those firms, we used data from Dun & Bradstreet in the UK and Creditreform in Germany. They are both leading credit rating and business information agencies in each country. All identified company records were subsequently screened to exclude those firms whose business activities suggested that they were not primarily engaged in producing and developing high-tech goods or services. As a result, 2,671 firms in UK and 5045 firms in Germany were retained as eligible for inclusion in the sample. In each country, we selected 2,000 firms using a stratified random sampling process (i.e. stratified by size class and service/manufacturing categorisation).

The Survey: The mail survey was started in October 1997. It resulted in 232 usable questionnaires for Germany and 362 for the UK. Despite the difference in response rates between the countries (24 percent of eligible firms in the UK; 14 percent in Germany), the response rates within the sampling strata were distributed in a similar way. This hints at a low selectivity bias in the response behaviour of firms. As we were interested in inferring from our sample values for the wider population of high tech young firms, we calculated weights for each strata taking into account the inclusion probability and the response probability. The inclusion probability accounts for the bias introduced through the deliberate over- or under-sampling due to the stratified random sampling process. It is calculated by dividing the number of firms by the number of firms in the adjusted (cleaned) Dun & Bradstreet and Creditreform samples per strata. Therefore, strata specific weights are calculated as the inverse of the product of inclusion probability and response probability per strata.

Descriptive Analysis

The means and standard deviations for the variables used in this study are summarised in Table 6.1. The most important message of this table is that the firms from both countries appear rather similar. The most obvious differences between the UK and Germany regard the age of the firm. This is simply due to the fact that data on East German firms were not available for start-ups in the years 1987-90. The majority of high-tech start-ups enter international markets in the first decade of their existence. Even when we consider that the share of internationally active firms could be subject to overestimation due to a response bias, we were nevertheless surprised by the large number of firms in our sample which had internationalised. The similarity between the samples is confirmed when looking at mean values. Both the German and the UK sample show similar characteristics with regard to various key variables, e.g. the distribution of firm sizes is similar both countries at the time of start-up and also at the time of the survey.

These similarities are confirmed by looking beyond the summary descriptive statistics. Figure 6.1 shows weighted, non parametric, kernel density estimates (a non-parametric estimation technique used to analyse distributions) for sales and employment growth. At first sight, we can conclude that the logarithms of the differences in sales and in employment levels is approximately normally distributed. Moreover, the distribution of growth rates seems not to differ much between Germany and the UK. Most of the (surviving) firms in both countries showed very impressive annualised sales revenue growth rates of between 25 and 35 percent. Employment growth is similarly distributed except that these growth rates were somewhat lower with the majority of firms falling within the 17-25 percent interval.

Table 6.1 Descriptive statistics regarding the UK and German data set

	Raw Data				Weighted data			
	UK		Germany		UK		Germany	
Variable	Mean/ Share		Mean/ Share		Mean/ Share		Mean/ Share	
West German firms			0.66				0.75	
East German firms			0.34				0.25	
ICT-Hardware	0.21		0.18		0.18		0.11	
Engineering	0.17		0.13		0.14		0.07	
Bio/Med/Life	0.09		0.08		0.07		0.05	
Other industries	0.26		0.31		0.22		0.18	
International sales	0.71		0.63		0.63		0.56	
Employment at start-up	4.5	(6.7)	5.9	(8.4)	4.0	(5.9)	4.7	(6.1)
Employment 1998	20.2	(23.7)	18.9	(21.2)	16.3	(21.4)	15.2	(18.4)
Age of Firm (1999)	7.1	(2.4)	6.5	(2.2)	6.8	(2.4)	6.1	(2.2)
Venture capital backed	0.11		0.09		0.10		0.09	
Public grants recipient	0.18		0.27		0.14		0.20	
Work experience abroad	0.53		0.31		0.52		0.31	
Work experience in MNU	0.51		0.35		0.48		0.35	
Education abroad	0.13		0.15		0.13		0.15	
Number of founders:								
2-3	0.43		0.28		0.44		0.29	
3-4	0.20		0.31		0.18		0.29	
5 and more	0.05		0.07		0.06		0.08	
R&D employment (as %)	20.8	(19.7)	19.6	(20.2)	22.8	(21.6)	23.0	(22.6)
Occasional R&D	0.27		0.31		0.31		0.36	
Permanent R&D	0.60		0.49		0.56		0.41	
Window of Opportunity								
Larger than 1 year	0.53		0.59		0.53		0.60	
Unknown	0.23		0.23		0.22		0.26	
High Customisation	0.30		0.35		0.32		0.30	
Age of Product	5.4	(2.5)	5.3	(2.2)	5.2	(2.5)	5.1	(2.2)
Share of Best Selling Product:								
30-60%	0.37		0.38		0.36		0.36	
60-80%	0.30		0.32		0.32		0.38	
80-100%	0.12		0.13		0.13		0.13	
Capital good	0.35		0.51		0.34		0.51	
Intermediate good / service	0.33		0.20		0.31		0.16	

Note: Standard deviation in brackets.
Source: LBS/ZEW (2000).

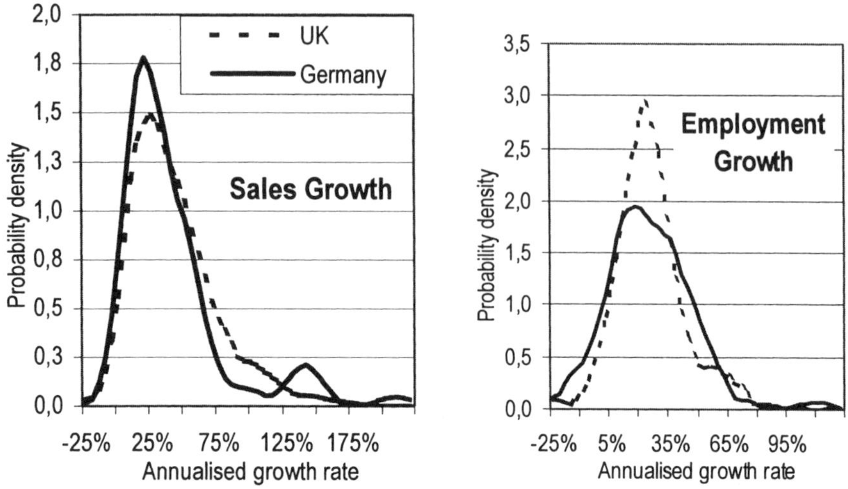

Source: LBS/ZEW (2000).

Fig. 6.1 Estimated distribution of sales and employment growth of high-tech start-ups by country

6.4 Results and Discussion

The average growth rates experienced by the firms in the sample were examined in relation to::

(a) (expected) sales in the current financial year and the first financial year in which the firms generated sales, and
(b) employment at the time of the survey and employment at start-up. Because of different ages of the firms in our sample, growth is best measured using 'average annualised growth rates':

$$G_i = \frac{\ln A_{t_{i2}} - \ln A_{t_{i1}}}{(t_{i2} - t_{i1})} \tag{6.2}$$

The growth rate of the variable A (sales or employment) between two time intervals t_2 and t_1 is calculated as the difference at these two points in time between sales and employment levels after taking logs divided by the length of time interval (measured in years). This formulation implicitly assumes an exponential growth path.

Estimation Procedures

Inferences about the determinants of firm growth might be biased if endogeneity existed among the independent variables. For example, if venture capitalists selected their investee firms based on previous track record, the causal relationship would run from (past) growth to venture capital involvement and not the other way round. The same argument can be used for internationalisation, which can be expected to be endogenous because strong (past) growth will more probably bring a firm to the limits of the domestic market. The consequence of this saturated home market will be that the growing firm is obliged to internationalise. Thus, internationalisation becomes a consequence of growth and not vice versa. In order to avoid those problems, we have used neither observed venture capital involvement nor observed internationalisation status. Rather, for the underlying observation, we use predictions of the latent variables from probit models on venture capital involvement, internationalisation status and public grants obtained. (Estimation results for these equations are available from the authors on request). Two approaches are used to assess the impact of internationalisation on growth. First, we estimate the model given in (6.1) by an instrumental variable procedure. Second, we transform the growth rate into a dummy variable in order to look only at the differences between slow growing and fast growing firms. In addition, both models are estimated for sales as well as for employment growth. Given that sales and employment growth rates should be related, we expect to find similar determinants of sales and employment growth.

Determinants of Firm Growth

The results of our regression models are presented in Tables 6.2 and 6.3. The former presents the results for the sales and employment growth models using standard OLS models with instruments for the internationalisation, venture capital and public grants status. Table 6.3 contains the probit model. Results for sales and employment growth turn out to be quite similar. Therefore we discuss results for both the sales and employment growth models together. We will highlight similarities and differences between both performance measures and interpret these findings in the light of theory and the existing literature.

International Sales: Firms with international sales showed higher growth rates than firms which operated only in the domestic market. Elasticity of the growth rate with respect to internationalisation was 13 percent. Thus, a 100 percent increase in the latent inclination to internationalisation would imply an increase in the average annual growth rate from 25 to 38 percent. Therefore, the effect of internationalisation on sales growth was quite remarkable in its significance. However, internationalisation only marginally affected employment growth. The results from the employment growth regression were statistically not different from zero. Taken together, the effect of internationalisation on sales growth and on employment growth imply a productivity enhancing effect of internationalisation. The growth motive of the owners or managers was confirmed by the observed growth rate differential between firms with international sales and firms without international sales.

Table 6.2 Sales and employment growth regressions – variable estimates

	Sales Growth		Employment Growth	
Exogenous variables	Coeff.	Asy. t-value*	Coeff.	Asy. t-value*
West Germany	-0.061	-1.98	-0.020	-1.09
East Germany	0.037	0.68	-0.011	-0.43
log (age)	-0.406	-6.30	-0.229	-6.40
log (sales first financial year)	-0.132	-7.55	-0.121	-12.46
Number of founders:				
2-3	0.045	1.55	0.009	0.53
3-4	0.120	2.93	0.036	1.90
5 and more	0.190	2.29	0.031	0.90
Shortage in competencies:				
Sale/Marketing	0.010	0.67	-0.001	-0.08
Production/R&D	0.018	1.05	0.014	1.36
Permanent R&D	0.064	2.35	0.022	1.43
Window of Opportunity:				
larger than 1 year	-0.014	-1.43	-0.031	-1.64
Not known	-0.038	-1.94	-0.049	-2.27
log (age of product)	-0.054	-1.89	N.A.	
Share of Best Selling Product:				
30-60%	0.053	1.65	N. A.	
60-80%	0.076	2.06		
80-100%	0.116	2.23		
Venture capital	0.056	0.67	0.044	0.97
Public grants	0.024	0.29	0.052	1.30
International sales	0.291	2.87	0.080	1.41
Constant	1.119	10.33	0.784	12.84
Summary statistics:				
Number of observations / R^2	503/ 0.25		528 / 0.36	
Specification Tests				
Functional Form Reset Test [1]				
F(24, 459) / p-value	1.14 / 0.30		0.60 / 0.92	
Heteroscedasticity [2]				
χ^2 / p-value	131.15 / 0.00		50.10 / 0.00	

Source: LBS/ZEW (2000).
N.A. = not available
* based on heteroscedasticity robust standard errors
[1] Cook-Weisberg test using powers of the fitted values
[2] Ramsey Reset test using powers of the exogenous variables

Table 6.3 Determinants of fast growth by firms – results using Probit models

	Sales and employment growth[2] fastest 25%		Sales growth fastest 10%[1]		Employment growth fastest 10%[1]	
Variables	Coeff.	t-value	Coeff.	t-value	Coeff.	t-value
West German firms	-0.208	-1.05	-0.350	-1.67	-0.297	-1.20
East German firms	0.275	1.00	0.262	0.92	0.477	1.65
ICT-Hardware	0.296	1.28	0.049	0.19	0.428	1.57
Engineering	-0.320	-1.21	0.104	0.40	0.150	0.51
Bio/Med/Life	-0.412	-1.08	-0.032	-0.09	-0.151	-0.38
Other industries	-0.210	-0.86	-0.578	-2.13	-0.080	-0.29
log (age)	-2.088	-5.48	-1.844	-4.70	-2.789	-6.18
log (no. empl. at start-up)	-0.729	-5.43	-0.353	-2.90	-1.189	-6.54
Number of founders:						
2-3	-0.256	-1.25	-0.159	-0.65	-0.139	-0.60
3-4	0.089	0.36	0.592	2.48	0.130	0.45
5 and more	0.446	0.99	0.714	1.87	0.800	1.48
Venture capital	0.363	1.25	0.094	0.30	0.116	0.33
Public grants	0.292	1.38	0.302	1.31	0.293	1.16
International sales	0.936	1.36	0.289	0.39	0.924	1.14
Permanent R&D	-0.066	-0.40	0.591	3.15	0.070	0.36
Best selling products (%):						
30-60%	0.188	0.72	0.124	0.44	0.240	0.78
60-80%	0.087	0.32	0.434	1.50	0.067	0.21
80-100%	0.695	2.20	0.344	0.93	0.566	1.52
Constant	2.781	4.51	1.441	2.36	3.750	5.21
Summary statistics:						
Number observations	503		503		528	
Wald χ^2	84.72		83.73		116.24	
Pseudo R^2	0.24		0.26		0.37	

Source: ZEW/WBS (1998).

[1] Fast growing firms are defined as those which belong to the fastest growing 10% (these obtain a value of 1, whereas all other companies have a value of 0).

[2] Firms belonging to the fastest growing 25% of enterprises in each growth dimension.

Therefore, internationalisation increased the returns to the initial investment in R&D and also human capital assets, both of which are necessary to enter high-tech markets. The lack of effect of internationalisation on employment growth should not be viewed as indicative of business failure. Rather, given the high risk exposure of a high-tech entrepreneur, the wealth-creating effect of internationalisation likely remains a more important personal goal than immediate employment growth. The larger international market enables firm to realise economies of scale. Furthermore, it is also clear from an inspection of the distribution of growth rates that a large share of the additional sales and employment generation is due to only a small number of firms. This seems to be especially true for the UK. Therefore, it is important to known whether or not the process of internationalisation contributed to the formation of these high growth/high potential firms. However, Table 6.3 shows that international sales is not a necessary condition for fast growth.

Country-specific effects: German start-ups showed a lower sales growth rate than UK start-ups. However, this sales growth differential was mainly due to the lower performance of West German companies which recorded on average a 6 per cent lower average annual growth rate than the UK firms. This clearly shows the influence of the macro-economic slump which hit West-Germany during the 1990s. In addition, based on case study evidence for a small number of our sample firm, it is also possible that a shorter pre-formation period resulted in smaller sales in the first financial year for the UK firms. This implies a larger potential for growth in the following years.

Start-up size and age of the firm: All models demonstrated a strong negative effect for the initial firm size on firm growth. This is compatible with the hypothesis that there is a minimum efficient scale and that firms are regularly founded at a sub-optimal size (see Ericson and Pakes 1995; Jovanovic 1992). This result is also in line with the majority of the existing economic literature on start-up growth (see Wagner 1992 for Germany, Dunne and Hughes 1994 for the UK). Hence, start-ups gain confidence in their growth potential, increase investment to reach their minimum efficient size. Our regression results show a strong negative effect for age on firm growth. This is in line with Ericson and Pakes' argument that firms gradually learn about their productivity after market entry.

Size of Founding Team and Shortages of Skills: Especially in the first years of a firm's existence, a larger human capital base can be view as a source of knowledge which can assist growth (see Brüderl *et al.* 1996). Conversely, it can also be argued that there is an increased chance that managers in a larger team will more likely be in conflict with each other resulting in growth reducing frictions (Eisenhardt and Schoonhoven 1990). However, our data was quite convincing: the larger the start-up team of owners/founders, the greater are the growth prospects of the firm. Venture capitalists' preference for team-based start-ups investments appears vindicated. In addition, we used the self-assessment of the present management to ascertain whether their company experienced severe skill shortages at the time of start-up. Yet, we do not identify a significant impact of shortages in management skills on firm growth.[1]

Research & Development: Sustaining investments in new technologies and new technological know-how is of major concern to high technology firms. Our results confirmed the large positive effects of R&D on sales growth. The estimated coefficient implies a 5-6 percent higher sales growth compared to both non R&D firms or firms which only occasionally conduct R&D. No effect of R&D on employment growth was found.

Window of Opportunity: Gaining profit from R&D, or from other forms of investment in new technologies, is best made when the firm can generate a unique (monopolistic) selling proposition. Product uniqueness was measured by the time period a competitor needs to market a product with similar characteristics at a competitive price. This competition-free time period is called the 'window of opportunity'.[2] We find that firms with a short window of opportunity exhibited larger sales and employment growth rates. An obvious explanation is that these firms must exploit their competitive advantage quickly in order to profit from innovation. In addition, firms with a longer window of opportunity appear to be especially cautious regarding their employment expansion. They seek to realise productivity gains with existing staff resources while exploiting their product based, competitive edge. This can be seen as a risk reducing response given that the duration of a product/market advantage cannot be guaranteed in an uncertain environment. This result is in line with Porter's (1979) argument that firms successfully occupying narrow strategic segments do not need to grow rapidly in order to survive in their chosen market.

Age of the Product: In rapidly changing markets, the age of the product may be more important for the firm's growth than the age of the firm itself. When we view high technology markets as being in a formative stage of evolution, the importance of the establishment of a 'dominant design' becomes evident (see Klepper 1996). Short product life cycles are increasingly typical for high-tech industries where old products frequently do not signal tried-and-tested quality, but out-of-date and superseded designs. Therefore, we would expect higher growth rates in companies whose best selling product is relative immature. This was confirmed by our estimates – sales growth declines as the product gets older. However, this result appears to be due to some 'outlier' firms which were active in highly volatile technology markets (Table 6.3). For the more typical firm, no

---

[1] Using a factor analysis on different possible management shortages (marketing, distribution, general, financial, production, R&D management) we isolated two types: shortages in technological know-how (e.g. production or R&D) and shortages in market related know-how (e.g. distribution, marketing). To evaluate whether a firm experienced a shortage of skill at the time of start-up, we used a 5-point Likert scale where 1 = 'Not at all' and 5 = 'Strongly'. The larger the resulting score, the greater the skill shortage.

[2] We differentiated between firms that had a competitive advantage expected to last longer or less than one year. A fairly large number of firms were not able to give reliable estimates of their 'window of opportunity'. These firms were treated as a separate group.

negative impact of product age on sales growth is obvious (Table 6.2). In addition, the age of the product had no significant impact on employment growth.

Product Diversification: Product differentiation was measured by the sales share of the best selling product. The smaller this share, the more a firm can be described as highly diversified. The results of our models suggest that specialisation has a sales growth enhancing effect. The larger the share of the best selling product, the larger was the observed sales growth rate of the whole firm. Therefore, product diversification is probably not a strategy that pays in early years. Diversifying across technologies or product markets is likely to result in a sub-optimal use of scarce resources.

Financing of Start-up by Venture Capital and Public Grants: Although the political focus of discussions on financing start-ups is primarily directed to the generation of more start-ups, some researchers have argued that the financing issue is also relevant for the growth process of young companies (e.g. Cressy 1996). However, empirical results on the impact of financing constraints on firm growth are rare. Case studies appear to support venture capital's positive effect on the growth of start-ups (see Oakey *et al.* 1988; Murray 1996). However, the evidence did not support the existence of financing constraints as neither venture capital backing nor the public grants enhanced the sales growth of our recipient firms. Likewise, we did not see a significant impact of these financing sources on employment growth.

6.5 Conclusions

Nearly all firms in our sample showed an impressive track record of sales and employment growth. However, we should remember that due to our sampling procedure, only firms surviving their first years are included, so the average growth rate of a complete cohort of new business is certainly lower that the average growth rate of our sample firms. It is well known from other studies that high-tech start-ups show a higher survival rate than other firms (Agarwal 1998). So, if non-surviving firms were also included in our data, the differences between technology-intensive and non-technology-intensive firms would be even more impressive. We found that internationally active firms have better sales performances than non-internationally active firms. Again, some caution is necessary when generalising this effect. As international business activities are probably more risky than purely domestic business activities, it may well be the case that the survivor bias leads to an overestimation of the positive growth effect generated by early internationalisation. This caveat calls for careful study of the relationship between internationalisation and firm survival. Such caution is particularly significant given the expectations held by many politicians and scholars regarding the employment-generating effect of start-ups.

Our results indicate that early internationalisation does not necessarily imply higher employment growth. Early internationalisation seemed to have positive effects on sales growth and competitiveness, but not on employment. Finally, while internationalisation may often occur by chance, our findings suggest that including a commitment to internationalisation in the business plan enhances subsequent success in foreign markets. This finding suggests that founders of high-tech firms should be more determinedly international in their vision and strategies from the very start of their planning if they wish to increase the economic success of their entrepreneurial efforts.

Appendix

Table A.1 Definition of high-tech industries

Aggregated industries	NACE Rev. 1	Short description according to NACE Rev.1
R&D intensive service industries	64.20; 72.20; 72.30; 72.40; 72.60; 73.10	Telecommunication, Computer Programming and Software Services, Data Processing, Misc. Computer Services, R&D in Natural Sciences and Engineering
ICT-hardware	30.01; 30.02; 32.20; 32.30	Office Equipment; Computers and other Information Processing Equipment; Television and Radio Transmitters and Apparatus for Telephony and Telegraphy; Television and Radio Receivers, Sound or Video Recording and Reproducing Apparatus
Engineering Industries	33.20; 33.30; 33.40	Electronic Instruments and Appliances for Measuring, Checking (except Industrial Process Control); Electronic Industrial Process Control Equipment; Optical Instruments; Photographic Equipment
Health and Life Sciences	24.41; 24.42; 33.10	Pharmaceutical Products and Preparations; Medical and Surgical Equipment and Orthopaedic Appliances
Misc. high-tech manufacturing	24.16; 24.17; 31.10; 31.20; 32.10; 35.30	Plastics and Synthetic Rubber in Primary Form; Electric Motors, Generators and Transformers; Electricity Distribution and Control Apparatus; Electronic Valves, Tubes and other Components; Aircraft and Spacecraft Manufacturing

References

Agarwal, R. (1998) Small Firm Survival and Technological Activity. Small Business Economics 11, 215-224

Bell, J. (1995) The Internationalisation of Small Computer Software Firms - A Further Challenge to Stage Theories. European Journal of Marketing 29(8), 60-75

Bernard, A.B., Jensen, J.B. (1999) Exceptional Export Performance: Cause, Effect, or Both? Journal of International Economics 47(1), 1-25

Bernard, A.B., Wagner, J. (1997) Export and Success in German Manufacturing. Weltwirtschaftliches Archiv 133(1), 134-157

Bloodgood, J.M., Sapienza, H.J, Almeida, J.G. (1995) The Internationalization of New High Potential Ventures: Antecedents and Outcomes. Frontiers of Entrepreneurship, Babson College, Wellesley MA.

Brüderl, J., Preisendoerfer, P., Ziegler, R. (1996) Der Erfolg neugegruendeter Betriebe. Duncker & Humblot, Berlin

Bürgel, O, Fier, A., Licht, G., Murray, G., Nerlinger, E.A. (1998) The Internationalisation of British and German Start-Up Companies in High-Technology Industries. ZEW Discussion Paper No. 98-34, Mannheim

Butchart R. (1987) A New UK Definition of High-Technology Industries. Economic Trends 400, 82-88

Caves, R.E. (1998) Industrial Organisation and New Findings on the Turnover and Mobility of Firms. Journal of Economic Literature 34(4), 1947-1982

Chabral, L. (1995) Sunk Costs, Firm Size and Firm Growth. Journal of Industrial Economics 43(1), 161-172

Clerides, S., Lach, S., Tybout, J.R. (1998) Is Learning by Exporting Important? Micro-Dynamic Evidence from Colombia, Mexico, and Morocco. Quarterly Journal of Economics 113(4), 903-947

Cressy, R. (1996) Are Business Start-ups Debt-Rationed? The Economic Journal 106(4), 1253-1270

Davis, S.J., Haltiwanger, J.C., Schuh, S. (1996) Job Creation and Destruction. MIT Press, Cambridge, MA.

Dunne, P., Hughes, A. (1994) Age, Size, Growth, and Survival: UK Companies in the 1980s. Journal of Industrial Economics 42(1), 115-140

Ebling, G., Janz, N. (1998) Export Behaviour and Innovation Activities in the Service Sector – Empirical Results for a Cross Section of German Firms, Mannheim, mimeo

Eisenhardt, K., Schoonhoven, C. (1990) Organizational Growth: Linking Founding Team, Strategy, Environment, and Growth among US Semiconductor Ventures, 1978-1988. Administrative Science Quarterly 35(3), 504-529

Ericson, R., Pakes, A. (1995) Markov-Perfect Industry Dynamics: A Framework for Empirical Work. Review of Economic Studies 62(1), 53-82

Jovanovic, B. (1982) Selection and Evolution of Industry. Econometrica 50(2), 649-670

Klepper, S. (1996) Entry, Exit, Growth and Innovation over the Product Life Cycle. American Economic Review 86(2), 560-581

Licht, G., Hipp, C., Kukuk, M., Münt, G., Janz, N. (1997), Innovationen im Dienstleistungssektor. Nomos, Baden-Baden

Lindqvist, M. (1991) Infant Multinationals: The Internationalization of Young, Technology-Based Swedish Firms. Unpublished doctoral dissertation, Stockholm School of Economics, Institute of International Business, Stockholm

McDougall, P.P., Oviatt, B.M. (1996) New Venture Internationalisation, Strategic Change and Performance: A Follow-up Study. Journal of Business Venturing 11(1), 23-40

McDougall, P.P., Shane, S., Oviatt, B.M. (1994) Explaining the Formation of International New Ventures: The Limits of International Business Research. Journal of Business Venturing 9(6), 469-487

Murray, G.C. (1996) A Synthesis of Six Exploratory, European Case Studies of Successfully-Exited, Venture Capital Financed, New Technology-Based Firms. Entrepreneurship Theory and Practice 20, 44-60

Oakey, R., Rothwell, R., Cooper, S. (1988) The Management of Innovation in High-Technology Small Firms. Pinter, London

Porter, M.E. (1979) The Structure within Industries and Companies' Performance. Review of Economics and Statistics 61(1), 214-227

Reuber, A.R., Fisher, E. (1997) The Influence of the Management Team's International Experience on the Internationalization Behaviour of SMEs. Journal of International Business Studies 28, 807-825

Roberts, M.J., Tybout, J.R. (1997) The Decision to Export in Colombia: An Empirical Model of Entry with Sunk Costs. American Economic Review 87(2), 545-564

Storey, D. J. (1994) Understanding the Small Business Sector, London

Sutton, J. (1998) Gibrat's Legacy. Journal of Economic Literature 35(1), 40-59

Wagner, J. (1992) Firm Size, Firm Growth, and Persistence of Chance: Testing Gibrat's Law with Establishment Data from Lower Saxony, 1978-1989. Journal of Small Business Economics 4(1), 125-131

Wakelin, K. (1998) Innovation and Export Behaviour at the Firm Level. Research Policy 26(4), 829-884

7 Survival, Growth, and Interfirm Collaboration of Start-Up Companies in High Technology Industries: A Case Study of Upper Bavaria

Johannes Hampe[1] and Martin Steininger[2]
[1] Dpt. Economics, Ludwig-Maximilians-University of Munich
[2] Technische Universität, Munich

7.1 Introduction

The theory of the firm is a central part of (neo)classical microeconomic analysis. In models of competitive markets, contestable markets and monopolistic competition, entries of new enterprises and exits of old enterprises change market structure and performance and are an important factor in reaching the long-term equilibrium in an industry. "Turnover processes are ubiquitous among plants and firms classified to an industry. They are also stable, explicable, and can be embraced within the traditional thinking based on market-equilibrium models that underlies the bulk of empirical research in industrial organisation." (Caves 1998, p. 1975).

In this chapter, working on the basis of such models, we examine the conditions for entries of new enterprises into a market and exits of old enterprises. Micro-economic and industrial economic text-books tend to deal with cases in which new enterprises fight for entry in a given market with existing firms. In these cases, the lower costs of the enterprises already in the market obstruct the entry of new enterprises. "A barrier to entry may be defined as a cost of producing (at some or every rate of output) which must be borne by a firm which seeks to enter an industry but is not borne by firms already in the industry" (Stigler 1968, p. 67).

Most of the German contributions to research on company foundation are quantitative studies in business economics in which empirical determinants of foundations within an ad hoc developed reference framework are described. The transaction cost theory of Coase (1953) and its improvement by Williamson (1975, 1989) supply a theoretical instrument to explain the foundation of firms. On this basis Picot *et al.* (1989) developed a theory which attempts to explain the foundation of a firm. In this approach, too, the strong concentration on cost-theoretical interdependencies causes difficulty in explaining the genesis of firms which develop completely new goods (technically) and hence form new markets.

In the long run, however, the foundations of technologically innovative firms are what advances the structural change and development of an economy.

"Many of the persistently most profitable firms in the United States are companies which came into existence along with the products with which they are most closely associated, e.g. Kodak, Gillette, Kellogg's, Gerber, Campbell Soup, Polaroid, Coca Cola, Wrigley, and Hoover" (Mueller 1991, p. 9). For such new enterprises, cost considerations are of smaller importance since they do not have to fight for market entry with competitors who are already present on the market. However, the same holds true for established firms that are successful in new markets with the continuing development of new products or even the complete conversion of their product programme. Traditional (conglomerate) companies (like Siemens or Nokia) have diversified into new markets, such as microelectronics and telecommunications. Some old enterprises from basic industry (above all the steel and mining sector) have switched to new products and new markets, especially in the telecommunication sector (e.g. Mannesmann has now been taken over by Vodafone). Other have established themselves in a different market like tourism (e.g. Preussag by taking over Hapag-Lloyd, TUI and Thomson Travel).

In this analysis, the relationship will be treated predominantly in the context of the product cycle models, which are also used to explain regional developments (Markusen 1985). On the one hand, the longer a firm exists in the market, the more it learns to decrease costs and increase efficiency. On the other, high profits can be obtained in the first phase of the product cycle, although the danger of failure is great, too. Empirical investigations have been able to show the influence of the product cycle phase in which the firm entered the market on its probability of survival (Agarwal and Gort 1996).

The research work reported here deals with the more pragmatic economic-political questions, and attempts neither to propose a general micro-economic theory of firm formation nor deal with the specific theories which try to explain the development of high-tech enterprises which enter the market in the first phase of the product cycle or follow basic innovations 'in swarms' (Schumpeter 1952) and form new industries. Our contribution is restricted to the analysis of the importance of new high-tech enterprises for structural change and the growth of employment in a region and to establishing factors for the development, survival and growth of these new firms. Since we regard only foundations within the high-tech area, we cannot predict differences in the founding, innovative and co-operative behaviour of firms in high-tech industries compared with others.

We will first describe the data sources which we had at our disposal and also explain the definitions used for high-tech firms, entries and exits. We then make an empirical analysis of survival probabilities of newly founded enterprises and their determinants. This is followed by the part of the work based on data from the survey, which deals with the innovative and co-operative behaviour of new firms. Because of limited space we will restrict ourselves to the description of the empirical results of the survey with regard to the co-operative and innovative behaviour and development of newly founded firms.

7.2 Data Sources and Definitions

The data sources used in this study are the data sets of the Chamber of Industry and Commerce for Munich and Upper Bavaria containing the registrations of businesses in selected high-tech industries, and a questionnaire given to some firms on this list. The Chamber of Industry and Commerce data set serves for the registration of potential members. Irrespective of the notification of the Chamber fees, everybody having registered a business receives a communication from the Chamber of Industry and Commerce as well as later the Chamber's journal four times a year. Therefore there is a constant examination of the list of addresses.

For the purpose of the analysis of the formation of firms, the disadvantages of the records at the Chamber of Industry and Commerce have already been discussed, particularly in the context of research work by the Institute for Sociology at the University of Munich which used the same data set (Brüderl *et al.* 1992). One problem is that new start-ups cannot be distinguished from the takeovers and shifts of existing firms. But since our analysis pays special attention to the regional effects, in our opinion all firm entries in a region provide a suitable starting point. On the basis of the traditional model of market equilibrium, all changes in the structure of companies in a region should in the long run result in an adjustment to the optimal allocation of factors of production. It has to be considered, however, that the registration of a business does not necessarily mean that the business activity is exercised. Pseudo registrations of businesses and the existence of second jobs cannot be detected. These are likely to be included particularly among the small businesses. In additional, as all managing partners in partnerships have to notify the Chamber, when non-contemporary notification occurs, allocation to the foundation of the same firm is not ensured. Because of the factors mentioned above a certain overestimation of foundations is probable. Nevertheless, we feel that – at least for the high-tech sectors chosen – the error rate should not be so large that it systematically distorts the statistical analysis. Many of the interviewed companies which at the time of foundation had no employees, except the founder, had in the meanwhile developed into 'real' firms.

Many recent studies on the foundation of firms have not used the Chamber of Industry and Commerce data, but the start-up panel (West) of the *Zentrum für Europäische Wirtschaftsforschung (ZEW)* based upon the CREDITREFORM data record (see Nerlinger 1998). CREDITREFORM records all new businesses in the register of companies, but only investigates them if there are inquiries about the creditworthiness of an enterprise. Thus on the one hand pseudo registrations of businesses are probably excluded. On the other hand, it can safely be assumed that certain foundations are underevaluated. According to Harhoff and Steil this underestimation concerns "... primarily the smallest businesses (so-called small traders)" (Harhoff and Steil 1997, p. 16).

We obtained the following data from the data of the Chamber of Industry and Commerce:

- name of firm and legal form of the company;
- location of the firm, available as the address with postal zip code. The

addresses were assigned to the four planning regions which form the districts used by the Chamber and for administrative purposes, and to different types of structural regions defined by the Federal Research Institute for Regional Geography and Regional Planning (BfLR);

- year, month, and day of the registration of the business, provided that this was before 01.01.1985, or was newly registered after 01.01.1985. In the following, we constitute this date as the date of foundation;
- year, month and day of exit of trade or ceasing of business activity. We used the exit of trade or an earlier date of rest as the date of abandonment;
- the size of firm, assigning it to one of thirteen size classes, namely 0 employee, 1-3 employees, 4-6, 7-9, 10-19, 20-49, 50-99, 100-199, 200-499, 500-999, 1000-4999, 5000-9999, 10000 and more employees;
- the classification of firms into the sectors, according to the five-digit classification of industrial sectors (WZ 93) of the Federal Statistical Office.

Our empirical analyses have concentrated on firms in the high-tech sector (see Table 7.1). A technology-intensive industry is defined as a high-tech industry if certain industry-specific input or output indicators are satisfied. The indicators adopted are those normally employed, e.g. expenditure on research and development (R&D), employees in R&D, patents, or share of turnover with product or process innovation. In the present investigation, we have classified firms into technology-intensive sectors (see Nerlinger 1998), based on the definition of 'technology-intensive' goods by OECD (Gehrke and Grupp 1994). Branches of trades referred to as (cutting-edge) high technology are those which have an intensity of R&D (expenditures on R&D referring to the turnover) of over 8.5 percent. These sectors are registered with five-digits in the classification of industry (WZ 79).

Table 7.1 High-tech sectors of economy: manufacturing

WZ 93	Industry
24.4	Pharmaceutical products
24.6	Miscellaneous chemicals [1]
30.020	Electronic computers
33.1	Surgical, medical and dental instruments
33.2	Engineering, laboratory instruments, scientific and research instruments, measuring and controlling instruments
33.40.2	Optical instruments and lenses
33.40.3	Photographic equipment and supplies [2]
35.3	Aerospace equipment manufacture

[1] This industry is counted by Gehrke and Grupp among the high-order technology sectors, but was included here because some high-tech products were registered among Miscellaneous chemicals (24.6).
[2] This industry by Gehrke and Grupp is counted among high-order technology.

The classification of industries in the data set which we used to analyse the probability of survival of firms was undertaken by the Chamber of Industry and Commerce. During the analysis of the questionnaire, this allocation was corrected according to the responses of firms with respect to the products manufactured by them. This led in particular to a shift of a small number of firms from the manufacturing to the service sector.

The industries listed in Table 7.1 were those with the most advanced manufacturing technology (excluding 23.30.0 – Nuclear material industry). As well as these industrial manufacturing sectors, we also considered selected technology-intensive service sectors, as in other recent research studies (Nerlinger 1998). According to WZ 93, this includes the industries listed in Table 7.2.

Table 7.2 High-tech sectors of economy: services

WZ 93	Industry	
72	Computer and data processing services	
73	Research and development laboratories	
74.2	Engineering services	} combined to one industry (74.2/74.3)
74.3	Surveying services	
74.4	Advertising [1]	

[1] This is not a technology-intensive industry, but was nevertheless included by us for purposes of comparison.

7.3 Variation in Survival and Exit across High-Tech Industries

The four planning regions located in the area investigated, Upper Bavaria, differ considerably in type – in terms of total population, rate of employment, and economic structure. Upper Bavaria contains a large agglomeration area (Munich), but also an urbanised area and two rural regions (see Table A1 in the Appendix). New firms are founded as two or three times as often in the region of Munich as in the others, but are closed just as frequently. This high correlation between entry and exit rates has already been mentioned in other studies (e.g. Dunne *et al.* 1988). In the service sector, the ratio between entries and exits since 1985 varies in the different regions between 3.5 and 3.1. In manufacturing the ratio differs rather more in fact between 4.1 and 2.6, depending on the sector (see Table A2 in the Appendix). Figs. 7.1 and 7.2, and Table A3 and A4 in the Appendix, show the great differences between the manufacturing and service sector in the relationship between entries and exits of start-up firms (since 1985) and exits out of the stock of firms founded before 1985. While the new formations in manufacturing led to a clear increase in the numbers of firms at the end of the 1980s/beginning of the 1990s, exits clearly outweighed the new entries from the mid 1990s onwards.

Only due to the large number of start-ups in the service sector is there an increase in the total number of firms, despite the continuous exit rate from the stock of enterprises founded before 1985 (see Fig. 7.3).

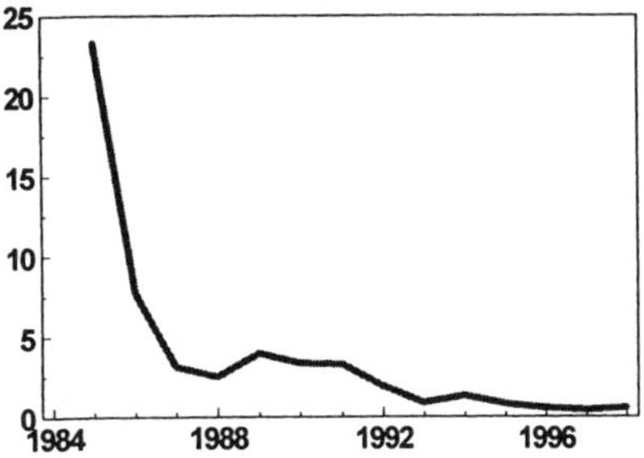

Fig. 7.1 Ratio entry to exit in (manufacturing sector), per year, 1985-1998

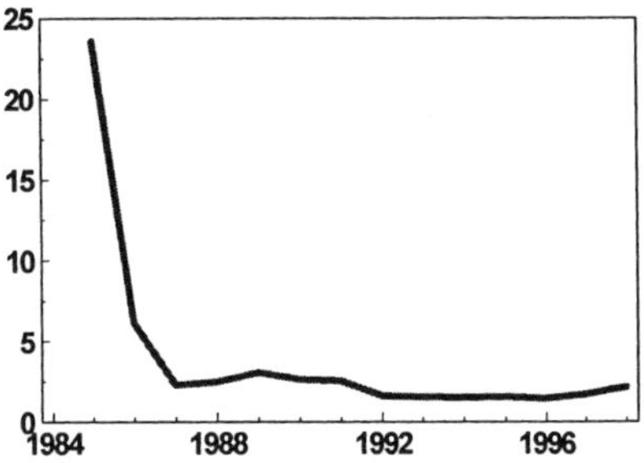

Fig. 7.2 Ratio entry to exit in (service sector), per year, 1985-1998

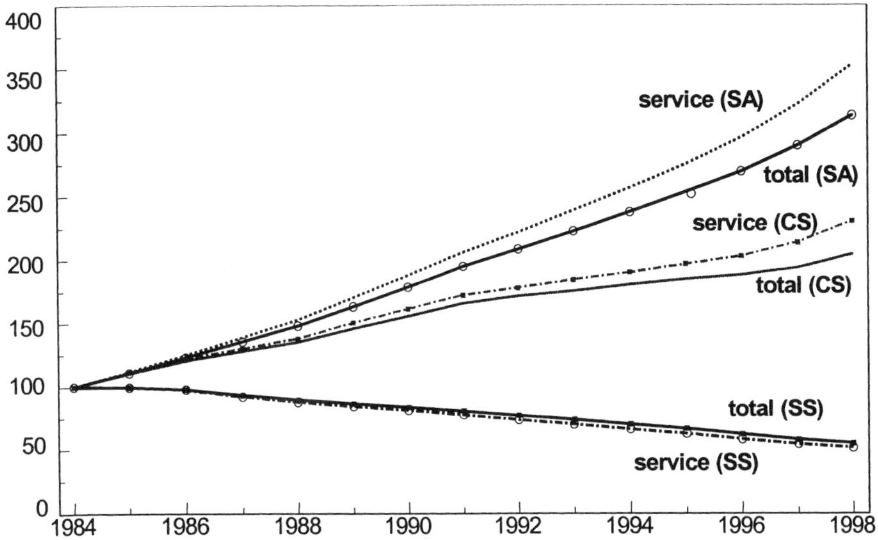

CS: current stock; SA: stock without exits; SS: stock without start-ups (1984 = 100).

Fig. 7.3 Number of high-tech firms (total, service sector) in Upper Bavaria

Longitudinal Aspects of Survival and Exit of High Technology Firms

Kiefer (1988) describes very clearly the need to develop statistical methods in order to analyse the duration of start-ups. Since not all firms die before the end of the observation period, and determinants of the length of life can change during the life span, one needs another method for the measurement of life duration than simply the number of months. The conditional probability that a firm will continue to exist when if it has already survived a certain time (e.g. one year) is of interest. The point at which a certain event occurs (here, the firm exit) is, in accordance to this assumption, subject to a certain probability distribution. As well as the survival function, we can use the hazard rate function to indicate the risk of a firm exiting at a given point in time after a certain duration of life.

Based on our data set on life duration – measured in months – of the over 7700 firms established during the study period (1985-1998), we used the standard method for estimating a survival function, i.e. the product limits estimator proposed by Kaplan and Meier. This was because "the product limits estimator provides an efficient means of estimating the survival function for right-censored data" (Klein and Moeschberger 1997, p. 85). Survival functions were calculated separately for subsets of the data (shown graphically in Figs. 7.4-7.11).[1]

Fig. 7.4. shows that the probability of a firm in manufacturing surviving a certain number of months is always greater than the probability of a firm in the service sector. The probability of a firm in manufacturing living longer than 100 months for example is about 67 percent, while in the service sector only approximately 59 percent survive. Fig. 7.5. shows clearly that firms with the legal form of limited liability company (GmbH) have a higher probability of survival than companies of all other legal forms. Here, however, also the sectoral affiliation has an effect. Fig. 7.6 shows that the life duration is longer on average in the region of Munich than in other regions. The probability of survival in the city of Munich, however, is below the average (Fig. 7.7).

Furthermore, it is remarkable that the probability of surviving a certain number of months is below average for pharmaceutical products (24.4) and advertising (74.4) (Figs. 7.8 and 7.9). In these sectors the exit rate was very high from the mid 1990s onwards. For the sectors engineering, scientific and research, instruments (33.2) and R&D laboratories (73) (Figs. 7.10 and 7.11) the survival rates were clearly above average.

Determinants of Survival and Exit of Start-up Companies

One of the stylised facts regarding the dynamics of industries that has emerged from empirical studies is that the survival rates of firms are positively related both to establishment size and age (e.g. Evans 1987; Phillips and Kirchoff 1989; Audretsch 1991). In addition to these results, the purpose of our study is to ascertain the relative importance of industry-specific variables and the characteristics of the region in explaining the time period between firm birth and its disappearance from economic activity.

---

[1] Estimations in this study were performed with the aid of "Stata Statistical Software, 6.0".

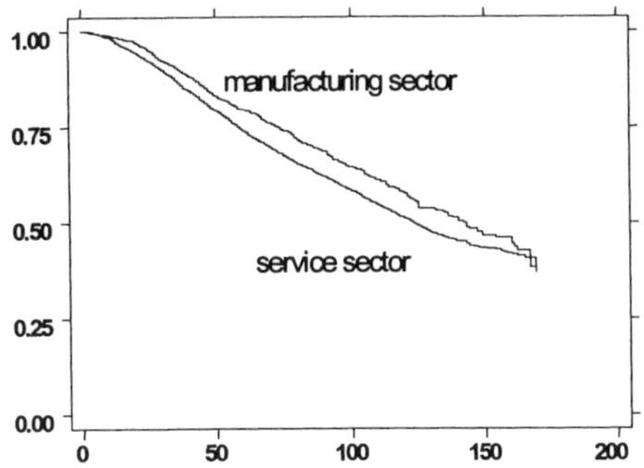

Fig. 7.4 Survival estimates, manufacturing vs. service sector

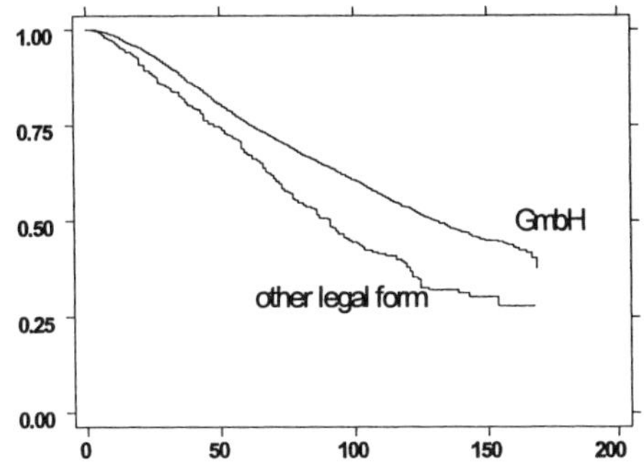

Fig. 7.5 Survival estimates, by legal form of start-up

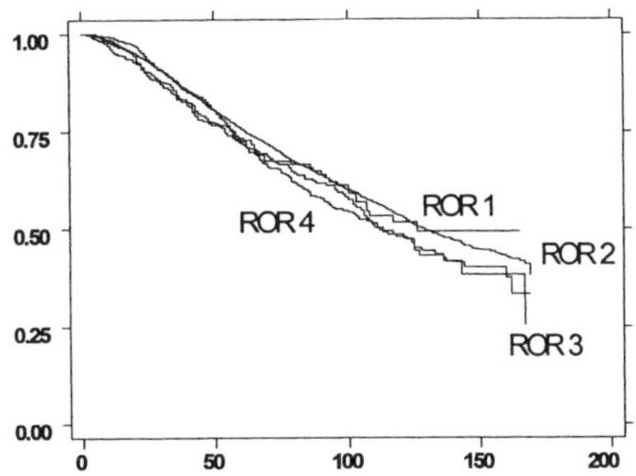

Fig. 7.6 Survival estimates, by regions

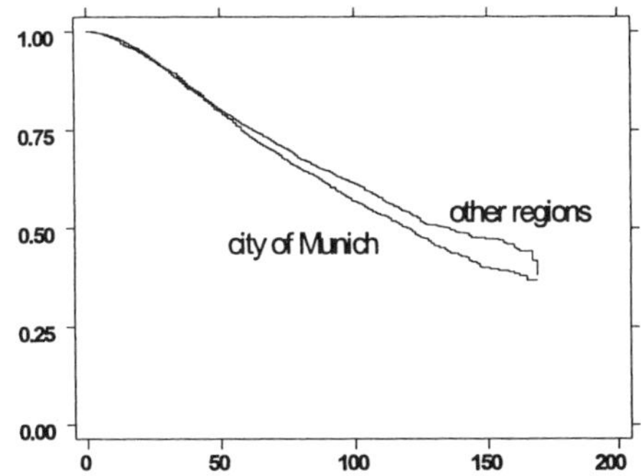

Fig. 7.7 Survival estimates, city of Munich vs. other regions

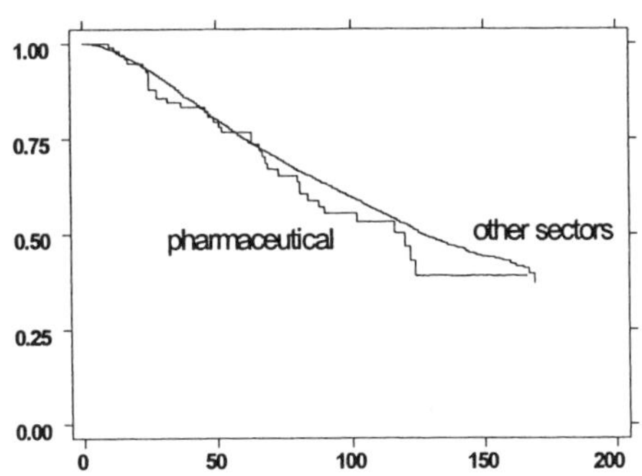

Fig. 7.8 Survival estimates, pharmaceuticals vs. other sectors

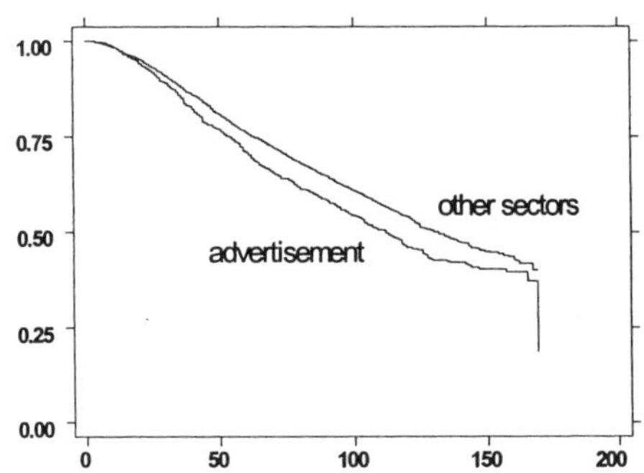

Fig. 7.9 Survival estimates, advertisement vs. other sectors

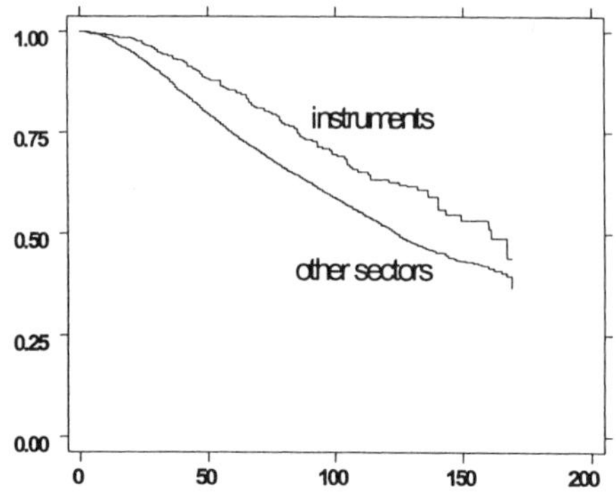

Fig. 7.10 Survival estimates, instruments vs. other sectors

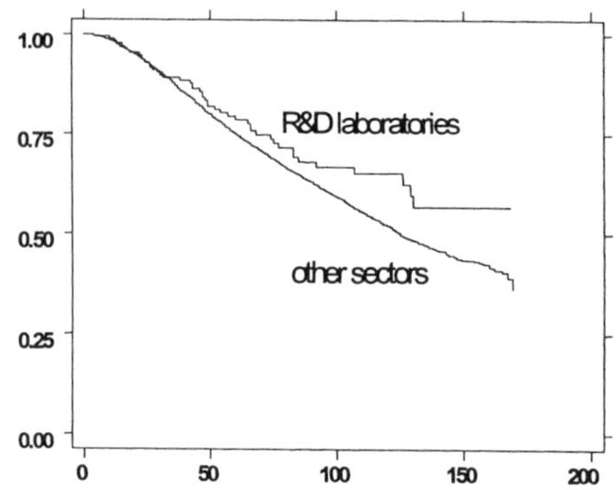

Fig. 7.11 Survival estimates, R&D laboratories vs. other sectors

Based on our data set, a hazard duration function for the start-up companies in the high-tech industry in Upper Bavaria was estimated and a comparison made between the manufacturing and service sectors. The most important figure in the analysis of duration is the length of time that elapses from the beginning of some event (entry) until its end (exit) or until the measurement is taken, which may precede termination. The hazard rate $\lambda(t)$ is the rate at which time periods are completed after duration t, given that they last at least until t.

Cox's (1972) approach to the proportional hazard model is a popular method of analysing the effect of covariates on the hazard rate. The model specifies that:

$$\lambda(t_i) = e^{\beta' X} \lambda_0(t_i) \qquad (7.1)$$

where λ_0 is the 'baseline' hazard, X is a vector of explanatory variables, and β is a vector of parameters.

The partial likelihood estimator provides a method of estimating β without requiring estimation of the baseline hazard λ_0. A variety of tests suggested that the proportionality assumption embedded in this model was appropriate to our data. A negative/positive coefficient can be interpreted as decreasing/increasing the value of the hazard function and therefore indicates a positive/negative relationship with survival. For a more detailed discussion see Cox (1975) and Kalbfleisch and Prentice (1980). The variables included in the X vector are described in Table 7.3.

Given that firm failure rates vary so extensively across industries, we now turn our attention to the determinants of the hazard rates and inspect the regression results from the Cox Proportional Hazards Model in Table 7.4. Firstly, the start-up size of the firms is found to be statistically significantly negatively related to the hazard rate. Only in size classes with a small number of firms the coefficients are not significant. In other words, the larger the firm's start-up size, the lower the risk of failure. Secondly, the t-ratios of the coefficients for the variable rural area measuring the characteristics of the region are statistically significant at the 95 percent level in the manufacturing sector and in all industries. The effect of settlement in a rural area (as opposed to an agglomeration area) increases the risk of failure by 33 percent (manufacturing sector) and 14 percent (total). Thirdly, the hypothesis that the legal form of the limited company (GmbH) (as opposed to partnerships) reduces the risk of exit can also be confirmed: On average for all branches the hazard rate for the 'GmbH' is about 34 percent lower. Fourthly, the t-ratios of the variable entry show no statistically significant result, the variable industry size is statistically significant at the 95 percent level in all industries, in the manufacturing and the service sector (e.g. for the manufacturing sector a one percental change in the number of existing firms in the industry increases the hazard rate by about 0.4 percent). Finally, our hypothesis that the exposure of new firms to risk tends to be greater in cyclical downturns can only be confirmed at the 95 (90) percent level of significance by altering the dummy variable with a lead of three months in the service sector (in all industries).

Table 7.3 Independent variables

Variable	Description
Branch of Trade	Dummy variables for each industry: 11 dummy variables (total) (respectively 7 (manufacturing) / 3 (service)), see Tables 7.1 (7.2)
Legal Form	Legal form of start-up firm at time of entry; classification to one of 3 classes: *Personengesellschaft (Einzelkfm., OHG, KG, GmbH&CoKG), GmbH, Aktiengesellschaft (AG)*
Region	Type of region: agglomeration area, urbanised area, rural area
Start-Up Size	Employment in firm at time of entry; classification to one of 6 size classes (0-3, 4-9, 10-19, 20-49, 50-99, 100+ employees)
Entry	Logarithm of number of new firms in branch of trade in year of entry of firm
Industry Size	Logarithm of number of all firms in each industry in year of entry
Business Cycle [1]	Dummy variable: 1: start-up in cyclical upturn, 0: start-up in cyclical downturn

[1] Industrial Output (mining and manufacturing) seasonally adjusted (Deutsche Bundesbank, various issues, and Statistisches Beiheft zum Monatsbericht 4, Saisonbereinigte Wirtschaftszahlen, Graph IV.2).

While the results of this study confirm many general findings of other authors (see e.g. Mahmood 1992; Mata and Portugal 1994; Audretsch and Mahmood 1995), they also point to the importance of establishment-specific, industry-specific and regional characteristics in shaping the post-entry performance of businesses.

Table 7.4 Regression results from the Proportional Hazards Model [a]

Independent Variables	Total	Manufacturing	Service
Branch of Trade	11 Industry Dummies [1]	7 Industry Dummies [1]	3 Industry Dummies [1]
Legal Form		Reference '*Personengesellschaft*'	
GmbH	0.659	0.616	0.660
	(-5.739)**	(-2.987)**	(-5.094)**
AG	1.315	0.877	1.441
	(1.295)*	(-0.294)	(1.514)
Region		Reference 'Agglomeration area'	
Urbanised area	1.043	0.916	1.073
	(0.391)	(-0.285)	(0.606)
Rural area	1.140	1.332	1.101
	(2.318)**	(2.254)**	(1.510)
Start-Up Size		Reference 'Size (0-3)'	
4-9 employees	0.663	0.545	0.700
	(-6.034)**	(-4.104)**	(-4.666)**
10-19 employees	0.574	0.505	0.596
	(-4.791)**	(-2.699)**	(-3.967)**
20-49 employees	0.769	0.606	0.851
	(-1.940)*	(-2.168)**	(-0.967)
50-99 employees	0.790	0.487	1.098
	(-1.060)	(-1.862)*	(0.345)
100 + employees	0.503	0.439	0.552
	(-3.574)**	(-2.774)**	(-2.344)**
Entry [2]	1.154	1.591	1.042
	(0.604)	(1.161)	(0.127)
Industry Size [2]	11.129	39.305	9.847
	(7.066)**	(4.040)**	(5.533)**
Business Cycle [3]	0.991	0.790	1.033
	(-0.148)	(-1.467)	(0.467)
Number of observations	7738	1150	6588
LR O²	283.77	111.26	177.62
Log of likelihood	-19333.25	-2446.79	-15823.23

[a] Exponentiated coefficients/hazard ratios are displayed. T-statistics in brackets.
* / ** Statistically significant at 90 / 95 percent level of confidence, two-tailed test.
[1] Industry Dummies statistically significant at the 95 percent level of significance.
[2] Hazard ratios of the logarithm of the number of new (all) firms, see Table 7.3.
[3] Altering the dummy variable with a lead of three months, the coefficient becomes statistically significant at the 90 (total) / 95 (service sector) percent level of significance.

7.4 Interfirm Collaboration, Innovation Activity and Growth of Start-Up Companies

The Survey

All firms in the selected industries of the manufacturing sector, and 10 percent of firms in the service industries received a postal questionnaire requesting information about characteristics of the firm, the main activity and date of foundation, co-operation, networks of co-operation and location factors, as well as innovation activities.

Out of a total of 1080 questionnaires, 182 were returned answered in a form suitable for the analyses, representing a good response rate of about 17 percent. Further information was gathered from 17 personal interviews held with entrepreneurs. This is not reported directly in the following sections, but has been incorporated in the conclusions from the questionnaires. Separation of responses according to industry, region and size of firm supports our assumption that the results of the survey are representative.

More than two thirds of the interviewed companies in manufacturing and more than four fifths in the service sector are located in the region of Munich. The sectors which are particularly strong technologically – pharmaceutical products and surgical, medical and dental instruments, computer and data processing services and R&D laboratories – in fact have above average representation in Munich. According to the date of foundation, many firms in the pharmaceutical products and surgical, medical and dental instruments sectors, as well as more than 50 percent of the service firms are young enterprises. Firms in the smallest size class (up to one employee) were recorded in our data only in the region of Munich, and firms founded before 1985 are heavily under represented in the region of Munich.

Due to the fact that we had information only on the allocation of firms to size classes at the times of the formation of the company and of the survey (end of 1998/beginning of 1999), we considered a jump in size classes (in the 13-digit scale) as a measure of employment growth. If a firm remained in the same size class or ascended only into the next one, this was regarded as 'stagnation'. In contrast, a strong employment dynamic was represented by that a company which skipped three or more size classes. It should however be mentioned that almost 50 percent of firms in both the manufacturing and service sector firms hardly grew in the study period. Pharmaceutical products and engineering, scientific and research instruments, computer and data processing services (software) and R&D laboratories grew the most – about 50 percent of the firms skipped two or more size classes.

Innovation Performance, Collaboration and Employment Growth

Using our data set, a probit model was used to specify a relationship between a binary (0/1) dependent variable (no co-operation/co-operation) and a set of covariates, gathered in a vector X, which explains the decision to co-operate with a firm or not. The set of parameters β reflects the impact of changes in X on the probability to co-operate. For a more detailed discussion see, for example, Greene (2000).

The variables included in the X vector are described in Table 7.5. Given that readiness to co-operate or not varies across firms and industries, we now examine the determinants of this decision and inspect the regression results (column I) from the probit model in Table 7.6.

Table 7.5 Independent variables

Variable	Description
Branch of trade	Dummy variable: 1:manufacturing sector , 0: service sector
Age	Age of firm (in years)
Region	Type of region: agglomeration area, urbanised area, rural area
Size	Current employment in firm (end of 1998/beginning of 1999); classification in one of 6 size classes, combining the 13 size classes of the survey (0-1, 1.5-6, 6.5-19, 20-99, 100-499, 500+ employees)
Input	Share of procurement of goods and services from local suppliers in South Germany (percentage)
Output	Share of sales of goods and services to local customers in South Germany (percentage)
Contact A	Dummy variable: 1: Contact with (former) firm/university/research institute, 0: none
Contact B	Dummy variable: 1: Contact with (former) team mate/alumni, 0: none
Experience	Dummy variable: 1: Entrepreneur has knowledge of the trade/industry, 0: none
R&D Dept.	Dummy variable: 1: R&D department, 0: none

First, the age of the firm is found to be statistically significant and negatively related to the dependent variable. Younger firms co-operate more often than older ones. Second, the t-ratio of the coefficient for the variable measuring the size of the firm is statistically significant at the 95 percent level. The effect of a rise in the size class of the firm increases the probability of co-operation by 11 percent. One-man companies co-operate least. Here, as indicated in the interviews as well, this was due in part to lack of interest but also lack of time, since a single person is not able to find time for co-operation activity at the beginning of a business project. In the size classes up to 19 employees, the proportion of co-operating firms doubles (from 40 to 80 percent), then it decreases slightly.

Table 7.6 Regression results from the Probit Model [a]

Independent Variables	I (Section Innovation Performance)	II (Section Co-operation Partner)	III (Section Co-operation Partner)
Branch of Trade	0.094	0.136	0.119
	(1.196)	(1.600)	(1.413)
Age	-0.020	-0.027	-0.017
	(-2.292)**	(-2.797)**	(-1.841)*
Region	Reference 'Agglomeration area'		
Urbanised area	-0.058	---	---
	(-0.441)		
Rural area	-0.027	---	---
	(-0.274)		
Size	0.110	0.077	0.075
	(2.970)**	(1.920)*	(1.839)*
Input	---	0.231	---
		(1.778)*	
Output	---	-0.138	---
		(-1.070)	
Contact A	---	---	0.092
			(0.977)
Contact B	---	---	0.223
			(2.369)**
Experience	---	---	-0.082
			(-0.526)
R&D dept.	---	---	0.105
			(1.326)
Constant	0.009	0.100	-0.081
	(0.076)	(0.706)	(-0.449)
Number of observations	182	182	182
LR O²	14.24	14.35	25.26
Log of likelihood	-94.45	-82.18	-77.44

[a] Coefficients are the change in probability. T-statistics in brackets.
* / ** Statistically significant at 90 / 95 percent level of confidence, two-tailed test.

Finally, the region and branch of trade are variables which were found to be not statistically significant. However, in the sectors miscellaneous chemicals, engineering, scientific and research instruments, as well as R&D laboratories, the proportion of co-operating firms is far above the average. An analysis of co-operating firms in different regions shows that there is more co-operation in the agglomeration area than in the rural regions. In the region of Munich the proportion of co-operating firms is much greater (72 percent), than in the other regions (about 60 percent), with the exception of the south east of Upper Bavaria (*Südostoberbayern*) where the level is 75 percent. The high degree of co-operation in this region can be explained by the concentration of the chemical industry, with a number of connected branch establishments belonging to the same holding.

Additional estimations, not included in this article, showed a significant relationship between the employment dynamic of firms and the probability of interfirm collaboration. Brüderl and Preisendörfer (1998) also found empirical confirmation for positive network effects in a study of new business ventures in Upper Bavaria. This relationship, however, may be influenced by special features of industries which could have a positive effect on both growth of employment and co-operation. Our analysis shows that the industries with above average co-operation – engineering, scientific and research instruments, and R&D laboratories – also have above average employment growth.

Likewise, the greater the growth of employment in a sector, the more likely the company is to carry out product innovations. It is not perhaps surprising that the sectors with the greatest share of innovating firms are also those with the greatest employment dynamic. The proportion of companies with innovations rises with their age. Since companies in the high-tech industries were founded generally on the basis of product innovations, it seems reasonable that there is less product innovation activity in younger firms. The size class of employment was found to have no influence on the range of innovation activity. In the manufacturing sector, there was a higher proportion of product innovations than process innovations, whereas in the service sector – with exception of the computer and data processing services (software) and R&D laboratories, the opposite was true.

The results give no hint of a dependency between co-operation and innovation activity, insofar as innovation networks between companies could not be detected. This conclusion was confirmed by the personal interviews with entrepreneurs, who did not recognise a (direct) relationship between their innovation activities and R&D co-operation. The proportion of innovating companies among co-operating firms is not greater than among non-co-operating firms. No evidence was found in our investigation of relations deriving from the 'local milieu' supporting innovation through co-operation networks, as described by the group of authors around Roberto Camagni – GREMI – Groupe de Recherche Européen sur les Milieux Innovateur (Camagni 1991). Our results confirm the scepticism expressed in other papers in relation to the importance of networks (Hellmer *et al.* 1999).

Co-operation Partner and Form of Co-operation

The interviewed companies co-operate very strongly in production, especially firms with a complementary production programme, but co-operation in R&D was also mentioned by more than half of the firms (see Table 7.7). Co-operation predominantly with universities takes place in R&D, this relation is greatest regarding the smallest firms.

Co-operation with suppliers from the manufacturing and service sector in nearly all industries is at least as frequent, and often more so, than co-operation with customers, with exception of pharmaceutical products. Already Oakey (1984) found in his study that input-output linkages of high technology firms were generally numerous, but that the importance of local customers was low. In our study proximity to ancillary industries, service firms, and R&D facilities was regarded as very important by nearly half of the firms, whereas close relations with customers in only a third of all cases. Our estimations of the probit model in Table 7.6 (columns II and III) confirm these results of our descriptive analysis: column II shows that input-linkages within South Germany are statistically significant at the 90 percent level, but output-linkages are not significant. An infinitesimal change of the firms' input-linkages lead to a 23 percent increase in the probability of co-operation.[2]

Table 7.6, column III, indicates that co-operation generally depends on the firm's age and size as well as contacts with former team mates or alumni. The existence of an own R&D department or knowledge of the trade/industry by the entrepreneur were not statistically significant. Links between companies and research centres have been analysed in several studies, most of them revealing that there is (mostly local) collaboration (see Prevezer 1997; Audretsch and Stephan 1996; Swann *et al.* 1998). In our study we found that co-operation with universities – a specific type of R&D co-operation – was particularly strongly cultivated in the following sectors: pharmaceutical products, surgical, medical and dental instruments, and R&D laboratories. This last sector comprises most of the biotechnology industry. Regarding both firm size and sector allocation this result is not surprising, since a high percentage of these new enterprises develops out of universities or research institutes. Additional regression results verify these observations. In relation to co-operation with universities, the firm's age or size are no longer statistically significant, but the existence of an own R&D department and contacts with the university or professor are statistically significant at the 90-95 percent level. A change of the dummy variable – contact with (former) team mate/alumni – increases the probability of co-operation by 22 percent. In this context, it should be mentioned that additional estimations of other types of co-operation (e.g. distribution, marketing, production) led to no universally valid results.

---

[2] Among co-operating companies, location of the partner in Munich/Upper Bavaria was reported as important by more than two thirds, location in the immediate neighbourhood, however, by only a quarter. These answers are fully comprehensible if one considers that the preferred form of co-operation for 80 percent of all firms is personal collaboration based on trust, whereas co-operation in a loose informal contact as well as in a common project is preferred by about 60 percent. If the co-operation is based on long-term written contracts (about 60 percent), the rights and obligations, and above all the allocation of the advantages of the co-operation, are usually laid down in detail.

Table 7.7 Size classes of employment and co-operation partner

Size class	Total no. firms	Co-operation (as %) R&D:	of which: Univ.	Distribution	Marketing	Production:	of which: Comple-mentary	Bottleneck
1	10	40.0	75.0	30.0	20.0	10.0	0.0	0.0
2	57	54.4	58.1	40.4	19.3	59.6	82.4	26.5
3	58	62.1	52.8	48.3	31.0	60.3	91.4	31.4
4	43	74.4	59.4	27.9	16.3	65.1	82.1	25.0
5	9	55.6	80.0	33.3	0.00	77.8	100.0	42.9
6	5	80.0	50.0	100.0	40.0	80.0	100.0	25.0

7.5 Conclusions

In this chapter, analyses of extensive data on start-ups and the survival of firms in high-tech industries have been combined with the results of a questionnaire sent to some of these firms to investigate their innovative and co-operative behaviour, and the growth of employment.

Our analysis of entry and exit, and hence the survival of firms in high-tech industries, has led firstly to confirmation of the hypotheses that differences exist between various industries in the life span of new firms, and the regional location is important for the probability of survival. Far more enterprises are founded in the service sector than in manufacturing, but many more of these start-ups fail to survive. The differences can be partly explained by the differences in the necessary capital endowment, but it should also be noted that the service sector also tends to develop new products, and therefore many new start-ups form part of a process of trial and error, in an attempt to find the exact market niche. The turnover of new firms is much higher in the conurbation of Munich than in the rural regions. The probable life duration of firms located within the urban agglomeration is greater than in rural areas, but firms in the city of Munich itself tend to have shorter lives. Those in the close surroundings of Munich clearly live longer than in the rest of Upper Bavaria. The high costs resulting from location in the centre of a conurbation are surely a reason for this difference. The higher proportion of service firms in the city is another, due to their lower average probability of survival than start-ups in manufacturing.

The results of the survival analysis were substantiated with an analysis of the determinants on the hazard rates of firms. In addition, it was confirmed that a larger number of employees at the time of foundation and the legal form of the limited company (GmbH as opposed to a partnership – *Personengesellschaften*) reduce the risk of exit.

The growth of employment in firms shows a sectoral and regional differentiation similar to that of life duration. Companies in dynamically growing industries, like engineering, scientific and research instruments (33.2) and research and development laboratories (73) have a life duration far above the average. Pharmaceutics are an exception, in that this sector, according to the answers of the interviewed firms, has a high employment dynamic, but the probability of survival is on an average lower than in other industries, especially in manufacturing. This results from the fact that our survey could not register the many exits in this industry from the mid 1990s onwards.

Co-operation is a form of organisation between market and firm hierarchy and consists of "relationships between firms (and other organisations), which are more than just spontaneous interchange relationships in the sense of buy/sale (arm's length transactions) ..." (Sydow 1992). This has been detected by us in different forms. But nevertheless rivalry still dominates, and co-operation between firms is predominantly laid down in precise written contracts. Our hypothesis, that co-operations between smaller firms is more frequent than between larger firms, was not confirmed. The opposite is in fact the case, because entrepreneurs in one-man firms found themselves unable to run time-consuming negotiations. They felt that delicate negotiations were inevitable in co-operation with other enterprises in order to protect their know-how (for similar research results, see Malecki and Tootle 1996).

The survey found that sectors with a large proportion of co-operating firms, e.g. engineering, scientific and research instruments, and R&D laboratories, have greater growth. The innovation activities, however, hardly differ between the high-tech industries analysed. The questionnaire confirmed the hypothesis that more innovations lead to a greater employment dynamism, but there was no obvious relationship between co-operation and innovation activities. Our interviews gave no indications that co-operation – except occasionally – was used to solve concrete technological problems, nor that co-operating entrepreneurs generally expect a faster growth or more innovations. Co-operation between start-up firms can rather be interpreted as a kind of mutual assistance, resulting predominantly from personal contacts and in the form of loose informal contacts. In the R&D sector, where co-operation is particularly frequent, the predominant form was co-operation with universities, where again personal relationships formed by the entrepreneurs in student and postgraduate periods played a significant role. These personal networks, particularly in the R&D sector, are the crucial reason for the higher proportion of co-operating companies in the region of Munich.

A further important result of our work is thus that co-operation networks formed with given goals rarely exist. The form of co-operation which develops from the environment of entrepreneurs and according to specific sector conditions should not be treated as equivalent to the type of innovation network which is described as catalyst of regional development in the literature (Camagni 1991) and for which rational means of control are supposed to exist.

Acknowledgements

The authors wish to express their appreciation for financial support from Deutsche Forschungsgemeinschaft – the German Science Foundation – in Bonn with grant No. FL 290/1-1, and from the Gesellschaft zur Förderung der regionalen und urbanen Strukturforschung – Association for the Promotion of Research on Urban and Regional Economic Structure – in Munich, who made the research project possible. We are also grateful to the Industrie- und Handelskammer für München und Oberbayern – Munich Chamber of Industry and Commerce – for providing data. We would like to extend our thanks to those who have helped us produce this study, Stefan Haindl, Patricia Walter, and Björn Hampe who coded the data or provided assistance in translating, data and word processing.

Appendix

Table A.1 Characteristics of the planning regions

	ROR 1 Ingolstadt	ROR 2 München	ROR 3 Oberland	ROR 4 Südostoberbayern
Type of region 1997	Urbanised area	Agglomeration	Rural area	Rural area
Population 1996 (in '000s)	420.4	2399.9	408.9	762.4
Employees 96 (in '000s)	132.4	992.3	118.4	235.5
Density of population				
1990	136	421	98	136
1996	148	436	103	146
Secondary sector				
1996 (as %)	54.7	29.7	40.6	46.6
Growth 1990-96 (as %)	-6.7	-18.4	-5.1	-5.4
Tertiary sector				
1996, in %	44.3	69.6	58.0	52.3
Growth 1990-96 (as %)	21.9	9.4	10.1	15.1
Highly qualified				
1996, in %	5.3	13.5	4.4	4.6
Growth 1989-96 (as %)	43.2	25.0	33.3	31.4

Source: Federal Research Institute for Regional Geography and Regional Planning (BfLR).

Table A.2 Entry/exit of start-up firms in the high technology sectors 1985-1998

	Entry		Exit		Entry/Exit	
	Services	Manufact.	Services	Manufact.	Services	Manufact.
ROR 1						
per population	0.67	0.11	0.19	0.026	3.5	4.1
per employment	2.11	0.34	0.60	0.083		
ROR 2						
per population	2.25	0.37	0.67	0.12	3.3	3.0
per employment	5.45	0.90	1.63	0.30		
ROR 3						
per population	0.89	0.20	0.27	0.071	3.3	2.8
per employment	3.08	0.70	0.92	0.25		
ROR 4						
per population	0.78	0.18	0.25	0.068	3.1	2.6
per employment	2.51	0.58	0.81	0.22		

Table A.3 Number of firm entries, exits and stock in the high-tech industries of the manufacturing sector in Upper Bavaria and the region of Munich (ROR 2)

	Upper Bavaria				ROR 2 (Munich)			
	Entry	Exit new firms	Exit old firms	Stock	Entry	Exit new firms	Exit old firms	Stock
pre 1985				1023				821
1985	93	1	3	1112	80	1	3	897
1986	93	0	12	1193	77	0	11	963
1987	90	0	29	1254	71	0	26	1008
1988	88	11	24	1307	73	10	21	1050
1989	87	8	14	1372	62	7	12	1093
1990	100	12	18	1442	78	7	15	1149
1991	124	18	20	1528	92	17	15	1209
1992	95	23	26	1574	73	16	22	1244
1993	55	36	26	1567	47	26	23	1242
1994	93	40	31	1589	68	34	26	1250
1995	74	51	41	1571	48	35	32	1231
1996	56	60	41	1526	43	46	33	1195
1997	49	63	52	1460	34	45	45	1139
1998	53	59	39	1415	39	49	29	1100
Total	1150	382	376		885	293	313	

Table A.4 Number of entries, exits and stock of firms in high-tech industries of the service sector in Upper Bavaria and the region of Munich (ROR 2)

	Upper Bavaria				ROR 2 (Munich)			
	Entry	Exit new firms	Exit old firms	Stock	Entry	Exit new firms	Exit old firms	Stock
pre 1985				2606				2284
1985	306	1	12	2899	268	1	10	2541
1986	338	3	52	3182	291	2	47	2783
1987	368	18	144	3388	309	17	126	2949
1988	357	36	109	3600	302	32	92	3127
1989	465	60	92	3913	381	52	81	3375
1990	463	95	81	4200	378	78	69	3606
1991	470	90	96	4484	386	76	83	3833
1992	407	150	103	4638	323	130	86	3940
1993	454	193	97	4802	353	150	82	4061
1994	455	199	102	4956	367	143	92	4193
1995	490	229	90	5127	400	198	78	4317
1996	530	248	114	5295	415	202	102	4428
1997	680	295	105	5575	539	229	91	4647
1998	805	299	75	6006	646	240	66	4987
Total	6588	1916	1272		5358	1550	1105	

References

Agarwal, R., Gort, M. (1996) The Evolution of Markets and Entry, Exit and Survival of Firms. Review of Economics and Statistics 78, 489-497

Audretsch, D.B. (1991) New-Firm Survival and the Technological Regime. Review of Economics and Statistics 60, 441-450

Audretsch, D.B., Mahmood, T. (1995) New Firm Survival: New Results Using a Hazard Function. Review of Economics and Statistics 77, 97-103

Audretsch, D.B., Stephan, P.E. (1996) Compagny-Scientist Locational Links: The Case of Biotechnology. American Economic Review 86, 641-652

Brüderl, J., Preisendörfer, P., Ziegler, R. (1992) Staatliche Gründungsfinanzierung und der Erfolg neugegründeter Betriebe. Industrie- und Handelskammer für München und Oberbayern, München

Brüderl, J., Preisendörfer, P. (1998) Network Support and the Success of Newly Founded Businesses. Small Business Economics 10, 213-225

Camagni, R. (ed.) (1991) Innovation Networks: Spatial Perspectives. Belhaven Press, London

Caves, R.E. (1998) Industrial Organisation and New Findings on the Turnover and Mobility of Firms. Journal of Economic Literature 36, 1947-1982

Coase, R.H. (1953) The Nature of the Firm. In: Stigler, G.J., Boulding, K.E. (eds.) Readings in Price Theory. George Allen & Unwin Ltd., London

Cox, D.R. (1972) Regression Models and Life Tables (with discussion). Journal of the Royal Statistical Society, Series B 34, 187-200
Cox, D.R. (1975) Partial Likelihood. Biometrika 62, 269-276
Deutsche Bundesbank (various issues) Statistisches Beiheft zum Monatsbericht 4, Saisonbereinigte Wirtschaftszahlen. Deutsche Bundesbank, Frankfurt
Dunne, T., Roberts, M.J., Samuelson, L. (1988) Patterns of Firm Entry and Exit in U.S. Manufacturing Industries. RAND Journal of Economics 19, 495-515
Evans, D.S. (1987) The Relationship between Firm Growth, Size and Age: Estimates for 100 Manufacturing Industries. Journal of Industrial Economics 35, 567-581
Gehrke, B., Grupp, H. (1994) Innovationspotential und Hochtechnologie – Technologische Position Deutschlands im internationalen Wettbewerb. Physica-Verlag, Hannover
Greene, W.H. (2000) Econometric Analysis. Prentice Hall, New Jersey
Harhoff, D., Steil, F. (1997) Die ZEW-Gründungspanels: Konzeptionelle Überlegungen und Analysepotential. In: Harhoff, D. (ed.) Unternehmensgründungen – Empirische Analysen für die alten und neuen Bundesländer. Nomos-Verlag, Baden-Baden
Hellmer, F., Friese, Ch., Kollros, H., Krumbein, W. (1999) Mythos Netzwerke. Edition Sigma, Berlin
Kalbfleisch, J.D., Prentice, R.L. (1980) The Statistical Analysis of Failure Time Data. John Wiley & Sons, New York
Kiefer, N.M. (1988) Economic Duration Data and Hazard Functions. Journal of Economic Literature 26, 646-679
Klein, J.P., Moeschberger, M.L. (1997) Survival Analysis. Springer-Verlag, New York
Mahmood, T. (1992) Does the Hazard Rate for New Plants Vary Between Low- and High-Tech Industries? Small Business Economics 4, 201-209
Malecki, E.J., Tootle, D.M. (1996) The Role of Networks in Small Firm Competitiveness. International Journal of Technology Management 11, 43-57
Markusen, A.R (1985) Profit Cycles, Oligopoly, and Regional Development. MIT Press, Cambridge, MA
Mata, J., Portugal P. (1994) Life Duration of New Firms. Journal of Industrial Economics 42, 227-245
Mueller, D.C. (1991) Entry, Exit, and the Competitive Process. In: Gerosky, P.A., Schwalbach, J. (eds.) Entry and Market Contestability: An International Comparison. Blackwell, Oxford
Nerlinger, E.A. (1998) Standorte und Entwicklung junger innovativer Unternehmen - Empirische Ergebnisse für Westdeutschland. Nomos-Verlag, Baden-Baden
Oakey, R. (1984) High Technology Small Firms. Palgrave, London
Phillips, B.D., Kirchoff, B.A. (1989) Formation, Growth and Survival: Small Firm Dynamics in the U.S. Economy. Small Business Economics 1, 65-74
Picot, A., Laub, U.D., Schneider, D. (1989) Innovative Unternehmensgründungen. Eine ökonomisch-empirische Analyse. Springer-Verlag, Berlin
Prevezer, M. (1997) The Dynamics of Industrial Clustering in Biotechnology. Small Business Economics 9, 255-271
Schumpeter, J.A. (1912) Theorie der wirtschaftlichen Entwicklung. Duncker & Humblot, Berlin
Stigler, G.J. (1968) The Organisation of Industry. Richard D. Irwin, Inc., Homewood, Ill
Swann, G.M.P., Prevezer, M., Stout, D. (1998) The Dynamics of Industrial Clustering: International Comparisons in Computing and Biotechnology. Oxford Univ. Press, Oxford
Williamson, O.E. (1989) Transaction Cost Economics. In: Schmalensee, R., Willig, R. (eds.) Handbook of Industrial Organisation, Vol. 1., North-Holland, Amsterdam
Williamson, O.E. (1975) Markets and Hierarchies. Macmillan, New York

8 Are There Too Many Innovation Centres in Germany?

Christine Tamásy
Department of Economic and Social Geography, University of Cologne

8.1 Introduction

Since the beginning of the 1980s young, innovative firms have been viewed in politics as a source of hope for the economy. This emphasis began with the studies by Birch (1979, 1987), who showed empirically that in the United States from 1969–1976 two thirds of all new jobs were created by firms with fewer than 20 employees or by newly founded firms. Examples of successful regional economies in the United States, like Silicon Valley in California, or Route 128 near Boston, also demonstrate that significant effects on employment and innovation at the regional level can stem from young, innovative firms. In contrast to the 1970s, when large corporations with significant market power were considered to be the motor of economic development, nowadays the importance of young, innovative firms in securing international competitiveness and solving problems on the job market is highlighted (see Kulicke *et al.* 1993). Due to their relatively small size and technological competence, such firms can react flexibly with respect to innovations and often adopt revolutionary new technologies like semiconductors, genetic engineering or biotechnology in the early stages of development, playing an important role in structural change (see Nerlinger 1998).

In the Federal Republic of Germany the growing interest in young, innovative firms is reflected in the allocation of government aid. For instance, federal R&D expenditures in the form of shared innovation risk with young technology enterprises rose between 1994 and 1998 (government proposal) from DM 73 million to DM 109 million (see BMBF 1998). Local governments have provided support primarily through innovation centres, which offer spatially-concentrated, reasonably-priced rental space, technical infrastructure and consulting services to young innovative enterprises during the difficult start-up phase. Since the establishment of the first innovation centre – the Berlin Innovation Centre (BIG) – in 1983, the German municipalities have founded approximately 200 similar establishments (see Fig. 8.1). The regional distribution of innovation centres in western Germany mirrors the technology policy of each state. For example, while Lower Saxony has only supported such facilities to a limited extent, states like North Rhine-Westphalia began quite early by investing heavily in innovation centres. Other states like Hesse have been catching up in recent years. Bavaria has developed a strong innovation and technology-oriented concept over the years. In eastern Germany the establishment of innovation centres following German reunification in 1990 was publicly funded by the former Federal Department of Research and Development (BMFT), a novelty for German technology policy. Massive state funding has led to a situation in which, in relation to the number of inhabitants and working population, East Germany has a higher concentration of innovation centres than West Germany (see Tamásy 1996).

In Germany, innovation centres have become a favoured political instrument and are predominantly built and supported by public funding. Based on the allocation of tax money, it would appear sensible to evaluate the efficiency of such funding, especially in view of the scarcity of resources in the public budget. Considering the number of business start-ups, it appears highly probable that there is now an oversupply of innovation centres. From 1993-1995 a total of 3,367 new businesses were founded in Germany, of which 1,262 were located in the new 'Länder' of eastern Germany (see Licht and Nerlinger 1997). On average this is equivalent to seven or eight business start-ups per county over a span of three years. Approximately every fifth business start-up in Germany takes place in technology-intensive fields of manufacturing. Thus, the number of innovative business start-ups is hardly sufficient to fully utilise all innovation centres over the mid to long term, particularly since only a certain percentage (the exact value is unknown) of new firms choose such centres as their start-up location. In addition, young innovative firms are over-represented from a regional perspective in the areas of industrial concentration and their near vicinity (see Nerlinger 1999). This means that chances of innovation centres to acquire a sufficient number of suitable renters from the surrounding area vary dramatically.

This chapter focuses on answering the two following central questions in this respect, by making an analysis of effectiveness. What levels of success have German innovation centres had based on their own goals? What factors determine the success (or failure) of innovation centres? Related studies already exist in Germany, but they only partially cover the main aspects relevant to an analysis of effectiveness (see Habersam *et al.* 1994; Pett 1994; Steinkühler 1994). Experience elsewhere, such as the evaluations of science parks in Great Britain and the USA, is helpful with respect to methodological considerations (see, for example, Luger and Goldstein 1991; Massey *et al.* 1992; Monck *et al.* 1988; Storey and Strange 1992; Westhead and Storey 1994; for a comprehensive overview see Behrendt and Tamásy 1998). One should bear in mind however that the numerous peculiarities of German innovation centres, for example the limited period of occupancy, the minimal participation of universities and the importance of municipal supporters, limit the validity of comparison with supposedly compatible facilities abroad (see Sternberg *et al.* 1997).

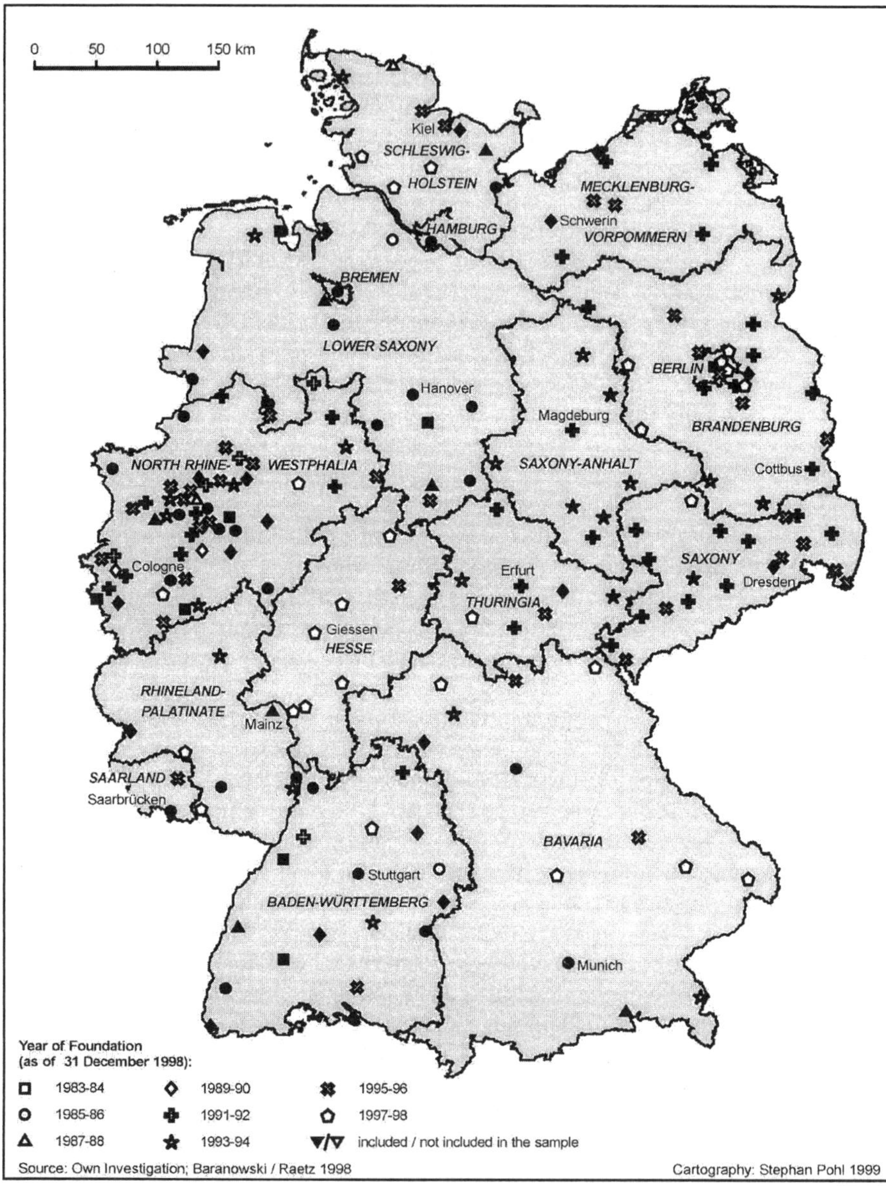

Fig. 8.1 Innovation centres in Germany

8.2 Study Design

The original data used in this study stems from an extensive research project – Evaluation of Innovation Centres in Germany – which was supported by the Deutsche Forschungsgemeinschaft (DFG) within the framework of the programme 'Technological Change and Regional Development in Europe', and the state Lower Saxony (graduate support). The methodology is based on a study from Sternberg (1988), in which a pool of 177 firms from 31 West German innovation centres were surveyed in 1986. The following goals have been pursued in the follow-up survey:

- to carry out a new survey of West German innovation centres within the framework of a cross-sectional analysis and, on the basis of the data available from the 1986 survey (see Sternberg 1988), to make a longitudinal sectional analysis. The main emphasis would be the comparison of two points in time (1986 and 1993–94) and the interpretation of any changes which emerged (see Behrendt 1996);
- to derive initial estimations of effectiveness from a cross-sectional analysis of young innovation centres in East Germany, in order to develop a basis for later longitudinal sectional analyses (see Tamásy 1996);
- to develop a cross-sectional analysis of successful firms which have left innovation centres and rate their time in the centres retrospectively (longitudinal sectional analysis) (see Seeger 1997).

The empirical basis of this investigation includes four partial surveys of 1,021 firms and 108 innovation centres allowing representative statements to be made about the landscape of German innovation centres.[1] The survey concentrated on the typical aspects and methods for analysing the effectiveness of instruments from technology policy (see Meyer-Krahmer 1989; for those applied to innovation centres see Tamásy 1999). The most important aspects of investigation include a clientele analysis, programme acceptance by target groups, intended and unintended effects, the learning curves, an evaluation of basic assumptions for the programme, the implementation and administration as well as the commercialisation of the supported projects. The key methods used for evaluating effectiveness are a before-and-after comparison and a control-group concept (within the basic group of 'innovation centres' and 'funded firms'). The substantive results of various individual projects are summarised by Sternberg *et al.* (1997).

[1] This analysis involved surveys of 108 innovation centres (of which 72 are in western Germany and 36 in eastern Germany) and 1,021 firms (585 are in western German innovation centres, 272 in eastern German innovation centres and 164 which had moved out of innovation centres). Thus, 92 percent of the innovation centres existing in 1993-94, 31 percent of the firms in innovation centres and 43 percent of the firms which have successfully departed innovation centres are considered.

8.3 The Concept of Innovation Centres

When the managers of innovation centres were asked to state the primary goals of the centres, their answers were generally: to support business start-ups, create qualified jobs and intensify of knowledge and technology transfers (in this order). Young, innovative firms are an ideal target group for promoting the transfer of technology and knowledge. This occurs almost automatically during the foundation process as a 'transfer from head to head'. In western Germany 'innovative founders' were considered to be part of the key target group in two thirds of the facilities (see Fig. 8.2), even though this share has declined since 1986 (by around 5 percent). In eastern Germany business leaders also identify 'innovative founders' as a key target group. Nevertheless, 'founders in general' were more frequently considered to be a key target group by eastern than by western German business leaders. An important distinction is that the establishment of small and medium-sized firms, which are not necessarily innovative, plays a key role in the 'new Länder' due to unfavourable underlying economic conditions. At the same time, the number of suitable potential renters is lower compared to western Germany. Therefore, in eastern Germany the chance of economic success of a firm applying to locate in an innovation centre is the most important criterion for selection, whereas in western Germany the central factor is still the technological orientation.

It should be pointed out that in German innovation centres there is no unambiguous definition of the terms 'young' or 'innovative', nor 'technology-oriented', and these are therefore subject to a broad interpretation. The operating authorities in both East and West attempt to avoid temporarily or permanently empty rental space due to financial constraints and political pressure for justification (e.g. by temporally extending existing rental contracts). That is why in approximately one quarter of the innovation centres a pragmatic selection of renters is practised. The demands on renters become more restrictive (with respect to technological orientation and years of operation), when a sufficient potential of acceptable firms is available.

The offer available in innovation centres is based on subsidised and, thus, inexpensive rental space and central services, which eases the difficult start-up phase of young, innovative firms by reducing the fixed costs (referred to in Sternberg 1988 as 'hardware'). The spectrum of central services includes meeting rooms, telecommunication services, copy facilities, secretarial functions and a central telephone operator, which are available in more than three-quarters of the facilities (see Fig. 8.3). Two-thirds of the innovation centres provide a cafeteria as a meeting place and centre for possible synergy effects. However, more specialised facilities, like computers for technical applications, laboratories and measuring instruments, are rarely offered due to their relatively high investment and operational costs. Private and/or public funding are not usually part of the central services of innovation centres.

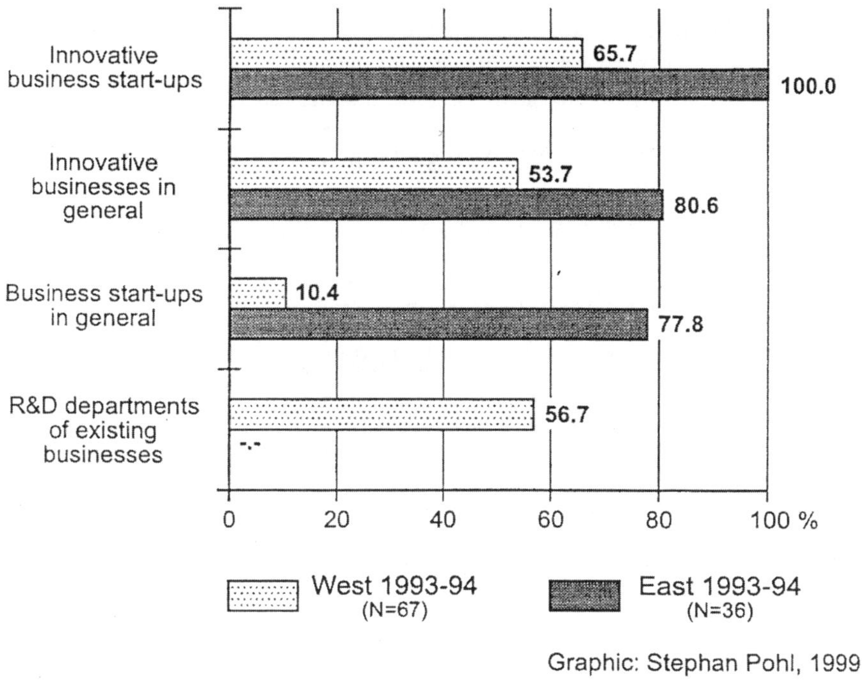

Fig. 8.2 Target groups of innovation centres

The truly innovative elements in the innovation centre concept are the consulting services ('software'). It is assumed that the founders of young, innovative firms normally possess technical qualifications, yet, at the same time they tend to lack expertise in marketing and management. A general consulting service for the founders of and the founding of firms is, therefore, available at no cost to the residents of practically all innovation centres. Contacts with specialised consultants and capital providers (e.g. seedcorn funding) outside the innovation centres are often included. Overall, the eastern German innovation centres possess better equipment and facilities than their western counterparts. This may well be because those responsible for planning the eastern German innovation centres achieved fast learning curves through support from their western partner facilities.

The rental space of innovation centres amounts to an average of 4,712 m^2 (1993-94; median: 2,600 m^2) in West Germany and 2,682 m^2 (1,725 m^2) in East Germany. In western German facilities the average rental space has increased in size by 1,567 m^2 since 1986. The current range extends from the smallest German innovation centre in Borna (Saxony) with 400 m^2 of rental space to the Industry and Technology Centre in Bonn (North Rhine-Westphalia) with 53,000 m^2.

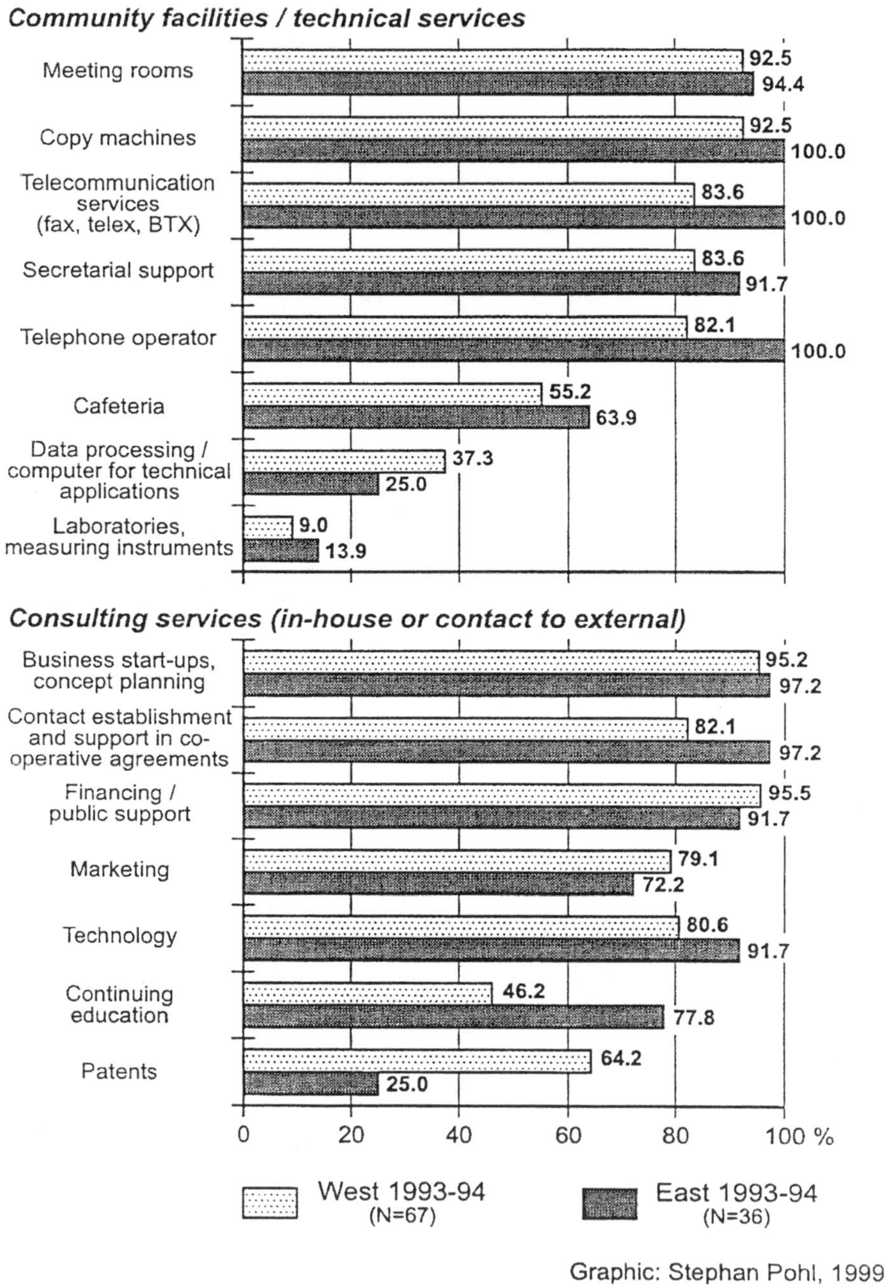

Fig. 8.3 Service supply in innovation centres

The latter can certainly be regarded as rather extraordinary with respect to the amount of rental space, and is not included in the average value given above. Around one-third of the innovation centres are constructing additional buildings and expanding. This is justified with the claim that the centres are currently not efficient enough. Rental space between 3,000 and 5,000 m^2 is considered necessary for an efficient innovation centre without state subsidies when full utilisation is reached. This minimal size of 3,000 m^2 is reached by only half the facilities in both East and West. If the degree of utilisation is considered, a quarter of the innovation centres in western Germany experienced under-capacity in the mid-90s especially in rural areas. In eastern Germany many innovation centres are still in the start-up and admission phase due to their newness (at the beginning of 1994 their average age was 2.6 years), whereas the level of utilisation of innovation centres with respect to rental space has achieved an average of 84 percent.

8.4 Support for Business Start-ups

The support function of innovation centres is their most important objective. The success of innovation centres in this respect depends upon the extent to which they are successful in motivating founders to enter the world of the self-employed. But the results show that only 3 percent of the business founders (West 1993-94: 5 percent; East 1993-94: 2 percent, Former Tenants 1993–94: 2 percent) would not have started their enterprises without the existence of innovation centres. Thus, the incentive effect of innovation centres proves to be quite low, since the number of technology-oriented firms has not been significantly increased as a result of the presence of such facilities. The majority of the founders accepted the support as an additional bonus. An evaluation of the merits of business funding is the duty of the innovation centre management, because firms behave rationally and consider financial support, when deciding on a business location.

It is worth considering whether innovation centres only provide an incentive to start-up businesses, or whether there are other positive effects on the development of businesses? Support for business development should be more positively judged, since the availability of rental space is the most decisive advantage for a business location (see Fig. 8.4). Rental prices in West German innovation centres have been slowly approaching corresponding local rents since the beginning of the innovation centre development in the 1980s. However, for two-thirds of the facilities the rents are still lower than local rents and assist the founders in reducing costs. In East Germany this situation applies to all innovation centres barring one exception. The typical flexibility of rental space also reduces the fixed cost burden, since the rental space can be adapted to the growth situation of a firm. In addition, the use of common facilities and technical services in innovation centres (e.g. offices, copy machines, meeting rooms) contributes to a reduction in material and operating costs of young firms. In East Germany, since German reunification, the shortage of legally secured production space (from the perspective of property and planning) has led to a situation in which the availability of rental space in innovation centres was considered to be of great importance as a locational advantage. This also applied to the technical infrastructure (e.g. adequate telephone networks), and consequently the innovation centres were quick to receive quality, high-value telecommunication facilities. Today, an oversupply exists with regard to the available space, and the communication infrastructure is now more modern than in West Germany.

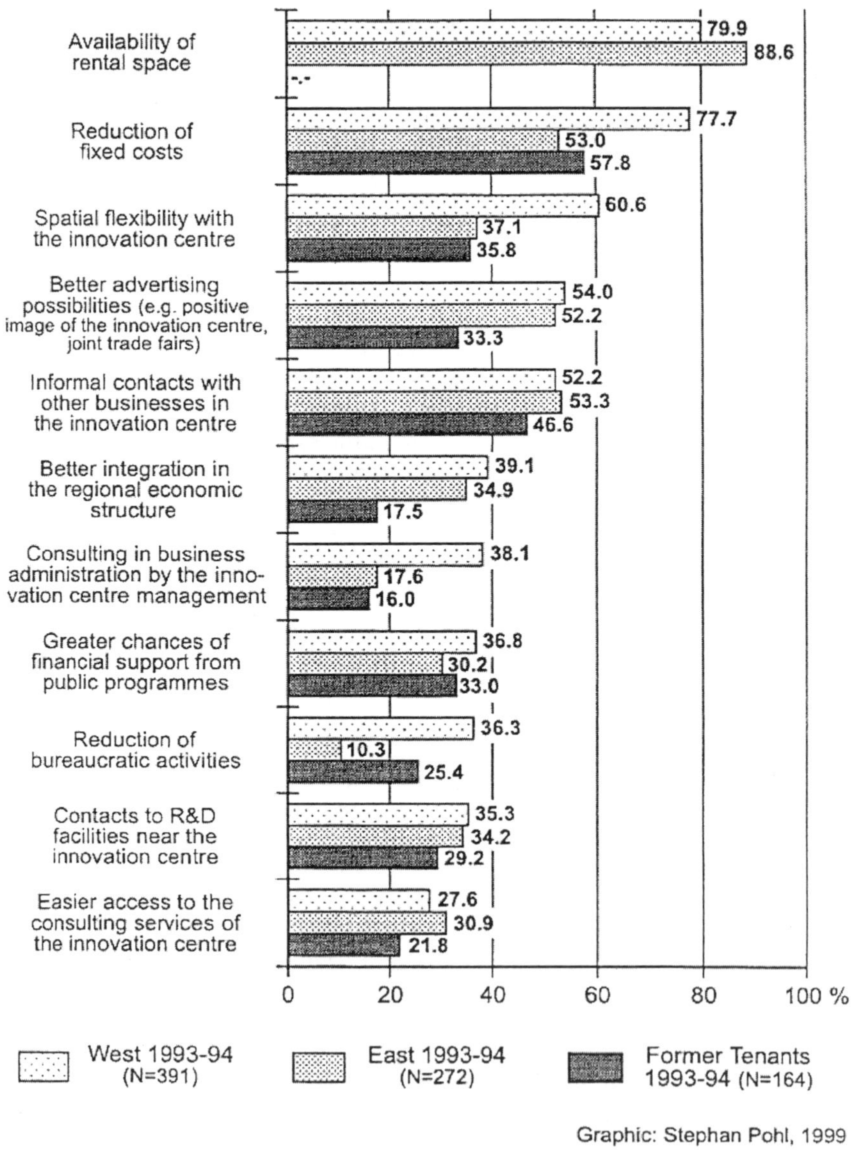

Fig. 8.4 Location advantages of innovation centres

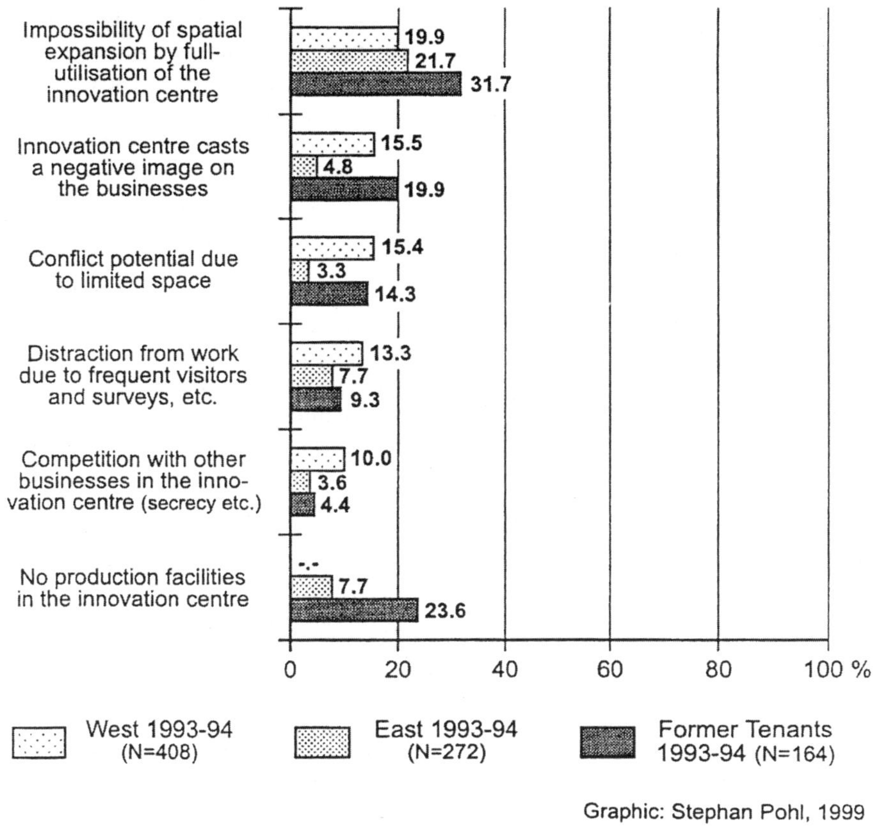

Fig. 8.5 Location disadvantages of innovation centres

According to the survey, the consulting services (as a central and innovative element of the innovation centre ideal) are of little significance for the development of firms and are rarely seen as an advantage of location in innovation centres. This includes the services provided by the management of innovation centres as well as the accessibility to services of facility supporters (e.g. chambers of industry and commerce, banks). More than half of the founders consider the services provided, such as the co-ordination of contact with public institutions and banks, continuing education and legal assistance to be 'unimportant' for the development of their firms. Their needs for assistance in business administration are typically fulfilled outside the innovation centres, which could be explained by the fact that there are often deficits in business management qualifications in the consulting teams. For example, only 16 percent of the eastern German managers of innovation centres had completed studies in business-related fields (in western Germany around 47 percent). It is also possible that the founders of firms are not sufficiently sensitised by the management of innovation centres. Therefore, the basic requirement of supplying the founders with essential information is not met and the need for consulting is underestimated. The question commonly asked in academics and politics about which service components in innovation centres are most important for new firms can be clearly answered: the physical (spatial) and facility infrastructure.

Nevertheless, there is in general good acceptance of innovation centres, since from the business perspective the benefits of settlement in an innovation centre outweigh the disadvantages (see Figs. 8.4 and 8.5). This high level of acceptance can be verified by the fact that only 9 percent of the firms (West 1993-94: 11 percent; East 1993-94: 1 percent, Former Tenants 1993-94: 17 percent) would *not* choose to locate in an innovation centre for a new business start-up. The 'work climate' too appears to be acceptable – the majority of those surveyed were content with their relations with the management of the innovation centres and the other firms there. 72 percent of the eastern German businesses and 50 percent of western German businesses co-operate with other renters in the innovation centres (this includes informal contacts and joint projects). The business network stemming from innovation centres continues (for the most part) even after departure from the centres. 46 percent of the firms which have departed the facilities successfully maintain their contacts with firms still in the centres and with other firms that have already left. The co-operative relations result partially from mediation activities of the innovation centre management. In this sense the centres can actually be seen as an intermediary in the information network and as a part of the innovative milieu.

But innovation centres can really only be considered successful if the firms receiving support achieve long-term sustainability. If the rate of insolvency is observed over time, it becomes clear that innovation centres do not significantly raise the sustainability of the supported firms. From 1986 to 1993-94 a total of 24 percent of the businesses went bankrupt and 5 percent were bought out. Forty-four percent of the firms successfully left the innovation centres; another twenty-seven percent still utilise the facilities. The level of bankruptcy corresponds to the results of other empirical studies on the sustainability of young, innovative firms (see e.g. Westhead and Storey 1994). In spite of the set rental period of three to five years, the period of actual support is very varied. 38 percent of the former tenants left the facilities prior to the end of the third year, thus not fully utilising the maximum period of support. At the same time 16 percent of the businesses remained for six or more years in the innovation centres, indicating that the principal of a rapid flow of firms in and out of the innovation centres is not upheld. The most significant motive for leaving the innovation centres is the inability to further expand within the facilities, which also represents the greatest locational disadvantage from the perspective of the firms. Discontentment with the services in the innovation centres (14 percent) or (specifically) with the centre's management (21 percent) played a role in the decision of firms to leave the innovation centres.

8.5 Creation of Qualified Jobs

For the management of innovation centres, the goal of 'creating qualified jobs' was ranked second in importance. The (quantitative and qualitative) employment effects of innovation centres arise directly in the supported firms and indirectly through multiplier effects. Suitable references for goal achievement include the number of employed and structure of employment by firms in innovation centres.

Of the businesses surveyed 93 percent possessed less than 20 employees in 1993–94 and can thus be considered small firms (see Fig. 8.6). The average number of employees following the start-up of operations in innovation centres – on the average after three years – climbed from 4.0 to 8.7 with a yearly growth rate of about 29 percent. On average the new eastern German firms reached an average of 6.4 employees and their western German counterparts 8.1, while for the former tenants a value of 14.3 was achieved. As expected, there was a positive relationship between the age of a firm and the growth in employment. This was however quite low (r-Spearman: 0.33 for a significance of 0.01) and was distorted by one exceptional value. In addition, the following features should be noted:

- in 6 percent of the firms the number of employees declined;
- in 28 percent of the firms the number of employees remained constant. These firms were normally either too small to reduce their personnel in periods of unfavourable business development, or the time frame from settlement in the innovation centre to completion of the questionnaire was rather short;
- the business development is very heterogeneous. 41 percent of the newly-created jobs were related to the top-five businesses in terms of growth.

In total, 2,597 businesses have settled in innovation centres creating 22,594 jobs. Statistically ascertainable effects on the German job market cannot be expected in the short or mid-term. At the same time the high share of university graduates, an average of 56 percent 1993-94 (West: 51 percent; East: 67 percent, Former Tenants: 54 percent), can be seen as evidence of a qualitative employment effect. Although at an absolute level it is comparatively small, it nevertheless contributes to the improvement of the regional employment structure. In eastern Germany, for example, a considerable proportion of the academic staff in innovation centres have risked entering into self-employment following the restructuring of the research landscape, or are employed as co-workers in such firms.

One should bear in mind that these figures must be interpreted as gross values. In order to determine the net employment effects, all jobs that would have been created without the innovation centres must be deducted from the statistic. Sternberg (1988) recommends that those jobs created by firms which had already existed for a long period of time prior to their settlement in innovation centres should be subtracted – this represents a quarter of the firms in West Germany. In the former East Germany young, innovative firms were not able to develop in the existing framework conditions, therefore the majority of enterprises in innovation centres are new business start-ups and young firms. Only 19 percent of the firms supported there had been in operation two or more years before entering an innovation centre. Thus 2,115 jobs (representing posts that would have been created without innovation centres) would have to be subtracted from the above value.

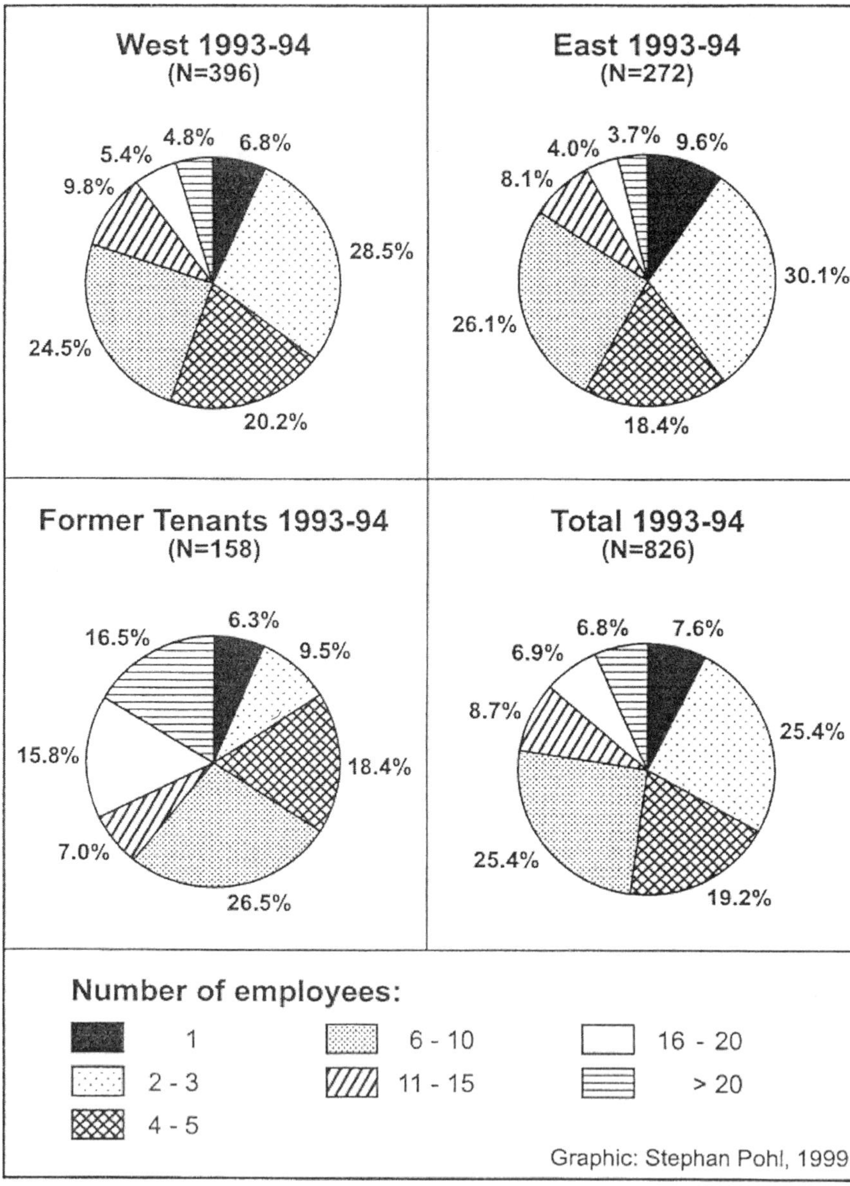

Fig. 8.6 Employment in firms in innovation centres – former tenants

8.6 Intensifying Knowledge and Technology Transfer

The impact of innovation centres on local knowledge and technology transfer in the sense of a speedy translation of new inventions into technologically superior products, processes or services is rather low. In most locations, innovation centres are not competitive due to shortcomings in consulting (see Section 8.4). Transfer of knowledge from one person to another is more effective and arises almost automatically after the founding of a firm. Innovation centres have little effect in this arena. The actual transfer service is performed by the founder, who transfers knowledge from incubator facilities to the new business start-up. The management of innovation centres perform the important function of selecting the truly 'innovative' firms, otherwise the technology transfer would not take place.

The target business group has been only partially reached with respect to innovative capability (See Table 8.1). At least one-third of the firms in innovation centres are active in low-value service sectors or commerce. This could be interpreted as a misappropriation of efforts if measured by the indicator of technological orientation. The firms in eastern German innovation centres are overall even less technology-oriented. There, the establishment of medium-sized firms, which do not necessarily have to be innovative or to develop and introduce 'regional' innovations into the eastern German market, is of key interest for innovation centres due to the unfavourable economic conditions.

Table 8.1 Technological orientation of firms in innovation centres – former tenants

Indicator	West		East		Former Tenants	
	No.	%	No.	%	No.	%
R&D Expenditures in % of Turnover (n = 320/233/164)						
- no R&D expenditures	41	12.8	83	35.6	81	49.5
- less than 3.5 %	8	2.5	20	8.6	6	3.5
- 3.5 % - 8.5 %	28	8.7	17	7.3	24	14.4
- more than 8.5 %	243	75.9	113	48.5	53	32.6
Main Activities of Firm (n = 406/272/164)						
- Research	67	16.5	50	18.4	16	10.2
- Development	218	53.7	124	45.6	80	50.6
- Production	106	26.1	56	20.6	59	37.3
- Trade	79	19.5	38	14.0	41	25.9
- Services	295	72.7	185	68.0	97	61.4
Patents (n = 404/272/164)						
- no patents	310	76.7	214	78.7	121	73.8
- 1 - 2	62	15.3	38	14.0	18	11.0
- 3 - 5	27	6.7	17	6.3	18	11.0
- more than 5	5	1.2	3	1.1	7	4.3

It is unlikely that suitable renters will be attracted from other regions due to the immobility of young innovative firms. Three-quarters of the founders had already worked in the same city or region before becoming self-employed. The 'incubators' may be research facilities (universities, colleges of applied sciences) with technical and natural science orientations, but more often are firms, where from 1993-1994 on average 56 percent of the new entrepreneurs were employed prior to founding a new business (West: 56 percent; East: 49 percent, Former Tenants: 52 percent). If no or few such facilities are located in regions with innovation centres (e.g. in rural areas in the periphery), the likelihood of the development of spin-offs or spin-outs is low.

The reason for the spatial immobility of founders is often the existence of information and contact networks in the private sphere and future business field, which lower the risk of business start-ups. Often contacts developed during university studies or employment offer a basis for later business relationships and deals. After leaving innovation centres, around 65 percent of the firms settle in the same city. An additional 23 percent of firms select their business location within 30 km from the city where the innovation centre is sited. In this case the smaller communities in the surrounding region benefit from the relocation of such businesses. The average distance of new business locations with a main site outside the city is 35.7 km from the innovation centre. Very few firms undergo an interregional business relocation, as property and rental prices play an especially significant role.

8.7 Conclusions

We conclude this chapter by listing a number of policy recommendations which derive from the findings of our survey of firms locating innovation centres in both the West and East of Germany.

a) Further Expansion of Innovation Centres Viable in only a few Locations

In most German regions, the potential of young innovative firms is too small and, overall, seems to be decreasing, which makes it impossible for them to promote the sustainable success of innovation centres. From a national, regional and local perspective, the number of innovation centres in Germany is too high to fully utilise all the facilities with respect to target groups. Many of the facilities in the East and West have reacted to the lack of demand by downgrading the admission criteria. They have reduced the technological requirements imposed on firms, have extended the period of stay or have abstained from using any selection criteria (as a final attempt). At several locations the innovation centres have already been closed. The likely reopening of innovation centres would increase the competition for scarce demand, if alternative concepts fail to be developed and new target groups are not addressed. An example of the need for caution is given by the density of innovation centres in North Rhine-Westphalia. This has resulted from state funding and has led to a high competitive pressure amongst the innovation centres.

b) Avoid Juggling with Names

The observable downgrading of admittance criteria due to the inadequate number of potential renters fitting the target group criteria has led to a situation in some innovation centres where the 'packaging' and claims made do not concur with the content and reality. The politicians and economic operators responsible should be aware that 'juggling with names' could worsen the image and chances of innovation centres in general. In a true innovation centre, the majority of firms should be young businesses whose activities are, first and foremost, aimed at creating new and improved products, processes or technical services.

c) Demand Instead of Supply Orientation

Innovation centres are poorly oriented to meet actual business demand. Many municipalities establish innovation centres hoping that the rental space and consulting services will automatically be utilised by a sufficiently large number of firms (supply-side policy). Before developing the concept of an innovation centre business location, regional analyses should be undertaken to quantify the needs of firms and entrepreneurs ex-ante and to determine what specific regional strengths and weaknesses exist. Such an analysis could well reveal that a realistic basis for the successful operation of an innovation centre does not exist (e.g. due to an absence of entrepreneurial or innovative potential). The simple availability of public funding should not be the reason why an innovation centre is established. If such an analysis leads to the conclusion that an innovation centre would have a good chance of success, the objectives of the parties involved and the location requirements of the region must be brought in line, in order to find a solution compatible with local demand (demand-side policy).

d) More Active, less Passive Support

For the renters, innovation centres offer the possibility of cutting costs and are thus effective in a passive sense. Raising the awareness of firms about problems and the need for consulting as a preventive measure against insolvency are part of the central duties of innovation centres. Solely managing the facilities (playing only a janitorial function) is inadequate for successfully establishing an innovation centre over the medium to long-term in a region. It is necessary to provide active support, which means that the motivation and education of potential entrepreneurs should occur, i.e. innovation centres should provide consulting prior to foundation of a business and contribute to their making a good start. In many business locations, the potential and actual founders are not known by the innovation centres. Contacts between technology-oriented firms and incubator facilities can improve interest in business start-ups, reduce information deficits, and lower inhibitions. It is particularly helpful when successful entrepreneurs are presented as models or examples through seminars or podium discussions. Such measures present self-employment as an alternative to the job market, can raise awareness about local innovation centres, improve their image and acceptance and, finally, provide rental space fitting the needs of particular target groups.

e) Expand the Perspective with Respect to the Funding of Business Start-ups

Today, service providers represent the largest group in innovation centres. Service providers make different demands (for example, on regional infrastructure) than inventors who wish to research new, high-value technological products in innovation centres, develop them as prototypes and produce them in small-scale production. The services in innovation centres must be adapted to meet the needs of the new clientele. The technology policy of the Federal Government, states and municipalities should avoid being over technology-oriented (concentrating only on high-tech firms). This is the basis of support in many innovation centres, but risks distorting the perspective of many cities and municipalities about what is realistically possible. An innovation policy is called for that includes today's expanding field of 'high level services'.

f) Specialisation only in Exceptional Cases

The specialisation of innovation centres in one or a few branches of business is only possible and sensible in very few facilities, because the total number of technology-oriented start-ups in many regions is insufficient for adequate utilisation based on target groups. The few successful innovation centres (e.g. Heidelberg) with a clear specialisation in one or a few technological fields are the exception to the rule. Achieving a definitive forecast of future fields of growth is another fundamental problem of technology policy. A concept can be considered pragmatic and promising when the business target group is shaped to meet local conditions. The goal is to find a sufficiently large group within a branch that is strong enough within the region and shows signs of growth possibilities.

g) Greater Consideration of Cost Aspects

The costs of building or renovating innovation centres totalled 1.3 billion DM (1993–94), of which DM 156.1 million were used in East Germany. In addition to these investment costs, the current operating and personnel costs, which are especially important in the medium and long term, must be considered. For the West German innovation centres, the current operating costs reached an average value of DM 1.0 million per facility per year, while in East German centres the figure was DM 455,000. Particularly in West Germany, many facilities were unnecessarily expensive (an average of 3,054 DM/m^2 rental space compared to East Germany's 1,617 DM/m^2), especially where they were supported by state funding. There appears to be a connection between the availability of state funding and investment costs for construction and renovation. In cases with less than 50 percent state funding, inexpensive renovation of old buildings prevails, in cases above 50 percent, more expensive new building construction dominates (4,245 DM/m^2), indicating a positive correlation of costs with the level of funding. Thus, the incentive structure of public funding appears to reward the construction of new buildings. Thus, it is recommended to include the maximum level of costs per m^2 in the guidelines for funding, in an effort to avoid negative unintended effects by municipalities. Lavishly built and equipped innovation centres can be rather counterproductive when they lead to negative reactions by the general public, visitors and renters (waste of tax money, etc.).

h) Division of Labour in Technology Transfer

Innovation centres appear to have a limited impact on the transfer of knowledge and technology within a region. Compared to other transfer facilities (e.g. innovation consulting offices at chambers of industry and commerce, transfer departments at universities) innovation centres are often not competitive in business terms due to a lack of consulting competency. An intra-regional division of labour should be set as a goal in an effort to avoid losses due to friction and competitive relationships. With respect to successful technology transfers, the unfulfilled need of firms in innovation centres is that of general business information like marketing, product innovation and financing. The management of innovation centres cannot be expected to function as a competent consultant in all fields due to the variety of possible problems, the heterogeneity among renters, as well as limited personnel and time. Consulting mediation in support of direct information transfers could lead to promising development. The management of an innovation centre would act in this case as a mediator between firms seeking assistance, on the one hand, and those offering support, on the other hand. Whether the external help stems from the innovation centre or outside is of little significance from the perspective of the firm. Those innovation centres successful in 'hooking up' firms to local and regional information and innovation networks play an important function.

i) Combination with High-Value Rental Space

The combination of innovation centres with high-value rental space has proven to be advantageous. It offers firms the possibility (even after leaving the innovation centres) to locate in the region or, better still, in the same neighbourhood, without time delays or having to sacrifice the services of the innovation centre and contacts with other firms there. Twenty-nine West German and sixteen East German innovation centres provide a physical and/or organisational link with a technology and business park (e.g. Dortmund, Cologne, Bremen, Dresden and Frankfurt/Oder). In this way, the effectiveness of regional economic effects from innovation centres is also secured in the medium and long-term.

j) Regular Measurement of the Success of Innovation Centres

Especially in the interest of those responsible for their management, every innovation centre should undertake some form of measurement of performance, preferably within the framework of a joint evaluation. However, such evaluations are only sensible, if clear, quantified goals are set and defined before the innovation centre begins operations, allowing for ex-post control at pre-established intervals. The goal-setting can save the time of justifying each step, and help to avoid unrealistic expectations developing among the public with respect to the effectiveness of innovation centres.

References

Baranowski, G., Raetz, G. (1998) Innovationszentren in Deutschland 1998/99. Mit Firmenbeschreibungen. Weidler Buchverlag, Berlin

Behrendt, H. (1996) Wirkungsanalyse von Technologie- und Gründerzentren in Westdeutschland. Wirtschaftswissenschaftliche Beiträge, Vol 123. Physica, Heidelberg

Behrendt, H., Tamásy, C. (1998) Bilanz eines Booms: Erfüllen Technologie- und Gründerzentren die politischen Erwartungen? Deutsche Analysen im Licht anglo-amerikanischer Untersuchungen. Geographische Zeitschrift 4, 34–51

Birch, D. L. (1979) The Job Generation Process. MIT Study on Neighborhood and Regional Change, Cambridge, MA

Birch, D. L. (1987) Job Creation in America. How our Smallest Companies Put the Most People to Work. Free Press, New York

BMBF (Bundesministerium für Bildung, Wissenschaft, Forschung und Technologie) (1998) Faktenbericht 1998 zum Bundesbericht Forschung. BMBF, Bonn

Habersam, M., Burmeister, K., Knoblauch, T., Colom, V., Sibum, D. (1994) Technologiezentren im Wandel. Wirkungsanalyse von Fördermaßnahmen des Landes Nordrhein-Westfalen im Bereich des Technologietransfers. Weidler Buchverlag, Berlin

Kulicke, M., Bayer, K., Bräunling, G., Ewers, H.-J., Gerybadze, A., Mayer, M., Müller, R., Wein, T., Wupperfeld, U. (1993) Chancen und Risiken junger Technologieunternehmen. Ergebnisse des Modellversuchs 'Förderung technologieorientierter Unternehmens-gründungen'. Physica, Heidelberg

Licht, G., Nerlinger, E. (1997) New Technology-Based Firms in Germany: A Survey of the Recent Evidence. ZEW-Discussion Paper no 97-18, ZEW Mannheim

Luger, M.I., Goldstein, H.A. (1991) Technology in the Garden. Research Parks & Regional Economic Development. University of North Carolina Press, London, Chapel Hill

Massey, D.M., Quintas, P., Wield, D. (1992) High-tech Fantasies. Science Parks in Society, Science and Space. Routledge, London

Meyer-Krahmer, F. (1989) Der Einfluß staatlicher Technologiepolitik auf industrielle Innovationen. Nomos, Baden-Baden

Monck, C.S.P., Porter, B., Quintas, P., Storey, D.J., Wynarczyk, P. (1988) Science Parks and the Growth of High-technology Firms. Croom Helm, London

Nerlinger, E. (1998) Standorte und Entwicklung junger innovativer Unternehmen. Empirische Ergebnisse für West-Deutschland. ZEW-Wirtschaftsanalysen, Vol. 27. Nomos, Baden-Baden

Nerlinger, E. (1999) Innovative Unternehmensgründungen in Deutschland: Ein Überblick über aktuelle Forschungsergebnisse und Trends. In: Bögenhold, D., Schmidt, D. (eds.) Eine neue Gründerzeit? Die Wiederentdeckung kleiner Unternehmen in Theorie und Praxis. Fakultas, Amsterdam

Pett, A. (1994) Technologie- und Gründerzentren. Empirische Analyse eines Instruments zur Schaffung hochwertiger Arbeitsplätze. Europäische Hochschulschriften, Vol. 1508. Peter Lang, Frankfurt/M.

Seeger, H. (1997) Ex-Post-Bewertung der Technologie- und Gründerzentren durch die erfolgreich ausgezogenen Unternehmen und Analyse der einzel- und regionalwirtschaftlichen Effekte. Hannoversche Geographische Arbeiten, Vol. 53, Lit, Münster, Hamburg

Steinkühler, R.-H. (1994) Technologiezentren und Erfolg von Unternehmensgründungen. Betriebswirtschaftslehre für Technologie und Innovation, Vol. 9, Deutscher Universitäts-Verlag, Wiesbaden

Sternberg, R. (1988) Technologie- und Gründerzentren als Instrument kommunaler Wirtschaftsförderung. Dortmunder Vertrieb für Bau- und Planungsliteratur, Dortmund

Sternberg, R., Behrendt, H., Seeger, H., Tamásy, C. (1997) Bilanz eines Booms – Wirkungsanalyse von Technologie- und Gründerzentren in Deutschland. Dortmunder Vertrieb für Bau- und Planungsliteratur, Dortmund

Storey, D.J., Strange, A. (1992) Where are They Now? Some Changes in Firms Located on UK Science Parks in 1986. New Technology, Work and Employment 1, 15-28

Tamásy, C. (1996) Technologie- und Gründerzentren in Ostdeutschland – eine regionalwirtschaftliche Analyse. Wirtschaftsgeographie, Vol 10, Lit, Münster

Tamásy, C. (1999) Evaluating Innovation Centres in Germany: Issues of Methodology and Empirical Results. International Geographical Union – Commission on the Organization of Industrial Space. Annual Residential Conference on "Promoting Growth: New Industries, Policies and Forms of Governance", Haifa and Beer Sheva, Israel, June 19-26

Westhead, P., Storey, D.J. (1994) An Assessment of Firms Located on and off Science Parks in the United Kingdom. HMSO, London

PART B: The Network Paradigm and Regional Development

9 The Regional Impact of Innovation Networks

Rolf Sternberg
Department of Economic and Social Geography, University of Cologne

9.1 Introduction, Method of Analysis and Clarification of Terminology

In recent years innovation networks have been adopted as an instrument of local development policy in many European cities. The main idea and hope behind this policy is that through such networks synergy effects will be created and innovation promoted, thus strengthening the competitiveness of the respective region. Numerous authors (e.g. Porter 1998) even maintain that intra-regional co-operation could become a locational factor for investors from outside the region. The high acceptance of the network concept among politicians derives at least partially from the many studies which explain regional development processes in terms of the so-called 'network paradigm' (see Cooke and Morgan 1993). A large number of recent studies in fact concentrate their analysis on the network idea, when explaining regional development. The 'Third Italy' has served as the most cited empirical proof of this kind of region in which intra-regional networking is well-developed and has led to economic success, as shown by Bathelt (1998).

In this chapter, we firstly examine the current theoretical concepts of regional development, discussing whether and to what extent they value innovation networks. In the following section, we then group together the results of empirical studies which analyse the connection between integration in networks and business success (and, thereby, implicitly regional growth as well). This is followed by an investigation of the role of intra-regional innovation linkages, using data from the European Regional Innovation Survey (ERIS). In conclusion, the political implications are illustrated and some unanswered research questions mentioned.

In the context of this study, innovation networks are considered to be linkages between businesses, politicians and researchers – the most important participants in innovation. A network is considered innovative when it continually restructures itself, remaining creative and open for new members (and excluding old members when necessary). According to Lundvall and Borrás (1998, p. 108), an innovative network represents "an explicit organisational co-operation and exchange arrangement aimed at the development of knowledge, products or services". The restriction to intra-regional networks is ignored here.

Innovation networks, as described above, belong to the group of economic networks with more than two participants and are characterised by four characteristics (see Kilper and Latniak 1996): benefit for the majority of the participants, dependency of the participants on resources controlled by others, formation of complex relationships in communication (requiring an openness of the various participants), and an informal and implicit method of functioning.

9.2 Main Theoretical Concepts

With regard to the relationship between innovation networks and regional development two partially-interdependent perspectives are conceivable. It can be argued that the spatial proximity of actors (as an input factor of business innovation – organisationally represented as innovation networks) leads to a higher innovation output from the respective participants, which results in positive impulses for regional development, taking the above assumptions as given. On the other hand, it could be claimed that successful regional development increases the likelihood of spatial clustering of innovation actors due to expected agglomeration economies. This would in turn lead to an improvement in innovation co-operation in the region. In this chapter we primarily explore the first hypothesis and thus the role of innovative linkages between various participants in innovation (businesses, politicians, financial institutions, research facilities). As a result, the function of spatial clustering is discussed, which can be seen in Fig. 9.1.

The analysis of innovation networks and their importance in regional development is neither new, nor solely limited to the field of economics (see Kamann 1998). The idea of innovation networks was already addressed in the theoretical studies of Marshall (1890), Weber (1929) and Schumpeter (1934), who stressed the advantages of inter-firm linkages for the businesses involved as well as for the location in which they operate. Their argumentation primarily concerns economies of scale and scope in the form of positive agglomeration economies. More recent institutional economic approaches (in particular Williamson 1985) emphasise inter-firm network arrangements as a transaction cost saving alternative (which is especially important in times of increasing vertical integration in production) to open markets and business-internal organisational hierarchies.

Since the eighties numerous explanatory approaches for dynamic regional development have arisen, sometimes with closely linked and sometimes highly conflicting characteristics. Despite all the differences between these approaches (the schools of thought of the various authors and their regional, national and disciplinary origins), common ground exists. They differ from earlier regional development theories and justify the claim of a change in paradigm regarding an explanation of the creation and growth of innovative businesses and products and the resulting effects for the region (Capello appropriately called it the 'network paradigm', see Table 9.1). Characteristics promoting consensus include the trend to post-Fordist rather than Fordist production and capital accumulation, the increasing importance of small firms, the relevance of regional framework conditions when considering the increased orientation toward the world market (globalisation and regionalisation). In particular, the new model of innovation involves a division of labour in the innovation process with numerous participants of equal status and varying information sources.

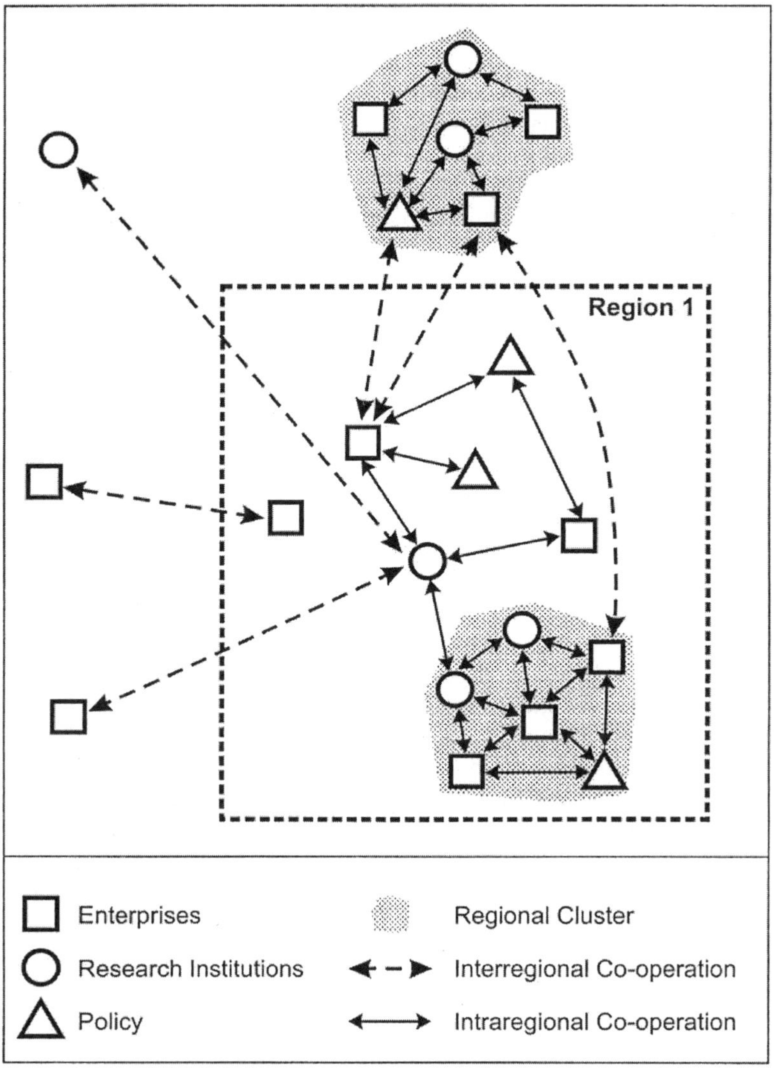

Fig. 9.1 Innovation networks and regional development: intra-versus interregional linkages

Previous crises and the restructuring of the global economy, as well as dramatic changes in production, competition and demand conditions (e.g. increased international competition, fragmented markets, growth of international debt and the level of savings, discontinuities in technological change resulting in economic uncertainty) made business networks consisting of interlinked small and medium-sized businesses with flexible specialised production structures ('vertical disintegration') seem suitable for securing regional growth and stability (see Piore and Sabel 1984). Such structures already exist in the regions of the 'Third Italy'. Innovation networks with a significant regional 'anchor' were viewed as a chance for endogenous regional development under new framework conditions.

Therefore the factors influencing the competitiveness of a region differ significantly from those factors considered as playing a decisive role in former models (formerly 'hardware', today 'software'). These characteristics are common to most of the newly-developed concepts following the era of large businesses, where the network idea is explicitly emphasised. In addition, both of the more recent concepts (i.e. the industrial district paradigm and the network paradigm) can be represented systematically as shown by Capello (1996) (see Table 9.1).

The central question is the entrepreneurial importance of innovation networks in a regional context, i.e. the causes and consequences (regional as well as participant-related) of spatial clustering by innovative businesses and activities. Neo-classical economists have formulated answers to this question with significant support from the theory of positive externalities. Even Porter (1998) used similar arguments to define his concept of comparative advantage in competition. The key arguments of the industrial district paradigm and the network paradigm go a step further. They include the qualitative and social aspects (e.g. trust) as determinants of economic decisions.

This concept will become clearer with a more detailed observation of the theoretical concepts which are used to explain the spatial concentration of innovative activities in their relationship to regional development (see Table 9.2). Thus, spatial concentration functions as a suitable object of study, since innovation networks (in the perspective of regional development) are most likely to arise in (sectoral) spatial clusters.

Innovation networks linking businesses and other participants in innovative activity at the regional level are central to most of these theories. For this reason the basic features of the theoretical statements about innovation networks are summarised here (for more detailed information on current research, see Fritsch *et al.* 1998). An innovation network, in the sense described above, is a central part of, but not identical to the innovative milieu, which can be defined as "the existing regional capacity, in a more institutional sense, that gives rise to the potential for innovation networks to flourish" (Lundvall and Borrás 1998, p. 108). Certainly the industrial district approach explicitly emphasises the relevance of innovation networks. Specific characteristics of businesses in industrial districts include their production for the same end (and world) market, their 'embeddedness' in a common cultural milieu (see Granovetter 1985, Dicken *et al.* 1994; Hirst and Zeitlin 1991) with collective assets and norms, highly intensive and primarily intra-regional networks based on reciprocity and trust between innovation actors

Table 9.1 Characteristics of economic paradigms since the 1960s

	The Large Firm Paradigm (c. 1960-1970)	The Industrial District Paradigm (c. 1970-1985)	The Network Paradigm (since c. 1985)
External conditions			
Macro-economic	Stable raw material prices, economic growth	Increasing raw material prices, high inflation rates, economic decline	Decreasing inflation rates stable exchange rates (at least until 1992)
Market conditions	Stable	Unstable	Unstable
Market competition	National	Mostly national	Global
Technology	Automated hardware	Reprogrammable fixed capital	Communications technology
Consequences on productions systems			
Production	Mass production	Small-batch, customised production	Diversified mass production
Decision-making	Perfect information	Uncertainty	Uncertainty
Competition factors	Low cost production	Local know-how specialisation	Control over complementary assets
Determinants of efficiency of economic system	Economies of scale	Economies of scope	Network externalities
Optimal firm size	Large	Small	Networked
Organisation of production	Vertically integrated	Vertically disintegrated	Quasi-vertically integrated
Theories			
Firm's growth	Internal growth (vertical integration)	Transaction costs	Co-operation agreements
Local and regional development	Development driven by external forces	Development from below approach	Global/local interface (Globalisation and regionalisation)
Organisation of firms in space	Transport costs (division of labour with multi-located firms)	Cluster of small firms	New management of territory

Source: adapted from Capello (1996) with minor changes.

Table 9.2 Overview of theoretical cluster approaches

	New Industrial Spaces	District Theory	Innovative Milieus	Porter's Cluster Concept	Systems of Innovation (national, regional)
Central hypothesis/actors	Vertical disintegration causes a spatial concentration of production	Local actors, embedded in a social-cultural milieu	A milieu as an organisation of networked actors	Firm strategies as a result of Porter's 'diamond'	System of institutional ties
Geographical coverage	Whole of core-periphery structures	Mainly success stories	Success stories (high-tech focus)	More competitive nations/regions	Broad coverage of areas with some innovative capability
Change in time	Windows of opportunity; lock-in effects > path dependency	Entrepreneurial; in social cultural background	Entrepreneurial	Created advantages, diamond interaction	Long waves > path dependency
Spatial clustering principle	Agglomeration forces > 'worlds of production'; untraded interdependencies	Embedding/ flexibilisation > 'localisation thesis'	Localised processes of learning	Local interaction between competitors, producers, customers, etc.	Largely as container; proximity facilitating buyer-supplier interaction
Role of networks	Negligible	Central	Central, especially intra-regional	Important	Important
Dominant actors	Large firms	Small firms, heavily embedded	Local entrepreneurs, politicians	Large firms	Institutions and their systems, entrepreneurs
Main policy implication	Limited scope; promoting first-mover advantages	Encouraging SMEs and flexibility	Improving learning milieu; encouraging networking	Indirect improving interaction of diamond factors	Institutions and network building
Representatives	Scott, Storper, Walker	Sabel, Granovetter, Marshall	Camagni, Aydalot, Maillat	Porter	Nelson, Lundvall, Freeman

> *indicates changing position*

Source: adapted from Lagendijk (1997, p. 22) with some changes

in the region, use of the newest highly productive technologies, the dominance of small and medium-sized enterprises, and an extreme intra-regional and intra-firm division of labour in the sense of specialisation in certain production phases (see Amin and Robins 1990; OECD 1994). All businesses located in industrial districts benefit from advantages due to the interaction of these factors since there are 'economies external to the firm but internal to the district'. This trust in common advantages of all parties in close co-operation makes the apparent contradiction between competition and co-operation understandable (see Sternberg 1998).

Following a period of predominantly positive evaluations of the industrial district concept (e.g. Becattini 1990; Brusco 1990; Garofoli 1991), a certain scepticism developed in the mid-nineties, especially with respect to its value as a general model of regional development or regional policy. The hopes of an era of "co-operative endogenous regional development" (Semlinger 1995, p. 15) should be seen in a relative sense, since exemplary regions like the 'Third Italy' or Baden-Württemberg have since lost some of their growth dynamism. There is an increasing number of indicators pointing to the fact that the development of these regional economies has not progressed according to expectations (see in particular Amin and Robins 1991; Bathelt 1998; Bellini 1996; Bianchi 1998; Grotz and Braun 1997a; Heidenreich 1996). Some of the characteristics once considered advantageous for regional economies in fact proved to be barriers to development in the process of adaptation to the globalising economy. In addition, many regional scientists assume that a limited number of regional economies possessing the features of industrial districts exist worldwide (see Simmie and Kirby 1998). As a result critics write about 'the networks myth' when describing regional development (see Hellmer *et al.* 1999). However, regarding the 'Third Italy', it should be considered that hitherto there have been no representative and empirical-based comparative studies on the regions within the heterogenous 'Third Italy' that could serve as a proof for the hypothesis of an overall economic decline. The same is true for industrial districts in general. There is a definite need for more empirical research in this field.

The recent theoretical debate has been characterised by a noticeable distancing from the industrial district theory in its pure form (e.g. renunciation of the emphasis on small businesses). The cause of successful regional development is increasingly seen as a mixture of cultural, social and institutional framework conditions, and less the result of hard economic and organisational factors such as product specialisation and extensive division of labour stemming from vertical disintegration. Terms like 'institutional thickness' (Amin and Thrift 1995), 'intelligent regions' (Cooke and Morgan 1994), the 'learning region' (Asheim 1996; Florida 1995; Morgan 1995), 'regional innovation systems' (Braczyk *et al.* 1998) and 'organisational learning' (Maskell and Malmberg 1995) correspond to the view that knowledge or know-how is the key to competitive businesses, and hence competitive regions, and that this knowledge can be acquired particularly well through collective learning. Even more recent studies on innovative milieus from the GREMI group concentrate on the milieu-specific causes of intra-regional networks, emphasising the importance of cultural features in regional development. They stress the role of the local/regional environment for the generation of innovation (see Bramanti and Maggioni 1997; Camagni and Capello 1997; Maillat 1998). This approach focuses on region-specific rules, conventions and social relationships. In this respect, a territorial production system is organised and controlled on the basis of a regional logic. To a certain extent the collective capability reserve ('Fähigkeitsvorrat', Maillat 1998) controls the cognitive abilities (and power to act) of participants in a region.

Another argument for the significance of collective learning processes permanently fed by intra-regional networks was recently introduced by Maskell *et al.* (1998) in the form of the so-called 'ubiquitification' process. This refers to the fact that formerly locally-specific production factors are more easily accessible worldwide in this era of internationalisation and globalisation. In other words, the source regions tend to lose their competitive advantage. Solely knowledge, which is hard to codify (and, thus, even more difficult to transfer), yet well-embedded in the regional innovation system, is immune to 'ubiquitification'.

An additional aspect of the importance of networks in the innovation process (but not necessarily intra-regional process) results from the new understanding of how innovations are created. In contrast to the linear innovation model with its clear succession of research, development, production and distribution, which was held for many years, it is now well accepted that it takes the form of a chain-linked model (Kline and Rosenberg 1986). This model recognises the possibility of feedback at any time from customers, producers, suppliers from the same or other industries or technological fields. However, these external sources are only utilised by businesses with access to innovation networks.

The numerous ideas for the further development of the industrial district and milieu approaches (or the attempt to introduce a dynamic element) emphasise that despite all other differences, knowledge-based economies are increasingly linked up. This implies the existence of various 'new combinations' between specialised businesses. In an effort to explain the economic dynamics of businesses and regions, it is no longer sufficient to observe individual businesses and their activities. Moreover, the regional (and wider) interaction field must be integrated into the analysis – the network concept remains the focal point. Consequently, network-oriented regional analysis should in the future take into greater consideration the systemic character of innovation in the sectoral-spatial clusters. So far, there fails to exist a complete concept which simultaneously makes an empirical test of the factors of influence and also analyses the reason why collective learning processes depend upon the deep embeddedness in a spatial context. The question of how innovative industry clusters must be structured to support high innovative capacity and employment growth by innovation cannot currently be answered with any conviction. Criticism of the industrial district approach described above was already expressed a number of years ago. For quite some time business administration has rejected a strong emphasis on the networking of innovative players in general, and also in relation to regions. In any case, many businesses today do not primarily pursue a maximisation of 'efficiency' (which would be possible through innovative co-operation), they attempt to maintain control over the market and their oligopolistic advantages (see Staber

1996). Lundvall and Borrás (1998) specify possible disadvantages for participants in innovation from network activity into four categories:

- networks can increase transaction costs, since considerable resources (economic, human, and temporal) are necessary for their foundation;
- collective utility can be reduced by the 'free-rider' behaviour of individual partners;
- networks can lead to the exclusion of various partners in the region;
- the power relationships of the participants in a network can be quite different (especially the prime position of large businesses, see Hancké 1998).

Maskell *et al.* (1998) also emphasise that closely integrated and successful innovation networks consciously or unconsciously introduce barriers to new (and often very innovative) businesses, thus raising the danger of lock-ins. The literature about the dangers of business or regional strategies aimed (primarily) at intra-regional innovation networks is extensive. Fürst and Schubert (1998) formulated three potential risks for regional development with particular regard to the studies from Grabher (1993) and his systematisation of various lock-in dangers as a result of intra-regional innovation networks:

- innovation networks can further a poor status-quo situation and hinder necessary changes ('sclerotic milieus', or 'structural conservation cartels' as in many old industrial regions);
- innovation networks can encounter restrictions, e.g. when they are managed from above (like state-run regional conferences ('Regionalkonferenzen');
- innovation networks can lead to over-proportionally high costs for members (e.g. entropic reproduction of 'round tables', which can lead to 'network noise' ('Netzwerkrauschen'), in other words numerous meetings and activities and little output due to the over-stimulation of participants).

As Fürst and Schubert claimed (1998), in some cases one could infer that the positive influence of innovation networks on regional development is highly dependent upon whether they represent an adequate combination of 'strong' and 'weak' ties (for the relevance of linkage intensities see Granovetter 1973 and the reaction of Grabher 1993, twenty years later). Strong ties promote the development of socio-emotional relationships and trust; on the contrary weak ties, without solid institutional connections but with numerous individuals of varying social backgrounds, are suitable for transmitting information.

This theoretical overview reveals that, due to the large number of concepts with innovation networks as their central theme, there is no clear answer to the question as to whether innovation networks positively influence regional development: "The richness of networks, combined with their distinctive duality of flexibility and control, makes them difficult to analyse (...) Researchers are grappling with difficult conceptual and operational issues, and no general theory is in place that would address the multiplicity and complexity of issues raised and integrate previous research into a theoretical whole" (Staber 1996, p. 2). To what extent an empirical answer can be given will be addressed in the following chapter.

9.3 Main Findings of the Empirical Research

The Relationship Between Innovation Networks and Firm/Regional Growth

Our analysis has been carried out in two steps. Firstly, we investigate whether sufficient empirical proof exists for the hypothesis that regions (and their actors) with strong innovation networks are economically more successful than regions without them.

Even today few empirical studies have been performed to examine the connection between the intensity of networking between innovation actors within a region and the economic and technological prosperity of the region. There are numerous case studies presented as positive examples of network-based regional development, but these are restricted to only a few regions (e.g. Emilia Romagna in northern Italy). Empirical analyses (Maskell and Malmberg 1995) and comparative regional studies (see Cooke and Morgan 1992) are exceptional, as are analyses of German regions outside of Baden-Württemberg (see a critical survey from Grotz and Braun 1997b). Previous studies have only been able to a certain degree to support or defeat central hypotheses like the positive correlation of strong intra-regional networks and the economic success of a region (see Signorini 1994). Among regions of high growth, it is possible to found examples with and those without intensive innovation networks (see a critique of the industrial district concept from Amin 1993). On the other hand, economically successful as well as economically depressed regions belong to the group of regions with innovation networks (for example, numerous old industrialised areas). In addition, interregional investigations have to deal with the fundamental methodological problem that at the origin of most economically successful regions today was an event that occurred many decades ago.

The concept of industrial districts has substantially lost importance as a general role model for regional development, although in the eighties it was found in part of the literature on regional economics. An evaluation of the empirical validity of the basic statement of this approach (see Sternberg 1995) shows the boundaries of local networks as a basis for regional development models in an era of flexible economies. The empirical evidence is restricted to a comparatively small number of success stories in the USA and Europe. Even in these case it can be seen that in R&D intensive industries, like biotechnology, the local and social 'embeddedness' of businesses and their networks diminishes with the maturity of the industry to the benefit of international and global linkages (see Tödtling 1994). The success stories are very heterogenous and include family and trade-oriented businesses of the Third Italy as well as relatively young high-tech regions like Silicon Valley. In spite of this heterogenity, a representative sample fails to exist. In the real world, regions intensively linked to large businesses or with absolutely no innovation networks are more numerous. Regarding maturity, however, it should not be forgotten that in recent past some of the established and successful industrial districts (including Silicon Valley) showed the ability to renew themselves when new technological opportunities arose. Start-ups play a significant role within this process. But in the end, ongoing technological change, especially in multimedia and bioinformatics, does not cause the genesis of new regions which were not already growth regions formerly, whereas in the past new technological opportunities favoured new industrial spaces.

The available literature shows at a glance the large number of current analyses of innovation networks that exist (for an overview see Arndt 2001, p. 52). These studies cover a wide spectrum of methods and approaches. One common element is the, more or less, explicit consideration of the range of forms of co-operation in innovation, as well as the connection between business success and the extent of co-operation. While the question of the forms of co-operation will be covered in the next section, this section discusses the variable 'firm success', which – referring to the sum of all firms – corresponds with regional success. The initial hypothesis, by which businesses have to acquire external knowledge in order to remain innovative and competitive, is verified by numerous empirical studies. Oerlemans *et al.* (1998), on the basis of a survey of 579 Dutch businesses, show that their innovation output is significantly influenced by their relationships to customers and suppliers. The EU Community Innovation Survey achieved similar results.

A joint project involving economic geographers and regional scientists was set up in 1996 as part of a research programme funded by the Deutsche Forschungsgemeinschaft on which this volume is based. This project attempted to quantify and evaluate the intensity of innovation networks and their significance for firm growth and regional development following a common method of analysis in eleven European regions[1]. The database of this European Regional Innovation Survey (ERIS) includes survey results from more than 8,600 manufacturing firms, business services and research institutions. First results from the three German regions of the first study phase are summed up in Sternberg (1999). In the summer of 2000 a special issue of 'European Planning Studies' (vol. 9, no. 4) was released containing a summarised version of several papers, in which data from all eleven regions is published. For the three German case study regions, the research team has already observed that a clearly positive relationship exists between the intensity of the link to innovation networks and the innovation output of the corresponding businesses (see Sternberg 1999).

The initial analyses of the ERIS database are now available covering the relationship between network integration and the growth of manufacturing firms in all study regions (see Arndt 1999). The comparison of co-operating and non-co-operating businesses shows clearly that businesses utilising co-operation in innovation as a strategic instrument enjoy more positive values for all four

[1] These regions include Alsace and Gironde (France), Saxony, Hannover-Brunswick-Göttingen and Baden (Germany), Stockholm (Sweden), Vienna (Austria), South Holland (Netherlands), South Wales (UK), Barcelona (Spain) and Slovenia. For a more detailed description of the ERIS approach see Sternberg (2000).

indicators selected (although not always at the same level of significance). Even though the causality cannot be clearly determined, mutual influence is plausible.

Table 9.3 Innovation co-operation and business success

	Businesses with innovation linkages (N=1.050)	Businesses without innovation linkages (N=250)	t-value
Share of turnover with new products in %	27.2	17.1	4.60**
Annual employment change in %	7.5	4.6	1.96*
Annual growth of turnover in %	15.4	12.4	1.82
Ratio of exports to turnover in %	26.3	14.3	6.77**

Significance level: * $p < 0.05$; ** $p < 0.001$
Source: Arndt 1999, European Regional Innovation Survey database.

On the basis of empirical research, it is difficult to establish whether external or intra-firm impulses are more important for innovation. The characteristics of innovation output are certainly an important factor, but not the sole source of business and regional success. A research project on the innovation linkages of SMEs in the Munich region supervised by the author (see Stenke 1999) revealed that, in line with expectations, indicators of innovation output correlate positively with those of business success (e.g. development of employment and turnover). Not only the number of network participants within the Munich region, but also the intensity of these contacts exhibit a highly significant correlation with the turnover of the businesses. With respect to the number of network participants, this relationship is also valid for percentage employment growth. It was therefore empirically shown that a strong, positive relationship exists between business success and the intensity or frequency of linkages to innovation networks. This result was not significantly influenced by other factors (for example, business or product age, innovation intensity).

Intra-Regional and/or Interregional Innovation Linkages?

The question of the geographical extent of networks is particularly interesting from the perspective of economic geography, as well as from the point of view of regional policy. The more important the regional share of a network, the greater the potential influence of local political measures and the stronger the regional effects of such networks.

Lundvall and Borrás (1998) claim that the regional dimension of innovation networks is being particularly decisive, since synergies (additional innovative utility) from common cultural, psychological or political perspectives can develop for those participants located in the same region and specialised in the same sector. The milieu and industrial district approaches also emphasise intra-regional linkages. Both concepts consider such linkages as playing a central role in the competitiveness of businesses and the region. In addition to the usual functions of networks, they fulfil a substitute function for insufficient or non-existent institutional decision structures, a mobilisation function as well as a forum and innovation function (identification of common problems) (see Fürst and Schubert 1998).

The relationship between intra-regional network and the region is mutual. It is clear that a higher share of regional rather than interregional network relationships leads to stronger regional effects. On the other hand, empirical research provides clues to the fact that the existence and quality of intra-regional network linkages is shaped to a large extent by the regional surroundings (see Cooke and Morgan 1993; Lundvall and Borrás 1998). Briefly, the logic behind this is the following: the permanent learning process of participants in innovation (within and outside an innovation network) is based on the continual exchange of knowledge – just as the collective creation and use of new knowledge is built on mutual trust. In this respect the spatial dimension of network activities is not a subsidiary factor, but rather a fundamental one. Networks function best as social organisms when they utilise all facets of tacit knowledge from regional interests and organisations. Tacit knowledge requires a substantial amount of trust and cultural understanding, which arises more easily through spatial proximity. This does not negate the existence and importance of interregional or global networks. Such networks are more formal in nature and exchange more codified knowledge.

There are a number of analysts who claim that the region represents the decisive level for collective learning and innovation networks, and who see concrete advantages for the future of regional development: "the emphasis on the region as a nexus of [learning] processes helps fix the idea of regional development as itself an evolutionary process" (Cooke and Morgan 1998, p. 82). This process helps avoid the danger of a path dependency, when all institutions of the region are involved.

The question of the spatial extent of innovation networks has been discussed in many empirical network studies (for an overview see Arndt 2001, p.60f). Without going into detail, a certain consensus can be observed. It is agreed that most individual businesses as well as the regions themselves must receive their impulses for growth from the local area *and* from the global arena. For a variety of reasons, the regional environment is important for business, product and regional development (possibly more important than maintained in many earlier paradigms). Therefore, intra-regional innovative linkages remain essential for most businesses in most regions even in this period of globalisation. But the globalisation of markets and production makes it necessary for innovation actors and regions to establish ties to the rest of the world. Without such connections the lock-in effects described above threaten to occur, resulting in path dependency for businesses and regions. In summary, this 'global/local interface' is defined as "the nexus between the forces which increasingly expose more firms to international, competitive markets and the structures and strategies which they adopt to compete successfully in those markets; and the local conditions, regulations and regimes which enable parts of or whole firms to export competitively into those international markets" (Simmie and Kirby 1998, p. 191).

An empirical verification of the global/local interface hypothesis (even though it is not named as such) is offered in several studies within the framework of the EU-TSER project 'Networks, Collective Learning and RTD in Regionally-Clustered High-Technology SMEs', in which networks of innovative SMEs in European regions were analysed (for an overview see the corresponding issue of 'Regional Studies', no. 6, 1999). Keeble *et al.* (1998) show that in the British case study regions of Cambridge and Oxford, technology-intensive businesses (with naturally strong innovation networks) possess above average ties to the global and local levels. Similar features can be observed for R&D-intensive businesses in Munich, the German case study region in the same project.

The empirical analyses quoted below are based on the European Regional Innovation Survey (ERIS). They underline the fact that for several European regions there are statistically representative results, concerning the question of the spatial extent of innovation linkages. When observing the three German regions from the ERIS project (Saxony, the 'research triangle' in Lower Saxony, and Baden), three clear conclusions can be drawn (see Sternberg 1999; Koschatzky 1999). First, in relation to the question as to whether intra- or interregional co-operation predominates, this is dependent upon the type of innovation actor. For public research institutions intra-regional linkages are more common, whereas manufacturing firms place more importance on interregional co-operation for innovation. Second, from the perspective of public research institutions, intra-regional cooperation is highly significant with businesses, whereas their ties with other research facilities are more likely to be interregional. Third, it emerges that innovation intensive firms exhibit a stronger emphasis on interregional linkages than less innovative firms.

If this analysis is extended to all ten European regions covered by ERIS (excluding Slovenia) and the innovation linkages of more than 1,000 manufacturing firms considered, one can see the characteristic patterns of the spatial range differentiated into the types of innovation actors (see Fig. 9.2 and Arndt 1999). Both Saxony and Gironde are characterised by a high share of intra-regional linkages. Considering the problems of the transformation region – Saxony – the extent of its spatial structure could be interpreted as a weakness of the regional innovation system. A second group of regions includes agglomeration regions, like Barcelona and Vienna, and those with a high share of international linkages, like Alsace and Wales, which represent regions with cost-oriented competitive advantages. A third group consists of regions shaped by a national orientation of co-operative relations – for example, the West German regions of Baden and Hannover-Brunswick-Göttingen. They benefit from the largest national consumer market within the EU. Both of these West German regions exhibit a similar spatial structure of co-operation, which can be interpreted as an indicator of the existence of national innovation systems. Following this reasoning, Saxony plays a special role due to its transformation process. The remaining regions fail to display clear spatial structures.

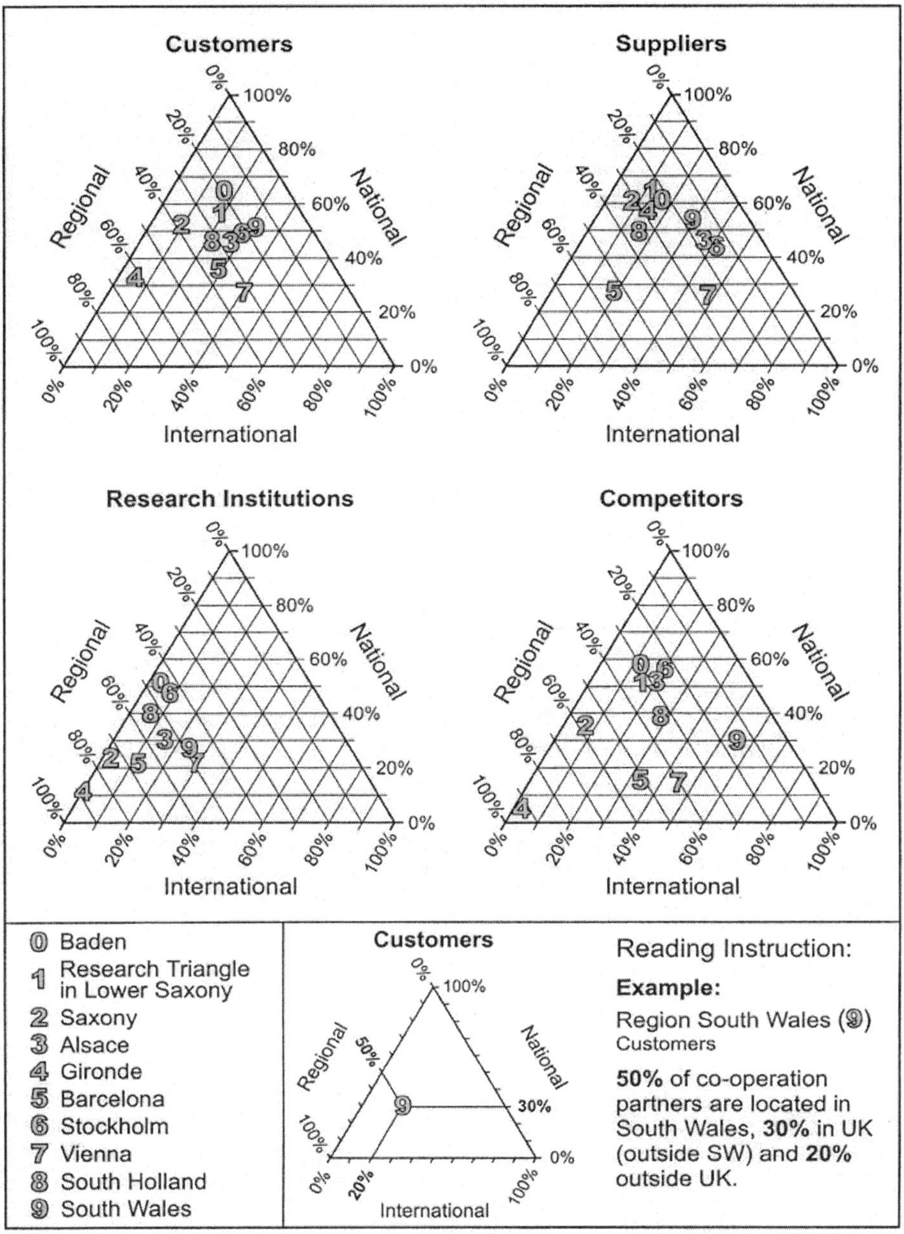

Source: Arndt (1999), European Regional Innovation Survey database.

Fig. 9.2 Range of innovation linkages of manufacturing firms in ten European regions

What conclusions be drawn from these results with respect to ties between the business and regional levels? ERIS provides results showing the connections between innovation networks and regional development for the various regions. Previously published results (based solely on the surveys of the three German regions in the sample) examine whether the existence and intensity of innovative linkages between regional innovation actors can be used as an indicator for the regions' innovativeness and, thus, implicitly their economic dynamism (see Sternberg 1999).

In relation to the share of manufacturing firms with external innovative linkages, only minor differences were found to exist between the three German case study areas. However, it is interesting that Baden, one of the most innovative German regions, has the lowest percentage, while Saxony has the highest. Hence, Baden's excellent R&D infrastructure is not reflected in the share of innovative manufacturing SMEs which have intra-regional contacts with research institutions (i.e. within Baden-Württemberg), although there is a high incidence of intra-regional linkages between innovative SMEs and customers and/or suppliers and/or competitors. By contrast, the technologically less advanced regional economies of the Lower Saxon 'research triangle' and of Saxony, have high shares of intraregional linkages with research institutions. Therefore, no statistical evidence can be found for the assumption that prosperous regions have stronger intra-regional linkages than less flourishing ones. However, it would seem that until now the predominantly local (intra-state) linkages between local firms and research institutions in the research triangle have had little effect on local small businesses in this region. So what is required for these links to contribute to an innovative milieu? The problem in this part of Lower Saxony is that one of the two sets of effects which should operate simultaneously in a true innovative milieu is lacking (see Malecki 1997b, p. 174): "Whereas proximity effects (reductions in costs because of quicker circulation of information and face-to-face contacts) obviously exist, the region suffers from underdeveloped socialization effects, related to collective learning, cooperation, and socialisation of risks".

In spite of the relevance of innovation networks, empirical research shows that the relationships between a region and the development of its businesses should be interpreted too narrowly – even in relation to linkages between innovation actors. Otherwise, one risks being accused of 'spatial fetishism'. Without exact knowledge of the socio-economic processes and framework conditions, the influence of a region on the relationship between networks and regional development cannot be clearly determined (Lagendijk 1997). Nevertheless, with reference to ERIS, it is clear that the more knowledge-intensive innovation activities of businesses, the greater the need for spatial proximity (specifically) and, in general, the greater the need for network integration (see Arndt 1999).

9.4 Policy Implications and Open Research Questions

A policy-oriented response to the relationship between innovation networks and regional development is based on the conclusions drawn in the first wave of ERIS empirically-based research on innovative linkages between manufacturing firms in European regions as formulated by Koschatzky and Sternberg (2000). Many attempts are in fact being made by governments in different nations and regions to foster regional economic development through the initiation and intensification of innovation networks (e.g. see Lagendijk 1999; Enright 1996). There is a broad belief among local economic policymakers that the number and the quality of intra-regional innovation networks can be increased by means of policy instruments. This assumption is supported by results of some recent qualitative research pointing to the significance of 'institutional thickness' (Amin and Thrift 1995) or the 'associational economy' depicted by Cooke and Morgan (1998). Finally, there is another fact that stresses the importance of policy: most of the regions with strong intra-regional innovation networks have strong and very active political institutions and actors (see Malecki 1997b).

Not only in relation to economic theory, but also in policy there has been a paradigmatic change during the last two decades, and hence the number of empirically-based assessments of policy approaches is still rather limited. This change can however be characterised as a decrease in the importance of 'hardware' components within regional economic policy (e.g. physical infrastructure) and a corresponding increase in the significance of 'software' components aiming to improve the non-physical conditions for co-operative ventures between innovation actors. In addition to EU projects (pre-competitive R&D support for international consortia, e.g. ESPRIT), several countries have implemented programmes designed to strengthen the software element, e.g. the Business-Oriented Technology Collaboration Scheme in the Netherlands or the very successful network programme in Denmark, as well as projects in the US (see Porter 1998 and Rosenfeld 1997 for an overview).

In Germany, the Federal Government has paid great attention to the regional level in the implementation of recent technology policy measures. Of special importance is the InnoRegio policy in the new federal states which, by initiating regional networks and supporting the development of innovative regional development strategies, aims to improve the employment situation and strengthen the comparative advantage of the new federal states. The same approach was followed some years ago by the rather successful BioRegio project, whose target was to initiate and support regional biotechnology clusters in Germany. The EU has also developed specific technology policy programmes for less developed regions that intend to initiate networks (e.g. the Regional Innovation Strategies).

A systematic and Europe-wide overview of early political attempts to initiate and foster innovation networks in the early 1990s drew four main conclusions (see Boekholt and Fahrenkrog 1993). First, the central broker function should be in the hands of a gatekeeper highly admired in the business community. Second, the development of innovation networks requires a certain awareness of the need for co-operation as well as trust and a substantial amount of time. Third, entrepreneurs do not invest time and money in the development of networks unless they expect clear profits for their businesses. Finally, science-led initiatives to promote innovation networks are rarely successful.

More recent experiences with the British Training and Enterprise Council (see Huggins 1998) reveal that such attempts will fail without trust between potential co-operation partners. The fear of competitive disadvantages connected with very intensive and strategically important co-operative arrangements – a popular argument with traditional economists – obviously serves as a fundamental barrier that cannot be overcome by spatial proximity alone. Even researchers with sympathy for the concept of regional innovation networks are sceptical about the possibility of generating innovation networks through policy instruments (see Lundvall and Borrás 1998). Experience in the Third Italy, with its regional clusters of small and medium-sized firms, strongly support the assumption that close connections between innovation actors are favourable to regional economic development, but they are extremely region-specific. Policy did play a major role in Third Italy's development, but due to specific socio-cultural conditions and other limitations, this cannot be viewed as a general model for regional development which can easily be transferred to regions in other countries, or even to other Italian regions (for a comprehensive and recent assessment of the Third Italy, see Bathelt 1998).

Even considering state-of-the-art research on innovation networks, it is not yet clear what policy instruments are necessary to successfully initiate co-operative ventures. According to the assessment of US programmes made by Malecki (1997a, p.84), one essential factor seems to be the existence of a network co-ordinator to act as "the hub and gatekeeper for the network of firms". This person could be either a consultant, an employee of the local economic development organisation or an entrepreneur. It is crucial for the success of such programmes that this person is well known and accepted in the region.

Because most of the policy attempts are rather new, many research gaps must be filled. In particular, it is not known (see Lagendijk 1999; Enright 1996) what is the correct balance between the different types of actors, what variations in the standard concept are needed for peripheral regions lacking strong institutions, and how the conflicting aims of national and regional policy can be solved (growth-orientation versus the reduction of spatial inequalities). In conclusion, the request of Enright (1996, p. 213) for more "ex-ante academic studies and ex-post policy studies" on innovation networks and regional clusters is worth considering – so far, most actors have travelled in the opposite direction.

References

Amin, A. (1993) The Globalisation of the Economy. An Erosion of Regional Networks? In: Grabher, G. (ed.) The Embedded Firm. On the Socioeconomics of Industrial Networks. Routledge, London, 278-295

Amin, A., Robins, K. (1990) The Re-emergence of Regional Economies? The Mythical Geography of Flexible Accumulation. Environment and Planning D, Society and Space 8, 7-34

Amin, A., Robins, K. (1991) These are not Marshallian Times. In: Camagni, R. (ed.) Innovation Networks: Spatial Perspectives. Belhaven Press, London, New York, 105-118

Amin A., Thrift N. (1995) Globalisation, Institutional 'Thickness' and the Local Economy.

In: Healey, P., Cameron, S., Davoudi, S., Graham, S., Madani-Pour, A. (eds.) Managing Cities: the New Urban Context. John Wiley and Sons, Chichester, 92-108

Arndt, O. (1999) Sind intraregional vernetzte Unternehmen erfolgreicher? Eine empirische Analyse zur Embeddedness-These auf der Basis von Industriebetrieben in zehn europäischen Regionen. Working Paper, Department of Economic and Social Geography, University of Cologne, 99-105

Arndt, O. (2001) Innovative Netzwerke als Determinante betrieblicher Innovationstätigkeit. Das Beispiel Süd-Wales/UK. Wirtschafts- und Sozialgeographisches Institut der Universität zu Köln, Köln. Kölner Forschungen zur Wirtschafts- und Sozialgeographie, 51

Asheim, B. (1996) Industrial Districts as 'Learning Regions'. A Condition for Prosperity? European Planning Studies 4, 379-400

Bathelt, H. (1998) Regionales Wachstum in vernetzten Strukturen: Konzeptioneller Überblick und kritische Bewertung des Phänomens 'Drittes Italien'. Die Erde 129, 247-271

Becattini, G. (1990) The Marshallian District as a Socio-economic Notion. In: Pyke, F., Becattini, G., Sengenberger, W. (eds.) Industrial Districts and Inter-firm Co-operation in Italy. International Institute for Labour Studies, Genf, 185-219

Bellini, N. (1996) Industrial Districts. Evolution and Change. European Planning Studies 4, 3-4

Bianchi, G. (1998) Requiem for the Third Italy? Rise and Fall of a too Successful Concept. Entrepreneurship and Regional Development 10, 93-116

Boekholt, P., Fahrenkrog, G. (1993) Public Measures to Support the Clustering and Networks of Innovative SMEs. Luxemburg (DG XIII, EIMS No.6)

Braczyk, H.-J., Cooke, P., Heidenreich, M. (eds.) (1998) Regional Innovation Systems. The Role of Governances in a Globalized World. UCL Press, London

Bramanti, A., Maggioni, M.A. (1997) The Dynamics of Milieux: The Network Analysis Approach. In: Ratti, R., Bramanti, A., Gordon, R. (eds.) The Dynamics of Innovative Regions. The GREMI Approach. Ashgate, Aldershot, 321-341

Brusco, S. (1990) The Idea of the Industrial District: Its Genesis. In: Pyke, F., Becattini, G., Sengenberger, W. (eds.) Industrial Districts and Inter-Firm Cooperation in Italy. International Institute for Labour Studies, Genf, 10-20

Camagni, R., Capello, R. (1997) Innovation and Performance of SMEs in Italy: The Relevance of Spatial Aspects. Paper Presented at the International Conference on Innovation and Performance of SMEs, Cambridge, March 17

Capello, R. (1996) Industrial Enterprises and Economic Space: The Network Paradigm. European Planning Studies 4, 485-498

Cooke, P., Morgan, K. (1992) Regional Innovation Centres in Europe. Report to Department of Trade and Industry, Cardiff

Cooke, P., Morgan, K. (1993) The Network Paradigm: New Departures in Corporate and Regional Development. Environment and Planning D 11, 543-564

Cooke, P., Morgan, K. (1994) Growth Regions under Duress: Renewal Strategies in Baden-Wurttemberg and Emilia-Romagna. In: Amin, A., Thrift, N. (eds.) Globalization, Institutions, and Regional Development in Europe. Oxford University Press, Oxford. 91-117.

Cooke, P., Morgan, K. (1998) The Associational Economy. Firms, Regions, and Innovation. Oxford University Press, Oxford

Dicken, P., Forsgren, M., Malmberg, A. (1994) The Local Embeddedness of Transnational Corporations. In: Amin, A., Thrift, N. (eds.) Globalization, Institutions, and Regional Development in Europe. Oxford University Press, Oxford, 23-45

Enright, M.J. (1996) Regional Clusters and Economic Development: A Research Agenda.

In: Staber, U.H., Schaefer, N.V., Sharma, B. (eds.) Business Networks. Prospects for Regional Development. De Gruyter, Berlin, New York, 190-214
Florida, R. (1995) Toward the Learning Region. Futures 27, 527-536
Fürst, D., Schubert, H. (1998) Regionale Akteursnetzwerke. Zur Rolle von Netzwerken in regionalen Umstrukturierungsprozessen. Raumforschung und Raumordnung 56, 352-361
Garofoli, G. (1991) Local Networks, Innovation and Policy in Italian Industrial Districts. In: Bergman, E.M., Maier, G., Tödtling, F. (eds.) Economic Networks, Innovation, and Local Development in Industrialized Countries. Mansell, London, 119-139
Grabher, G. (1993) The Weakness of Strong Ties: The Lock-in of Regional Development in the Ruhr Area. In: Grabher, G. (ed.) The Embedded Firm. On the Socioeconomics of Industrial Networks. Routledge, London, 255-277
Granovetter, M. (1973) The Strength of Weak Ties. American Journal of Sociology 78, 1360-1380.
Granovetter, M. (1985) Economic Action and Social Structure. The Problem of Embeddedness. American Journal of Sociology 91, 346-364
Grotz, R., Braun, B. (1997a) Limitations of Regional Network-orientated Strategies for Manufacturing Industries. Erdkunde 51, 43-51
Grotz, R., Braun, B. (1997b) Spatial Aspects of Technology-Oriented Cooperation: Examples from the German Mechanical Engineering Industry. Regional Studies 31, 545-557
Hancké, B. (1998) Trust or Hierarchy? Changing Relationships Between Large and Small Firms in France. Small Business Economics 11, 237-252
Heidenreich, M. (1996) Beyond Flexible Specialization: The Rearrangement of Regional Production Orders in Emilia-Romagna and Baden-Württemberg. European Planning Studies 4, 401-420
Hellmer, F., Friese, C., Kollros, H., Krumbein, W. (1999) Mythos Netzwerke. Regionale Innovationsprozesse zwischen Kontinuität und Wandel. Sigma, Berlin
Hirst, P., Zeitlin, J. (1991) Flexible Specialisation versus Post-Fordism: Theory, Evidence and Policy Implications. Economy and Society 20, 1-56
Huggins, R. (1998) Local Business Cooperation and Training and Enterprise Councils: The Development of Inter-Firm Networks. Regional Studies 32, 813-826
Kamann, D.-J.F. (1998) Modelling Networks: A Long Way to Go. TESG 89, 279-297
Keeble, D., Lawson, C., Lawton Smith, H., Moore, B., Wilkinson, F. (1998) Internationalisation Processes, Networking and Local Embeddedness in Technology-Intensive Small Firms. Small Business Economics 11, 327-342
Kilper, H., Latniak, E. (1996) Einflußfaktoren betrieblicher Innovationsprozesse – Zur Rolle des regionalen Umfeldes (Determinants of Firms' Innovation Activities – On the Role of the Regional Environment). In: Brödner, P., Pekruhl, U., Rehfeld, D. (eds.) Arbeitsteilung ohne Ende? Von den Schwierigkeiten inner- und überbetrieblicher Zusammenarbeit. Mering (Hampp), München, 217-240
Kline, S.J., Rosenberg. N. (1986) An Overview of Innovation. In: Landau, R., Rosenberg, N. (eds.) The Positive Sum Strategy. National Academy Press, Washington, 275-305
Koschatzky, K. (1999) Innovation Networks of Industry and Business-Related Services – Relations between Innovation Intensity of Firms and Regional Inter-Firm Cooperation. European Planning Studies 7, 737-757
Koschatzky, K, Sternberg, R. (2000) R&D Cooperation in Innovation Systems – Some Lessons from the European Regional Innovation Survey. European Planning Studies 8(4), 487-502
Lagendijk, A. (1997) From New Industrial Spaces to Regional Innovation Systems and beyond. How and From Whom Should Industrial Geography Learn?. CURDS Discussion Papers 10, Newcastle.

Lagendijk, A. (1999) The Emergence of Knowledge-Oriented Forms of Regional Policy in Europe. TESG 90, 110-116
Lundvall, B.-Å., Borrás, S. (1998) The Globalising Learning Economy: Implications for Innovation Policy. European Commission, DG XII, Luxemburg
Maillat, D. (1998) Vom 'Industrial District' zum innovativen Milieu: Ein Beitrag zur Analyse der lokalisierten Produktionssysteme. Geographische Zeitschrift 86, 1-15
Malecki, E. (1997a) Entrepreneurs, Networks, and Economic Development: A Review of Recent Research. Advances in Entrepreneurship, Firm Emergence and Growth 3, 57-118
Malecki, E. (1997b) Technology & Economic Development. Longman, Harlow (2nd edition)
Maskell, P., Eskelinen, H., Hannibalsson, I., Malmberg, A., Vatne, E. (1998) Competitiveness, Localised Learning and Regional Development. Routledge, London
Maskell, P., Malmberg, A. (1995) Localised Learning and Industrial Competitiveness. University of California, Berkeley Roundtable of International Economy, Berkeley
Morgan, K. (1995) The Learning Region: Institutions, Innovation and Regional Renewal. CASS, Cardiff
OECD (1994) Globalisation and Local & Regional Competitiveness. Paris
Oerlemans, L.A.G., Meeus, M.T.H., Boekema, F.W.M. (1998) Do Networks Matter for Innovation? The Usefulness of the Economic Network Approach in Analysing Innovation. TESG 89, 298-309
Piore, M.J., Sabel, C.F. (1984) The Second Industrial Divide. Basic Books, New York
Porter, M. (1998) On Competition. Harvard Business School Publishing, Boston
Rosenfeld, S.A. (1997) Bringing Business Clusters into the Mainstream of Economic Development. European Planning Studies 5, 3-23
Semlinger, K. (1995) Industrial Policy and Small-firm Cooperation in Baden-Württemberg. In: Bagnasco, A., Sabel, C. (eds.) Small and Medium-Size Enterprises. Pinter, London, 15-30.
Signorini, L.F. (1994) The Price of Prato, or Measuring the Industrial District Effect. Papers in Regional Science 73, 369-392
Simmie, J., Kirby, M. (1998) Innovation and the Theoretical Base of Technopole Planning. Progress in Planning 49, 159-198
Staber, U. (1996) Networks and Regional Development: Perspectives and Unresolved Issues. In: Staber, U.H., Schaefer, N.V., Sharma, B. (eds.) Business Networks. Prospects for Regional Development. De Gruyter, Berlin, New York 1-23
Stenke, G. (1999) Governance Structure and SME/Large-Firm Relationships in an Innovative Milieu – Evidence from a European Core Region. Working Paper, Department of Economic and Social Geography, University of Cologne, Köln, 99-104
Sternberg, R. (1995) Die Konzepte der flexiblen Produktion und der Industriedistrikte als Erklärungsansätze der Regionalentwicklung. Erdkunde 49, 161-175
Sternberg, R. (1998) Technologiepolitik und High-Tech Regionen – ein internationaler Vergleich. Lit, Münster, Hamburg. Wirtschaftsgeographie 7 (2nd edition).
Sternberg, R. (1999) Innovative Linkages and Proximity – Empirical Results from Recent Surveys of Small and Medium-sized Firms in German Regions. Regional Studies 33, 529-540
Sternberg, R. (2000) Innovation Networks and Regional Development – Evidence from the European Regional Innovation Survey (ERIS): Theoretical Concepts, Methodological Approach, Empirical Basis and Introduction to the Theme Issue. European Planning Studies 8(4), 389-408
Tödtling, F. (1994) Regional Networks of High Technology Firms – The Case of the Greater Boston Region. Technovation 14, 323-343

10 Innovation Activities and Networks in Metropolitan Systems of Innovation: Empirical Findings from Barcelona, Vienna and Stockholm [1]

Javier Revilla Diez
Department of Economic Geography, University of Hannover

10.1 Introduction

Metropolitan regions are increasingly coming to be seen as regional development engines in a globalising world (Huggins 1997). On the one hand, as traditional approaches have explained, metropolitan regions are able to facilitate agglomeration economies in the form of urbanisation and localisation economies for their actors. On the other, they function as gateways to other regions, thus linking the local actors with national or international ones. With respect to innovation, these two aspects are becoming more and more meaningful, as the innovative capacity of firms depends not only on their own R&D capabilities. The opportunity of a firm to co-operate with external partners, such as customers, industrial suppliers, producer service firms, research institutes and competitors during innovation processes becomes an important locational factor which reduces risks and uncertainties and leads to collective learning (De Bresson and Amesse 1991; Lakshmanan and Okumura 1995; Malecki and Oinas 1999; Hudson 1999, Crevoisier 1999). Due to their size, metropolitan regions offer a variety of potential network partners to local firms, ensuring synergies creating new knowledge and resulting in technological progress. For these reasons such regions can be interpreted as metropolitan innovations systems (MIS), as an example of a regional innovation system as described in Revilla Diez (forthcoming) and Fischer *et al.* (2001).

Besides these agglomeration economies, metropolitan regions are characterised by a high degree of openness. Metropolitan regions are frequently locations for multinationals, either foreign or domestic, as well as innovative SMEs and research institutes which are linked to co-operation partners worldwide. In the case of multinationals, there is a clear tendency for utilising several home bases instead of one headquarters. This means that multinationals establish a global

[1] This contribution draws heavily on Revilla Diez (forthcoming).

network of production plants and R&D centres which are closely interrelated. As a consequence, multinationals in a metropolitan region are involved in a constant exchange of ideas and experience with outside co-operation partners. Innovative SMEs, for example in biotechnology or telecommunication, have to cooperate internationally. The complexity of innovation processes in these two branches compels local firms to have immediate access to leading firms and research institutes. Research institutes themselves are strongly engaged in international co-operation projects and connected with international science networks.

Although from general discussion, there have been no specific studies analysing the importance of metropolitan innovation systems using a rigorous methodology to compare different metropolitan regions. This chapter presents the findings of a comparison between the metropolitan innovation systems of Barcelona, Vienna and Stockholm based on data from the European Regional Innovation Survey. The aim of this project was to shed light on how innovative actors co-operate within metropolitan innovation systems. The empirical analysis was designed to answer the following questions:

i. How does the innovation capacity and performance across the metropolitan innovation systems surveyed compare with the EU average?
ii. How different is the innovation capacity of the manufacturing firms across the metropolitan innovation systems surveyed?
iii. How important is external co-operation for manufacturing firms, producer services and research institutes, and to what extent does spatial proximity matters for co-operation networks?
iv. What is the role of producer service firms within metropolitan innovation systems? Do they differ in their own R&D capacities and in supporting manufacturing firms innovation activities across the case study regions?
v. How important are research institutes for businesses within metropolitan innovation systems?
vi. How are framework conditions in metropolitan areas with respect to innovation evaluated by businesses?
vii. How open are the metropolitan innovation systems surveyed?

The database of the European Regional Innovation Survey (ERIS) was compiled within the framework of the extensive research programme 'Technological Change and Regional Development in Europe', funded by the Deutsche Forschungsgemeinschaft. In a joint project involving the University of Hannover, the University of Cologne, the Technical University of Freiberg and the Fraunhofer Institute for System Analysis, postal surveys were conducted in eleven regions across Europe. Written questionnaires were sent to the most important actors in regional innovation systems, i.e. manufacturing firms, producer services and research institutions, in order to analyse their innovative and networking activities. In the case of the manufacturing survey, firms belonging to manufacturing sectors 15–36 according to the EU classification of economic activities (NACE) were selected (Fritsch *et al.* 1998; Sternberg 2000).

The producer service survey covers producer service firms in Computer Software (hardware consultancy, software consultancy and supply, data processing, database activities, NACE 72.1-72.4), Technical Consultancy (architectural, engineering and related technical consultancy, technical testing and analysis, NACE 74.2, 74.3), Business Consultancy: business and management consultancy (NACE 74.14) and Market Research and Advertising (market research and public opinion polling, advertising, activities of trade fairs, exhibitions, and congress organizers, NACE 74.13, 74.4, 74.8). The survey of research institutes, i.e. universities and other research institutions, covered the fields of Architecture, Construction, Surveying, Biology, Chemistry, Medicine, Mathematics, Informatics, Physics, Electrotechnology, Mechanical Engineering, Economics, Social and Geo-Sciences. In order to obtain a detailed insight into the research and network activities of the research institutions, the questionnaire was sent to the departmental level or, if these units were too large, to separate research groups.

In order to garantee a high degree of comparability, the same basic actor-specific questionnaires were used in all the regions surveyed (Fritsch *et al.* 1998). We focus in this chapter on the results relating to the three metropolitan regions Barcelona, Stockholm and Vienna. The data collection was co-ordinated jointly by Folke Snickars from the Royal Institute of Technology in Stockholm, Manfred Fischer of Vienna University of Economics and Business Administration, and Pere Escorsa from the Polytechnic University of Catalonia. The three regions were defined from a functional perspective, including the industrial hinterland as well as the city core area, where the producer services and research institutions are mainly located. The metropolitan region of Barcelona therefore comprises the communities of Barcelona, Baix Llobregat, Valles Occidental, Valles Oriental and Maresme. The metropolitan region of Stockholm includes the province of Stockholm, Uppsala, Södermanslands, Örebro and Vastmanlands, while the metropolitan region of Vienna consists of the city of Vienna and the districts of Baden, Bruck an der Leitha, Gänserndorf, Korneuburg, Mödling, Tulln and Vienna Umgebung. Table 10.1 gives an overview on sample sizes and response patterns. Overall, the survey data for all three metropolitan regions was representative of the total population.

Table 10.1 Metropolitan innovation survey

	Metropolitan Innovation System of:		
	Vienna	Barcelona	Stockholm
Manufacturing firms:			
No. responding firms	204	394	451
Share of responding firms	23%	15%	24%
Producer service firms:			
No. responding firms	185	105	334
Share of responding firms	29%	18%	26%
Research institutes:			
No. responding research units	290	148	173
Share of responding firms	45%	35%	50%

In the following sections we look in turn at the findings of the survey in relation to the points listed above.

10.2 The Metropolitan Innovation Systems of Barcelona, Stockholm, and Vienna in the European Context

The three metropolitan innovation systems surveyed vary significantly in their innovation capabilities. However, these differences are already clear when one compares the national innovation systems. Table 10.2 summarises the strengths and weaknesses of the three national innovation systems. With respect to innovation, Sweden is the most successful country. Sweden occupies the top position in the EU with respect to the gross expenditure on R&D (GERD) and the number of researchers per 10,000 workers. The private sector in Sweden is the driving force within the national R&D system. Nearly 68 percent of all expenditure on R&D comes from the business sector. As a result, the Swedish patent applications at the European Patent Office are twice as high as the European average. Interestingly, in Sweden foreign ownership of domestic inventions is lower than in Austria and Spain, but at the same time Swedish ownership of foreign inventions is markedly higher than in the two other countries. This shows that the Swedish R&D system has a solid base within the country, and that Swedish multinationals are highly competitive in an international perspective too, able to control inventions outside the country.

With respect to innovation indicators, Austria is in second place. Although the country has one of the highest levels of per capita income within the European Union, its R&D system shows several weaknesses. Not only is the input in R&D – measured as the share of gross expenditure on R&D – below the EU average, but the active participation of the business sector in R&D activities is also very limited. Contrary to Sweden, it is the public R&D system which plays the leading role in the innovation system. The high proportion of foreign ownership of domestic inventions demonstrates the attractiveness of Austrian research capacities for multinationals. But at the same time it illustrates the heavy dependence of the innovation system on foreign R&D efforts. Austrian firms are not able to control inventions abroad in a substantial manner. As a whole, the Austrian R&D system is not able to achieve high innovative outputs. The patent indicator clearly underlines the weak position at international levels.

The Spanish innovation system lags some way behind the two other countries, although the Spanish economy has been able to achieve high economic growth rates since joining the EC. This catching-up process was, among other factors, heavily based on foreign investment. But Spain has still not reached the EU average in terms of per capita income. In comparison to Sweden, which can be labelled as an inventor country, the Spanish economy is much more an applier of new knowledge, whereas Austria lies in between. The Spanish indicators on R&D expenditure lie significantly below the EU average. Like the Austrian case, the participation of businesses in R&D is rather low, resulting in a high proportion of foreign ownership of domestic inventions. In terms of patent data, the distance from the knowledge and technology intensive economies is even bigger.

The differences revealed at the national level are also present at the regional level (see Table 10.3). The metropolitan innovation system of Stockholm seems to be much more innovative than those of either Vienna or Barcelona. The strengths of the Stockholm innovation system can be seen in the high number of patent applications at the European Patent Office. One explanation could be high the expenditure on R&D which is twice that of Vienna or Barcelona. Another explanation could be the much higher qualification levels of the population in the metropolitan region of Stockholm. 38 percent of the population aged 25-64 have completed a university level education. As a consequence, scientists and researchers are far more numerous in business enterprise in Stockholm than in Vienna and Barcelona.

Table 10.2 Comparison of National Innovation Systems

	GDP per capita (as % of US)	GERD	Researchers per 10,000 labour force	Business enterprises	Patents applied for at EPO per capita	Foreign ownership of domestic inventions[a]	Domestic ownership of foreign inventions[b]
	1997	1997		1997	1996	1993-95	1993-95
Sweden	70	3.9	86 (1997)	67.7	187	10.0	10.4
Austria	79	1.5	34 (1993)	49.3	95	20.9	8.2
Spain	55	0.9	33 (1997)	44.7	11	16.6	4.1
Germany	75	2.3	59 (1995)	61.6	186	6.9	4.6
United Kingdom	70	1.9	51 (1996)	49.5	69	23.0	11.3
France	73	2.2	61 (1996)	48.5	95	8.9	5.8
USA	100	2.7	74 (1993)	64.3	78	5.0	8.8
Japan	84	2.9	92 (1997)	73.4	103	3.0	1.8
OECD	75	2.2	55 (1995)	62.3		8.2	8.1
EU	70	1.8	50 (1996)	52.8	94	6.5	3.5

[a] Share of patent applications to the European Patent Office owned by foreign residents in total patents invented domestically.
[b] Share of patent applications to the European Patent Office invented abroad in total patents owned by country residents.
Source: Eurostat 1999; OECD 1999.

The metropolitan system of Vienna follows Stockholm in terms of innovativeness, and the per capita income – as for Austria as a whole – is significantly higher than in the two other metropolises. But the R&D output measured in patent applications demonstrates that this former European knowledge centre has declined in importance. The weak contribution of the private business sector to the metropolitan innovation system is expressed in low business expenditure on R&D. Surprisingly, the proportion of highly qualified work force is even lower than in the metropolitan region of Barcelona.

The metropolitan system of Barcelona is the leading Spanish region in business R&D, but in an international perspective this position has to be seen in relative terms. The region has been quite successful in attracting foreign investments and in achieving high economic growth since the Spanish entry to the EC in 1986. In only 10 years, the region has succeeded in reaching the European average in per capita income. The innovative output measured in terms of patents is still far behind the leading European regions, and is comparable to the output of the Vienna metropolitan system. Again, the most serious factor impeding a higher innovative performance is the weak business sector. But efforts at improving the higher education system seem to be paying off. The proportion of university level qualified work force is already higher than in Vienna.

Table 10.3 Comparison of Regional Innovation Systems in six countries

	Barcelona (Catalonia)	Stockholm	Vienna	Ober-bayern	Iles de France	Greater London	EU
GDP per capita (EU=100) 1996	99	123	167	157	160	140	100
Unemployment rate 1997	17.4	7.9	5.9	4.8	10.7	9.7	10.7
Educational level of the population aged 25-59 (total %)							
Low	63	17	22	20	34	45	41
Medium	17	45	63	52	38	24	40
High	19	38	15	27	29	31	20
Total number of patents, EPO 1995	136	522	162	1339	2222	242	33651

Source: Eurostat 1999.

10.3 Variations in the Innovative Capacity of the Manufacturing Firms Surveyed

The innovation capacity of the manufacturing firms surveyed differs significantly between the three metropolitan innovation systems. Differences not only across industrial branches but also within the branches are notable (see Table 10.4). The innovation performance of manufacturing firms was measured in terms of both input and output indicators. When input indicators such as R&D personnel and the R&D expenditure ratio are analysed, manufacturing firms in the metropolitan regions of Vienna and Stockholm have much higher values than the firms in the metropolitan region of Barcelona. The differences become very clear in the case of high-tech sectors, reflecting the backwardness of the Spanish metropolis. In all the three regions, the highest R&D personnel ratio can be found in the sector of electrical and optical equipment. But again, the Viennese figure is more than double that of Barcelona.

Table 10.4 R&D characteristics of surveyed manufacturing firms 1994-1996

	Barcelona		Stockholm		Vienna	
	R&D Personnel ratio[a]	R&D Expenditure ratio	R&D Personnel ratio[a]	R&D Expenditure ratio	R&D Personnel ratio[a]	R&D Expenditure ratio
Industrial Sector:						
Textiles & Clothing	60.6	4.12	52.6	10.0	19.8	5.79
Food Industry	17.0	9.68	25.4	0.9	27.7	1.75
Wood, Paper & Printing	15.8	0.75	54.1	2.5	9.2	1.55
Chemicals	76.1	4.48	70.2	4.3	48.3	6.53
Electrical & Optical Equipment	107.1	4.69	144.0	9.5	255.3	16.03
Basic Metals & Metal Products	54.3	4.21	31.8	2.8	29.2	2.37
Machinery & Transport	67.5	3.98	117.1	14.1	30.5	5.52
High Technology	74.0	4.2	119.0	9.2	132.9	10.58
Employment Size:						
≤ 49	70.9	5.87	86.9	4.4	56.5	2.79
50 – 99	78.1	4.98	85.9	5.9	31.6	3.15
100 – 499	33.6	2.24	68.8	3.8	35.3	4.28
≥ 500	63.9	4.57	92.0	12.5	127.2	10.30
Total	61.8	4.3	84.0	7.1	96.0	8.2

[a] per 10,000 employees
Source: European Regional Innovation Survey 1997.

With respect to R&D expenditure ratio, the picture across the regions is less distinct. In the metropolitan region of Barcelona the most R&D intensive sector is the food industry, which is one of the few sectors in the Barcelonese economy in which domestic firms reach international levels of competitiveness in terms of R&D capabilities and strategies. In Stockholm, the sector with the most intensive R&D expenditure is machinery and transport equipment, one of the major industrial sectors of the local economy, and in Vienna it is the electrical and optical equipment sector. Beside these sector differences, the size of the manufacturing firms influences the R&D input levels. Whereas in the metropolitan systems of Stockholm and Vienna large firms with more than 500 employees have the highest R&D input levels, in Barcelona it is the small and medium sized firm with less than 100 employees. The relatively poor commitment of large firms in Barcelona to R&D is a consequence of the low number of domestic multinationals. The number of multinational headquarters is distinctly higher in Stockholm and Vienna.

The overall innovation capacity of manufacturing firms also needs to be examined in terms of output indicators such as the innovation rate or the share of turnover from product innovations (see Table 10.5). Contrary to the results obtained so far, manufacturing firms in Barcelona achieve the highest number of new product developments, followed by Stockholm and Vienna. With respect to the share of turnover from product innovations, the metropolitan region of Vienna is the most innovative, followed by Barcelona and then Stockholm. The relatively good results for Vienna and Barcelona are the consequence of the catching up process. In the past, as indicated above, these two were not among the most innovative regions of Europe. The increased competition since their membership in the European Union has forced firms to invest more heavily in R&D in order to improve product quality and develop new products.

10.4 Manufacturing Firms' Innovation Networks

The two most important research objectives of the empirical surveys carried out in the three metropolitan regions were to assess the importance of external co-operation within innovation processes, and determine the role of spatial proximity for such co-operation. The network paradigm postulated by Cooke and Morgan (1993) implies that networks have the function of linking innovation actors, resources and activities within and between innovation systems, enabling the exchange of information and knowledge, and facilitating learning processes. Overall, manufacturing firms in all the regions surveyed proved to be strongly involved in innovation networking. The innovative activity of firms was not solely based on in-house capabilities. The results obtained clearly demonstrate the importance of external cooperation in innovation processes in both manufacturing and producer service firms (see Table 10.6).

Table 10.5 Innovation activities of surveyed firms 1994-1996

	Barcelona		Stockholm		Vienna	
	Innovation rate[a]	Share of turnover by product innovations	Innovation rate[a]	Share of turnover by product innovations	Innovation rate[a]	Share of turnover by product innovations
Industrial Sector:						
Textiles & Clothing	99.4	0.47	340.9	0.68	65.8	0.13
Food Industry	13.2	0.07	22.9	0.11	33.7	0.28
Wood, Paper & Printing	129.6	0.15	62.6	0.20	19.3	0.04
Chemicals	73.4	0.15	37.7	0.06	36.8	0.19
Electrical & Optical Equipment	139.6	0.33	36.3	0.45	6.4	0.51
Basic Metals & Metal Products	130.9	0.20	28.0	0.13	12.0	0.57
Machinery & Transport	6.9	0.47	23.6	0.38	4.3	0.53
High Technology	34.1	0.37	29.4	0.26	12.8	0.43
Employment Size:						
≤ 49	176.2	0.22	170.6	0.24	134.9	0.13
50 – 99	106.4	0.29	54.8	0.31	86.5	0.16
100 – 499	77.0	0.22	20.8	0.11	6.5	0.35
≥ 500	4.0	0.37	10.7	0.34	2.3	0.45
Total	49.4	0.33	30.0	0.22	15.2	0.43

[a] denotes number of new products per 10,000 employees.
Source: European Regional Innovation Survey 1997.

Interestingly, the most important co-operation partners for manufacturing firms are customers, suppliers and producer service firms (rather than research institutions). For the producer service firms surveyed, industrial customers and other producer service firms were the major co-operation partners. Vertical co-operation partners along the value chain are much more likely to be involved in innovation networks than horizontal co-operation partners, like research institutes and competitors. The spatial range of networking tends to differ for vertical and horizontal co-operation partners. Spatial proximity appears to be much more important in horizontal linkages between manufacturing firms and research institutes or competitors than in vertical linkages, where co-operation is undertaken with partners far over larger distances. It can be stated that the network pattern of the manufacturing firms was much more complex than expected. Co-operation partners were commonly found both in spatial proximity and at larger distances, reflecting the need to make use of local, and also national or even international knowledge sources.

Table 10.6 Co-operation partners of innovating manufacturing firms

	Barcelona	Stockholm	Vienna
Percentage of manufacturing firms with co-operation partners (% of all firms)	78	64	63
Co-operation partners of manufacturing firms: [a]			
Customer	69	75	52
Supplier	56	37	37
Producer Services	61	45	60
Competitors	23	18	23
Research institutes	23	34	23

[a] as % of all co-operating manufacturing firms.
Source: European Regional Innovation Survey 1997.

However, against this general picture there are significant differences depending on the size, industry sector and innovativeness of firms. Small manufacturing firms tend to be less involved in innovation networks than large firms. Manufacturing firms with high innovative performance have stronger connections with co-operation partners than less innovative ones. With respect to branches, the results underline the importance of external co-operation for technology and knowledge intensive industries, which also co-operate more often with horizontal co-operation partners than the low tech industries.

Between the three innovation systems, significant differences can be distinguished in the degree of external co-operation of manufacturing firms. The metropolitan region of Barcelona has the highest percentage of manufacturing firms involved in networking, followed by the metropolitan region of Stockholm and then Vienna. The high share of Barcelona can be explained by two factors. First is the importance of small and medium-sized firms, which have a long tradition of networking among themselves, and second, the presence of multinationals which ususally have frequent exchange with their headquarters and other research and production sites worldwide. In the more mature (in economic terms) metropolitan regions of Stockholm and Vienna, the percentages of co-operating manufacturing firms are lower and quite similar, which may be an indication of a lesser need to co-operate due to better in-house R&D capabilities.

10.5 The Role of Producer Service Firms

Producer service firms play a crucial role in supporting innovation activities in industry. In the metropolitan region of Vienna, producer service firms were the most important external co-operation partner for the manufacturing firms surveyed. In the metropolitan regions of Stockholm and Barcelona, they follow in second position after customers. This illustrates that producer service firms have a leading position within an innovation system. Their innovative capabilities and capacities are decisive for the functioning of an innovation system, whether at the national, regional or local scale.

As for manufacturing firms, the innovative performance of the producer service firms surveyed was analysed through numerous indicators (see Table 10.7).

Table 10.7 Selected R&D characteristics of surveyed firms in producer services 1994-1996

	Barcelona		Stockholm		Vienna	
	R&D Expenditure ratio	R&D Personnel ratio	R&D Expenditure ratio	R&D Personnel ratio	R&D Expenditure ratio	R&D Personnel ratio
Service Sector:						
Computer software	9.7	15.0	5.7	23.7	4.3	11.2
Technical consultancy	4.2	17.2	4.9	6.1	5.4	25.4
Business consultancy	6.0	12.6	2.5	17.8	3.1	4.0
Market research and advertising	2.5	6.5	4.7	20.4	3.7	8.0
Employment Size:						
≤ 19	10.3	24.4	7.4	24.6	5.0	15.3
20 – 49	6.1	28.0	2.3	16.3	3.1	13.6
50 – 249	4.1	3.7	5.6	16.0	3.9	20.9
≥ 250	1.7	10.8	4.8	13.0	5.0	3.8
Total	7.7	10.8	4.7	15.4	3.6	12.3

Source: European Regional Innovation Survey 1997.

Again, similarities and differences across the metropolitan regions can be distinguished. However, when input indicators like R&D expenditure or the R&D personnel ratio are considered, a number of common features prevail among the knowledge-intensive business services. According these indicators, the two most important service sectors are computer software and technical consultancy. In the metropolitan region of Stockholm, the sector of computer software has the highest R&D inputs for both indicators. In the metropolitan region of Barcelona, the R&D expenditure ratio is highest in computer software, the personnel ratio in technical consultancy. In the metropolitan region of Vienna, technical consultants are the most R&D intensive service firms. Compared to Stockholm and Barcelona, the Viennese computer software firms fall behind in terms of R&D inputs. With respect to firm size, it can be stated that in Stockholm and Barcelona small firms with less than 20 employees have the highest input indicators. Only in Vienna is the highest personnel ratio reached by firms with 50 to 249 employees.

10.6 The Importance of Research Institutes

Overall, it is necessary to re-assess the great importance of research institutes in business innovation processes often claimed by the literature on the subject (Revilla Diez 2000). The results of the survey clearly showed that vertical co-operation partners, such as buyers and suppliers, and also service providers situated close to businesses, hold a higher status in support of business innovation processes than do research institutes. In addition, the survey proved quite clearly that, in contrast to the usual hypothesis, as far as business co-operation partners are concerned, the favoured co-operating partners are above all medium-size and large firms. Small businesses are rarely reached by the research institutes. When manufacturing firms co-operate with research institutes, they demonstrate a higher preference for neighbouring institutions. Research institutes themselves co-operate intensively at a national and international scale. The active participation in international science networks allows them to fulfil a gateway function. Through their contacts they are able to transfer internationally available information and knowledge to local firms.

Despite this general picture, differences across the three metropolitan innovation systems are profound. In contrast to Vienna and Barcelona, manufacturing firms in Stockholm make significant use of research institutes (see Table 10.8). Large manufacturing firms with more than 500 employees were the most important co-operation partners for the Stockholm research institutes. In Vienna, the large manufacturers are the preferred co-operation partners of research institutes. Only in Barcelona do research institutes co-operate intensively with small manufacturing firms with fewer than 100 employees. Taking into consideration the high number of multinationals in Barcelona, this result shows that local research units are not able to provide knowledge resources for these global players. In other words, the decisive factor for multinationals locating in Barcelona is not the knowledge-base found in local research institutes.

One reason for the lower participation of research institutes in innovation networks could be the mismatch of technology fields. In Table 10.9 it can be clearly seen that the specialisation patterns of manufacturing firms and research institutes vary significantly. Research institutes tend to have patterns of specialisation that produce few complementary effects for local businesses, and vice versa. But interestingly, the mismatch is highest in the Stockholm metropolitan innovation system. In contrast to the innovation system of Barcelona and Vienna, the Stockholm research institutes are intensively engaged in technology fields which are new to the industrial fabric. In Barcelona and Vienna, the research institutes are much more likely to be involved in technology fields with an existing industrial base. While the role of research institutes in Stockholm is more to push manufacturing firms into new and highly potential technology fields, research institutes in Vienna and Barcelona assist manufacturing firms in their technology fields in order to augment their R&D capabilities.

Table 10.8 Co-operation of research institutes with firms

	Barcelona	Stockholm	Vienna
Cooperation with firms [a]	71	64	55
Employment size of firms[b]			
≤ 49	29	3	20
50 – 99	27	15	15
100 – 499	20	24	19
≥ 500	24	58	46
Total	100	100	100

[a] Percentage of research institutes co-operating with firms.
[b] Size distribution of firms co-operating with research institutes as %.
Source: European Regional Innovation Survey 1997.

10.7 Assessment of Regional Framework Conditions

The assessment of framework conditions by the manufacturing and producer service firms surveyed allow us to reach some conclusions on the strengths and weaknesses of the regional infrastructures with respect to innovation support. In all three metropolitan regions, regional supply factors like transport and telecommunication infrastructure and R&D related factors like the availability of qualified staff were evaluated positively (see Table 10.10). Poor assessments, on the other hand, were given to network factors like the willingness of research institutes and firms to co-operate and to political/institutional factors like the local economic policy. But besides this general picture, variations can be distinguished across the three regions and between manufacturing and producer service firms, expecially in the case of poor assessments.

In the metropolitan region of Barcelona, manufacturing firms stated that the supply of capital, the low willingness of research institutes and firms to co-operate, and local economic policy seem to be constraints to innovation activities. Producer services firms assessed the same factors as being problematic. In the metropolitan region of Stockholm, firms' willingness to cooperate and the supply of capital were evaluated negatively. In the case of producer service firms, a major shortcoming was considered to be local economic policy and the lack of willingness of research institutes to co-operate. In the metropolitan region of

Vienna, manufacturing firms complained about poor consultancy and the lack of willingness of research institutes to co-operate. Both factors were also evaluated negatively by the producer service firms.

Table 10.9 Relevance of technology fields for innovations in research institutes and manufacturing firms

	Barcelona		Stockholm		Vienna	
	Res.	Manuf.	Res.	Manuf.	Res.	Manuf.
	a	b	a	b	a	b
Technology fields [1]						
Biotechnology-pharmaceuticals	15	11	31	9	18	14
Chemistry	18	31	19	24	12	23
Power engineering	10	14	19	24	16	18
Information and communication technology	40	25	31	41	30	28
Aircraft and spacecraft	7	1	6	3	5	2
Medical and health engineering	14	6	18	11	21	10
Micro-opto electronics, laser	10	8	6	19	8	10
New materials	21	47	14	55	25	52
Production and process engineering	27	60	24	65	17	62
Sensor engineering, measuring and control technology	23	22	16	40	19	31
Environmental engineering	35	20	19	35	24	22
Traffic and transport engineering logistics	7	14	9	26	14	28

[1] Technology fields according to the ISI classification.

a: percentage of research institutes co-operating intensively in the respective technology field with manufacturing firms.

b: percentage of manufacturing firms co-operating intensively in the respective technology field with research institutes.

Source: European Regional Innovation Survey 1997.

Table 10.10 Assessment of framework conditions

	Assessment by[a]			
	Manufacturing firms		Producer service firms	
	Poor	Good	Poor	Good
Metropolitan region of:				
Barcelona	1. Supply of capital	1. Transport infrastructure	1. Consultancy offers	1. Supply of capital
	2. Willingness of research institutes to co-operate	2. Availability of staff in scientific sector	2. Willingness of research institutes to co-operate	2. Availability of staff in scientific sector
Stockholm	1. Consultancy offers	1. Transport infrastructure	1. Willingness of research institutes to co-operate	1. Availability of clients
	2. Willingness of research institutes to cooperate	2. Telecom-munication infrastructure	2. Local economic policy	2. Availability of suppliers
Vienna	1. Willingness of firms to cooperate	1. Availability of staff in business sector	1. Supply of capital	1. Telecom-munication infrastructure
	2. Supply of capital	2. Telecom-munication infrastructure	2. Willingness of firms to cooperate	2. Transport infrastructure

[a] Only the two most important factors are listed.
Source: European Regional Innovation Survey 1997.

10.8 The Degree of Openness

The degree of openness of a metropolitan innovation system is directly linked to whether it fulfils a bridging function between the local and national economy, and between the internationally most competitive regions in the world. As discussed in the introduction, metropolitan regions are increasingly seen as global, national and regional development engines. The importance of the metropolitan regions of Barcelona, Vienna and Stockholm for the national and regional economies is undoubtedly high. In order to analyse the gateway function of metropolitan regions, the external co-operation links of manufacturing firms, producer service firms and research institutes were surveyed. Table 10.11 shows that all three metropolitan innovation systems have a high degree of openness. A large proportion of the co-operation partners of all the actors surveyed were located locally, but at the same time the firms co-operate substantially at the national or the international level. Research institutes, especially, were often linked to national and international knowledge resources. Interestingly, the geographical scope of the co-operation seems to depend on the type of co-operation partner. When producer service firms co-operate with manufacturing firms, a stronger national or international orientation can be expacted. When the producer service firms co-operate with research institutes, the metropolitan level is likely to be more important.

Table 10.11 Geographical distribution of co-operation partners

	Barcelona				Stockholm				Vienna			
	MS[a]	PS[b]		RI[c]	MS[a]	PS[b]		RI[c]	MS[a]	PS[b]		RI[c]
		MS[a]	RI[c]			MS[a]	RI[c]			MS[a]	RI[c]	
Level:												
Metropolitan	38	33	46	30	32	32	31	23	32	34	48	27
National	32	45	22	40	43	43	42	44	22	30	25	23
International	30	22	32	29	25	25	27	34	46	36	28	50
Total	100	100	100	100	100	100	100	100	100	100	100	100

[a] MS = manufacturing firms
[b] PS = producer service firms
[c] RI = research institutes
Source: European Regional Innovation Survey 1997.

10.9 Summary and Conclusions

The analysis of the three metropolitan regions – Barcelona, Vienna and Stockholm – has provided interesting insights into the innovative activity and networking of the most important actors within regional innovation systems. Across the three metropolises, a number of significant similarities and also differences emerged. With respect to the seven research questions listed in Section 10.1, the following conclusions can be drawn.

Firstly, the innovative capacity of the metropolitan innovation systems differ markedly, reflecting the differences already visible in a comparison of the national innovation systems. The metropolitan region of Stockholm is one of the most innovative regions in Europe, with R&D activities basically carrieed by businesses in the private sector. In Vienna, a former world leader in respect to innovations, the R&D performance is very much concentrated in the science sector. Local businesses are relatively weak in terms of innovativeness. Barcelona is by far the least innovative of these metropolitan regions, although like Vienna, since joining the European Community, the innovation system has been rapidly transforming to meet international levels of competitiveness.

In terms of R&D inputs, Vienna and Stockholm have much higher rates than in Barcelona, but firms in Barcelona are catching up. The innovative output measured in terms of turnover accounted for by new or improve products indicates that Barcelonese firms are changing their products in order to match market needs more successfully. With respect to firm size, in Vienna and Stockholm large firms are much more involved in R&D activities than in Barcelona. In the Spanish metropolis the SMEs are especially R&D oriented.

External co-operation in innovation processes is a common feature of the firms surveyed, but this is not the only source of own innovations. R&D capabilities and knowledge gained through own product and production experience is a precondition for successful co-operation. Interestingly, across the regions, the vertical co-operation partners such as customers, industrial suppliers and producer service firms dominate the external co-operation networks of manufacturing firms. Spatial proximity of co-operation partners is important, but at the same time many manufacturing firms have co-operation partners also outside the region. Whereas the firms in Stockholm and Vienna tend to co-operate more with partners outside the region, in Barcelona the firms surveyed were much more regionally oriented.

It emerged that producer service firms play a crucial role in the metropolitan innovation systems surveyed. Across the regions, they are intensively engaged in supporting manufacturing innovation activities. They support innovation activities especially in neighbouring firms. In comparison to co-operation partners such as customers, industrial suppliers or producer services, the role of research institutes for the innovation processes of manaufacturing firms was relatively weak. The greatest importance of research institutes can be observed in Stockholm. The two other regions still face some difficulties in linking the science sector with the business sector.

The assessment of the framework conditions conducive for innovations by the firms surveyed showed that regional supply factors like infrastructure or availability of suitable work force are not perceived as obstacles for own innovation activities. Interestingly, poor assessments were given to network factors like the willingness of research institutes and firms to co-operate, and political institutional factors like the local economic policy.

The gateway function of metropolitan innovation systems was underlined by the geographical location of co-operation partners. Across the regions, besides being linked to lokal cooperation partners, the co-operation of manufacturing firms, producer services and research institues at the national and international level predominate. Research institutes in particular are characterised by a high degree of international co-operation.

References

Crevoisier, O. (1999) Innovation and the City. In: Malecki E., Oinas P. (eds.) Making Connections – Technological Learning and Regional Economic Change. Ashgate, Aldershot, 61-77

De Bresson, C., Amesse, F. (1991) Networks of Innovators: A Review and Introduction to the Issue. Research Policy 20, 363-379

Fischer, M., Revilla Diez, J., Snickars, F., Varga, A. (2001) Metropolitan Systems of Innovation: Theory and Evidence from Three Metropolitan Regions in Europe (Advances in Spatial Science). Springer-Verlag, Heidelberg

Fritsch, M., Koschatzky, K., Schätzl, L., Sternberg, R. (1998): Regionale Innovationspotentiale und innovative Netzwerke, Raumforschung und Raumordnung 4/98, 288-298

Eurostat (1999) Sechster periodischer Bericht über die sozio-ökonomische Lage und Entwicklung der Regionen der Europäischen Union. Amt für amtliche Veröffentlichungen der Europäischen Gemeinschaften, Luxemburg

Hudson, R. (1999) The Learning Economy, the Learning Firm and the Learning Region: A Sympathetic Critique of the Limits to Learning. European Urban and Regional Studies, 6, 1, 59-72

Huggins, R. (1997) Competitiveness and the Global Region: The Role of Networking. In: Simmie, J.M. (ed.) Innovation, Networks and Learning Regions. Jessica Kingsley Publishers. London, 101-123

Lakshmanan, T., Okumura, M. (1995) The Nature and Evolution of Knowledge Networks in Japanese Manufacturing. Papers in Regional Science. The Journal of the RSAI 74(1) 63-86

Malecki, E., Oinas, P. (eds.) (1999) Making Connections – Technological Learning and Regional Economic Change. Ashgate, Aldershot

OECD (1999) Benchmarking the Knowledge Base Economy. Paris

Revilla Diez, J. (forthcoming): Metropolitan Innovation Systems – A Comparison Between Barcelona, Stockholm, and Vienna. International Regional Science Review.

Revilla Diez, J. (2000) The Importance of Public Research Institutions in Innovative Networks – Empirical Results from the Metropolitan Innovation Systems Barcelona, Stockholm and Vienna. European Planning Studies, 8 (4), 451-463

Sternberg, R. (2000) Innovation Networks and Regional Development – Evidence from the European Regional Innovation Survey (ERIS): Theoretical Concepts, Methodological Approach, Empirical Basis and Introduction to the Theme Issue. European Planning Studies, 8 (4), 389-408

11 Networking of Small Firms: Is the Region a Knowledge Source for Innovation?

Knut Koschatzky and Andrea Zenker
Fraunhofer Institute for Systems and Innovation Research, Karlsruhe

11.1 Large and Small Firms in the Innovation Process

The debate about whether small or large firms are more innovative, and whether size is a useful criterion for distinguishing the differences in the intensity and kind of innovative activity is not a recent phenomenon. It can be traced back to the pioneering work of Schumpeter, who in his early work emphasised the risk-taking behaviour of pioneer entrepreneurs in enhancing the supply of innovative solutions (Schumpeter 1911). He later argued that large firms can devote more resources to systematic research and development (R&D) and are therefore more innovative than small firms due to scale advantages (Schumpeter 1942). These two hypotheses were summarised by Freeman in the models of entrepreneurial innovation (Mark I) and of large-firm managed innovation (Mark II) (Freeman 1982).

An important aspect of studies analysing innovation processes in firms (e.g. Nelson and Winter 1982) is therefore the relationship between firm size and innovative activity. One common result of the studies carried out during the 1970s and 1980s was the conclusion that innovation intensity increases with firm size up to a certain point and then decreases again, forming an inverted U-shaped curve. Although these studies produced variations concerning the trend and exact turning point of the inverted U-curve, depending on the data used for the analysis, the innovation indicators and the business units observed, the general pattern was believed to be stable (see Frisch 1993 for a summary of various input and output-oriented studies).

Small firms and the role they play in job creation and economic development came into the limelight during the 1980s, following empirical evidence emerging from several North American and European regions. In the United States, between 1969 and 1976 two-thirds of all new jobs were created by start-ups and firms with under 20 employees (Birch 1987). Also in many other countries and regions, small firms were shown to contribute to regional and employment growth (Aydalot 1986; Camagni 1991; Keeble 1997; Piore and Sabel 1984; Pyke *et al.* 1990; Sengenberger and Pyke 1992). The decentralisation of entrepreneurial functions and the creation of smaller production units, as well as outsourcing and other strategies for improving the core competencies of companies, led to an increase in the number of smaller firms during the 1980s and to the assumption that small firms adjust more efficiently to market volatilities. Evidence for the importance of small firms was provided by the SPRU innovations database, according to which small firms were not only responsible for more innovation than their share of R&D expenditure would imply, but also for a larger share of innovations than would be expected from their share of employment (Pavitt *et al.* 1987; Tether *et al.* 1997).

Not surprisingly, in the late 1980s and early 1990s the contribution of small firms to innovation was the subject of several publications (e.g. Acs and Audretsch 1990). Although these studies found some evidence that small firms are more innovative than large firms, one of the major conclusions was that the degree of innovativeness mainly depends on the industry. The innovation rates of both small and large firms depend on the level of capital intensity. In capital-intensive, advertising-intensive, concentrated and highly unionised industries, larger firms are more innovative than smaller ones, although the innovative activity tends to decrease as the level of concentration in an industry increases. On the other hand, in highly innovative industries composed predominantly of large firms, the innovative advantage is held by the smaller firms (Acs and Audretsch 1990).

By reclassifying the firms originally listed, the SPRU database now suggests that "...the relationship between innovative intensity and enterprise size in the manufacturing sector (tends) to be not U-shaped but J-shaped, with only the largest enterprises introducing a disproportionately large share of the innovations" (Tether *et al.* 1997, p. 31). While pointing to the limitations of his analysis, Tether came to the conclusion in another study using the SPRU database that by taking the average value of an innovation, measured in terms of revenue, "... the interpretation that small firms are more innovative (or more efficient innovators) than large firms because they have introduced a larger number of innovations relative to their employment is unsound" (Tether 1998, p. 742). There is also no evidence for particularly rapid growth among the small firms included in the database between 1975 and 1983.

All the results presented so far lead to the conclusion that size alone is not sufficient for distinguishing innovative firms, but that a number of internal features, as well as the nature of the innovation process itself are also relevant. As Frisch (1993) concludes in his study, there is no optimal firm size for innovation. The innovative potential of a firm depends, among other factors, on its risk-taking propensity, which itself depends on the structure and behaviour of the management (Barkham *et al.* 1996). It is also linked to the firm's absorptive capacity, which concerns its ability to exploit, evaluate and utilise external knowledge for innovation (Cohen and Levinthal 1990). Whether a firm is large or small, the bigger its knowledge base and the greater its capacity to absorb this knowledge into the organisation, the better its ability to innovate (Le Bars *et al.* 1998). Among the elements contributing to the knowledge base are the internal and external communication structures, R&D, production experience and the learning capacity of the staff. In this respect, the so-called 'gatekeeper' undertakes an important interface function. Firms which tend to centralise access to external information and its distribution can run into problems, especially under conditions of rapid and uncertain technical change (Cohen and Levinthal 1990). Allowing more people access to innovation-relevant knowledge reduces the risk of not being able to monitor important technical information. For its internal diffusion, it is also essential for technicians to translate it into a language which can be understood by other members of the firm.

The importance of spatial and cultural proximity as a prerequisite for the exchange process depends on the kind of knowledge concerned. It is generally argued that as codified knowledge can be transferred over long distances at low costs, spatial proximity between transmitter and receiver is not necessary. The exchange of tacit knowledge, on the other hand, requires interpersonal contacts involving verbal and non-verbal communication and is therefore sensitive to the spatial and cultural distance (Arnold and Thuriaux 1997; Foray and Lundvall 1996; see also Saviotti 1998). The overall potential of a firm for knowledge exchange is influenced by the sum of distances to the various partners it interacts with. Firms which can minimise this distance should have an advantage over others, which will either be unable to transfer (tacit) knowledge, or only at higher costs.

One strategy is therefore to locate in a place where there is a large selection of possible knowledge sources. This is the reason for the attraction of large urban areas (agglomerations), which are characterised by the concentrated availability of localised knowledge, innovation-related spillovers and other generic assets (Storper 1995; Storper 1997). On the other hand, agglomerations do not necessarily offer a beneficial innovative environment for all industries, because cumulative processes based on the existing economic structure of a region tend to predetermine the location of modern economic activities (Coe and Townsend 1998). Non-core regions too can generate growth conditions and provide a favourable innovation climate (Scott 1995; Storper 1997). There is empirical evidence that firms in fact adapt to their regional environment by applying different innovation strategies. For example, in regions where the supply of skilled labour is limited, labour is substituted by capital (Meyer-Krahmer 1985).[1] It can therefore be concluded that the regional environment in which a firm is embedded has at least some impact on its access to information and knowledge and on its ability for collective learning (Keeble and Wilkinson 1999; Lawson and Lorenz 1999), especially when the firm is small and unable to manage complex networking relations, so that the spatial range of networks is mainly confined to the region itself (Klein Woolthuis *et al.* 1998).

Although small firms may have the ability to exploit internal and external knowledge for innovation, larger firms in general have a stronger resource base with respect to human capital, capital and economic power, and can therefore make better use of national and international knowledge sources than small firms.

---

[1] See also Keeble, who concludes that "... firms in peripheral regions may actively try to compensate for and overcome environmental handicaps by pro-active engagement in research and development to an even greater degree than their counterparts in core regions" (Keeble 1997, p.289).

This emerges in empirical studies of networks which show that larger firms are engaged in more diverse and spatially distant networking relations than smaller firms (Backhaus and Seidel 1998; Sternberg 1998). This pattern is often closely linked with the market reach of firms – generally small firms receive a higher share of turnover from local and regional markets, while larger firms have a greater propensity to be engaged in international business relations.

In the recent literature on industrial innovation, the main issue is not whether small or large firms are more innovative, but the role each plays in the innovation process. The growth in the number of small firms during the 1980s is not seen as an independent process, but is attributed to the decentralisation strategies of large firms (Camagni and Capello 1997; Sengenberger and Pyke 1992). The outsourcing of entrepreneurial functions by larger firms has increased their flexibility, allowing them to react more quickly to changing market conditions. Small firms are a major source for new products and processes, but due to their limited financial resources they are often confined to the first phase of the innovation process. Large firms, on the other hand, tend to be engaged in gradual technological change, imitation and diffusion, often adopting the incomplete innovations of small firms and bringing them to the market (Frisch 1993). They make incremental innovation and carry out more process-oriented research and development than smaller firms (Cohen 1995). Mass production enables larger firms to achieve learning effects, but also leads to path dependence and tends to bind them to a technological trajectory, impeding flexibility.

According to the research work presented above, the relationship between firm size and the intensity and kind of innovative activity undertaken can be summarised as follows:

- There is ample evidence that small firms are not *per se* more innovative than larger firms, although small firms that perform R&D tend to be more innovative than large firms and also generate a larger number of innovations per unit of R&D input.
- The number of firms that do not innovate or that were not engaged in R&D is relatively high among small firms and declines with size. Large firms are more innovative with respect to the share of firms with R&D.
- An optimal firm size for innovation does not exist.
- Innovation varies between firms, between sectors and between markets.
- Innovation activity depends on the risk aversion of firms, their absorptive capacity, knowledge base, their competencies in organising innovation processes, their learning abilities and information channels and their access to and handling ability of external knowledge.
- Small and large firms play different roles in the innovation process.
- Small firms are the engine of new technological development, but are often unable to complete innovations because of limited resources.
- R&D activity in large firms is more directed towards incremental innovation and process developments, since the budget for process R&D rises somewhat more with size than the budget for product R&D.

These findings emphasise the different roles played by large and small firms in the innovation process. It is of course not merely size which makes the distinction between the activities and behaviour of firms. However, firms with similar structural characteristics tend to group around a particular size. So, in this study, size will be used as a substitute for structural characteristics and for classifying firms according to their different attributes.

So far, most of the empirical studies dealing with firm size and innovation have involved only the manufacturing sector. One important result already reported is that innovative activity depends on the industrial sector. It would be interesting to discover whether this finding can also be transferred to the service sector. In other words, can evidence of similarities and differences in the nature of innovative activity be found between service sectors, and also between manufacturing industry and the service sector. Research on innovation in services, especially in business-related services, started only quite recently (Bellini 1998; Koschatzky 1999; Licht *et al.* 1996; Miles *et al.* 1994; Strambach 1995; Wood 1995). Although there are far fewer studies for services than for manufacturing industry, it would seem worth comparing at least some innovation and networking characteristics of manufacturing and business-related service firms.

It is therefore the objective of this chapter to discover whether the size of a firm significantly affects its innovative behaviour and co-operation pattern, and whether there are differences between manufacturing firms and business-related service firms, for which only a few innovation studies exist. For both manufacturing and service firms the following research questions should serve as guidelines for the empirical analysis:

1. What innovation strategies are applied typically by large and small firms?
2. What external information sources are used by these firms and how is the distribution of this information within the firm organised?
3. What kind of knowledge and knowledge sources are used for innovation by firms, and what is the spatial range of innovation networking? Are there differences between small and large firms in information and knowledge acquisition and the spatial range of networking in different types of regions?
4. Are there similarities in innovation behaviour between small manufacturing and small service firms, or do they differ significantly in terms of innovation, irrespective of size?
5. What conclusions can be drawn for regional innovation policy with respect to small firms innovation and regional supply supporting factors?

The chapter is structured as follows. Section 11.2 describes the methodology and the data sources used for empirically testing the above research questions. The empirical analysis for manufacturing and business-related service firms is presented in Section 11.3. Conclusions from this analysis, especially with respect to regional innovation policy, are then presented in Section 11.4.

11.2 Data and Methodology

The data used for this analysis originate from the European Regional Innovation Survey (ERIS) carried out among mainly small and medium-sized manufacturing and business-related service firms in several German and other European regions during 1995 and 1998.[1] The present chapter presents data from Baden, i.e. the western part of Baden-Württemberg, and from south-east Lower Saxony, comprising the cities of Hannover, Braunschweig and Göttingen (for details see Backhaus and Seidel 1997; Koschatzky and Traxel 1997; Koschatzky 1997). These include a range of different types of region, e.g. the automobile regions in eastern Lower Saxony, the service-oriented Expo 2000 urban region of Hannover and the technology region Baden. In accordance with the official German planning region classification of 1991, a differentiation has been made between three types of functional regions, i.e. central, urban regions (e.g. Hannover, Karlsruhe), intermediate regions (e.g. Freiburg, Göttingen), and rural regions (e.g. the Black Forest region Schwarzwald-Baar-Heuberg).

Usually in classifying small, medium-sized and large firms, the threshold applied for separating SMEs from large firms is 500 employees, although some studies define large firms as having a minimum of 2,000 employees. In the present study, a different approach was applied with respect to the size distribution and company characteristics. First of all, only firms which recorded at least some innovative activity and related interactions were included in the analysis. Secondly, as the average size of manufacturing firms was 265 employees (median 97 employees) and service firms 44 employees (median 3 employees), it was necessary not only to apply different definitions of large and small, but also to relate this to the structural characteristics of the sample firms.

In order to divide the sample into size classes taking into account the firms' structural characteristics, co-operation behaviour and expected future development[2], a homogeneity analysis was performed. This type of analysis uses plot outputs to represent the relationships between variables in few dimensions, which makes it possible to describe structures or patterns in relationships which would otherwise be difficult to detect.[3] Homogeneity analysis is based on optimal scaling and assigns scores to the categories which best account for associations between the variables. Consequently, the output indicates similar categories of variables and can serve as a basis for characterising and classifying the sample.

---

[1] This survey was carried out jointly by the Fraunhofer Institute for Systems and Innovation Research Karlsruhe, the Department of Economic Geography at Hannover University, the Chair for Economic Policy at the Technical University Bergakademie Freiberg, and the Department of Economic and Social Geography at University of Cologne, supported by a research grant from the Deutsche Forschungsgemeinschaft.

[2] These variables include the number of employees with university degree, co-operation with other economic actors, the sector of activity and expected changes in R&D activities and the number of employees.

[3] Thus, homogeneity analysis can be described as principal component analysis for nominal data.

For manufacturing firms, the size variable discriminated well in both dimensions of the analysis. Out of the total sample of 398 firms, 173 were defined as small (up to 40 employees) and 225 as large (more than 76 employees) (see Fig. 11.1).

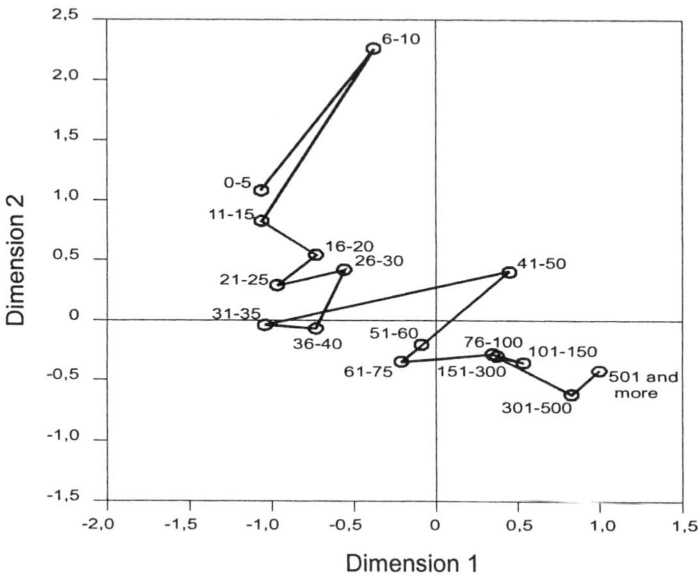

Fig. 11.1 Homogeneity analysis for classifying manufacturing firms by size

The sample of service firms comprises 174 firms. Resulting from the homogeneity analysis, 95 were defined as small service (up to 3 employees) and 79 defined as large (more than 21 employees). Tables 11.1 and 11.2 give an indication of the size distribution among industries and types of location: SF stands for small firm and LF for large firm. It should be pointed out that the firms referred to as large in this study are small compared to the definitions used in many other innovation studies, and that this definition differs between service and manufacturing firms.

While for manufacturing firms the industrial mix between small and large firms is statistically insignificant (according to the χ^2 test) and therefore branch effects on firm behaviour can mostly be neglected (though the industrial mix between the three types of region varies considerably), the industrial composition between small and large service firms differs significantly. The consultancy sector in particular is dominated by small firms, unlike engineering services where far more large firms can be found. Although this could justify demand sector specific analyses, the sample size is too small for a sectoral and regional breakdown for each of the variables. We therefore abstained from this analytical step.

The empirical analysis in the following section is based on cross-tabulations and χ^2 tests as these were considered to be more appropriate than multivariate statistics. Among the independent variables included, for example, in regression models to reflect the firms' characteristics, regional characteristics and networking activity, the last does not usually contribute much to the total model (Koschatzky 1998). To synthesise the results, we included pertinent categories for both size groups in further homogeneity analyses in order to be able to 'map' the most important knowledge acquisition and networking characteristics of small and large manufacturing and service firms. This analysis complements bivariate χ^2 tests by illustrating associations between the most important categories of variables.

Table 11.1 Distribution of small and large manufacturing firms according to industry and type of region

Industry [1] (% of firms)	*Total*		*Central*		*Intermediate*		*Rural*	
	SF (n=173)	LF (n=225)	SF (n=50)	LF (n=65)	SF (n=73)	LF (n=115)	SF (n=50)	LF (n=45)
Food	2.3	5.3	2.0	9.2	4.1	5.2	0.0	0.0
Textile	2.9	5.3	0.0	0.0	2.7	8.7	6.0	4.4
Wood	19.1	13.8	14.0	10.8	24.7	15.7	16.0	13.3
Plastics	15.0	17.3	22.0	26.2	16.4	16.5	6.0	6.7
Metal	13.9	11.1	16.0	7.7	8.2	11.3	20.0	15.6
Machinery	24.9	28.4	26.0	21.5	24.7	29.6	24.0	35.6
Electronics	22.0	18.7	20.0	24.6	19.2	13.0	28.0	24.4
χ^2	0.301		0.404		0.381		0.890	

(1) Aggregation of NACE codes 15 - 36.

Table 11.2 Distribution of small and large service firms according to industries and type of region

Industry [1] (% of firms)	*Total*		*Central*		*Intermediate*		*Rural*	
	SF (n=95)	LF (n=79)	SF (n=47)	LF (n=40)	SF (n=31)	LF (n=29)	SF (n=17)	LF (n=10)
Computers	26.3	22.8	27.7	22.5	22.6	27.6	29.4	10.0
Accounting	6.3	11.4	2.1	10.0	6.5	6.9	17.6	30.0
Consultancy	36.8	11.4	40.4	12.5	35.5	10.3	29.4	10.0
Engineering	30.5	54.4	29.8	55.0	35.5	55.2	23.5	50.0
χ^2	0.000		0.007		0.138		0.273	

(1) *Computers:* Computer and related activities (NACE 72); *Accounting:* Legal activities, accounting, book-keeping and auditing activities, tax consultancy (NACE 74.11 and 74.12); *Consultancy:* Market research, business and management consultancy activities, advertising (NACE 74.13, 74.14, 74.4); *Engineering:* Architectural and engineering activities and related technical consultancy, technical testing and analysis (NACE 74.2 and 74.3).

11.3 The Empirical Analysis

Innovative Activity

It emerged that differences do exist between small and large manufacturing firms in the kind of innovative activity carried out. While 30.6 percent of small firms carried out only product innovation, the figure was 11.6 percent for the large firms. More than 84 percent of the large firms reported a combination of product and process innovation compared with 63.0 percent of the small manufacturing firms. No such distinction is possible between small and large service firms. The slight differences which can be seen in Table 11.3 are statistically insignificant. It may be however that the definition of service innovation was not as well understood by the firms interviewed as for manufacturing innovation (although explained in the questionnaire). The fact that large manufacturing firms are more strongly engaged in process innovation, as pointed out in the first section, can be indirectly confirmed by our analysis.

Table 11.3 Kind of innovative activity of large and small firms

Manufacturing firms			*Service Firms*			
Kind of activity [(1)] (% of firms)	SF (n=173)	LF (n=225)	*Kind of activity* [(2)] (% of firms)	SF (n=95)	LF (n=79)	χ^2
Only product innovation	30.6	11.6	New service	61.1	63.3	0.762
Only process innovation	6.4	4.0	Improved service	56.8	62.0	0.489
Both product and process innovation	63.0	84.4	New/improved processes	67.0	60.8	0.392
Total	100.0	100.0				
χ^2	0.000					

(1) Measured according to R&D expenditure.
(2) Share of firms which implemented this kind of innovation.

The amount of research and development (R&D) activity is generally measured in terms of the share of R&D expenditures in total turnover or the share of R&D personnel in total employment (Pfirrmann 1994). For manufacturing firms, the survey confirms that a higher share of small firms have no R&D personnel compared with large firms, but a higher share also have over 8.1 percent R&D employees (see Table 11.4). This is statistically significant for the total sample and for all three types of region, i.e. also in rural areas. Large firms are relatively strong in the size classes up to 8 percent R&D employment share, and in absolute terms employ far more people in R&D activities than small firms (also statistically significant). The same holds true for the service firms, although the differences between small and large firms are statistically less significant. This outcome indicates the relatively diversified pattern of innovation activities in small firms. With respect to their size, small innovative firms (in manufacturing and services) devote more financial and human capital resources to R&D than large firms. In absolute terms, however, large firms have a greater R&D potential than small firms.

Table 11.4 R&D intensity of small and large firms

	Share of R&D personnel in manufacturing firms							
Share as % of personnel	*Total* SF (n=173)	LF (n=225)	*Central* SF (n=50)	LF (n=65)	*Intermediate* SF (n=73)	LF (n=115)	*Rural* SF (n=50)	LF (n=45)
Nil	11.6	8.0	12.0	7.7	11.0	8.7	12.0	6.7
< 3%	8.7	39.6	10.0	33.8	8.2	41.7	8.0	42.2
3 - 8%	41.6	32.0	32.0	33.8	43.8	32.2	48.0	28.9
> 8 %	38.2	20.4	46.0	24.6	37.0	17.4	32.0	22.2
χ^2	0.000		0.011		0.000		0.002	

	Share of innovation expenditure in service firms							
Share as % of turnover	*Total* SF (n=95)	LF (n=79)	*Central* SF (n=47)	LF (n=40)	*Intermediate* SF (n=31)	LF (n=29)	*Rural* SF (n=17)	LF (n=10)
< 3.5 %	22.1	30.4	27.7	27.5	19.4	37.9	11.8	20.0
3.5 – 8 %	29.5	41.8	27.7	42.5	32.3	41.4	29.4	40.0
> 8 %	48.4	27.8	44.7	30.0	48.4	20.7	58.8	40.0
χ^2	0.022		0.271		0.066		0.628	

For manufacturing firms, information is also available for the *regularity of R&D*, which might be interpreted as routine innovation reflecting path dependence (Dosi 1982). 19.7 percent of the small firms and 28.9 percent of the large ones are permanently engaged in research work aimed at finding new technical and organisational solutions. This strong orientation of large firms towards research is statistically significant at the 5 percent level. Development processes, which reflect a continuous improvement of products and processes, are carried out by most of the firms (Table 11.5). Only 3.5 percent of the small firms (and 0.4 percent of the large ones) did not perform any development work at all. Permanent development processes seem to be a characteristic of large firms (80.4 percent), while for more than 40 percent of the small firms development is only an occasional option. As postulated in the literature, large firms seem to follow trajectories which are defined by systematic and continuous R&D activities.

The *first research question* can therefore be answered as follows:

- Innovation in small manufacturing firms is more focused on product innovation than on a combination of product and process innovation (as in large firms). Small manufacturing and service firms invest a higher share of expenditures and personnel in R&D and innovation, but the absolute input of large firms is greater.
- More small manufacturing firms carry out development work on an occasional basis (only when needed), while large firms are permanently engaged in development, reflecting routines in innovative behaviour.

Table 11.5 Continuity of development of small and large manufacturing firms and according to type of region

Continuity (% of firms)	*Total*		*Central*		*Intermediate*		*Rural*	
	SF (n=173)	LF (n=225)	SF (n=50)	LF (n=65)	SF (n=73)	LF (n=115)	SF (n=50)	LF (n=45)
Never	3.5	0.4	4.0	0.0	0.0	0.9	8.0	0.0
Occasionally	41.6	19.1	42.0	21.5	43.8	16.5	38.0	22.2
Permanently	54.9	80.4	54.0	78.5	56.2	82.6	54.0	77.8
χ^2	0.000		0.011		0.000		0.023	

Information Co-ordination

Information is an essential basis for knowledge. It is the source of knowledge creation and knowledge formalisation. Information consists of a flow of news which can be divided into single parts ('bits'), which are added to the knowledge base, thereby altering it (Nonaka 1994). For a firm to be innovative, it is crucial to have access to recent information and to channel information flows efficiently within the firm in order to create knowledge which is specific and relevant to the needs of the user.

In Section 11.1 it was argued that decentralised information handling favours creativity and innovation. The *way in which innovation activities are co-ordinated* gives an indication of how the gatekeeper function is organised. As can be seen from Table 11.6, innovation activities in small manufacturing firms are mainly centrally co-ordinated (94.7 percent of firms), while nearly 40 percent of large firms a decentralised co-ordination strategy is applied. This behaviour is largely independent of the kind of the regional environment. Only in rural areas did more large firms in the sample favour centralised co-ordination (71.1 percent compared to an average of 62.7 percent). This could be attributed to differences in the regional industrial mix, since the machinery industry is over-represented in rural areas (35.6 percent of large firms against the average of 28.4 percent), while the plastics industry is underrepresented (6.7 percent compared to 17.3 percent).

The different kind of gatekeeping activity in small and large firms may have influenced the more negative assessment of small firms concerning their access to external knowledge. While 11 percent of the small firms said they faced obstacles in accessing external knowledge, only 3.3 percent of the large firms had a similar problem. When information transfer and related activities are monopolised, the knowledge base and innovative potential of a firm depend strongly on the absorptive capacity of the gatekeeper. In cases where this is low it could have negative effects on the learning and knowledge-building abilities of the firm. Due to their size, small manufacturing firms suffer more from inefficient centralised gatekeeping than large manufacturing firms which have, according to the figures in Table 11.6, also other options in organising information processing processes.

Table 11.6 Structure of information and innovation co-ordination in small and large manufacturing firms according to type of region

Type of co-ordination (in %)	*Total*		*Central*		*Intermediate*		*Rural*	
	SF (n=173)	LF (n=225)	SF (n=50)	LF (n=65)	SF (n=73)	LF (n=115)	SF (n=50)	LF (n=45)
Corporate co-ordination	3.6	22.2	2.0	21.5	6.9	27.8	0.0	8.9
Decentralised co-ordination	1.8	15.1	2.0	18.5	1.4	11.3	2.1	20.0
Centralised co-ordination	94.7	62.7	95.9	60.0	91.7	60.9	97.9	71.1
χ^2	0.000		0.000		0.000		0.001	

For innovation it is not only important by whom information is distributed and how, but also which information sources are used. In this respect, Table 11.7 should answer the question whether there are clear differences between small and large firms in accessing *external information sources*. For manufacturing firms, the two most important information sources for product innovation are customers and exhibitions. With customers, it is learning by using and related information flows which play a major role, while selective and autonomous information search are important when information is picked up at exhibitions. For these two sources, large and small firms act in a similar way.

Major differences were found however with respect to competitors, suppliers and research institutes. All three sources are considered far more important by large firms than small ones. In the case of competitors, this might have something to do with trust and diversification. Large firms with a broader product spectrum and less dependence on a few strategic products have more freedom in entering into information exchange with competitors than small firms. The knowledge base and absorptive capacity of a firm is also related to its ability to co-operate with research institutes (Rosenberg 1990; Hicks 1995). In our sample many more large firms rate research institutes as an important information source than small firms (significant at the 1 percent level). Technical services are the least important information source for both small and large firms. It can be concluded that the information spectrum of large firms is more diversified than that of small firms.

Table 11.7 Importance of external information sources for small and large manufacturing firms

Information source [(1)] (in %)	*Product Innovation*				
	SF		LF		χ^2
	(n=173)	Rank	(n=225)	Rank	
Customers	90.2	1	91.1	1	0.749
Exhibitions	72.3	2	75.1	2	0.520
Literature	69.4	3	69.3	4	0.995
Competitors	59.0	4	71.1	3	0.011
Suppliers	44.5	5	56.0	5	0.023
Research	20.8	6	36.9	6	0.001
Services [(2)]	19.7	7	22.7	7	0.467

[(1)] Rated important and very important for innovation (multiple answers allowed).
[(2)] Engineering and planning bureaux.

With respect to the *second research question,* it can be stated that small manufacturing firms are characterised by strong centralised information and innovation co-ordination, with a high dependence on the knowledge-base and absorptive capacity of the gatekeeper. In large firms, information flows are more decentralised. According to the concept of the absorptive capacity of a firm, this supports innovativeness and reduces the risk of not being able to monitor and process relevant information. Compared to the large firms, small manufacturing firms acquire less information from competitors, suppliers and research institutes, while other information sources are used to a similar extent.

Knowledge Exchange by Networking

While information networking does not demand close relations, innovation networks are rather different. They can be defined as a loose, informal institutional arrangement by which firms seek to reduce uncertainty, to enter into learning processes, to gain access to complementary knowledge and exchange know-how and knowledge with their network partners (DeBresson and Amesse 1991; Koschatzky 1998; Powell 1990). It is this knowledge transfer function which makes innovation networks so important for both large and small firms. Especially for small firms external linkages play an important role in accessing complementary knowledge (Laranja 1998).

A distinction is usually made between vertical networks, with an integrated value chain of customers and suppliers, and horizontal networks providing links with other firms and research institutes. The degree of freedom to search for partners is greater in horizontal than in vertical networks as the latter are more production based.

Depending on the kind of information and knowledge exchanged within the networks, relationships can be organised informally or formally. In the questionnaire used for the empirical study, only linkages which served for innovation purposes were considered relevant (i.e. conventional producer-supplier linkages without any reference to innovation were not analysed). Loose contacts and exchange of experience were assumed to be informal relationships, while co-operation in joint projects or pilot applications usually demand formal arrangements. Depending on the complexity of the networking activity, different competencies are needed for the management and handling of these external relations. Firms without appropriate network management are unable to make sufficient use of network advantages and can lose the trust of their network partners (Ritter 1998; Koschatzky and Zenker 1999).

The manufacturing firms in the sample were asked with which partners they co-operate in innovation processes beyond the usual business relations. These relationships were classed as vertical co-operation (with customers and suppliers), horizontal co-operation (with other firms and research institutes) and co-operation with service companies as a special case of knowledge support. *Vertical innovation networks* were rated to be most important. 71.7 percent of small and 78.2 percent of large firms found this type of relationship of great importance for innovation support (Table 11.8). There was no significant variation between large and small firms or for the three types of region.

Due to its production-based nature, vertical networking mostly consists of existing business relations which are exploited for innovation purposes. This kind of collaborative activity does not differ significantly between small and large firms and is also independent of the type of region.[1] The spatial range of these networks does not vary significantly between the two types of firm. Large firms show a slightly higher interregional orientation, while small firms co-operate a little more with partners from the same federal state. This pattern is not affected by the type of region in which a firm is located.

---

[1] Using the same database, but including data from Saxony, Fritsch (1999) found that for vertical co-operation "... not only the propensity to have at least one co-operative relationship, but also the number of co-operative relationships increases with size" (p. 12). This is indirectly supported by our results, which reveal a slightly higher percentage share for large firms, although the differences are statistically insignificant.

Table 11.8 Importance and spatial range of vertical networking by large and small manufacturing firms according to type of region (% of firms)

Importance/ Spatial range	*Total*		*Central*		*Intermediate*		*Rural*	
	SF (n=173)	LF (n=225)	SF (n=50)	LF (n=65)	SF (n=73)	LF (n=115)	SF (n=50)	LF (n=45)
No co-operation	27.2	20.9	30.0	18.5	23.3	23.5	30.0	17.8
Less important	1.2	0.9	0.0	1.5	2.7	0.9	0.0	0.0
Very important	71.7	78.2	70.0	80.0	74.0	75.7	70.0	82.2
χ^2	0.323		0.253		0.608		0.165	
Regional	40.5	35.6	36.0	30.8	38.4	38.3	48.0	35.6
Interregional	40.5	42.2	40.0	41.5	43.8	45.2	36.0	35.6
$\chi^{2\,(1)}$	0.317		0.554		0.990		0.220	
$\chi^{2\,(2)}$	0.724		0.868		0.853		0.964	

(1) For regional networking: within the same federal state.
(2) For interregional networking: outside the federal state.

In relation to vertical networking, no significant differences exist between small and large firms either in the intensity, the spatial range, or the kind of collaborative activity (Fig. 11.2). For both small and large firms, the major purposes of vertical networks are informal contacts and the undertaking of joint projects, which are usually based on contracts and therefore formally organised. The exchange of experience is usually more informally organised. Co-operation in pilot applications ranks fourth. It can thus be seen that vertical networks are not only a collaborative arrangement for the exchange of informal information and knowledge, but are also used for joint research, development and application in which mutual learning processes occur.

A totally different pattern was found for *horizontal networking* with other firms and research institutes. Not only was horizontal co-operation rated as less important than vertical relationships, but the differences between small and large firms were statistically significant (59.0 % the former had no horizontal co-operation at all). While 64.9 % of the large firms considered these networks important, the figure for small firms was only 34.1 % (see Table 11.9). Since horizontal relations are characterised by a high degree of freedom, firms can select between different partners, but have to carry out this search on their own and also have to establish trustworthy relationships. This is sometimes a costly and time-consuming process which requires competencies in network management and knowledge processing. Usually, networking is not a one-way process, but a mutual interaction to which each partner brings specific knowledge. This requires a knowledge base interesting to others. All these requirements favour large firms in establishing horizontal innovation networks.

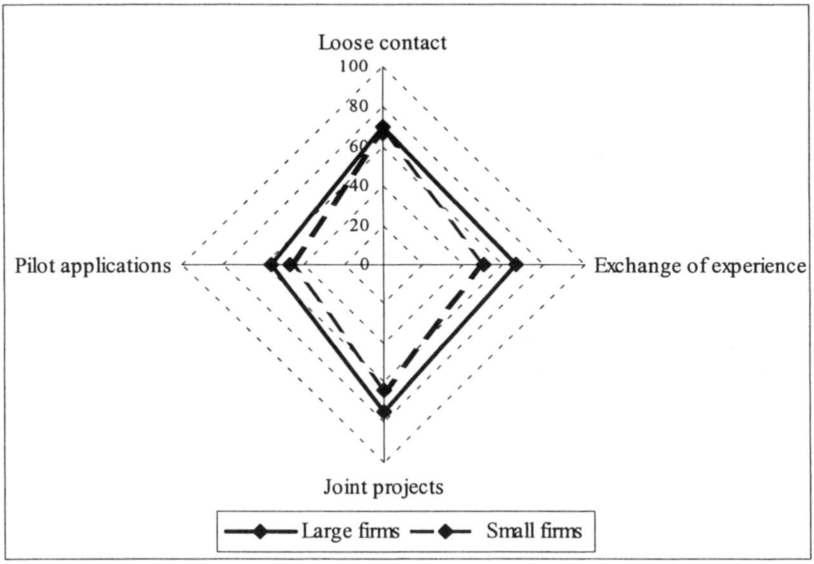

Fig. 11.2 Important and very important forms of vertical co-operation (% of firms)

Table 11.9 Importance and spatial range of horizontal networking by small and large manufacturing firms according to type of region (% of firms)

Importance/ Spatial range	*Total*		*Central*		*Intermediate*		*Rural*	
	SF (n=173)	LF (n=225)	SF (n=50)	LF (n=65)	SF (n=73)	LF (n=115)	SF (n=50)	LF (n=45)
No co-operation	59.0	32.9	50.0	24.6	63.0	38.2	62.0	31.1
Less important	6.9	2.2	12.0	0.0	1.4	3.5	10.0	2.2
Very important	34.1	64.9	38.0	75.4	35.6	58.3	28.0	66.7
χ^2	0.000		0.000		0.004		0.001	
Regional	12.7	22.7	16.0	24.6	11.0	20.0	12.0	26.7
Interregional	11.7	21.3	16.0	26.2	11.0	17.4	6.0	24.4
$\chi^{2\,(1)}$	0.011		0.260		0.104		0.069	
$\chi^{2\,(2)}$	0.006		0.191		0.227		0.011	

(1) For regional networking: within the same federal state.
(2) For interregional networking: outside the federal state.

With respect to co-operation with research institutes, the general differences between large and small firms in the approach to horizontal networking become evident (see Fig. 11.3). Firstly, small firms are much less involved in relationships with research institutes. Large firms, on the other hand, make strategic use of diploma theses as a kind of knowledge exchange but also, more importantly, for personnel acquisition. Other major forms of co-operation are joint R&D projects, in which there are bilateral learning processes, and the placing of research projects with institutes. The joint use of equipment does not play a major role for large firms, but seems to be relatively important for small firms.

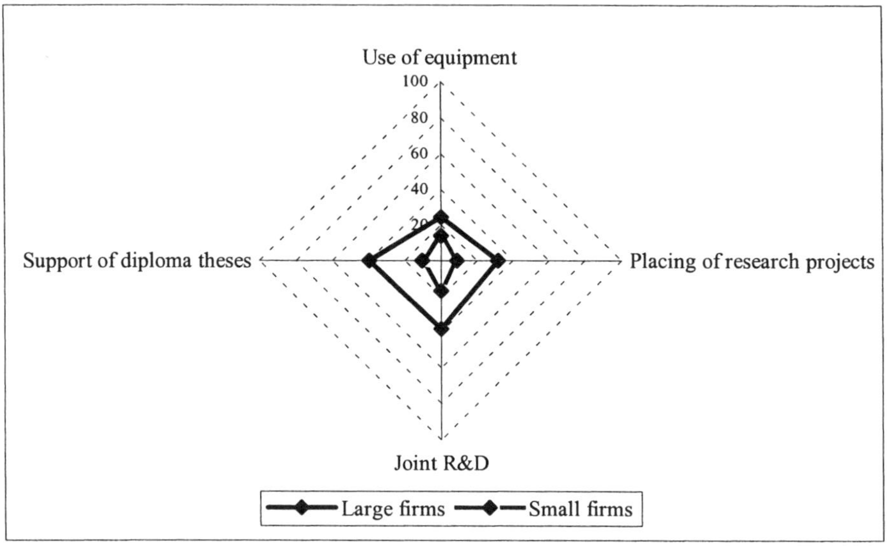

Fig. 11.3 Important and very important forms of horizontal co-operation with research institutions (% of firms)

Compared to vertical networks, where no regional differentiation was found, the importance rating for horizontal networks also discriminates between the types of region. Firms seem to establish more horizontal relations in central regions than in the two other types of region. This could possibly be attributed to the larger supply of possible co-operation partners due to urbanisation economies. On the other hand, the shares of interregional networking are also higher compared to the average. So the greater activity in horizontal networking of small and large firms located in central regions seem to be a characteristic of this type of region.[1] With respect to the spatial range of horizontal co-operation, it can be clearly stated that large firms are more actively engaged in both regional and interregional networking. In central and intermediate regions the differences are not pronounced enough to be statistically significant, while they are in rural regions and the total sample. Especially in the rural areas, only a few small firms have interregional

[1] In his analysis of 1,000 small and medium sized manufacturing and service enterprises, Keeble (1997) similarly found greater collaborative activity in central regions. In his study over twice as many metropolitan service firms reported collaborative arrangements compared to service firms in peripheral regions.

collaborative relationships, while many large firms are engaged in both regional and interregional interaction. The figures do not provide an explanation for this collaborative behaviour, but it can at least be concluded that horizontal networking activities differ slightly with respect to the type of the regional environment of the firm.

As well as manufacturing firms and research institutions, business-related service firms are playing an increasing role in knowledge creation and exchange. This is the case not only for organisational and social innovations, but for technological innovations as well (Muller and Zenker 1998). Because of the intensive linkages between manufacturing and service firms, the supply of innovation supporting services plays a crucial role in the stimulation of regional innovation activity (Bellini 1998; Cappellin and Nijkamp 1990; Coffey and Polèse 1987; Wood 1995). In our sample 84.4 percent of the large and 59.5 percent of the small manufacturing firms availed of technical and advisory services for innovation purposes (see Table 11.10).

Advisory services comprise accounting and business consultancy, and technical services computer-related activities and engineering. It is clear that large firms make more use of the complementary knowledge base that service firms can offer than small firms. Small firms seem to use advisory services than technical ones, suggesting that they acquire less technical information and knowledge from external sources. There are not great differences between the regions, but there is less distinction in the collaborative behaviour between small and large firms in rural areas than elsewhere.

Table 11.10 Networking with service companies by small and large manufacturing firms according to type of region (% of firms)

Collaborative activity	*Total*		*Central*		*Intermediate*		*Rural*	
	SF (n=173)	LF (n=225)	SF (n=50)	LF (n=65)	SF (n=73)	LF (n=115)	SF (n=50)	LF (n=45)
No co-operation	19.1	7.6	16.0	6.2	23.3	8.7	16.0	6.7
With advisory services only	20.2	7.1	22.0	7.7	19.2	5.2	20.0	11.1
With technical services only	1.2	0.9	4.0	0.0	0.0	0.9	0.0	2.2
By both types	59.5	84.4	58.0	86.1	57.5	85.2	64.0	80.0
χ^2	0.000		0.006		0.000		0.177	

Small manufacturing firms have a much closer spatial range in their interaction with service companies than large firms. This applies to networking with advisory and technical services in the three types of region, except in the rural areas where there is a greater use of technical services outside the region (see Table 11.11). In interacting with advisory services, many small firms limit their search radius to their region, so 68.4 percent (in intermediate regions up to 75.0 percent) co-operate with partners from the same area. Large firms have a wider search radius and are more selective in choosing their partners. Nearly 55 percent have complementary linkages with advisory and technical services from within and outside the region.

Although the high regional percentage share recorded for small firms using advisory services would suggest a limited ability for longer distance interaction, this is not the case for technical services. The share of small firms which co-operate only with technical partners from outside their own region (32.4 %) is higher than for the large firms (23.7 percent). Especially for small manufacturing firms, the search radius does not seem to depend only on the availability of local services, but on personal contacts and trust as well. These were considered to be more important for legal activities and tax accounting than for other kinds of co-operation such as software support. Between the regions there are only slight deviations in the spatial range of co-operation. Large firms in central regions for example have a slightly higher regional co-operation than the average. This might reflect the better service supply, but the tendency is not statistically significant.

Table 11.11 Share of regional and interregional networking of large and small manufacturing firms with service firms by type of region (% of firms)

	Co-operation with advisory services							
Range of co-operation	*Total*		*Central*		*Intermediate*		*Rural*	
	SF (n=136)	LF (n=197)	SF (n=39)	LF (n=58)	SF (n=56)	LF (n=98)	SF (n=41)	LF (n=41)
Only in region	68.4	28.9	69.2	32.8	75.0	27.6	58.5	26.8
Only outside	8.8	16.2	7.7	10.3	3.6	17.3	17.1	22.0
In and outside	22.8	54.8	23.1	56.9	21.4	55.1	24.4	51.2
χ^2	0.000		0.002		0.000		0.011	
	Co-operation with technical services							
	SF (n=102)	LF (n=190)	SF (n=29)	LF (n=55)	SF (n=42)	LF (n=98)	SF (n=31)	LF (n=37)
Only in region	35.3	21.6	31.0	23.6	38.1	19.4	35.5	24.3
Only outside	32.4	23.7	34.5	12.7	31.0	28.6	32.3	27.0
In and outside	32.4	54.7	34.5	63.6	31.0	52.0	32.3	48.6
χ^2	0.001		0.020		0.030		0.373	

With respect to *research question 3* the empirical findings suggest the following:

- Vertical networking and interactions with service firms are more important knowledge sources for manufacturing firms than horizontal co-operation, irrespective of firm size.
- In vertical networks, small and large firms behave similarly, so size is not a discriminating factor for this kind of knowledge exchange. There are also no regional influences on vertical networking activities. No clear dependence on the quality of the regional environment could be detected.
- Large firms make much more strategic use of additional expert knowledge by accessing horizontal networks than small firms. The latter seem to rely more on production based (vertical) relations. This is especially the case in central regions which positively influence the propensity to co-operate. In rural areas, small firms are less integrated in horizontal networks, perhaps because of a limited supply of possible co-operation partners.
- Small manufacturing firms co-operate significantly more with partners from the same region than large firms which have a higher share of complementary, i.e. regional and interregional network relations. Due to this stronger regional embeddedness, small firms are more dependent on the availability and quality of regional knowledge sources, while large firms try to minimise co-operation risks by selecting partners from several regions.
- The knowledge exchange pattern is only slightly affected by the regional environment. The type of region in which a firm is located plays a role only for horizontal networking activity, in that small manufacturing firms in rural areas are less engaged in interregional co-operation.
- Large service firms find spatial proximity more important in interactions with industrial clients compared with small firms. As these results are statistically insignificant, they only reflect a tendency.

To confirm the knowledge acquisition and networking pattern of the firms, a homogeneity analysis was carried out to see whether the results obtained by cross-tabulations and χ^2 testing hold also true for interrelated variables. Limiting the analysis to two dimensions, the discrimination measures per variable for manufacturing and service firms are shown in Table 11.12.

It can be seen that for the manufacturing firms size (SIZE) is a discriminating variable in that large firms are more engaged in horizontal networking (both regionally and inter-regionally; REG_HOR, INTREG_HOR). They also have more interregional co-operation with service firms (INTREG_SERV) and co-operation with research institutes (COOP_RESEAR). Small firms, on the other hand, are more regionally oriented, both with respect to co-operation behaviour and markets. The type of region in which the firm is located (REGION) discriminates more in relation to the second dimension, which points to the importance of vertical networking. In this respect, firm size plays only a minor role compared to the first dimension.

In the two-dimensional plot, although not reflected by the coefficients, decentralised innovation co-ordination is more closely linked to large than small firms. For the service firms, size (SIZE) and the type of region (REGION) are not discriminating factors. A clear distinction between small and large service firms and their collaborative behaviour is therefore not possible. Nevertheless, the plots show that service firms which often co-operate with other services also co-operate quite often with research institutes. Those which mainly use vertical information sources from within their region also have a high share of industrial clients from the same region. All in all, the homogeneity analysis confirms the results already derived from descriptive statistics, showing that networking behaviour differs especially between small and large manufacturing firms. The discrimination measures also make it clear that for service firms the firm size (as defined in this study) is far less a discriminating factor in information exchange and innovation co-operation than for manufacturing firms.

Table 11.12 Discrimination measures for manufacturing and service firms

Manufacturing firms	*Dimension*		*Service firms*	*Dimension*	
Variables	*1*	*2*	*Variables*	*1*	*2*
REGION	0.027	0.201	REGION	0.010	0.051
REG_VERT	0.105	*0.642*	COOP_SERV	*0.540*	0.118
INTREG_VERT	0.145	*0.506*	COOP_RESEAR	*0.334*	0.176
REG_HOR	*0.323*	0.072	CLIENT_RANGE	*0.578*	*0.335*
INTREG_HOR	0.387	0.035	REG_VERTINFO	*0.297*	*0.501*
REG_SERV	0.151	0.002	REG_HORINFO	0.198	*0.380*
INTREG_SERV	*0.336*	0.053	REG_OTHERINFO	0.248	0.226
COOP_RESEAR	*0.260*	0.055	TURNOV_RANGE	0.099	*0.267*
TURNOV_RANGE	0.133	0.145	SIZE	0.023	0.000
COORD_INNO	0.168	0.165			
SIZE	*0.351*	0.192			

11.4 Summary and Conclusions

The empirical analysis has shown that there are more similarities between small manufacturing and small service firms than between small and large manufacturing firms. In their information and co-operation activities, small and large service firms behave fairly similarly. This seems to be an indication that, at least for the firms in our sample, size is a significant variable for differentiating the structural and behavioural characteristics of firms, especially within the manufacturing sector. This is less true among service firms. Based on the findings of this study, we would seem justified in concluding that small firms depend more on regional information and knowledge sources for their innovative activity than larger firms.[1]

[1] In this respect, our results seem to follow a general pattern, since also Feldman (1994) came to a similar conclusion for firms from the United States. She states that: "small firms rely more on external sources of input to the innovation process" and "small

An interesting question which arises is whether the stronger regional embeddedness of small firms affects their innovative and economic performance. If it is influenced positively, there seems no need to support small firms with region-specific innovation policy measures. If they face problems because of their stronger dependence on regional networking, innovation policy support seems justified in order to reduce their disadvantages compared to large firms.

For small firms in general, the innovation literature would seem to answer this question with: "it depends". The results of the present study allow a tentative reply. Our analysis indicates that firms in intermediate and rural areas seem to face more problems in innovation than those in central regions, which have a more favourable innovation climate. Due to the shorter range of their network contacts, small firms cannot compensate for knowledge deficits in their regional environment in the same way as large firms. However, small firms in central regions can benefit from a better supply of knowledge sources through regional networking, and are also more engaged in interregional networking, especially in horizontal knowledge exchange. These may depend on each other, but this assumption could not be tested empirically.

Small firms in intermediate and rural areas have fewer possibilities of interacting with partners from outside the region and are more strongly embedded within their region. This reduces their knowledge input to regional resources and to knowledge acquired by independent learning (e.g. from technical literature). In the light of the argument that information and knowledge are important prerequisites for innovative activity, and regarding the perception of the regional environment, it may be assumed that small manufacturing and service firms especially in intermediate and rural areas are discriminated against in knowledge access compared to firms in central regions. On the other hand, this should not automatically imply negative impacts on the innovative performance of small firms located outside the metropolitan cores. At least with respect to innovation intensity, our analysis found no major difference compared to firms located in central areas. This supports findings of other empirical studies, which conclude that firms in peripheral areas are not less innovative, but simply apply different innovation strategies (Keeble 1997).

The present study has not attempted to answer the question as to which policy support measures are most appropriate. This would require more detailed analysis of knowledge access and processing by small firms. On a general level, however, the results of the empirical study suggest that regional innovation policy should aim to improve:

- the capacity for independent learning in small manufacturing and service firms,
- the knowledge accessing and knowledge processing abilities of small manufacturing and service firms,

---

businesses have a less well developed internal R&D capability than their larger counterparts and thus rely more heavily on external R&D from universities" (p. 370).

especially those located in intermediate and peripheral areas. This would not only improve the firms' learning abilities, but also qualify more firms in intermediate and peripheral areas to become network partners at a regional and interregional level.

References

Acs, Z.J., Audretsch, D.B. (1990) Innovation and Small Firms. MIT Press, Cambridge MA

Arnold, E., Thuriaux, B. (1997) Supporting Companies' Technological Capabilities. Technopolis Ltd, Brighton

Aydalot, P. (ed.) (1986) Milieux Innovateurs en Europe. GREMI, Paris

Backhaus, A., Seidel, O. (1997) Innovationen und Kooperationsbeziehungen von Industriebetrieben, Forschungseinrichtungen und unternehmensnahen Dienstleistern: Die Region Hannover-Braunschweig-Göttingen im interregionalen Vergleich. Hannoversche Geographische Arbeitsmaterialien 19, Universität Hannover, Hannover

Backhaus, A., Seidel, O. (1998) Die Bedeutung der Region für den Innovationsprozeß. Raumforschung und Raumordnung 56, 264-276

Barkham, R., Gudgin, G., Hart, M., Hanvey, E. (1996) The Determinants of Small Firm Growth. An Inter-Regional Study in the United Kingdom 1986-90. Jessica Kingsley Publications, London

Bellini, N. (1998) Services to Industry in the Framework of Regional and Local Industrial Policy, Paper presented at the OECD Conference on Up-Grading Knowledge and Diffusing Technology to Small Firms: Building Competitive Regional Environments, May 28-29, Modena (mimeo)

Birch, D.L. (1987) Job Creation in America. How Our Smallest Companies Put the Most People to Work. The Free Press, New York

Camagni, R. (ed.) (1991) Innovation Networks. Spatial Perspectives. Belhaven Press, London, New York

Camagni, R., Capello, R. (1997) Innovation and Performance of SMEs in Italy: The Relevance of Spatial Aspects. Paper presented at the International Conference on Innovation and Performance of SMEs, Cambridge, March 17

Cappellin, R., Nijkamp, P. (1990) The Role of Space in Technological Change. In: Cappellin, R., Nijkamp, P. (eds.) The Spatial Context of Technological Development. Avebury, Aldershot, 1-13

Coe, N.M., Townsend, A.R. (1998) Debunking the Myth of Localized Agglomerations: The Development of a Regionalized Service Economy in South-East England. Transactions of the Institute of British Geographers 23, 385-404

Coffey, W.J., Polèse, M. (1987) Trade and Location of Producer Services: A Canadian Perspective. Environment and Planning A 19, 697-711

Cohen, W. (1995) Empirical Studies of Innovative Activity. In: Stoneman, P. (ed.) Handbook of the Economics of Technological Change. Blackwell, Oxford, 182-264

Cohen, W., Levinthal, D.A. (1990) Absorptive Capacity. A New Perspective on Learning and Innovation. Administrative Science Quarterly 35, 128-152

De Bresson, C., Amesse, F. (1991) Networks of Innovators. A Review and Introduction to the Issue. Research Policy 20, 363-379

Dosi, G. (1982) Technological Paradigms and Technological Trajectories. Research Policy 11, 147-162

Feldman, M.P. (1994) Knowledge Complementary and Innovation. Small Business Economics 6, 363-372

Foray, D., Lundvall, B.-A. (1996) The Knowledge-Based Economy: From the Economics of Knowledge to the Learning Economy, Employment and Growth in the Knowledge-based Economy. OECD, Paris, 11-32

Freeman, C. (1982) The Economics of Industrial Innovation (2nd edition). Pinter, London

Frisch, A.J. (1993) Unternehmensgröße und Innovation. Die schumpeterianische Diskussion und ihre Alternativen. Campus-Verlag, Frankfurt

Fritsch, M. (1999) Co-operation in Regional Innovation Systems. Freiberger Working Papers, 10, TU Bergakademie, Freiberg

Hicks, D. (1995) Published Papers, Tacit Competencies and Corporate Management of the Public/Private Character of Knowledge. Industrial and Corporate Change 4, 401-424

Keeble D. (1997) Small Firms, Innovation and Regional Development in Britain in the 1990s. Regional Studies, 31, 281-293

Keeble, D., Wilkinson, F. (1999) Collective Learning and Knowledge Development in the Evolution of Regional Clusters of High Technology SMEs in Europe. Regional Studies 33, 295-303

Klein Woolthuis, R., Schipper, D., Stor, M. (1998) How Entrepreneurial Networks Can Succeed: Case from the Region of Twente. In: During, W., Oakey, R. (eds.) New Technology-Based Firms in the 1990s. Vol. IV, Paul Chapman, London, 112-124

Koschatzky, K. (1997) Entwicklungs- und Innovationspotentiale von unternehmensnahen Dienstleistungsbetrieben in Baden. Ergebnisse einer Unternehmensbefragung, Arbeitspapier Regionalforschung 10, Fraunhofer ISI, Karlsruhe

Koschatzky, K. (1998) Firm Innovation and Region: The Role of Space in Innovation Processes. International Journal of Innovation Management 2, 383-408

Koschatzky, K. (1999) Innovation Networks of Industry and Business-Related Services: Relations between Innovation Intensity of Firms and Regional Inter-Firm Co-operation. European Planning Studies 7, 737-757

Koschatzky, K., Traxel, H. (1997) Entwicklungs- und Innovationspotentiale der Industrie in Baden. Erste Ergebnisse einer Unternehmensbefragung. Arbeitspapier Regionalforschung 5, Fraunhofer ISI, Karlsruhe

Koschatzky, K., Zenker, A. (1999) Innovative Regionen in Ostdeutschland – Merkmale, Defizite, Potentiale. Arbeitspapier Regionalforschung 17, Fraunhofer ISI, Karlsruhe

Laranja, M. (1998) Entrepreneurial Innovation Networks: Small Firms' Contribution to Collective Innovation Efforts. In: During, W., Oakey, R. (eds.) New Technology-Based Firms in the 1990s, Vol. IV, Paul Chapman, London, 62-70

Lawson, C., Lorenz, E. (1999) Collective Learning, Tacit Knowledge and Regional Innovative Capacity. Regional Studies 33, 305-317

Le Bars, A., Mangematin, V., Nesta, L. (1998) Innovation in SME's: The Missing Link. Proceedings of the High-Technology Small Firms Conference, 6th Annual International Conference Vol. 1, University of Twente, Twente, 307-324

Licht, G., Kukuk, M., Kuhlmann, S., Hipp, Ch., Münt, G., Smid, M., Hess, D. (1996) Innovationstätigkeit im Dienstleistungssektor. Empirische Analyse der Erhebung 1995. ZEW, ISI, Mannheim, Karlsruhe

Meyer-Krahmer, F. (1985) Innovation Behaviour and Regional Indigenous Potential. Regional Studies 19, 523-534

Miles, I., Kastrinos, N., Flanagan, K., Bildebeek, R., Den Hertog, P., Huntink, W., Bouman, M. (1994) Knowledge Intensive Business Services: Their Roles as Users, Carriers and Sources of Innovation. PREST, Manchester

Muller, E., Zenker, A. (1998) Analysis of Innovation-oriented Networking Between R&D Intensive Small Firms and Knowledge Intensive Business Services. Proceedings of the High-Technology Small Firms Conference, 6th Annual International Conference, Vol. 1, University of Twente, Twente, 175-203

Nelson, R., Winter, S.G. (1982) An Evolutionary Theory of Economic Change. Harvard University Press, Cambridge, MA
Nonaka, I. (1994) A Dynamic Theory of Organizational Knowledge Creation. Organization Science 5, 14-37
Pavitt, K., Townsend, J., Robson, M. (1987) The Size Distribution of Innovating Firms in the UK: 1945-1983. Journal of Industrial Economics 35, 297-316
Pfirrmann, O. (1994) Die Bestimmung Regionaler Innovationsdisparitäten. Raumforschung und Raumordnung 52, 203-211
Piore, M.J., Sabel, C.F. (1984) The Second Industrial Divide. Possibilities for Prosperity. Basic Books, New York
Powell, W.W. (1990) Neither Market nor Hierarchy. Network Forms of Organization. In: Staw, B.M., Cummings, L.L. (eds.) Research in Organizational Behavior, Vol. 12. JAI Press, Greenwich, 295-336
Pyke, F., Becattini, G., Sengenberger, W. (1990) Industrial Districts and Inter-Firm Co-Operation in Italy. International Institute for Labour Studies, Geneva
Ritter, T. (1998) Innovationserfolg durch Netzwerkkompetenz. Effektives Management von Unternehmensnetzwerken. Gabler Verlag, Wiesbaden
Rosenberg, N. (1990) Why do Firms do Basic Research (With their Own Money)? Research Policy 19, 165-174
Rothwell, R. (1989) Small Firms, Innovation and Industrial Change. Small Business Economics 1, 51-64
Saviotti, P.P. (1998) On the Dynamics of Appropriability, of Tacit and of Codified Knowledge. Research Policy 26, 843-856
Schumpeter, J.A. (1911) Theorie der Wirtschaftlichen Entwicklung. München [8th edition: (1993) Duncker Humblot, Berlin]
Schumpeter, J.A. (1942) Capitalism, Socialism and Democracy. New York [German version, 4th edition: (1975) Francke, München]
Scott, A.J. (1995) The Geographic Foundations of Industrial Performance. Competition and Change 1, 51-66
Sengenberger, W., Pyke, F. (1992) Industrial Districts and Local Economic Regeneration. Research and Policy Issues. In: Pyke, F., Sengenberger, W. (eds.) Industrial Districts and Local Economic Regeneration. International Institute for Labour Studies, Geneva, 3-30
Sternberg, R. (1998) Innovierende Industrieunternehmen und ihre Einbindung in intraregionale versus interregionale Netzwerke. Raumforschung und Raumordnung 56, 288-298
Storper, M. (1995) The Resurgence of Regional Economies, Ten Years Later: The Region as a Nexus of Untraded Interdependencies. European Urban and Regional Studies 2, 191-221
Storper, M. (1997) The Regional World. Territorial Development in a Global Economy. New York, Guilford Press
Strambach, S. (1995) Wissensintensive unternehmensorientierte Dienstleistungen. Netzwerke und Interaktion. Am Beispiel des Rhein-Neckar-Raumes. Lit, Münster
Tether, B.S. (1998) Small and Large Firms: Sources of Unequal Innovations? Research Policy 27, 725-745
Tether, B.S., Smith, I.J., Thwaites, A.T. (1997) Smaller Enterprises and Innovation in the UK: The SPRU Innovations Database Revisited. Research Policy 26, 19-32
Wood, P. (1995) Business Services, the Management of Change and Regional Development in the UK: A Corporate Client Perspective. Working Paper Series 23, University of Cambridge, Cambridge

12 R&D Co-Operation Between Public Research Institutions: Magnitude, Motives and Spatial Dimension

Michael Fritsch[1] and Christian Schwirten[2]
[1] Faculty of Economics and Business Administration, Bergakademie Freiberg
[2] Bundesverband deutscher Banken, Berlin

12.1 Introduction

Universities and other kinds of publicly funded research institutions constitute important knowledge sources for innovation activities in private firms[1]. A vast body of theoretical literature has analysed the relationship between publicly funded research institutions and the private sector (see for example Bonaccorsi and Piccaluga 1994; Etzkowitz 1998; Gee 1993; Lee 1996; Onida and Malerba 1989). Correspondingly, numerous empirical studies have demonstrated that public research establishments do not exist in 'ivory tower' isolation, but are to a considerable degree involved in private sector innovation activities (see Audretsch and Stephan 1996; Faulkner and Senker 1994; Fritsch and Schwirten 1999; Mansfield 1995; Mansfield and Lee 1996; Meyer-Krahmer and Schmoch 1998; Van Dierdonck *et al.* 1990).

However, not all the knowledge transferred from a particular research institution to a firm is generated by the research institution itself. Clearly, there is not only a division of innovative labour between public research institutions and private firms, but also between different public research establishments. Researchers working in publicly funded institutions like universities usually share the knowledge they have generated with other researchers via publications or presentations and discussions at conferences. In many cases, public research establishments co-operate closely and create knowledge jointly. However, until now there has been little investigation of co-operation within the academic sector

[1] The term 'publicly funded research institutions' encompasses all research establishment that are financed to a considerable degree by the state. In Germany this includes all universities and *Fachhochschulen* (universities with a particular focus on applied studies in engineering, business and other subjects areas) as well as non-university research institutes like those of the Max-Planck or the Fraunhofer Society which are not part of the higher education system.

(see Georghiou 1998; Geuna 1998; Katz and Martin 1997). This contribution aims to reduce the gap.

While most of the previous research in this field has concentrated on co-authored scientific papers that may represent the result of joint research, here we investigate research co-operation directly. Our data has been gathered through postal questionnaires in which we asked publicly funded research establishments about their co-operative relationships. In the next section, we give a brief description of the database. The empirical evidence presented in Section 12.3 concentrates on three issues: a) the frequency of co-operation between public research establishments and reasons for non-collaboration, b) the number of collaborators and their spatial distribution, and c) the motives for research co-operation with other public research institutions. Finally, in Section 12.4 some conclusions are to drawn concerning the division of labour within the sector of publicly funded research.

12.2 Database

Our analysis is based on data gathered by postal questionnaires sent to publicly funded research establishments in three German regions.[1] The main aim of this survey was to investigate the role of public research institutions in regional innovation systems. It focused particularly on the importance of spatial proximity for a division of innovative labour within innovation systems and on differences with regard to the impact of public research institutions between the regions examined. These three regions all have a long-standing manufacturing tradition, but vary in several respects:[2]

- Baden, the western part of the State of Baden-Wuerttemberg, is a rather prosperous region characterised by far above-average performance with regard to innovation. The region has a reputation for possessing a network of transfer institutions which function well and facilitate knowledge flows between academic institutions and private sector firms, as well as co-operative networks

---

[1] The study was designed as a joint project involving four teams, all founded by the Deutsche Forschungsgemeinschaft. The research institutions and their respective project leaders are: Department of Economic Geography at the University of Hannover (Prof. Dr. Ludwig Schätzl), Department of Economic and Social Geography at the University of Cologne (Prof. Dr. Rolf Sternberg), Fraunhofer Institute of System Analysis and Innovation Research in Karlsruhe (Dr. Knut Koschatzky, Prof. Dr. Frieder Meyer-Krahmer) and the Faculty of Economics and Business Administration at the Technical University Bergakademie Freiberg, Research Unit Innovation Economics (Prof. Dr. Michael Fritsch). In addition to the survey of public research institutions, separate questionnaires have been sent out to manufacturing enterprises and suppliers of business-oriented services in the regions as a base for investigating the role of these types of actors in the division of innovative labour.

[2] For a detailed analysis of the innovation performance in these three regions, see Fritsch, *et al.* 1999.

among private firms (Cooke 1996; Heidenreich and Krauss 1998; Semlinger 1993). Baden is recognised as having a distinguished entrepreneurial culture. The share of small establishments is considerably above the national average.

- The region Hannover-Brunswick-Goettingen comprises most of the State of Lower Saxony which, like Baden, is located in West Germany. The region has a high share of employment in 'old' large scale industries (e.g. automobiles, steel), so the proportion of employment in new, innovative industries is comparatively low. Despite various policy attempts to improve innovation performance in this region, the innovation system is said to have considerable deficiencies (Schasse 1995).
- Saxony is one of the new German States that, until 1990, formed the socialist German Democratic Republic (GDR), which was characterised by a centrally planned economic system. The region has a long tradition in manufacturing, particularly in the mechanical engineering industry. Under the socialist regime, the region was dominated by very large and relatively inflexible economic entities that were then split up into smaller units during the privatisation process that took place after German unification in 1990.

The questionnaire was sent out to universities, *Fachhochschulen* and to publicly funded non-university research institutions. There are important differences between these three types of institutions. At the universities, research is conducted by professors as well as by teaching assistants (usually with a contract up to five years) and Ph.D. students. Quite frequently, grants from other public sector institutions or contracts with private firms provide additional research capacity.

Professors at the *Fachhochschulen* have considerably higher teaching loads than university professors and therefore have much less time for conducting research. Furthermore, there are almost no teaching assistants employed and no Ph.D. students, since *Fachhochschulen* are not entitled to grant a doctoral degree. The primary mission of the *Fachhochschulen* is education of students, mainly in the field of engineering and business administration. Ambitious research agendas are rather the exception at these institutions.

The non-university research institutions (excluding the *Fachhochschulen)* comprise several types, such as establishments belonging to the Max-Planck and the Fraunhofer-Society. Some of these institutions are financed primarily by appropriations from the state, while others rely more on research contracts with private firms or compete for public research funds. Even though a certain number of Ph.D. students conduct their research at such institutions, in general non-university research institutions are little involved in educational activities.

Due to resource constraints, our survey included only those scientific disciplines which could be expected *a priori* to be of high potential relevance for innovation activities in private firms.[1] At the universities and the *Fachhochschulen*, each

---

[1] These disciplines were: architecture, construction engineering, biology, chemistry, computer sciences, energy/environment/traffic, electronics, geology, mechanical engineering, material sciences, mathematics, medicine, physics, process engineering and economics.

professorship in the selected disciplines received one questionnaire. Non-university research institutions where asked to fill in one questionnaire for the whole establishment.[1] The information gathered focussed on the extent and structure of the research activities and in particular R&D co-operation with private firms as well as with other public research establishments (the questionnaire is reproduced in Fritsch *et al.* 1997).

Our data set comprises 1,020 responses classified as 'usable'. Of these questionnaires, 709 (69.5 percent of all responses) were from professorships at universities, 208 (20.4 percent) from professors at the *Fachhochschulen* and 103 (10.1 percent) from non-university public research institutions.[2] The overall response rate amounted to about 41 percent.

12.3 Empirical Evidence

Frequency of Co-Operation

In 80.4 percent of all cases in our sample, the respondents stated that they had collaborated with other public research establishments in the period 1993-95.[3] This rate was highest (96.1 percent) for the non-university research institutions followed by the universities, for which the proportion amounted to 85.9 percent. However, only slightly more than half of the professors at *Fachhochschulen* (53.8 percent) reported inter-research collaboration in the respective period. This low percentage can be mainly explained by the high teaching load and scarcity of research resources at this type of research institution. The largest difference between scientific disciplines with regard to co-operation with other research institutions occurred at the universities, where inter-public research collaboration was reported most frequently in biology/chemistry/medicine (94 percent of all responses). The lowest share of co-operating establishments was found in the field of economics (only 67 percent of all cases).

---

[1] These institutions vary considerably in size. To send more than one questionnaire to each institution would have required the identification of the appropriate subentities. Unfortunately, this was not possible due to the limited resources available for the research project. We account for differences between the various types of research institutions by reporting all the results separately for universities, *Fachhochschulen*, and non-university public research institutions.

[2] The 709 responses from universities consist of 172 from Hannover, 159 from Baden, and 378 from Saxony. The majority of responses from *Fachhochschulen* (164 cases) came from Saxony, only 44 were from the Hannover region. With respect to the non-university research institutions, Hannover accounts for 30 responses, Baden for 27, and Saxony for 46.

[3] In our questionnaire, 'collaboration' comprised a variety of activities: general information exchange, generation of new ideas, joint conduct of research projects, personnel transfer, and common usage of laboratory equipment.

Table 12.1 Reasons for non-collaboration with other research institutions

Reason for non-collaboration	Percentage of non-collaborating research institutions
No necessity	44.0
Harmonisation too difficult	23.2
Other research establishments are more competitors than partners	20.2
Unusual in our field of research	14.9
Others	31.0

The non co-operating research institutes were asked why they had not collaborated with other publicly funded research establishments (see Table 12.1). In 44.0 percent of these cases, respondents stated that they simply felt no necessity to do so. This answer was given least frequently by the professors at the *Fachhochschulen,* who seem to feel the greatest pressure for co-operation, while none of the non co-operating extra-university institutes considered this a reason for non co-operation. Of all non co-operating establishments in our sample, only 23.2 percent refrained from collaboration because of difficulties with regard to harmonisation or co-ordination. None of the extra-university institutes mentioned this as a reason for non co-operation.

20.2 percent of the respondents that had no co-operative relationship with other public research institutes replied that one reason for not collaborating has been that other research establishments are perceived as being competitors rather than partners. However, there are interesting differences between the three types of research institutions. At the *Fachhochschulen*, only 15.4 percent of the professors gave this reason for not co-operating. In contrast, 50.0 percent of the extra-university research institutes regarded other public research establishments more as competitors than potential partners. This can be explained in part by the need of many non-university research institutes to earn a relatively high proportion of their budgets through research contracts with private firms or by competing with other research establishments for public funds.

Only 14.9 percent of all non co-operating establishments cited as a reason for not collaborating the fact that collaboration is unusual in the respective research field. Remarkably, none of the non-university institutes mentioned this motive. The share or university professors who found collaboration with other public research establishments unusual, was relatively high in the social sciences, in engineering sciences and in architecture, whilst this motive was largely unimportant in the fields of mathematics, physics, biology and in medicine. The most frequently named 'other motive' for non-collaboration were 'lack of time' or 'lack of resources'. In particular, professors at *Fachhochschulen* very often considered this a bottleneck for co-operation with other research institutes.

Number and Geographic Distribution of Co-Operation Partners

The number of co-operating partners does vary significantly between the different types of institutions that maintain collaborative relationships with other publicly funded research establishments. On average (median value) university professors collaborated with six partners (see Table 12.2). In Saxony the number of co-operation partners was slightly lower than in the other regions. Professors at *Fachhochschulen* had far fewer partners (only three), with no differences between Hannover and Saxony.[1] Not only did professors at *Fachhochschulen* co-operate less frequently with other public research institutions (as shown in the previous section), but when they co-operated, they also had a smaller number of partners. Thus, the integration of *Fachhochschul* professors within the scientific community appears to be weak in a double sense.

The rather large number of co-operation partners of non-university research institutions (14 partners on average) was to be expected due to the relatively large amount of research conducted there. Researchers in these institutions normally have no significant teaching load and are therefore able to devote a large proportion of their time to research. Moreover, many of the non-university research institutions have a larger number of personnel than professorships at a university or *Fachhochschule*.

Table 12.2 Number of co-operation partners in all regions (median values)

	Universities	Fachhochschulen	Non-university research institutions
Hannover	7	3	14
Baden	7	-	12.5
Saxony	6	3	15
All regions	6	3	14

One focus of our analysis was the importance of spatial proximity between co-operating research institutions. Fig. 12.1 shows the spatial distribution of the collaboration partners. The spatial categories that were used to characterise the location of co-operation partners were the 'same region', the 'rest of Germany' and 'abroad'.[2] Regarding *university professors*, Baden is the region with the most

[1] Differences between the three regions are greater when the mean is used instead of the median. The mean number of co-operation partners at universities (*Fachhochschulen*) is 15.9 (9.3) in Hannover, 10.6 (-) in Baden and 6.9 (4.7) in Saxony. Due to resource restrictions no questionnaires were sent to *Fachhochschulen* in Baden.

[2] It should be noted that in each of the regions, the category 'same region' had to be defined individually. In Saxony the region is identical with the Federal State of Saxony while the

widespread research networks geographically. In Baden, on average 42 percent of all co-operation partners were located abroad. Though the share of regional partners was similar to that of the other two regions (32 percent in Baden versus 32 percent in Hannover and 31 percent in Saxony), co-operative relationships of university professors in Baden were less spatially concentrated, since in the Baden survey the category 'same region' comprises an area roughly twice as large as in Saxony and Hannover (see note 1 on previous page).

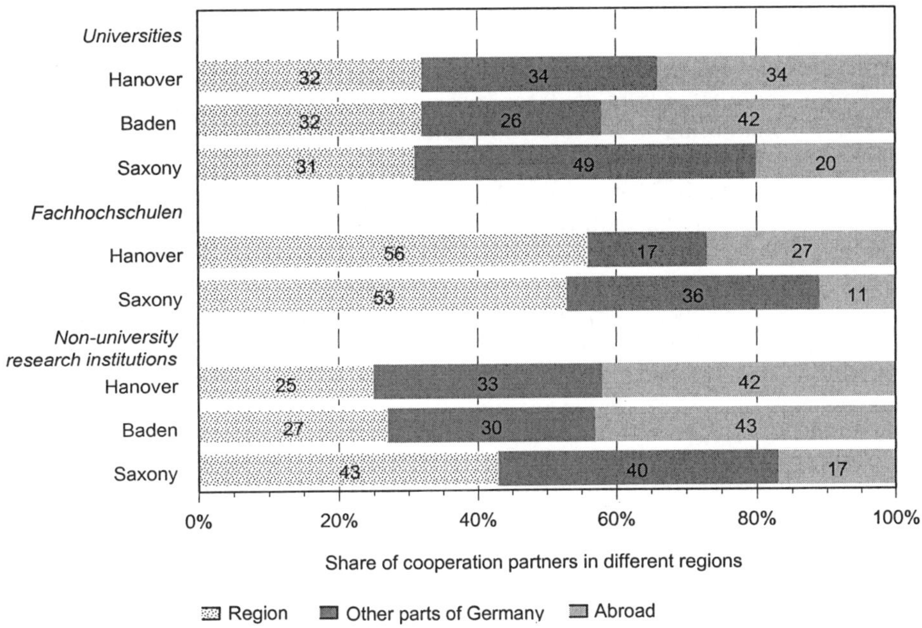

Fig. 12.1 Regional distribution of co-operation partners

The proportion of collaboration partners coming from within the same region was significantly higher in the case of *Fachhochschul* professors than university professors. More than 50 percent of the public research establishments which *Fachhochschul* professors collaborated with were located in the same region. The

---

Hannover region (Hannover-Brunswick-Göttingen) constitutes only a part of the respective Federal State (Lower Saxony). These two regions are of roughly comparable size. Hannover-Brunswick-Göttingen (Saxony) accounts for 5.1% (5.6%) of the German population and 4.3% (3.1%) of the manufacturing employment in Germany. In Baden the 'region' was defined as the state of Baden-Württemberg. This area is considerably bigger than the other two regions. It comprises 12.6% of Germany's population and 18.3% of the overall manufacturing employment (see Niedersächsisches Landesamt für Statistik 1996).

share of foreign co-operation partners was also comparatively low. Of all types of research institutions, the *non-university research establishments* had the smallest proportion of co-operation partners located in the same region. The highest share of regional partners (43 percent) was found in Saxony.

Interestingly, in Saxony all three types of research institutions had a much lower share of foreign partners than in the other two regions. This indicates that Saxony's public research establishments are rather poorly integrated into interregional contact and research networks. A possible consequence is that the ability of the regional innovation system to absorb internationally available scientific and technological knowledge may be relatively weak. The relatively low percentage of professorships in Saxony that maintain co-operative relationships with research establishments located abroad suggests a similar conclusion. While in Baden, about 80 percent of all professorships at universities had at least one co-operative relationship with a foreign research institution, this proportion is only 61 percent in Saxony. A similar picture arises with regard to professors at *Fachhochschulen*. In Saxony only 34 percent of the respondents reported some co-operation with foreign partners, while in Hannover this share amounted to 45 percent. The sharpest contrast with regard to the existence of co-operative relationships to partners located abroad could be found among the non-university research establishments. In Baden and in Hannover, nearly all of the non-university research establishments maintain at least one such relationship to a foreign partner (92 percent in Baden, 91 percent in Hannover), while this share amounted to only 61 percent in Saxony.

Motives for Collaboration

According to our survey, co-operation among research institutions is not driven by a single dominant motive (see Table 12.3). Generally, we found only very small differences between the three types of research institutions concerning the motives. The most important reason for maintaining a co-operative relationship to another research establishments was to gain ideas for own research projects. More than half of the respondents (55.3 percent) declared this issue to be very important.[1] Gaining access to financial sponsorship tied to co-operation with other public research establishments was the second most important motive (29.6 percent). Interestingly, of all three types of public research institutions in our sample, non-university research establishments stated most often that this motive (financial sponsorship) played some role though only few respondents in this category considered this motive to be *very* important. Obviously, for most of the non-university research establishments, public financial sponsorship did not seem to be a primary source of motivation for establishing a collaboration with other research institutions.

[1] For each motive the respondents could choose between three possible answers ('disagree', 'agree', 'strongly agree') regarding the importance of a motive.

Table 12.3 Motives for collaboration with other research institutions

Motives for collaboration	Percentage of research institutions that 'strongly agreed' with the respective motive
Ideas for research work / thematic additions	55.3
Financial sponsorship only available for collaboration	29.6
Insufficient own equipment or budget capacity	23.7
Raising own profile	12.1
Others	8.3

Overcoming insufficient research capacities by collaborating with other public research establishments played a very important role in only one out of four cases and, thus, turned out to be less significant than expected. This motive was slightly more important for the *Fachhochschulen,* but differences between the three types of research institutions were essentially small. Raising the institution's own profile ranked fourth among all motives for establishing co-operation with other research institutions and was therefore the least important motive. However, one cannot completely rule out that in some cases the responses with regard to this motive do not reflect the whole truth, as some respondents might not have wanted to appear vain! Furthermore, in several cases, being well known might also be a prerequisite for an agreement on joint projects rather than one of its consequences.

Those research institutions that co-operated with other public research institutes were asked to estimate the intensity of this collaboration[1] according to the different types of partners. One of the partner types given in the questionnaire was an 'alliance of research establishments commonly sponsored by the European Union'. Correlation analysis between the type of collaboration partner and the motives for collaboration yields some interesting results (Table 12.4).

We found that the motive 'to gain inspiration for research projects' was significantly and positively correlated with the intensity of collaboration with other research institutions, but not with the intensity of co-operation within EU supported research alliances. Accessing financial aid is significantly and positively correlated with both types of co-operation partners, though the correlation is somewhat stronger for EU-funded consortia. To compensate for insufficient research capacities seems of relatively little importance for co-operation within alliances sponsored by the EU, since we found a significantly negative correlation coefficient for the relationship between the rating of this motive and the intensity of collaboration in an EU-sponsored framework. Interestingly, the respective coefficient of correlation is significantly positive for co-operation with other

[1] This estimation was made using a three grade scale ranging from 'hardly intensive' to “very intensive”.

research institutions, indicating that these relationships are more appropriate for bridging resource gaps. No systematic relationship exists between the type of partner and the desire to become better known.

Table 12.4 Correlation coefficients between partner and reason for collaboration

	Alliance of research establishments sponsored by EU	Other research establishments
Importance of collaboration motive:		
Ideas for research work / thematic additions	0.01	0.21**
Financial sponsorship only available for collaboration	0.17**	0.11**
Insufficient own equipment or budget capacity	-0.10*	0.10*
Raising own profile	-0.02	0.08

Spearman rank-correlation coefficients, n = 560.
** statistically significant at the 1% level.
* statistically significant at the 5% level.

These results raise serious questions with regards to EU funding of research collaboration. Its aim is to make research more fruitful and productive by inducing co-operation, yet from our results it appears that such co-operation is mainly motivated by the availability of financial sponsorship and not by insufficient own capacity or the desire to gain additional knowledge on specific themes. On average, the co-operation induced did not help to overcome problems of insufficient capacity. Moreover, the scientific value added of EU sponsored co-operation appears to be rather low.

12.4 Conclusions

Our analysis shows that collaboration between research establishments is rather widespread, especially among university departments and non-university research institutions. A relatively high share of collaboration is located within the same region, indicating the importance of spatial proximity for establishing and maintaining co-operative relationships with other research institutions. However, a high concentration of co-operation partners within the same region may indicate a low degree of integration within international knowledge transfer networks and corresponding division of innovative labour. Therefore, the pronounced concentration of co-operation with regional research establishments which we found in Saxony may work as a disadvantage for the innovation system there.

Furthermore our study raises some serious questions concerning the EU funding of international alliances of research establishments. As desirable as international co-operation might be, to stimulate such collaboration in a reasonable way seems to be a difficult task. Our analysis shows that co-operation within EU-supported research alliances is strongly motivated by financial considerations, while the exchange of ideas would seem to play only a minor role.

References

Audretsch, D.B., Stephan, P.E. (1996) Company-Scientist Locational Links: The Case of Biotechnology. American Economic Review 86, 641-652

Bonaccorsi, A., Piccaluga, A. (1994) A Theoretical Framework for the Evaluation of University-Industry Relationships. R&D Management 24, 229-247

Cooke, P. (1996) The New Wave of Regional Innovation Networks: Analysis, Characteristics and Strategy. Small Business Economics 2, 159-171

Etzkowitz, H. (1998) The Norms of Entrepreneurial Science: Cognitive Effects of the New University-Industry Linkages. Research Policy 27, 823-833

Faulkner, W., Senker, J. (1994) Making Sense of Diversity: Public-Private Sector Research Linkage in Three Technologies. Research Policy 23, 673-695

Fritsch, M., Broeskamp, A., Schwirten, C. (1997) Oeffentliche Forschung im saechsischen Innovationssystem – Erste empirische Ergebnisse. Working Paper 97/2, Faculty of Economics and Business Administration, Technical University Bergakademie, Freiberg

Fritsch, M., Franke, G., Schwirten, C. (1999) Innovation in Manufacturing Industry – An East West comparison. In: Fritsch, M., Brezinski, H. (eds.) Innovation and Technological Change in Eastern Europe: Pathways to Industrial Recovery. Edward Elgar, Cheltenham 167-183

Fritsch, M., Schwirten, C. (1999) Enterprise-University Co-operation and the Role of Public Research Institutions in Regional Innovation Systems. Industry and Innovation 6, 69-83

Gee, R.E. (1993) Technology Transfer Effectiveness in University-Industry Cooperative Research. International Journal of Technology Management 8, 652-668

Georghiou, L. (1998) Global Co-operation in Research. Research Policy 27, 611-626

Geuna, A. (1998) Determinants of University Participation in EU-funded R&D Co-operative Projects. Research Policy 26, 677-687

Heidenreich, M., Krauss, G. (1998) The Baden-Württemberg Production and Innovation Regime: Past Successes and New Challenges. In: Braczyk, H., Cooke, P., Heidenreich, M. (eds.) Regional Innovations Systems. UCL Press, London

Katz, J.S, Martin, B.R. (1997) What is Research Collaboration? Research Policy 26, 1-18

Lee, Y.S. (1996) 'Technology Transfer' and the Research University: A Search for the Boundaries of University-Industry Collaboration. Research Policy 25, 843-863

Mansfield, E. (1995) Academic Research Underlying Industrial Innovations: Sources, Characteristics and Financing. Review of Economics and Statistics 77, 55-65

Mansfield, E., Lee, J.-Y. (1996) The Modern University: Contributor to Industrial Innovation and Recipient of Industrial R&D Support. Research Policy 25, 1047-1058

Meyer-Krahmer, F., Schmoch, U. (1998) Science-Based Technologies: University-Industry Interactions in Four Fields. Research Policy 27, 835-851

Niedersächsisches Landesamt für Statistik (1996) Kreiszahlen: Ausgewählte Regionaldaten – Ausgabe 1996, Niedersächsisches Landesamt für Statistik, Hannover

Onida, F., Malerba, F. (1989) R&D Co-Operation Between Industry, Universities and Research Organizations in Europe. Technovation 9, 131-195

Schasse, U. (1995) Produkt- und Prozess-innovationen in Niedersachsen (Product and Process Innovation in Lower Saxony). In: Ulrich Schasse and Joachim Wagner (eds.) Erfolgreich produzieren in Niedersachsen, Hannover: Niedersächsisches Institut für Wirtschaftsforschung (NIW-Vortragsreihe, Bd. 10), 61-82

Semlinger, K. (1993) Economic Development and Industrial Policy in Baden-Württemberg: Small Firms in a Benevolent Environment. European Planning Studies 1, 435-463

Van Dierdonck, R., Debackere, K., Engelen B. (1990) University-Industry Relationships: How Does the Belgian Academic Community Feel About it? Research Policy 19, 551-566

13 Creative Milieus and Regional Networks: Local Strategies and Implementation in Case Studies in Bavaria

Jörg Maier and Frank Obermaier
University of Bayreuth

13.1 Preliminary Considerations

Changing conditions in the economy, in technology and in society are requiring new creative ways to achieve competitive development. Since the period of economic construction which ended with the 1960s, there has in Europe been a noticeable decline in the growth potential to be shared around. This situation has been exacerbated by the competition created within the Single Market due to the opening of borders and the elimination of international barriers to factor mobility. All this has resulted in the so-called 'competition of the regions'.

In terms of the strategic concepts behind regional policy, it has led to a shift from a growth-oriented system to a more stock-oriented endogenous system. High priority is given to the ability of regional enterprises to cope with structural change through their innovative capacity. This led in the 1980s to the emergence of 'innovation-oriented' regional policy (Ewers 1990). The core of this strategy is to accelerate the diffusion of innovations, even in rural areas, through the decentralised provision of hard infrastructure, such as centres of technology transfer, universities and public research institutions, as well as through support to small and medium-sized businesses (SMEs). Experience with technology and innovation centres in the new Federal States (see Franz 1996) show that the mere existence of infrastructure facilities is not sufficient to generate success in innovative development.

In the more recent approaches, the role of the regional surroundings in favouring the innovative capacity of enterprises has been increasingly acknowledged, stimulated by successful development in regions like the 'Third Italy' or Silicon Valley (see e.g. Hahn *et al* 1994; Hassink 1994). These areas have illustrated the importance not only of sound infrastructure, but also the potential and ability of a region to exploit it. In this context, the activity of businesses, politicians and other designers of regional development, comes increasingly into focus. According to this perspective, people do not act in isolation, but within their economic and social 'milieu'. In this situation, classical regional research approaches lack explanatory power in comparison with concepts which prescribe an independent function for the milieu factor, accompanied by strategies which attempt to further the qualitative attraction of the area in the form of a 'culturalised regional policy' (Häußermann and Siebel 1993).

13.2 Creative Milieus as a New Approach in Regional Research

The 15 research teams belonging to GREMI (Groupe de Recherche Européen sur les Milieux Innovateurs) have been working since 1985 on the development of the milieu approach. This approach focuses on the success of regions in coping with structural change, emphasising in particular the significance of the regional environment in the development of innovation-directed behaviour by businesses. The potential for technological change and the nature of the regional milieu are perceived as being closely bound together (Camagni 1991a). The concept has been described as the "embedding of businesses in their regional environment" (Grabher 1993b, p. 4).

In contrast to the traditional view of economics, GREMI has defined the milieu as a central factor in the development of innovation, rather than just an exogenous background condition (Bramanti and Senn 1991). Not only are regional facilities and structural characteristics seen as crucial, but the way in which they are exploited is also a vital element. This is positively influenced by the existence of 'networking' between facilities and actors in a region (Fromhold-Eisebith 1995). The economic success of individual regions is explained in terms of the social interactions, synergy effects and collective learning processes which characterise a milieu: "Creativity and continuous innovation are seen as the result of a collective learning process, fed by such social phenomena as inter-generational transfer of know-how, imitation of successful practices and technological innovations, interpersonal face-to-face contacts, formal or informal co-operation between firms, tacit circulation of commercial, financial or technological information" (Camagni 1991a, p. 1).

'Networking', as a form of organisation between the individual actors, is a precondition if the milieu is to exercise an influence on the innovative ability of the actors. A fundamental feature of networks is the co-operation of actors who have the same objectives, and whose co-operation is characterised by an atmosphere of trust, without sacrificing their independence. Thus, networks are located between two extremes: at one pole there is a completely symmetrical exchange relationship between equal partners, which can be broken at any time, and at the other, there is a one-sided dependence and power relationship within a fixed hierarchy (Kaman 1991).

As mentioned above, networks are nourished by the existence of immaterial elements such as trust, latent knowledge and a common consciousness of values. Given these preconditions, the positive effects of a creative milieu can develop, including the reduction of uncertainty in decision-making and the generation of common learning effects, which can lead to the creation of specific regional know-how.

In this chapter, we focus on regional milieu conditions as decisive determinants of the regional ability to adapt and innovate. The successful functioning of a milieu lies in the creativity of the regional context within which the businesses are embedded. The kinds of innovation which are of interest to us are therefore the new features of the regional milieu (e.g. the establishment of a technological transfer facility), processes of political decision-making (e.g. new negotiation solutions) and new forms of organisation. In other words, the factors which qualitatively describe the locational factors of the region, and which Ratti has called 'supporting space' (Ratti 1991). By this expression, he meant the relational framework of businesses which falls outside the normal market relations regarding the acquisition of production factors (e.g. personnel, information, know-how, capital) and strategic relationships with partners, competitors or customers (e.g. exchange of information, cooperation, strategic alliances). As shown in Fig. 12.1, supporting space overlaps the usual framework of the functional relationships 'production space' (in particular the spatial distribution of products) and 'market space' (the nature of the market in question). It also includes strategic relationships with regional authorities, institutions and facilities.

In this context, there is an interesting relationship between innovative behaviour and strategic areas of business. Whereas local relationships are of prime importance particularly for 'incremental innovations' (improvements), adaptive innovations require an orientation towards the 'market space', and radical innovations need an orientation towards the 'production space' (Ratti 1991).

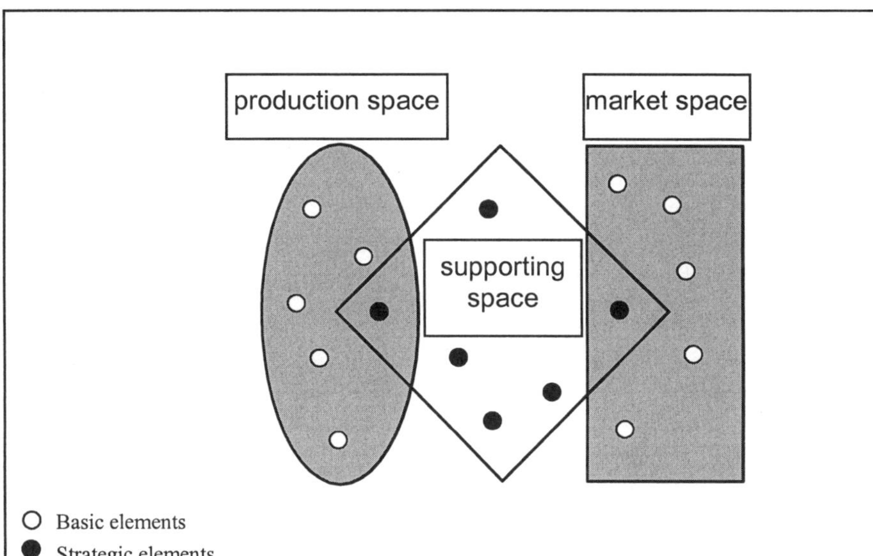

Source: Adapted from Ratti 1991.

Fig. 13.1 Strategic activity areas of enterprises

Bramanti and Senn (1991) view these connections in a dynamically evolutionary way. Using the concept of production life cycle, they claim that businesses apply different strategies and, thus, fall back on different strategic areas, with the type of innovation activity following the above pattern. Seen from the point of view of economic policy, innovations evolving from local relationships would thus be of little value to businesses at the end of their life cycle. The question therefore arises whether promotion of the supporting space should be an objective.

The supporting space is especially important for SMEs, as they often do not have access to the resources which would enable them to adopt innovations on their own. It acts as a source of information, particularly for radical innovations. There are three important conditions for the development of supporting space: a particular economic structure (e.g. the size and field of businesses), positive locational factors (e.g. transport infrastructure, quality of life) and synergy effects (e.g. research facilities, risk capital, availability of staff) (Ratti 1991).

The regional work culture, which can be defined in a simplified way as the attitude of the population towards work, is crucial with regard to acquiring qualified personnel. The existence of training programmes is, of course, an important factor. However, many professional schools provide specialist knowledge, rather than across-the-board management knowledge. This has shown itself to be a handicap, especially in the old industrialised areas such as Upper Franconia with its ceramics and textile industries or the Swiss Jura region with its clock-making industry. The concentration of training within traditional areas of knowledge can hinder the development of new knowledge and new requirements, e.g. micro-electronics in process technology or strategic market research for the placement of products (for comments on the Jura region, see Glasmeier 1994).

When capital is required, the acceptance of risk by capital providers is an important factor in a creative milieu. If the establishment of new partnerships is necessary, the existence of entrepreneurial qualities can be important. Here, the institutional landscape, including administrative, educational and research facilities, is significant. But although the number of such institutions in a region is significant in achieving the necessary 'critical mass', it is the quality of such facilities which is the decisive element. An open-minded public administration working according to modern management principles can be more helpful for SMEs than tradition-bound chambers of commerce, 'ivory tower' universities or large research facilities conducting basic research. The critical feature of these institutions it would seem is not so much their function as technology providers, as their quality of open-mindedness towards ideas and new suggestions, together with a lack of restriction on the transfer of information.

A creative milieu should, therefore, not be viewed solely from the perspective of technology-orientated innovative networks, but rather in terms of the ability of regional actors and decision-makers to network with businesses and research facilities in order to exploit and develop existing potential. Rural and peripheral regions, in particular, often do not possess the material preconditions to establish technology-orientated milieus due to their lack of facilities and infrastructure. In densely populated urban areas, it is more likely that these preconditions will exist, but here the boundaries of the networks are relevant. This can lead to a situation where an alignment towards technology-promoting structures is not always desired or strenuously pursued, and established social structures are marginalised by networks, as shown by Grabher in the case of the Ruhr (Grabher 1993a).

13.3 Milieu Factors

The discussion in this section is directed to the question of which milieu factors are relevant with regard to their empirical measurability, since there is often a certain lack of clarity of definition concerning the milieu approach. This question is only briefly mentioned in empirical studies on creative milieus (see e.g. Camagni 1991b; Maillat *et al.* 1994, Grotz and Braun 1993, Maillat *et al.* 1995; Fromhold-Eisebith 1995). These studies focus mainly on the results which are intended to assist the further development of the milieu approach. Fromhold-Eisebith (1995) correctly require attention to be dedicated to the details of definitions as an essential element of the milieu approach.

It is difficult to achieve a complete and homogenous definition of all relevant factors, since research interests in the framework of the milieu approach are too diverse. For example, while the early work of the GREMI group concentrated on the significance of innovation networks (see Aydalot and Keeble 1988), German economic geography concentrates on high-tech regions (e.g. Sternberg 1995) and only the more recent work by GREMI is beginning to give greater emphasis to the importance of the milieu (Camagni 1995). We thus discuss milieu relevant factors primarily in terms of:

- innovation and contact behaviour of enterprises,
- material and institutional factors of the regional milieu,
- immaterial factors,
- network connections in the regional milieu and effects as indicators of a creative milieu.

Innovation and Contact Behaviour of Businesses

A question which is crucial for the development of a creative milieu is to what extent enterprises, as actual innovators, are 'milieu capable', i.e. to what extent they are interwoven with the regional milieu. In classic examples, such as the 'Third Italy' or Silicon Valley, it has been shown that small and medium sized enterprises (SMEs), in particular, are embedded in intensive network relationships which stimulate the development of innovations. The starting point is primarily how willing the enterprises are to pursue an innovation strategy designed for co-operation and networking. The reason for such an innovation strategy is founded in the innovation process. According to Malecki (1990, p. 123), following the considerations of Schumpeter, this is not necessarily linear, and is often discontinuous. However, SMEs in particular have difficulty generating the money to pay for the necessary research and development (R&D) to carry out an innovation, e.g. to support R&D departments. Malecki in fact attributed great importance to informal gains of information: learning-by-doing and learning-by-using as cost reducing information strategies. At the core of this 'externalised' innovation strategy is the establishment of contact networks with providers of technology and information, such as facilities for technological transfer, (regional) economic associations and unions, or data banks. With this externalised innovation behaviour, contacts established by the entrepreneurs gain significance. If these behavioural patterns are oriented at a regional level, the function of a creative milieu in reducing uncertainties and generating local learning processes can be achieved. Hence inclusion within supra-regional innovation networks needs to be taken into consideration as a precondition for gaining external knowledge (Malmberg *et al.* 1996).

Inclusion of the regional level in the innovation and contact behaviour of enterprises therefore presents an important precondition for a creative milieu. Enterprises which make little use of their regional environment to gain information can only make a small contribution to the development of the creative milieu and are not 'milieu capable'. An example of this would be enterprises possessing internalised' innovation facilities, e.g. their own R&D departments, or which do not have relationships with the regional environment, or whose contact partners are chosen at random, according to strictly functional rather than spatial aspects. By contrast, enterprises looking for contacts at a regional level and which therefore contribute to the diffusion of latent knowledge – the 'tacit' knowledge of a region – are described as milieu capable.

Material and Institutional Factors of a Regional Milieu

In the literature, the material factors regarding a regional milieu are Maillat *et al.* 1994. The term 'material factors' includes those factors which constitute the regional starting conditions, i.e. the structural preconditions which form the framing conditions for a creative milieu. The distinction between material factors and institutional factors is not clear-cut and is not elucidated in the literature (see the criticism by Fromhold-Eisebith 1995). Nonetheless, it is possible to regard the structural (economic) starting conditions as including the material factors and the facilities provided by the supporting space (Ratti 1991), i.e. those facilities in a region which help to generate, process and achieve regional innovations and economic performance, as defined by institutional factors.[1]

[1] Here, a material term for institutions is being applied. Factors such as 'communal values and perceptions of norms' which also belong to the concept of 'institutional thickness' (Amin and Thrift 1994a), fall under 'immaterial milieu factors'.

Immaterial Factors

Whereas it seems feasible to establish the definition of the material factors of a regional milieu, in the sense of regional starting conditions and institutional factors, the definition of other important factors belonging to the milieu approach is more difficult. For example, determining the constitution, mentality or attitudes of regional actors towards development is problematic: these are factors which give information about the quality of the 'supporting space'. In this context, it is necessary to ask to what extent region-specific mentalities or historical developments, for instance, exercise an influence on the regional milieu, regarded as a common economic and work culture. These aspects have hitherto been little discussed in existing works on creative milieus. A closely related question is how the effect of such groups can be qualitatively evaluated. One has to fall back on the terms 'willingness to deal' and 'development consciousness' as the basis for a regional problem solving competence.

Developing the conditions for high economic dynamism seems to require a corresponding basic social attitude in addition to a market-orientated structure and appropriate economic policy. This basic attitude cannot be taken for granted. Furthermore, it is often cultivated via a long-term historical process, from which a particular work and economic culture has evolved.

Permanent, long-term and current influences all mould and affect the individual and also collective modes of thought and perspective (Miegel 1991). The climate or specific geographical position of a mountain region, for instance, can be regarded as a permanent influence. Historically determined power structures and the religious atmosphere would be listed among the long-term influences. The current politics or prevailing laws belong to the current influences. The fact that these influencing factors assume different forms, depending on the region, mean that regionally-diverse mentalities and attitudes evolve. These different modes of thought and perception express themselves through regionally-diverse tendencies and behaviour regarding one's profession, family or income. The tendencies and behaviour solidify into a 'culture'.

Such an economic and work culture expresses itself in attitudes to work (Grüske 1992). Individual attitudes towards performance, creativity, acceptance of risks, technological progress, and so on, are included here. When economically-relevant attributes are more developed in one region than in another, they will enable that area to achieve superior economic performance. Additional factors also play a role in the development of a region, e.g. structure, size of businesses, materials and infrastructure. Yet, generally speaking, the hard infrastructural factors that can be identified as ubiquitous resources can explain regional disparities only to a certain extent. "The quality of 'soft' locational factors, the quality of life offered by a region, the mentalities and the life styles of the population, the industrial relationships, the organisation of political institutions and their style of politics thus become crucial preconditions for successful regional development" (Häußermann and Siebel 1993, p. 219).

Buchholz (1995) is right when he criticises the notion that subjectivity when evaluating the factor economy and work culture limits its expressiveness and transferability. It is however difficult to precisely define the effect of individual factors on a creative milieu. A mixture of different work and economic cultures, as they are called by Buchholz, can cause the dominant mentalities in conurbations to be relativised. While taking these possible limitations into consideration, the population's attitude towards work, historical administrative developments or the individual willingness to perform can, nevertheless, be important qualitative determinants which help account for region-specific differences and, thus, influence the form of a creative milieu.

The question of development consciousness and the willingness to act within a region is closely connected to the features of an economy and the work culture (Derenbach 1988). But how does an active economy and work culture actually express itself? Does it attempt to reinforce its own position, leading inevitably to confrontation and barriers between actors, or is it used to encourage broad regional development? According to the creative milieu approach, the objective should be to achieve regional development, considering the predominant importance of community values or network connections. In contrast, in the economy and work culture, it is only particular people who design the developments, i.e. specific decision-makers are generally involved. The relevant circle of persons is thus limited to a small cross-section of actors who take decisions on behalf of the regional population.

Therefore, as a first step, it is necessary to define those persons considered as decision-makers regarding regional economic questions. Sociological studies in the US have dealt with this topic since the 1930s. It was for example developed by the Chicago School under the term 'community-power-group research' and deals with the influence of local elites on communal policy decisions (compare Maier and Kreitmayr 1979). In the 1980s, these descriptive approaches were extended to take into account the regional origin of decision-makers as a criterion for endogenous regional development in relation to regional self-confidence (compare Meier-Dallach 1987a, 1987b).

In the context of the discussion of the role of decision-makers in creative milieus, the findings of research on elite groups are insufficient. Questions such as the willingness to take decisions or risks, or those regarding attitudes to co-operation cannot be answered using this approach. Even though decision-makers may have a distinct regional consciousness, it cannot be concluded that they will take on a leading pro-active role. On the contrary, when using the term 'regional self-confidence' in the sense of 'identity', 'tradition consciousness', etc., there are overtones of a preservation mentality, which aims to retain the habitual and block the new. This leads to a lack of flexibility and willingness to consider external information and hence to redefine existing structures, which is necessary for innovative and adaptive ability. Consequently, it is personal factors in particular which define the role of decision-makers in the process of structural change. Following Derenbach (1988), social/psychological factors, e.g. development consciousness, willingness to act, and motivation, should be recognised as positive for the milieu.

Psychological or social criteria for decision-makers within a creative milieu approach indicate that it is desirable that they should have the ability to recognise and solve latent or manifest problems and, thus, to improve the innovation and adaptive capacity of the region. This ability to solve problems comprises two components (Runco 1994): problem finding and problem solving. In the literature on the topic of problem solving and creativity, the problem solving process begins with the definition of the problems (Franke 1980). But this implies that problems can be perceived and recognised as such. However, in so-called 'sclerotic' milieus (Läpple 1994) where the situation is complex, problems are often not acknowledged. They are perceived as a danger to the status quo, and are therefore 'ignored'. The starting point for the problem solving process is, thus, situated in the ability to search for and perceive problems. In order to emphasise the pro-active character of a creative milieu and its significance for the structural competitiveness of a region, it is important that not only the perception of problems, but also the identification of possible fields of action should be discussed, i.e. the initiative in regional development should be seized.

According to Derenbach, the perception of problems depends on individual, decision-forming behaviour. The general target policy in industrial society adopted by regions is that of job creation. At the same time, however, not every region possesses the same means for achieving such (pre-defined) targets. In order to escape this dilemma, there are three behavioural strategies which determine decisions from a social/psychological perspective (see Derenbach 1988, p. 261):

- escaping the situation (i.e. migration),
- resigned behaviour, allowing risky actions only when 'damage-limitation' is expected, or
- willingness to act, enabling targets to be reached through ideas and initiatives, despite disadvantageous situations.

Decisions are taken according to the chosen approach. The quality of the evaluation of regional potential and regional structures is an element which will determine whether regional development is positive or not. Regional decision-makers who aim at effective use of the potential of the region, offer better preconditions for positive regional development than decision-makers characterised by a resigned attitude. The possibility of developing a creative milieu is also influenced by the underlying attitude.

The functions of creativity and problem-solving processes are closely related. Creativity within the problem-solving process partly determines the quality of the output, regarding innovation and the adaptability of a region. Creativity can be perceived as the starting point for the ability to innovate: "Creativity refers to the generation of novel ideas – innovation to making money with them" (Schneider 1993, p. 87).

Anderson (1985) attempts to bring about a transfer of individual creativity-promoting conditions to the meso level of the region. In this context, he regards creativity as a 'social phenomenon'. According to this interpretation, creativity does not develop within organisations, but between organisations and consequently within a regional milieu. Taking the example of Vienna as the intellectual centre of Europe around the turn of the century, Anderson speaks of a 'creative region'. Creative regions are characterised by five features (Anderson 1985, p. 19):

- extensive existing competence,
- rich academic and cultural activities,
- dense region-internal and externally oriented communicative strands,
- communal perception following dissatisfied needs, and
- general structural instabilities which lead to communally perceived insecurities.

The concept of Anderson, however, leaves it unclear to what extent these conditions actually lead creative output to develop. The above features could actually result in such a milieu cutting itself off, due to the pressure created by the instabilities and insecurities mentioned. Whether it did so would depend on how far the individual micro conditions in favour of creativity were activated in the face of this pressure. Creativity at the regional meso level thus depends on the willingness of regional actors to take initiatives and the simultaneous design of individual micro conditions in order to generate ideas – if it is accepted that creativity originally takes place at the micro level, i.e. of the individual or small group.

13.4 Empirical Analysis

The Methodological Approach

The significance of milieu factors for regional development has been analysed within the framework of four case studies in Bavaria. The empirical investigations are based on the analysis of statistical documents and literature, a written questionnaire sent to businesses, as well as interviews carried out by experts with representatives of political bodies, administration, institutions, businesses and associations. The selection of the regions was orientated primarily by questions regarding the 'critical mass' of creative milieus, as well as the possible overlapping of several milieus in one location.

The 'critical mass' refers to a certain settlement size which allows one to assume a high degree of centrality and the corresponding facilities. To our knowledge, critical mass has not been defined exactly in this sense in the literature. The boundaries can only be drawn in a normative way, but this conforms with the case study character of the investigation. According to the Regional Policy Plan for Bavaria, the critical mass should correspond to medium-sized centres, with a threshold of at least 7,300 non-agricultural jobs. The minimum is also determined by the requirements for classification as medium-sized centres of the Regional Policy Plan for Bavaria – among others, the presence of a grammar school, trade schools, facilities for major cultural and social events, craft firms with varied goods, authorities and courts, a supply of free-lance professionals and services in different economic fields, a range of shopping options for satisfying higher demand for goods (see LEP Bavaria 1994, p.44). Subsequently, the regions under consideration were regarded as being sufficiently large even if they lacked academic or technology facilities. The districts of Deggendorf in Lower Bavaria and Kulmbach in Upper Franconia were selected.

In order to investigate whether more than one milieu overlapped in a single location, cases have to be selected which possess a high 'milieu potential' with regard to human capital, institutions etc. due to their size (measured in terms of population). Thus, cities with well over 100,000 population which also possess supra-regional functions (e.g. in education, administration, economics, politics), can be considered. One can assume that overlapping milieus are most likely to be found in cities due to the concentration of these functions. Transferred to Bavaria, this would mean that three possible examples exist, i.e. Munich, Nuremberg and Augsburg. In this case, Augsburg and Nuremberg were selected.

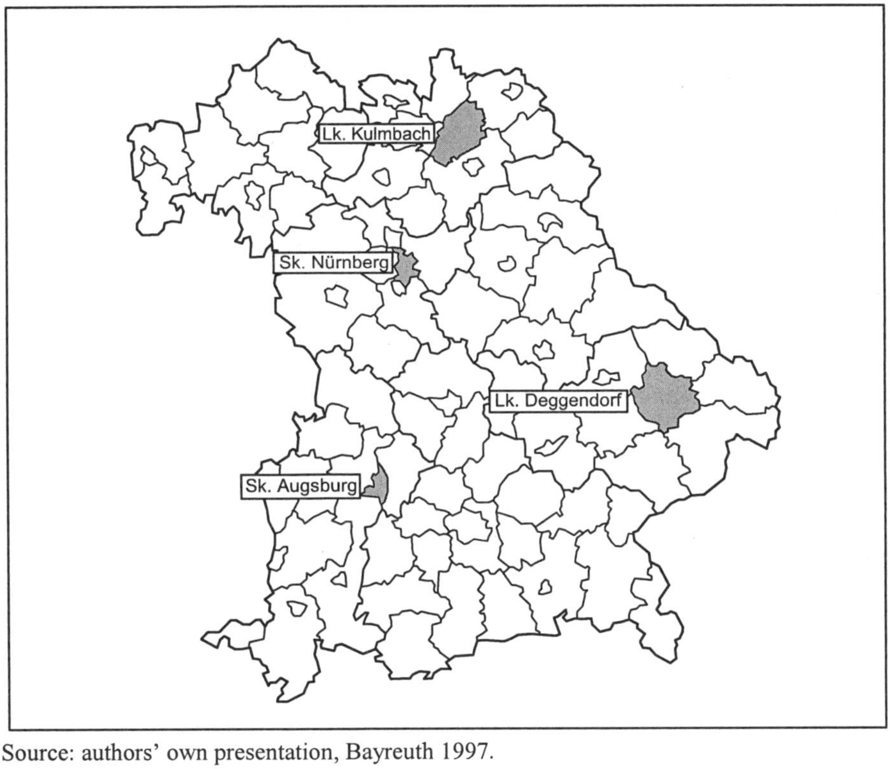

Source: authors' own presentation, Bayreuth 1997.

Fig. 13.2 Selected case study regions

The Deggendorf Case Study

The district of Deggendorf has about 112,000 inhabitants (of which the town Deggendorf has 28,000 citizens) and is a region which experienced structural economic problems for decades due to the dividing effect of the Danube. Only with the creation of infrastructure such as the A92 motorway, as well as larger industrial settlements from the 1960s and 1970s onwards, were the first impulses given to development, which reached a temporary peak recently with the establishment of a specialised institute of higher education. The high development consciousness in the region, the existence of several people with initiative, the resulting positive competition between the most important decision-makers and their sometimes excellent connections to the political centres of power in Munich, proved to be a growth-generating force.

A significant part of the development, however, lives and dies with particular personalities. Development can be characterised as making up for lost time and is being directed towards continuous growth. There are signs of sporadic stagnation ('pauses in the development'). The regional actors are to some extent aware that continuous growth is not possible. It must be seen whether the region is able to manage the status quo as dynamically as growth. Various discussion partners were pessimistic concerning this, as the decision-makers did not have any strategies at their disposal in the case of setbacks. The decision-maker networks are built up hierarchically, which is a basic problem, but this does not have a negative effect because of the mentalities (open-mindedness, enthusiasm) of the decision-makers and the spur of competition between the mayor and council.

Within the region there are dense networks connecting administration, the economy and institutions, which are characterised by the intensive exchange of information. Thus, ideas are quickly put into practice. The networks, however, lead to very little synergetic effect in the entrepreneurial area. Co-operation in the construction field is limited to work associations on large building sites. Communal development activities are also not evident, as companies are orientated towards their market requirements. Furthermore, the necessary critical mass for the establishment of business networks and, thus, of a region-specific technical culture, is absent. Here, the institute of higher education can be an instigator. It functions as an information broker and improves the locational factors for businesses, e.g. by providing knowledge through the working group banks and general environment. It cannot yet be judged to what extent training, technology transfer and new businesses are leading to specific knowledge in the region (e.g. facility management). The ability of businesses to innovate is limited by their adaptability in framing conditions and their recognition of market opportunities in the context of a learning region. If these area-transcending abilities are seen as more positive for the competitiveness of a region, from a structural economic perspective, than dependence on area-specific knowledge, then the milieu in the district of Deggendorf can be judged as very creative.

The Kulmbach Case Study

The district of Kulmbach, with a population of about 78,000 – including its economic centre, the town of Kulmbach, with a population of about 28,000 – is the third biggest location for the food and semi-luxury food industry in Bavaria. This area possesses facilities which represent 'supporting space', such as the Federal Institution for Meat Research (BAFF), the Specialist School for Food Technology and the initiative 'know-how transfer and co-operation in the food field of the region Kulmbach' (KKL). In addition to this sector, the textile and clothing industry, as well as engineering, are of regional significance, but have experienced major structural problems in recent years. The marketing of the region as a centre of competence for the food industry indicates the possible existence of an 'industrial district', particularly since essential preconditions for a competitive location in the sense of its supporting space are present, with relevant research, education and technology-transfer facilities.

In spite of this, the empirical analysis demonstrated that a distinct creative milieu could not be identified from the materially or institutionally necessary preconditions. Only the immaterial components, such as ideas, mentality, innovation behaviour, co-operation tendency, willingness to act or development consciousness proved to be sufficient preconditions for a creative milieu. The results show that these immaterial factors, with a few exceptions, are present in Kulmbach in such a form that they possibly block a creative milieu. A crucial feature seems to be the existence of traditional patterns of thought, which are orientated towards self-interest and prevent co-operation and regional innovation. It may be possible for the KKL to break these structures in the entrepreneurial field. In the political field, the town of Kulmbach, in particular, is attempting to introduce new forms of dialogue. Following the resignation of a former councillor, named by the protagonists interviewed as an integrator and central driving force, it is not yet possible to recognise a regional guiding figure. Thus, a vacuum has developed, producing noticeable development blockages related to attitude. In the case of the Kulmbach district, present development impulses do not evolve via regional consensus, but – partly by operating with external institutions – through individual initiatives or through 'forced' co-operation under external pressure.

The Cities of Augsburg and Nuremberg as Case Studies

The conurbation of Augsburg, with about 700,000 inhabitants, is an economically strong area encompassing the leading branches of engineering, vehicle technology and computer production, despite the decline of the former significant industries of textiles and clothing. Furthermore, Augsburg is a location for regionally important institutions such as the Chamber of Industry and Commerce for Augsburg and Swabia, or the Swabian regional government. As a formerly 'free town', Augsburg can look back on an important history which saw it as the most important industrial town in Bavaria up to the 19th century. More recent drives for development are being provided by the initiative KUMAS of the Bavarian state government, with the aim of developing Augsburg into a competence centre for environmental technology.

During discussions with experts, it was evident that there was a regional character trait of actors being reluctant to co-operate. This was revealed as a crucial obstacle in the use of facilities in the supporting space. There also exists regional networks, corresponding to the size of the conurbation area. In particular, networks can be found in association with the Chamber of Industry and Trade (IHK) for Augsburg and Swabia, which have understanding with the discussion partners, and at the same time networks sympathetic to trade unions were also named. In contrast to the thesis that, due to clearly distributed power potentials, several milieus may exist in conurbation areas, the empirical analysis gave the impression that further milieus have difficulty in developing alongside the networks dominated by the IHK. The regional and local elites are also essentially based around the IHK in Augsburg. They include powerful entrepreneurs with the potential for supra-regional influence.

Networks, in the sense of creative milieus, i.e. system-transgressing networks, are found only to a limited extent. This might be a reason why ideas generated endogenously are judged critically and why there is no culture of constructive discussion. Again, regional mentalities/peculiarities play a part as obstructive factors. In particular, the lack of openness, intra-regional competition and a certain ponderousness were mentioned in the interviews. By way of summary, the preconditions for a creative milieu in the Augsburg region exist but only to a limited extent. Institutional factors and also material preconditions are present, but there are several hindering factors in the field of the immaterial milieu. Finally, an external impulse, such as KUMAS, could increase the capacity of the regional milieu, but only provided that broader active groups are included in order to gain positive learning effects, as well as to make the generation of regional specific knowledge in the field of environmental technology possible.

The second example of a major city, the conurbation area of Nuremberg is the seventh biggest conurbation centre in the Federal Republic, with about one million inhabitants. Nuremberg has encountered many major economic and structural employment problems over the past fifteen years, particularly in the regionally important branches of electro-technology, manufacture of office machines, vehicle technology and engineering. Nuremberg is an exhibition town and seat of important facilities for the supporting space, such as the Chamber of Industry and Commerce for Middle Franconia, several institutes of higher education and academies, as well as an international airport.

The empirical analysis carried out in Nuremberg showed that there are sufficient material and institutional preconditions, in a quantitative sense, for the establishment of a creative milieu. The influence of the local mentality and personal characteristics, however, show that these are not sufficient to actually create a creative milieu. An essential limiting feature is the way institutes of higher education are dependant on particular personalities. As these institutes are central hubs of innovation networks, this results to only a certain extent in region-specific effects. The most important centres for innovation, including SME, have differing relationships with large companies. As far as the innovation potential of the Nuremberg region is concerned, it should also be noted that, although the institutes of higher education have hitherto had limited involvement with KMU, future prospects exist in this area.

Regional or local political behaviour, accompanied by a certain conservative and cautious basic attitude among the actors, according to the statements of the discussion partners, mean that the creative richness of ideas is not fully exploited. Regarding the role attributed by EUREK to Nuremberg as 'gateway' to Central and East Europe, local attitudes could be a great disadvantage, since it has not been possible to establish an open-minded image. These image problems in the region have been recognised and a regional marketing association was set up at the instigation of the private sector.

With regard to the creative milieus in this major city and their relationships with each other, a hierarchical system can be noted. In principle, our interviews showed that the actors in Nuremberg are current concentrating on discussion about developing regional fields of competence. Many professional activities are also connected to these structural political regional activities. The influential medium-sized business milieu was to some extent seen as less innovative with respect to accepting unusual ideas. This does not mean, however, that unusual ideas do not find fertile ground. It was possible to identify networks which are creating niches for the realisation of their ideas, thus gradually eroding the intractable structures of the elites and substituting them with innovative elites.

Brief Evaluation of the Case Studies

The empirical analysis of the case studies of Deggendorf, Kulmbach, Nuremberg and Augsburg, conducted following the creative milieu approach, showed that there are signs of different kinds of creative milieu being established in the respective regions. These contribute in different ways to the competitive and innovative ability of each region. However, 'model' creative milieus are not perceivable in any of the case studies, except for some segments in which individual milieu factors have been established. More specifically:

- In the Deggendorf region, the immaterial factors, willingness to act and development consciousness could be considered central factors aiding regional development, although the material starting conditions, for instance in the form of a dense economic structure, limit the establishment of a region-specific body of knowledge. Signs of a creative milieu are distinctly evident via the activities of the facilities in the supporting space.
- The Kulmbach region, as a centre of the food industry, demonstrates good material starting conditions for the establishment of a regional production system. However, the empirical analysis showed that the immaterial milieu factors proved to be an obstacle for establishing a creative milieu. On the one hand, this is demonstrated by the unwillingness of small and middle-sized businesses to co-operate and, on the other, by the limited degree of regional self-awareness, which often hampered a regionally structured course of action for the design of regional competition and innovation.

- In the case study of Nuremberg, it became apparent that the effects of material and institutional milieu factors, which are adequate, are conditioned by immaterial factors. Due to the influence of mentality and personality characteristics of the protagonists (particularly, the lack of willingness to take action), the potential for the creation of a creative milieu is not fully realised. However, initial signs for the establishment of a creative milieu are distinctly visible, which accounts for the change in political style. The networking of regional actors in an economic forum, as well as the formation of various entrepreneurial networks around initiated network interchanges should be considered of primary importance.
- A distinctive feature of the Augsburg case study is the negative influence of immaterial milieu factors in establishing creative milieus. On the one hand, they tend to cement existing power constellations which impede the endogenous creation of ideas and innovations in the context of structural change. On the other hand, there is limited use of opportunities from the extended supporting space due to the influence of mentality and personality factors. Consequently, given the low overall network intensity, only a few exchange relationships between regional networks could be noted.

Thus the empirical analyses show clearly that the elements of a creative milieu, and in particular the immaterial milieu factors, can make an essential contribution to innovative regional development within the context of structural change.

13.5 The Importance of Creative Milieus for Regional Development

What conclusions can be drawn from the importance of creative milieus for regional development?

Seen from the perspective of material factors, the institutions present in the supporting space are a primary precondition for regional development as they can act as designers of regional development via their decision-making potential. The form of the institutions is ideally measured in terms of regional development potential, for instance as regards their technology intensity. But in the end, it is the *performance* of the institutions which determines their contribution within the supporting space. However, what contribution do such institutions make? Do they function within the framework of their 'duties' or do they contribute to the improvement of regional competition and innovation ability via extended activities? This latter function is based on the realisation that the involvement in structural change needs to go beyond what is required purely by duty. With regard to the organisational field of action and the resources of individual institutions, networking and co-ordination between them is particularly important. The function of regional institutions in the supporting space can only be considered sufficient if these additional functions are carried out and if networks are established to this end.

As far as technological change is concerned, such networks provide enhanced performance the more they succeed in integrating businesses or in developing business networks, aiming at increasing innovative entrepreneurial ability. Lack of success occurs because businesses are only partly willing to co-operate, or simply because the critical mass of 'milieu-able' businesses is missing in a region – the performance of these networks being limited to reducing insecurity via network internal exchange or information transfer. Only if businesses accept the additional role of creating innovative ideas, being involved in a learning process and creating region-specific knowledge, will larger scale results occur.

The empirical analyses showed that only few regional entrepreneurs were integrated in such networks. Although the need for innovation is recognised, regional partnerships have been established only reluctantly, mainly for mentality-related reasons. Expectations of the effects of a creative milieu should not be set too high where *direct* effects of increase in innovation of regional businesses are concerned. There is lack of success, particularly in thinly populated areas, because the critical mass is not reached. However, the question arises as to whether the tendency towards co-operation, for example industrial districts where it is strongly developed, does not represent a black box for the qualitative establishment of creative milieus, as it is little influenced by regional political measures and, thus, limits the scope for strategic use of the creative milieu concept.

It thus becomes evident that the creativity potential of a regional milieu is, in the end, highly dependent on immaterial factors. The ability of the region to compete and innovate is primarily determined by the acknowledgement by regional actors of their ability to 'design' the regional environment through structural change (according to Derenbach, 'development consciousness'). An innovation-promoting process promises success if it succeeds in integrating the various groups involved in regional development – such as businesses, associations, chambers of commerce or trade unions – in the process of designing the environment. Grabher (1993b) has shown that this type of 'open' procedure can decisively reduce the restrictions and reservations. Such 'blockage coalitions' or hindering alliances can, in the end, limit the ability of these procedures to be innovative in adapting a region to the requirements of structural change. This refers not only to the technological ability to innovate but also, in particular, the organisational ability to innovate in the form of creating system-transgressing networks, like regional conferences or strategic round tables.

In addition to these power-related restrictions, further person-related restrictions can be determining factors of influence. Even when there exists a basic willingness to co-operate in system transgressing-networks, if the motivation to design the regional environment is absent ('willingness to act'), there may be constraints on a successful outcome. It became apparent that this was a decisive factor. For instance, although the economic-historical development of a region can account for a particular attitude of regional actors, e.g. in the activities of 'innovative elites', a change of consciousness can be achieved through continuous and long-term networking. It is not possible to judge in general which of these factors of influence will be dominant in a given region. Therefore, the concept of the creative milieu, which per se emphasises regionally different development processes, cannot have general application, but has to relate to the particularities of a region in terms of its situation.

The Possibility of Planning Creative Milieus

To what extent creative milieus can actually be planned and, thus, applied strategically as political options, needs to be viewed under different aspects, since a so-called 'milieu orientated regional policy' is made up of different components. Maier and Rösch (1996) attempt to summarise the requirements of a milieu-oriented regional policy by means of different elements (see Table 12.2).

Table 13.1 Elements of a milieu-oriented regional policy

Milieu-Oriented Regional Policy		
1. Traditional regional policy = facilities with classical production and location factors	2. Innovation oriented policy = regional networks	3. Culturalised regional policy = socio-cultural environment
– Traffic infrastructure – Communication infrastructure – Provision and disposal – Training and educational facilities – Business space – Communal economic support	– Technology transfer – Co-operation network (technology forums etc.) – Consulting firms – Support of new firms – Risk capital trusts – Industrial districts (KMU networks)	– Regional identity – Cultural institutions (clubs, associations) – Leisure and recreation potential – High environmental and quality of life standards – Cultural sponsorship – Town and regional marketing – Numerous social activities – Leading personalities – Administrative culture

Source: Maier and Rösch 1996, p. 198.

The table shows that elements of traditional and innovation-orientated regional policy are complemented by culturalised regional policy which includes, in particular, soft and ultrasoft elements. According to this milieu-oriented policy, the three policy fields presented have to interlock and used in parallel for the design of a creative milieu. While measures exist for improving the material resources in a region, the constraint of scarce public funds (e.g. decentralised university policy, regional risk capital trusts), which generally seem to apply, means that the political capitalisation of the material elements of creative milieus is often limited.

The establishment of a decentralised network of institutes of higher education, for instance, can provide a crucial knowledge and development incentive for the relevant locations. However, it is difficult to overcome the obstacle of generating an entrepreneurial 'critical mass' for developing regional specific knowledge. As long as the entrepreneurial location policy or market forces do not allow an agglomeration of critical mass within a region, planning attempts to artificially create such an agglomeration will be expensive or ineffective. Forming regional networks, furthermore, presupposes that the actors to be incorporated in a network are willing to co-operate. Policy can only encourage, enlighten and motivate. It is not possible to 'plan' whether regional co-operation via networks ultimately takes place. At the same time, the question arises whether the willingness of regional actors to act can be increased by planning. Here, the dilemma which becomes evident is that the creative milieu approach focuses at the meso level (concerning in particular networks, and the facilities of the supporting space). In order to influence the individual willingness to act, the creative milieu needs to be considered at the micro level of regional actors. Due to the absence of political instruments, this is not possible, as psychological elements are involved. These – as in an individual case – cannot be applied at a planning or political scale.

One of the most crucial factors for the establishment of a creative milieu is the individual willingness to act, which is based on the individual development consciousness. This makes planning more difficult, particularly if historically moulded mentalities and behaviour are involved. The creative milieu approach can thus show and explain regional development in the form of obstacles or success factors on the material and immaterial level, but strategic solutions are not offered. Regional comparisons are also not possible using this approach because of the different starting conditions. Thus, it also becomes evident that a centrally controlled ability to plan the creative milieu cannot be applied as a development factor. Likewise, the approach does not enable statements to be made about the external framework conditions under which regions act, since only region-internal factors are analysed. The fact that region-external framing conditions also influence the regional ability to compete and innovate is due to enterprises and institutions being embedded in globalised processes.

The creative milieu approach should, thus, essentially be seen as a descriptive device for presenting the situation within a region through milieu-oriented aspects. But if it is desired to strengthen the region's ability to innovate and compete, then further concepts concerning the regional ability to learn and adapt – within a creative milieu aspect – are necessary. These will be discussed, with consideration of the 'learning region' approach, in the following section.

13.6 The Concept of the Learning Region: An Approach to Increase the 'Milieu Consciousness' of Regional Actors and Enterprises?

Without wanting to connect this concept too strongly with the term learning, it should be pointed out that, in the empirical analysis, the willingness to co-operate of businesses was seen as a generation question. In many places, the traditional patterns of running a business – hostile to co-operation – are breaking down. This is explained by the experts interviewed in terms of the changed training methods of the present generation of managers, connected with the trend to acquire qualifications, e.g. in marketing or strategic business management, in addition to traditional (technical) professional training. If 'learning' is understood as the ability or willingness of regional actors to question traditional patterns of action and behaviour and to be open-minded towards new patterns, the first signs of an increased learning ability seem to be visible.

According to Butzin (1996), networking via telecommunications technologies with their constant and spatially independent access to knowledge and know-how (e.g. via the Internet), has contributed to strengthening the learning capacity of regional actors. Yet, exchange between people so that they can increase their ability to learn is only possible in limited ways (e.g. via newsgroups), with the result that regional networks are necessary to enable transmission and discussion of acquired knowledge through the possibility of face-to-face contacts. The willingness and ability of a region to establish regional networks is, thus, an important catalyst of learning capacity.

Butzin's approach implies, however, that regional actors have already recognised the use of networks. MacLeod (1996) begins from a prior standpoint. The learning capacity of regional actors is, according to him, dependent on a basic cultural change in society, as the learning capacity is dependent on non-economic factors concerning the family, education and training. New concepts acquired in particular through professional training would, thus, provide fertile ground for learning capacity and, therefore, milieu ability. Networks help to implement and propagate what is learnt within a region (Morgan 1997). Decentralised forms of employment and training policy adapted to a specific region have, accordingly, a special function. In the framework of the Bavarian job market fund, regional bodies design instruments for the job market according to the principles of self-organisation in order to improve the regional situation via co-operative projects. Institutions such as chambers of commerce, associations, local labour exchanges etc. have the function of 'learning laboratories' (Morgan 1997, see also @Huggins 1998 in relation to the English Training and Enterprise Council TECH) and, thus have a central function in incentivating regional development.

If the regional ability for development and innovation is understood in terms of these aspects of learning capacity, the creative milieu approach could become strategically important, as regional learning capacity is again defined by the qualitative establishment, in particular, of immaterial milieu factors such as development consciousness and willingness to act.

References

Amin, A., Thrift, N. (1994a) Holding down the Global. In: Amin, A., Thrift, N. (eds.) Globalization, Institutions, and Regional Development in Europe. Oxford University Press, New York 257-260

Anderson, A. (1985) Creativity and Regional Development. Papers of the Regional Science Association 56, 5-20

Aydalot, P., Keeble, D. (eds.) (1988) High Technology Industry and Innovative Environments: The European Experience. Routledge, London

Bramanti, A., Senn, L. (1991): Innovation, Firms and Milieu: A Dynamic and Cyclic Approach. In: Camagni, R. (ed.) Innovations Networks: Spatial Perspectives. Belhaven Press, London, 57-62

Buchholz, T. (1995) Regionale Netzwerke und Kreative Milieus - Theoretische Ansätze, empirische Befunde und regionalpolitische Konsequenzen. Unveröffentlichte Diplomarbeit am Lehrstuhl für Wirtschaftsgeographie und Regionalplanung der Universität Bayreuth

Butzin, B. (1996) Kreative Milieus als Elemente regionaler Entwicklungsstrategien? Eine kritische Wertung. In: Maier, J. (ed.) Bedeutung kreativer Milieus für die Regional- und Landesplanung. Arbeitsmaterialien zur Raumordnung und Raumplanung, Heft 153, University of Bayreuth, 9-38

Camagni, R. (1991a) Introduction: From the Local "Milieu" to Innovation Through Cooperation Networks. In: Camagni, R. (ed.) Innovation Networks: Spatial Perspectives. Belhaven Press, London, 1-9

Camagni, R. (1991b) Local "Milieu", Uncertainty and Innovation Networks: Towards a New Dynamic Theory of Economic Epace. In: Camagni, R. (ed.): Innovation Networks: Spatial Perspectives. Belhaven Press, London, 22-32

Camagni, R. (1995) The Concept of Innovative Milieu and its Relevance for Public Policies in European Lagging Regions. Papers in Regional Science 4, 317-340

Dehrenbach, R. (1988) Regionales Entwicklungsbewußtsein und Handlungsbereitschaft. Raumforschung und Raumordnung 5-6, 258-264

Ewers, H.-J. (1990) Regional Economic Development and Innovation-oriented Measures: Summary and Perspectives. In: Ewers, H.-J., Allesch, J. (eds.) Innovation and Regional Development. de Gruyter Press, Berlin, 337 – 340

Franke, H. (1980) Problemlösen und Kreativität. Bratt- Insitut für Neues Lernen, Goch

Franz, P. (1996) Technologie- und Gründerzentren als Hoffnungsträger kommunaler Wirtschaftsförderung in Ostdeutschland. Raumforschung und Raumordnung 1, 26-35

Fromhold-Eisebith, M. (1995) Das "kreative Milieu" als Motor regionalwirtschaftlicher Entwicklung. Geographische Zeitschrift 1, 30-47

Glasmeier, A. (1994) Flexible Districts, Flexible Regions ? The Institutional and Cultural Limits to Districts in an Era of Globalization and Technological Paradigm Shift. In: Amin, A., Thrift, N. (eds.) Globalization, Institutions, And Regional Development in Europe. Oxford University Press, New York, 118 – 146

Grabher, G. (1993a) Wachstums-Koalitionen und Verhinderungs-Allianzen. Informationen zur Raumentwicklung 11, 749-758

Grabher, G. (1993b) Rediscovering the Social in the Economies of Interfirm relations. In: Grabher, G. (ed.) The Embedded Firm. Routledge, London, 1-31

Grotz, R., Braun, B. (1993) Networks, Milieux and Individual Firm Strategies: Empirical Evidence of an Innovative SME Environment. Geografiska Annaler B 3, 149-162

Grüske, K.-D. (1992) Außerökonomische Faktoren und regionale wirtschaftliche Entwicklung. In: Görgens, E., Tuchtfeldt, E. (eds.) Die Zukunft der wirtschaftlichen Entwicklung - Perspektiven und Probleme. Paul Haupt, Bern, 449-474

Häußermann, H., Siebel, W. (1993) Die Kulturalisierung der Regionalpolitik. Geographische Rundschau 4, 218-223

Hahn, R., Gaiser, A., Héraud, J.-H., Muller, E. (1994) Innovationstätigkeit der Unternehmen und regionales Umfeld. Raumforschung und Raumordnung 3, 193-202

Hassink, R. (1994) Regionale Innovationsförderung im Vergleich. Raumforschung und Raumordnung 2, 105-115

Kamann, D.J.F. (1991) The Distribution of Dominance in Networks and its Spatial Implications. In: Bergman, E.M., Maier, G., Tödtling, F. (eds.) Regions Reconsidered. London, 115-125

Läpple, D. (1994) Zwischen gestern und übermorgen. In: Kreibich, R. (eds.) Bauplatz Zukunft - Dispute über die Entwicklung von Industrieregionen. PRO, Essen

MacLeod, G. (1996) The Cult of Enterprise in a Networked, Learning Region? Governing Business and Skills in Lowland Scotland. Regional Studies 8, 749-755

Maier, J., Kreitmayr, E. (1979) Karlsfeld - Strukturbild einer Stadt-Rand-Gemeinde unter Berücksichtigung bestehender sozialräumlicher Kontakte und Konflikte. Arbeitsmaterialien zur Raumordnung und Raumplanung, 1, Bayreuth

Maier, J., Rösch., A. (1996) Chancen und Möglichkeiten eines kreativen Milieus für die Stadt- und Regionalentwicklung. Gutachterliche Stellungnahme im Auftrag des Bayerischen Staatsministeriums für Landesentwicklung und Umweltfragen. University of Bayreuth, Bayreuth

Maillat, D., Crevoisier, O., Lecoq, B. (1994) Innovation Networks and Territorial Dynamics: A Tentative Typology. In: Johansson, B., Karlsson, C., Wertin, L. (eds.) Patterns for a Network Economy. Springer, Berlin, 33-52

Maillat, D., Lecoq, B., Nemeti, F., Pfister, M. (1995) Technology District and Innovation: The Case of the Swiss Jura Arc. Regional Studies 3, 257-263

Malecki, E.J. (1990): Promoting and Inhibiting Factors in the Regional Development System. In: Ewers, H.-J., Allesch, J. (eds.) Innovation and Regional Development. de Gruyter Press, Berlin, 123-147

Malmberg, A., Sölvell, Ö., Zander, I. (1996) Spatial Clustering, Local Accumulation of Knowledge and Firm Competitiveness. Geografiska Annaler B 2, 85-97

Meier-Dallach, H.-P., Hohermuth, S., Nef, R. (1987a) Zur Berücksichtigung regionaler Sozialstrukturen und Identitäts- und Verhaltensmuster in der Raumentwicklungspolitik. Informationen zur Raumentwicklung 7-8, 451-463

Meier-Dallach, H.-P., Hohermuth, S., Nef, R. (1987b) Regionalbewußtsein, soziale Schichtung und politische Kultur. Informationen zur Raumentwicklung 7-8, 377-393

Miegel, M. (1991) Wirtschafts- und arbeitskulturelle Unterschiede in Deutschland. Bertelsmann Stiftung, Gütersloh

Morgan, K. (1997) The Learning Region: Institutions, Innovation and Regional Renewal. Regional Studies 5, 491-503

Ratti, R. (1991) Small and Medium-sized Enterprises, Local Synergies and Spatial Cycles of Innovation. In: Camagni, R. (ed.) Innovations Networks: Spatial Perspectives. Belhaven Press, London, 172-184

Runco, M.A. (ed.) (1994) Problem Finding, Problem Solving, and Creativity. Ablexs Publishing, Norwood

Schneider, H.-D. (1993) Wie fördert man Innovationsbereitschaft? Management Zeitschrift 12, 87-90

Sternberg, R. (1995) Wie entstehen High-Tech-Regionen? Geographische Zeitschrift 1, 48-63

14 The Biotech Region of Munich and the Spatial Organisation of its Innovation Networks

Jürgen Oßenbrügge and Christian Zeller
University of Hamburg

14.1 Introduction

Biotechnology is often seen as one of the new leading technologies of the 21st century. Although the claims are often exaggerated, there is no doubt that there has been a remarkable wave of successful commercialisation processes and intensified research and development leading to a fast differentiation into many different technologies and applications. Economically, the most important are the new pharmaceutical products resulting from the discovery of new active substances and technologies such as genomics and gene therapy. These innovation processes are organised by public research centres as well as small biotech firms and big pharmaceutical multinationals.

The economic exploitation of biotechnological knowledge as a motors of regional growth are to be found in the U.S., especially in the San Francisco Bay Area. But biotechnology has been a very dynamic industry in Germany too. According to market observations, the number of companies rose from about 150 in 1996 to 279 in early 2000. Most of the European start-ups in this sector and the second highest share of specialised biotechnology firms and employees are located in Germany (Schitag Ernst & Young 1998; Ernst & Young 1999; 2000a; 2000b). Within Germany, biotechnology companies are clustered in a few regions such as Munich, the upper Rhein, Heidelberg and Mannheim in Southern Germany, Frankfurt, the middle Rhein, Berlin and Hamburg.

The BioRegio Contest is often given as an explanation for the recent dynamism in Germany. The German Federal Ministry of Education, Science, Research and Technology proposed this contest in 1995 in order to promote the commercialisation of biotechnology, asking the regions to compete against each other using regional concepts of biotechnological specialisation. The reasoning behind this competition was to promote applied research and commercialisation at state level by encouraging regional actors and resources. The BioRegio Contest has been considered a very successful operation by many of the actors involved and independent observers. Indeed, Prof. Winnacker who was involved in the contest, is now president of the Deutsche Forschungsgemeinschaft.

The rapid growth of the industry and the successful implementation of commercialisation incentives were the main motivation behind the present research project, whose aim is to understand the spatial dimension of the biotech industry (Oßenbrügge 2001; Zeller 2001a, 2001b). In this chapter, we outline the preliminary results, emphasising conceptual problems and initial answers to the question of whether this industry represents an identifiable regional system of innovation (as defined by Cooke 1998; Howells 1999).

14.2 Theoretical Context: Input-Output Relations and Untraded Interdependencies

The existing literature on regional variation in technological change and economic competitiveness offers a wide range of explanatory concepts. There is a multi-perspective debate stressing different components which are seen as key elements for understanding why innovative forms of the knowledge-based economy grow faster in one region than another. Such explanatory concepts include creative milieus (e.g. Maillat 1996), the debate about national or regional systems of innovation (Edquist 1997; Bracyk *et al.* 1998; Archibugi *et al.* 1999), the California school of increasing returns (Scott 1995; Storper 1997) or the regional innovation policy approach. Within this growing body of literature three basic questions are of major importance:

- The first question is related to the paradox finding that alongside the ongoing process of time-space-compression, regional variation is becoming a major feature of the world economy. Though some of the basic concepts explaining regional growth are well elaborated, the question remains open why certain regions offer qualities for structuring the world economy within the process of globalisation.
- The second question is related to innovation. While early approaches to the phenomena of innovation were characterised by the idea of technology push or demand pull, linear models have in recent years been replaced by interactive models. Though multi-actor-networks and complex forms of interaction offer better insights into innovation processes, there is no clear understanding either of the actions of persons and institutions, or of the rationality that contributes to the evolution of a collective and systemic process.
- Finally, many authors emphasise that regional development is path dependant and that each region therefore has an individual trajectory. Change should be understood "as an evolutionary path in which each step moves one away from a past that cannot be recovered and that limits future directions" (Storper and Walker 1989, p.113). The concept of path dependency rests on the assumption of positive feedback mechanisms, e.g. to alleviate technological choices in any certain situation.

These basic questions are not independent, but connected and involve various fields. An integrative perspective has been elaborated by Michael Storper. His concept of material and relational assets defines pathways of regional development as a special combination of technological as well as organisational change and learning processes. While material assets are well known agglomeration advantages, relational assets are derived from uncodified knowledge and untraded interdependencies. The economic process is seen as "conservation and co-ordination, the subjects of the process not as factors but as reflexive human actors" (Storper 1997, p. 28).

Rather than provide a comprehensive critique of Storpers' approach, we just outline those material and relational assets worked on in our regional case studies. Our basic assumption is that "knowledge inputs used in commercialisation may be embodied in human, institutional and facility form. These types of resources are relatively immobile and place-specific" (Feldman 1994, p. 20). Therefore they facilitate regional specialisation and represent starting points of regional pathways. Of major importance, according to Dosi (1988) and Feldman (1994) are:

- Public research institutions as main centres of knowledge creation. Though this kind of research is open to the public, and research results are spread into the scientific community very quickly, the location of research institutions plays a significant role for the evolution of a regional system of innovation (through personal contacts, spin-offs, research co-operation, learning-by-doing, specialised manpower, etc.).
- The existence of external economies of scale and scope (pooling of specialised manpower and other factors of production).
- The increased complexity of innovation suggests that other sources of information besides public research centres are very important, e.g. the co-presence of related industry and specialised business services. The concept of interactive innovation presupposes high density of information, multiple decisions and opportunities for different actors to come together to facilitate commercialisation (learning by interacting).
- Avoidance of uncertainty as a major motivational background. This explains why actors in the private economy are prepared to exchange information and reinforce different forms of co-operation. In the case of biotechnology, the risk reduction strategy is highly plausible, as uncertainty avoidance saves new technological inventions and also allows control over the commercialisation process.

The material and relational assets of a region are interwoven. Without 'soft' communication there will be no 'hard' co-operation; without an infrastructure of research institutions and research firms beyond a critical threshold there is no diversity of interaction and no knowledge spillovers. Against this general background we try to identify those concrete assets which operate within the biotechnology sector in Germany. Because of an obvious spatial concentration of biotech firms, we wanted to know whether the Munich cluster is an example of a 'regional world of innovation' as it is called by Storper (1997).

14.3 Research Project Design and Method

The subject and theoretical orientation of our analysis imply the combination of various methods and procedures in a complex research design. In general, our aim was to reveal the embeddedness and network integration of important biotechnological actors in their social, political and economic environment, consisting of competitors, clients, suppliers, consultants as well as economic and political institutions. To identify innovative input-output systems, two starting points or levels of analysis can be distinguished analytically. On the one hand, the rationale of the principal actors in the innovation systems and, on the other, the innovations of new products and processes themselves. Both levels are interwoven, but in this study the actor specific perspective will dominate (see Fig. 14.1).

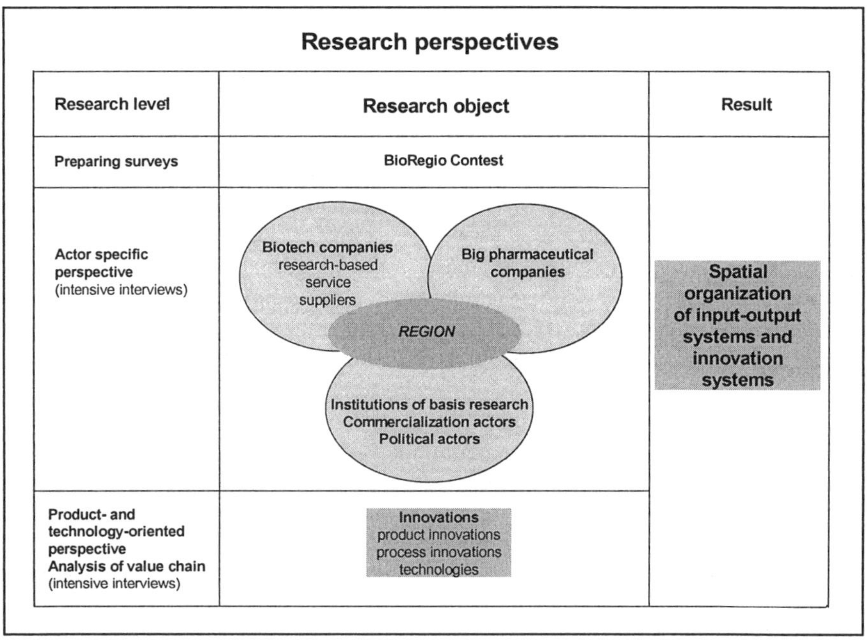

Fig. 14.1 Levels of analysis

The value chain is a useful tool for locating biotech actors (see Porter 1996; Howells and Wood 1993). It describe the steps taken from the original idea to the market. These steps can be internalised within one firm or organised in a complex externalised actor-network.

The development process from the discovery of active therapeutics substances to the market is illustrated in Fig. 14.2. Value creating activities within one firm or network of firms are characterised by research, development, production and commercialisation of a product. In the context of biotechnology, quite distinct transactions may constitute these input-output relations, such as:

- the sequence of activities to produce a product or a service within a firm;
- the purchase of raw materials, intermediate products, means of production and services necessary in the value-creating process;
- in-licensing or out-licensing of patent rights;
- a service for analysing substances.

Such input-output system are simultaneously innovation systems, if relations generate additional knowledge, new products, technologies and processes.

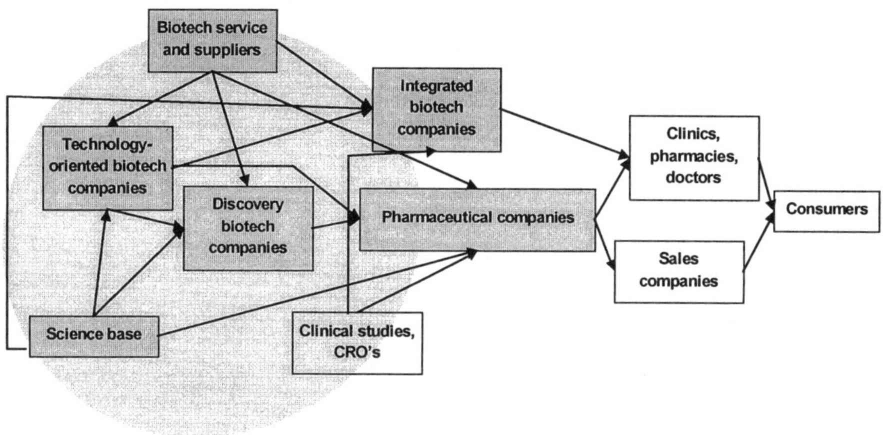

In order to understand the rationale of the actors involved and the interrelations between them, our approach was to carry out intensive interviews with major actors in biotech innovation systems (Healey and Rawlinson 1993; Schoenberger 1991; Markusen 1994). Our analysis focused on the biotech firms, the relationships among them and also with other actors such as the science base, suppliers, users, commercialisation and political actors.

14.4 The Biotech Region of Munich: Networks and Scale

The region of Munich has been among the strongest agglomerations in Germany in terms of economic development over the last two decades. After World War II the region was transformed from an agricultural and residential area to an industrial region based on machinery, cars, electro-technical, fine mechanics and optics which were integrated by cross-section sectors, such as aerospace, military equipment and micro-electronics. Of central significance was the electronic company Siemens which had shifted from Berlin to Munich after World War II (Sternberg 1995).

Munich is characterised by intensive economic networks based on a collaboration between production sites, private and public research institutions. The R&D potential is excellent. Since the creation of the Federal Republic, Munich profited from a large number of Federal orders and subsidies, especially from the Research and Defence Ministries. Eleven out of sixty Max Planck Institutes are located in Munich, and six out of thirty-five Fraunhofer Institutes.

More recently a shift to research, administration and headquarters functions has occurred. Munich benefits from an excellent image regarding the quality of life as well as the industrial and company-friendly policy. Therefore it is not surprising that the Bavarian technology policy succeeded in promoting biotechnology, although related industries such as pharmaceuticals are not very strong in Munich. The amount and diversity of biotech firms and institutions contribute to attractive location conditions being generated.

Political Actors in Biotechnology and Promotion Policy

In the course of the "Zukunftsoffensive Bayern" (an offensive approach to future development in Bavaria), the state government launched several incentives and investments financed by an extensive privatisation of public assets. Biotechnology was chosen as one of the priorities for promotion activities. The location of Martinsried near München gained particular attention in the sense of regionalised technology policy under the principle of 'strengthening of the strong'. The focus on the location of Munich metropolitan area should increase its attractiveness for new biotech firms and venture capital firms, provoking a multiplier effect following the example of the biotech clusters in the U.S.A.

The building of important institutions of basic research such as the gene centre, the Max-Planck-Institute for Biochemistry and other centres preceded the commercial promoting of biotechnology. Two recent instruments of the biotech promoting policy have to be emphasised:

a) The Biotech Innovation and start-up Centre of Martinsried (IZB) was built in 1994 and afterwards extended several times. It offers laboratory space for start-up companies and other useful internal and external infrastructure. Later on, attempts to enter formal co-operation and informal networking between the companies and other actors, especially research institutes in the neighbourhood were facilitated. Some of the companies interviewed are located in the IZB.
b) Bio^M AG is a direct result of the BioRegio Initiative and was founded in 1997 to support the biotech region Munich. Bio^M AG raises and offers seed capital and co-ordinates grants of the BMBF. Bio^M AG helps start-up projects individually in relation to business planning, management, linkages with collaboration partners and questions of patents and licensing.

The Science Base (Universities and Research Institutes)

A starting point for the creation of a biotech region are institutions of basic research working on relevant issues in biotechnology, molecular biology and genomics. In Munich the most important of these institutions are the Max-Planck Institute for Biochemistry, the Gene Centre and the Ludwig-Maximilian University. These institutions have formed a substantial basis for several firms founded after 1993. The regional science basis has been extended by two Fraunhofer-Institutes and GSF-Neuherberge, in additional to the Max Planck Institutes and Technical University of Munich.

The technology and knowledge transfer between the research institutes and the business sector are organised by means of direct collaboration, patent licensing and personal relationships with the companies in the region and outside the region. Traditionally, Boehringer Mannheim has entered a broad range of agreements with universities and research institutes in the region. Companies such as MediGene, Connex, Domed, BayKG, Micromet, Microgen, Pulsion and Switch are spin-offs from the LMU, Morphosys, Toplab and Sugen Inc. (USA) are spin-offs from the MPI.

Large Pharmaceutical Companies Active in Biotechnology

In general, the chemical-pharmaceutical industry is far less important in Munich than in other regions like Rheinland and Rhein-Neckar. However Boehringer Mannheim has run important biotechnological production facilities in Tutzing and Penzberg since 1950. At these sites around 2000 employees were employed before the acquisition by the Swiss pharmaceutical giant Hoffmann-La Roche in 1997.

Boehringer Mannheim had already invested huge amounts in the modernisation of research and manufacturing facilities before the take-over by Roche. In the meantime, the research centre in Penzberg has been integrated into the global research networks of Roche. It is now one of six 'centres of excellence' of the pharmaceuticals division with special responsibilities in the areas of oncology and diagnostics. Besides Roche, Aventis (formerly Hoechst Marion Roussel) is also involved in genomics research in Martinsried and is located in the immediate neighbourhood of the well-known biotech company MediGene.

The Biotech Companies

On the basis on the principal activities in the value-creating process of therapeutics and diagnostics, a typology has been elaborated which takes the core competence of the firm as central distinguishing feature (Table 14.1). This typology of firms allows a better understanding of typical collaboration agreements which are legal forms of input-output-relations. The collaboration agreements represent always specific forms of division of labour. An understanding of their spatial pattern enables us to grasp the spatial organisation of part of the externalised input output relations. This method allows us to describe the spatial integration of the major actors in a biotech cluster.

Table 14.1 Typology of biotech companies

Research	Development	Production
Research-based and discovery firms Technology-oriented firms Research for new discovery and screening technologies used in identification of target molecules and genes. Application of the technologies to specific therapeutic areas depends also on the collaboration partners.	**Firms and institutions in (pre-)clinical development** The clinical studies phase I, II and III surmount the possibilities of small biotech firms. To process these parts of the value chain, a variety of agreements can be entered into between biotech and pharmaceutical firms.	**Production-based firms** Production-based firms produce active substances in GMP-quality for development purposes (clinical studies) and for markets after approval.
Discovery-oriented firms Research in the areas of discovery of active substances and identification of target molecules and genes for specific diseases.	**Contract Research Organisations** Organise and process parts of pre-clinical and clinical studies. Specialised in costly tests and the issue of special certificates.	
Information-oriented firms Information-oriented firms offer services in the field of information production and transfer, especially databases, and activities in *rational drug design and bioinformatics.*	**Hospitals** Hospitals are the central partners for clinical studies.	
(Biotechnological) suppliers and service firms		
Service firms Service firms analyse e.g. substances, molecules and DNA sequence on behalf of large firms, biotech firms and research laboratories, etc. They can also be active in quality control of therapeutic active substances.		
Biotechnological and non-biotechnological suppliers These very varied firms are mostly specialised in specific products in the sense of niche producers. They produce (biotechnological) devices and intermediates (e.g. chemicals, gels, laboratory hardware, proteins, monoclonal antibodies).		
Production means and auxiliaries firms These firms produce biotech-based analytical, screening, diagnostics devices and technologies which are used in research and development. Depending on the technology intensity of the products certain activities can also be categorised in the group of technology-based firms.		

The Commercialisation Actors

Companies in the area of finance, legal firms and consultancies are of great importance in creating an appropriate biotech-friendly business climate in a region. We refer to these actors with the term 'commercialisation actors'. Many institutions are involved in supporting the financing of biotech companies, especially venture capital firms such as ATLAS Venture GmbH, Techno Venture Management Gesellschaft mbH (TVM), Apax Partner & Co. and the Life Sciences Ventures GmbH. Investment firms, such as Bayerische Kapital Risikobeteiligungsgesellschaft mbH and the Bay BG, both supported by the State of Bavaria are also important. Patent attorneys are another group of indispensable commercialisation actors.

As Munich is the location of the German and European Patent Agency, a broad range of specialised knowledge can be found in Munich. About 70 percent of all patent lawyers in Germany are located in Munich. This facilitates the organisation of the legal protection of intellectual property necessary for the commercialisation process.

Collaboration as a Form of Input-Output Relations

A typology of collaboration opens a way to better understanding of the major input-output-relations in and between companies and institutions. They can only be identified on the basis of a detailed knowledge of the firm and intensive interviews. A characterisation of the various types of collaboration makes it possible to seize the externalised input output relations in the context of a whole innovation system. The internalised input output relations remain hidden behind the doors of the firms.

Neither input-output systems nor innovation systems need to have regional expression. Spatial input-output-relations of a company can be illustrated in a very simplified way in the following figure suggested by Markusen (1994). The most important input and output relations of MediGene, which is one of the most innovative and successful biotech companies in Munich, are shown in Fig. 14.3. *MediGene* pursued three strategic activities in 1999. Interestingly some of the most strategic inputs and outputs are organised on a transatlantic scale.

Innovation-oriented collaboration is normally an exchange relationship lasting several month or years. Collaboration for the common development of a technology or an active therapeutic substance requires a high level of obligation and dense exchange of information between partners. Such an agreement often consists of very distinct transactions extending over a long period. In the course of such agreements new knowledge is created which benefits both partners. At the same time the innovation process is marked by considerable uncertainty.

The form of financial returns to the customer consist of 'milestone payments' to royalties and weighty capital investment in the biotech firm. Collaboration to produce services in biotechnology are more likely to be short term, although there are also long term orders. The customer normally pays a clearly defined work of the supplier. Such a input-output relation involves little uncertainty. The agreement takes the form of an order or a purchase. There is normally no significant interlocking of capital.

Clinical studies are normally carried out in close collaboration with hospitals. In the course of the outsourcing of such studies, a market for so-called Contract Research Organisations (CRO) has evolved. 'Late stage' biotech firms (such as *MediGene*), which develop their own therapeutics, depend on a close collaboration with partners in the field of clinical studies.

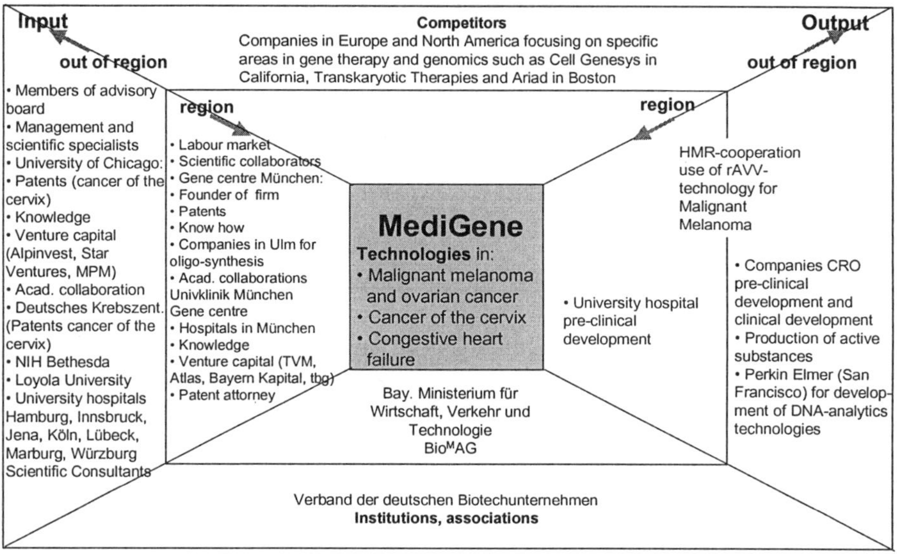

Fig. 14.3 Input-output relations of a biotechnological firm: the example of MediGene in 1999

At the moment, biotech firms are not normally able to carry out up-scaling processes for the production or even the industrial manufacturing of the active substances. A special market has been developed meanwhile in this area. In Germany some companies, such as Rentschler and Thomae (a subsidiary of Boehringer Ingelheim) have focused on biotechnological production of therapeutic active substances. But none of these firms is located in the region of Munich.

Input-output relations between biotech firms and commercialisation actors are normally not focused on the direct activity in research or production. Especially for those companies focused on value intensive and specialised products and technologies a co-operation with venture capital firms and patent attorneys can be very decisive to secure the capital and the legal safety. These input-output-relations are important components of the whole innovation system.

Collaboration with academic research institutions are an instrument of knowledge transfer into the commercialisation sphere of the companies. The collaboration can take various forms – ranging from licensing and financing of grants to close collaboration in common research projects – depending on the object and conditions.

Purely market-oriented agreements can be very diverse. They may manifest themselves in a sharing of the markets and/or licensing of patent rights. Or a pharmaceutical company may achieve control over the development and marketing rights of a product based on an active substance identified by a biotech firm. Further on, we observe that biotech firms sell marketing rights to each other and thus neutralise competition. In so doing, entry barriers of new markets are reduced for the partners.

14.5 Spatial Structure of Input and Output Relations

In this section, we look firstly at the input factors including of the workforce, technology and knowledge, and capital. We then discuss the various devices and means of production, the intermediate products and services.

The Workforce

A highly qualified workforce and the know-how linked to this workforce are decisive input factors for research-oriented firms. There are several factors which have contributed to the creation of a critical mass of researchers in molecular biology and biotechnology in Munich. The establishment of research institutes, such as the Max Planck Institute and the Gene Centre, as well the longstanding existence of companies such as Boehringer Mannheim, have contributed to the development of a specialised workforce. Although to a certain extent highly skilled specialists can be recruited at a European or North Atlantic level, the existence of a specialised labour market is seen as being very important for the promotion of the biotech companies. Also the service-oriented firms are dependant on qualified and specialised personnel, but not as exclusively as the research-oriented firms.

All companies and institutions attempt to increase the qualifications of their employees. In this way the general level of knowledge is improved and a qualified workforce created which may serve other firms when people change their workplace. Employees, firms and institutions therefore contribute to cumulative regional processes of 'learning-by-doing'.

Technology and Knowledge

Knowledge and technology are strategically the most important inputs for research-based biotech firms. Innovative firms obtain technological knowledge mainly from the persons they employ or with whom they collaborate. A very important input factor is the know-how related to the setting up and management of a company. Start-ups are often based on existing teams of scientists who knew each other already before the creation of the new firm. This illustrates that mutual understanding and trust is a crucial factor in the early stage of a biotech company, and is an element which suggests that spatial proximity to the science base and similar companies may facilitate the start-up process of biotech firms.

On the other hand, technological knowledge may be acquired through in-licensing of patents from almost anywhere. Research-oriented firms such as Morphosys, MediGene, Genome Pharmaceuticals Corporation, Micromet and Connex draw strategic technological inputs from Europe and North America. Later, technologies or substances are developed in the course of co-operation agreements with large pharmaceutical companies which normally acquire the rights to commercialise them. The agreements can assume very distinct economic and legal forms. The various levels of outputs and knowledge are often packaged in very complex contracts. The most advanced companies in Munich and Rheinland are focused on such specialised, high quality and complex technologies that the potentially interested partners have to be found on a North Atlantic or Triad level.

Service-oriented firms, such as Toplab, or supplier firms such as Microcoat normally acquire their technology inputs by purchasing or leasing them. The transfer of highly specialised knowledge through collaborators, consultants and patents is less relevant here than with research-oriented firms. Likewise the production and output of technology and knowledge is less important.

Capital

Without considerable capital, even the most innovative researchers cannot set up a company. Most research-oriented firms rely on venture capital. This is especially true for those companies involved in North Atlantic competition such as Morphosys, MediGene and GPC. From the mid 1990s the financing situation has improved remarkably and important venture capital companies have in the meantime located in Munich.

More recently, companies have benefited from state grants from Bavaria. Seed capital came from institutions in the region, the BioRegio Initiative and the European Union. But companies pursuing an international strategy also have to guarantee financing on a international basis. Highly innovative firms begin very early to pursue an international strategy. Partnership with well-known venture firms which are internationally active increases the credibility of the company in terms of technologies and the product pipeline. This can improve the chance of entering an important long term co-operation agreement with a pharmaceutical company.

Entering collaboration agreements with pharmaceutical multinationals is usually a strategic aim of research-based biotech firms. After a phase of financing primarily based on venture capital, such agreements offer the basis to secure the existence of the company for several years. Companies assume that they can only adopt a development which has already been tackled by US models several years before, by pursuing very aggressive and international financing strategies. Private placements and finally the initial public quotation on the stock markets are further components and stages in the financing strategy of a highly specialised research-oriented biotech company.

In contrast, less advanced companies and less internationally oriented firms depend more on regional and national financial sources. The personality of the entrepreneur can be of central significance. To avoid dependency or guardianship from venture capitalists, a company can intentionally rely on own capital resources and classical forms of loan capital. In a similar way, service-oriented firms in the field of laboratory services finance themselves through credits and own capital. Venture capital is less important because the expected profits are much smaller than for successful research-oriented biotech firms. Finally, it can be concluded that the availability of seed capital, the existing of financing institutions and venture capital companies in the region can be of great importance, especially during the setting up of companies.

Devices and Means of Production

Although it could be assumed that research-based companies share some means of production with other companies, we found only few examples of such co-operation in the IZB and in the Max Planck-Institute. The same holds true for service-oriented and biotech supplier firms regarding the question of procurement of devices and means of production. Equipment is usually purchased or leased. But the enormously high costs of such equipment, as for proteomics or mass spectrometrics, require very careful planning of the firm's expansion.

Intermediate Products

For research-based biotech firms, especially those which focus on the development of technologies or bioinformatics, classical physical intermediate products are much less important than knowledge and technologies. The geographical origin is of no significance for the procurement of specialised biochemicals, monoclonal antibodies or other biological molecules. The inputs of specialised intermediate and auxiliary products may have the character of mass products, which can be purchased in many places, whereas some intermediate products such as biochemicals and reagents are important inputs of service firms and biotech suppliers firms. These products may be important outputs in R&D processes in other biotech and pharmaceutical companies. Although we have defined some of the important transactions between companies in this field, a specific spatial context of these transactions could be identified.

Services

Technology and discovery-oriented biotech firms normally procure analytical services, DNA-sequencing and other laboratory services from biotech and other companies specialised in this activities. Our research gives evidence for the assumption that spatial proximity to the customers can be very useful for service-oriented biotech firms as it allows the fast and correct handling of specialised orders. Spatial proximity allows intensification of the division of labour between clients and service firms, though it is difficult to estimate its precise importance.

14.6 Conclusions

Since Munich is one of the winning regions of the BioRegio Contest, it is not surprising that the region contains a technological and institutional infrastructure which has an extraordinary potential for developing a national biotechnological innovation policy. Our conclusions will address four aspects, summarising the main findings of our analysis, and relating to the conceptual questions posed in the introductory section.

a) Relations Between Inputs and Outputs

The exchange of input and outputs can take very different forms depending on the conditions, business sector and market structure involved. While input-output systems of supporting firms, such as service and supplier firms, are characterised by market exchange, there is a wide variation in the relationships between research-oriented biotech companies and pharmaceutical multinationals, ranging from hierarchies to market exchange. Depending on the complexity of the joint project, the collaboration agreements may combine almost all forms of transaction, such as licensing, purchase, capital investment, milestone payment, royalty and leasing. It is however decisive that such collaboration agreements represent exchange relations over a period of several years. Overall, it is very difficult to generalise the findings of our study. However, the conclusion is suggested that the huge transaction expenditures involved in arranging such long term and sweeping contracts are signs of the importance of untraded relations between the actors.

b) The Significance of Untraded Dependencies and Relational Assets

The significance of untraded relations may be illustrated by following two examples. Mainly in the early stages of a company's life, untraded and tacit knowledge can be of great importance. Entrepreneurs need a shared perception and knowledge of scientific, market, financing and management issues related to the growth perspectives of their firms. A remarkable amount of this knowledge cannot be purchased. It has to be created within specific social contexts of the research community itself. This means that proximity and clustering favours the creation of such untraded dependencies, which lead finally to relational assets in a specific region.

The second example emphasises the co-operation required between biotech firms and large pharmaceutical companies. In this case, untradable relations are a necessary condition to conclude a complex collaboration agreement. Both partners need to have a shared perception of the business perspectives, the goals and major milestones of a common project. In other words, they have to trust to each other. Such a mutual understanding is necessary to fulfil jointly the common goals in business activities. But this suggests that regional coexistence does not play a crucial role, because most large scale collaboration between biotech and pharmaceutical companies is entered into on a European or North Atlantic scale.

Both examples illustrate different space concepts of firms. While for small and less specialised biotech companies, proximity is relatively important in order to organise their crucial input and output relations, larger, advanced and highly specialised companies focusing on high value added technologies and products, organise a 'time-space-compression'. For the latter, it is necessary to manage operations beyond the regional and national scale.

c) The Importance of Regional Governance

There are remarkable feedback loops between regional governance and the creation of new firms. In the case of Munich, we found a Bavarian 'governance spillover' based on experience of the development of high technology cluster in the region (electronics and aerospace). This knowledge has been successfully turned into the promotion of a biotechnology pathway, i.e. into successful institutions assisting the commercialisation process. Examples are the foundation of a technology and life science park and the Bio^{M}AG, which has been established and organised through a public/private partnership. Moreover this knowledge has been responsible for creating a friendly public biotechnology 'climate'. The strong political and institutional support for building up a 'business community' (Cooke 1998) has led to new start-ups in the region. In so doing, existing barriers to the risky commercialisation process are reduced. This is our strongest argument in favour of a 'regional world of innovation'. But there are some counter arguments too, especially with regard to intra-regional learning processes.

d) Regional Specialisation as a Source of Extra Profit for Transnationals

Young biotechnology firms which have been successful over the recent years are characterised by collaboration contracts with large multinationals in the pharmaceutical industry. This means that major incentives for developing new products and technologies are observed or even controlled by actors outside the region. In this major area of invention and development of new products, regional actors are integrated in global networks which are organised by powerful oligopolies. The transnationals therefore operate within the region and use local competence without being forced to contribute to the evolution of regional assets. Seen in this way, regional relational assets are an important factor for the re-organisation of transnationals, because they allow the internalisation of results from R&D activities conducted by external partners. The former research director of Roche, Jürgen Drews, even sees the possibility that the large pharmaceutical enterprises will in the future conduct the commercialisation process, leaving the research basis to public research centres and a multitude of small research companies, which may (but not necessarily) be bound together within regional innovation systems (Drews 1998). Though it is rather improbable that the large companies will give up their own science base and their potential to conduct their own R&D, the future growth of 'externalised' R&D companies is highly likely.

In the form of a conclusion, we should like to emphasise two arguments regarding the concept of 'regional systems of innovation'. Firstly, the innovation processes of highly specialised and advanced technologies takes place at a North Atlantic or triad level. Any company active in such areas needs to situate its strategies at the triad scale. Regional and national contexts play a minor role.

Secondly, the mode of regulation and political power relations are still constituted at a national level. In the context of global competition, states try to implement national innovation policies in order to build and attract high value added sectors in their sphere of influence. That means that the BioRegio Contest is primarily an expression of a national innovation policy which is adjusted to regional conditions and calls for the participation of regional actors.

Innovative biotech clusters are the result of an appropriate perception of regional actors concerning the relations between global scientific and economic conditions and the potential of a region. Therefore, the local social and cultural context permitting such a perception is the sphere where untraded relations and tacit knowledge evolve, and where we can find evidence of a regional innovation system. But the regional scale in itself does not explain the dynamic observed within certain regions or within the biotechnological sector. Though we would agree that proximity matters, it is just one aspect of different and interacting scales of innovation.

References

Archibugi, D., Howells, J., Michie, J. (1999) Innovation Policy in a Global Economy. Cambridge University Press, Cambridge

Bracyk, H.-J., Cooke, P., Heidenreich, M. (1998) Regional Innovation Systems. The Role of Governance in a Globalized World. UCL Press, London

Cooke, P. (1998), Introduction: Origins of a Concept. In: Bracyk, H.-J., Cooke, P., Heidenreich, M. (eds.) Regional Innovation Systems, the Role of Governance in a Globalized World. UCL Press, London, 2-27

Dosi, G. (1988), The Nature of the Innovative Process in Technical Change and Economic Theory. In: Dosi, G., Freeman, C., Nelson, R., Silverberg, G., Soete, L. (eds.) Pinter Publishers, London, 221-238

Drews, J. (1998) Die verspielte Zukunft: Wohin geht die Arzneimittelforschung? Birkhäuser, Basel

Edquist, C. (ed.) (1997) Systems of Innovation. Technologies, Institutions and Organizations. Pinter, London.

Ernst & Young (eds.) (1998) European Life Sciences 98: Continental Shift. The Fifth Annual Ernst & Young Report on the European Life Sciences Industry. Ernst & Young International Ltd, London

Ernst & Young (eds.) (1999) European Life Sciences 99: Communicating Value. Sixth Annual Report. Ernst & Young International Ltd., London

Ernst & Young (eds.) (2000a) Evolution. Ernst & Young's Seventh Annual European Life Sciences Report 2000. Ernst & Young International Ltd., London

Ernst & Young (eds.) (2000b) Gründerzeit: Ernst & Youngs Zweiter Deutscher Biotechnologie-Report 2000. Ernst & Young, Stuttgart

Feldman, M.P. (1994) Geography of Innovation. Kluwer Academic Publishers, Boston, MA

Healey, M.J., Rawlinson, M.B. (1993) Interviewing Business Owners and Managers: A Review of Methods and Techniques. Geoforum 24, 339-355

Howells, J. (1999) Regional Systems of Innovation. In: Archibugi, D., Howells, J., Michie, J. (eds.) Innovation Policy in a Global Economy. Cambridge University Press, Cambridge, 67-93

Howells, J., Wood, M. (1993) The Globalisation of Production and Technology. Belhaven Press, London

Maillat, D. (1996) Vom 'Industrial District' zum kreativen Milieu. Beitrag zur Analyse der gebietsgebundenen Produktionsorganisation. Working Paper, Neuchâtel University

Markusen, A. (1994) Studying Regions by Studying Firms. Professional Geographer 46, 477-490

Oßenbrügge, J. (2001) Regionale Innovationssysteme: Evolution und Steuerung geographischer Formen der wissensbasierten Wirtschaft. In: Schwinges, R., Messerli, P. Münger, T. (eds.) Innovationsräume: Woher das Neue kommt – in Vergangenheit und Gegenwart. vdf, Hochsch.-Verl. an der ETH, Zürich, 85–101

Porter, M.E. (1996) Wettbewerbsvorteile: Spitzenleistungen erreichen und behaupten (deutsche Übersetzung von Competitive Advantage, 1985). Campus, Frankfurt am Main

Schitag Ernst & Young (1998) Aufbruchstimmung: Erster Deutscher Biotechnologie Report, Stuttgart, May, 78

Schoenberger, E. (1991) The Corporate Interview as a Research Method in Economic Geography. Professional Geographer 43, 180-189

Scott, A.J. (1995) The Geographic Foundations of Industrial Performance. Competition and Change 1, 51-66

Sternberg, R. (1995) Technologiepolitik und High-Tech Regionen – ein internationaler Vergleich, Lit-Verlag, Münster

Storper, M. (1997) The Regional World. Territorial Development in a Global Economy. The Guilford Press, New York

Storper, M., Walker, R. (1989) The Capitalist Imperative. New York, Basil Blackwell

Zeller, C. (2001a) Clustering Biotech: A Recipe for Success? Spatial Patterns of Growth of Biotechnology in Munich, Rhineland and Hamburg. Small Business Economics 17, 123–141.

Zeller, C. (2001b) Die Biotech-Regionen München und Rheinland. Räumliche Organisation von Innovationssystemen und Pfadabhängigkeit der regionalen Entwicklung. In: Grotz, R., Schätzl, L. (eds.), Lit-Verlag, Münster

15 Organisational Innovations in Different Systems of Innovation: A Comparison of Germany and UK

Simone Strambach
University of Stuttgart

15.1 Changing Perspectives on Innovation and Innovation Processes – A Systemic View

Organisational innovations at the level of the firm are not a recent phenomenon. This can be seen from the broad scientific debate about Fordism and Taylorism and the large amount of research on the flexible specialisation of firms carried out since Piore and Sable (1984) first spoke about the Second Industrial Divide. Early work concentrated mainly on new organisational principles applied to production systems and processes which enable firms to exploit numerical and functional flexibility so that they can respond to changes in market and demand conditions.

However, in the 1990s there was a fundamental change in the quantitative and qualitative dimensions of the new modes of organisation. Compared to earlier years, there was not only a rapid succession of different organisational models and principles, but there were also organisational innovations which went far beyond production and production-related functions. These affect all the functional areas of firms and include organisational relationships and procedures involving suppliers, co-operation partners, as well as customers. The aim of organisational innovations is no longer just to increase the functional and numerical flexibility of firms, it is also to increase their strategic flexibility. Through decentralising and empowering company units and functions, the rapid recombination and separation of whole functional areas is possible. Organisational restructuring has increasingly led to the breaking up of the traditional company structure, with strongly hierarchical and functionally determined subdivisions, resulting in a fragmentation of production and service chains.

New forms of organisation in firms are directed not only towards material transformation processes, but also non-material interactions and communications within the firm and at its interfaces with the environment. This kind of innovation influences the way the internal and external know-how resources are used and integrated, and how they influence the organisational learning capacity. These resources are now often seen as the intangible dimension of the innovative capacity of the firms.

The acceleration of change in the globalisation process, combined with shortening innovation cycles and knowledge half-life, requires firms to expand their capacity for continuous change. Organisational learning processes are becoming important for creating and maintaining competitiveness. Although organisational innovations are highly firm specific, it would seem that differences in modes of organisation are rooted in national systems of innovation, as can be seen from studies in evolutionary institutional economics.

Studies made in the 1990s of national and regional innovation systems have shown that the environment in which innovation takes place is very important for the firms' innovation processes. These studies have made a significant contribution to a process-oriented systemic view of innovations. Innovations are understood as the result of cumulative interaction and learning processes involving different actors, and it is clear that these are related to the institutional and socio-cultural context in which the actors are embedded.

National and regional governance structures, existing business structures, and the socio-cultural framework all influence innovation processes at the micro level. Innovation systems are characterised by particular operating conditions which are formed by both formal institutions and relationships and informal socio-cultural institutions. These conditions are structurally relatively stable. They include social rules, cultural norms and habits developed over a long period which are difficult to quantify. The systemic operating conditions are also subject to dynamic change, nevertheless, a distinction can be made between these and operating conditions which change in the short run and which are more likely to be found at the micro level of the firm. The systemic conditions have a substantial impact on the extent to which firms can make innovation decisions and on the kind of innovation which they introduce (see Edquist 1997, 1999; Lundvall 1992). This is the main argument of the systemic approach.

The aim of this chapter is to analyse the effects of different systemic socio-economic contexts on the processes of interaction and learning in relation to organisational innovation in firms. The German and British systems have different patterns of economic structures, industrial relations, research and education and training systems, labour market institutions, and governance structures. A comparative study of organisational innovations in Great Britain and Germany is interesting because this type of innovation would appear to have been introduced earlier in the British system. Many of the models for organisational innovation in the 1990s, like lean management or business process re-engineering, originated in North America and were imported from there to European countries. The large international consulting firms played a major role in this process (Eims 1996). There is plenty of evidence which suggests that organisational ideas were taken up first in Britain. The similarities in the innovation systems of the Anglo-Saxon economies (Porter 1991), and the fact that the countries are socio-culturally close have probably been contributing factors here.

International comparative studies have shown that the absence of organisational innovations in Germany contributed to the loss of competitiveness and innovativeness in the early 1990s. Because of the path dependence of learning processes and the inertia of institutionalised structures, it is very difficult to reconstruct existing organisational structures and processes. It seems that, in the past, the institutional arrangements of the national system reinforced the focus on technological reorganisation at the firm level. This meant that the non-technical potential for increasing productivity, such as firm and work organisation, was not sufficiently exploited (Bender 1996; Dreher *et al.* 1995; Priewe 1997). Drawing on empirical studies of industrial companies, Meyer-Krahmer (1999) speaks of 'organisational conservatism' when referring to management that is unwilling to adopt new concepts.

Against this background, the present study considers two questions:

- what differences can be established between the innovation patterns of firms in the two countries?
- to what extent are these differences rooted in the systemic conditions of the different innovation systems?

The chapter is organised as follows: in the Section 15.2 the understanding of organisational innovations and their specific characteristics will be outlined, in order to define this type of innovation for empirical research. Section 15.3 focuses on the empirical results of a survey of firms in the two countries, examining differences and similarities in organisational innovation patterns. Here, the relationship between the institutional environment and the innovation processes of the firms is analysed. The Section 15.4 concentrates on the policy dimension and looks at some implications for innovation policy following from the empirical results.

15.2 The Multidimensional Character of Organisational Innovations – Towards a Definition

To date, there is no generally accepted understanding, such as an international standard, to facilitate the systematic study of organisational innovations beyond national boundaries. The situation is different with innovations in technological products and processes. Although the revised OECD Oslo Manual[1] explicitly stresses the importance of organisational innovations for economic performance and the ability of firms to innovate, this handbook providing guidelines for investigating innovations is mainly concerned with the two Schumpeterian categories, technological product and process innovations (TPP). Capturing organisational innovations is very difficult both empirically and conceptually.

[1] The Oslo Manual, OECD/EUROSTAT (1997) Proposed Guidelines for Collecting and Interpreting Innovation Data, is one of the OECD's method handbooks – it is also known as the Frascati Handbook.

As stated by the OECD, "Organisation is a critical dimension of innovation, but its measurement appears to be very difficult both conceptually and in practice. Moreover organisational change is highly firm-specific, making it still more difficult to summarise in aggregate, sector or economy-wide statistics. As a consequence, organisational innovation has not been included in the measures recommended in the body of the manual." OECD/EUROSTAT (1997, p. 43). This makes it important to conceptualise organisational innovation as the object of study and to define the most important characteristics of this type of innovation.

Using the traditional microeconomic three-part division of innovations into product, process and organisational innovations, any significant improvements in, or the reorganisation of, the organisational structure of a firm – the structural and process organisation – is usually assigned to the last category (see, for example, Pleschka and Sabisch 1996). In addition to structural organisational changes, this innovation category also includes the implementation of new techniques of management and leadership, such as quality management systems, and major changes in the orientation of the firm's strategy.[1]

Although these definitions may at first appear clear, they are unsatisfactory for an empirical study of organisational innovations, because they cannot describe the complexity and various facets of this innovation category. It is not always possible to separate organisational innovations from technological ones. National and international studies have since shown that technological innovations often are combined with organisational changes and vice versa (see Bellmann *et al.* 1996; OECD 1996; Freeman 1998). The results show that *interdependence between technological and organisational innovations* should be considered as a major characteristic of organisational innovations. For example, the use of modern information and communication technologies plays an important role in helping to restructure processes in process oriented re-engineering (Hammer and Stanton 1995), as it is this innovative information technology that makes it possible to implement the new structures.

Another factor is the *process character* of organisational innovations which causes broad areas of overlap between the categories of process and organisational innovations. In many cases, organisational innovations are at the same time process innovations, or at least the two are closely linked. Examples here are the introduction of Total Quality Management Systems (TQM), the implementation of cross functional teamwork, and the reorganisation of business practices. It is often not easy to recognise organisational innovations in empirical studies because they are classified as process innovations. The process character of organisational innovations is also one of the reasons why it is very difficult to record and measure this kind of innovation. The boundaries between organisational modification, organisational change, and organisational innovation are fluid, as these changes can occur in a radical fashion or more slowly in an evolutionary process.

---

[1] Other writers refer to these as 'management innovations'. Here, they are included under the heading of 'organisational innovations'.

Furthermore, they may relate to the company as a whole, or just to single departments, units or teams and thus can vary considerably in *breadth* and *depth*. Following King and Anderson (1995), the term organisational innovations should be used if they are new for the 'social' setting in which they are introduced (the team, the department, the company as a whole) and if their effects are both intentional and public.[1]

Organisational innovations are not only closely interwoven with technological innovations, they also have a *social dimension*, because they touch on the human aspects of companies. Changes in the organisation of work and the content of work require changes in the behaviour of employees. Organisational innovations are the result of learning processes and successful changes in attitude. If, for example, a firm reorganises its business practices in order to put more emphasis on its customers, not only must the work processes restructured and technological systems changed, there must also be changes in the thinking and values of its employees. Institutional structures of organisations based on past learning processes provide an orientation for action, just as the firm culture provides patterns for perception, interpretation, and understanding which result from social interaction (Luhmann 1964; Schein E. 1995; Schein A.H. 1996). For this reason, depending on the magnitude of the organisational innovation, structural changes will be linked with a more or less deliberate reinterpretation of past norms and values. This social and socio-cultural dimension of innovations is an important – though not always obvious – component of organisational innovation.

Table 15.1 Characteristic features of organisational innovations

Features			
Scope of the innovation	Team/department	Company as a whole	Beyond the company
Dimension of the innovation	Strategic change	Structural change	Socio-cultural change
Implementation	Evolutionary	Mixed forms	Radical

Source: own compilation.

It is therefore obvious that organisational innovation is a much broader concept than technological innovation (see Table 15.1). The rest of this study will use the following definition as starting point. *An organisational innovation can be understood as a significant change in strategy, structure and culture of an organisation, which can vary in the speed of its implementation (from evolutionary to radical including mixed forms which combine evolutionary and radical elements) and/or its scope (team to whole company, beyond the company).*

[1] Thus only those changes that have substantial effects on the organisation, or part of it, come under the heading of organisational innovations (Kimberley 1981).

The advantage of this definition is that it also takes into account the essential characteristics of organisational innovation just described. It is also sufficiently open to capture the various firm-specific features of organisational innovations.

15.3 Organisational Innovations in London and Stuttgart in the 1990s – Empirical Results

Sample and Methodology

The structural difference between the study areas – the Stuttgart region in Baden-Württemberg in Germany and the Greater London region in south-east Britain – was the reason for their selection. Stuttgart, whose structure is still dominated by industry, can be considered representative of the German innovation system, while the service economy of the London region is representative of the advanced structural changes in the British economy.

A mixed method was adopted to analyse organisational innovations in Germany and the UK. First, a standardised written questionnaire was used to obtain primary information about organisational innovations that took place in the 1990s. In a second step, qualitative face-to-face interviews with firms, politicians and intermediary institutions were carried out in both countries. The response ratio is show in Table 15.2, and the response by sectors in Table 15.3.

Table 15.2 Response rate

	Stuttgart region (absolute)	London region (absolute)	Total (absolute)
Questionnaires	27	23	50
Interviews*	21	22	43
Total replies	48	45	93
Total Sample	141	147	288
Response rate %	34.7 %	30.6 %	32.3 %

* in addition to the interviews with the companies, 11 further interviews were conducted with intermediary institutions in both countries.
Source: own data.

The firms were selected using the 'theoretical sampling' method. A statistical probability theory sampling procedure could not be used as there are no data sources, either for Germany or for Britain, which contain valid information about the implementation of organisational innovations, allowing the parent population to be determined. This is why representativeness could not be the criterion for inclusion in the study, as it was in the case with the quantitative method. Instead, the criterion had to be how suitable the cases were for answering the theoretical questions. The present study used two criteria for the inclusion of firms – the branch and size of the firm. Firms were chosen from the branches typical of the respective regions in both the industrial and service sectors. A minimum firm size of 150 employees was set because organisational innovations are especially important for larger firms. The particular structures of small and very small firms means that their organisational problems can often be solved on an ad hoc basis.

Table 15.3 Response by sectors

Sectors	Stuttgart region		London region		Total
	absolute	%	absolute	%	absolute
Manufacturing industries	30	62.5	22	48.8	52
Service industries	18	37.5	23	51.2	41
Total	48	100	45	100	93

Source: own data.

Number and Types of Organisational Innovations Implemented by German and British Firms

The organisational innovations of the 1990s, such as total quality management systems, implementation of process oriented re-engineering, or empowerment of units of the firm, are changes which do not only involve the technological optimisation of material transformation processes. Essentially, these kinds of innovation alter the interaction and communications relationships within the firm and at its interfaces with the environment. The particular kind of firm organisation influences the way external and internal know-how resources are integrated, how the competencies are linked and how their applications take place. Organisational innovations therefore influence the learning capacity of the firm. As the results of the survey show, this kind of innovation is increasingly relevant to the firm's ability to adapt to rapid changes in its markets and environment, and the growing intensity of international competition. In the years 1989-1998, firms in both countries made a major organisational change every two to three years, which corresponds to an average of 4.3 changes implemented by each firm. There are no significant country-specific differences in the average number of organisational innovations implemented between Germany (4.5 changes) and Great Britain (4.1 changes). In both countries, only 2.2 percent of the firms had carried out none of the organisational restructuring measures listed in Fig. 15.1.

If we differentiate the projects implemented by type of organisational innovation, we find that the most common innovation is the introduction of a total quality management system (TQM). 84 percent of firms in the sample have changed their organisation to focus on quality. This means that we can speak here of a change that is already well established. Priorities in both Germany and Great Britain in the 1990s were total quality management systems (TQM), followed by lean production/lean management, downsizing, and process-oriented re-engineering. The components of these measures are rather similar and include customer orientation, full understanding of quality, orientation towards processes, decentralisation of decision-making and communication structures, and the development of human resources in order to increase performance. It can be concluded that both countries consider the same organisational principles appropriate for increasing the adaptability and productivity of the firms in the present period of structural change.

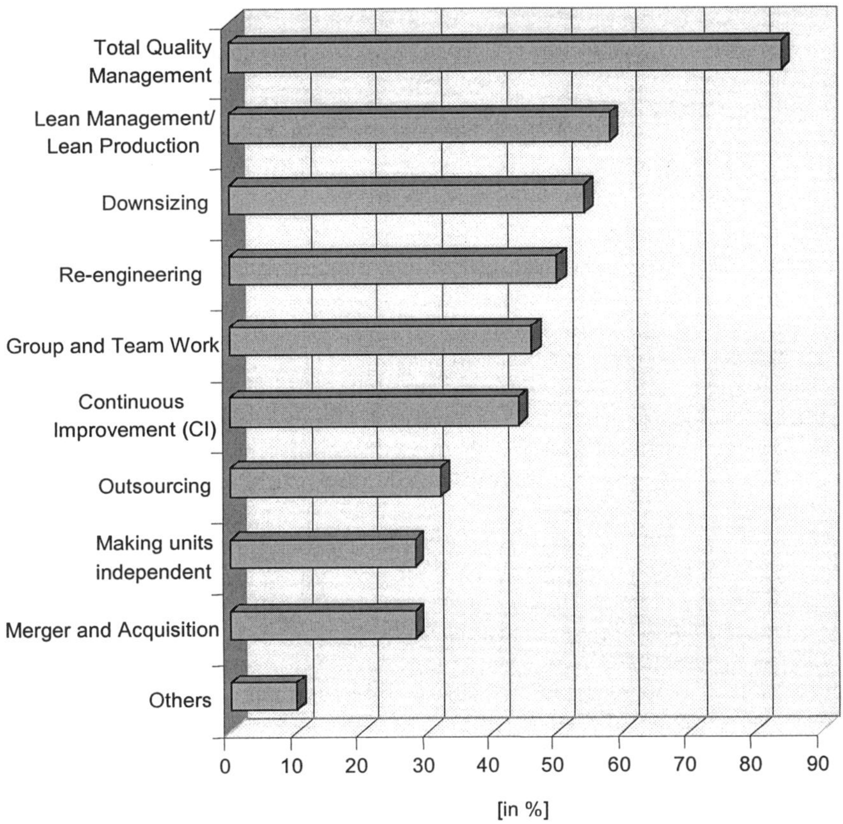

Fig. 15.1 Organisational changes implemented

The interviews carried out in the firms showed that in both Britain and Germany organisational changes do not only take place sequentially, they are sometimes carried out in parallel. It is often a case of 'both at once' rather than 'either/or'. Firms link and combine different organisational restructuring principles, for example TQM with process-oriented re-engineering and downsizing. Different models are often used in different parts of the same firm, although these are sometimes based on contradictory principles, and hence reduce their effectiveness. Moreover, the people in the firm responsible for the changes tend to interpret and implement the models differently. Firms can implement TQM as a higher level framework within a process of change which affects the whole firm, or they can introduce TQM as a subsidiary concept as part of a much more comprehensive innovation concept (e.g. lean management).

A major finding of the study therefore is that the importance and content of individual organisational innovations are determined by the firm-specific context in which they are introduced and applied. Compared to technological innovations, which for maximum performance are also adapted to the individual company, organisational innovations are to a much higher degree social constructs, whose content has to be seen as context dependent. Organisational innovations therefore cannot simply be imitated or copied from other firms. This may also explain why their diffusion and implementation is often so difficult.

Increased Market Competition as the Main Stimulus for Organisational Innovations

There are many reasons why the firms surveyed implemented organisational innovations. However, in all cases, the trigger was a crisis situation. The nature of the event varied and had different causes, but was nevertheless perceived by the firms as a crisis and hence a problem situation.

Management and organisational research has shown that processes of organisational learning and innovation may be introduced as a reaction to external environmental changes and the resulting insecurity, but factors internal to the organisation may also be responsible for their introduction (Chandler 1990; Dodgson 1993). In many cases, internal and external factors influence one another and are closely interrelated. One main point emerges clearly when firms talk about the problem situations they see as inducing change: the importance of external factors. Problem situations internal to the firm were given as the reason for organisational learning processes less frequently than external factors.

Increasing competition and the serious economic recession at the start of the 1990s were quoted by firms in both countries as major reasons for introducing organisational adaptations. In most cases, changes were made necessary by tougher competition, shrinking markets, a declining customer base, and the resultant fall in earnings. In addition, there were increasing pressures on prices caused by international competition. Quantitative economic indicators, such as sales revenue and profits, were what made most of the firms aware of the existence of a problem situation requiring action.

Customers' new requirements provided the second important external incentive for organisational innovations, especially for supplier chains. This applied particularly to quality-related innovations. Customers, directly or indirectly, encourage their suppliers to set up particular quality control systems in their organisations. These can include quality control by certification according to ISO

9000 or systems defined by the customers themselves. The automobile industry, which appears to exert considerable pressure on its suppliers in relation to quality, is a key branch in this respect. This was found to be the case in both Germany and Britain. In the Stuttgart region, the demands of the car manufacturers were a major reason for the implementation of quality management systems by firms in electronics and the mechanical engineering, which produce specialised equipment for the car manufacturers. The suppliers in Great Britain, who in many cases had already met the British quality standard (BS 5750) by the late 1980s, cited pressure by their most important customers as the reason why they introduced standardised control systems, corresponding to the international standard ISO 9000, in order to obtain this certification as well.

This shows that it is mainly pressure from the organisation's environment that makes the need for organisational changes and innovation apparent. As this pressure increases, so too does the willingness to change. This is illustrated by a machine tool manufacturer in the Stuttgart region, which as late as 1998 did not have a standardised quality management system as part of their organisation. The reasons given for this were as follows: "Our international competitors are not yet certified, and our customers do not yet demand certification, otherwise we'd have to catch up. The strength of our company is our international market presence, but our structures have been neglected so far, i.e. there have been few organisational changes. However, we do have a problem in that many interfaces are not efficiently integrated." (Interview D: 19).

The company supplies a niche market and 99 percent of its sales come from the export of customer-specific machines to Asia. The company's positive economic situation means that it is not willing to introduce organisational innovations, even though internal problems are seen to be quite important. This result accords with a pilot study of the international transfer of organisational innovations. The study makes the general observation that firms which had some awareness of a crisis situation were more open to implementing the processes of change (EIMS 1996). The interviews showed not only that external pressure is the main trigger/stimulus for learning processes – which could be called adaptive learning – they also showed that there were differences in the depth and intensity of the organisational processes of learning and innovation so triggered.

Interaction and Learning Processes at the Firm Level: the Integration of Internal and External Knowledge in Organisational Innovation Processes

Firms largely rely on external expertise for the complex learning processes associated with organisational innovations. In both countries, 80 percent of the firms which participated in the written survey used external knowledge to different degrees and from various areas of knowledge in the implementation of organisational innovations. The percentage was even higher for the participants in the interviews. By far the most common way of obtaining new knowledge is to 'buy' expertise primarily from private knowledge-intensive service firms. This results in a transfer of knowledge between the consulting firms and their clients. By contrast, relatively few firms in Germany or Britain acquired external knowledge by employing specialists with innovative know-how and experience with processes of organisational innovation.

Universities as well as research and technology organisations were seen as the important actors in innovation systems. Differentiated technology and knowledge transfer institutions are characteristic of the innovation systems in both the countries.

There are many different research and technology institutions which carry out a wide range of tasks and services including basic research, technology transfer, and applied research. In Germany, these intermediary institutions have a long tradition and are mainly industry and technology oriented. Numerous regional science studies have shown that the widespread decentralised knowledge and technology transfer structure in Baden-Württemberg is a major strength of the regional innovation system (Cooke and Morgan 1994; Pyke and Sengenberger 1992). In the research area, the most important actors at the local level were considered to be universities, technical universities, the Max-Planck Institutes and Fraunhofer Institutes. In the area of technology and knowledge transfer, the Steinbeis Foundation, the German Economy Rationalisation Committee, and the Chambers of Industry and Commerce were seen as important actors.

Since the end of the 1980s a number of organisations have been created in the UK whose task is to support the capacity of firms to innovate at the local level (Bennett *et al.* 1994). The institutions cover research and technology transfer and also provide support in the fields of training and management issues. Universities, colleges, business schools, government laboratories, business links, training and enterprise councils (TEC's), and enterprise agencies were identified as functionally equivalent institutions in the UK.

In order to discover the role played by these intermediary institutions in organisational innovation processes, the firms were asked about their utilisation of, and participation in such institutions. In Table 15.4, the answers have been aggregated under the heading 'public and semi-public institutions'. The survey indicated that knowledge obtained from public and semi-public institutions was far less relevant then private sources. None of the firms surveyed, in either the Stuttgart or London regions, had had assistance only from public or semi-public institutions. A number of firms used this in conjunction with assistance from private suppliers, in most cases as part of certification processes, since the certificates are obtained from these institutions. Public institutions play a minor role in the intermediation process and therefore in the transfer of knowledge.

Knowledge transfers in the context of organisational innovation processes mostly take place in the private market, directly between the customers and knowledge-intensive service firms.[1] One reason is certainly that organisational innovations do not primarily need pure technological knowledge – other areas of knowledge in the fields of economics and the social sciences are also important for innovative problem-solving. The close connections between the firms

[1] Current studies of technology transfer in Germany have shown that these take place mostly between the customers, technology-using firms, and suppliers, whereas the suppliers of technology are mostly other firms (Reinhard and Schmalholz 1996).

surveyed and external knowledge-intensive service suppliers shows how very relevant external expertise and competencies from different areas of knowledge are for organisational innovations. Among those involved are not only business and management consultants with competence in the organisation and management of firms, but also knowledge-intensive service firms from other knowledge fields. These include firms which can provide external knowledge in data processing, training and further education, and technical engineering (see Table 15.5). The kind of knowledge required, which goes beyond individual disciplines and fields, cannot normally be obtained from public institutions.

Table 15.4 Firms' external knowledge sources in organisational innovation processes

External institutions	Number of cases	%
Private knowledge-intensive business services	40	80
Public and semi-public institutions	9	18
Private and public institutions	9	18
Private institutions only	31	62
Public institutions only	0	0
Private knowledge-intensive business services belonging to own firm group	8	20
No external knowledge	10	20

Source: own data.

Table 15.5 Use of external knowledge-intensive services

Area of knowledge	Absolute	%
Organisation and Management	22	56.4
Data processing	16	41.0
Further education, training	11	28.2
Technical engineering services	10	25.6

Source: own data.

These indicators show the multi-dimensional character of organisational innovations, the interdependence of organisational and technological changes and the resulting higher demands on employees. Various external firms are involved in the projects, which take on a wide range of roles and the differing functions associated with them. The set of roles ranges from information suppliers, and catalysts who mobilise internal sources, to diagnostic, training, and process associated functions. These roles are normally filled by different suppliers, but they may also be filled by a single consulting firm which switches roles in the course of the innovation process. The number of external service and consulting firms involved depends on the extent and scope of the projected changes and also the size of the firm and the organisation-internal knowledge. Table 15.6 provides a general outline of the extent to which external firms are involved. Especially for large companies and company-wide changes, the range can extend to more than 20 external knowledge carriers.

Table 15.6 Number of external knowledge-based service companies

Number of external companies	Number of occurrences	%
1 - 2	13	44.8
3 - 4	11	37.9
5 - 10	3	10.4
> 11	2	6.9
N*	29	100.0

* 11 of the 40 companies who used external service companies did not indicate how many.
Source: own data.

The number and the different branches and fields of knowledge of the external firms involved show the complex interaction and communication processes associated with organisational innovations which occur within and between firms. The kind and amount of external knowledge required often shows up only during the innovation process. A detailed analysis of the learning processes is beyond the scope of this chapter. However, it can be said that there was a large variance in the results for the same organisational innovation in different firms, both in Stuttgart and the London region. It is obvious that the quality of the results is strongly influenced by the quality of the interaction and learning processes which occur during implementation. The results of the organisational innovation projects are determined by the quality of the two main actors – the customer and the service firm. The competence and experience of the latter is important, but so too is the ability of the customer to use the external knowledge and integrate it into the organisation. Not least, the ability of both actors to successfully design the interaction process is essential.

Differences in Organisational Innovation Patterns: Earlier Adaptation and Shorter Implementation Stages in British Companies

A lack of organisational innovation proved to be a crucial factor in the loss of competitiveness by German companies at the start of the 1990s (Naschold 1994, 1996; Braczyk 1994). Various efforts were made to implement technical innovations, but organisational innovations were neglected, as is shown by comparisons between companies in the USA and Japan (Jürgens and Naschold

1994; Schienstock 1997). International comparisons of the structural changes at the macroeconomic level indicate that, in Germany, business-related service functions in particular tend not to be transferred to outside firms. The significant difference is not in the general services deficit, but in the different institutional organisation of business-related service functions (DIW 1996; Strambach 1997a). The business services segment is also under represented in Baden-Württemberg compared to the national level. Even in 1997 Baden-Württemberg was not yet at the national level, its business services share of employment at 5.5 percent was a little lower than the average (Strambach 1997b, 1998). Empirical studies on the outsourcing behaviour of firms in Baden-Württemberg conclude that outsourcing has only taken place on a small scale and that a large potential still exists (see Zahn *et al.* 1996). Empirical research in Baden-Württemberg's major industrial branches indicate that by focusing mainly on technological reorganisation, the non-technical potential for increasing productivity has long been neglected (Braczyk and Schienstock 1996; Cooke 1996; Morgan 1996).

Certainly, regional innovation systems are not simply small scale national systems, since they combine elements that are specifically regional, national and even international. But the corresponding empirical indicators at the national and regional level let suggest that it is the framework of constraints and incentives of the national infrastructural institutional set-up, industrial relations, the labour market institutions and the education and training system, that determine the innovation patterns of organisational innovations.

There are significant differences between Germany and Britain in the timing of the implementation of three kinds of organisational innovation – the introduction of cross-functional group and teamwork, process oriented re-engineering, and outsourcing. The greatest difference (as shown in Table 15.7) was in the area of outsourcing. More than 87 percent of the firms which introduced outsourcing in the 1990s were German, while only 12.5 percent were located in Britain.
Numerous indicators suggest that this difference is the result of a catching up process by firms in the Stuttgart region. Looking at the years in which outsourcing was implemented, it is obvious that none of the German firms in the study made this kind of organisational change in the late 1980s. 1993 is the earliest year mentioned for outsourcing by firms in the Stuttgart region. Further evidence can be deduced from the organisational structures of the firms. 68 percent of the firms which had an above average number of internally differentiated functional areas were German and less than a third were British.

Comparing the two countries over the period in which TQM was introduced shows that 60 percent of the firms which had begun to introduce this far reaching change before 1991, i.e. relatively early, are located in Britain. Moreover, at the start of the 1990s, more British firms than German firms were implementing TQM. Only in the second half of the 1990s did German firms have a larger share (see Fig. 15.2). These results show that firms in the London region implemented TQM earlier than those in the Stuttgart region.

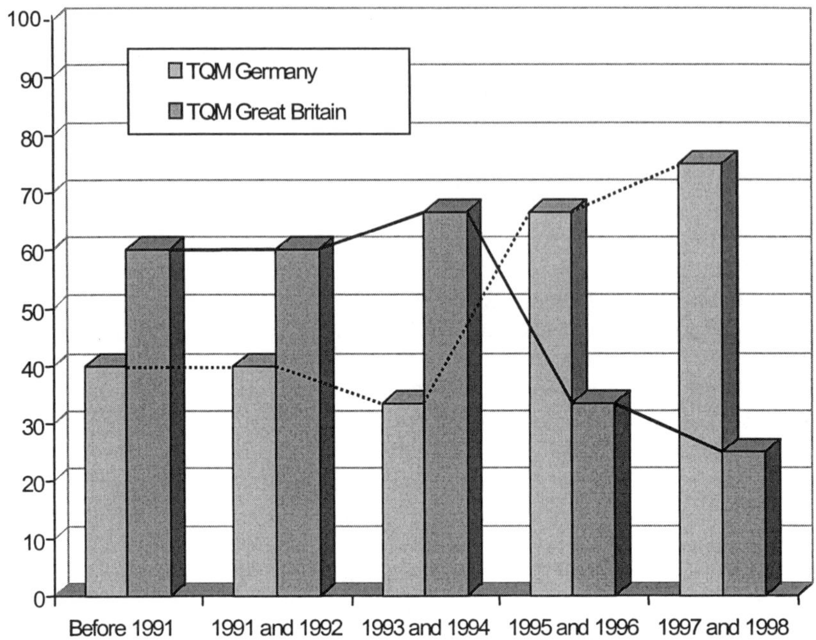

Fig. 15.2 Percentage of companies in Germany and Britain which implemented Total Quality Management in the 1990s

Table 15.7 Organisational innovations implemented in Germany and Britain in the 1990s

Organisational innovations	Projects Total	Germany %	Britain %
Total Quality Management TQM	42	52.4	47.6
Continuous Improvement systems	22	50.0	50.0
Lean Production/ Lean Management	29	55.2	44.8
Downsizing	27	55.6	44.4
Cross-functional group and teamwork	23	60.9	39.1
Process-oriented re-engineering	25	60.0	40.0
Making units independent	14	50.0	50.0
Outsourcing	16	87.5	12.5
Mergers and Acquisitions	14	42.9	57.1
Others	5	80.0	20.0
Total Projects	217	57.1	42.9

Source: own data.

The proportion of German firms which implemented process-oriented re-engineering projects is 20 percent higher than that of British firms. Here too, a catching up process seems to have taken place. According to a survey by the Fraunhofer Institut für Arbeitswirtschaft und Organisation (Fraunhofer Institute for Labour Economy and Organisation) only 5 percent of the firms surveyed in Germany were implementing re-engineering projects in spring 1994. However, 45 percent claimed that they were planning such projects and 50 percent were discussing possible projects (Bullinger *et al.* 1994, Fraunhofer Institut für Arbeitswirtschaft und Organisation 1995). The results of the present study show that, only four years later, the share of firms involved in re-engineering had increased twelve-fold. It can thus be said that process orientation as a basic principle of design and organisation has now become widely accepted among German firms. These results also throw some light on the speed with which organisational innovations have spread.

Organisational innovations generally take a long time to implement. Even though the time needed is influenced by the extent and scope of the individual measures, it can nevertheless be seen from Table 15.8 that most projects took on average from two to three years to complete. Picot and Böhme (1995), who examined business process re-engineering projects, also found that while in some cases more than four years were necessary, the average period was two years.

Table 15.8 Average time taken to complete projects of organisational change

Organisational innovations	Duration in years and months
Total Quality Management TQM	2.7
Continuous Improvement systems CI	1.8
Lean production/ Lean management	2.8
Downsizing	2.0
Cross-functional group and teamwork	2.2
Process-oriented re-engineering	3.1
Making units independent	3.3
Outsourcing	1.8
Mergers and acquisitions	2.3

Source: own data.

A marked difference emerged between the two countries in terms of the time taken to complete innovation projects. British firms indicated significantly shorter implementation times for the various organisational innovations. According to the average project times shown above, British firms took six months less time for TQM and CI projects. For outsourcing and process-oriented re-engineering, the times were respectively eight and seven months shorter. The biggest difference between British and German firms is with the introduction of lean production/lean management. The completion time for these projects in Britain is more than one year less than the average for the firms as a whole.

In summary, it can be said that by the end of the 1990s there was no evidence, either from the survey or the interviews, that the German firms were still lagging behind with regard to organisational innovations, at least from a quantitative point of view. The situation had clearly changed since the early 1990s when there was much discussion about their competitiveness. However, the empirical results show that, with regard to the *time dimension*, the patterns of innovation in the two countries are different. It is clearly evident that the British firms tend to adopt the organisational innovations earlier, and the more rapid completion, which stems from shorter implementation stage, indicates that the organisational learning processes are different.

From a systemic point of view firms' organisational learning processes take place in the interaction with their institutional environment. The question now arises of how much the different innovation patterns in the two countries are related to the different socio-economic frameworks and the systemic features of the innovation systems in which the firms are embedded.

The Influence of Institutional Contexts on Organisational Innovation Processes: Different Labour Institutions and Management Cultures

The different labour relations and labour market conditions faced by the firms in the two countries provide one answer to the question of which factors are responsible for the differences outlined above. In Britain the deregulated labour market allows organisational restructuring measures to be implemented quickly and flexibly, although this often has drastic consequences for employees. For example, this is shown by the following quote of the manager of an industrial supplier for large electronics and telecommunications companies in London:

"Since much of value added in the current businesses is labour, we pay much attention to downsizing (or increasing) the workforce in line with the business cycles. Decisions in this respect are based on the forward order book. It allows a quicker reaction than the management accounts which only look at the past. *Reducing the work force* is relatively simple since those who have been with the company for less than two years *only require one week's notice*. The notice period increases by one week for each subsequent year. Following the downturn in 1996, the company introduced lean management by cutting three of the middle management positions." (Interview UK: 8).

The conditions under which German firms operate are different because the laws which govern the labour market, providing protection from dismissal and the right of employees to co-determination, limit the firms' scope for action. The works councils must be informed about dismissals and have the right to be consulted about restructuring (Ebbinhaus and Visser 1997). Extensive organisational innovations usually modify existing work rules, working hours, and wage structures. The works councils have a co-determination right in these matters and are required to participate as representatives of the interests of the employees. In contrast to Britain, the institutional regulation of labour relations in

Germany means that the interest groups affected must be informed and negotiate an agreement before organisational innovations can be implemented. This interaction process takes far more time than a 'top down' strategy, where only the efficiency of the firm is considered, and more time than a short-term market oriented strategy, that considers only the requirements of the market, both of which are possible in Britain due to the deregulated labour relations.

Other explanations for the shorter implementation periods for organisational innovations in Great Britain are the different work and management cultures, which have been observed in many comparative international studies of European business systems and analyses of the respective corporate governance structures (Becker and Vitols 1997; Heidenreich 1998; Hickson 1993; Lane 1992; Soskice 1996; Whitley 1992; Whitley and Kristensen 1997).

In Great Britain conflicts have traditionally been resolved to a much larger extent at the firm level. The different institutional regulation of employer-employee relations means that negotiations at the branch level are relatively unimportant. The system makes higher demands on management in terms of its responsibility for human resources management. Involving colleagues, dealing with opposition and conflict, and motivating workers, whose job mobility is high, are abilities which have far more influence on the education and career paths of managers in Britain than in Germany. The value of a general management education, which is reflected in the institution of the 'Business School', shows that management know-how is valued far more highly in the British system than in the German system.[1] By contrast, management in Germany is not considered to be a separate generally definable activity that can be learned (Lane 1992, 1997; Heidenreich 1998). The results of comparative empirical studies show that the organisation of work and the 'management culture' in Germany are influenced more by specialised expertise, mostly technical and technological. Management as such is not considered a specific function, it is carried out by managers who have mostly attained their positions and functions in the firm by virtue of their technical qualifications (Lane 1992; Warner and Campell 1993).

These differences are particularly relevant for organisational innovations which require a far greater knowledge of management and social skills than technological innovations, since they involve initiating restructuring processes and the guidance and accompanying of the complex learning processes, which cut across various functions and interfaces. Knowledge of economics and the social sciences is thus crucially important for organisational innovations. The need to integrate social skills and management know-how with technological education and training only began to be widely discussed in Germany in the early 1990s (Mai 1994; Weber and Seltz 1994). Human resource management has, in contrast, been an integral part of the British system for many years. These differences in the work and management cultures, and the resulting differences in action orientation, must be seen as explanatory factors for the shorter implementation times of the organisational innovation projects.

---

[1] For a historical view of German management education see Kipping (1998).

15.4 Conclusions – Some Implications for Innovation Policy

Organisational innovations are associated with complex interactions and learning processes both within and between firms. Although the firms in the two countries consider the same organisational principles – customer orientation, full understanding of quality, process orientation, as well as the decentralisation of decision-making and communications structures – to be suitable for increasing flexibility and productivity, these have very strong firm-specific features. The decision to introduce such an innovation is the starting point for learning and adaptation processes at different levels and dimensions of the firm. At the end of the process, the organisational innovation implemented is often different from the model planned at the start. The organisational learning processes connected with the changes ultimately not only define the specific details of the innovation, they also determine whether the performance potential of the innovation can be exploited.

A question can now be asked with regard to innovation policy. Is it necessary to include organisational innovations as a factor in the development strategies relating to innovation policy at the European, national, and regional levels?

Interventions in the area of innovation and technology policies in recent decades have focused primarily on technology and research-intensive areas of the economy. On the other hand, in the emerging 'knowledge economy', value creation and competitiveness appear to be increasingly linked with the production of new knowledge, involving the access to and reconfiguration of knowledge from all over the world. Thus the ability to learn and to innovate is becoming crucially important even for traditional industries and the so-called low and medium tech industries (OECD 1996; Lundvall and Borras 1998; Lundvall and Johnson 1994; Malmberg and Maskell 1999). The intensification of international competition in the current situation of global structural change, and the external pressure on firms, deriving from rapidly changing markets and new demands from customers, require the ability both to respond to change and to be creative. This is one of the main reasons for integrating organisational innovations with innovation policy strategies. They make an initially 'intangible' contribution to increasing the ability of firms to innovate and learn. This is apparent in dimensions other than the classical short-term cost-oriented efficiency calculations. The strategic effects of reorganisation measures, such as increased customer satisfaction, positive effects on employee motivation, and the ability to react more quickly to qualitative market changes, are only realised in the medium to long run. The large number of organisational measures examined in this study, and also numerous empirical case studies (Andreasen *et al.* 1995) show the importance of these innovations for increasing the flexibility of firms and their ability to react and adapt.

It is now clear that an essential task for innovation policy interventions is to create awareness of the importance and relevance of organisational innovations for the firms' ability to learn and innovate, and also an awareness of the multi-dimensional character of this kind of innovation. They are not only linked to organisational and technological changes in structures and processes, they also have a definite socio-cultural dimension. It requires major changes in the employees' attitudes and behaviour. Especially firms which have only limited experience with organisational innovations tend to overlook or underestimate the importance of the socio-cultural changes required for the success of the innovation, as this study shows. It cannot be assumed that companies are aware that the parallel, mutually supportive development of strategy, structure and culture is essential for organisational innovation projects. Here we have an important field of action for political actors – to increase the knowledge of the importance of socio-cultural innovation on a wide basis.

This leads to a further question. What kinds of measure are usually appropriate to promote the initiation of complex innovation processes? Without going into action concepts here, it is nevertheless obvious that the tasks go far beyond the present forms and instruments of technology transfer and scientific-technical collaboration. The challenge for the political actors is to initiate the firms' self-organising and learning processes in the area of organisational innovations. The different innovation patterns in firms in Great Britain and Germany indicate that the systemic conditions in which the firms are embedded the different country-specific industrial relations and labour market regulations, and the different work and management cultures, strongly influence the collective interaction and learning processes. In contrast to the USA, Europe has a large variety of different national and regional innovation systems. Measures to promote organisational innovations can only be effective if they are adapted to the particular institutional context of an individual innovation system. Political actors could, for example, develop institutional leading models to document and disseminate the importance of values. Stimulus for organisational learning processes could proceed from this kind of leading model in the environment of the firm. Such models (in German called 'Leitbilder') would be able to take on orientation, motivational and co-ordination functions for firms in the context of complex organisational innovation processes, and provide support for self-organising processes.

Acknowledgements

The author is grateful for the financial support provided by the Deutsche Forschungsgemeinschaft as part of the research programme 'Technological Change and Regional Development in Europe'. Particular mention should be made of the help given by Dr. Matthais Kipping of the University of Reading, for his support with the collection of data in the UK and for the fruitful discussions at the empirical stage of the project.

References

Andreasen, L., Coriat, B., Den Hertog, F., Kaplinsky, R. (eds.) (1995) Europe's Next Step: Organisational Innovation, Competition and Employment. Frank Cass, Ilford

Becker, C., Vitols, S. (1997) Innovationskrise der deutschen Industrie? Das deutsche Innovationssystem der neunziger Jahre. In: Naschold, F., Soskice, D., Hancké, B., Jürgens, U. (eds.) Ökonomische Leistungsfähigkeit und institutionelle Innovation: das deutsche Produktions- und Politikregime im globalen Wettbewerb. Edition Sigma, Berlin, 251-268

Bellmann, L., Düll, H., Kühl, J., Lahner, M., Lehmann, U. (1996) Flexibilität von Betrieben in Deutschland. Ergebnisse des IAB-Betriebspanels 1993-1995. Beiträge zum OECD-Projekt "Flexible Enterprise" Institut für Arbeitsmarkt- und Berufsforschung, Nürnberg.
Bender Ch. (1996) Innovation By Half-Measures in German Manufacturing. Critique of Industrial Restructuring from the Perspective of Social Innovation. Journal of Industry Studies 3(3), 153-162
Bennett, R.J., Wicks, P., McCoshan, A. (1994) Local Empowerment and Business Services. Britain's Experiment with Training and Enterprise Councils, London
Braczyk, H.-J. (1994) Organisationswandel und Regulationsstruktur – Das Beispiel Baden-Württembergs. In: Weber, H. (ed.): Lean Management – Wege aus der Krise. Organisatorische und gesellschaftliche Strategien. Gabler Verlag, Wiesbaden, 103-122
Braczyk H.-J., Schienstock, G. (eds.) (1996) Kurswechsel in der Industrie. Lean Production in Baden–Württemberg. Kohlhammer Verlag, Stuttgart
Bullinger, H.-J., Roos, A., Wiedmann, G. (1994) Amerikanisches Business Reengineering oder japanisches Lean Management? Office Management, July, August, 14-20
Chandler, A.D. (1990) Scale and Scope: The Dynamic of industrial Capitalism. Harvard University Press, Cambridge Mass.
Cooke, P. (1996) Der baden-württembergische Maschinenbau: Regionale Antworten auf globale Bedrohungen. In: Braczyk, H.-J., Schienstock, G. (eds.): Kurswechsel in der Industrie. Lean Production in Baden-Württemberg. Kohlhammer Verlag, Stuttgart, 52-68
Cooke, P., Morgan, K. (1994) The Regional Innovation System in Baden-Württemberg. International Journal Technology Management 9, Nos 3/4, 394-429
DIW 1996: Keine Dienstleistungslücke in Deutschland – Ein Vergleich mit den USA anhand von Haushaltsbefragungen. DIW–Wochenbericht, No. 14/1996. Berlin, 221-226
Dodgson, M. (1993) Organizational Learning: A Review of some Literatures. Organization Studies 14(3), 375-394
Dreher, C., Fleig, J., Harnischfeger, M., Klimmer, M. (1995) Neue Produktionskonzepte in der deutschen Industrie: Bestandsaufnahme, Analyse und wirtschaftspolitische Implikation. Physica Verlag, Heidelberg
Ebbinhaus, B., Visser, J. (1997) Der Wandel der Arbeitsbeziehungen im westeuropäischen Vergleich. In: Hradil, S., Immerfall, S. (eds.) Die westeuropäischen Gesellschaften im Vergleich. Leske+Budrich, Opladen, 333–376
Edquist, Ch. (1997) Systems of Innovation: Technologies, Institutions and Organizations. Printer, London, Washington.
Edquist, Ch. (1999) Innovation Policy – A Systemic Approach. In: Paper Presented at The European Socio-Economic Research Conference: The Globalising Learning Economy. Major Socio-Economic Trends and European Innovation Policy. April 28-30. Brussels
Eims/European Commission (1996) International Transfers of Organisational Innovation. EIMS Publication, No. 45
Fraunhofer Institut für Arbeitswirtschaft und Organisation (1995) Business Reengineering: Aktuelle Managementkonzepte in Deutschland: Zukunftsperspektiven und Stand der Umsetzung. Fraunhofer Institut für Arbeitswirtschaft und Organisation, Stuttgart.
Freeman, Ch. (1998) The Economics of Technical Change. In: Archibugi, D., Michie, J. (eds.) Trade, Growth and Technical Change. Cambridge University Press, Cambridge, 16-54
Hammer, M., Stanton, S. 1995: Die Reengineering-Revolution: Handbuch für die Praxis. Campus-Verlag, Frankfurt, New York
Heidenreich, M. (1998) Arbeit und Management in den westeuropäischen Kommunikationsgesellschaften. In: Hradil, S., Immerfall, S. (eds.) Die west-

europäischen Gesellschaften im Vergleich. Leske+Budrich, Opladen, 289-232

Hickson, D. (ed.) (1993) Management in Western Europe. Society, Culture and Organization in Twelve Nations. De Gruyter, Berlin, New York.

Jürgens, U., Naschold, F. (1994) Arbeits- und industriepolitische Entwicklungsengpässe der deutschen Industrie in den neunziger Jahren. In: Zapf, W., Dierkes, M. (eds.) Institutionenvergleich und Institutionendynamik. Jahrbuch des Wissenschaftszentrum Berlin für Sozialwissenschaft. Edition Sigma, Berlin, 239-270

Kimberley, J. R. (1981) Managerial Innovation. In: Nystrom, P., Starbuck, W.H. (eds.) Handbook of Organizational Design (1). Oxford University Press, Oxford, 81-104

King, N., Anderson, N. (1995) Innovation and Change in Organizations. Routledge, London

Kipping, M. (1998) The hidden Business Schools. Managment Training in Germany since 1945. In: Engwall, L., Zamagni, V. (eds.): Management Education in Historical Perspective. Manchester University Press, Manchester, New York, 95-110.

Lane, Ch. (1992) Management and Labour in Europe: the Industrial Enterprise In Germany, Britain and France. Aldershot.

Lane, Ch. (1997) The Governance of Interfirm Relations in Britain and Germany: Societal or Dominance Effects? In: Whitley, R., Kristensen, P.H. (eds.): Governance at Work. The Social Regulation of Economic Relations. Oxford University Press, Oxford, 62-85

Luhmann, N. (1964) Funktionen und Folgen formaler Organisation. Duncker & Humblot, Berlin.

Lundvall, B.-A. (1992) National Systems of Innovation: Towards a Theory of Innovation and Interactive Learning. Printer, London

Lundvall, B.-A, Borras, S. (1998) The Globalising Learning Economy: Implications for Innovation Policy. European Commission, Studies Targeted Socio-economic Research, Luxemburg

Lundvall, B.-A., Johnson, B. (1994) The Learning Economy. Journal of Industry Studies, 1(2), 23-42

Mai, M. (1994) Engpaß Ingenieurqualifikation. Anstöße zu einer notwendigen Reform. In: Weber, H. (ed.) Lean Management – Wege aus der Krise. Organisatorische und gesellschaftliche Strategien. Kohlhammer Verlag, Wiesbaden, 145-155

Malmberg, A., Maskell, P. (1999) Localized Learning and Regional Economic Development. European and Regional Studies 6(1), 5-8

Meyer-Krahmer, F. (1999) Der Prozeßcharakter von Innovationen In: Meyer-Krahmer, F., Lang, S. (eds.) Geisteswissenschaften und Innovationen. Physica Verlag, Heidelberg, 45-57. (Technik, Wirtschaft und Politik, 35)

Morgan, K. (1996) Umkehrung der Zermürbung. In: Braczyk, H.-J., Schienstock, G. (eds.) Kurswechsel in der Industrie. Lean Production in Baden-Württemberg. Kohlhammer Verlag, Stuttgart, 245-268.

Naschold, F. (1994) Das deutsche Wirtschaftsmodell auf dem Prüfstand. Herausforderung an Politik und Wirtschaft in den 90er Jahren. Landeszentrale für politische Bildung Baden-Württemberg: Der Bürger im Staat 44 (2), 133-138

Naschold, F. (1996) Jenseits des baden-württembergischen 'Exceptionalism': Strukturprobleme der deutschen Industrie. In: Braczyk, H.-J., Schienstock, G. (eds.) Kurswechsel in der Industrie. Lean Production in Baden-Württemberg, Kohlhammer Verlag, Stuttgart, 184-212

Nelson, R. (ed.) (1993) National Innovation Systems. Oxford University Press, Oxford

OECD (1996) Employment and growth in the knowledge-based economy. Paris

OECD, EUROSTAT (1997) The measurement of scientific and technological activities. Proposed guidelines for collecting and interpreting technological innovation data. Oslo Manual. Paris

Picot, A., Böhme, M. (1995) Zum Stand der prozeßorientierten Unternehmensgestaltung in Deutschland. In: Nippa, M., Picot, A. (eds.): Prozeßmanagement und Reengineering: Die Praxis im deutschsprachigen Raum. Campus-Verlag, Frankfurt, 227-247

Piore, M.J. and Sable, C. (1984) The Second Industrial Divide. Basic Books, New York.

Pleschak, F., Sabisch, H. (1996) Innovationsmanagment. Schäffer-Poeschel Verlag, Stuttgart

Porter, M.E. (1991) Nationale Wettbewerbsvorteile: erfolgreich konkurrieren auf dem Weltmarkt. Droemer Knaur, München

Priewe, J. (1997) Die technologische Wettbewerbsfähigkeit der deutschen Wirtschaft. Stärken, Schwächen, Innovationsdefizite. Berlin. Discussion paper FS II 97-203, Wissenschaftszentrum Berlin für Sozialforschung

Pyke, F., Sengenberger, W. (1992) Industrial Districts and Local Economic Regeneration. International Institute for Labour Studies, Geneva.

Reinhard, M., Schmalholz, H. (1996) Technologietransfer in Deutschland: Stand und Reformbedarf. Schriftenreihe des ifo Instituts für Wirtschaftsforschung, 140. Berlin, München

Schein, A.H. (1996) Culture: The Missing Concept in Organization Studies. Administrative Science Quarterly 41, 229-240

Schein, E. (1995) Unternehmenskultur: ein Handbuch für Führungskräfte. Campus-Verlag, Frankfurt, New York.

Schienstock, G. (1997) The Transformation of Regional Governance: Institutional lock–ins and the Development of Lean Production in Baden–Württemberg. In: Whitley, R., Kristensen, P.H. (eds.): Governance at Work. The Social Regulation of Economic Relations. Oxford University Press, Oxford, New York, 190-208

Soskice, D. (1996) German Technology Policy, Innovation, and National Institutional Frameworks. Discussion paper FS I 96-319 Wissenschaftszentrum Berlin für Sozialforschung, Berlin

Strambach, S. (1997a) Wissensintensive unternehmensorientierte Dienstleistungen – ihre Bedeutung für die Innovations– und Wettbewerbsfähigkeit Deutschlands. Deutsches Institut für Wirtschaftsforschung (DIW), Vierteljahreszeitschrift, 66(2) Berlin, 230-242

Strambach, S. (1997b) Die Rolle wissensintensiver unternehmensorientierter Dienstleistungen im Strukturwandel der Region Stuttgart. In: Gaebe, W. (ed.) Struktur und Dynamik in der Region Stuttgart. Verlag Eugen Ulmer, Stuttgart, 82-97

Strambach, S. (1998) Knowledge-intensive Business Services as an Element of Learning Regions – The Case of Baden-Württemberg. CD-ROM 38th Congress of the European Regional Science Association August 28 - September 1, Vienna

Warner, M., Campell, A. (1993) German Management. In: Hickson, D. (ed.) Management in Western Europe. Society, Culture and Organization in Ttwelve Nations. De Gruyer, Berlin, New York, 89-108

Weber, H., Seltz, R. (1994) Zwischen 'Over-engineering' und 'Lean Construction' – Zum Wandel von Organisation und Qualifikation von Ingenieuren. In: Weber, H. (ed.): Lean Management – Wege aus der Krise. Organisatorische und gesellschaftliche Strategien. Kohlhammer Verlag, Wiesbaden, 157-187

Whitley, R. (1992) European Business Systems: Firms and Markets in their National Contexts. Sage, London

Whitley, R., Kristensen, P.H. (eds.) (1997) Governance at Work. The Social Regulation of Economic Relations. Oxford University Press, Oxford, New York.

Zahn, E., Soehnle, K., Hertweck, A. (1996) Auswirkungen des Outsourcing von Dienstleistungen in der Region Stuttgart. Industrie- und Handelskammer Region Stuttgart, Stuttgart.

16 Environmental Management in Manufacturing Industry: A Comparison Between British and German Firms

Boris Braun and Reinhold Grotz
Geographisches Institut, Bonn University

16.1 Introduction

In years to come, environmental performance will be an increasingly important factor in determining the competitive success of manufacturing companies. The demands of the environmental challenge will require considerable changes in the organisation of firms, as they have to respond to an ever-tightening environmental legislation and to the needs of more environmentally aware consumers, investors and employees. The 'greening of industry' will also have long-term consequences for technological change and regional development. This paper intends to explore one facet of these profound changes – the adoption of environmental management systems (EMS) by manufacturing companies in the United Kingdom and Germany. More specifically, the study aims to compare British and German manufacturing establishments which have successfully implemented the European Eco-Management and Audit Scheme (EMAS).

The two countries have often been regarded as opposite poles in the spectrum of responses to the environmental challenge. While Germany is generally perceived to be among the leaders in the 'greening of industry', Britain is mostly seen as a laggard and has gained an image as the 'Dirty man of Europe' (Porrit and Winner 1988). Recent studies challenge this simplistic view, but confirm the notion that Germany has created greater pressures for private companies to take environmental action (Gordon 1994; James *et al.* 1997; Peattie and Ringler 1994). According to these studies, there are a number of reasons for the relative advantage of the German system, most importantly:

- more stringent regulation;
- a consensus-oriented political culture and a political system more open to environmental protection;
- greater decentralisation of political power allowing all tiers of government to develop environmental policies;
- more widespread concern amongst the German public;

- competitive strategies which focus on high quality and high value products, making extra costs easier to bear;
- a well-developed and politically influential environmental technology sector;
- a system of corporate financing and governance which fosters long-term decision-making perspectives and closer interaction with external stakeholders.

Without doubt, national approaches to the environmental issue are still different at both government and company levels. Some analysts argue that German regulations are not only more stringent, but create a major competitive advantage, too (e.g. Braun 1998; Porter 1996, Porter and van der Linde 1996). This is said to occur through the existence of a larger and more advanced environmental technology sector and first mover advantages for other industrial sectors, since over time German standards are often adopted in the rest of Europe. On the other hand, the United Kingdom has led the way in the development of environmental management standards (EMS) and was the first country in the world to adopt a national EMS (BS 7750) in the early 1990s. A major stimulus to environmental consciousness in the United Kingdom has been a general desire to reduce costs or to find markets for recycled goods. The introduction, in particular, of the Landfill Tax in October 1996 stimulated a more market-seeking behaviour by industrial waste generators.

There are three more general trends which are tending to close the gap between the two national systems. These are a partial 'levelling up' of environmental regulation under the growing influence of European legislation, the changing economic circumstances under the pressure of globalisation, and the concept of sustainability which seems to be more influential in the United Kingdom than in Germany.

Set against this background, the aim of this paper is to compare the economic and technological relevance of recently implemented EMS within British and German manufacturing firms. Within this framework we are particularly interested in the external effects on environmental strategies and their spatial dimensions. Our analysis is based on both the stakeholder (Donaldson and Preston 1995, Freeman 1984) and the network approach (Cooke and Morgan 1993). As both concepts have been widely discussed in recent publications, their conceptual basis does not need to be presented in detail. The concepts are based on different traditions in economic research, but both highlight the external determinants of corporate development and the relevance of non-market relationships.

Basic elements of the network approach are co-operative agreements based on a certain extent of mutual trust. This co-operation may be of regional or non-regional character. The stakeholder approach was initially a (normative) business management concept which tried to overcome simple input-output models by emphasising the role of the environment in which firms operate. Stakeholders can be defined as any person or organisation who affects or is affected by the way a company manages its business. In other words, stakeholders have a 'stake' in the business, and demand to influence company decisions that affect them (Grafé-Buckens and Hinton 1998). In order to be successful, enterprises have to find a sustainable balance between various stakeholder demands, e.g. from shareholders, employees, customers, banks, environmental organisations or the state. Despite its normative character, the stakeholder concept can also be used as an empirical tool to analyse external demands on management decisions (e.g. Dyllick and Belz 1995). We do not aim to discuss the theoretical virtues of the network and stakeholder concepts here. They rather serve as an analytical framework for our empirical approach.

Several questions arise in the light of these theoretical concepts and the current debate on EMS:

1. What is the role of environmental stakeholders in the process of corporate greening? Are there any significant differences between Britain and Germany?
2. What are the differences in environmental performance of British and German manufacturers?
3. How cost-effective are EMS? How far are economic and environmental benefits related?
4. What are the firm-specific and the external factors which influence the performance of EMS with regard to ecological, technological and economic goals?

16.2 The Evolution of Environmental Management

The late 1980s saw growing interest in the concept of corporate environmental auditing around the globe. Although the most remarkable progress was made in Europe in the early 1990s. The British BS 7750 became the point of reference for international efforts to set standards for corporate environmental management. The BS 7750 itself was based on the best-known quality standard, the ISO 9000 series, also developed by the British Standard Institution (BSI) in the early 1980s (BS 5750).

All three management standards are similar in that they focus on procedures of achieving objectives rather than on the objectives themselves. The progress that has been obtained over the years resulted in the publication of the EMAS by the European Communities in June 1993 and the ISO 14000 series (environmental management) by the International Standard Organisation in September 1996. Today, there are two standards by which European enterprises can achieve formal certification of their EMS: EMAS and ISO 14001. Both standards are comparable in their major objectives. Both emphasise the importance of business ethics and a continuous improvement of environmental performance. EMAS and ISO 14001 differ in spatial scope (European versus global), organisational approach (site versus organisation), and obligations for public information.

With respect to the latter aspect the EMAS is the more demanding standard, as it requires the publication of an environmental statement. However, many companies perceive the two systems as complementary rather than as exclusive. The European Eco-Management and Audit Scheme (Council Regulation 1836/93) has been available for voluntary participation since April 1995. It basically works as an external control and validation of internal policies, programmes, management systems, and audit cycles (Fig. 16.1). It sets no physical targets, requiring only compliance with existing national environmental standards.

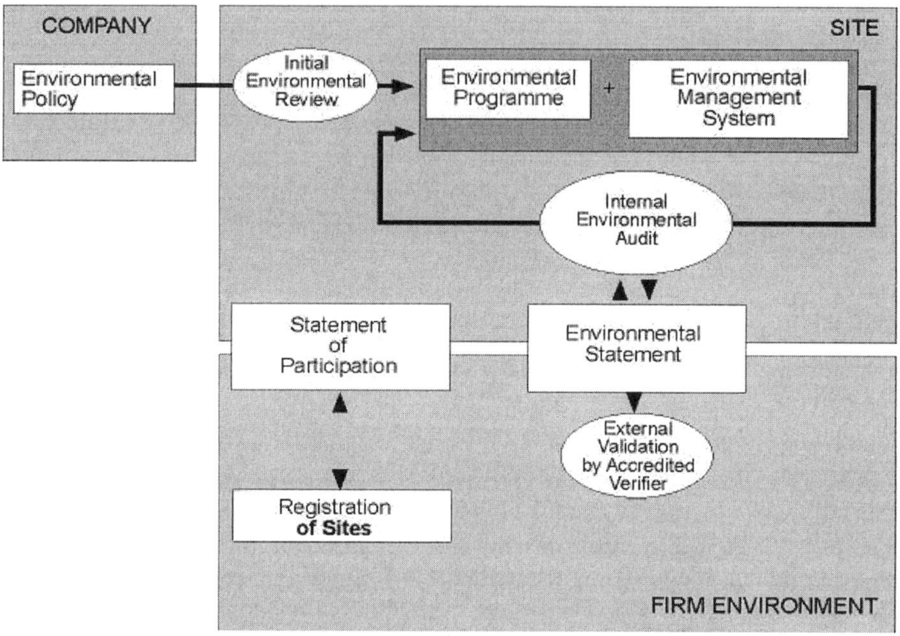

Fig. 16.1 The EMAS process: elements, audit cycles and validation

From 1995 onwards, German industry has been particularly keen to adopt EMAS. In other European countries, including the United Kingdom, the uptake has been considerably slower. Meanwhile, three out of five registered sites within the European Union are located in Germany. When figures are adjusted for population or manufacturing jobs, however, the German dominance gives way to a whole group of countries with high rates of adoption, including Austria, Sweden, and Denmark (Braun and Geibel 2000). There are, on the other hand, countries with extremely low participation rates such as Portugal, Greece and Italy. These differences are partly a consequence of the varying pace of the member states in establishing the national prerequisites necessary to administer the system. Some member states have also implemented measures to promote small firm participation (i.e. grants, supported pilot projects).

Apart from these different regulatory and financial frameworks, there are other reasons for national differences in the adoption of EMAS by private companies. In the United Kingdom, the national standard BS 7750 which later was converted into ISO 14001, proved to be more attractive to firms than EMAS. As a result, the number of companies with ISO 14001 in the United Kingdom is still higher than in Germany. Due to a more decentralised certification system, it is difficult to get accurate data on the global acceptance of ISO 14001. Recent estimates of the International Standards Organisation (ISO 1999) from December 1998 reveal that Japan leads in terms of absolute numbers of certificates (1,542), with the United Kingdom second (921) and Germany third (651).

However, it is important to recognise that some large international customer firms consider ISO 9000 and ISO 14001 to be rather low-quality standards. These firms impose higher ones, obliging smaller suppliers to meet these standards. There may therefore be some under-reporting of quality and environmental standards. Britain's greater openness to foreign investment may mean that this neglect of ISO standards in favour of higher corporate ones is more widespread in the United Kingdom than in Germany.

16.3 Methodological Aspects of the Study

Our analysis is based on two different samples. The first sample compares the environmental management of British and German manufacturing establishments in a matched-pairs design.[1] A matched-pairs design is useful in this case because it controls for independent variables which might distort a comparison of two sub-samples. Key explanatory variables are controlled by matching respondents in pairs on these variables. For this reason, this method is preferable to random sampling if one wishes to test specific comparison-based hypotheses with small samples. Although the design as such is quite simple, it is highly dependent on the identification of adequate match criteria and the availability of sufficient numbers of pairs which meet these criteria (Peck 1985). The approach has been used widely in medical and psychological sciences and has also been employed in economic geography (e.g. O'Farrell *et al.* 1995).

The matching of manufacturing establishments in Britain and Germany was done as closely as possible with respect to products, industry, ownership characteristics, employment size, annual turnover, and age. In July 1998, 60 EMAS sites were registered in the United Kingdom. In 37 manufacturing establishments interviews were conducted and 33 were selected for matched-pairs analysis. The British sub-sample was matched with 33 German manufacturing establishments, which were comparable with respect to the selected characteristics (see Table 16.1). Data was obtained from interviews with environmental managers. Statistical tests indicated no significant difference between the two sub-samples with respect to the criteria. Hence, it may be concluded that neither age, ownership, size nor type of industry contribute to an explanation of between-establishment differentials in the two countries. A comparison of standard

[1] Matched-pairs research designs require specific statistical tests. Adequate non-parametric tests for matched data are the *sign test* and the *Wilcoxon's matched-pairs signed rank test.* The sign test can be applied to ordinal and even nominal data. The Wilcoxon test is more effective when both, sign and magnitude of differences, are available and the data are organized in ordered classes (O'Farrell and Hitchens 1988, p. 67). If variables are dichotomous in nature, then *McNemar's test* will be appropriate.

performance indicators (earnings, employment growth, turnover growth, etc.) revealed that the British firms were slightly more successful than their German counterparts. Although these differences in business performance are not statistically significant, they reflect the more favourable business climate in the United Kingdom during the 1990s.

Table 16.1 Industry and employment size of manufacturing firms sampled

	Matched-pairs British/German		Representative German sample	
Industry	pairs	%	no.	%
Food, beverages	-	-	47	12.2
Textiles, clothing	-	-	10	2.6
Wood products, furniture	-	-	36	9.4
Paper, printing	4	12.1	33	8.6
Chemicals, chemical products	15	45.5	57	14.8
Rubber and plastic products	2	6.1	29	7.5
Fabricated metal products	3	9.1	65	16.9
Machinery, transport equipment	3	9.1	50	13,0
Electrical machinery, electronics	2	6.1	37	9.6
Other	4	12.1	21	5.5
Employment size	pairs	%	no.	%
0 – 50	7	21.2	64	16.6
51 – 250	14	42.4	123	31.9
250 – 500	6	18.2	73	19.0
> 500	6	18.2	83	21.6
Not stated	-	-	42	10.9
Total	33	100.0	385	100.0

Source: Survey of British and German manufacturing establishments 1997/98.

Matched-pairs analysis is an effective tool to deduct differences between paired sub-samples, but it is not oriented towards the estimation of population parameters or statistical modelling. For this reason, it was decided to carry out a second sample survey of manufacturing establishments. This sample was based on a representative postal survey of German sites validated according to EMAS. The total number of validated German sites in December 1997 was 1,030. In 35 sites of these personal interviews were conducted instead of a postal survey. In addition, 66 sites were excluded from the postal survey, because they were only small branch plants of large companies and the EMS was administered and controlled by the company headquarters. A questionnaire was mailed to the remaining 929 sites in late 1997 and early 1998. A total of 429 business establishments returned the questionnaire, representing a 46 percent response rate. As for the present study we were interested in only manufacturing establishments, we ended up with a sample of 385 cases. The sample was still large enough to guarantee representative results. A comparison between the responding sites and the parent population on several control variables indicated that the structure of the respondents does not differ significantly from the parent population.

The representative German sample, as well as the matched-pairs, include a wide range of industries. But as the total number of respondents in the matched-pairs sample is small, we can only present reliable branch-related results for the chemical industry (15 pairs).

16.4 National Differences and Similarities – Empirical Results

Our empirical results are presented in four parts. Firstly, consideration is given to various stakeholders and their influence on environmental management. Secondly, the role of inter-firm networking will be briefly analysed. The third section examines the costs and benefits of environmental management. Fourthly, the comparative matched-pairs study will be completed by a closer examination of factors determining the successful implementation of environmental management. For statistical reasons, this last analytical step is based on the representative sample of German manufacturing establishments.

Influences of Stakeholders on Environmental Activity

In order to gain more precise knowledge of the influence of contextual factors on environmental management we asked environmental managers to access the influence of different stakeholders on their company's environmental activities, according to a scale from 1 (very low) to 5 (very high). The results basically confirm the central assumption of the stakeholder concept that the management of companies is influenced by a wide array of different interests and interest groups. However, the hypothesis that German firms are generally more exposed to environmental stakeholder demands cannot be confirmed. On the contrary, the comparison of British (UK) and German (G) firms reveals that the national differences in the relevance of specific stakeholders are not very pronounced (Table 16.2). Significant differences between the two sub-samples exist only with respect to owners and shareholders. To a lesser extent, some differences are evident for banks, insurance companies, suppliers, wholesalers, and retailers.

The ranking according to the relevance of particular stakeholder demands differs in detail. German environmental managers judged governments and state authorities to be the strongest influence. UK environmental managers stated them to be the second strongest influence. This demonstrates the crucial role of environmental regulation and the dominance of traditional compliance strategies within private enterprises, especially in Germany. On the other hand, British firms are rather dominated by the interests of shareholders and owners. This is probably more a reflection of their general shareholder value orientation than an indication of more environmentally responsible capital owners. This view is partly confirmed by the relatively modest importance of other financial stakeholders (banks, insurance companies). The postulated 'greening of the money markets' is obviously not a major force for the greening of manufacturing enterprises, either in the United Kingdom or in Germany.

Table 16.2 Relevance of stakeholders for environmental activities of British and German manufacturers

Stakeholder	Pairs	Rank UK	Rank G	Difference UK	Difference G	Significance Sign	Significance Wilcoxon
Owners, shareholders	26	1	3	+	-	**	*
Government, authorities	32	2	1	-	+	n.s.	n.s.
Employees	30	3	4	o	o	n.s.	n.s.
Customers	30	4	2	-	+	n.s.	n.s.
Trade, industry associations	30	5	7	+	-	n.s.	n.s.
Banks, lenders	26	6	12	+	-	n.s.	*
Local community	29	7	9	o	o	n.s.	n.s.
Media	29	8	6	-	+	n.s.	n.s.
Insurance companies	27	9	5	-	+	*	n.s.
Environmental organisations	29	10	8	-	+	n.s.	n.s.
Suppliers	30	11	14	+	-	n.s.	*
Universities, research institutes	28	12	15	+	-	n.s.	n.s.
Competitors	28	13	10	o	o	n.s.	n.s.
Wholesalers and retailers	25	14	11	-	+	n.s.	*
Political parties	29	15	16	o	o	n.s.	n.s.
Consumer associations	29	16	13	-	+	n.s.	n.s.

Matched-pairs comparison: + higher values in sub-sample, – lesser values in sub-sample.
Levels of significance: * 10%, ** 5%, *** 1%, n.s. not significant.
Source: Survey of British and German manufacturing establishments 1997/98.

In general, the survey results reveal that internal stakeholders (owners, shareholders, employees) and the state are still the most relevant forces for environmental action. Market-oriented stakeholders (e.g. customers, consumer associations, suppliers) show a relatively inconsistent picture. The importance attached to customers indicates a growing relevance of environmental issues within the supply chain. The influence of more diffuse and diverse environmental stakeholders (media, environmental organisations, local communities etc.) is still moderate, though growing because of an increasing environmental awareness in the general public. This may quickly change under certain conditions. The harsh reaction of environmental groups, the media and the general public in Germany during the Brent Spar affair serves as a case in point. Moreover, the results for the environmentally sensitive chemical industry differ from the overall picture. Chemical plants in Germany are significantly more affected by demands of customers, insurance companies, environmental organisations and the media than their British counterparts.

In this context one could ask whether general stakeholder demands result in a notable interest in EMS and the EMAS validation of specific firms. Considerable national variations emerged, when we put a relatively general question: "How would you assess the perception of the EMAS by the general public?" The answers of German firms suggest that they are more optimistic than their British counterparts (Table 16.3). This assessment is a reflection of the positive image of EMAS in German business circles.

Table 16.3 Perception of EMAS by general public according to manufacturers

					Significance	
	Pairs	G > UK	G = UK	G < UK	Sign	Wilcoxon
Chemical industry	14	14	0	0	***	***
All industries	32	26	5	1	***	***

Level of significance: *** 1%.
Source: Survey of British and German manufacturing establishments 1997/98.

In order to gain more stakeholder-related information, we asked environmental managers to assess the stakeholders' level of interest in their EMS. The ranking is not very different from the one in Table 16.2, except for the considerably lower ranks for the media and the local community. This applies to Britain as well as to Germany. The limited interest of the local community in EMS is somewhat disappointing, given the fact that the local dimension has been central for the formulation of EMAS. All aspects considered, differences between the two countries prove to be relatively minor, though German employees and competitors show more interest in EMS than their British counterparts. Qualitative information from the interviews also indicates that German employees might be more aware of the importance of environmental issues within the firm than British ones.

Reconsidering these empirical results, it becomes clear that external stakeholders' demands and the rise of environmental awareness in the general public have become influential forces for a 'corporate greening'. Nevertheless, government regulations and market-driven stakeholder demands remain dominant. This is true for the British as well as for the German context, suggesting that the importance of national differences is indeed decreasing.

The Role of Information Exchange and Inter-firm Networks

A critical public assessment is widely seen as a major impetus behind the increase in environmental activity. Right from the start, communication about environmental or ecological issues between companies as well as between companies and their stakeholders has been in the focus of the protagonists of corporate greening (e.g. Vollmer 1995). For example, EMAS demands the publication of an environmental statement in order to communicate firm-related environmental issues to different groups of stakeholders. The number of environmental statements distributed may serve as a simple quantitative indicator for the degree of environmental communication which takes place between the firms and the outside world. The total number of distributed statements is quite different from firm to firm mainly depending on size, industry and the timing of validation. On average, German enterprises have distributed more environmental statements than British firms (Table 16.4). Moreover, German firms use environmental statements more actively to inform external stakeholders, particularly within the supply chain. German environmental managers see the environmental statement as important and beneficial to the operations of their firm. Their British colleagues, on the other hand, are more sceptical often stressing the danger of disclosing too much information.

Table 16.4 Number of environmental statements distributed by manufacturers

	United Kingdom		Germany		Wilcoxon
	Median	Max.	Median	Max.	Sig.
Total	300	4000	675	6200	*
In response to inquiries	100	1550	100	1000	n.s.
On own initiative	125	3800	375	6000	**
Own initiative as % of total	42	98	80	100	**

Levels of significance: * 10%, ** 5%, n.s. not significant.
Source: Survey of British and German manufacturing establishments 1997/98.

The exchange of specific information between co-operating firms is as important as the provision of general information to external stakeholders. Studies on industrial networks and innovative milieus frequently stress the point that intensive inter-firm co-operation and communication favours the quick adoption of organisational and technological innovations (Camagni 1991; Maillat 1998). Given the innovative character of environmental management, a close relationship between inter-firm co-operation and environmental performance might be expected. In fact, there is an intensive exchange of information on environmental issues on a regional as well as on a non-regional level. Only 12 percent of the British and 17 percent of the German manufacturing establishments in the matched-pairs sample do not maintain a regular exchange of information with other firms on environmental issues (Table 16.5). This suggests that inter-firm co-operation and information exchange may be closer in the field of environmental protection than in other fields of business.

Table 16.5 Regular exchange of information on environmental issues with other firms

	Matched-pairs sub-samples				Representative	
	United Kingdom		Germany		German sample	
	no.	%	no.	%	no.	%
Local and regional levels	6	18.2	8	26.7	90	24.1
National and international levels	4	12.1	8	26.7	57	15.2
Exchange on all spatial levels	19	57.6	9	30.0	123	32.9
No exchange	4	12.1	5	16.6	104	27.8
Total	33	100.0	30	100.0	374	100.0

Source: Survey of British and German manufacturing establishments 1997/98.

British firms are slightly more active in inter-firm information exchange than their German counterparts, especially on a local and regional level. Even though the level of statistical significance is low (McNemar: $p = 0.119$), these differences indicate more fundamental contrasts in the environmental innovation systems. The British 'green business clubs' (e.g. Business Environment Association East Midlands, Cumbria Business Environmental Network, North London Business Environment Network) do not really have an equivalent in Germany. They are local or regional support networks which consist of a group of organisations or individuals who are able to offer assistance, advice or other forms of support (Holt *et al.* 1998). These networks are based on a co-operative partnership between a range of interested organisations and tend to contain one or several 'model firms'. Very often they also include public institutions, commercial environmental consultants and universities. Where possible, networks act both as consultants to private firms, thus earning income, and as applicants to the European Union for environmental projects which supply additional near-market income for them. They are frequently represented in European environmental networks even though they are not legitimate, democratic representative bodies of the normal kind.

Comparable networks are still rare in Germany. One successful example of regional co-operation is the '*Modellversuch Hohenlohe*' in the northern part of Baden-Württemberg. It consists of a formalised network of about 250 companies which concentrates on the exchange of information on environmental protection, especially in the field of waste management.

The function of green business clubs in the United Kingdom is served in Germany in part by the Chambers of Industry and Commerce. While the

Chambers are quite important in the German context, they count for little in the United Kingdom. The fact that membership is compulsory for German firms gives the Chambers a very prominent and central position in regional economic affairs. Moreover, the German Chambers were given the right to register the sites that have been EMAS validated. For this reason, the evolution of EMS has further reinforced the already strong position which the German Chambers of Industry and Commerce hold within regional information networks.

Costs and Benefits of EMS

In the long term, EMAS as an instrument of environmental policy will only be successful if it leads to ecological, economic or technological gains. Therefore, we will briefly analyse three important dimensions for a successful implementation: cost-efficiency, resource consumption and technological innovations.

Cost savings depend on the specific situation in each company. While some firms show net losses from having implemented an EMS, others show considerable gains. The costs for the implementation of an EMS as well as the participation in EMAS were significantly higher in Germany (Table 16.6). The number of establishments which have been able to achieve cost reductions through environmental management also differs between the two countries. British companies have been considerably more successful in saving money. There are three main reasons for greater cost-efficiency of the British firms:

1. Costs of bureaucratic overheads are lower in the United Kingdom. As this is also true for labour costs in general, British firms find themselves in a better position to reduce their annual expenditures for running an EMS.
2. British firms are more experienced with environmental management standards and management standards in general. BS 7750/ISO 14001 as well as ISO 9000 certifications were awarded more frequently and significantly earlier than in Germany. The majority of British firms implemented EMAS after they were already certified according to ISO 9000 and BS 7550/ISO 14001. Most of the German firms did not have any experience with environmental management standards before they decided to adopt EMAS. This lack of experience meant that German firms needed to rely more frequently on expensive external consultations.
3. Most importantly, EMS of British firms are highly oriented towards cost-effectiveness. Saving costs is a central impetus behind their efforts, whereas German firms put more emphasis on finding better technical solutions for specific environmental problems. German legislation and many private companies traditionally focus on the best available technology. This approach often leads to high absolute standards in environmental protection, but raises questions about the cost-effectiveness of many measures.

The representative sample of German firms provides a closer look at the cost-effectiveness of environmental management. 57 percent of the surveyed manufacturing establishments claimed that they were able to achieve cost reductions within the first year after the system came into operation. In many cases greater cost-effectiveness had been achieved by optimising the production process – resulting mainly in a reduction of energy inputs and of harmful by-products. For a majority of sites, however, the total expenses for establishing and running the system still exceeded cost reductions. Despite the optimistic expectations of many German consultants and scholars (e.g. Günther 1998), it can take years until the investment of a company in environmental management starts to pay off.

Table 16.6 Costs and cost savings as results of environmental management

					Significance	
	Pairs	D > UK	D = UK	D < UK	Sign	Wilcoxon
Costs of implementation:						
Internal costs	21	16	0	5	**	***
External costs	24	20	0	4	***	***
Total costs	21	15	0	6	*	***
Costs after implementation:						
Annual costs	16	10	0	6	n.s.	n.s.
Annual cost savings	18	1	4	13	***	***
Cost-effectiveness [a]	12	2	0	10	**	***

[a] annual cost savings minus annual costs.
Levels of significance: * 10%, ** 5%, *** 1%, n.s. not significant.
Source: Survey of British and German manufacturing establishments 1997/98.

Cost reductions are generally related to a more efficient use of natural resources. The issue of resource consumption is a decisive criterion if one wants to assess the quality of EMAS as an instrument of environmental policy. Such an evaluation, however, is not easy to accomplish because in many cases there is a lack of reliable data on resource and energy consumption, emission of specific pollutants, etc. For this reason, our data can provide only a rough indication of the environmental effects of EMAS. Firms in the British sub-sample seem to be have been more successful in reducing the overall resource consumption than those in the German sub-sample. But due to the small size of our sample and missing data, the differences are not statistically significant and should be interpreted with care.[1] The slightly higher rates of reduction of resources achieved by British

[1] Due to the inherent characteristics of the matched-pairs survey, the British sub-sample may be somewhat more biased towards 'positive examples' than the German one, which was drawn from a much larger population of EMAS validated manufacturers.

manufacturers in recent years are possibly no more than a reflection of the closing of the former gap which existed between German and British firms.

A statistically more reliable picture emerges from the German sample. About one third of the surveyed adopters of EMAS in Germany were able to reduce their total resource consumption between 1995 and 1998. This reduction applies to the consumption of water (35 percent), fuel oil (31 percent), electricity (24 percent), natural gas (20 percent), and petrol (15 percent). More important than the reduction in absolute terms is the reduction in relation to output. The percentage of sites which managed to achieve economies in relative terms is considerably higher (68 percent), because most plants increased their output in monetary and physical terms. It is, however, almost impossible to determine or quantify the exact impact of EMS on the overall resource consumption. Qualitative information provided by interviewees in Britain and Germany suggests that the actual impact of EMS should not be overestimated.

Technological innovations are another dimension of EMS. In relation to the effect of environmental management on product and process innovations, there are no significant differences between the United Kingdom and Germany (Table 16.7). Due to the process-oriented nature of EMAS, innovations are mainly achieved through the way in which products are manufactured. In some cases, the adoption of environmental management resulted in a substantial change in the manufacturing processes. By contrast, product innovations were relatively minor and mostly related to changes in the manufacturing process.

Table 16.7 Innovations generated by EMS

	Matched-pairs sub-samples				Representative	
	UK		Germany		German sample	
Business establishments with:	no.	%	no.	%	no.	%
Product innovations only	1	3.1	2	6.1	22	5.8
Process innovations only	14	43.7	17	51.5	154	40.7
Product and process innovations	6	18.8	4	12.1	43	11.4
No innovations	11	34.4	10	30.3	159	42.1
Total	32	100.0	33	100.0	378	100.0

Source: Survey of British and German manufacturing establishments 1997/98.

It became obvious that environmental management has the potential to combine ecological and economic gains. However, not all firms have been able to actually profit from this so-called 'double dividend'. The next section will deal with factors explaining the success of EMS.

16.5 Determinants for Successful Environmental Management

The following analysis is based on the representative German sample. This is because matched-pair samples do not allow statistical modelling and many decisive parameters do not significantly differ between British and German firms. Logistic regression was used to estimate the impact of different internal and external parameters on the successful implementation of EMS. The logistic regression model is basically a non-linear transformation of an ordinary linear regression which lessens problems such as heteroscedasticity or multicollinearity. While the dependent variable must have a binary format, variables of all scales are accepted as independent variables (Agresti 1996). In our logistic regression models, successful implementation of environmental management is described by the dependent variables COSTRED (Model 1) and RESOURCE (Model 2). Both models are designed to measure economic (reduction of running expenses for raw materials, energy, waste treatment etc.) and environmental effects (decrease of energy and raw material consumption). A third dependent variable, INNOVATE (Model 3), serves as an indicator for innovation processes initiated by environmental management.

Our basic hypothesis is that successful implementation of environmental management is positively connected with favourable internal (experience with management systems, environmental commitment, economic viability, etc.) as well as external factors (urbanisation and agglomeration effects, network integration, external consultation etc.). The full set of selected indicators and variables is presented in Table 16.8. Due to a stepwise backward exclusion of variables with $p > 0.2$, only statistically relevant parameters were included in the logistic regression models.[1]

The logistic regression results are presented in Table 16.9. This table includes regression coefficient estimates (B) and their significance as well as partial correlation coefficients (R) to indicate the covariate's contribution to the overall model. Positive B-coefficients indicate an increasing probability, and negative B-coefficients a decreasing probability of positive values of the dependent variable. All models are significant at the 1 percent level according to model chi-square statistic. The percentages of correct predictions are not very high, but still acceptable. The results of the logistic regression models can be summarised as follows.

Model 1: The probability of actually achieving cost reductions increases significantly when a business establishment manages to reduce its overall resource consumption (RESOURCE) and to generate environmental product and process innovations (INNOPROD, INNOPROC). Experience already gained with management systems (ISO9000, EARLY) is another, although less significant component which is positively related to the ability to cut costs. General internal

[1] In the calculations, ENERGY, INDUSTRY, RESEARCH, WESTEAST, AGGLO and STAKE were excluded from all three models, due to their limited explanatory power.

factors prove to be less influential (INDUSTRY, GROUP, PROFIT, etc.). The more complex impact of the employment size deserves a closer look. From additional chi-square tests, it becomes obvious that medium-sized enterprises (50 to 500 employees) are more successful in saving costs than either very small or very large manufacturing establishments. Moreover, the regression results reveal that firms do not depend too much on their external environment. Only the integration in regional information networks (NETREG) has a significant effect on cost savings.

Table 16.8 Variables of the logistic regression models

Dependent variables:	
COSTRED	Running expenses reduced by EMS (yes = 1, no = 0)
RESOURCE*	Relative decrease of energy and raw material consumption, selected inputs (water, electricity, gas, fuel oil, petrol) (yes = 1, no = 0)
INNOVATE	Product or process innovations as a result of EMS (yes = 1, no = 0)
Independent variables – environment-related internal factors:	
EARLY	Adoption of EMAS before July 1996 (yes = 1, no = 0)
INNOPROD**	Environmental product innovations (yes = 1, no = 0)
INNOPROC**	Environmental process innovations (yes = 1, no = 0)
ISO9000	Additional ISO 9000 certification (yes = 1, no = 0)
ISO14001	Additional ISO 14001 certification (yes = 1, no = 0)
ENERGY	On-site-usage of renewable energy (yes = 1, no = 0)
Independent variables – general internal factors:	
INDUSTRY	Dummies for 12 different industries (yes = 1, no = 0)
GROUP	Subsidiary or branch plant (yes = 1, no = 0)
SIZE	Number of employees
PROFIT	Profit situation, scale from 1 (very poor) to 5 (excellent)
RESEARCH	R&D expenditure as percentage of total turnover
Independent variables – external factors:	
WESTEAST	Location in the old or the new Länder (West = 1, East = 0)
AGGLO	Location type (urban agglomeration = 1, rural area = 0)
NETREG	Regular exchange of information with other companies on environmental issues, local and regional levels (yes = 1, no = 0)
NETNAT	Regular exchange of information with other companies on environmental issues, national and international levels (yes = 1, no = 0)
CONSULT	Assistance by external environmental consultant(s) (yes = 1, no = 0)
SUPPORT	EMAS process supported by public funds (yes = 1, no = 0)
STAKE	Median of the strength of stakeholder demands (min. = 1, max. = 5)

* also an independent variable in model 1, ** not tested in model 3.

Model 2: Environmental gains (RESOURCE) are harder to predict from the given set of independent variables than cost savings. According to Model 2 only two variables significantly influence the probability of achieving reductions in the overall resource consumption. Decreasing resource consumption obviously depends on quite specific and very individual parameters (experience, market-opportunities, technology, machinery, etc.). These parameters are difficult to measure due to their diverse and often problem-oriented, pragmatic character. Nevertheless, the positive sign for PROFIT tends to confirm the assumption that there is a close correlation between economic success and environmental progress. At first sight, the result for CONSULT is surprising, as the influence of external consultants is inverse of that expected. A plausible explanation for this could be that consultants are commissioned primarily by firms which have difficulty in establishing a working EMS. Experienced and successful firms, on the other hand, are mostly able to implement an EMS without the help of external consultants.

Table 16.9 Logistic regression results

Independent variable	Dependent variable								
	COSTRED			RESOURCE			INNOVATE		
	B	Sig.	R	B	Sig.	R	B	Sig.	R
RESOURCE (+)	0.683	***	0.203		Not tested			Not tested	
INNOPROD (+)	0.758	***	0.159		-			Not tested	
INNOPROC (+)	0.396	**	0.112		-			Not tested	
EARLY (+)	0.502	*	0.083		-			-	
ISO9000 (+)	0.438	*	0.059	0.261	n.s.	0.012		-	
ISO14001 (+)		-			-		0.329	**	0.100
GROUP (-)		-			-		-0.336	**	-0.095
SIZE (o)	-0.001	**	-0.107		-			-	
PROFIT (+)		-		0.433	**	0.093	0.404	**	0.099
NETREG (+)	0.442	**	0.129		-			-	
NETNAT (+)		-		0.220	n.s.	0.011	0.331	**	0.104
CONSULT (+)	0.355	n.s.	0.041	-0.457	**	-0.104		-	
SUPPORT (+)	-0.250	n.s.	0.000		-		-0.238	n.s.	-0.034
Constant	0.570	n.s.		-0.677	n.s.		-1.018	n.s.	
Number of cases	194			194			272		
Model Chi-Sq. [df]	44 [9]	***		15 [4]	***		25 [5]	***	
Correct predictions	71.3	%		71.0	%		68.1	%	

In brackets: expected sign of regression coefficient.
B: Regression coefficient; R: Partial correlation coefficient.
Levels of significance: *10%, **5%, ***1%, n.s. not significant.
Source: Survey of German manufacturing establishments 1997/98.

Model 3: The ability to generate technological innovations seems to be primarily influenced by the degree of commitment to environmental management (additional ISO 14000 certification), economic success (PROFIT) and the integration in national or international information networks (NETNAT). As expected, subsidiaries or branch plants are less successful when it comes to technological innovations (GROUP). None of the other variables has a significant impact.

From the logistic regression models, a number of more general findings emerge. These are supported by qualitative information from firm interviews. Most of the findings are relevant not only for the German, but for the British context too:

- Firm-internal determinants are more important for successful implementation of environmental management than external factors such as location characteristics or stakeholder demands. In particular, firms in peripheral locations are not significantly disadvantaged.
- General firm characteristics such as size, industry or product range have only a limited impact on successful environmental management. Irrespective of these long-term structural characteristics, firms have enough room to find individual windows of environmental opportunity. Yet experience matters, especially where the economic aspects of environmental management are concerned.
- Economic and environmental success prove to be closely related in all three models. Our findings tend to confirm the optimistic hypothesis of a positive interrelation between environmental and economic gains for the firm (Fritz 1995; Hurt and Ahuja 1996).
- Networking between manufacturing enterprises proves to be a crucial factor for successful implementation of environmental management. Additional chi-square tests also reveal significant direct relations between information exchange and innovation. Local networks for the exchange of environmental information seem to be especially important for cost savings, whereas national and international networks are more important for technological innovations.

16.6 Concluding Remarks

A comparative study conducted by James *et al.* (1997) conclude that, on average, German companies are still better environmental performers than those in the United Kingdom. However, they also mention that the picture is not a consistent one and that the gap in environmental performance is steadily closing. Peattie and Ringler (1994) also found that British companies are at no real competitive disadvantage in terms of their organisational commitment to 'greening. Our empirical results basically confirm the conclusions of these earlier studies. With regard to the performance of EMS, German firms have no significant advantage over British ones. Both countries have their own patterns of strengths and weaknesses. The main advantage of British firms lies in their better understanding of modern management instruments and their ability to combine environmental progress with cost-efficiency. German firms, on the other hand, normally maintain higher technological standards of environmental protection. Moreover, they benefit from the greater environmental awareness of employees, customers and consumers. Nevertheless, it should be borne in mind that our survey covered only manufacturing establishments that had already implemented EMS. For this reason, our findings are not applicable to British or German manufacturers as a whole.

In the light of the theoretical concepts applied, our results suggest the following conclusions:

- Nationally differentiated stakeholder demands are influencing corporate environmental behaviour significantly. German firms are rather more exposed to environmental pressure from stakeholders than their British counterparts, but the relative importance of national differences is decreasing.
- Market-driven stakeholder demands and government regulations play an important role for the development of environmental strategies of manufacturing enterprises. The greater diffusion of external stakeholders (media, environmental organisations etc.) are gaining importance, too.
- Internal characteristics and individual abilities of firms are dominating determinants of their environmental performance. But the diffusion of environmental know-how is also supported by inter-firm networking, especially in the case of Britain. Spatial characteristics such as agglomeration and urbanisation effects are of minor importance.
- Successful environmental management is positively related to economic competitiveness and is encouraging innovations within manufacturing firms. Due to its process-oriented character environmental management induces mainly process innovations.

It is certainly too early to fully assess the environmental and economic effects of EMAS and the corresponding ISO 14001 standard. Our empirical evidence suggests that environmental management has the potential to reduce costs as well as ecological side effects of production. However, the full potential still remains untapped in most companies. For example, only a minority of manufacturing firms in Britain and in Germany are designing their products according to the requirements of sustainability. Freight transport is almost entirely road-based and the use of renewable energy is limited. Manufacturing companies in both countries have become considerably cleaner during the last decade, but they still have a long way to go before they can justly call their production 'sustainable'.

References

Agresti, A. (1996) An Introduction to Categorical Data Analysis. Wiley, New York

Braun, B. (1998) Locational Response of German Manufacturers to Environmental Standards. Tijdschrift voor Economische en Sociale Geografie (TESG) 89, 253-263

Braun, B., Geibel, J. (1999) The Implementation of Environmental Management: A Milestone in Firm Development? In: Van Dijk, J. & Pellenbarg, P.H. (eds.) Demography

of Firms. Spatial Dynamics of Firm Behaviour. Nederlandse Geografische Studies 262. Utrecht, Groningen, 285-302
Camagni, R. (ed.) (1991) Innovation Networks: Spatial Perspectives. Belhaven Pinter, London
Cooke, P., Morgan, K. (1993) The Network Paradigm: New Departures in Corporate and Regional Development. Environment & Planning D 11, 543-564
Donaldson, T., Preston, L.E. (1995) The Stakeholder Theory of the Corporation: Concepts, Evidence, and Implications. Academy of Management Review 20, 65-91
Dyllick, T., Belz, F. (1995) Anspruchsgruppen im Öko-Marketing. Eine konzeptionelle Erweiterung der Marketing-Perspektive. Umweltwirtschaftsforum 3, 57-61
Freeman, R.E. (1984) Strategic Management: A Stakeholder Approach. Pitman, Boston
Fritz, W. (1995) Umweltschutz und Unternehmenserfolg. Eine empirische Analyse. Die Betriebswirtschaft 55, 347-357
Gordon, J. (1994) Environmental Policy in Britain and Germany: Some Comparisons. European Environment 4, 9-12
Grafé-Buckens, A., Hinton, A.-F. (1998) Engaging the Stakeholders: Corporate Views and Current Trends. Business Strategy and the Environment 7, 124-133
Günther, K. (1998) Betriebliches Umweltmanagement setzt sich in der Praxis durch. Ergebnisse der UNI/ASU-Umweltmanagementbefragung 1997. Umweltwirtschaftsforum 6, 16-20
Holt, D., Anthony, S., Viney, H. (1998) Greening SMEs in the United Kingdom: Partnerships, Alliances and Support Networks. Paper presented to the 7th International Conference of the Greening of Industry Network "Partnership and Leadership: Building Alliances for a Sustainable Future", Rome, November 15-18
Hurt, S.L., Ahuja, G. (1996) Does it Pay to be Green? An Empirical Examination of the Relationship Between Emission Reduction and Firm Performance. Business Strategy and the Environment 5, 30-37
ISO – International Standard Organisation (1999) The ISO Survey of ISO 9000 and ISO 14000 Certificates – eighth cycle. http://www.iso.ch/infoe/8thcyclesurvey.pdf
James, P., Prehn, M., Steger, U. (1997) Corporate Environmental Management in Britain and Germany. Anglo-German Foundation, Layerthorpe
Maillat, D. (1998) Vom 'Industrial District' zum kreativen Millieu: Ein Beitrag zur Analyse der gebietsgebundenen Produktionsorganisationen. Geographische Zeitschrift 86, 1-15
O'Farrell, P.N., Hitchens, D.M.W.N. (1988) Inter-firm Comparisons in Industrial Research: The Utility of a Matched Pairs Design. Tijdschrift voor Economische en Sociale Geografie (TESG) 79, 63-69
O'Farrell, P.N., Hitchens, D.M.W.N., Moffat, L.A.R. (1995) Business Service Firms in Two Peripheral Economies: Scotland and Ireland. Tijdschrift voor Economische en Sociale Geografie (TESG) 86, 115-128
Peattie, K., Ringler, A. (1994) Management and the Environment in the UK and Germany: A Comparison. European Management Journal 12, 216-225
Peck, F.W. (1985) The Use of the Matched-Pairs Research Design in Industrial Surveys. Environment and Planning A 17, 981-989
Porrit, J., Winner, D. (1988) The Coming of the Greens. Fontana, London
Porter, M. (1996) America's Green Strategy. In: Welford, R., Starkey, R. (eds.) Business and the Environment. Earthscan Publications, London, 33-35
Porter, M., van der Linde, C. (1996) Green and Competitive: Ending the Stalemate. In: Welford, R., Starkey, R. (eds.) Business and the Environment. Earthscan Publications, London, 61-77
Vollmer, S. (1995) EG-Öko-Audit-Verordnung. Umwelterklärung. Anforderungen, Hintergründe, Gestaltungsoptionen. Springer, Heidelberg

PART C: Sectoral Studies

17 Innovations and Regional Development: Human Capital and Knowledge Transfer as Driving Forces for Spatial Clustering in the Semiconductor Industry of East Germany

Michael Plattner
Philipps-Universität Marburg

17.1 Introduction

The current transformation from an industrial to an information society has triggered intense debate about the probable spatial consequences. In this context, the regional sciences have emphasised the importance of innovation and regional linkages for economic competitiveness and stability. There is some evidence that despite increased use of communication technologies, the process of innovation can lead to the creation of sectoral and spatial clusters (Audretsch and Feldman 1995; Enright 1996; Krugman 1991). But alongside these centripetal localisation forces, strong centrifugal forces from international competition also appear to influence economies. Despite some positive effects, processes of fragmentation tend to trigger off various frictions (Altvater and Mahnkopf 1999). Taking a systemic and dynamic point of view, it would seem that the centripetal forces are driven by regional integration, while the centrifugal forces are driven by global integration.

Here, innovation is understood as the knowledge-intensive response of organisations to socio-economic change with respect to the division of labour within the client, producer and supplier chain. The aim of this chapter is to discuss the relevance of human capital and knowledge transfer for the spatial concentration of sector-specific activities, using the semiconductor industry in East Germany as a case study. The thesis is that face-to-face contacts are necessary for the above interactions. As stated by Audretsch and Feldman, "while the cost of transmitting *information* may be invariant to distance, presumably the cost of transmitting *knowledge* and especially *tacit knowledge* rises along with distance" (Audretsch and Feldman 1995, p.4). In this sense, spatial proximity and human capital are especially relevant for the operational use of knowledge and the incorporation of information into knowledge (Feldman and Florida 1994).

We have attempted to answer the following questions. How important are intra- and inter-regional interactions and human capital regarding technological innovations? How intensely are knowledge transfer and human capital tied to an area? Can the evolution of clusters be explained by forms of interaction based on regional potential?

17.2 A Sectoral Concept for Spatial Innovation Research

Since the division of labour is based on internationalised processes, not only does production follow a chain of value added functions, but so does knowledge generation and innovation. All these functions focus on organisations[1] (Bea and Göbel 1999), which are connected to each other in a value system, as underlined in Porter's value chains (Porter 1990). The production chain proposed by Dicken (1998) follows a similar concept. However, the process of production as well as the process of innovation is undertaken in a local, regional and global context, and some regional chains of production as well as chains of innovation arise from it. These are discussed in terms of network and system approaches[2].

It should be assumed that a region portrays economic processes from a spatial point of view. We could consider it as a cluster in which many processes depend on each other. This enables us to explore the interactions between organisations and the changing structure of a region. The related organisations can be seen as a set of connected structural and functional elements[3], activating as well as utilising the global and regional potentials of production and innovation. Since processes of production and innovation overlap, an analytical model could be seen as a 'System of Innovation and Production' [SIP] (see Fig. 17.1). In the endogenous growth model of Romer (1990), human capital and knowledge are considered to be essential parts of a production system (Clar *et al.* 1997). Following this concept, we need to define the geographical level of interactions focusing on knowledge intensive technology transfer and human abilities.

Knowledge Intensive Technology Transfer

Technology transfer is one of the main supporting factors for innovation processes. The necessary transfer between the members of organisations includes specific technology knowledge, as well as scientific and applied activities (Gibbons *et al.* 1994; Nonaka and Takeuchi 1995). This implies that the transfer of knowledge for purposes of innovation is encoded through informational communication (direct and indirect) and also material interaction (the flow of goods and services). It can be seen as a complex chain of innovation with vertical, horizontal and informational complements (Feldotto 1997). The degree of

---

[1] Enterprises, public institutions, R&D facilities, education and financial institutions.

[2] Cooke 1998; Edquist 1997; Fraunhofer-ISI 1999; Fritsch 1998; Fritsch *et al.* 1998; Koschatzky 1998; Lundvall 1988, 1992; Nelson 1993; OECD 1996, 1999.

[3] The spatial order of the economy can be divided into a) the formal structure or structural elements as organisations, and b) the functional relations or functional elements as material and informational interactions.

significance for innovation depends on the extent of the interaction. Both synergetic as well as co-operation effects are therefore based on the transfer of knowledge through informational contacts and material use. The process is a combination of inter- and intra-plant knowledge generation to create and sell new goods. However, the effects of the underlying co-ordination mechanism are not sufficiently recognised. Bearing this in mind, the following theses need to be examined. First, the forward and backward input/output from suppliers and customers and their influence over innovation are equal in a spatial perspective (vertical complement). Second, the use of equipment and services is spatially relevant because their influence is more innovative than that of other segments (horizontal complement). Third, even if the use of new media increases, the informational inputs and their influence over innovation do not lead to spatial equality (informational complement).

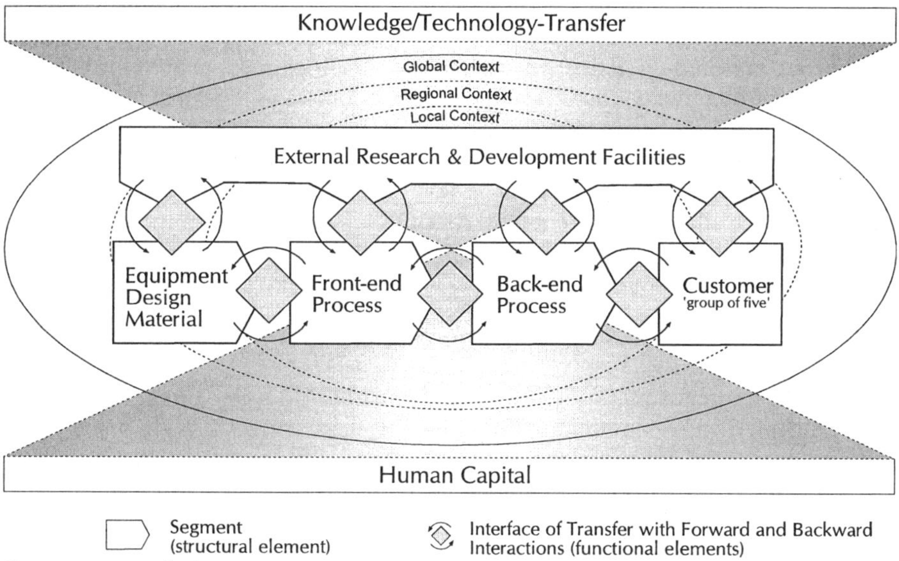

Source: own analysis.

Fig. 17.1 Sectoral System of Innovation and Production [SIP]

Human Capital Based Transfer

Human capital is one of the key factors for production and innovation. Being innovative does not only mean selecting the right information, but also making the right decisions. Both are based on "knowledge, skills, competence and other attributes embodied in individuals that are relevant to economic activity" (OECD 1998: 3). The availability of high quality human capital is therefore particularly relevant for innovation. However, the possibility of synergy arises not only from geographical proximity, but equally from functional relationships between the segments of the SIP. A communication flow between employees exists through different kinds of organisations. Public, private and hybrid organisations interact according to their own targets and interests. One of the main achievements of employees within the private sector is the creation of new goods and services. The communication between them enables the transfer of coded 'general human capital', but there is also tacit knowledge known as 'specific human capital' (Blechinger and Pfeiffer 1997). The latter is not coded and not transferable without the relocation of the person concerned. The transferability comes with spatial, social and occupational mobility. Additionally, the transaction cost decreases if the frictions of interaction can be kept low.

Given the growing importance of human capital in a knowledge-based economy, the following points have to be taken into account. First, the majority of innovation is generated by employees within their firm (Reinhard and Schmalholz 1996). Second, the preservation and formation of human capital is particularly important during the process of transformation in post-communist countries. The regional absorption of immobile labour occurs with a time lag, since the system is in transformation and will be only partly reconfigured. Third, the value of human capital is measured in terms of occupation, qualifications, and the ability to improve qualifications. Therefore, formal education and informal occupational experience produce knowledge and help to generate innovation, while the production of knowledge is closely related to the human ressources active in regional organisations. The process of innovation will promote the growth of a spatial cluster with a concentration of activities typical of a given industrial sector (Englmann and Walz 1995; Walz 1997).

17.3 The Case of the Semiconductor Industry in East Germany

The surge of innovations in the fifth Kondratieff cycle promotes existing endogenous potential through interactions typical of several industrial sectors. If these sectors stay inactive, the potential fails to be realised. The functional elements of a SIP play a crucial role for the economy of a region. The geographical proximity of these structural elements can reflect the joint efforts of entrepreneurs to generate innovations, promote dynamic growth and foster regional development. But proximity is not the only important factor for the formation of a cluster, the material and informational interactions also have an influence. However, the proximity effect can be used efficiently by locating new firms within a given cluster.

The semiconductor production system has been chosen for the sectoral concept of this research as it is highly innovative. East Germany was chosen for several reasons. First, economic transformation can be understood as a national process of innovation. As well as the creation of new goods, processes, sales and support co-ordination, almost every enterprise was newly founded after the re-unification of Germany. Second, the industrial policy of the Democratic Republic as well as the Federal Republic saw the semiconductor industry as a driving force for both national and regional development. Since production and product development in the semiconductor industry in East Germany was lagged behind, scientists and engineers always compared their efforts with those undertaken in non-socialist countries. Third, since unification the restructured semiconductor firms compete internationally. They are currently being pushed by the global integration of high-tech industries. Fourth, the division of labour has changed profoundly and is now linked to the global industry. Fifth, sectoral tradition and path dependence can be observed by comparing the locations of old and new semiconductor firms (see Fig. 17.2).

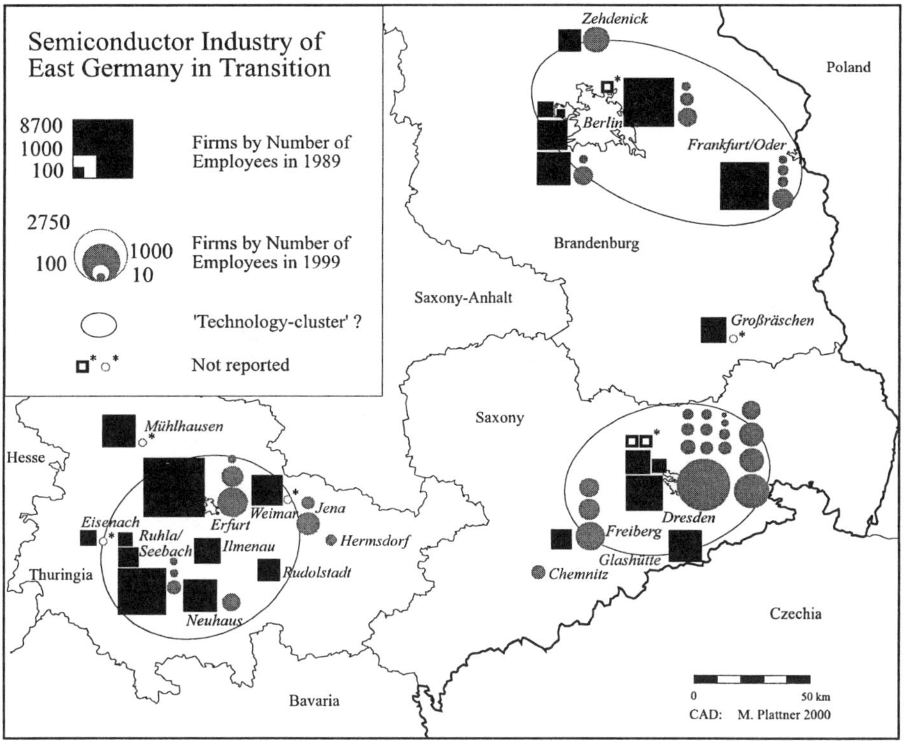

Source: Survey 1999; Stinglwagner 1989.

Fig. 17.2 Transition of the semiconductor industry in East Germany, 1989, 1999

The current spatial pattern depends on the trends of technological integration and disintegration. Division of labour enables the spatial separation of production steps into the segments of the semiconductor SIP[1]. The aim of this study is to find

[1] Production of basic material (silicon wafers), design of IC (Integrated Circuits), front-end processes (fabrication of wafers), back-end processes (assembly/packaging), equipment supplier, microelectronic customers (group of five), related R&D and educational institutions as well as further services (consulting, finance).

out whether human capital and knowledge transfer are driving forces for regional development. The analysis is based on data from a field survey carried out between May and July 1999. Interviews were conducted with the CEOs of 38 out of 41 East German semiconductor firms (i.e. 93 percent), hence the replies are highly representative. All kinds of SIP segments are located in the area, but every segment needs specific human resources[1], financial[2] and special services for supply as well as the disposal of chemicals and water. Beside these factors, various types of hierarchical relations cause technological and perhaps also spatial differentiation (see Fig. 17.3).

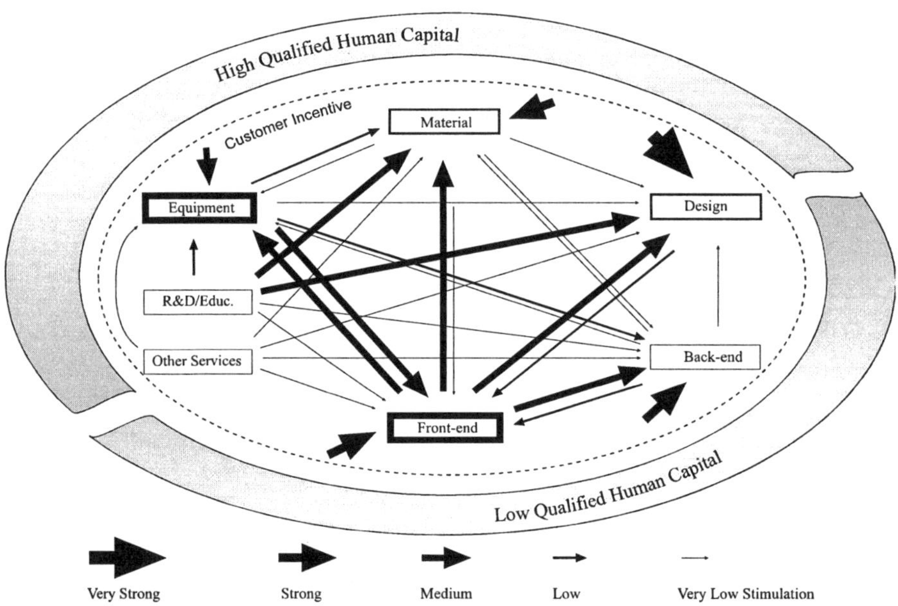

Source: Survey 1999.

Fig. 17.3 Interactions by stimulation of innovation between segments of the SIP

1 Highly qualified human capital for design and production, low qualified human capital for production, assembly and packaging, intensive interaction between service, production, research/qualification and knowledge of customer needs.

2 To support the huge financial investments for building up clean-rooms and hook up production.

17.4 SIP Interactions in a Spatial Perspective

In order to investigate the concept mentioned above, the differences in location of the structural elements (companies with more than 50 percent of turnover in one segment of the system of innovation and production) have to be observed. The SIP segments are clustered in a new way compared with the previous situation (see Fig. 17.4) with a large proportion located in and around Dresden. Seven out of eight equipment producers, three out of four material producers, a large number of R&D facilities (private and public), as well as almost half the design firms and front-end producers started their activities there. Only the companies with a mainly back-end function are underrepresented. At least half (21) of the forty one firms are located in Dresden. Another quarter is located in Frankfurt/Oder and another in Erfurt. Before unification, Erfurt was the centre of the semiconductor industry. Now, after ten years of transformation, Dresden has taken over this position.

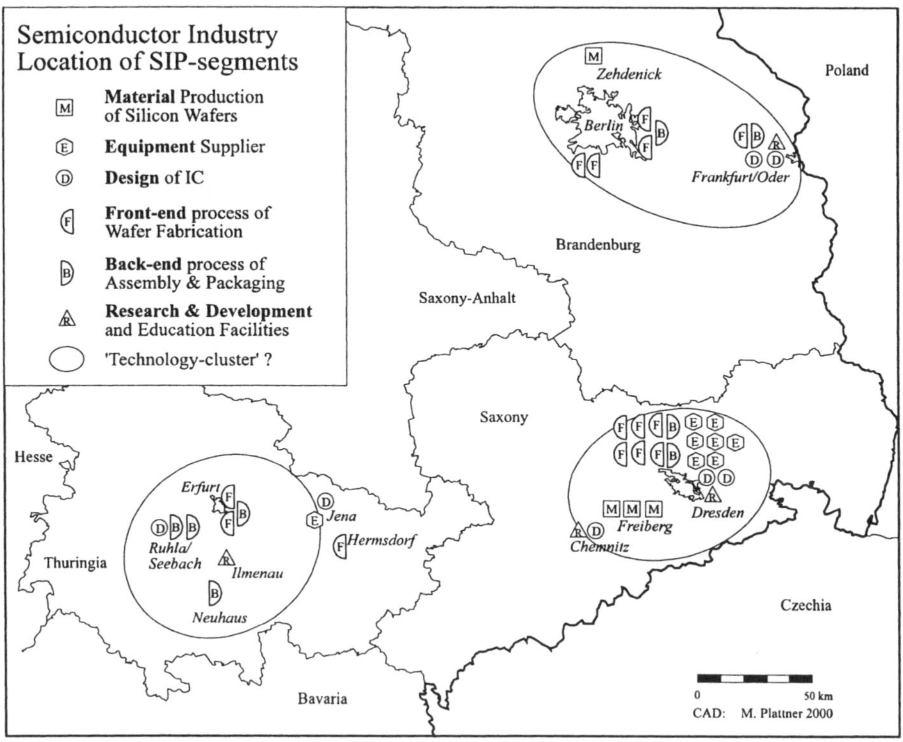

Source: Survey 1999.

Fig. 17.4 East German semiconductor industry and location of the SIP segments

We shall now describe the spatial shift of structural elements in terms of employees and turnover. The semiconductor start-up companies which began their activities during the first half of the 1990s had a total of 3,537 employees and by 1998 had doubled their personnel. However, core start-ups of semiconductor firms in the former GDR have had decreasing employment rates during the last ten years. Until 1998 Thesys (the former core of Kombinat-Microelectronic-Erfurt), ZMD (former ZMD-Dresden) and SMI (former core of Semiconductor-Frankfurt/Oder) had to reduce their staff by 23 percent, even though the turnover of the three mentioned firms rose. One explanation of the annual loss of staff lies in the domain of public policy.

Public policies support companies in order to maintain or increase the level of know-how of personnel. Thus, they help to make human capital more competitive in the labour market. But the strategy could not prevent a brain drain of highly qualified people and the dismissing of 52,836 workers. Regarding the type of privatisation and also the regional scope, there were differences in the development of firms. The number of new firms set up not only differs regionally (see Fig. 17.2), but also their profit levels and personnel.

While the number of employees and turnover increased dramatically in Dresden, there was a fall in the number of new firms in and around Erfurt, Frankfurt/Oder and Berlin (former TV-electronics). Due to the arrival of global players such as AMD and Siemens/Infineon, Dresden's new semiconductor industry grew faster than at the other locations. The growth of semiconductor firms in and around Erfurt was very slow between 1989 and 1999. They had an increase of only 8 percent in employees and 18 percent in turn over. On the other hand, firms in Frankfurt/Oder and Berlin-Brandenburg doubled the number of employees (up by 221 percent), but increased turnover by only 38 percent. The movement of the semiconductor centre to Dresden and a clustering tendency can be observed (see also Fig. 17.2, Fig 17.3, Fig 17.5a). It is interesting to examine whether the SIP segments cluster functionally too.

Vertical Input/Output Interactions

We now look at the forward and backward input/output from suppliers and customers and their influence on innovation to see whether they are spatially balanced. These interactions can be understood as vertical complements. We need to analyse the relations between the segments of the SIP: firstly, the forward and backward input/output of goods and services, and secondly their material and informational influence on innovation.

It emerged that the average forward and backward input/output differs from a spatial perspective. The output interactions reveal global integration while the input interaction are regionally integrated (see Fig. 17.5b). This spatial tension is typical of a globalised export-oriented sector such as the semiconductor industry. The material input/output relations for specific SIP segments are spatially varied. The input of materials, design and equipment derives mainly from international firms, while front-end and back-end products are used by regional firms. The output towards material and design firms, but also to front-end and back-end firms, are once again international. On the other hand, the output towards equipment producers is mainly regional (see Fig. 17.5c).

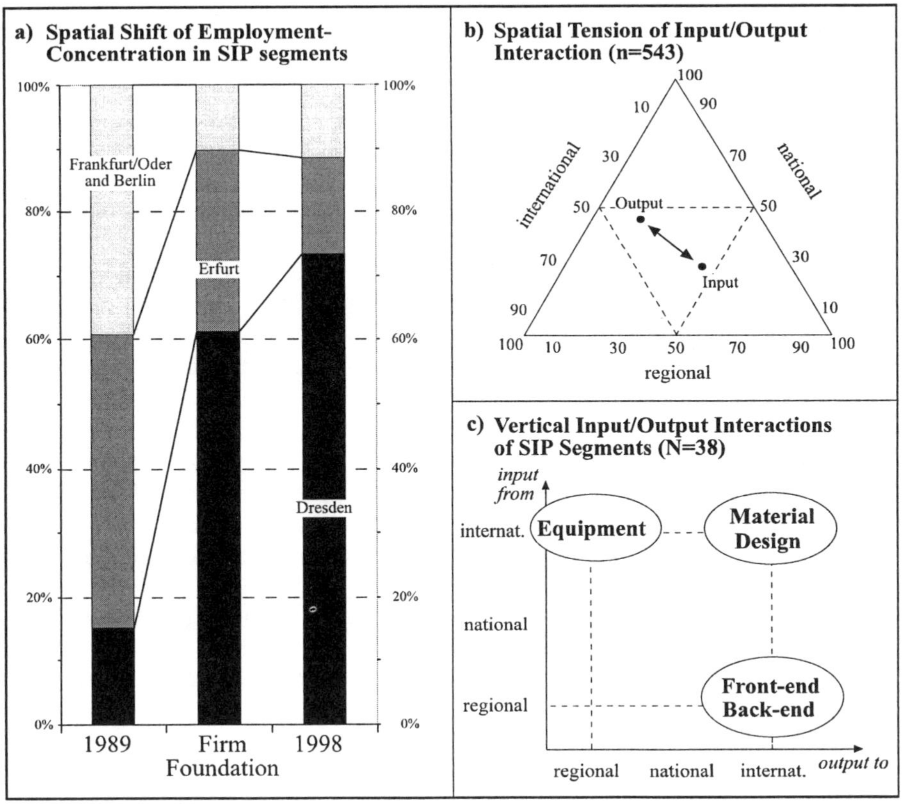

Source: Survey 1999.

Fig. 17.5 Changing spatial pattern of employment and vertical input/output interaction

The semiconductor firms within the SIP receive equipment principally from suppliers with recognised expertise. Since the equipment suppliers are branches of the leading international firms or joint ventures, they are competitive enough to support the international integrated front-end and back-end firms. The input from and output towards material and design firms are mainly embedded in the global context. The firms' output of products to front-end as well as back-end firms are competitive, so their sales are mainly international and the demand regional. It can be seen that the material forward and backward input/output are not equal in spatial perspective, but possibly neither is their influence over innovation.

A significant difference between regional and national influence as well as between regional and international influence over innovation indicates that the interaction pattern for regional and international purposes is very similar. The 'group of five' customers (firms in consumer electronics, information technology, machine and industrial, automotive, precision tools/optics) as well as the front-end firms each have more than 25 percent of influence. Furthermore, the equipment and design firms take over 10 percent of influence. The contribution of back-end and R&D facilities is less then 10 percent. Not taking the 'group of five' in account, the design and material firms take their stimulation principally from R&D as well as from front-end companies. The equipment producers take it mainly from front-end and other equipment companies, the back-end from design and front-end and the front-end from equipment and other front-end firms. Each segment of the SIP has therefore its own pattern of stimulation over innovation (see Fig 17.3).

Concerning input and output relations by material and informational interactions, the influence over innovation differs spatially. About 60 percent of the intra-regional (n = 149) material input has no influence, while 58 percent of the informational input does. About nine out of ten material inputs from firms outside the region (n =185) have no influence over innovation (88 percent), but four of ten informational interactions are of influence (42 percent). Almost all output relations are of influence over innovation (95 percent; 199 out of 209). Intra-regionally (n = 72) there is no significant difference by type of interaction, but inter-regionally (n = 137) over half the interactions are of material influence (52 percent) while every fourth interaction has an informational influence over innovation.

Each segment of the SIP has a typical spatial pattern of input and output interactions. This can be also seen as a result of different absorption levels. The stimulation over innovation fluctuates between intra- and inter-regional input/ output interactions. The informational influence in the case of input interaction is higher than the material one and increases for inter-regional interactions. Distance is therefore compensated for by various mechanisms (e.g. travelling, use of information technology). In the case of output relations, a spatial differentiation for informational and material influence over innovation cannot be observed, but it is dominated by material interactions. The equipment and IC (Integrated Circuits) design firms portray a specific pattern, representing a part of the SIP.

Horizontal Equipment and Design Interactions

As explained above, the input/output interactions of equipment and design firms are highly relevant for the stimulation of innovation. They develop a typical spatial pattern of interaction within the SIP. Therefore, we need to examine the horizontal complement of these interactions (see Fig.17.6a).

Qualified employees are necessary for building up and maintaining machines and interpreting IC-related knowledge generation through the segments of the SIP. In the case of ASIC (application specific IC) production, they are custom made and the design firms receive their innovation input mainly from front-end production and related R&D. The input from design-firms derives mainly from international firms, and the output towards design-firms is international, too.

Through the demand as well as through informational contacts they have a strong impact on front-end firms. Their activities are closely related to the customers of the 'group of five'. Furthermore, the front-end firms have a tight link to the equipment suppliers. The latter are principally responsible for the successful process of production. Their engagement in close co-operation is a dynamic factor within the SIP and leads to a high degree of co-ordination. Moreover, the process of mass production is based on pre-manufactured design-modules as well as machines. The whole process depends heavily on the availability of human resources.

The equipment firms mentioned above are often branches or international joint ventures, but are at least suppliers of regional firms. Their support activity concerns material as well as information influence (see Fig. 17.6b). An overall differentiation between material and informational influence is significant at a regional level. These interactions regarding innovation involve the generation of additional information through 'group of five' customer relations. The national interactions involving innovation are more materially oriented, while the regional ones are again more information oriented. This is a result of the various modes of involvement into the process of production. The geographic proximity facilitates informational influence over innovation of equipment firms as well as design firms, but the interaction is very heterogeneous. Geographic proximity helps solve problems through long term personal relations. Face-to-face contacts are necessary, and incorporated into the division of labour and the flow of goods and services. Therefore, both material and informational horizontal interaction have a clear influence over innovation.

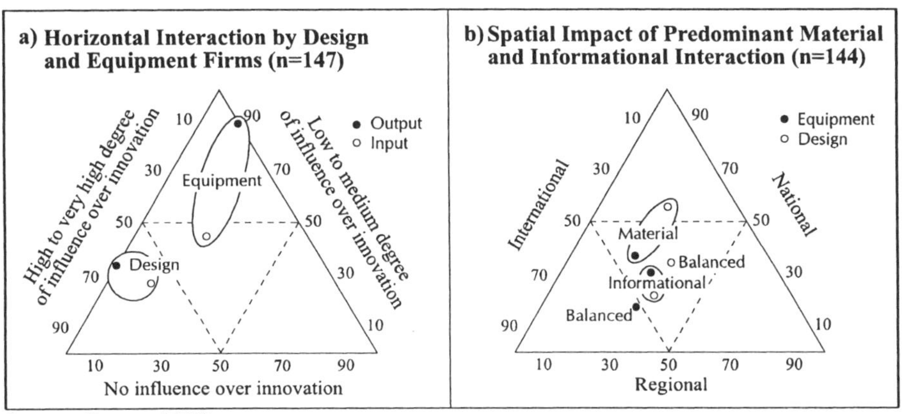

Source: Survey 1999.

Fig. 17.6 Influence of horizontal interactions over innovation in a spatial perspective

Informational Influence over Innovation by Input/Output Interaction and Further Personal Contacts

Even though the use of new media and communication technology is increasing, the informational inputs and their influence over innovation do not lead to spatial equality at either the regional or global level. In the last two sections, we have shown that the influence over innovation depends on the division of labour, while material interactions smooth the way. Regional interchange of goods and services are the basis for the informational complement of those interactions.

The fundamental education of the staff determines the potential in a knowledge-based economy to catch up with competitors during the process of innovation as well as transformation. A high level of human capital derives from applied both knowledge and experience. Nearly half (46 percent) the employees of the SIP firms surveyed have a university degree and almost all of them were formerly employed within the semiconductor industry of the GDR. In addition, Siemens/ Infineon, Semiconductor300 and AMD employ experts from the region and all over the world. In contrast, SME employees have years of sectoral and regional working experience and therefore a high level of pragmatic problem-solving competence. The highest share of personnel with university degree is found in the design firms, the lowest in the material firms (see Fig. 17.7a). It should be mentioned that the design firms are mostly small engineering companies, while the material producers are medium sized enterprises. The latter need more non-academic staff with practical experience in production.

The assumption that the information exchange through face-to-face contacts has superior relevance for innovation has to be examined. The highest level of informational influence on innovation is a result of intra- and inter-regional output interaction. A high impact was also recorded for the inter-regional input relations and other inter-regional personal contacts. Furthermore, intra-regional input interaction as well as the intra-regional personal contacts have an influence on innovation (see Fig. 17.7b). Therefore only in output relations would informational interaction seem to have a high regional impact on innovation. Even if (regional) personal face-to-face contacts occur frequently, the high level of influence derives from the functional relations between the structural elements of the SIP. In this case, it is important to find out which segments are already successfully linked intra-regionally.

The highest level of intra-regional informational interaction is towards equipment and design firms. But incorporation of innovation derives from input as well as output relations. Producers of silicon wafers are mainly intra-regionally connected by input relations, while the back-end and front-end firms are principally linked regionally through the informational output relations. The regional consulting and financial services as well as the customers have only a low influence over innovation (see Fig. 17.7c).

On the other hand, the inter-regional interactions have a high informational impact through the links to services (input), material (output) and design firms (input/output) as well as customer relations (personal contact). Personal contacts are less important for interaction with equipment, front-end, back-end and design firms. For the material producers, inter-regional personal contacts and input interaction have less influence over innovation (see Fig. 17.7d). This indicates that informational influence over innovation is not balanced spatially if we differentiate between the SIP segments.

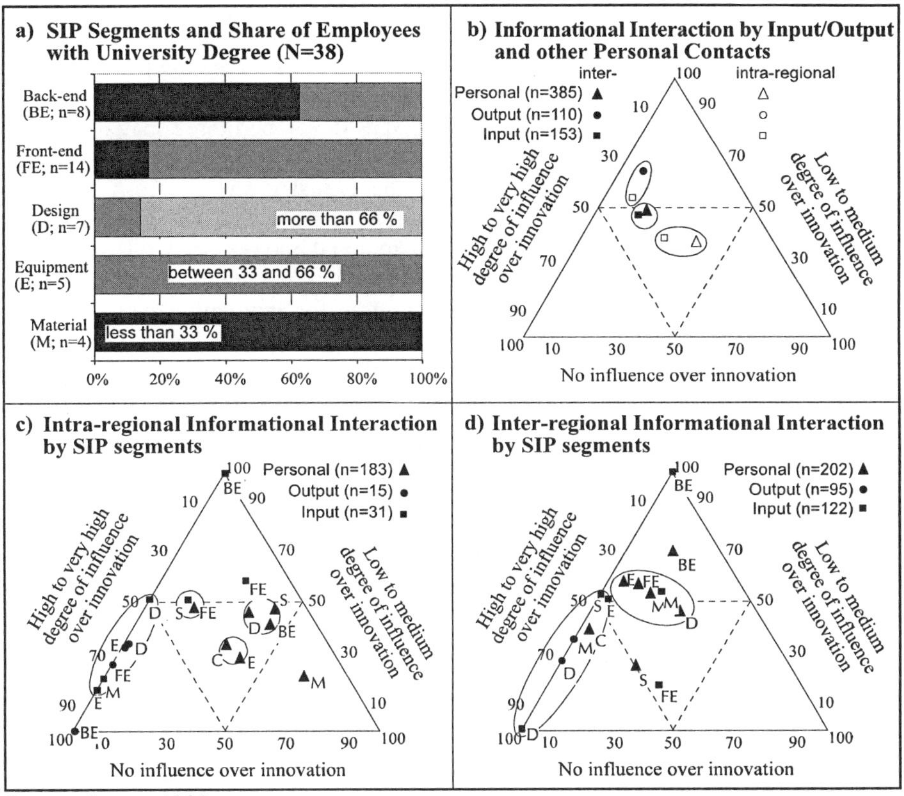

Source: Survey 1999

Fig. 17.7 Informational influence on innovation by SIP segments

17.5 Conclusions and Outlook

At the end of the 20th century, national economic systems are being strongly affected by the forces of globalisation. Industrial locations are undergoing change due to the new economic conditions. Parallel to this globalisation scenario, a more fundamental socio-political change is leading to a reappraisal of existing economic areas. In East Germany, the spatial conglomeration of industry is shifting as a result of the dissolution of the old locational patterns and the founding of new enterprises. The process of the transformation from industrial to post-industrial patterns can be therefore analysed and classified in a geographical context. Many spatial and temporal processes of change are emerging within the organisation structures of enterprises. On the one hand, a process of fragmentation is taking place and, on the other, a process of concentration due to the changing forms of interaction between different segments of the SIP (System of Innovation and Production). As human capital is very important for technological innovations, the question investigated in this chapter is whether human capital and knowledge transfer are driving forces behind spatial clustering in the semiconductor industry of East Germany.

The semiconductor industry of the former GDR developed three spatial clusters. Within these, sectoral concentrations emerged by incorporating human capital into the new start-ups. The main activities of the industry shifted from Erfurt to Dresden. By taking the structural elements in account, we find evidence of path dependence. Observing the intra- and inter-regional input/output relations, it is clear that the material and informational as well as personal interactions have changed profoundly. Not only does the stimulus for innovation comes mainly from inter-regional relations, but output interactions show a higher level of global integration than input interactions. However, the spatial interaction differs less between regional and international relation than between regional and national ones. The structural pattern behind the interaction will be therefore reflected by a sectoral and spatial cluster.

The pattern of spatial interaction of the different SIP segments vary because of their specific needs and opportunities. The equipment firms are of intra-regional relevance while the design firms are mainly of interregional relevance. Both introduce the world product standards into regional firms though in different ways. The equipment firms co-operate with regional front-end and back-end firms to carry out the production process, while the design firms locate the customer needs in a global perspective. In contrast, informational inputs and the influence of further personal contacts over innovation lead to a partial balance in a spatial point of view. But, it has to be taken into account that their influence over innovation is less than the interaction through the concrete input/output relations. Even if face-to-face contacts occur frequently, the high level of influence derives principally from the functional relations between the structural elements of the SIP.

Additional perspectives for regional development lie in strengthening the functional interaction within a given region. Moreover, cyclical informational and material relations between the SIP segments can foster regional development. But there are still some questions remaining, such as what level of regional interaction is needed to be successful, what kind of hierarchical relations exist and why a spatial shift of the main semiconductor activities resulted in East Germany.

References

Altvater, E., Mahnkopf, B. (1999) Grenzen der Globalisierung. Ökonomie, Ökologie und Politik in der Weltgesellschaft. Westfälisches Dampfboot, Münster

Audretsch, D.B., Feldmann, M.P. (1995) Innovative Clusters and Industry Life Cycle. WZB Discussion Papers, Berlin
Bea, F.X., Göbel, E. (1999) Organisation. Lucius & Lucius, Stuttgart
Blechinger, D., Pfeiffer, F. (1997) Qualifikation, Beschäftigung und technischer Fortschritt. ZEW Discussion Paper, Berlin
Clar, G., Doré J., Mohr, H. (eds.) (1997) Humankapital und Wissen. Grundlagen einer nachhaltigen Entwicklung. Springer, Berlin
Cooke, P. (1998) Global Clustering and Regional Innovation: Systemic Integration in Wales. In: Braczyk H-J, Cooke, P., Heidenreich, M. (eds.) Regional Innovation Systems. UCL Press, London, 245-262
Dicken, P. (1998) Global Shift: Transforming the World Economy. Paul Chapman, London
Edquist, C. (ed.) (1997) Systems of Innovation: Technologies, Institutions and Organizations. Pinter, London
Englmann, F., Walz, U. (1995) Industrial Centres and Regional Growth in the Presence of Local Inputs. Journal of Regional Science 35, 3-27
Enright, M.J. (1996) Regional Clusters and Economic Development: A Research Agenda. In: Staber, U., Schaefer, N., Sharma, B. (eds.) Business Networks. Prospects for Regional Development. De Gruyter Studies in Organization 73, Berlin/New York, 190-214
Feldmann, M.P., Florida, R. (1994) The Geographic Sources of Innovation: Technological Infrastructure and Product Innovation in the United States. Annals of Association of American Geographers 84(2), 210-229
Feldotto, P. (1997) Konzeptionen und institutionelle Voraussetzungen für ein regionales Innovationsmanagement. Raumforschung und Raumordnung 4/5, 305-315
Fraunhofer-ISI (1999) Innovation Networks – Concepts and Challenges in the European Perspective. Proceeding of the Conference, November 18-19, Karlsruhe
Fritsch, M. (1998) Das Innovationssystem Ostdeutschland: Problemstellung und Überblick. In: Fritsch, M., Meyer-Krahmer, F., Pleschak, F. (eds.) Innovation in Ostdeutschland. Potentiale und Probleme. Physica-Verlag, Heidelberg, 3-20
Fritsch, M., Koschatzky, K., Schätzl, L., Sternberg, R. (1998) Regionale Innovationspotentiale und innovative Netzwerke. Raumforschung und Raumordnung 4, 288-298
Gibbons, M., Limoges, C., Nowotny, H., Schwartzmann, S., Scott, P., Trow, M. (1994) The New Production of Knowledge. Sage, London
Koschatzky, K. (1998) Firm Innovation and Region: The Role of Space in Innovation Process. International Journal of Innovation Management 2(4), 383-408
Krugmann P (1991) Geography and Trade. MIT Press, Cambridge, MA
Lundvall, B.A. (1988) Innovation as an Interactive Process: From User-Producer Interaction to the National System of Innovation. In: Dosi G., Freeman C., Nelson R., Silverberg, G., Soete, L. (eds.) Technical Change and Economic Theory. Pinter, London, 349-369
Lundvall, B.A. (1992) (ed.) National Systems of Innovation. Pinter, London
Nelson, R.R. (1993) National Innovation Systems. A Comparative Analysis. Oxford University Press, Oxford
Nonaka, I., Takeuchi, H. (1995) The Knowledge-Creating Company. How Japanese Companies Create the Dynamics of Innovation. Oxford University Press, Oxford
OECD (1996) The Knowledge-Based Economy. OECD Working Papers IV(50), Paris
OECD (1998) Working Group on Innovation and Technology Policy: Facilitating International Technology Co-operation: Proceedings of the Seoul Conference, October 13-14, 1997, Paris
OECD (1999) Managing National Innovation Systems. Paris
Porter, M.E. (1990) The Competitive Advantage of Nations. Macmillan, London

Reinhard, M., Schmalholz, H. (1996) Technologietransfer in Deutschland – Stand und Reformbedarf. Duncker und Humblot, Berlin (Schriftenreihe des Ifo-Instituts für Wirtschaftsforschung; Nr. 140)
Romer, P.M. (1990) Endogenous Technological Change. Journal of Political Economy 98, 71-202
Stinglwagner, W. (1989) Die zentralgeleiteten Kombinate in der Industrie der DDR: Überblick und detailliertes Branchenprofil des Industriezweiges Elektrotechnik/ Elektronik. Gesamtdt. Inst., Bonn
Walz, U. (1997) Humanressourcen und wirtschaftliche Entwicklung von Regionen – Möglichkeiten und Grenzen regionaler Wirtschaftspolitik. In: Clar, G., Doré, J., Mohr, H. (eds.) Humankapital und Wissen. Grundlagen einer nachhaltigen Entwicklung, Springer, Berlin, 295-304

18 Correlation Between the Innovative Behaviour of Biotech Firms and Regional Development

Rainer Voß[1,2], Martina Brandt[2], Ulla Große[2] and Frank Hartmann[2]
[1] Technische Fachhochschule Wildau
[2] Institut für Regionale Innovationsforschung, Berlin

18.1 Introduction

The globalisation trend has been accompanied by growing recognition that the generation and implementation of innovations is much more strongly influenced by regional conditions and protagonists than had previously been thought, and that innovations in turn have a more or less direct effect on regional development. This is the case when innovation creates regional markets – for example by meeting a demand for renewal of regional development resources – which can contribute to solving regional problems. This in turn produces qualitatively better conditions for innovation. Innovation may also lead to reduced demands on regional development resources, making them available for forward-looking planning of vocational and social processes in the region (Voß and Hartmann 1994). This presupposes that the firms, and others actively involved in the innovation process, are aware of the connections between innovation and regional development. Also that they draw up their own appraisal of the connections, and then plan their own behaviour so that it corresponds to these more closely.

Small and medium-sized technology firms are believed to play a special role in innovation, because they can turn the latest research results into business products and services very quickly, reacting flexibly to specific customer requirements. As for SMEs in general, their internal composition means that they are characterised by a high degree of dependency on external resources. And since their products are in competition with established technologies, or even may substitute them in the future, there are additional demands on managing innovative behaviour, increasingly assuming the character of milieu management.

Our own investigations to date suggest that the need to intensify these processes of resource exchange, and thus also the possibility for feedback to regional development, is particularly pronounced in the field of biotechnology, and even more so in environmental biotechnologies. For this reason the investigation has concentrated on land reclamation and 'biomethanisation' applications.[1] These technologies are politically highly relevant, highly regulated, subject to the attentions of economic, technology, environmental, agricultural, science and health policy, and touch a wide range of interests. They also include a range of technological variants, and can be put into practice on different scales. The two processes differ in a number of important ways, such as the degree to which they are established, the complexity of the process and the process management requirements.

Two of the new Federal States were selected for the study, because many regional development problems tend to occur simultaneously and in heightened form in the ex-Democratic Republic of Germany. The regional protagonists prioritise regional effectiveness when creating, stimulating and using the research, technology and business potentials required to solve these problems.

18.2 Aims of the Project

In its most general sense, the innovative behaviour of firms involves the specific way firms react to changes in demand, to the competitive situation, developments in research and technology, resource availability, and their own rationalisation needs in relation to developing marketable products and processes. It concerns how the firm tackles the process of recombining resources, demand and its own products and services both internally and in relation to its milieu (Voß 1996).

Project-related innovative behaviour by a firm is basically unique in each case, otherwise it would not lead to innovation. This uniqueness also results from the diversity and development dynamic of resources, the needs and demand, and the multitude of possible combinations thereof. All the same, it can be assumed that there are basic patterns of innovative behaviour, which are determined by the effect of particular factors on the innovation process, and by the origin and development of the firm. This applies in particular to the internal factors influencing company development, which consist primarily of the firm and its staff. In addition, there are also milieu protagonists (such as customers, suppliers, competitors, R&D institutions, banks, official bodies and local authorities) which play a decisive role in the development of external resources. This makes it necessary for the firm to increase its direct and indirect influence on the milieu protagonists.

In this project we have studied various innovation projects by environmental biotechnology firms in the regions of Berlin-Brandenburg and Saxony, in order to investigate the extent to which the innovative behaviour of the firms:

- is regionally contextualised;
- directly or indirectly touches on the interests of regional protagonists;
- can be orientated to the solution of regional development problems.

---

[1] Biomethanisation (also referred to as 'biogas' in the following) involves the anaerobic fermentation of organic waste to produce biogas fuel (in a biogas plant).

18.3 Method of Investigation

Various approaches for investigating innovative behaviour of firms were considered for the design of the empirical method (Perlitz *et al.* 1989; Kilper *et al.* 1990; Schwitalla 1993; Latniak and Rehfeld 1994; Felder *et al.* 1995, Heinemann *et al.* 1995; König and Speilkamp 1995). Empirical studies can produce very contradictory conclusions.[1] They normally relate to the analysis of various input indicators (e.g. annual investment and innovation spending, proportion of staff in R&D) or output indicators (patents, proportion of new products and processes, etc.). This type of approach to innovative behaviour (which is mostly not technology-specific) assumes that the existence of particular internal and external factors in a particular quality and quantity is generally advantageous for innovative behaviour of firms.

In the present project we have also used a factor-based approach, but combine it with a behaviour-oriented approach. The aim is to describe and explain innovative behaviour in technological fields, and to identify approaches for regional development management. By focusing on the innovative behaviour of firms in combining external and internal resources, it is assumed that the existence of intensive resource exchange processes indicates possibilities of influence and a starting point for regional orientation and effective innovative behaviour. In connection with the analysis of the influence of regional milieus on innovative behaviour of firms, the study also investigated whether networking activity by the protagonists can be ascertained.

The investigation comprised eight case studies of complex innovation processes in biotechnology firms. Two firms specialising in land reclamation and two biomethanisation firms were selected from each region. Due to the importance accorded to the behaviour of milieu protagonists for the realisation of innovations, each case study covered not only the innovating company, but also all the regional protagonists directly or indirectly involved in the innovation process. This made it necessary to hold a total of 66 interviews with experts. The wealth of complex empirical data was then compressed and evaluated in order to:

- prepare innovative behaviour profiles of the eight firms studied;
- prepare technology-specific and region-specific intensity profiles of the influencing factors;
- characterise the properties and interrelationships which could be classified objectively;
- appraise the extent to which the factors can be influenced by regional protagonists, and the effects of innovative behaviour on regional development.

---

[1] For this reason Maas calls for a conceptional framework which allows existing knowledge and new findings about innovative behaviour to be systematised (Maas 1990).

18.4 Profiles of the Innovative Behaviour of Firms

The condition of the eight firms investigated is typical for biotechnology firms involved in land reclamation and biomethanisation (biogas) in the New Federal States. It allows a differentiated and representative explanation of the innovative behaviour of these companies, and the formulation of some general conclusions. The internal factors differ in intensity, because the study covers a range of different types of enterprise: newly founded firms and older firms with longer business and biotechnology traditions, independent and subsidiary firms, small firms with just nein staff and medium-sized firms with 490, firms which concentrate on one biotechnology process as well as firms where biotechnology is only one aspect of their business.

We evaluated the intensity of the firms' involvement with each of the nineteen factors which influence innovative behaviour in order to prepare innovative behaviour profiles. Fig. 18.1 shows the example of two biogas firms in Saxony. In this field of technology each firm was found to have a highly firm-specific innovation behaviour profile in relation to the innovation projects, even where the firms are similarly constituted. On the other hand, greater similarity of the profiles was found among land reclamation firms. In order to explain this finding, a characterisation and analysis was carried out, first of the factor properties and the relationships between factors, and subsequently of the degree to which these can be influenced by regional protagonists.

18.5 Characterisation of the Factors Influencing Innovative Behaviour

Considering criteria such as whether a factor if present or not present, or quantitatively more or less intense is insufficient to determine the functionality of the factors influencing innovative behaviour. For this reason the following behaviour-relevant characteristics of the factors (properties and interrelationships) were included in the evaluation:

- Technology-specific relevance and regional intensity;
- Interrelationships between influencing factors;
- Variability (availability of external factors through just one milieu protagonist, or through many);
- Degree to which individual factors can be influenced by business and/or milieu protagonists and the time-scale of this influence (short, medium or long term), referred to as their 'influenceability'.

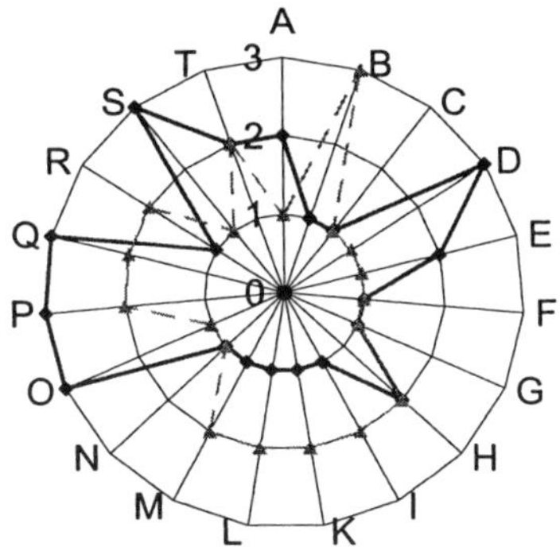

Intensity of firms' involvement with factors which influence innovative behaviour:
1 = low, 2 = medium, 3 = high
——— firm 1
– – – firm 2

External influencing factors:
A - Regional demand
B - National demand
C - Statutory provisions
D - Approval and enforcement practices
E - Financing
F - Acceptance
G - Research potential
H - Technical infrastructure
I - Representation of interests
K - Intensity of competition (biotechnology)
L - Intensity of competition (alternative methods)
M - Developments in science and technology
N - Technological knowledge of milieu protagonists

Internal influencing factors:
O - R&D capacity
P - Plant and equipment
Q - Biotechnology know-how
R - Size of firm
S - Proportion of biotechnology in firm's activities
T - Capital resources

Fig. 18.1 Innovative behaviour profiles of two biogas firms in Saxony

All factors were evaluated with reference to innovative use of the investigated technologies under current conditions using a three-point scale (1-low, 2-medium, 3-high) (Voß and Hartmann 1995; Voß *et al.* 1995; Große *et al.* 1995). This showed that technological knowledge and acceptance were significantly more important for firms in the field of biomethanisation than for land reclamation firms. The regional significance of the external influencing factors on the innovative behaviour of the land reclamation firms was almost identical in the two regions investigated (the presence of many abandoned polluted areas from lignite mining and processing; polluted abandoned military sites; few reclamation contracts awarded due to the poor financial situation of potential clients; environmental protection, civil engineering and/or biotechnology experience in the firms; and possibilities for using relevant research results from the region through research co-operation). However, the regions differ greatly in the intensity of the factors influencing the innovative behaviour of biogas firms. In Saxony, for example, regional demand, approval and enforcement practices, and acceptance were less intense. Unlike Brandenburg, Saxony already had strong capacities in plant engineering and research before the reunification of Germany. After 1990, although the problems were similar, biological treatment of waste and recycling was apportioned a different role in each state. While Saxony favoured other technologies despite its traditions, several government departments in Brandenburg made biotechnology a priority of technology policy. In the final phase of the project, the state administration's attitude to the importance of biotechnology for waste treatment started to change in Saxony too.

Innovative firms are forced to act when external factors of great technology-specific relevance are regionally weak, having the effect of hindering investment. In Brandenburg such a discrepancy existed only in the statutory provisions, while in Saxony it also encompassed approval and enforcement, financing, and technological knowledge of milieu protagonists.

The networked thinking method was used to analyse and standardise the relationships between the influencing factors, and to quantify the influenceability between and within the external and internal influencing factors. The graphic portrayal of the results (see Fig. 18.2) shows clearly the degree to which a single factor influences and is influenced by other factors. The factors can bc characterised accordingly as active, passive, inert or dynamic. The results shown in Fig. 18.3 demonstrate that the effect of many external factors is mediated by internal factors, and that the conditioning of external factors is often significantly influenced by external factors.

From the point of view of the project's behaviour-orientated approach, the ability of the regional protagonists to influence the factors on the one hand, and on the other, their perception of this ability, form the principal linkages between influencing factors and innovative behaviour. Alongside the objective regional contextualisation of the influencing factors, there is also a subjective regional contextualisation influenced by the behaviour of the regional protagonists.

All the appraisals for characterising influencing factors were combined to create factor profiles. Comparison of these profiles (the example in Fig. 18.4 shows the 'Approval' and 'Regional Demand' factors for land reclamation) make it clearer how diverse the factors and their influenceability are (influenceable by whom, in what timeframe, by altering other factors, etc.).

18.6 Innovation-Relevant and Innovation-Orientated Behaviour of Milieu Protagonists

The innovative behaviour of a firm is not shaped solely or predominantly by the existence or the intensity of particular external and internal influencing factors, but also by the attitude to relevant milieu protagonists, and by their own behaviour. The diversity and intensity of attitudes to milieu protagonists found in the innovating firms confirms the special importance of milieus for innovation in small and medium-sized firms. Because milieu protagonists develop and manage external resources which are vital for innovation, they have, from the point of view of the innovating firm, innovation-relevant behaviour. In a specific case clients, suppliers, competitors, R&D institutions, authorities, funding bodies, local authorities or others can control information and/or material and financial resources which can support the innovative project, or may even make it possible in the first place.

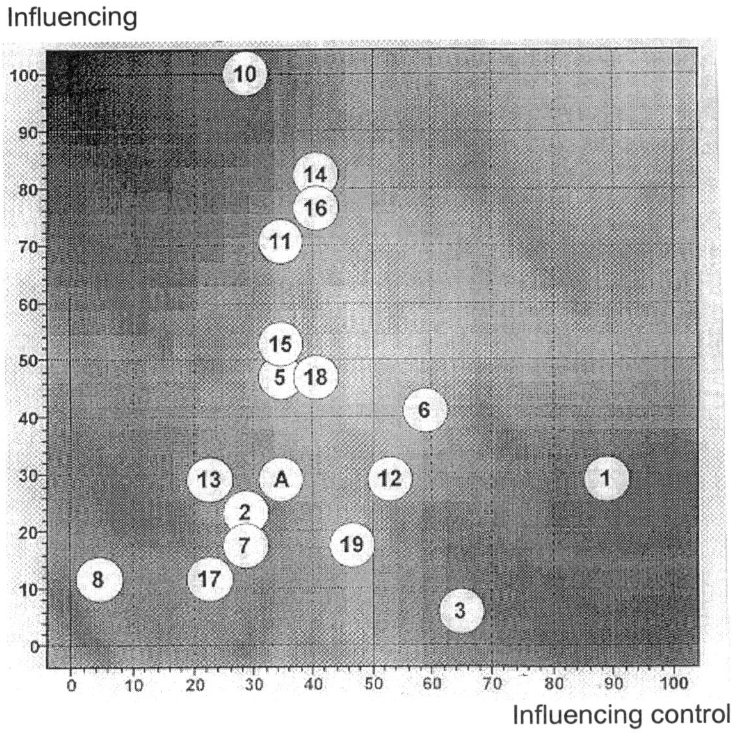

1	Regional demand	11	Intensity of competition (altern. methods)
2	National demand	12	Development in science and technology
3	Statutory provisions	13	Technology knowledge of milieu protag.
A 4	Approval and enforcement practice	14	R&D capacity
5	Financing	15	Plant and equipment
6	Acceptance	16	Biotechnology know-how
7	Research potential	17	Size of firm
8	Technical infrastructure	18	Prop. of biotechnology in firm's activity
A 9	Represent. of interests	19	Capital resources
10	Intensity of competition (biotech)		

Fig. 18.2 Degree to which a single factor influences and is influenced by others

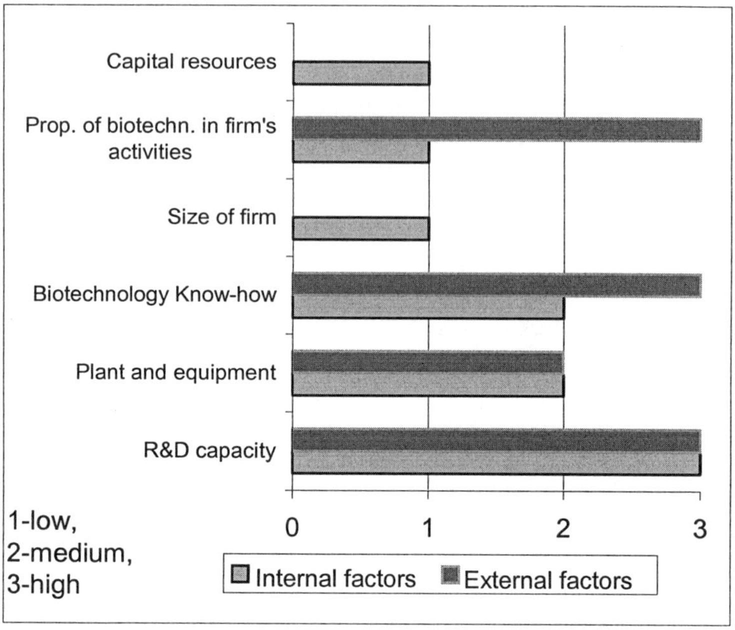

Fig. 18.3 Influenceability of internal factors (within other internal or external factors) for land reclamation

This does not mean that these protagonists are themselves aware of their (potential) role. And even if they have recognised the innovative relevance for the firm, their own interests (or a framework which restricts their activities, etc.) may be an obstacle to their willingness and ability to facilitate the innovative process of a firm in the required quality, quantity and timeframe.

The firm must attempt to transform the innovation-relevant behaviour of these protagonists into innovation-orientated behaviour, or in certain cases to prevent or delay this transformation (by influencing competitors, legislature, etc.). The firm must perceive not only the behaviour of the individual protagonist, but also interrelations in the behaviour of milieu protagonists, as the first step in developing ways to indirectly influence innovation-promoting and innovation-inhibiting influencing factors. Often the innovating firm will have to invest a great deal of time and energy in dealings with the respective resource-holder, if it is to achieve a mutually advantageous exchange of resources and thus transform innovative-relevant behaviour of milieu protagonists into innovation-orientated behaviour. This fundamental relationship between protagonist behaviour and the entrepreneurial innovation process is illustrated in Fig. 18.5.

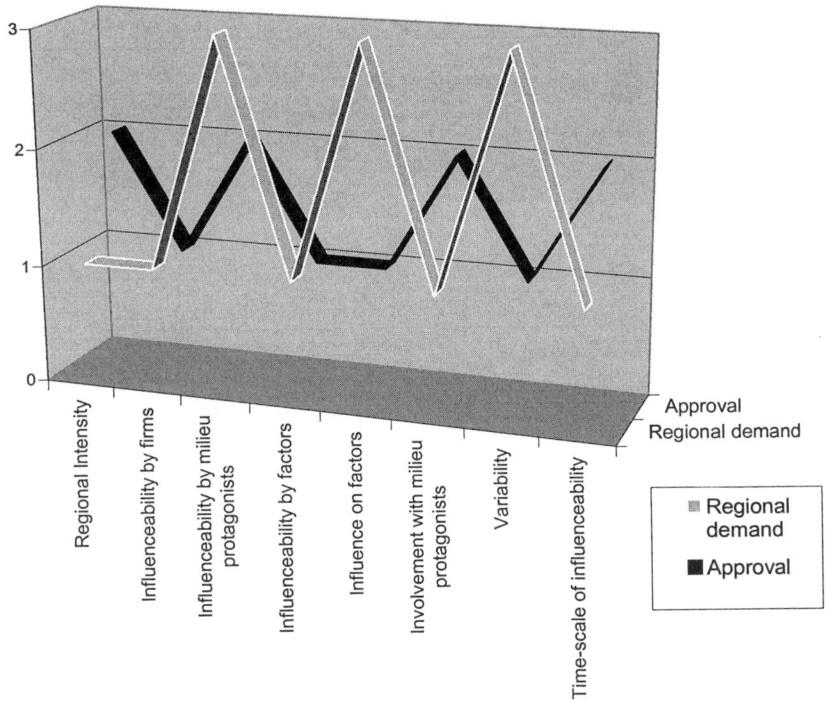

Fig. 18.4 Profiles of factors 'Approval' and 'Regional Demand' for land reclamation

The intensity of contacts between the firm and the milieu protagonist, and the chances of success for the firm to effect innovative behaviour on the part of the milieu protagonist largely depend on:

- whether, when and how the firm and the resource-holder become aware of one another;
- the relevance accorded by the firm to the respective external resources and the protagonists controlling them;
- the willingness and ability developed by the firm to orient the resources of other protagonists to its own innovation process by linking its innovation process to theirs; and
- what interest the resource-holder has in reciprocal exchange of resources or provision of exploitable resources to the firm, and what relevance this has for the resource-holder's own goals.

Firms and milieu protagonists may themselves be protagonists, or they may influence factors which they do not themselves hold. Their approach to participation in networks will be determined by which of these two alternatives is the case.

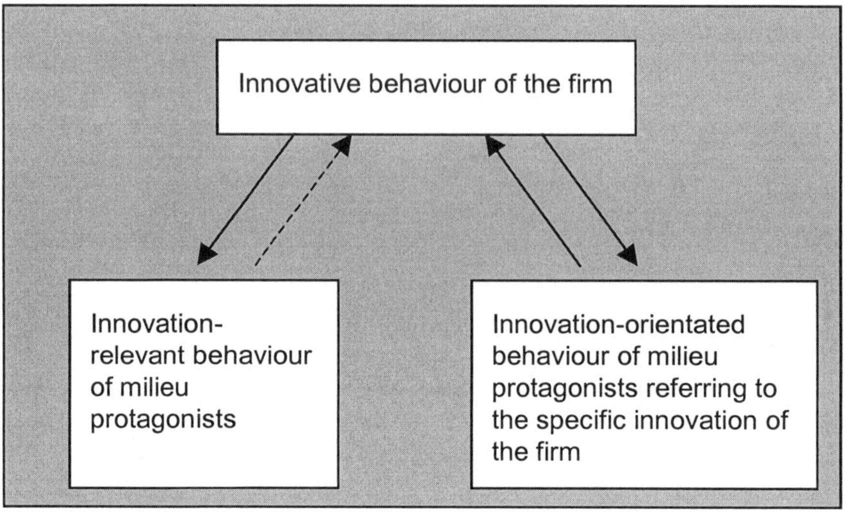

Fig. 18.5 Protagonist behaviour and entrepreneurial innovation process

18.7 Innovative Behaviour and Networks

To describe the innovation-orientated relationships between firms and milieu protagonists, there are a number of theoretical approaches which investigate the role of networks (for example, Camagni 1991; Fritsch 1992). Under dynamic milieu conditions, networks are a particularly suitable organisational form for perceiving, shaping, co-ordinating and influencing the innovation-relevant behaviour of protagonists.

The behaviour-orientated approach of this project implies an understanding of networks through an attempt to explain network behaviour in terms of the protagonists' differing perceptions of factor dependencies. Network relationships are understood as relationships between protagonists for the purpose of putting innovation projects into practice. They extend beyond contractual and thus relatively permanent co-operative relationships. In the two fields of applied biotechnology investigated, protagonist networking was found only in biomethanisation. This has two primary causes: on the one hand, the number of innovation-relevant protagonists involved in this field is significantly greater than in land reclamation. On the other, the problems in putting innovations into practice are generally significantly greater than in land reclamation, and are also regionally differentiated – greater in Saxony than in Brandenburg.

Managing the extremely large number of milieu contacts needed by a biogas firm requires a great deal of effort, and is almost impossible for a small firm. Often innovative biogas firms do not operate alone, but in close co-operation with partners who have a vital interest in the success of the innovation project (engineering firms, farmers, marketing agencies, consulting engineers, financing firms, other domestic and foreign biogas firms).

In the innovation process, Saxon plant engineering firms are confronted with a milieu which is almost 'hostile' to innovation. There is low acceptance of biogas technology, preference for alternative methods, considerable difficulties in the approval process, and lack of willingness by other protagonists to recognise or support the interests of the innovating firm. Deficiencies in knowledge about biogas were one important reason for this. The typical hindrances for 'land reclamation' – such as weak regional demand, lack of statutory provisions, and financing problems – also played a role for biogas.

For these reasons biogas firms participate in networking with the aim of reducing the technological, planning and market risks for their innovation. In the innovation projects investigated empirically, these functions attributed to innovation networks (Kowohl 1998) played a positive role for the firms involved. Unlike the case of land reclamation, other groups of protagonists (as well as the biotechnological plant engineering firms) were also affected by the negative constellation of innovation-relevant factors (e.g. operators of agricultural and waste disposal facilities, consulting engineers, local authorities), and recognised a mutual interest in eliminating these obstacles. In some Saxon biogas projects a type of division of labour in the milieu work developed between the involved protagonists. Although the investigated alliances differed in their composition, all those involved in the biogas project acted together to win the milieu protagonists to an innovation-orientated attitude.

Clearly, for networking to take place, a number of protagonists must share a particular awareness of problems and positive assessment of their influenceability. Protagonist networking will only arise where, for example, those concerned recognise that many of the obstacles to innovation arise through poor acceptance of the technology in the region, and acknowledge that their own abilities are insufficient to overcome them. The networking process intensifies when, apart from the innovating firms, other protagonists are also affected by the obstacles. The initiative for networking does not necessarily come from the innovating firms. In the field of biogas, the role played by consulting engineers is at least as great.

These network-forming effects are triggered by the innovative behaviour of the biotechnology firms and their influence on the behaviour of milieu protagonists. When a transformation from innovation-relevant to innovation-orientated behaviour is achieved in a large number of milieu protagonists, the effects multiply. Their intensity can be greater and longer-lasting when the innovative behaviour of a firm leads to the creation of innovation alliances or innovation networks.

18.8 Conclusions and Outlook

The assumption that investigating the (direct and mediated) influence of external and internal factors is not sufficient to describe and explain technology-specific and region-specific innovative behaviour led the authors to devise a behaviour-orientated approach. This involved including in the investigation the milieu protagonists' own appraisals of the factors they 'manage'.

This step enhanced the description of innovative behaviour, but on its own contributed little to explaining innovative behaviour and identifying management approaches. For this reason it was necessary to unite a factor-orientation with a behaviour-orientation in the analysis. On the factor side, bridging between the factor and behaviour components of innovation conditions is made possible by the ability of firms and/or particular milieu protagonists to influence the conditions directly and indirectly. On the behaviour side, the bridge is created by the processes of perception and appraisal of both the factors and their influenceability. The innovative behaviour of the firm develops through this complex process, involving the transformation of milieu protagonists' innovation-relevant behaviour into innovation-oriented behaviour.

In this context an innovation condition is always simultaneously:

- a factor with a particular character and a particular intensity;
- the perception of this factor and;
- the behaviour of protagonists towards it, and thus toward other protagonists who also have a relationship with the factor.

Further theoretical consolidation of the concept and its operationalisation, with the aim of shaping the behaviour of firms and milieu protagonists to allow more effective management of innovation processes at the level of the firm and the region, will be the subject of future research projects. The issues to be investigated include, for example, the connection between innovative behaviour and regional diffusion of technologies, the relationship between stability and renewal in innovative behaviour patterns, the influence of altered innovation conditions on the behaviour of firms and milieu protagonists, and the time-dependency of perceptions, appraisals, reappraisals and changes in behaviour.

References

Camagni, R. (ed.) (1991) Innovation Networks: Spatial Perspectives. Pinter, London

Felder, J. *et al.* (1995) Innovationsverhalten der deutschen Wirtschaft. ZEW-Dokumentation 95-03, Mannheim

Fritsch, M. (1992) Unternehmens-"Netzwerke" im Lichte der Institutionenökonomik. Jahrbuch für Neue Politische Ökonomie 11, Tübingen, 89-102

Fürst, D., Kilper, H. (1993) Die Innovationskraft regionaler Politiknetzwerke. Gelsenkirchen

Grabher, G. (1994) Lob der Verschwendung. Redundanz in der Regionalentwicklung. Ein sozioökonomisches Plädoyer. Edition Sigma, Berlin

Große, U., Hartmann, F., Voß, R. (1995) Marktpotentiale und Unternehmensanforderungen für mittelständische Unternehmen in Mecklenburg-Vorpommern und Brandenburg im Zuge der Anwendung von Biotechnologien. Abschlußbericht RKW-Projekt

Heinemann, F. *et al.* (1995) Das Innovationsverhalten der baden-württembergischen Unternehmen. ZEW-Dokumentation 95-05, Mannheim

Kilper, H. *et al.* (1990) Regionale Gestaltungsnetzwerke und betriebliche Innovation. Bericht des Institut für Arbeit und Technik 2, Gelsenkirchen

König, H., Spielkamp, A. (1995) Die Innovationskraft kleiner und mittlerer Unternehmen. ZEW-Dokumentation 95-07, Mannheim

Kowohl, U. (1998) Innovationsnetzwerke. Deutscher Universitäsverlag, Wiesbaden

Latniak, E., Rehfeld, D. (1994) Betriebliche Innovation und regionales Umfeld – Erfahrungen in NRW. Arbeit no. 3, vol. 3, 238-253

Maas, C. (1990) Determinanten betrieblichen Innovationsverhaltens. Theorie und Empirie. Berlin: Duncker und Humblot. Volkswirtschaftliche Schriften no. 399, 20

Perlitz, M., Löbler, H. (1989) Das Innovationsverhalten der mittelständischen Industrie. Poeschel, Stuttgart

Schwitalla, B. (1993) Messung und Erklärung industrieller Innovationsaktivitäten. Physica-Verlag, Heidelberg

Voß, R. (1996): Innovationsmanagement in kleinen mittelständischen Unternehmen – Ansatzpunkte für ein Forschungskonzept mit Beratungsoptionen. Wissenschaftliche Beiträge der TFH Wildau 1, 85-93

Voß, R., Hartmann, F. (eds.) (1994) Biotechnologiepotentiale für die Entwicklung Sachsen-Anhalts. IRI-Schriften, vol. 2. IRI, Berlin

Voß, R. *et al.* (1995) Regionale Voraussetzungen und Wirkungen der Biotechnologieanwendung untersucht in den Bundesländern Brandenburg und Sachsen-Anhalt. Abschlußbericht DFG-Projekt

19 Locational Effects of Innovations in Information and Communications Technology on Food Retailing in Germany

Sven Henschel
Institute of Geography, Humboldt University, Berlin

19.1 Introduction

Over the last three decades, food retailing has undergone far reaching structural change. This process is characterised by a change in store type, a concentration of business enterprises and an enormous increase in sales area. The reasons for these changes can, on the one hand, be found in specific processes affecting the business, such as changes to cost structure and changes in the basic conditions within society, especially with regard to demand behaviour. On the other hand, a particularly significant role has been played by the introduction of innovations, which have led to wide-ranging transformations. The adoption of self-service, for example, has massively transformed retail structure and has therefore been a contributory factor in the extension of the sales area, with consequent new concepts of store type. In addition, social developments such as the rising standard of living which, among other things, has been marked by a growing level of motorization and improved refrigeration facilities, have encouraged these processes and led to a sales orientation.

The changes have led firstly to internal modifications within businesses regarding the merchandise process linkages expressed, for example, via a standardised product range in all branches of one retail business. Secondly, the process has changed the location patterns of food retailing. The internal changes have primarily affected merchandise and logistics through the uniform product range policy, which itself has resulted in extensive standardisation. Thus the changes in location pattern have been marked by a significant decrease of network density with, on average, a larger sales area per branch and finally by the genesis of an additional trade network including car-oriented and disintegrated locations. These transformations have been accompanied by reduced costs and a sales orientation. Both individuality and service within food retailing have been greatly reduced.

Further rationalisation of trade-internal processes has helped enforce innovations in information and communication technologies. Their effect can be seen in the widespread new orientation in the field of merchandise and logistics.

Zentes (1991) writes about the increased computerisation in retailing at the beginning of the nineties.

This development was brought about by he introduction of electronic data cash desks, scanners, microcomputers, together with data transmission. These form the components of product management systems (PMS). The massive spread of computer-based PMS has led to more efficient stock management, differentiated customer focus and matching logistic solutions.

19.2 The Product Management System

The product management system has been primarily discussed in publications concerned with business management. The reasons for this are mainly due to the cost-orientated approaches that led to the development of PMS. Contemporary PMS can be referred to as the merchandise process system, which includes only the physical process of transportation of goods. The latter is the basis for the product management system, characterised principally by the direct control and regulation of trade through electronic data processing (EDP).

The processing of merchandise can be divided into different aspects, including the physical, administrative and direct handling of goods (Ebert 1986). All these aspects are connected within a PMS. Varying definitions can be found in the literature. A common feature is the integrated approach adopted in the systems.

Table 19.1 gives in chronological order a number of definitions of PMS illustrating its development and potential for the trading business. Ebert (1986) criticises the definitions given by Birther, as well as a definition published by IBM, which assume that PMS necessarily incorporates the use of electronic data processing (EDP). Ebert claims that PMS have been in existence since the origin of commercial relations. This opinion follows the definitions given by Steckenborn (1981). However, traditional PMS would fulfil only a rudimentary function in the present German business situation. It is through the use of EDP that the PMS has become more universally applicable, as well as having a high degree of flexibility and allowing information processing. The definition given by Hertel (1999) is the first to embody an information and planning process model that extends beyond the purely merchandise-processing aspect, thereby introducing a new quality of PMS. Thus it is Hertel who currently does most justice to the complexity of the processes taking place in the field of retailing.

The significance of computer-aided product management systems lies in their complex data intensity. Thus a very wide range of different processes within a trading business can be data-processed and analysed.

The processing information on merchandise gained from a product management system provides details of the following (Simmet 1990):

- the supplier;
- the incoming-goods date;
- the outgoing-goods date;
- the item type and quantity;

- the supply price;
- the checkout process;
- the inventory.

Furthermore, additional information about the customer can be gained. For example:

- the time of sale (day, time);
- the purchase sum;
- the item type and quantity and thus corresponding connected purchases;
- mode of payment;
- sex;
- age;
- social status (last 2 points only if customer cards or membership cards exist).

Table 19.1 Definitions for product management systems in the literature

Steckenborn (1981)	"A product management system is an integrated system for accounting, invoicing and information management".
IBM	"A product management system is integrated and supports merchandise processing with the help of EDP"
Birther (1982)	"Product management systems are computer-aided methods designed to rationally process the data acquisition and processing routines that accompany merchandise movements, together with the resulting communication and information systems".
Zentes (1983)	"...Product management systems represent the informational side of product-related logistics in trade; in this respect they are closely linked to the system of physical distribution, i.e. to the flow of goods. Implementing integral merchandise processing requires that all merchandise occurrences are completely recorded and evaluated".
Theuer (1983/84)	"Product management systems encompass all measures that are implemented in separate commercial entities and on the basis of inter-company co-operation in order to improve the design and control of the flow of merchandise, information and vouchers."
Ebert (1986)	"A product management system is the sum of all of the information and decision processes within the trading concern, that are directed towards the merchandise".
Hertel (1999)	"A product management system is a model of all the business processes within a commercial enterprise; it consists of a merchandise process model, a disposition process model, an invoice process model as well as an information and planning process model".

This information is recorded by mobile data terminals in the incoming-goods area or by scanner cash desks at the point of sale (POS). A further current development consists of the possibility for data interchange using data carriers or data networks. During the last few years a wide range of innovations have been introduced in this field. Thus today's high-performance computer technology allows data and information about programme changes to be transferred from the mainframe to chain-store computers. Conversely, all transactions are transmitted to the mainframe. This system of distributed data processing (DDP) facilitates cost savings as a result of homogeneous systems in which information management and computer activities are centrally controlled.

In a 1994 study conducted by the Europäisches Handelsinstitut (EHI – European Institute of Trade), 17 US and European commercial enterprises were questioned about the cost and use of scanned data. The results showed that there is generally a favourable cost/benefit ratio (Fig. 19.1).

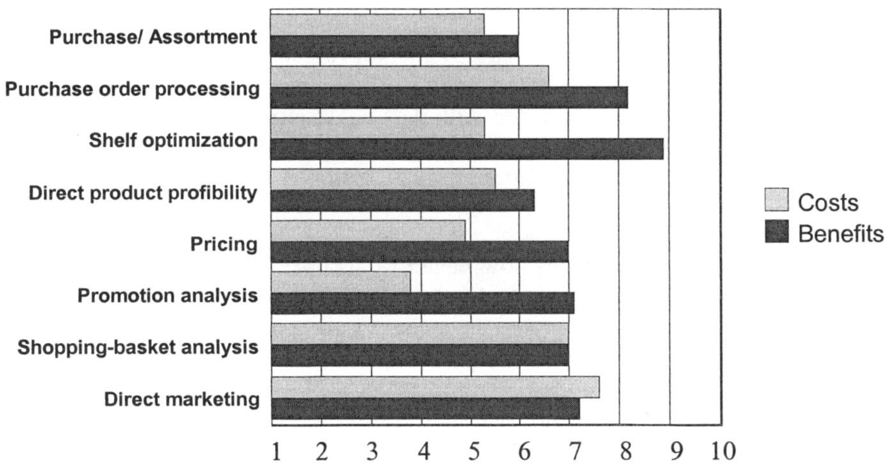

Source: EHI 1994, p. 18

Fig. 19.1 Cost/benefit assessment of scanner data provided by assessed companies

It became apparent that there was scope for rationalising business-intensive processes such as purchasing, shelf optimisation, purchase order processing, pricing and promotion analysis. Developments in the use of scanner technology show further potential for innovations over time.

Developmental Stages in Businesses with the Introduction of Scanner Systems

The extensive introduction of scanner technology that occurred during the second half of the eighties prompted the Deutsche Handelsinstitut (DHI - German Institute of Trade) to conduct a study in the early nineties on the implementation and use of scanner technology. In the mid-nineties, the European Institute of Trade (EHI) (Gerling 1994) performed a more detailed follow-up of this study and compared the developmental state of German industry with that internationally. In the latter study it was possible to work out developmental phases and trends, which provided a good overview of the use of this technology. Furthermore, the results of this research project indicated developments which are opening up potential new areas for the use of scanner data.

1st phase: As early as the end of the eighties, the rationalisation of job sequences in branch offices – such as more efficient pricing, faster checkout processing and lower inventory differences – already justified the investment expenditure that had been made on the full-scale application of scanner technology[1]. Furthermore, parts of companies had to be reorganised in order to make effective use of the potential of PMS. This included the acquisition and maintenance of items as well as data transmission to the marketplace. Thus a uniform cost advantage was achieved in all locations, even though this exclusively concerned internal business processes.

2nd phase: The demand for sales data by market research institutes and suppliers opened up scope for scanner technology outside the individual company. The problems that arose were associated with data aggregation, data quality and their systematisation. This meant enormous additional expense for companies, because information on every existing variation of a particular item had to be precisely identified and stored.

3rd phase: Belatedly, companies now began to also use the available information for their strategic decisions. Thus individual departments and field posts were set up with the exclusive task of processing and evaluating point of sale (POS) data.

4th phase: The potential for successfully using scanner data was analysed and implemented in certain areas such as shelf optimisation, purchasing or pricing. In this phase it thus became necessary to create fast, simple and flexible access to the scanner data for defined groups of people. Furthermore, staff qualifications had to be improved.

5th phase: This is the phase in which scanner data was applied within automatic decision systems that deal with the manufacturer/dealer relationship as well as the dealer/logistics-service relationship. It is primarily here that Efficient Consumer Response (ECR) and Electronic Data Interchange (EDI) were able to open up new value-added potential (Töpfer 1996). After highly efficient corporation-internal structures had been established, future potential was found in processes external to the corporation.

---

[1] Falling hardware and installation costs made full-scale applications possible. For example in 1982 there were 67 scanner installations installed thoughout the Federal Republic. In 1994 this figure reached 15000 installations.

6th phase: Corporation-external processes such as customised marketing gained acceptance on the basis of scanner technology. Furthermore it is mandatory to perform site optimisation at existing locations. Site-specific specialisation with standardised and automatic corporation-internal processes facilitate a wider range of distinguishing strategies in business.

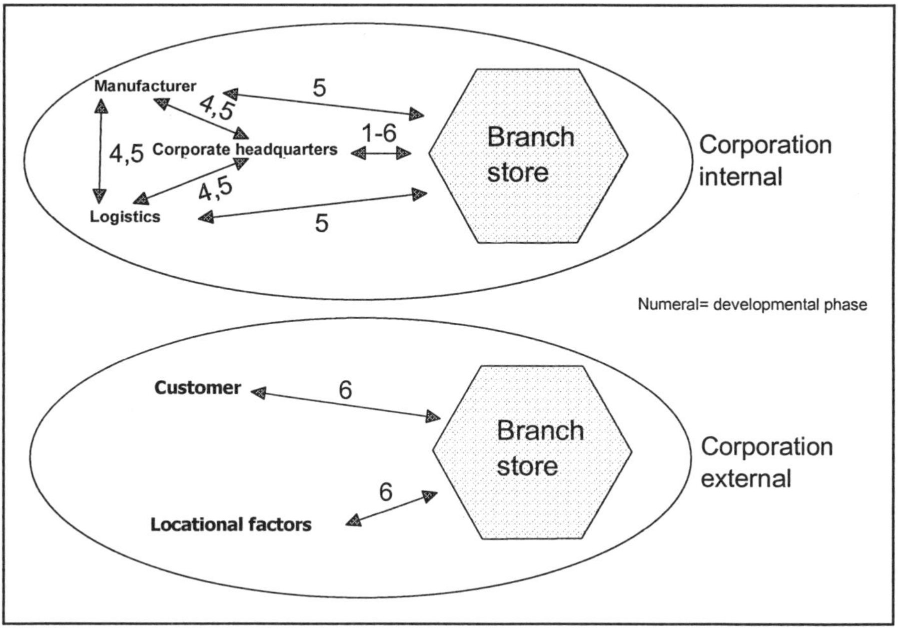

Fig. 19.2 Innovation potential in business

Success Potential of Product Management Systems

The phases in the application of scanner technology show the success potential of computer-aided PMS. These can be subdivided into the areas of rationalisation, management, co-operation and marketing (Zentes 1984).

With the massive introduction of scanner cash desks in Germany towards the end of the 1980s, it was primarily pricing, improvement in checkout accuracy and reduction of inventory differences, in other words mainly corporation-internal **rationalisation potential** that was exploited.

It was only following the second and third phase that the strategic significance of the **management potential** of PMS was recognised. Decision-making was facilitated and made more effective through the availability of scanner data so that better based decisions in the areas of assortment (shelf optimisation) and price could be reached. Strategic objectives such as store-type positioning and the development of new sales markets were also affected. The management level is currently gaining greater significance in PMS because additional external information (on the customer and environment) is flowing into the product management system thus facilitating business policy decisions. In the course of this development, there has been a centralisation of the complex decision-making processes such as procurement, logistics and sales.

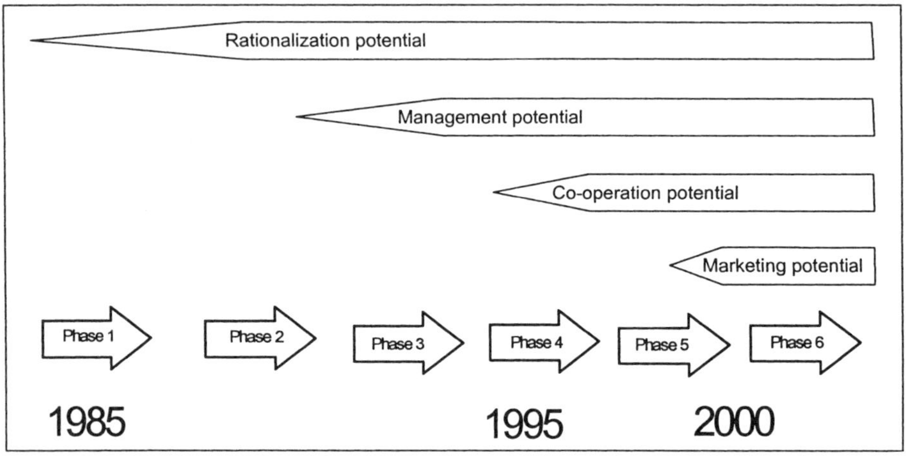

Source: based on Gerling 1994.

Fig. 19.3 Success potential for PMS compared with the introduction of scanner technology

Exploitation of the **co-operation potential**, which gained significance during the fourth and fifth phase, requires the retail sector, manufacturers and logistics services to have a high degree of confidence and to be able to compromise. This confidence is a decisive basis for implementing automatic decision systems. The strategy of Efficient Consumer Response (ECR) is gaining enormous significance. Cost savings can be obtained by shortening processes and accelerating object flows in conjunction with enhanced customer orientation. Furthermore there is internal and external data exchange via electronic data interchange (EDI).

The Internet, intranet and extranet provide the technical basis for co-operation between manufacturers and the trade sector, i.e. business to business (b2b). It serves primarily as a communication platform between computers, but also gives all participants the opportunity for data access in almost real time. According to the OECD, at present around 80 percent of e-commerce is b2b. This means that in this field too, it is the internal potential that is being exploited first, resulting in reduced costs and increased efficiency.

For example, suppliers of Wal-Mart in the USA can access Wal-Mart's own database down to the level of branch-store sales data. It is thus possible for the manufacturer to use production capacities more economically and to plan and apply the distribution systems more efficiently. However Wal-Mart will not be implementing this system for its German branch offices before 2001.[1] It is an absolute necessity for the retail sector that the sales data for specific product groups be available at all times.

As a next step, high priority is being given to recording the need-orientated demand-pull effect emanating from the customer. This facilitates flexible, order-oriented production and an adapted distribution system by means of automatic order and delivery execution. The aim of these solutions is to design the delivery chain more efficiently so that tied-up capital is reduced and customer needs can be better serviced.

Within the food industry, logistic implementation is achieved via regional storage facilities but also, increasingly, via central storage facilities, the aim being to have a low level of storage volume.[2] With their know-how, professional service providers can assure bundled product deliveries and delivery services more cost-effectively. It is necessary to have permanent communication between the groups involved within the trade operation, i.e. head office/ branch office/ manufacturer/ logistics service provider.

During the introductory phase of scanner cash desks, very little significance was attached to the opening up of **marketing potential**. Only after data from the point of sale (POS) had been sold to suppliers and market research institutes did the industry recognise the strategic importance of target-group oriented marketing. However at this time, the company-internal improvement of potential was still the main focus. When data begins to be acquired at the POS and customer cards are slowly introduced, it is possible to gather hitherto inaccessible quantitative and qualitative customer information (primary data). It is through these means that customer-specific marketing becomes based on the buying characteristics of individual customers, and ultimately leads to a greater customer tie-up and to increases in turnover. A 'trading up' of marketing follows.

A further aspect is online marketing, in which an integrated PMS forms the interface. In the retail food industry, because of the relatively low level of advertising required, the Internet provides an additional marketing platform and, at the same time, an electronic salesroom. This makes it possible to provide a type of selling that is independent of time and place. Additionally, certain user-defined offers can be transmitted online to the customer. Electronic trade of foodstuffs is currently still a long way from being profitable. However, the introduction of these systems promotes the service concept as well as making the performance of individual commercial enterprises transparent. The provision of information to the customer is the main focus at present. This may affect certain products or prices but also business conditions and locations, the potential customer can thus use the information offered to determine his own preferences. As real purchasing for the most part takes place in a retail store, once preferences have been established,

---

[1] Lebensmittelzeitung No. 50/1999, Deutscher Fachverlag, Frankfurt a. Main, p. 32.

[2] Here the trend is towards multi-storage capability, i.e. the same assortments are stored in several storage facilities and are regionally distributed (see Hertel 1999).

these are very slow to change. By moving online shopping in this area too, it will become easier to discern certain preferential patterns of customer purchasing behaviour and to adapt the offers made accordingly. In addition, due to the need for transparency between the offers made by various dealers on the net, it will be easier for customers to choose the most competent supplier for their own particular needs.

However, electronic trade will not displace stationary retail trade. Rather, it will provide a complementary offer since it facilitates customised online marketing.

19.3 Location Effects

The rationalisation and optimisation strategies of the above processes have led to highly efficient procurement and sales policies in the retail food industry. During the first phase this mainly affected the corporation-internal developments and processes. Currently it is increasingly affecting strategic enterprise decisions as well as store-type optimisations. These include an improved delivery relationship between the manufacturer, dealer and logistics service provider as well as faster internal communication between the branch offices and the company headquarters with respect to volumes sold.

A further step will be improved marketing using a target-group orientated sales policy and optimisation of locations. The reason for this is that the implementation of rationalisation potentials will decrease as the corporation-internal processes become more efficient. Additional potential can be found in the corporation-external factors such as the customer and location factors. These two aspects are in fact, closely related because the type of customers and their purchasing behaviour are an essential location factor. A target-group oriented marketing policy means that defined target groups of the existing customer base as well as potential customers living in the catchment area must be sought out and supplied with specific information. The location potential is thus examined more closely and addressed more directly. Furthermore, suitable locations are increasingly scarce and are therefore subject to increased exploitation pressures.

The quality of a location depends on the corresponding location factors and store type. During its life cycle, the store type is subject to change, expressed in trading-up or trading-down strategies. The course of this process depends on the expansion of the specific store type and its penetration in the local marketplace. A further decisive characteristic is the location itself and, in particular, its quality, as well as the development of the surrounding environment. In addition to a sound concept for the store type, the latter contributes significantly to the success of the branch store. However the location and corresponding environment are subject to constant change over time. This change affects a large number of location factors, which, independent of the branch store, are in themselves subject to change. These include:

- changes in the catchment area;
- new competitors;

- changes in the socio-demographic and socio-economic structure;
- changes in transport connections;
- development of new residential areas;
- long-term construction measures which lead to a temporary devaluation of the location and thus alter consumer preferences;
- image;
- flow of pedestrians;
- coupling potential;
- possibilities for communication with the customer.

The last point is likely to attain great significance in the future. Location factors generally progress slowly and gradually. For many outlets this means a creeping process of change. As location analyses are primarily conducted for new establishments or sometimes following extensive modernisation, there is usually no adaptation of the store-type concept to the changing locational potential.

Information processing offers a considerable but still mainly unused potential for location evaluation. This is corporation-external because communication can be found at the interface between the branch office and the location factors. Developing this potential requires regular and repeated location evaluation for the individual branch offices. In the evaluation process, the location factors of the outer environment are related to the location factors of the closer environment and customer structures, so existing and future developments of the store type and location can be evaluated, or new establishments in comparable locations compared.

With the increase in branch-office structured companies in the retail food industry, personal contact with customers was lost. This also meant that there was no longer information available about changes in the environment and in the status of customers. Through social identification with his customers and the location, the single outlet enterprise was able to receive this information, which could then be implemented.

With increased selling space and the expansion of the catchment area, social identification between the dealer/branch office and the location was also lost. But it is this identification which originally allowed a dealer to adapt to the creeping changes in the location or his customers.

The increasing number of complaints heard in the industry about the difficulty of assessing customer buying behaviour is a direct result of increases in store size, branch offices, similar offers and similar marketing concepts in the retail trade. As the branch network increases, dealers operate less and less in a location-specific manner, instead being mainly cost sensitive. Currently this is leading to ruinous price competition within the retail food industry. This strategy is applied to all branches simultaneously, with the same low price levels in all outlets irrespective of the specifics of the particular locations.

Locational optimisation is the next step after implementing highly efficient structures within the corporation-internal processes. Due to the 'qualitative jump', this development leads to an accelerated concentration process within the trade, which results in a stronger polarisation between highly specialised businesses on the one hand and turnover-oriented multi-business operations on the other. A further effect is the increase in market entry barriers due to high investments in information and communication technologies for new participants in the industry. This relates in particular to know-how regarding data maintenance and security as well as data evaluation.

19.4 Regional Effects

Within the framework of a research project of the Deutsche Forschungsgemeinschaft (DFG), the spatial effects and trends in the retail food industry were examined with the use of new information and communications technology in the municipal areas of Hannover and Leipzig. The prospects of success of this technologies for food retailers were also analysed, and in 1998 a complete record of the data concerning retailers made in the study areas, defined as the cities of Hannover and Leipzig and the surrounding suburban areas[1].

In Hannover the development of retail trade remained constant from the fifties onwards, with unchanging social and economic background conditions. This development was influenced by a persistent change in the structure of retail trade. At the same time location patterns formed which corresponded to the prevailing stage of development of the structural change. In this way hypermarkets and self-service department stores, for instance, experienced a period of growth in the seventies. This occurred in parallel with heavy migration of the resident population into the suburbs of West German cities. A new type of retail outlet – the discount market – began to gain ground in the mid seventies. In the old German states, this kind of outlet ended its growth stage at the beginning of the nineties and has now reached market saturation, leading the retailers in this sector to adopt various strategies in order to make themselves more prominent. This process has been further stimulated by a high concentration of retail firms within the food industry providing several kinds of outlet.

Retail development in Leipzig took place in two periods. The first in the German Democratic Republic (GDR) was from the beginning of the 1950s until 1989/1990. Typical characteristics of this period can be said to be the strong state influence, a limited variety of retail outlets and a very dense retail network of small food outlets in an exclusively primary retail network. The second period commenced in 1989/90 coinciding with the passing of the socialist economic system and establishment of a market economy. The transformation of the social system led to far reaching restructuring of retail trade in the new German states. This led to the implementation of West German retail structures over a period of a few years, and was characterised by a high concentration of firms providing several store types, a large number of branches and generally larger premises (see Table 19.2). The establishment of new retail outlets resulted in new location patterns. Unlike the old German states, the development time for these new

---

[1] Only communities bordering directly on the municipality were considered.

location patterns has been very short and so the potential for certain store types in the Leipzig area have not been exhausted to the same extent as in Hannover.

a) The Cities of Hannover and Leipzig

An analysis of the data shows a contrast in the distribution of different store types in the two cities (Fig. 19.4). Retail outlets with small premises, in particular the neighbourhood stores in Leipzig, have a very large market share in comparison with Hannover. In contrast, the market share of discount supermarkets in Leipzig is much lower than that of Hannover. The distribution of other store types shows only small deviations between the two cities.

The reasons for the unequal distribution of these two types of retail outlet lie in the different development of the retail food industry. In Hannover, the neighbourhood store was replaced in several stages of structural change, firstly by the self-service market, then the supermarket and finally the discount market. At present in many areas of the city the discount market is assuming the function of local food provision with a standardised range. The quantity and distribution of this type of retail outlet is present in a high density network within the city.

In Leipzig the discount supermarket is far less dominant in relation to other kinds of retail outlet than in Hannover. The large market share of neighbourhood stores is striking. This can be accounted for by two factors. Firstly, because these new store types have been present on the local market for a relatively short time and have consequently not yet achieved market saturation or full development. Secondly, the retail network in the GDR, which was dominated by two kinds of retail outlet, the neighbourhood store and the supermarket[1], has had after-effects on the retail food industry. Moreover, the opening of small retail food outlets appeared to many people in the East German states an opportunity to make themselves independent with little know-how.

In future development, it is likely that the market share of neighbourhood stores will be eroded by the discount market, as with regard to costs, logistics and marketing, this store type has higher potential than a family-run business.

The percentage share of sales space of the various types of retail outlet in the two cities confirms once again the different stage of development of store types with regard to the life cycle model (Fig. 19.5). The small retail outlets as well as supermarkets and hypermarkets in Leipzig have a greater local market presence than in Hannover due to their predominance in the old retail network of the GDR. The discount market was still in a period of growth in 1998 and had not reached the level of market saturation as in Hannover. The highest percentage share of selling space in Hannover is accounted for by discount markets and self-service department stores, followed by hypermarkets. This corresponds to the stage of development in which branches offer increasing sales space and standardisation of products.

---

[1] The retail outlet 'Kaufhalle' has a retail area of 350-1200 sq. m. and is comparable to a supermarket or small hypermarket.

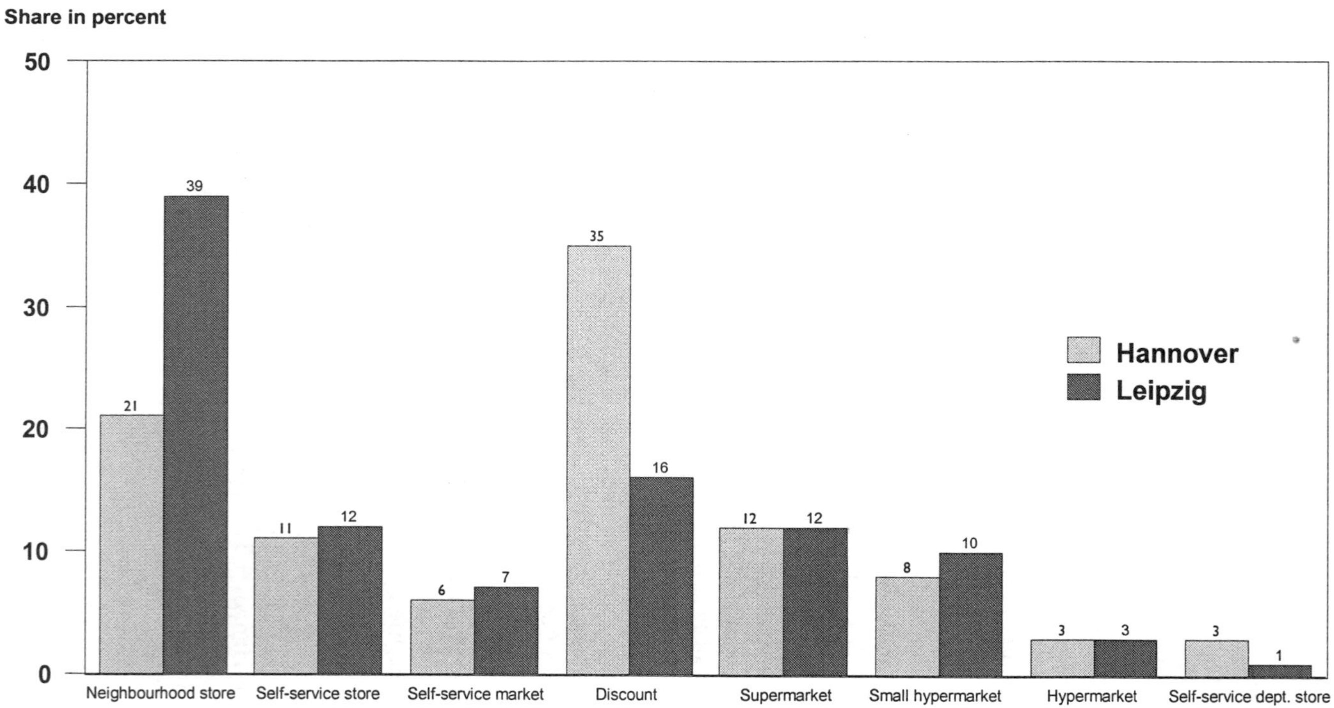

Source: own survey.

Fig. 19.4 Percentage market share of various store types in Hannover and Leipzig

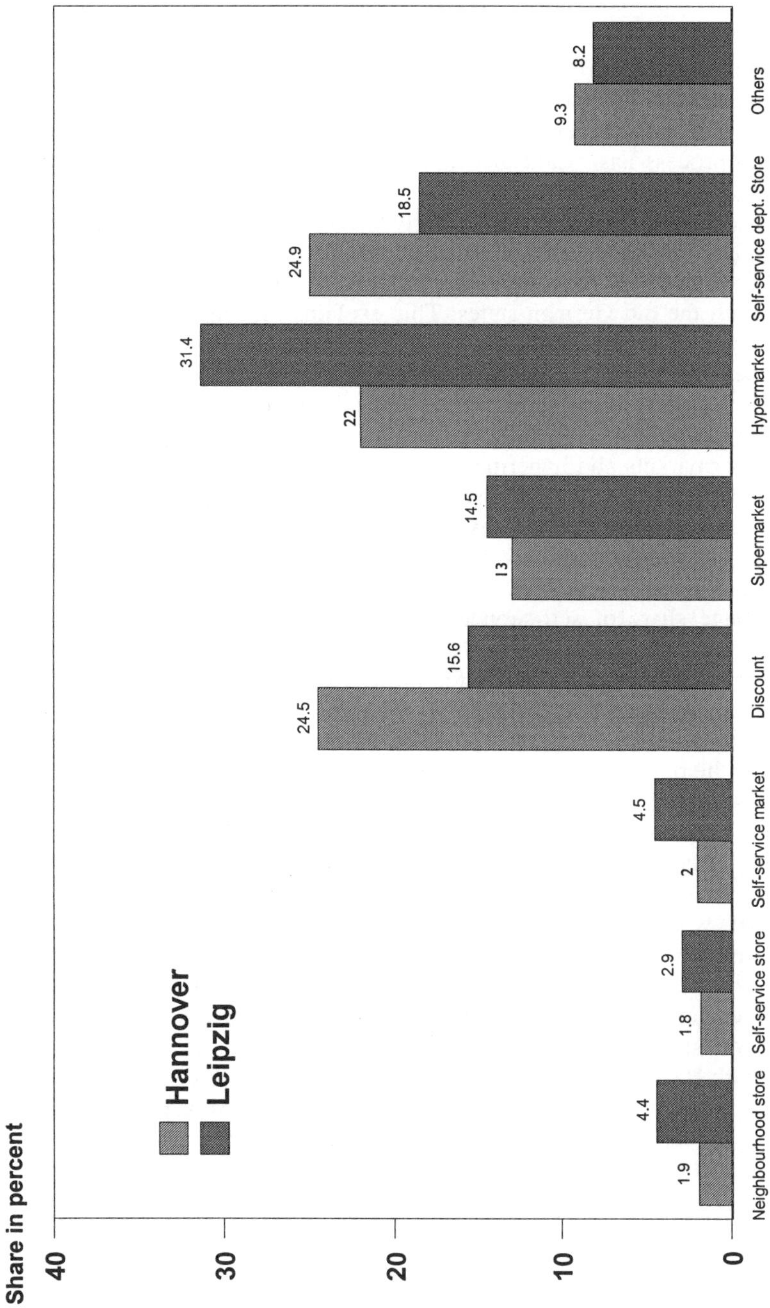

Source: own survey.

Fig. 19.5 Percentage share of sales space by store type in Hannover and Leipzig

b) The Suburbs of Hannover and Leipzig

In the areas surrounding the two cities, the discount market has the largest market share in Hannover and the neighbourhood store in Leipzig. In the latter, however, a smaller market share of supermarkets and hypermarkets to the benefit of the discount market can be clearly seen (Fig. 19.6).

This imbalance can likewise be traced back to the short time over which locational patterns have developed in the area surrounding Leipzig. The rapid transformation process has meant that new retail outlets with large sales area or price-aggressive outlets were established on new premises which were not integrated into the old network (still clearly present). Another feature was the almost complete absence of suburbanisation processes in the GDR and consequently weak retail structure in areas directly surrounding large cities in comparison with the old German states. This explains the small market share of retail outlets such as supermarkets and small hypermarkets. Hypermarkets with a size of between 1500 and 2999 sq.m. were completely absent in the area around Leipzig. The most prominent store type in the suburbs of Hannover in terms of quantity is the discount market, followed by small outlets with premises of under 400 sq.m., supermarkets and hypermarkets. This distribution is a consequence of both structural change, with the discount market being the most intensively expanding store type over the last few years, and the steady suburbanisation of housing since the 1960s, with new retail outlets ensuring the local provision of food in suburban areas.

The percentage share of self-service department stores (SSDS) is noticeably higher in both suburban areas than in the cities themselves, which is explained by the preference of this kind of outlet for locations outside the city centre. The percentage share of sales space clearly shows the significant presence of SSDS and discount supermarkets (Fig. 19.7). In Leipzig, the high percentage of SSDS by sales space can be put down to a number of reasons. One is that this type of outlet had the largest growth in the first transformation phase. Thus it was the first to be present on the local market and influenced the preferences of the 'new customers'. The relatively large catchment area of this type of outlet further reinforced this effect. Since suburbanisation did not take place in the GDR it was more difficult for retail outlets with a local catchment area to enter the market in suburban areas.

This occurred with the beginning of suburbanisation of the resident population, accompanied by the completion of new residential areas. The principal store type in these new residential areas is the discount supermarket and to a lesser extent the supermarket or small hypermarket. The high percentage share of SSDS in comparison with Hannover results from the establishment of fewer outlets of other types in the area surrounding Leipzig. The high share of supermarkets and hypermarkets in the suburbs of Hannover is connected to the suburbanisation which occurred in the seventies. During this period, these store types grew rapidly and were considered innovative within the setting of structural change.

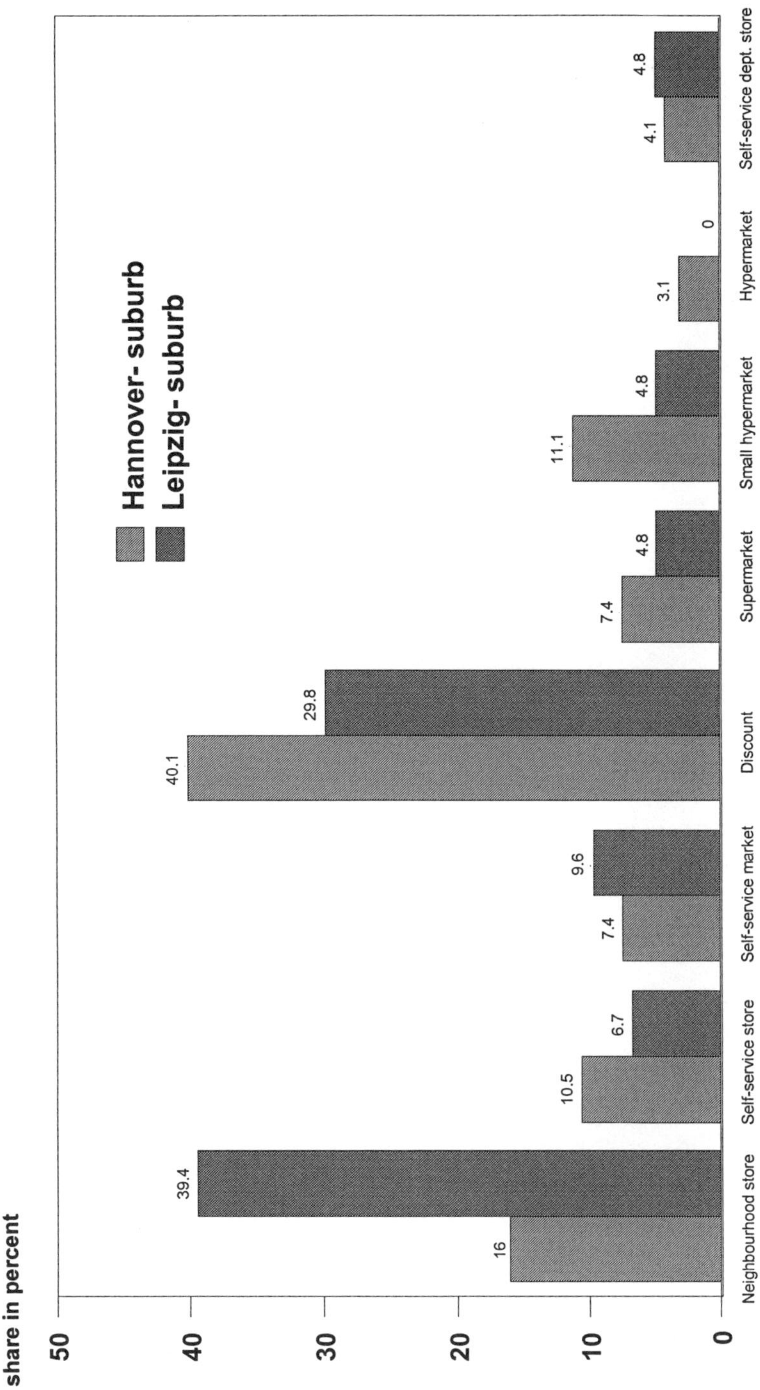

Source: own survey.

Fig. 19.6 Percentage share of various store types in suburbs of Hannover and Leipzig

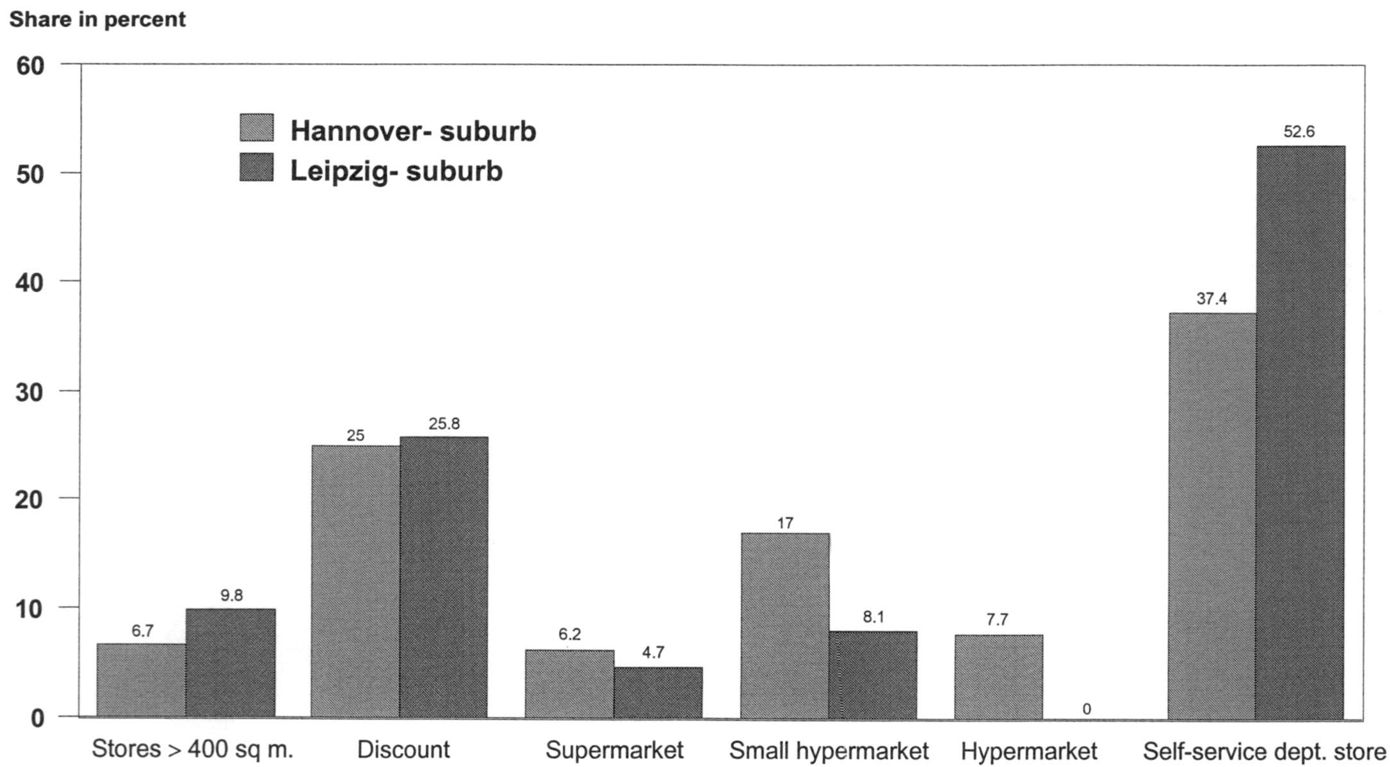

Source: own survey.

Fig. 19.7 Percentage share of sales space in suburbs of Hannover and Leipzig by store type

The provision of food sales space per head of population is about the same in the two cities (Fig. 19.8). The structural difference between the two cities is the larger average retail space of discount markets in Leipzig, with premises of up to and including 3000 sq.m. (Table 19.2). The number of branches with such large premises in Leipzig is smaller, and the share of price-aggressive discount markets is markedly lower, but the overall provision of floor space is only slightly less.

The food selling space in the suburbs of both cities was found to be 0.51 sq.m. per head in the Leipzig region compared with a value of 0.37 sq.m in the Hannover region. The greater provision in the suburbs of Leipzig can be traced back to the massive expansion of large retail outlets at the beginning of the nineties. This is further reinforced by the low level of suburbanisation which has led to greater polarisation, with small retail outlets and discount supermarkets on the one hand and large SSDS on the other. Supermarkets and hypermarkets will have difficulty gaining ground in the area surrounding Leipzig, because discount markets show optimal growth potential in the compensatory suburbanisation phase, due to their low prices and better cost structure.

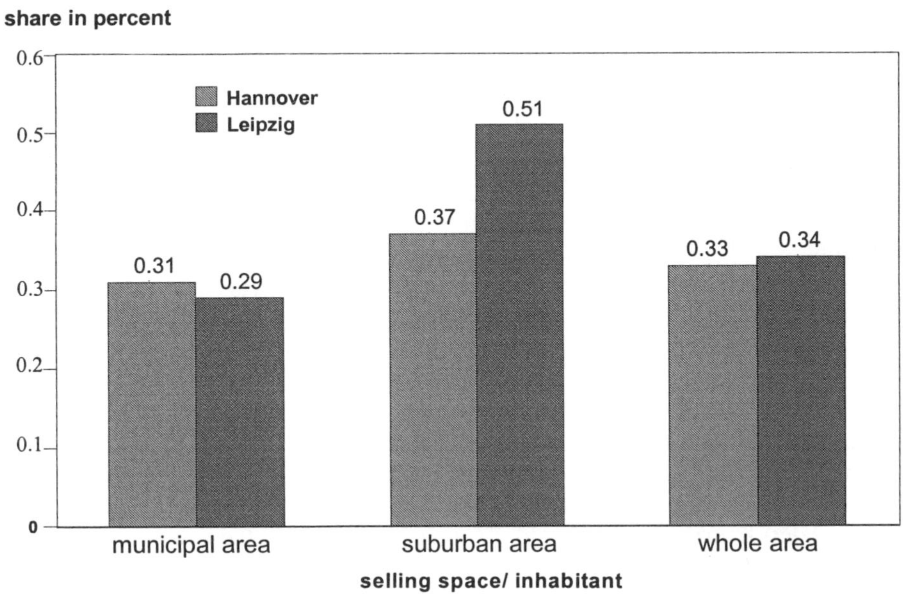

Source: own survey.

Fig. 19.8 Share of food sales space per head of population in the study areas

c) Effects on Geographical Location of New Potential resulting from Adoption of Information and Communications Technologies

Analysis of the data has shown that the different historical development trends in the retail trade in the two areas have resulted in different structures and networks within the retail food industry. Factors that are becoming important for enterprises are a particular size and a diverse structure of stores and on average a larger sales area per outlet. This is due to the more favourable cost-benefit ratio of investment in new information and communication technologies and their increasing use.

The table shows that outlets in the metropolitan area of Leipzig have much higher average sales areas than elsewhere. An exception was the absence of hypermarkets in the greater Leipzig area, due to the lack of suburbanisation, as well as the absence of self-service department stores in the city centre because there was a lack of suitable areas with clear ownership conditions. Furthermore, in the restructuring process in the city of Leipzig, only supermarkets and hypermarkets outlets that had the highest sales were able to survive. In both areas studied, only the larger chain stores were equipped with scanners (Table 19.2).

The supermarkets and hypermarkets in the city of Leipzig have a special position. As a result of their geographical location, most of these outlets still date back to the time when Leipzig was part of the GDR. Most of these chain stores have only survived until now because of their low and stable costs, such as extremely low rental charges due to old leases.

Table 19.2 Average sales space of major food retailing store types in sq. metres

	Discount Store	Super-market	Small hypermarket	Hypermarket	Self-service dept. store
Hannover	**407** (*423*)	**563** (*606*)	**1054** (*1063*)	**1707** (*1774*)	**4954** (*5550*)
H.-suburb	**463** (*474*)	**620** (*620*)	**1130** (*1134*)	**1851** (*1851*)	**6412** (*7489*)
Leipzig	**579** (*587*)	**647** (*631*)	**1120** (*1101*)	**1771** (*1700*)	**4916** (*5095*)
L.- suburb	**551** (*566*)	**627** (*664*)	**1072** (*1072*)	No data	**6854** (*6854*)

Figures in bold represent all stores, in brackets stores with scanner cash desks.
Source: own survey.

Currently, almost 72 percent of all retail food stores in the city of Hannover and greater Hannover, including discount markets with scanner equipped cash systems, have a sales area exceeding 400 sq.m. The figure for the city of Leipzig and greater Leipzig area rises to 77 percent. Most of these are chain stores belonging to only a few different companies, but their share of the retail food store market is as high as 90 percent in both Hannover and Leipzig.

Overall, the retail food stores in the city of Hannover are more extensively equipped with scanners then their counterparts in Leipzig. Although the stores in Hannover have a somewhat smaller average sales area in terms of size, they have a higher potential for data processing due to their use of scanners. However, the relatively limited use of scanner technology in supermarkets and hypermarkets within the study area of Hannover is noticeable. The city parallels the nation-wide tendency, that these two types of retail store are of diminishing importance.[1]

[1] See Lebensmittelzeitung No.3/2000. Deutscher Fachverlag, Frankfurt a. Main, p. 56

Hannover's advanced position within the restructuring process affecting the retail food industry resulted in the early introduction of so-called 'trading-up' strategies of single outlets on the local market. These strategies focus on both cost reduction and the improvement of services for customers. Another important aspect of these strategies is the evaluation of different store locations. Through the analysis of the data received from the scanners, a diversified and precise knowledge of the local market of each single store is available and helps to position the store better within the market.

In the city of Leipzig, the self-service department stores and hypermarkets are well equipped with scanner technology. The discount market store-type has introduced scanner technology to a lesser extent. With regard to this, it is worth noting that the restructuring process in food retailing in the city of Leipzig is still at a early stage compared to the city of Hannover, hence the density and spread of discount markets in the city of Hannover is much lower then in Leipzig. The local market in the city of Leipzig is therefore less diversified. The best opportunities for successful use of data from scanner-operated cash systems are large-scale self-service department stores and the somewhat smaller hypermarkets.

There was no evidence in terms of geographical location within the urban area that chain stores were equipped to differing extents with scanner technology. Therefore, the average size of a single chain store still seems to be a more important factor than location in determining whether or not modern information and communication technologies are introduced.

In the suburban areas of both cities, Hannover as well as Leipzig, the situation is the opposite of that in the cities themselves (see Fig. 19.9). All types of stores in Greater Leipzig are very well equipped with scanner technology. In fact, the majority of these stores are on newly developed sites (built after the political changes in the GDR) or have very large sales areas in the food sector (see Fig. 19.8). Therefore, stores in this area began to use strategies of diversification earlier than the stores in the urban areas of the city.

Chain stores with scanner technology have a very high share of the total amount of available sales area in both study areas (see Figs. 19.9 and 19.10). Hence, the majority of the players in the food retail sector are basing their future development strategies on the analysis of data received from the use of scanners.

19.5 Conclusions

After the successful implementation of computerised information systems involving merchandise, enormous short and medium term potentials opened up in all fields of business, initially combining to reduce internal variable costs. The goal was to standardize and automate the company's internal procedures as far as possible. In the medium and long term the external potentials of retail food companies will change. This will particularly affect marketing and business strategies. It will be possible to differentiate food retailing to a significant extent, offering user-defined and customer-specific supply at the level of specific locations. In spite of a high degree of standardisation, retail outlets will be attractive and individual. However, investment in product management systems

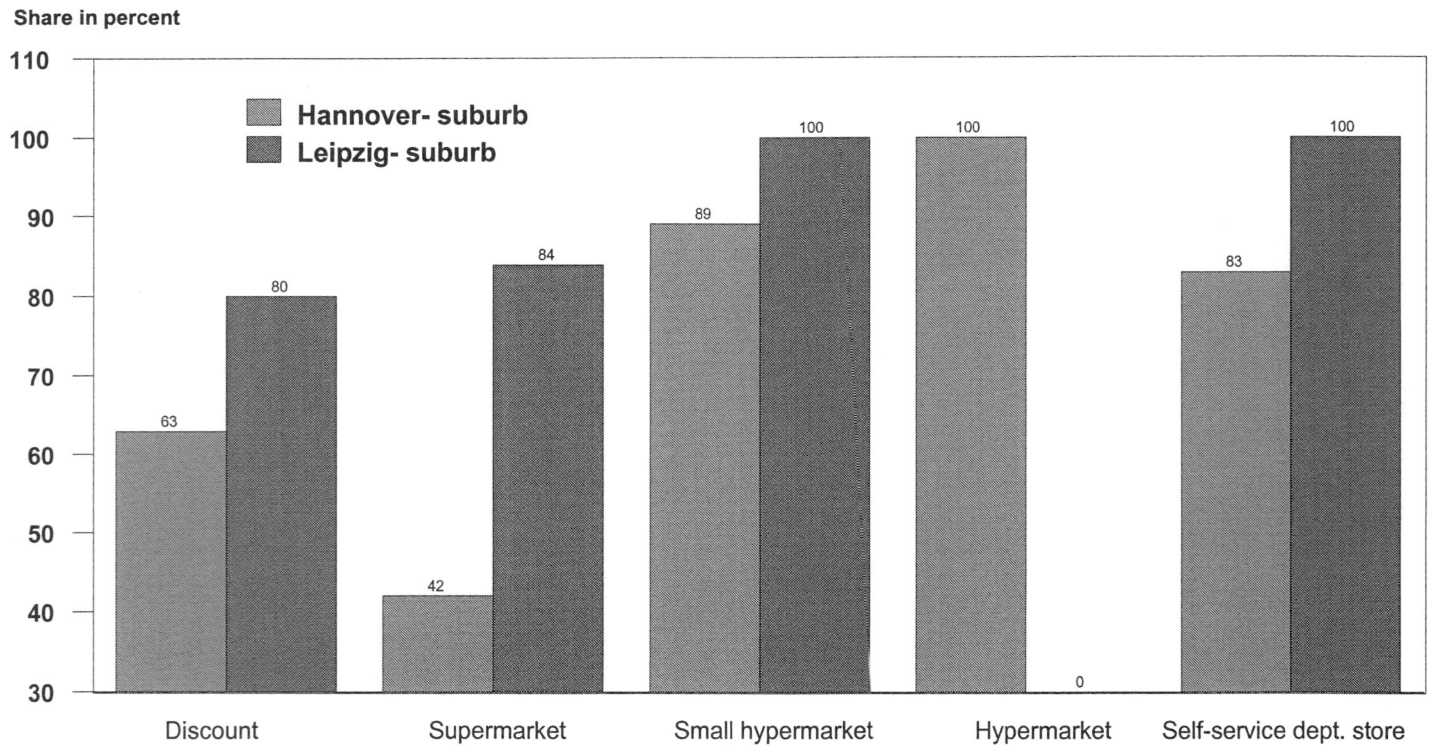

Source: own survey.

Fig. 19.9 Percentage share of selling space with scanner cash desks in the suburbs of Hannover and Leipzig

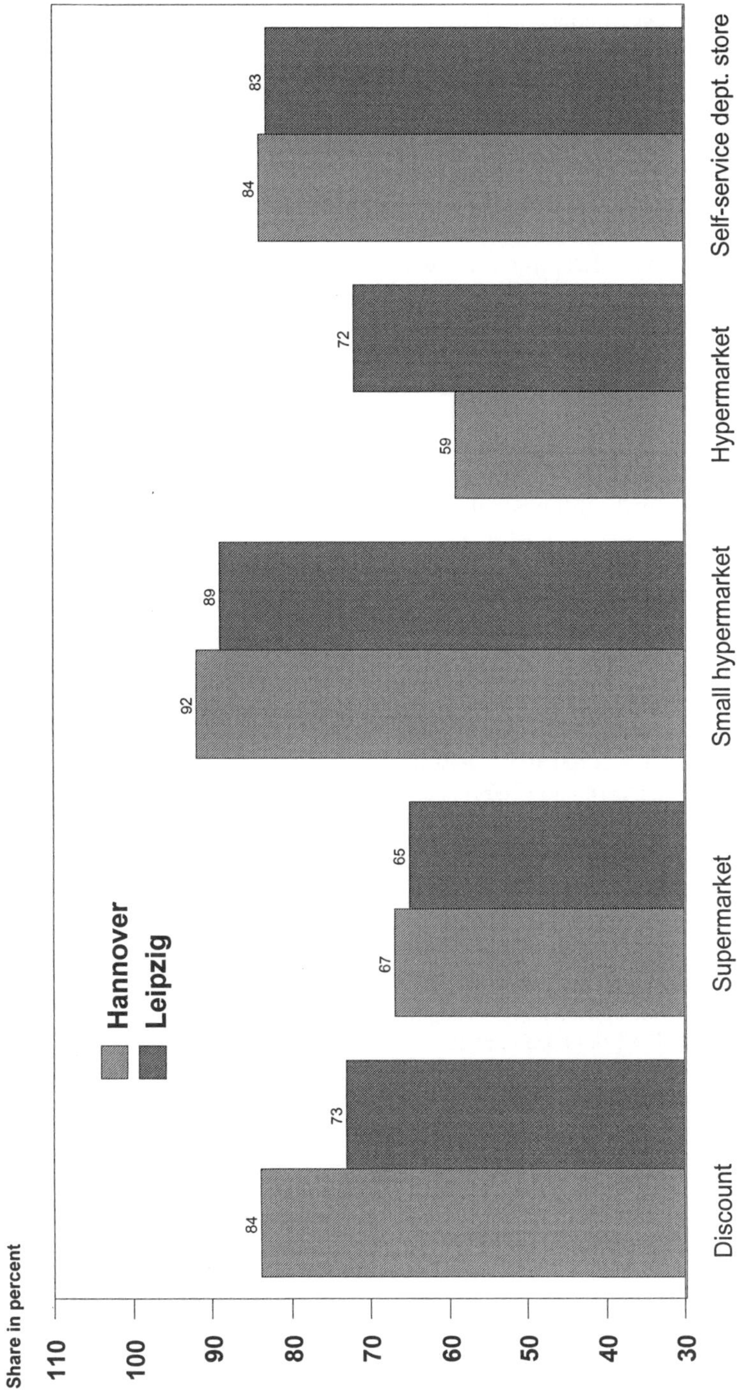

Source: own survey.

Fig. 19.10 Sales space of outlets with scanner cash desk in the cities of Hannover and Leipzig

with high capital cost is required. This will favour large companies and further reinforce the process of concentration.

The size and the location of stores parallels the stages of development within the retail food sector in terms of store density and store type. Due to high competition or excess selling space in some market areas, better equipment in the form of a scanner cash desk is advantageous. It is thus possible to achieve strategic gains in positioning more location-specific store types.

This means locational developments should use point of sale data to recognise and compare specific location potentials. Due to the availability of data, the players in the food retail sector have new opportunities to guide their future prospects in terms of geographical location so as to increasingly focus on product lines oriented towards the needs and demands of the local market.

Customer-specific focusing of a location gives stores far greater scope to operate and compete than if they just focus on product prices or the size of selling area. If a player in the retail food sector grows to a certain size, specialisation with cost-efficient and standardised ranges can occur. In fact, store locations having a supposedly disadvantageous position can transform into a higher quality operation and thereby effectively influence the pattern of the network of stores in the retail food sector.

References

Birther, M. (1982) Art. Warenwirtschaftssysteme (WWS). In: Falk, B., Wolf, J. (eds.) Das große Lexikon für Handel und Absatz. Verlag Moderne Industrie, Landsberg a. Lech, 837

Ebert, K. (1986) Warenwirtschaftssysteme und Warenwirtschaftscontrolling. In: Ahlert D. (eds.) Schriften zu Distribution und Handel, Lang, Frankfurt am Main, 52-58

Gerling, M. (1994). Scanning: Anfang einer neuen Ära. Enzyklopädie des Handels-Scannersysteme. Europäisches Handelsinstitut EHI, Köln, 10-22

Hertel, J. (1999) Warenwirtschaftssysteme. Physica, Heidelberg

IBM Ein paar Worte über den Handel. Stuttgart

Lebensmittelzeitung No. 50/1999. Deutscher Fachverlag, Frankfurt/M.

Lebensmittelzeitung Nr.3/2000. Deutscher Fachverlag, Frankfurt/M.

Simmet, H. (1990) Neue Informations- und Kommunikationstechnologien im Marketing des Lebensmitteleinzelhandels. Poeschel, Stuttgart

Steckenborn, I. (1981) Teil fürs Ganze.In: Rationeller Handel 04/81, 9

Theuer, G. (1983/84) "Brainstorming" Zur integrierten Warenbewirtschaftung im Großhandel. Der Markt 88/83/84.Verlag für Kapitalanlage und Marketing, Stuttgart, p. 146

Töpfer, A. (eds.) (1996) Efficient Consumer Response-ECR. 1. CPC Trend Forum. CPC Deutschland, Mainz

Zentes, J. (1983) Grundbegriffe des Marketing. Poeschel, Stuttgart

Zentes, J. (1984) Neue Informations- und Kommunikationstechnologien in der Marktforschung. Springer, Berlin

Zentes, J. (1991) Computer Integrated Merchandising-Neuorientierung der Distributionskonzepte im Handel und in der Konsumgüterindustrie. In: Zentes, J. (eds.) Moderne Distributionskonzepte in der Konsumgüterwirtschaft. Pöschel, Stuttgart, 4

20 Technological Change in the German Packaging Industry: Structure, Behaviour and Performance

Hans-Dieter Haas and Sven Siebert
Institute of Economic Geography, University of Munich

20.1 Introduction

Structural changes affecting entire branches of industrial activity or regions are not processes which normally occur suddenly. Due to the fact that systems and their elements are continuously evolving, human activities as well as applied techniques and technology are exposed to continuous adaptational stresses. Space and time serve as organising and linking dimensions for the individual elements of the supersystem[1]. There is no general theory to date on possible correlations between technical change and the spatial distribution of its actors, so it seems difficult, "...to identify specific spatial effects, since they are interconnected within the process of changes in economic structures in a multi-faceted way, as well as interlinked to economic and political forms of regulation, and to social and cultural processes of change" (Läpple 1989, p. 219).

At the same time, continuous debate on location issues show that research and the application of techniques[2] and 'technologies' are one of the key factors in highly developed societies. In recent decades, the application of technique as a basic prerequisite of the modern production and distribution of goods has, almost unnoticed, turned one specific industrial branch of activity – packaging – into a 'key branch'. The post-industrial service society would be inconceivable without the packaging industry (see Haas 1991). Packaging enables a sophisticated spatial division of labour, separation of production and consumption as well as the expansion of markets.

---

[1] In general, the supersystem refers to the whole range of physical and non-physical processes in the world's ecosystem (including social and economic systems).

[2] The expression 'technique' will be used here to denote 'real technique', i.e. applied technological knowledge. The expression 'technology' implies the total process in all its aspects, including organisation (Uhlmann 1978; Ropohl 1979). Thus the expression 'technology' integrates development of necessary knowledge (R&D) as well as the practical application of the resulting knowledge.

In this context, technological change[1] is considered a substantial element in positive regional development. However, it is necessary to consider the question of unintended and often negative consequences. Public opinion has come to regard 'packaging' as one of the representative features of the environmentally harmful 'throw-away society' (see Haas and Siebert 1993). There have been numerous discussions about a 'sustainable economy' focused at the specific regional level. In this context, technological change has come to signify successful structural change for modern economic systems. In many ways, it is seen as a prerequisite for the preservation of a competitive economy and also as an essential developmental factor for individual regions and branches of industrial activity.

The question also arises whether the packaging industry is being subjected to radical changes caused by 'external' impacts (Verpack V[2]), or is just undergoing normal development within the framework of general technical, economic and social progress.

The empirical analysis presents a profile of the packaging industry, covering the different packaging producers and materials. A detailed examination is made of the consequences of adapting processes of packaging and restrictions on its use and how this affects the overall system and its elements, as well as the region specific effects which could be expected during this process. The study focuses on the economic, spatial and social correlations of technologies connected with the industrial production of packaging, and the consequences which can be expected from increasing restrictions based on environmental concerns.

20.2 The Packaging Industry

Due to the wide range of discussions on environmental policy throughout Germany and the closely related question of waste legislation, packaging[3] as a

---

[1] Therefore the general definition of 'change' shall be defined as the changing of specific parameters within a fairly long-term perspective (evolution). Short-term or even sudden radical change (revolution) are distinguished from continuously ongoing processes of change, based on permanent repetition and continuation.

[2] Verpack V (literally in English 'Pack V') is a widely used abbreviation for the German Regulations for Avoidance of Packaging Waste (deutsche Verordnung über die Vermeidung von Verpackungsabfällen = Verpackungsverordnung).

[3] Packaging is a collective definition for any kind of external wrapping of goods. It serves both as a container and as protection during transport. In a narrower sense, it defines packaging material and aids made from one or more agents. Packaging agents are basic materials, e.g. carton, glass, plastics from which packaging material and aids can be produced by moulding. Packaging material is therefore a product made from packaging agents shaped as boxes, cans, bottles, etc. Packaging agents constitute the main part of the packaging, serving as a container for the product, with the product being partially or completely enclosed. The overall function of the packaging is achieved through use of so-called 'packing aids', e.g. ribbon, tape or labels, Thus, the 'package' is made up of the packing and packaging, involving packaging material and aids, in addition to the item itself.

product and service has been a recent target. Problems of environmental pollution and the growing difficulties of waste disposal have placed the packaging industry in the midst of public criticism. Actors such as legislators, producers and distributors have tried to meet this criticism via the reduction or replacement of specific agents used. Nevertheless, it remains undisputed that packaging remains an irreplaceable functional element[1] within the production and consumption system. Thanks to packaging, a considerable number of consumption goods such as fluids, gases, powders, and also long-distance goods, become transportable and commercially viable (see Ritter 1994).

The packaging business does not really fit the definition of an 'industry' as normally understood (see Stillwell 1991). It can only be considered in a very general way as a horizontal system of enterprises offering a variety of highly substitutable products to a common market (Bain 1968). A wider conception of the 'packaging business' encompasses the design, production, distribution and use of packaging agents and packaging machinery. Only the actual production of packaging material and machinery can strictly be referred to as the 'packaging industry'[2] (DIN 1991). The packaging business is a special case as it functions as an entity linking together almost every area of industry as well as interlinking different sectors (enterprises, households, etc.). Therefore it would be better classified as a 'production service'. According to MUT, "Packaging as well as packed material are interrelated, which means that if it were not possible to produce individual packaging, the distribution and in effect the production of that specific product would not be possible at all" (MUT 1991, p. 26).

One result of this development is the continuing concentration of packaging in the food and luxury foodstuff sector[3], together with the loss of local and regional production and distribution. Nuhn states that, "The small scale production chains and supply areas are beginning to [...] disappear more and more and are leading to completely new production and distribution relationships" (Nuhn 1993, p. 146). However, large chains are increasingly taking over dominant market positions.

---

[1] The general function of packaging is protection, storage and transportation. This is however supplemented by a variety of 'added' functions, such as advertising and assuring service, as well as 'convenience' functions (portioning, processing, etc.). The particular elements of functional packaging (packing material, locking, etc.) depend on the packaging service desired. However, the choice of packaging agents, shapes and the production procedures adopted by packaging producers and users is restricted by the specific characteristics of the item itself (e.g. its state of aggregation, weight, sensitivity, etc.) and are subject to continuous technological change (Runge 1993).

[2] The expression 'packaging industry' remains somewhat problematic. No such industrial branch is independently listed in official statistical surveys or other current classifications (SYPRO, NACE, ISIC). In addition, it frequently involves small enterprises with less than 20 employees, adopting a craft approach. Moreover, most producers of packaging machinery consider themselves governed by the standards and requirements of general mechanical engineering. Statistically they are included in this category.

[3] In Germany, the main players in the food industry are Unilever (total turnover DM 10 bn), Coca Cola and Nestlé (each DM 7 bn total turnover), with brands accounting for between DM 1 bn (Iglo/Unilever) and almost DM 2 bn (Coca Cola).

Although the European food industry is still structured on a medium scale basis[1], business is driven by a small number of large companies. Combines like Metro, Aldi and the large department store groups, whose 1993 sales lie between DM 3 billion (Norma), DM 27 billion (Aldi) and DM 56 billion (Metro Group), make use of their enormous purchasing power to determine the product range offered as well as product packaging. It is rare for packaging companies to be interlocked within this controlling system. Only worldwide operating combines, such as Pechiney in France (the world's largest packaging company with about DM 10 billion turnover per year), or the German VIAG Corporation and its affiliates Schmalbach-Lubeca (metal), VAW (aluminium), Gerresheimer (glass) and PWA (compounds) are capable of imposing their own ideas. Even the largest packaging machinery producer, Bosch, with its turnover of DM 580 million is classified medium size.

In re-unified Germany the packaging industry is a medium size market sector employing about 500,000 people and producing goods worth up to DM 100 billion – depending on the limiting values chosen – and represents a 4 percent share of GNP (Klöckner 1992, RGV 1988). Because of the large number of small and medium scale enterprises, the highly diversified division of labour, the large number of 'in-line packagers'[2] and the non-uniform product spectrum, there exists no specific official statistical survey on this sector of the economy. The packaging sector fundamentally consists of the production of packaging machinery, the production and design of packaging and packaging aids as well as the process of packing (wrapping) itself.

In general it can be stated that the German packaging industry is fairly heterogeneous. There is a small number of (European) combines and numerous medium scale enterprises. There is fierce competition in the different market sectors, which is increased by the market power of the main customers. On the one hand, individual agents compete in their key markets; on the other hand, there is substitution competition between individual packing materials or between different packaging systems (e.g. single use versus multiple use). Nonetheless, new packing material combinations (e.g. compounds) have recently seemed to be encouraging greater co-operation in some market sectors.

For the first time in history, the German legislature made use of its legislative power according to §14 of the AbfG (Waste Regulation) of the Regulations on Avoidance of Packaging Waste (Verpack V), which had quite restrictive effects on the packaging industry and its associated branches. Subcontractors and the retail

---

[1] A completely different view results from looking at individual market sectors. For example, while the food and luxury foodstuff industry in Germany is in general much less concentrated than in France or Britain, its market for long-life bakery products, coffee and tea, sugar and processed fish can be considered highly concentrated (Borrmann and Michaelis 1990).

[2] 'In-line procedures' can be understood as the packaging manufacture and the actual packing and packaging of the product at the same place, usually either where the product is produced or in specialised packing facilities. There, packaging is shaped, filled and sealed on only one machine 'just-in-time'.

trade are obliged to take back any transport packaging or sales packaging material. In addition, as an alternative to the firm's obligation to take back the packaging material, public containers can be used for the disposal of sales packaging (Dual System). To be exempted from these obligations, it is necessary to comply with defined identification and use quotas and to maintain multiple-use systems. For this purpose, industry has established a venture called "Der Grüne Punkt – Duales System Deutschland – Gesellschaft zur Abfallvermeidung und Sekundärrohstoffgewinnung mbH (DSD)[1]. The DSD manages the classification and sorting of sales packaging material in co-operation with private and municipal waste disposal facilities and is financed by the license fees from labelling with the 'Green Dot'. In order to be eligible to use the Green Dot label, users have to guarantee that they will re-use packaging material appropriately. The Green Dot demonstrates to the consumer and retailer that a product producer is participating in the dual system. Re-use itself is carried out by the packaging producer and specialist companies.

The charge to producers via license fees was originally independent of the specific material, i.e. it was a flat rate for all packaging agents. The volume of individual packaging material was the determining factor. But given the differing ease of reuse of different packaging materials, license fees were later adjusted according to the packaging agents used and thus adapted to current trends. This differentiation of costs was intended to raise prices, provide an economic incentive and – if done correctly – to penalise packaging materials which are difficult to reuse. As a result such materials have become much more expensive (e.g. plastics, compounds). Recent process improvements (hydration) and administrative changes (Advanced VerpackV, EC Directives) are beginning to show the desired effects as regards materials (plastics) and packaging solutions (throw-away items). In environmental discussions there is some criticism of these effects, however.

20.3 The Structural Perspective

In order to properly examine the interconnection of the packaging industry and its associated activities, it is necessary to consider cause and effect issues at all levels: the large-scale level (the whole politico-economic system), medium-scale level (organisations, companies) and small-scale level (actors, projects) (Jokisch and Lindner 1982; Ritter 1991). In this analysis, the economy and society with all its participating elements and interrelations, are treated as one system[2]. This system

[1] In English: The Green Dot – German Dual System – Company for Waste Reduction and Recycling Inc.

[2] The science of systems defines a system as consisting of a quantity of elements, their interrelations with each other and the environment in general (see Hall and Fagen 1956), with the concrete definition and boundaries of the system and its elements depending on the formulation of the question. The levels or subsystems are highly dependent on exchange with each other, material as well as energy. In the material domain the term '(industrial) metabolism' is used (Neef 1969, Ayres and Simonis 1993), and in the non-material domain 'neuronal communication' (Jantsch 1992).

and its sub-systems have one goal: survival. Preservation of the system is possible only by continuous structural adaptation, which means that differences, frictions, conflicts etc. drive the evolutionary processes.

Technological change is the trigger[1], the means and the consequence of short-term adjustments and long-term processes of change. Technological change can thus be more broadly defined as the origination, application and distribution of new know-how relating to the production and distribution of goods. An analysis of the correlations is carried out following a so-called "Multi-Level Analysis' (Dörrenbächer 1992) (see Fig. 20.1) in order to identify the detailed component aspects of the factors involved and to be able to examine individual influential factors at the appropriate level in relation to their interchange (see Pachner 1992). This approach sees 'global' trends, regional disparities and sectoral patterns as an interrelated structure with interchanges between frame conditions, competition, regional milieus and individual entrepreneurial decisions (Schlütter 1992). According to Hahn and Gaiser, "The management of structural-technological change on the entrepreneurial level as well as regional expansion of the economy" should be the focus of attention when considering social structures, organisations and processes (Hahn and Gaiser 1994, p. 60).

When interlocking becomes more complex, the medium level (market/region) begins to apply. However, it is not technological change *per se*, which causes spatial variations, but the functional changes made possible by specific technologies (De Koning and De Smidt 1990). Thus, the way society uses space also determines present and future patterns and creates a type of feedback which characterises such complex systems. A representative example of these correlations is the way waste is treated (Storbeck 1982).

From an empirical point of view, the hypothesised positive correlation between technological change and regional prosperity is not proven. For a product category such as packaging, which has no use as an isolated item and is highly dependent on the demand for the goods to be packaged, statements on such effects can only be determined by looking at economic sectors closely related to the packaging industry. This is becoming more important as the present flow of information, material and value does not depend on entrepreneurial limits, regional or state borders.

Structural approaches focus on power, influence and the social status of the economic subjects. They cannot be considered to have homogeneous characteristics and differ in their growth and regional agglomeration (Neef 1950). Although the structure-related perspective seems to be more like a fixed statement[2], the present analysis makes use mainly of features found in the 'structure-agency' approach, or the 'structure-conduct-performance' framework, which enables the behaviour of individuals or organisations to be interpreted as

[1] The analysis of technological change takes account of the alteration of the individual characteristics of a technical system, and should therefore be assessed with respect to technical and economic, as well as social, ethical and ecological criteria (Jaeckel and Grupp 1991).

[2] See the detailed discussion by Juen (1992).

though working like a hinge, linking the politico-economic structure and system performance (Schlütter 1992). Input or process variation in production leads to an altered value for the region; which again affects the sectoral and regional structure, and may finally lead to modified production parameters within companies. Application of the so-called 'structure-conduct-performance' approach (SCP) of industrial economics allows us to examine this mechanism empirically (Bain 1968). Proceeding from the frame conditions and specific structure of a market ('structure'), the behaviour of market participants ('conduct') is first studied and finally the results from market processes ('performance') are analysed. The SCP model (see Fig. 20.1) is therefore comparable to the 'structure-agency' approach, which also considers the acting participant as a mediator between processes of structural change (Schlüter 1992).

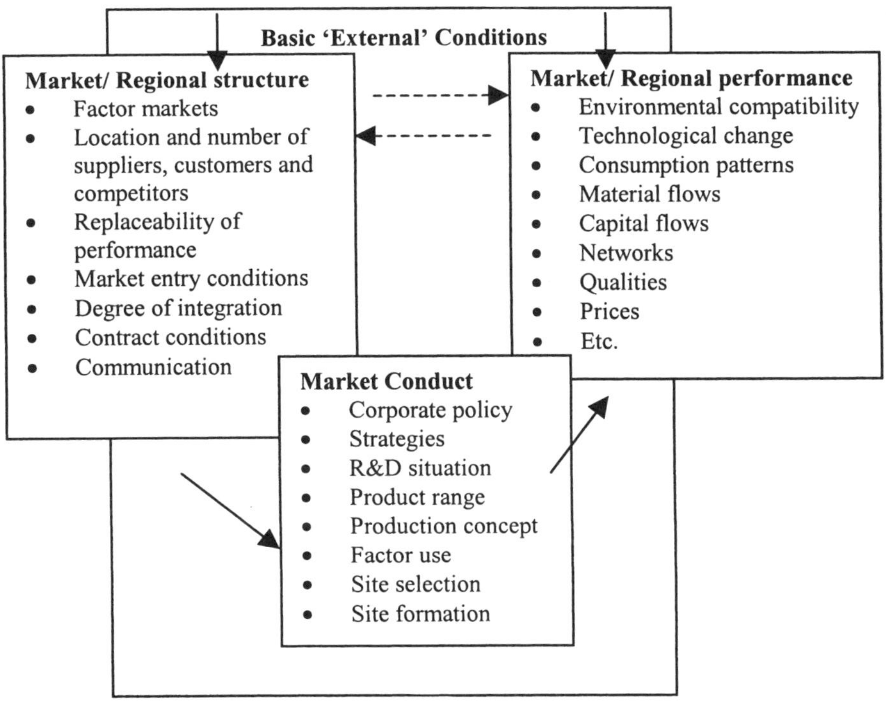

Source: Siebert 1995.

Fig. 20.1 Modified 'structure-conduct-performance' approach

a) The Large-Scale Level

The conditions of the system at a large-scale level are determined by the prevailing economic and social structure, which has a controlling influence but changes only gradually. This structure encompasses environmental conditions as well as institutions or political principles. Likewise, so-called 'global' trends[1] and growing global environmental problems merge together with the 'superstructure'.

However, impacts on nature deserve special attention on all levels, especially in this present context. The knowledge that environmental damage does not halt at regional or national borders has led to a completely new conception of environmental politics.[2] The concept of 'packaging regulations', as introduced in Germany, has been copied throughout Europe.[3] Not only in Europe, but world wide, administrative decision-makers have been constantly releasing new environmental standards, e.g. EMAS or ISO 14000.

b) The Medium-Scale Level

System conditions at the large-scale level largely determine business decisions on small-scale issues. "Structures on the medium-scale level act as a buffer in case of friction and stabilise the supersystem" (Ritter 1991, p. 175). On the medium-scale level, specific regional structures and processes therefore play an important role. This applies for the functional medium-scale levels (market) as well as the territorial (spatial). Thus, for example, it could happen that, because of altered frame conditions, material procurement (supply) and/or distribution areas have to be greatly modified. Companies in particular sectors of packaging might even have to seek new varieties of their preferred raw material, which may not be available in the close neighbourhood. Other firms, in order to remain competitive in their area of activity, may have to switch to a completely different system (e.g. multiple-use) and participate in a supra-regional pool. This means that spatial structures begin to reflect the politico-economic system, and they might be altered at any time by particular groups of actors. In the end, the determining 'ecological' dimension of the economy is defined at this level, since environmental problems and performances will initially operate at the medium-scale level.

---

1 For example, the international division of labour, the so-called 'globalisation' of markets, the reduction and professionalisation of jobs (Kern and Schumann 1984), new regional production systems (Leborgne and Lipietz 1990) or 'flexible specialisation' (Piore and Sabel 1985).

2 In addition to a number of regional conferences on the environment, mention should be made of Resolution 44/228 of the UN General Conference in 1989 and the so-called 'Rio Declaration' (Agenda 21) of June 1992 (BMU). An essential measure would be the implementation of environmental considerations into other political areas and at all levels.

3 Comparable license systems exist in Austria (Altstoff-Recycling AG), Belgium (FOSTPLUS) and France (Eco-Emballage) as well as Poland, Portugal and Spain.

Because of the close relationship between environmentally damaging activities and economic consequences, growth-oriented regional policies have to be questioned and possibly reconsidered (Nuhn and Ossenbrügge 1984). Issues of technological change and effects at the non-spatial medium-scale level can be considered in a similar way. Sector analyses of a variety of branches indicate a demand-oriented technology push[1]. In the packaging business, this was driven by well-funded companies, mostly in the plastics industry. Since the packaging regulations came into force in Germany and then other European countries, it has been possible to observe a demand-pull situation, which has determined the course of technological development, stimulated by the problem situation at the market level. As stated by Badke, "the direction of technological progress in a sector can be exclusively explained by the development of sector-specific demand for consumer goods" (Badke 1990, p. 3), thus emphasising the importance of market structure through technological change.

c) The Small-Scale Level

If we consider technological change as the mover of structural change in economies, including both the regional and sectoral elements (Schlütter 1992), the adaptation processes must be analysed with different criteria. The question would be, for example, whether the shift from tender-oriented mass production towards demand-oriented small-scale manufacturing also affects the packaging industry in the same way, and what role government regulations and regulatory policies play with respect to production concepts or adaptive processes.

In order to be able to forecast the behaviour of actors in the market, the strategies followed by business, technologies applied and location questions must be studied and linked with interchanges on the regional level. Environmental policies must also be considered as they are an increasingly important factor in business adaptation processes. Since government regulation is becoming an increasingly decisive factor, with customers and markets becoming more and more sensitive to environmental issues, businesses are being forced to respond to these demands. Recognition by a company of its obligations and an ecologically motivated adaptation (Andersen 1999) can often lead to market success and even radical change as well.

The characteristics of technological change on the small-scale level can be derived from the conditions of a functioning competitive economy and can indicate changes in productive power, organisation and logistics (Lempa 1990). Environmentally guided business options show, for example, that damage limitation can be achieved through effective mediation of a company's position (lobbying, PR), even at the level of an individual company (Blazejczak. 1993). Strategic measures only make a small difference in the short term, but can lead to organisational and technological improvement. The relatively low average cost

---

[1] While the 'technology-push hypothesis' is based on the proposition that technical know-how is generated relatively independently of concrete applications, the 'demand-pull hypothesis' suggests that the demand side determines the R&D process (Badke 1990).

burden due to regulatory environmental directives is the result of fairly quick adaptation by companies. This is enhanced by quantifiable environmental policies and a generally high social acceptance. Favourable reactions are provided by policies (communities, states, EC, etc.). In this case, even minor cost variations may cause locational shifts (Blazejczak 1993).

20.4 Structure, Behaviour and Performance of Elements

a) Correlation Between Basic Conditions, Market Structure and the Entrepreneurial Environment

The representative businesses[1] considered to date are fairly diverse – the range of small and very small businesses display all the characteristics of polypolistic competition. Most of the companies are traditional firms, some over a hundred years old, which have developed their accumulated know-how in an evolutionary, rather than revolutionary manner. Except for the area of artificial packaging material and aids, young and particularly innovative businesses are to be found almost exclusively among packaging services (labelling systems, packaging software, utilisation concepts). The overall market structure has, as expected, hardly changed at all over the years. Now as before, it basically comprises two groups: a small number of international large combines and numerous highly specialised small and medium-sized regional or national, companies. Only occasionally are companies willing and able to expand at the rate of their customers' growth. Since the foundation of the Federal Republic of Germany, the packaging market has become a classic buyer's market, whose requirements are largely controlled by big brands and chains. The only exceptions are some types of specific packaging systems (e.g. Tetrapack) or at times of unpredicted political events (e.g. the reunification of Germany). The latter temporarily led to shortages of the preferred packaging in the refreshment beverage segment, with consequent alteration of market power relations, but it was only a temporary phenomenon.

The packaging regulation (Verpackungsverordnung) did not however change the structural conditions. A number of orientation problems arose in the initial years after the introduction of these regulations, affecting market participants in much the same way. Although the companies themselves intended to contribute to the waste avoidance concept, a basic decision-making foundation was lacking. It was not only the confusion over the definition of 'sales' packaging, 'temporary' packaging and 'transportation' packaging which led to uncertainty, but also the chaotic situation which resulted when *Dual System Germany Inc.* radically altered the license fee structure in just a few years. Since the 'Green Dot' licenses have a decisive impact on the costs and benefits of a packaging system, this has greatly influenced adaptation strategies in the packaging industry.

---

[1] The businesses examined operated with an average of 66 employees. The total range was from 5 to 320 employees, with 80% employing fewer than 100 people.

All parties involved have been equally affected by, for example, the enormous pressure on time and costs resulting from higher technical, market-related and government requirements (see Table 20.1). The situation of strict market focus, with consequent short production runs, greatest possible flexibility and higher demands for environmental protection and quality, requires small and medium-size companies to be more efficient at identifying value when producing, filling and packing goods. Meeting growing market demands for highly diversified packaging systems faster and more flexibly, combined with the tendency to finalise products as late as possible, shifts an even greater responsibility onto the packaging industry. The so-called 'pack-in-time-system', in which the item is held in stock at a relatively low level of processing, and packaging carried out as close to the customer as possible, leads to smaller and smaller runs and custom-made solutions in an often integrated production sequence.

Table 20.1 General innovation factors in the packaging industry (multiple responses)

Factor	Most important	Second most important	Third most important	Total
Competition	25.0%	10.7%	0.0%	35.7%
Buyer power	25.0%	3.6%	14.3%	42.9%
Ecology	14.3%	3.6%	3.6%	21.4%
Legal conditions	10.7%	3.6%	0.0%	14.3%
New markets	7.1%	14.3%	10.7%	32.1%
License fees	7.1%	14.3%	0.0%	21.4%
Consumer behaviour	7.1%	3.6%	7.1%	17.9%
Other	3.6%	21.4%	28.6%	28.6%

Source: Siebert 1995.

On the other hand, systems of use and disposal came and went so rapidly during the trial period that the sector became quite confused. Lack of consistency over financial issues and difficulties for the DSD due to cartel legislation, have led to a situation where the original packaging industry, the target of the regulation, hardly considers itself represented at all. The sector showed little awareness or concern about developments relating to the environment and recycling in the early 1990s. This accounts for the ineffective lobbying activity undertaken and lack of concerted action by the industry.

The insignificant degree of formal and informal interconnections within the sector can be attributed to the extraordinary 'tight', i.e. highly competitive, nature of the packaging industry, which allowed packaging of any kind to become a type of general commodity. This fact, among others, is one reason why hardly any wider, technology-based regional differences could be observed. Regional differences only occur when generated by demand and/ or specific traditions. Examples are the French and German mineral water industry (e.g. PET one-way in France and multi-use glass in Germany) or the German beer industry (various glass and can systems in the North, standardised refundable bottles in the South). These demand-related conditions lead to a corresponding supplier structure in the packaging industry.

The packaging industry in the new German Länder (regions of the former German Democratic Republic) illustrates how important socio-political conditions can be for the technological development of spatial structures. It was not personal preferences acting with an anonymous market that shaped the structures, but rather a prescriptive plan which deliberately made the rules within well defined 'market' segments and interconnections at conventional production locations. The feedback of a well-functioning system was disconnected, with the result that the total collapse of the system literally turned the entire territory of the former German Democratic Republic (GDR) overnight into a completely residual entity.

b) Market Behaviour and Adaptation on the Small-Scale Level

The business and production concepts found in individual companies are as diverse as in the entire sector or market structure. Their strategies – if one can define the widespread 'muddling through' of most packaging companies as such – are, firstly, highly dependent on the base material used, i.e. the packaging material.[1] All actors share an inclination towards so-called 'flexible diversification' or a 'just-in-case strategy', in order to ensure business survival. Options include speciality production and minor ranges, along with shifting mass production into existing or just purchased subsidiary firms.

A typical characteristic of all small and medium-size companies is the 're-insourcing' of formerly outsourced value-adding steps (e.g. CAD, DTP, and the like) in order to cut costs. Certainly, great technological changes have taken place, even if induced by sources outside the packaging industry. The innovations in materials originated mostly in the chemical, metal and paper industries, and are the main factor driving the reorganisation of packaging companies (see Table 20.2). Even small companies are forced to adapt their behaviour to the supply side, and this can only encourage the trend towards use of highly complex and sophisticated pre-materials.

The question of 'environmentally appropriate' packaging is extremely complex, not only for small businesses. Since hardly any enterprise is capable of offering a packaging service independent of the packaging material issue, most small enterprises do not seem able to cope with the contradictory arguments of the overall environmental discussion. Except for plastics processing firms, individual

---

[1] The market behaviour of packaging machinery producers, which are also considered, is more likely to be subsumed in that of the mainstream machinery or tool manufacturing firm, so statements regarding the latter mostly apply to the packaging material segment.

general managers in charge have not grasped the environmental problem of packaging, or they see it as too severely constrained by economic pressures. There is thus a tendency to behave defensively rather than proactively, and market success is often regarded as pure 'windfall profit'. For example, some sectors, e.g. paper or cardboard processing packaging businesses, and also certain areas of the plastics business, have hardly contributed anything themselves to achieve success on the market. Their success has resulted from the incidental 'ecological correctness' of the packing agent or packaging system they use. Avoidance and use-specific advantages of specific materials (e.g. paper-based packaging) and systems (e.g. multi-use trays made from plastic materials) were not discovered and effectively made use of by the packaging industry but by the users of packaging. The revolution in packing logistics has been triggered by the customers. Thus, one can consider it as a typical case of a 'demand-pull' rather than 'technology-push' phenomenon.

Table. 20.2 Technological innovation factors in the packaging industry

Factor	Most important	Second most important	Third most important	Total
New materials	29.6%	7.4%	3.7%	40.7%
Computerisation	22.2%	0.0%	3.7%	25.9%
New machines	14.8%	22.2%	0.0%	37.0%
New controls	11.1%	11.1%	18.5%	40.7%
New procedures	11.1%	3.7%	3.7%	18.5%
Other	7.4%	7.4%	0.0%	15.8%

Source: Siebert 1995.

In discussions on packaging-related environmental issues, sensibility to environmental questions can often be seen to depend on the size of the enterprise. The larger enterprises tend more often to recognise that they are affected by the discussion on packaging and associated regulations than smaller enterprises. But the perception of the situation and the manner of reacting to it are highly dependent on company culture and the employee's qualifications[1]. In this context, factors specific to materials used, production or even region affect the small-scale level. It is in the medium-size area that 'key enterprises' using adaptation processes can mostly be found. While small businesses, struggling for survival, are forced to merely react to economic issues, large enterprises have the option of avoiding economic or environmental obligations via technological measures. Medium-scale

[1] See also the treatises of Andersen (1999) and Oddkjell (1997).

of technical equipment or material) as are the larger or smaller ones. While for the latter, this dependence seems unavoidable, for the larger ones it only seems to be a management issue. Medium-scale enterprises seem to prefer to depend on the 'trial-and-error' principle and thus adapt procedures to their own needs.

This internal adaptation to innovation being introduced into the packaging industry can be considered a typical process. In particular, key elements of technological development, outside a company's own field, lie in the area of general improvements in materials as well as new development and production techniques (CAD, CIM, etc.). Additional direct effects from innovations in micro-electronics or general mechanical engineering affect the packing machinery industry as well. The rapid improvement of the CNC area has led the entire packaging industry to undertake total computerisation of production. Innovative solutions are found internally, especially as a result of precision work (e.g. folding, filling, etc.) and developments in machinery for packaging producers.

It is surprising that measures to develop re-use of old and secondary raw materials are not a higher priority, as almost all enterprises state that material costs represent the most important factor in production. From a statistical viewpoint, average material costs exceed even salary and capital costs. Labour costs are much more dynamic in nature, especially in rural areas, likewise rental costs in urban areas. Here, packaging businesses differ little from general economic trends.

The way the examined enterprises chose their location, partly due to the classic criteria of raw material and energy availability (e.g. the glass and aluminium industry), is quite deep-seated. But the reasons for this persistence are not so much due to traditional location factors as to the personal sphere[1]. The majority of people in top positions would not wish to consider moving away, even if a decision not to move results in severe locational problems. While it seems much less of a problem for producers of packaging machinery, with their goods of comparatively high value, to remain in their traditional location in close vicinity to an area of conventional mechanical engineering (e.g. Baden-Württemberg), this does not seems to be at all valid for producers of packaging material. Their products are highly sensitive to transport costs and they have put themselves in enormous commercial difficulty by sticking to the same location strategy, a feature which seem to be typical for the entire sector.

c) Market and Regional Effects on the Medium-Scale Level

In contrast to France, for example, hardly any regional branch clusters[2] can be found in Germany. This makes it difficult to empirically identify regional effects

---

[1] Quite often, the choice of location by one-man businesses can be derived from the particular circumstances of historical foundation or present ownership (see Ritter 1992). Emotional ties to the location, children attending a specific school and a set of other personal reasons lead to a decisive persistence of location once chosen.

[2] The best known example would probably be 'Packaging Valley' in the Champagne region, where 236 businesses employ 15,000 people and achieve a yearly turnover of about 13

here. Some branches appear to be located in given areas, such as producers of packaging machinery in the Osnabrück area, in Hessen and Baden-Württemberg, or the agglomeration of paper and cardboard processing companies in the south of the former German Democratic Republic (Saxony). However, none of these agglomerations can be considered particularly outstanding locations for the packaging industry. They are rather the result of agglomeration benefits (packaging – mechanical engineering) or of vertical integration (packaging material – packaging agents) within the packaging chain.

Indeed, within the course of business cycles, material-specific benefits and setbacks occur, but reasons for existing regional differences in waste disposal or utilisation pressure, do not emerge. Perhaps this is due to the generally low interest in the subject. As the Bavarian example[1] clearly shows, spatial distribution patterns in the packaging business follow the valence (perceived value) of the product. Thus, packaging services (research, development, enhancement, and trade) prevail in large urban agglomerations, whereas packaging material producers seem to prefer settling in small towns or medium-sized centres, and those companies which mostly improve products can often be found in structurally more disadvantaged areas (e.g. near the former East-West German border). However, still noticeable regional differences between businesses in the new regions of former GDR and those of West Germany can be traced back to their differing cultural experiences, e.g. with regard to resource use.

The direct and indirect effects of change in the packaging industry can be seen to differ considerably between regions, not only in a technology-related way. Packaging companies do not usually react very differently to actors in other sectors as far as phenomena such as effects on employment due to automation and on-site rationalisation are concerned. But because of their particular size and regional distribution, some differences can be found. For example, for non-urban small businesses subject to change, low skill jobs can be significantly affected, while larger companies in urban agglomerations, with a variety of highly skilled jobs, do not affect the regional employment market so severely, independent of the sector considered. In two other respects, the packaging industry also differs from other sectors of the economy: Above all, the sector can be considered an amplifier of economic trends, just following the course of existing economic sectors, without itself triggering either positive or negative trends.

Apart from areas where earlier structural conditions continue to have effect (e.g. in the former German Democratic Republic), the regional employment market is mainly influenced by internal business decisions and market behaviour (see Weber 1980, 1993). Whilst in the new *Länder*, for example, about two thirds of firms had to alter either their form, their production concept or their product range because of the temporary upheaval – and as many as half of them had to make changes in some or even all these areas – significant changes seem to have been the exception in West German firms. It seems rather strange that the latter seem to follow

---

billion French francs. In the days of the German Democratic Republic, such 'artificial' clusters existed in the form of combines (Kombinate).

[1] See USIV 1994 and Siebert 1995.

completely different rules. The companies either come up with a different range, while not really changing how they run their business, or they buy or sell whole parts of their business, but then stick to the original product range offered. When the range was completely altered, as was observed in all the cases examined, this led to a completely new production concept. Usually this meant a shift from producing component elements to producing a complete product, or from mass-production to individual manufacture. Apart from the consequences for the employment market, effects on suppliers and sales relations have to be considered too in this case (see Fig. 20.2). Despite all the dynamic change and region-specific characteristics, a general trend towards enhancing business relationships seems to prevail. This 'extensification' can be described quantitatively (a higher number of customers) as well as spatially (greater distances), according to the general economic trends of increasing specialisation, concentration and internationalisation.

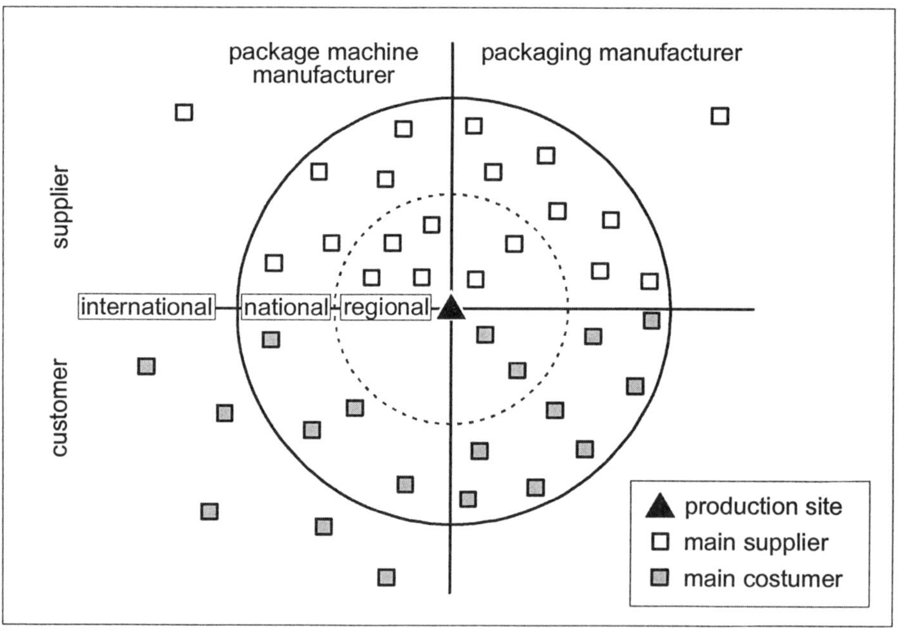

Source: Siebert 1995.

Fig. 20.2 Regional interlocking between supply and market

20.5 Outlook

Is the packaging industry undergoing radical change? Outsiders tend to answer this question in the affirmative. But where exactly is the 'rupture', at what level is it occurring, at what point in time and what are factors causing it? The SCP multiple-level analysis used in the underlying empirical study (Siebert 1995) allows both the elements and actors of the examined sector to be determined without losing sight of the bigger picture. However, this multi-layered reality results in a rather evolutionary structural change, i.e. a change without significant ruptures.

The expected 'revolution' in the packaging market, which it was thought would be prompted by the German Packaging Regulations, seems hardly to have taken place at all. Despite the fact that estimates made on behalf of the Federal Environment Ministry (Bundesumweltministerium) have revealed declines in annual production of about 3 to 4 percent since the regulations came into effect, this trend hardly offsets the growth rates between 1989 and 1991 after re-unification (see Fig. 20.3). There was a decrease of only about 2 percent in the price-adjusted retail turnover in the period examined (Runge 1994). Some market segments certainly experienced losses or gains which are difficult to place within the general survey. Looking a bit closer, this is not really surprising, since conditions at the large-scale level (environmental consciousness, Verpack V, division of labour, etc.) hit a varied and disorganised medium-scale market whose actors can only react with a certain time lag and in a limited way due to the structure of the sector. Undoubtedly, there can be a material link between the individual elements ('metabolism'), without the need to propose a corresponding information structure ('network'). Within the same market segment at the same location, the identified adaptation behaviour of firms (proactive versus defensive) can unfold as either a planned or an unplanned process.

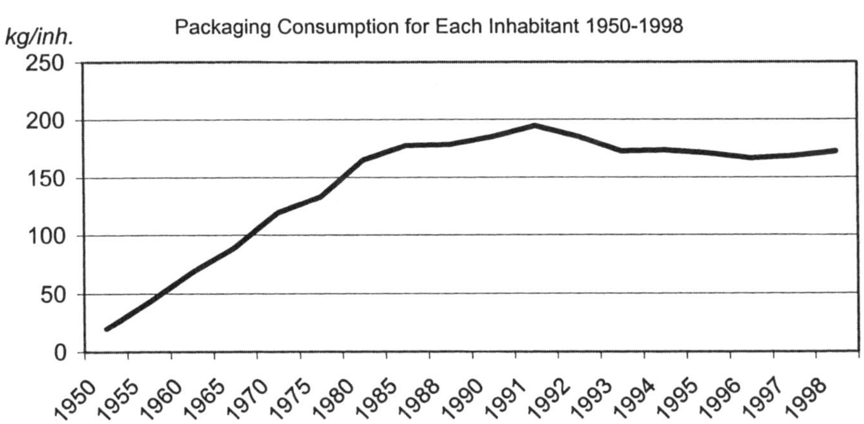

Source: GVM 1999, Klöckner 1992, own calculations.

Fig. 20.3 Specific packaging consumption in Germany from 1950 to 1998

This kind of self-organisation means that the incoming system information (e.g. increase of license fees for a particular packaging agent) can be interpreted individually by the entrepreneurs at the small-scale level. Partly conflicting, slightly chaotic adaptation processes can be noticed. There is no common association, nor sector-typical contacts through the entire packaging chain from design to disposal. There have been some efforts to meet the new environmental standards by using thinner material or completely new packaging agent combinations, but these factors are undoubtedly overshadowed by more significant influences like the competitive situation, power relations and other structural conditions on the medium-scale level. Additionally, there are regional and cultural differences in the demand for certain types of one-way glass and multiple-way packaging in South Germany as against a preference for plastics or metal in the north of the country. Packaging producers are usually dependent on packaging agents and do not offer a general service called 'packaging' which would allow them to select the ideal individual packaging agent combination; they are also dependent on regional differences such as mentioned above. The packaging business has turned from a seller's to a buyer's market and regional effects are driven by demand.

As a result of environmental obligations, it is possible to see characteristics of a 'planned economy', e.g. requirements by authorities targeting specific technologies, materials and systems. On the other hand, a kind of fragmentation of environmental constraints also exists, with environment-related decisions being assigned to individual entrepreneurial responsibility. Voluntary activities in this sector, as for example ISO 14000, EMAS etc., point in this direction. The desired performance profiles of common packaging materials can in fact be achieved by the present material standards: hardly any totally new specifications are required at all. Work still remains to be done on environmental questions, with regard to the required closure of material cycles.

The 'winners' or 'losers' resulting from these changes cannot be assigned to the particular levels being considered. Thus, it is difficult to quantify the overall impact of, for example, producers of synthetic packaging material being obliged to shut down their business for environmental reasons in order to improve the local and 'global' environmental quality, if this causes the region to suffer economically. In general, this accounts for the spatial-functional differentiating processes considered. On the one hand, differences at the large-scale level are balanced by the ubiquity of the packaging industry, on the other, polarisations at medium-scale level are amplified by the development of an urban-rural decline in the packaging industry. This trend is to some extent balanced, whether desired or not, by a new spatial-functional differentiation in urban as well as in rural disposal areas. Further differences result from problems being shifted, e.g. the transfer of the disposal question to the consumer (Green Dot), the packaging situation to logistics (traffic density) or to other environmental issues (energy issues, greenhouse effect).

All in all, the heterogeneity noted in this sector is an indication of high system flexibility and self-organisation. This suggests that the sector structures are stable. Indeed, the system requirements are subject to change themselves. In former times, the determining parameters were exclusively technical (e.g. how can vacuum wrapping be achieved?) Recently, the importance of technical-economic criteria (e.g. how can specific requirements be met most effectively?) has increased, triggering the processing of synthetic packaging materials (how can packaging material be produced and disposed of in an environmentally acceptable way?). In the process the market is often distorted by subsidy-like systems (DSD).

Nonetheless, if the analysis is taken beyond levels or system elements, a survey of the results reveals that everything is interlinked and thus, virtually everything affects everything else. Each cause has major effects and side-effects, but even the slightest side effect is a cause of yet other effects. Systemic frameworks – like the SPC approach followed here – do not exclude effects at any level and interpret reality as a paradox, whose contradictions and force fields can, in the end, be supportive of further innovations (Hormann 1995).

References

Andersen, M.M. (1999) Trajectory Change Through Interorganisational Learning. On the Economic Organisation of the Greening of Industry. Copenhagen (Dissertation)

Ayres, R.U., Simonis, U.E. (1993) Industrieller Metabolismus. Konzept und Konsequenzen mit umfassender Bibliographie. WZB-papers, FS II 93-407, Berlin

Badke, M. (1990) Eine Theorie des technischen Fortschritts, Empirische und theoretische Untersuchung des gesamtwirtschaftlichen Produktivitätsfortschritts in der Bundesrepublik Deutschland. Kovac, Hamburg

Bain, J.S. (1968) Industrial Organisation. Wiley, New York, London, Sydney.

Blazejczak, J. (1993) Umweltschutz und Industriestandort: der Einfluß umweltbezogener Standortfaktoren auf Investitionsentscheidungen; Forschungsbericht 10103162. UBA-Berichte 93, 1, Berlin

BMU (Bundesministerium für Umwelt und Reaktorsicherheit) (ed.) (no year) Konferenz der Vereinten Nationen für Umwelt und Entwicklung im Juni 1992 in Rio de Janeiro. Dokumente. Agenda 21, Bonn

Borrmann, C., Michaelis, J. (1990) Lebensmittel im europäischen Binnenmarkt. Veröffentlichungen des HWWA-Instituts f. Wirtschaftsforschung, Hamburg

DIN (Deutsches Institut f. Normung e.V.) (ed.) (1991) Verpackung: Terminologie, Prüfung, Maßordnung, Markierung, Kennzeichnung, Lieferbedingungen, Normen. Berlin, Köln

Dörrenbächer, P. (1992) Unternehmerische Anpassungsprozesse. Ein Industrie-geographisches Arbeitsmodell, dargestellt am Beispiel der Saarbergwerke AG. Arbeiten an dem Geogr. Inst. d. Universität d. Saarlandes, Bd.38, Saarbrücken

Glenz, W.W. (ed.) (1984) The Plastics Industry in Western Europe. Facts and Figures. Hanser, Munich

GVM (Gesellschaft für Verpackungsmarktforschung) (ed.) (1999) Verpackungsverbrauch 1990-1998. Wiesbaden

Haas, H.-D. (1991) Tagung "Duale Abfallwirtschaft" – Eine Einführung. In: Haas, H.-D. (ed.) Duale Abfallwirtschaft. Tagung des Arbeitskreises "Entsorgung und Rohstoffrecycling", Dec 6-7, 1990, München. Münster u. Hamburg, 1-7

Hahn, R., Gaiser, A. (1994) Aktuelle Innovationsprozesse im verarbeitenden Gewerbe. Beispiele aus dem Maschinen- und Fahrzeugbau sowie der Elektroindustrie im Raum Bodensee-Oberschwaben. Zeitschrift für Wirtschaftsgeographie 38(1/2), 60-75

Hall, A.D., Fagen, R.E. (1956) Definition of a System. General Systems Yearbook 1, 18

Haas, H.-D., Siebert, S. (1993) Mutation en République Fédérale d`Allemagne, d`une société de gaspillage à une société de recyclage. Revue Géographique de l`est 2, 89-105

Hormann, J. (1995) Management am Scheideweg. Süddeutsche Zeitung 278, December 2-3, V1-25

Jaeckel, G., Grupp, H. (1991) Raster Prinzipieller Auswirkungen des Technischen Wandels auf Wirtschaft, Gesellschaft und Umwelt. TAB, Beobachtung der technisch-wissenschaftlichen Entwicklung, TAB-Arbeitsbericht 4/91, Bonn, 19-25

Jantsch, E. (1992) Struktur. In: Seiffert, H., Radnitzky, G. (eds.) Handlexikon der Wissenschaftstheorie. Dt. Taschenbuch Verl. München, 326-329

Jokisch, R., Lindner, H. (1982) Technologischer Wandel in Gesamtdarstellungen. Probleme seiner Strukturierung für die Frühindustrialisierung. In: Jokisch, R. (ed.) Techniksoziologie. Suhrkamp Frankfurt/M., 160-183

Juen, C. (1992) Die Theorie des sektoralen Strukturwandels. Konzeptionelle Grundlegungen, Probleme und neuere theoretische Ansätze zur Erklärung des sektoralen Strukturwandels. Lang Bern, Frankfurt/M, New York

Kern, H., Schumann, M. (1984) Das Ende der Arbeitsteilung? Rationalisierung in der industriellen Produktion. Bestandsaufnahme, Trendbestimmung. Beck, München

Klöckner, H. (1992) Verpackung – Fluch oder Segen? Verpackungswirtschaft der BRD 1950-2000. Gladenbach

Koning, J.W. de, Smidt, M. de (1990) Technological Development and Spatial Effects: Research Results and Hypothesis. In: Heide, H. der (ed.) Technological Change and Spatial Policy. Nederlandse Geografische Studies 112. Amsterdam, 33-55

Läpple, D. (1989) Neue Technologien in räumlicher Perspektive. Informationen zur Raumentwicklung 4, 89, 213-226

Leborgne, D., Lipietz, A. (1990) Neue Technologien, neue Regulationsweisen: Einige räumliche Implikatioen. In: R. Borst (ed.) Das neue Gesicht der Städte. Theoretische Ansätze und empirische Befunde aus der internationalen Debatte. Birkhäuser, Basel, 109-129

Lempa, S. (1990) Flächenbedarf und Standortentwicklung innovativer Technologie und Logistik unter besonderer Berücksichtigung des Logistik-Konzeptes Just-In-Time in der Automobilindustrie. Münchner Studien zur Sozial- und Wirtschaftsgeographie 36. Kallmünz, Regensburg

MUT (Programmgruppe Mensch, Umwelt. Technik im Forschungszentrum Jülich) (1991) Aktuelle und zukünftige Konflikte im Bereich der Hausmüllentsorgung in der Bundesrepublik Deutschland. Gutachten im Auftrag des TAB. Jülich

Neef, E. (1950) Landesplanung und geographische Forschung. Berichte zur dt. Landeskunde 7, 1949/1950, 310-332

Neef, E. (1969) Der Stoffwechsel zwischen Gesellschaft und Natur als geographisches Problem. Geographische Rundschau 21, 12, 69, 453-459

Nuhn, H. (1993) Auflösung regionaler Marktsysteme und Konzentrationsprozesse in der Milchwirtschaft der BRD. Zeitschrift für Wirtschaftsgeographie 37, 3/4, 93, 143-150

Nuhn, H., Oßenbrügge, J. (1984) Räumliche Konflikte im Hamburger Hafenerweiterungsgebiet. Sozioökonomische und ökologische Auswirkungen einer wachstumsorientierten Regionalpolitik. In: Schätzl, L. (ed.) Regionalpolitik zwischen Ökonomie und Ökologie. Jahrbuch d. Geographischen Gesellschaft zu Hannover, SH. 11, Hannover, 129-162

Oddkjell, V. (1997) Ökologischer Wandel in der Getränkekartonindustrie. Haupt, Bern

Pachner, H. (1992) Räumliche Strukturen der Vermarktung landwirtschaftlicher Erzeugnisse in Württemberg. Struktur- und funktionsräumlicher Ansatz zum Verständnis von Vermarktungswegen und Marktregionen als Gestaltungselemente der ländlichen Raumes. Erdkundliches Wissen 106, Stuttgart

Piore, M., Sabel, C. (1985) Das Ende der Massenproduktion. Wagenbach, Berlin

RGV (Rationalisierungs-Gemeinschaft Verpackung im RKW e.V.) (ed.) (1988) Produktionsmenge und Produktionswert der Verpackungsindustrie in der BRD und Berlin (West) 1986-1987. Eschborn/Ts.

Ritter, W. (1991) Allgemeine Wirtschaftgeographie. Eine systhemtheoretisch orientierte Einführung. Oldenbourg, München

Ritter, W. (1992) Vorwort des Herausgebers. In: Gros, U. (ed.) Einfluß der Unternehmensorganisation auf den Standort von Zweigbetrieben. Nürnberger Wirtschafts- u. Sozialgeographische Arbeiten, Bd. 45. Nürnberg

Ritter, W. (1994) Welthandel. Geographische Strukturen und Umbrüche im internationalen Warenaustausch. Wiss. Buchgesellschaft, Darmstadt

Ropohl, G. (1979): Eine Systhemtheorie der Technik. Zur Grundlegung der Allgemeinen Technologie. Hanser München, Wien.

Runge, M. (1993) Verpackungen im Spannungsfeld von technisch-wirtschaftlichen und ökologischen Anforderungen. In: Runge, M., Schricker, G. (eds.) Die Verpackungsverordnung. Umsetzung in die Praxis. Heusenstam, St. Gallen, 13-38

Runge, M. (1994) Milliardengeschäft Müll. Vom Grünen Punkt bis zur Müllschieberei. Argumente und Strategien für eine andere Abfallpolitik. Piper München, Zürich

Schlütter, L. (1992) Globaler technologischer Wandel und regional-sektorale Produktionskonzepte in Schwellenländern. Theoretischer Zusammenhang und empirische Darlegung am Beispiel der südkoreanischen Bekleidungsindustrie. Urbs et Regio 60, Kassel

Siebert, S. (1995) Verpackungswirtschaft im Umbruch. Eine Empirische Studie zu Wechselwirkungen von Umweltauflagen, technologischem Wandel und Regionalentwicklung im wiedervereinigten Deutschland. WRU-Berichte 4, München

Stillwell, E.J. (ed.) (1991) Packaging for the Environment. A Partnership for Progress. New York

Storbeck, D. (1982) Gesellschaft und Raum. In: ARL (ed.) Grundriß der Raumordnung. Verl. der ARL Hannover, 1-15

Uhlmann, L. (1978) Der Innovationsprozeß in westeuropäischen Industrieländern. 2: Der Ablauf industrieller Innovationsprozesse. Duncker&Humblot Berlin, München

USIV (Umweltentlastende Systeminformationen im Gesamten Verpackungswesen) (1994) Auswertung der Datenbank USIV für das Land Bayern. unveröff. Manuskript, Köln

Weber, J. (1980) Der Unternehmer als Entscheidungsträger regionaler Arbeitsmärkte. Bayreuther geowissenschaftliche Arbeiten, Bd. 2, Bayreuth

Weber, W. (1993) Die Relevanz kleiner und mittlerer Betriebe für die Struktur und Entwicklung ländlicher Räume in der Bundesrepublik Deutschland sowie regionalpolitische Konsequenzen. Arbeitsmaterialien zur Raumordnung und Raumplanung, 125, Bayreuth

21 The Changing Organisation of Production in the European Horticultural Sector and the Influence of Technology

Barbara Lenz
Institute of Geography, University of Stuttgart

21.1 Restructuring in the Primary Sector

Restructuring of the organisational and spatial production patterns in the primary sector is a development which is running parallel with changes in the other economic sectors, especially the sector of industrial goods production. In the course of this development, the functions of both enterprises and production locations have become increasingly differentiated due to the fact that, even in the primary sector, the product no longer represents a single 'unit' which is manufactured at one enterprise and one location. Instead, the product has been broken down into various elements so that it is possible to prepare and process it at different enterprises and different locations. Due to this segmentation of production, the individual enterprise has more options for specialisation, i.e. for the assumption of specific functions within the overall production process, which thus takes on a chain-like pattern. This development is especially pronounced in flower and ornamental plant cultivation which today is marked by highly differentiated production and distribution chains.

Among the framework conditions having supported this development, new technologies have played a particularly significant role (Gordon 1995). In addition to production technologies, there are also organisation-supporting information and communication technologies which are no longer used selectively in individual enterprises for rationalisation purposes, but are restructuring the overall organisation of production and distribution along the value added chain of a product (Littek and Charles 1995; Porter 1991).

The segmentation of production and distribution processes is accompanied by an increase in the opportunities for new locations which are able to bring their special competitive advantages to bear. For quite some time subtropical and tropical locations with favourable natural conditions and low labour cost have been clearly gaining in importance for horticultural production. The final markets, which have considerable spending power, are in Central Europe and North America. For example, imports of flowers and ornamental plants from non-European countries to Europe increased from DM 4.5 billion in 1985 to almost DM 12 billion in 1997, reaching as much as a third of the sales value within the European Union for individual products, especially cut flowers such as roses, carnations and gerbera.

Today, the flow of goods within the chains is connecting enterprises and locations with highly diverse structures, assigning them specific functions in the framework of overall production. As a result, locations emerge which vary greatly with regard to their functional range. Another major factor are the regional markets. Several questions arise in this context. In what manner do different types of enterprises contribute to the overall production, what rules can be deduced for the structure of production chains and how can these rules be substantiated? By endeavouring to answer these questions, in this chapter we aim to contribute to the discussion about the restructuring of primary production in organisational and spatial terms. It provides an analysis of the functional changes in horticultural production in Europe and gives examples to illustrate the types of inter-business flows of goods characterising contemporary European horticulture, the changes these flows of goods have undergone and the role of technological development in this context. To this end, the production and distribution chain within flower and ornamental plant cultivation is described, and the reasons for its entrepreneurial and spatial patterns are examined. Depending on the product, three main chains can be identified. Even though the organisational pattern of these chains is basically subject to the same principles, it is also influenced by the way in which the enterprises use the framework conditions of their locations – also by using certain technologies – to optimise their production.

21.2 Changes in Functions of Enterprises in Primary Production

Explanations for changes in the functions of enterprises within primary production can be grouped into two different categories according to the view adopted. On the one hand, there is the view that functional changes result mainly from the reduction of primary production into a kind of 'rump production' which has the exclusive function of providing raw materials to the processing industry. Changes in agricultural enterprises are explained by the impact of downstream production and distribution (Bowler 1992; Nuhn 1999). On the other hand, is the view which focuses on functional change as the result of an increasing distribution of tasks within rump production. Tasks are distributed with the aim of stepping up production and lowering costs by employing more efficient methods. Rationalisation is achieved by synchronising work processes and biological growth processes which in traditional agricultural production do not coincide, and where the utilisation capacity of labour and fixed assets is subject to considerable limitations. Synchronisation is based on the standardisation of growth and ripening processes by employing a variety of technological and biological procedures. With their help, it becomes possible to stagger production batches in such a way that seasonal phases with a low labour demand are eliminated and, simultaneously, output can be scheduled for a specific point in time. The smooth interplay of the various production stages is ensured by standardising the product and its components (for animal production see, for example, Dauce and Guigueno 1984; Troughton 1986; Windhorst 1984 1989).

In this system of standardised mass production, the functions of an individual enterprise are reduced to a narrow section within the overall production process. An individual enterprise assumes more comprehensive sections of overall production only in the case of a non-standardised niche production. The specific section of overall production in which an enterprise specialises depends on the operational preconditions and the framework conditions of the location.

21.3 Primary Production as a Vertical Chain

The segmentation of production leads to a distinct vertical production pattern in the primary sector. Production within an individual enterprise constitutes one link in a chain whose pattern consists of controlled and monitored growth processes which are spatially and organisationally separated from each other for economic reasons. Various models have been created to describe such a production pattern. One is the model of the 'value added chain' which has been studied in detail mainly by Porter (1991), others are the 'production chain' and the 'filière' which have been discussed primarily in the English and French-speaking areas (e.g. Edgington and Hayter 1997; Lambooy 1991; Lenz 1997; Monfort 1983; Morvan 1982; Stoffaes 1980). In all cases, the chain model aims to describe the structure of a larger production context with the aim of providing the opportunity to compare different types of production contexts or temporary development stages of one and the same production context.

Porter's value chain refers to the system of activities within an enterprise. By optimising these activities, the enterprise gains a competitive edge: "An enterprise is more than the sum of its activities. The value chain of an enterprise represents an interdependent system or a network of activities which are interconnected by *links*" (Porter 1991, p. 64). Here, the value added chain is not merely an analytical concept but the basis of well-planned, specific entrepreneurial actions where a 'set' of individual activities is subject to repeated optimisation and, thus, restructuring. However, the chain is limited to an internal context, and connections reaching beyond the individual enterprise, e.g. suppliers or distribution channels, are grouped together by Porter into the 'value system' as a 'larger flow of activities'.

In contrast, the models of the production chain and filière specifically comprise illustrations of inter-business connections above the level of the individual enterprise. The filière constitutes the more comprehensive model of the two because it expressly includes production *and* distribution up to the final market. This approach is based on the assumption that the distribution, or the kind of access to the final market, significantly influences the entire upstream production chain. This aspect is also emphasised by authors who have specifically examined the effect of distribution chains on production (Hörmann 1992; Barrett *et al.* 1999).

In addition, chain models make it possible to show physical and non-physical input to each segment of the chain. However, the approach which backs up the present analysis, concentrates on the segmentation of the product throughout the chain.

The empirical analysis on which this chapter is based uses the production and distribution chain as an analytical pattern. This is to guarantee a perspective which is committed consistently to the overall context of production and distribution up to the final market. Such a perspective is useful because the arrangement of the enterprises as a pattern in the chain is not random but depends on the operational structures which in turn may influence the functional changes within the chain. The aspects which need to be explained are the *organisational* segmentation of the chain on the one hand, and its *spatial* segmentation on the other. The organisational segmentation of the chain is the result of enterprises with different structures and different functions being combined to form a temporary production and distribution system. In order to explain this system which, for the primary sector, is comparatively simple and mainly linear, we study the various individual entrepreneurial structures which contribute to the manufacturing and distribution of a final product. Once the structures and functions of the individual enterprises involved have been understood, we can explain the organisation of the entire chain, i.e. the relations and interconnections between the enterprises. To complement this analysis, the spatial segmentation is examined. Its pattern is the result of linking several business locations with the aim of manufacturing a final product. The spatial distribution of the chain segments depends to a large extent on how hard and soft location factors, political, economic and social conditions as well as demand factors influence the decisions of the personnel involved within the enterprises.

21.4 Historical Development of Traditional Horticultural Locations

Although the cultivation of ornamental plants designed for a middle-class clientele can look back on a tradition of almost two centuries, consumption of ornamental plant products within all strata of society began only in the 1950s and 1960s (Flicoteaux 1996; Bitsch and Ludwig 1992). Since then, cut flowers and indoor plants have become products for which there is a regular demand from large sections of the population. Due to growing spending power in the highly industrialised core countries in Europe, new sales opportunities have arisen for horticultural products. Currently, in Germany alone – the European market with the highest sales volume – bulbs, cut flowers, indoor and garden plants as well as nursery products with a value of almost DM 12 billion are sold annually to the final consumers (AIPH 1998).

Against this background of continuously increasing demand, production in Europe has expanded significantly over past decades, but with different consequences for the individual countries where production takes place. Based on the spatial distribution at national level, the Netherlands, Italy, Germany and France represent the main European countries producing flowers and ornamental plants, with the Netherlands clearly outstripping their competitors in terms of growth and volume of production. In the field of ornamental plant cultivation alone, the Dutch horticultural industry achieved a boost in production value of 700 percent in the period from 1970 to 1995. This means that the value of Dutch ornamental plant production exceeds even that of the entire US production (Fig. 21.1).

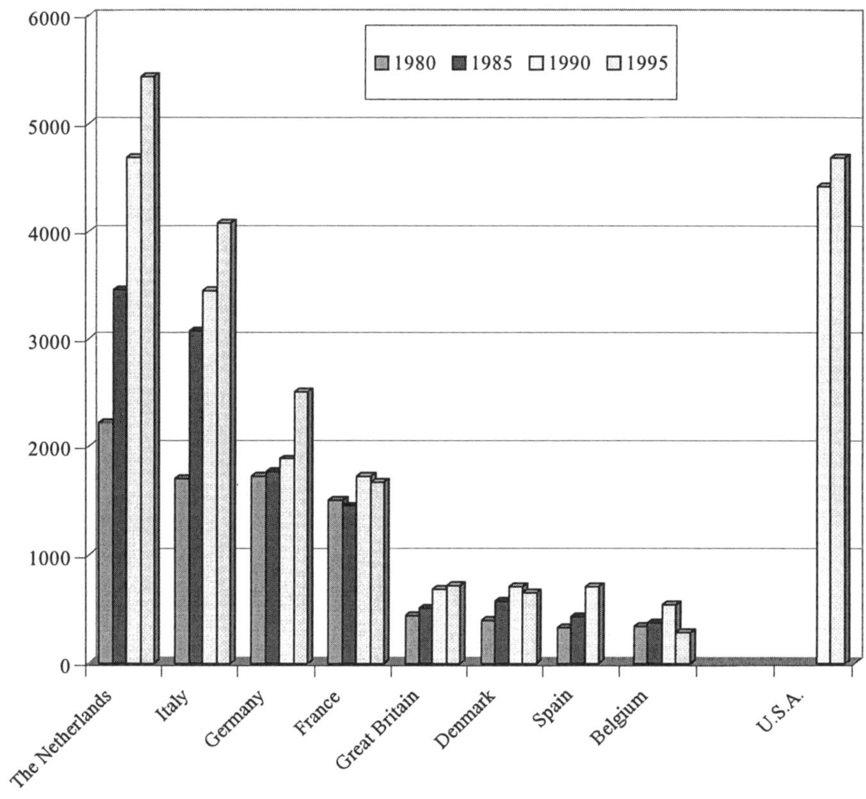

Source: AIPH Yearbook of the International Horticultural Statistics 1998.

Fig. 21.1 Development of production values in European and US ornamental plant cultivation between 1980 and 1995

Until well into the first half of the 20th century, the geographic location of horticultural businesses was determined by the proximity of production and consumption locations. Thus, the circle of commercial horticultural locations – which is still evident even today in the vicinity of the larger cities in Europe – was created around the turn of the century (Böhm 1988). One reason for this proximity was that horticultural products were difficult to transport. Moreover, production was oriented towards an urban clientele with the necessary income and consumption habits – which are preconditions for the sale of high-quality fruit and vegetables as well as of flowers and ornamental plants. It was only after the decline of the agriculturally self-sufficient population and the general increase in income after World War II that a comprehensive demand for horticultural products and especially flowers and ornamental plants emerged.

In the same period, production expanded for the first time in Central Europe and South European regions. A major precondition of this development was the existence of unlimited export and import possibilities within Europe. Most of the southern locations which were integrated into the Central and North European market at an early point in time were also tourist regions, so their infrastructure was well developed and they had good traffic connections to the northern markets. This applied in particular to Italy, southern France and Tenerife.

Until well into the 1970s, the southern locations fulfilled a seasonally complementary function, especially when it came to the cultivation of cut flowers such as carnations and roses. An additional function was assumed quite early by these locations, namely the production of cuttings, primarily pelargonium cuttings, to satisfy the growing demand for bedding and balcony plants. The production of cuttings in the south offers two advantages: one is the superior quality of the plants, but even more important are the cost-saving effects which are obtained mainly because the production of cuttings takes place during months when there is very little light in the mid latitudes, i.e. from December to April. This made it possible to offer the fully grown pelargoniums to the final consumer in time for the beginning of the 'balcony season' in May. Production at southern locations entails both considerably lower energy costs and lower cost of labour.

The spatial shifts in production were accompanied by several waves of adaptations in the operational structures. The first such wave occurred in the middle of the 1970s as a result of the rise in energy costs, both in the Netherlands and in the adjacent countries (Avermaete 1975). It is easy to understand the strong influence of energy costs on the development in the enterprises when one takes into consideration that in the case of glasshouse cultivation, even under the relatively favourable conditions in the Netherlands, these costs make up 13 to 15 percent of the total costs of the enterprises (author's own estimates for the period from 1987 to 1992 based on figures of the Landbouw-Economisch Instituut, Central Bureau Voor de Statistiek 1994).

Table 21.1 Prices of different types of energy in Germany (without VAT)

	1970	1980	1990	*1991*	1994
Light fuel	25.9	125.7	94.9	*100*	77.6
Natural gas	29.1	82.3	85.6	*100*	88.1
Electricity	42.9	72.8	101.1	*100*	101.4

Source: Bmelf (1995).

As an alternative to spatial shifts in production, a large number of the Central European businesses implemented rationalisation measures, for example by introducing EDP control into production (AIPH Business Report 1982, 1983). These measures aimed at reducing labour costs, which represent about one third of total costs and are continually increasing. For example, at DM 22.34 per hour, the hourly rate of pay for a horticulture foreman in Germany in 1994 was nominally 392 percent higher than in 1970. Also in 1994, the pay for a semi-skilled worker in the horticultural sector amounted to about DM 25.00 per hour in the Netherlands, to DM 8.00 to 10.00 on the Canary Islands, and to about DM 1.00 per day (!) in an African country.

In contrast to the production of cut flowers, cuttings and young plants, the production volume of pot plants remained stable in Germany, Belgium, Denmark, Great Britain and the Netherlands throughout the 1980s, and in some cases the volume even grew significantly. There are several reasons for the stability or even growth in the pot plant production in Central and North Europe. The reason which is most important in spatial terms is the proximity to the market. This aspect constitutes a cost advantage in pot plant production because the products entail high transportation costs due to their volume and weight. Moreover, pot plant production also offers a number of operational advantages which can be achieved in a highly individual manner, depending on the resources which enterprises have at their disposal.

In general, considerable shifts have occurred in Europe regarding the cultivation of flowers and ornamental plants. However, these shifts did not affect the entire range of production. Because of the differentiation of operational functions, they applied only to those parts of production which are associated with high labour and/or energy costs. This development can be summarised roughly as follows. A shift in production locations occurs in those areas which produce labour and energy-intensive products whose value is high in comparison to the transportation costs. Thus, shifts occur in the production of cuttings and young plants as well as of various cut flowers, but not with regard to pot plants which have relatively high transportation costs. Consequently, these products continue to be manufactured in the vicinity of the place of consumption. Based on the cost relationships and changes in costs, we have now obtained a plausible pattern of explanation for the organisational and spatial changes in the flower and ornamental plant cultivation both on the national and the regional level.

Simultaneously, the technologies which play a significant role in the above mentioned contexts are beginning to emerge. They include both internal and external technologies. The internal technologies comprise *horticultural-specific* methods, mainly greenhouse technologies which, in combination with electronic data processing, include the automation of difficult tasks. (For example, one of these tasks is the sorting of plants according to quality characteristics. This activity, which is very labour-intensive if not automated, must be accomplished several times in the course of the production process. By repeatedly grouping together uniform batches, plants with the same characteristics are treated in the same manner. In the end, the customer is supplied with large batches of highly uniform plants.) In general, it can be observed that the development of mechanical technologies is accompanied by biotechnological progress which in turn considerably enhances the effects of mechanical innovations. This phenomenon is illustrated in the field of energy-saving measures, where research into plant behaviour and the cultivation of types and versions with lower energy consumption or a more flexible energy intake constitute an important element in the framework of energy saving (Hendriks 1990). In addition to instances of rather spectacular technological progress, innumerable small innovations have been made, e.g. simple mechanical improvements in irrigation and internal transport, which nonetheless can have a significant impact on operational efficiency.

There are also technologies which are *not specifically oriented toward horticulture*, above all electronic data processing, which is used not only in production but also as a planning, control and administration tool where it produces significant rationalisation effects. These internally employed technologies are complemented by external technologies, especially transportation and cooling techniques. Thus, a shift in production to locations with lower energy costs was possible only after an end-to-end cooling chain was available. The management of transportation in the horticultural sector represents a complex system involving not only the means of transport, but also techniques to render the product fit for transportation in the specific means of transportation. A large number of highly specialised technologies has been developed to meet the specific requirements of individual products to ensure that they will withstand the transportation period in the best manner possible. Consequently, one of the focal points of the technological advancement in horticulture today are the fields of goods packaging and transportation methods, as well as the improvement of the interfaces between the available transportation routes and means.

21.5 Foundations of the Empirical Analysis

Proceeding from the finding that the organisational and spatial development of European horticulture is based on a differentiation of functions, the question arises as to how this functional change is reflected at the level of the individual enterprise and which position this individual enterprise assumes in the production chain. Our analysis of businesses and their specific functions in the production and distribution chain is based on an empirical study of 81 horticultural enterprises located at Landbouwgebied Amstelland en Aalsmeer in the Netherlands (22 businesses), Tenerife and Gran Canaria in the Canary Islands (35 businesses) and in the Stuttgart region in Germany (24 businesses). These locations were selected for the analysis on the reasonable assumption that different combinations of production factors, technologies and locations would be evident in the three regions, while interconnections among these locations would be manifest as well. All three regions have been focal points of production at the national level for a number of years, and all of them include businesses of different sizes.

The analysis was strongly quality-oriented and based on guideline interviews. It comprised horticultural businesses in the market gardening sector which specialised in ornamental plant production, including businesses at all production stages (e.g. breeding, production of cuttings, production of young plants, raising, production of cut flowers), but excluding retailers who only buy raw products (plants raised at the nursery until they are ready to be sold to the final customer) or finished products (plants ready to be sold). As a result, nurseries with a sales volume of which more than 50 percent was generated by self-marketing were not taken into consideration.

The operational structures considered in the study are highly varied, ranging from small businesses with a greenhouse area of less than 0.5 hectare and a staff comprising a few family members to large-scale enterprises with production areas of up to 110,000 sq.m. under high glass frames and a permanent staff of more than 100. The sample is made up mostly of pure greenhouse nurseries in the lower and medium-size categories, i.e. with areas under glass frames of up to 10,000 sq.m. and 10,000 to 50,000 sq.m. respectively. About 30 percent of the businesses interviewed are open-air nurseries with much more extensive workable land. As could be expected, the majority of open-air cultivation nurseries are located on the Canary Islands.

21.6 Functional Interconnections and Use of Technology

Product and Location

The interviewed businesses can be assigned to the following product groups: 'slow growing pot plants,' 'cut flowers and greenery', 'bulbs and tubers' and 'bedding and balcony plants'. In this grouping process, it becomes evident that there are focal points of production at the various geographic locations: the product groups are divided among the locations in the way that was to be expected given the general development of the flower and ornamental plant cultivation in Europe (Fig. 21.2). However, it also becomes evident that the production range is relatively broad at each of the locations.

For example, slow growing pot plants (foliage plants such as *ficus, sansiveria*) and cut flowers as well as cuttings and young plants are produced mainly on the Canary Islands, i.e. at a location where long periods and large quantities of natural light and natural heat are available. In contrast, flowering pot plants (e.g. African violets, begonias) as well as bedding and balcony plants are produced at locations relatively close to the place of consumption, i.e. in the Stuttgart or Aalsmeer regions, because of the high transportation costs involved. Production of cuttings and young plants is important at all locations, but is characterised by a spatial distribution of the individual production tasks. While cultivation of the parent plants and production of unrooted cuttings takes place mainly on the Canary Islands, rooted cuttings are cultivated in Northern Europe, in the vicinity of the nurseries which produce raw and finished goods for the final consumer market.

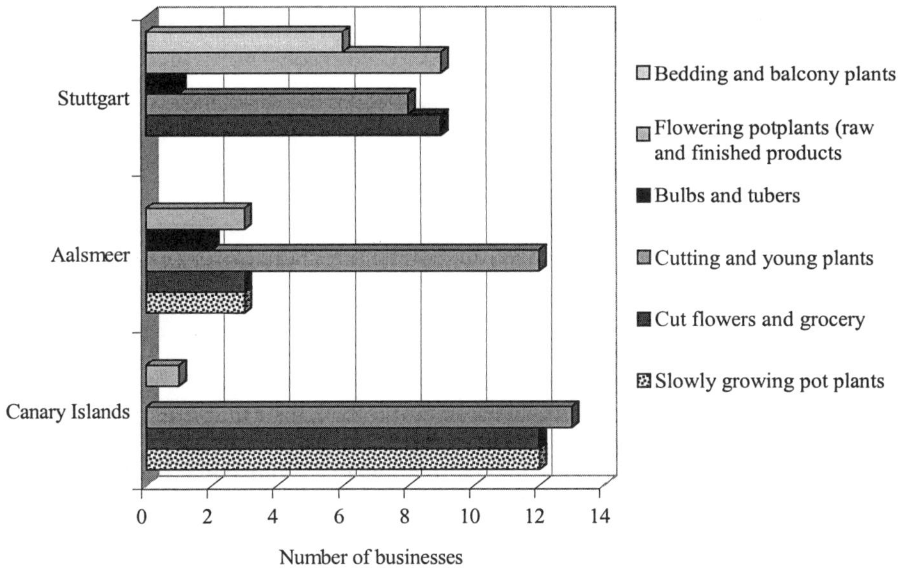

Fig. 21.2 Focus of production in interviewed businesses by location

Individual Businesses and their Function in the Chain

Through an analysis of the individual enterprises, it was possible to directly reconstruct several, sometimes highly divergent chains. In the following, the principles governing the functional structure within the overall production cycle are illustrated, using the cultivation of pelargoniums as an example. Firstly, the organisational and spatial pattern of the chain is described, followed by an explanation of its functional pattern based on the structures of the businesses involved and the framework conditions at the locations. The employment of technologies by the businesses belonging to the chain is also taken into consideration. Subsequently, we discuss whether any laws governing the chain pattern can be identified, the explanations which substantiate such rules, and what future developments can be expected on the basis of the current structure of the chain.

The Production and Distribution Chain of Pelargoniums

Pelargoniums are a product whose production has been characterised for a relatively long time by a distinct distribution of tasks among several businesses. Based on the empirical analysis, the production cycle can be divided into as many as eight stages, which are as follows:

(1) Breeding of new sorts and varieties;
(2) Production of so-called 'elite material', i.e. virus-free and high-quality plants to create a basic stock;
(3) Propagation of elite cuttings to create a new stock;
(4) Detaching of cuttings from the parent plants;
(5) Rooting of cuttings by placing them in substrate;
(6) Growth of rooted cuttings into young plants;
(7) Growth of young plants into 'raw products', i.e. into a stage where the flowering has not yet commenced but the growing of buds has just begun;
(8) Raising of plants until they reach the stage of 'finished products' ready to be sold.

With regard to the *entrepreneurial structure* of the chain pattern, there is generally a single company which is responsible for performing stages (1) to (5), although in organisational terms the different tasks are assigned to spatially separate businesses. Individual functions may even be outsourced to businesses which do not belong to the group. For example, the production of elite material in the Netherlands is usually outsourced to private or semi-public laboratories which also issue official certificates. Thus, outsourcing does not only serve to reduce costs by utilizing external know how, it also offers a competitive advantage by providing a certificate of good quality. In the production of cuttings, tasks are also outsourced simply to eliminate excessive workloads or to expand production without having to expand one's business as well. Outsourcing of this type is accomplished by large enterprises on the Canary Islands by providing smaller nurseries with their parent plants and tasking them exclusively with the detachment of the cuttings. The product is transferred, i.e. sold, to another, independent enterprise, usually when it has reached the stage of rooted cutting. From here on, all subsequent production stages are generally performed by separate and legally independent enterprises.

The *operational structures* within the chain are characterised by the circumstance that breeding and production of cuttings take place exclusively in large operational units, with small enterprises assuming only the function of satellites, if any, during these production stages (see above). Large businesses are also mainly responsible for producing young plants. In contrast, raw and finished goods are produced in large as well as in small and medium-sized businesses.

There are essentially two factors which account for the way in which production is organised among enterprises with different structures. On the one hand, there is the possibility of profiting from economies of scale which increase along with the size of the enterprise and becomes especially significant when the workflow is highly standardised and human labour can be replaced by automation. This applies above all to the production of cuttings, where the raising of rooted cuttings and also of young plants has been turned into a highly automated process. In general, the same level of automation is also possible in the following production stages. However, because this work is less labour-intensive, automation does not have such a significant effect, and so production at these stages is in the hands of smaller and medium-sized businesses.

The second factor constitutes the ability of businesses to distribute specific tasks internally. This ability depends on the size of a business. Cost-intensive operational areas such as research and development (R&D) can be set up only by large enterprises which gain a competitive edge by utilising the results of their organic R&D activities. This is why innovations – especially in the field of selection and breeding – achieved by small nurseries are developed into marketable products in the context of co-operation projects with large, market-dominating firms. Especially in the Netherlands, successful breeding results obtained by small businesses are marketed with the help of large partners. Thus, the small businesses gain indirect access to the market, while the large companies can purchase additional, know how-intensive products.

The *spatial pattern* of the chain begins with businesses in the Aalsmeer and Stuttgart regions where both breeding and production of elite material takes place. These businesses send their elite cuttings to a southern location where the stock of parent plants for the production of unrooted cuttings is established. The cuttings then root at a location in the Aalsmeer and Stuttgart regions. With regard to the subsequent production stages, the tasks are distributed among several locations, with production moving ever closer to the final consumer market in the course of the production cycle (Fig. 21.3).

The spatial pattern of the chain can be explained essentially by looking at the major cost factors of the individual production stages, to which the costs incurred by transportation between the stages must be added (Fig. 21.4). Thus, the production stages involving a high demand for land and energy as well as for semi-skilled workers are situated at southern locations – if the transportation costs of the respective product do not use up the cost savings resulting from the shift in production. Since transportation costs rise with the increasing volume and weight of the product in the course of its cultivation, production shifts to the vicinity of the retailers, who initially may still be found close to the cutting nurseries. However, production of finished products is mostly located in the immediate vicinity of the final consumer market. In the case of pelargoniums, this development is the result not only of the transportation costs, but also of the difficulties related to transporting this tender product. In this context, a relatively new phenomenon has been observed recently. The disadvantages arising for producers located far away from the market because of the limited transportability of the finished product are eliminated by offering raw products to the final consumer before the beginning of the season. As a consequence, production of finished goods is taken out of the business chain and shifted to the final consumer.

The Significance of Use of Technology for the Functional Structure of the Production Chain

So far, the study has shown that the segmentation of the overall production process into separate production stages is based on economies of scale in the individual businesses which, in the case of high labour costs, promotes the use of technology. Consistent with this finding, it was observed in our study that the degree to which technology is used increases commensurately with the size of the business and the labour costs at the location. However, in addition to the rational justifications for the use of technology given by the interviewed businesses, another element – formulated by Freeman in his thesis about national and regional technology paradigms – must also be taken into consideration. This element is rational only to a limited extent. Freeman regarded these paradigms as a "set of guiding principles which become the managerial and engineering 'common sense' for each major place of development" (Freeman 1982, p. 449). Whereas the Dutch enterprises consider the use of modern technology as necessary in order to achieve the highest possible level of rationalisation, businesses in the Stuttgart region prefer simple solutions involving less technology. On the Canary Islands, the regional technology paradigm can be described as almost anti-technology.

Fig. 21.3 Spatial segmentation of pelargonium production

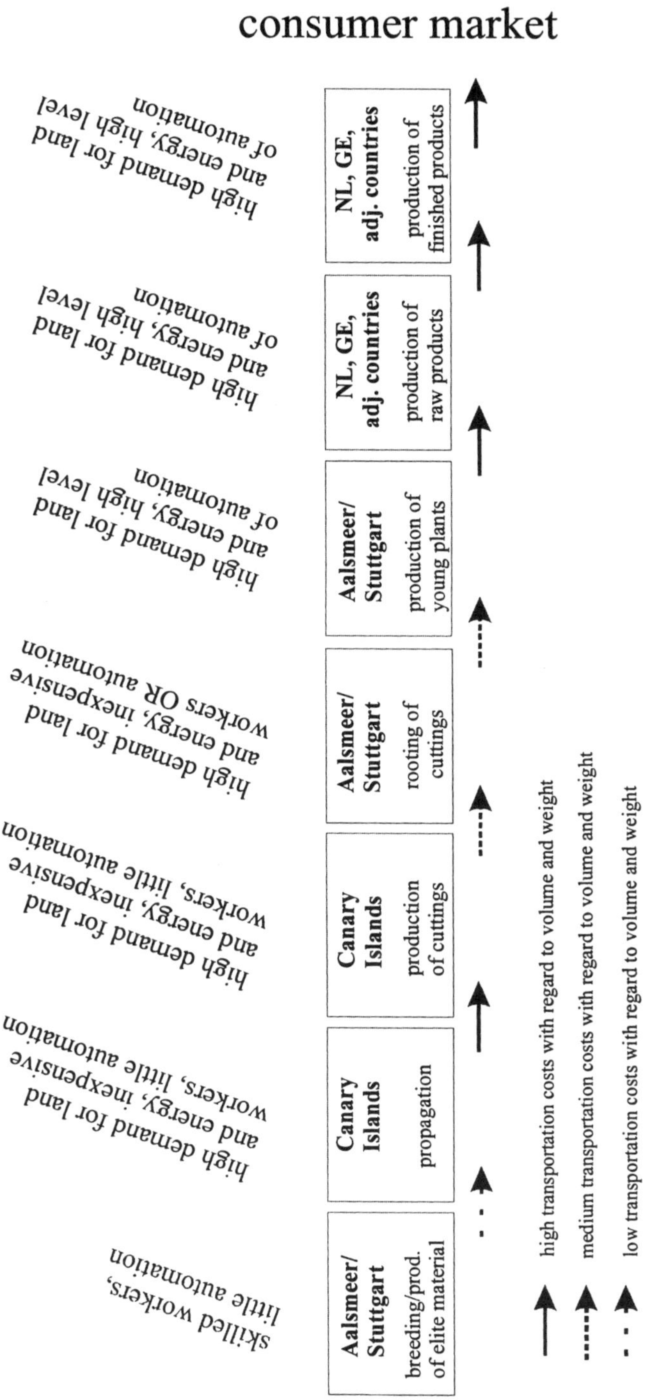

Fig. 21.4 The significance of different cost factors for the production of pelargoniums

There is yet another reason for the regional differences in the use of technology, namely the environment of the businesses concerned. This becomes clear from the example of the Aalsmeer region, where horticultural production forms a cluster together with firms from the secondary and tertiary sector. This cluster supports a wide range of innovations in horticultural production (concerning for example irrigation, ventilation, and temperature control). The use of information and communications (I&C) technologies in the flower and plant production of the Aalsmeer region illustrates the strong impetus horticultural enterprises can receive from outside for the employment of new technology. Marketing institutions like the great flower auctions as well as state agencies and associations offer important online information and transaction services to the enterprises. The auctions assume the task of marketing the product online from the producer via the auction to the buyer, with the result that neither the buyer nor the seller has to be physically present at the marketing site. In addition to the auctions arranged by the co-operatives, there are also auctions organised by private industry which promote the use of modern I&C technologies (primarily PCs integrated into electronic information networks). Although the use of technology is of course based on economic factors, it is also facilitated because the businesses are generally willing to make use of these instruments. A similar cluster does not exist on the Canary Islands, and in the region of Stuttgart it is incomplete.

In contrast to the internal technologies, transportation and communication technologies represent 'enabling technologies' which are oriented primarily toward facilitating an optimal utilisation of the global range of locations. In this situation, the range of global locations available serves as a substitute for the employment of technology in the existing businesses. Yet it also means that businesses which use technologies only to a small degree must have modern technologies available at least in those fields where they need to establish links to the upstream or downstream production stages. In the case of pelargoniums, the main use of technology is for cooling the plants in order to preserve the ability of the detached cutting to root later on. Consequently, all businesses on the Canary Islands are equipped with modern technological systems for transport preparation and transportation so that a continuous cooling chain can be established. This includes not only the branch businesses of German, Dutch and British companies, but also the independent or co-operative nurseries in the cut-flower sector which sell their products in the Netherlands or Germany.

In this context, it is obvious that new organisational and spatial structures established with the help of specific technologies are strengthened by orienting the advancement of those technologies for quite some time toward an optimisation of the newly created interconnections. For example, Dutch and German firms involved in the production of cuttings have recently been able to outsource tasks to locations even further away because the transportation technology has now reached the standard necessary to transfer the products over even longer distances without risking qualitative losses. However, the cost factor, especially labour and energy costs, still remains the major reason for shifting production to distant locations here as well, while goals such as company expansion carry the same weight only in the larger firms.

The Production Chain and Business Size

Based on the example of pelargonium production and its segmentation into spatially separate businesses, it is possible to deduce several rules which govern the structure of the production chain. A particularly striking aspect is the way in which the businesses of various sizes are distributed along the chain (see Fig. 21.5).

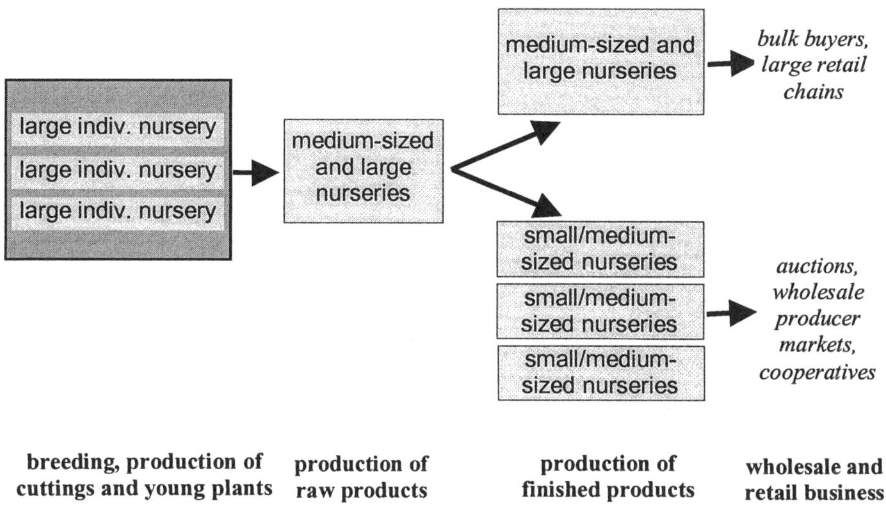

Fig. 21.5 Operational structures in the production chain

The first stages of production are characterised by the dominance of large multi-business companies with large operational units. Production in these stages requires specific know how. Research and development efforts are necessary in order to obtain this know how, and only large companies can accomplish such efforts. Production is subject to a division of labour, with a highly automated and thus technology-intensive part at a Central European location and another location involving only little automation and technology, but offering favourable framework conditions regarding the costs of energy and labour.

Most of the firms involved are internationally active companies with considerable shares in their production segment's global market. By dominating the early stages of production, these companies influence production along the entire chain in many ways, for example with regard to the production techniques used in the downstream businesses, and especially with regard to the strict standardisation of the product range on offer. In the case of some products, this influence is so strong that 75 to 80 percent of the global output of a specific sort is based on a small number of cuttings which were cultivated in the breeding nursery in the Netherlands.

The central part of the production chain comprises single-business enterprises of various sizes, with medium-sized and large nurseries making up the majority. The smaller nurseries working in this part of the chain are usually situated close to the market and sell their products to regional wholesalers or to retail nurseries only when they have reached the stage of finished products. The scope of internal technology employment varies depending on the size of the nursery. Whereas large businesses have automated most of the work processes, small and medium-sized nurseries tend to use technology only to a small degree. At the same time, however, there are remarkable differences between the various locations. These can be accounted for by the influence of the respective business environments and by some kind of 'common sense' among the producers with regard to the need to use technology in production.

In the subsequent chain segments, both large and small businesses are involved in overall production. The dominating business size depends on the available options for automating the production and, to an even greater degree, on the ways in which the products can be marketed.

The size of the business is influenced by the respective sales market and the customer type. Thus, when the producers have a contractual guarantee to sell their products to large retail chains or wholesalers, which in turn sell mostly to bulk buyers, the final production stages in the chain are dominated by large businesses. In contrast, the production of small and medium-sized nurseries is located closer to the market for regional buyers, such as specialised retailers or wholesale producer markets. The market niche exploited by the smaller enterprises in the framework of standardised mass production consists of selling plants which have been forced to a fairly highly-developed stage. Such plants can be raised only in the immediate vicinity of the market because they are very tender and hence difficult to transport. As they are so delicate, it would be too risky to cultivate large batches.

In conclusion, the rules governing the structure of a chain as illustrated by pelargonium production can be summarised as follows:

- Large firms occupy those segments of the chain where cost advantages can be obtained by automation or a shift in production. The specific strategy chosen depends mainly on the relation between the cost factors of energy + labour and the transportation costs.
- Small and medium-sized businesses can be found primarily in those segments of the chain where market niches, which cannot be serviced by the large enterprises, can be exploited. Here, the small and medium-sized businesses have to maintain a production that is particularly close to the market.

Similar principles can also be established for other production chains. However, a comparison leads to the remarkable finding that specifically in the production of cut flowers, large firms tend to occupy the entire chain with their spatially separate businesses. The reason for this phenomenon is that, given the particularly rapid changes in fashion trends in the cut flower market, information about the market and market trends constitutes central know how that is essential for both production and breeding. Thus, by generating this information itself, the firm aims at obtaining a competitive advantage in the market. This strategy also offers the possibility to achieve greater stability and reduce the marketing risk involved in the production of cuttings and young plants by controlling marketing up to the final market.

The operational structure of the chain varies with regard to its spatial stability. For example, large businesses make use more often of the possibility of shifting production spatially, whereas smaller businesses must do without this alternative. It is a disadvantage that, particularly for small firms, cannot be offset by the employment of technology. Thus, in those areas where businesses of various sizes are involved in production, it is to be expected that structural changes will take place, whereas in those areas where large firms dominate production there will be a more pronounced trend to shift production to other locations. The answers given by the interviewed businesses already point to such a development.

21.7 Summary

The objective of this paper was to study production in the primary sector as a chain of single operational activities arranged in a logical order. The explanation for the chain pattern is based primarily on the relationship between operational structures and location conditions as regards the individual business. In this context, it has also emerged that particular business sizes are typical of specific segments of the pattern. Technological progress is especially important for the spatial and organisational division of labour in those cases where alternative locations are not available, i.e. in particular when the weight and volume of the product entail high transportation costs. It is mainly the large firms which employ technology to obtain advantages. Smaller businesses try on the other hand to find market niches.

The restructuring processes in horticultural production can be illustrated with the model of a production chain. By analysing and explaining such a chain it is possible to identify those sectors where primarily *structural changes* are to be expected, and those sectors where *spatial shifts* are to be expected. It can be demonstrated that the functional segmentation of horticultural production has led to stable and unstable locations. Locations which can currently be described as relatively stable are either in the vicinity of the market or characterised by a high input of know how into production. With regard to locations characterised by a wide variety of functions, a functional differentiation is to be expected over the medium term, during which production stages involving a low level of technology will disappear as the result of shifts in production.

References

AIPH-Union Fleurs (1998) Yearbook of the International Horticultural Statistics. Institut für Gartenbauökonomie der Universität Hannover 46
AIPH-Business Report 1982/83
Avermaete, U. (1975) Gevolgen van energiekostenexplosie voor onze internationale concurrentiepostie in de tuinbouw. Tuinbouwberichten, 39(5), 199-201
Barrett, H.R., Ilbery, B.W., Browne, A.W., Binns, T. (1999) Globalization and the Changing Networks of Food Supply: The Importation of Fresh Horticultural Produce from Kenya into the UK. Transactions of the Institute of British Geographers 24(2), 159-174
Bitsch, V., Ludwig, S. (eds.) (1992) Einflussfaktoren auf die Entwicklung des Gartenbaus und deren zukünftige Veränderungen aus ökonomischer Sicht. Arbeitsberichte zur Ökonomie im Gartenbau, Institut für Gartenbauökonomie der Universität Hannover
Böhm, H. (1988) Gartenbau und Landwirtschaft in der Umgebung von Bonn. Arbeiten zur Rheinischen Landeskunde 58, 225-246
Bowler, I.R. (1992) The Industrialization of Agriculture. In: Bowler I.R. (ed.) The Geography of Agriculture in Developed Market Economies. Longman Scientific&Technical, Essex, 7-30
Bundesministerium für Ernährung, Landwirtschaft und Forsten (BMELF) (1995) Statistisches Jahrbuch über Ernährung, Landwirtschaft und Forsten, Münster-Hiltrup
Dauce, P., Guigueno, L. (1984) Aux origines de la modernisation et de l'intensification de l'agriculture en Bretagne. Aviculture industrielle et vulgarisation agricole à Saint-Jean-Brévelay, 1950-1965. Norois 31(124), 541-557
Edgington, D., Hayter, R. (1997) International Trade, Production Chains and Corporate Strategies: Japan's Timber Trade with British Columbia. Regional Studies 31(2), 149-164
Flicoteaux, A. (1996) Géographie du pélargonium en France. Acta Geographica 108/IV, 67-74
Freeman, C. (1982) The Economics of Industrial Innovation. Pinter, London
Gordon, R. (1995) Globalization, New Production Systems and the Spatial Division of Labour. In: Littek, W., Charles, T. (eds.) The New Division of Labour. Emerging Forms of Work Organisation in an International Perspective. DeGruyter, Berlin/New York, 161-207
Hendriks, L. (1990) Current Status of Environmental Research on Potted and Bedding Plants in Europe with Special Emphasis on Temperature. Acta Horticulture 272, 71-79
Hörmann, D.M. (1992) Der Structure-Conduct-Performance-Ansatz (SCP) zur Beurteilung vertikaler Produktions- und Absatzsysteme. In: Storck, H. (ed.) Gartenbauökonomie – heute und morgen. Institut für Gartenbauökonomie der Universität HannoverPublisher Hannover, 82-87
Lambooy, J.D. (1991) Complexes, Formation and Networks. Nederlandse Geografische Studies 132, 15-23
Landbouw-Economisch Instituut/Centraal Bureau voor de Statistiek (1994) Tuinbouwcijfers. S'Gravenhage, Voorburg
Lenz, B. (1997) Das 'filière' -Konzept als Analyseinstrument der organisatorischen und räumlichen Anordnung von Produktions- und Distributionsprozessen. Geographische Zeitschrift 85(1), 20-33
Littek, W., Charles, T. (1995) Introduction. In: Littek, W., Charles, T. (eds.) The New Division of Labour: Emerging Forms of Work Organization in an International Perspective. DeGruyter Berlin/New York, 161-207

Monfort, J. (1983) A la recherche des filières de production. Economie et statistique 151, 3-12

Morvan, Y. (1982) Réflexions sur le contenu et le destin d'un concept: la filière. Entreprises et Organisations. Mélange en l'honneur de Jeanne Krier. Economica 6, 131-164

Nuhn, H. (1999) Auflösung regionaler Produktionsketten und Ansätze zu einer Neuformierung: Fallstudien zur Nahrungsmittelindustrie in Deutschland. Arbeitsberichte zur wirtschafts-geographischen Regionalforschung 2

Porter, M.E. (1991) Nationale Wettbewerbsvorteile. Erfolgreich konkurrieren auf dem Weltmarkt. Droemer-Knau, München

Stoffaes, C. (1980) Filière et stratégie industrielle. Annales des Mines 1, S, 9-20

Troughton, M.J. (1986) Farming Systems in the Modern World. In: Pacione, M. (ed.) Progress in Agricultural Geography. Croom Helm, London, 93-123

Windhorst, H.-W. (1984) Strukturwandlungen und räumliche Prozesse in der US-amerikanischen Geflügelwirtschaft. Geographische Zeitschrift 72, 225-244

Windhorst, H.-W. (1989) Die Industrialisierung der Agrarwirtschaft. Strothe, Frankfurt am Main. Also: http://www.dehne.de/interess/gartenb.htm.

22 How Culture Determines Regional Economic Trajectories: The Changing Landscape of European Costume Jewellery Production

Thorsten Hülsmann[1], Jürgen Pohl[1] and Norbert Rehle[2]
[1] Department of Geography, University of Bonn
[2] FAST, Gesellschaft für angewandte Softwaretechnologie, Munich

22.1 Introduction

Recent theoretical research on the economic and technological development of European regions is widely based on the concept of the 'industrial district'. Industrial districts are seen, on the one hand, as innovative units *per se* and, on the other, as relics of a pre-modern economic system, now out of date in a time of 'footloose industries' and a globalised world economy.

Most recent studies have focused on dynamic regions with high rates of technological and product innovation. Our study, however, follows the work of Maillat *et al.* (1995) which investigates the change and adaptability of the local production systems of one industry. Our interest therefore lies neither in a single region, nor in branches which are traditionally innovative such as the media, advertising, biotechnology or high-tech production in general. We have explored processes of innovation in a relatively low tech industry and have focused on the process of change and structural adjustment undergone by firms and the local production system.

The starting point of the research was the observation that new technologies in the centres of European costume jewellery production have adapted in different ways and with different economical consequences. For both historical and technological reasons, the production of costume jewellery in Europe is to a large degree concentrated in industrial districts. Placing emphasis on the costume jewellery production regions within Europe, not only the product, but also other variables like the production process, labour organisation and distribution are relatively constant. The regions in question are Jablonec nad Nisou (in the Czech Republic), Kaufbeuren-Ostallgäu (Germany), Enns-Oberösterreich (Austria), and Minorca (Spain) (see Fig. 22.1). The main purpose of the study is to describe the different forms of structural change in these regions and to explain the interrelations between economic and socio-cultural processes. Due to our broad definition of innovation as product innovation, the nature of the decision structure affecting innovation in the field of technology and organisation, it is necessary to focus in the whole network, that is the regional level. Communication processes, interactions and interrelations between organisations and actors need to be observed.

In addition, it is necessary to consider the institutional setting of norms, routines and conventions, since these influence innovative action, though in many cases they are not easy to define. 'Mentality' (Miegel 1991), 'regional consciousness' (Becattini 1990), 'reflexive regional identity' (Grabher 1994) and other terms are used to describe this regionally-based cultural dimension. At a general level, Granovetter has described it as 'embeddedness', claiming that economic behaviour is mostly embedded in interpersonal networks (Granovetter 1985).

Fig. 22.1 The European regions of costume jewellery production

22.2 The Research Study

The methodological basis of the study was strongly influenced by the need to take into consideration the non-economic aspects referred to above. This meant that it was necessary to choose a mixture of methods which combined elements of statistical analysis, analyses of historical sources, participant observation, narrative interviews and interviews with experts. We therefore tried to include the maximum variation of perspectives in order to cover as many facets as possible and to understand the organisational structure of the costume jewellery industry. Within the regions examined, the research team visited several firms and interviewed 45 employers. 17 representatives of regional organisations and 16 homeworkers in Jablonec nad Nisou and Kaufbeuren were also interviewed. These interviews were supplemented by continuous participant observation by one of the team members, who worked as a representative of the Association of German Fashion Jewellery Producers. Statistical data was obtained from governmental organisations and industrial sources.

The following section investigates the significance of institutions in this context. We ask whether regionally-bounded institutions are useful, or a hindrance, in coping with the increasing destabilisation of conditions resulting from the globalised economy. By examining developments in different costume jewellery regions, we wish to emphasise that the ability to introduce innovations is for the most part dependent on specific regional institutions, understood as hegemonial patterns of interpretation (in the sense of Antonio Gramsci).

22.3 Regional Institutions and Innovation

Our initial position corresponds with most 'system of innovation' approaches which have in common an emphasis on the role of institutions. Institutions are seen as central elements and are therefore included within the array of potential determinants of innovation (Lundvall 1992; Nelson and Rosenberg 1993; Carlsson and Stankiewicz 1995).

Institutions consist of "persistent and connected sets of rules, formal and informal, that prescribe behavioral roles, constrain activity, and shape expectations" (Storper 1997, p. 268). A feature common to all kinds of institution is that they give order to expectations and allow actors to act under conditions of uncertainty. In other words, institutions help the individual by establishing certain fundamental behaviour or routines. The problem of how institutions manage the balance between totality and permissiveness is seen as question of mediation between the inside and outside (Glasmeier 1994). The image of the regional economy as a cell, enclosed by a semi-permeable membrane, provides an illustration of this process. The membrane produces cohesion and security of action on the inside, but at the same time facilitates the diffusion of information and innovative impulse from inside to outside and vice versa. Provided that the system in fact works in this way, it supplies the conditions for institutional change.

Continuing with this image, the aim of our investigation is to study the process of construction or deconstruction of this 'membrane', and hence the power-geometries and politics in the regional context. The cultural dimension of the regional economy as a 'collective memory' seems to have great importance in relation to these constructions. Collective memory refers to the institutionalisation of tradition, which needs a permanent reconstruction of the memory through social interaction. This means that there is a circularity between conventions and institutions. These conventions are the source of ontological security. All institutions which dominate social action over a long period or over distance are transporting a 'myth'. This myth ensures that they will not be confronted with any doubts about the effectiveness of their norms. The myth reduces contingency and gives collective action sense and security. If regional networks are seen as social institutions, the establishment of such a myth through the collective memory means that the rules and norms which regulate the network will be automatically accepted. In other words, institutions can only function successfully if the rules and sanctions are integrated into the conventions that guide peoples' behaviour.

Recalling what has already been said above about innovation, it can be assumed that the socio-culture and historical location is in the end responsible for innovation or its prevention (see Fig. 22.2). Innovations are regarded as the introduction of new knowledge or new combinations of existing knowledge into the economy. This means that innovations are mainly regarded as the result of interaction. In our fields of study, such interaction takes place for the most part in normal everyday economic and non-economic life. Further, we regard innovation as a cumulative process (Edquist and Johnson 1997). Institutions affect interactions between people and habits, which partly contribute to the cumulative nature of learning processes. We therefore need to discover the forces binding individuals into interactions that allow or stimulate them to create economically viable innovations.

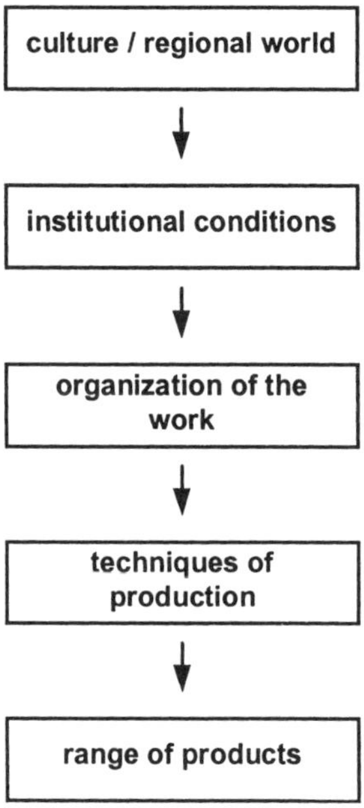

Fig. 22.2 From the regional world to the product

22.4 Costume Jewellery Production in Europe

In this section we describe the structure of the costume jewellery industry in the various regions surveyed. The importance of the industry differs according to the regional economy concerned. Whereas in Enns there are 40 firms in the sector, in Jablonec there are over 700, with a total of 600 and around 12,000 employees respectively. While in Enns the turnover is around 10m. euros, in Kaufbeuren-Neugablonz it is 200m. In both Enns and Kaufbeuren-Neugablonz the production of costume jewellery is one industry among many others, but in Minorca it is nearly the sole source of income besides tourism. In Jablonec too, the local economy is dominated by the production of costume jewellery. We now look at some of the main characteristics of the industrial structure of the four districts examined.

Vertical Disintegration

Most of the firms in all four regions do not have more than five in-house employees. Their small size is made possible because of an extreme division of labour. This point is made clear with the example of Jablonec in the Czech Republic shown in Table 22.1. About 93 percent of firms have fewer than six employees and 65 percent have no employees. The ten enterprises with more than 100 employees are remnants of the pre-1989 socialist system which continue to exist because the general wage level is lower than in the other European regions.

Table 22.1 Number of costume jewellery production firms in the region of Jablonec in 1998 by number of employees

No. of employees	No. of firms	%
500 - 4499	2	0.3
100 - 499	8	1.1
50 - 99	5	0.7
25 - 49	4	0.5
20 - 24	3	0.4
10 - 19	16	2.2
6 - 9	14	1.9
1 - 5	201	27.6
0	475	65.2
Total	728	100

Source: Ceský Statistický Úrad 1998.

In the costume jewellery industry, marketing, technology and labour-market circumstances are fundamental to survival and the reason for the predominance of small firms. Permanently changing styles and the dependency on broad fashion trends, mean that costume jewellery production is marked by short production runs which preclude economies of scale. Short-term cyclical changes are therefore far more common than in other sectors. These sometimes abrupt changes make firms particularly vulnerable during economic downturns, and underline the importance of a functional institutional setting which can be essential to interchange and therefore competitiveness. This is in fact, according to Marshall, one of the main reasons for the existence of industrial districts (Bathelt 1998).

The individual phases of production in the various districts are integrated within a regional network. As described by Lazerson (1990) in relation to the knitwear industry in the region of Modena, Italy, there are many small and very small enterprises specialising in specific techniques, materials or phases of production. As well as these producers of semi-finished products, there are also distributors and producers of finished products.

Putting-out of Work

Within the costume jewellery production process, there are several highly labour-intensive phases. This has led to a tendency to put work out. In Kaufbeuren (Germany), as in the other regions examined, the number of workers operating from home is nearly as high as those working within the firms (see Fig. 22.3). This is why the local production system has sufficient workforce at its disposal at times of surges in demand.

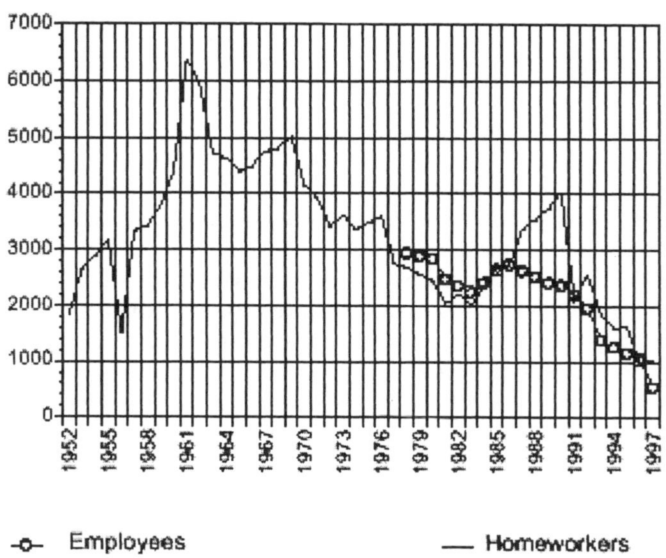

Source: Job centre Kempten 1998, Bavarian Ministry of Employment 1998.

Fig. 22.3 Number of employees and workers operating from home in Kaufbeuren-Ostallgäu in 1998

Each enterprise holds a specific position within the regional production system. Becattini describes it as "localised division of labour, which is neither diluted in the general market, nor concentrated in one firm or in just a few firms" (Becattini 1990, p. 40). Due to its functional rationality, the production system depends on two socially determined elements. The historical development and specific unity of the district which establish structural conditions allowing large numbers of individuals to operate small firms or to work from home with minimal organisational resources. In addition, many individuals possess specific skills and family resources, therefore providing a large reserve of labour available for self-employment. Another important element of the local production system is the ability of the manufacturers to produce fashion-ready designed products in small numbers. The whole regional labour market is therefore highly flexible and the boundaries between manufacturers, employees and those working from home, or between part-time and full-time workers are fluid.

Entrepreneurship

The division of labour and flexibility described above refers mainly to the production of costume jewellery. Traditionally, the most important 'institution' in each region is the entrepreneur as exporter or, in Minorca, the commercial travellers called 'viajantes'. Their position is of great significance, because it functions as a kind of gatekeeper to the market and controls the production activities. If the manufacturers and their employees can be considered the 'performing elements', the entrepreneurs are the customers. This is not, however, only an economic division of labour, but has far-reaching interrelations as far as social life is concerned.

Regional Identity

Within industrial districts there are interrelations between economic activities and social life which have been referred to as 'reflexive regional identity' (Grabher 1994) or 'regional consciousness' (Becattini 1991). It is widely accepted that industrial districts are characterised by a wide variety of informal agreements and relations which are only weakly formalised. Moreover, the firms tend to have both competitive and co-operative relations at the same time. These relations can only exist because opportunistic behaviour is limited, due to the existence of trust and the importance of reputation. In addition, the concept of 'civil' behaviour is shaped directly by the concept of regional identity, as a mixture of collective identity and efficient politics.

Civil behaviour, in the context of imagined communities, implies the activation of solidarity and reciprocal aid in informal relations. Both trust and a shared sense of community are basic factors in the cultural context already mentioned in the previous section. In the case of Kaufbeuren in the Allgäu and Enns-Oberösterreich, the shared sense of community derives from the events after 1946, when most German inhabitants were expelled from Sudetenland. This led to the former production system of Gablonz, in the present-day Czech Republic, being re-established in Kaufbeuren-Neugablonz in Germany and Enns in Austria. The 'myth' surrounding the re-foundation of the industry is a key element in the current economic climate and behaviour. In the case of Jablonec, one element in the myth is the sense of pride deriving from the former world-wide reputation of Gablonz, the place of origin of costume jewellery production in Europe.

The history of the costume jewellery production in Minorca, on the other hand, has oriented the present in an entirely different way. The powerful position of the 'viajantes' in the past was seen as the reason for decline in the industry. The myth of the manufacturers in Minorca is therefore their 'liberation' from the viajantes and the establishment of their own independence. Re-orientation, in a positive sense, led to the foundation of an Association of Manufacturers in 1972, which promotes joint presentations by Minorcan costume jewellery manufacturers. The activities of the Association culminated in the foundation of a Fair, 'Eurobijoux and Accessories', held annually on Menorca since 1994. The Association has also been able to obtain substantial public funding – the total amount of support received in 1997 was around 400,000 euros.

22.5 Changing Landscapes: The Difficult Transition of Culture and Institutions Towards a Competitive Future

As we have seen above, culture and institutions are regulatory mechanisms that help to keep a regional system flexible. Due to the immense pressure of the world market and very high labour costs on the production side, the European costume jewellery regions have been forced to make radical structural changes since the early 80s. These structural changes have concerned organisational processes, such as distribution, as well as institutional changes. This section illustrates the liabilities which derive from sectoral dominance of a region's economic base. It also shows how complex relationships and rigidities influence the ability to break with prior industrial traditions and develop new capabilities. We examine how the institutions and institutional relationships are evolving during a period of heightened international competition and change.

Locational Patterns

Over the period from 1980 to 1999, there has been a massive drop in the number of costume jewellery firms in Oberösterreich and Ostallgäu, and an only slightly less dramatic fall in Minorca (figure 22.4). In Jablonec, the number of firms remained stable until in 1990, when there was a large number of new start-ups.

The trajectories concerning the output and turnover differ from region to region. In the 1980s the turnover increased in all regions, while at the beginning of the 1990s a large decline took place in Ostallgäu and Oberösterreich (see Fig. 22.5). In the former, the number of employees dropped from 3000 in 1978 to 500 in 1997. In Jablonec, the production of costume jewellery fell because of the loss of the important market of the former Soviet union and the beginning of deep restructuring in the whole regional production system. Only in Minorca has turnover consistently risen, except in the year 1993.

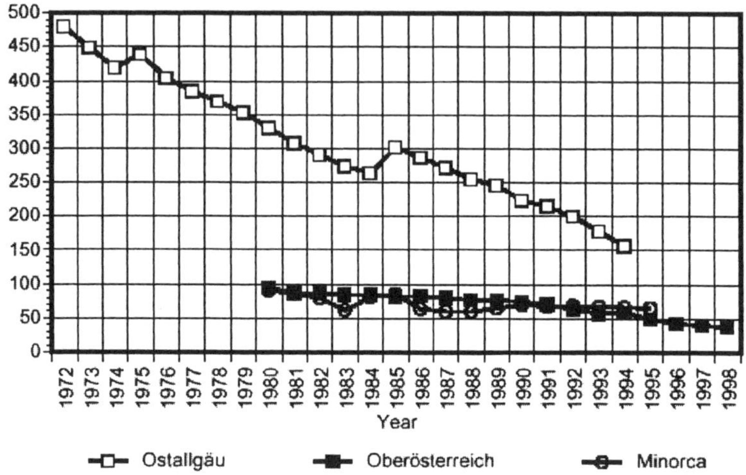

Source: Bundesverband der Gablonzer Industrie e.V., Wirtschaftskammer Oberösterreich, Confederación de Asociaciones Empresariales Baleares.

Fig. 22.4 Number of firms of costume jewellery production in Ostallgäu, Oberösterreich and Minorca

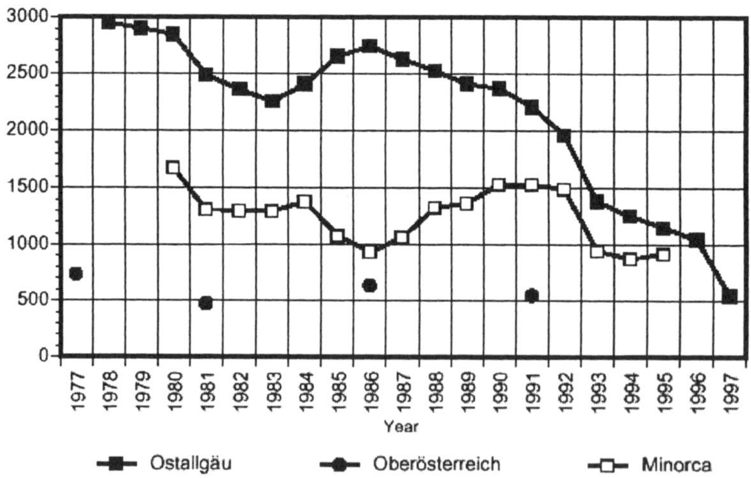

Source: Bundesverband der Gablonzer Industrie e.V., Wirtschaftskammer Oberösterreich, Confederación de Asociaciones Empresariales Baleares.

Fig. 22.5 Number of employees

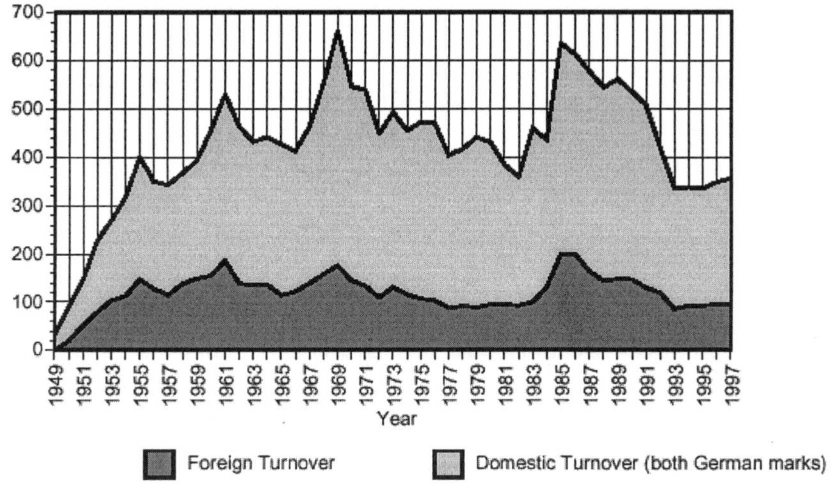

Source: Bundesverband der Gablonzer Industrie e.V.

Fig. 22.6 Turnover in Kaufbeuren-Ostallgäu 1948-1997, in million German marks

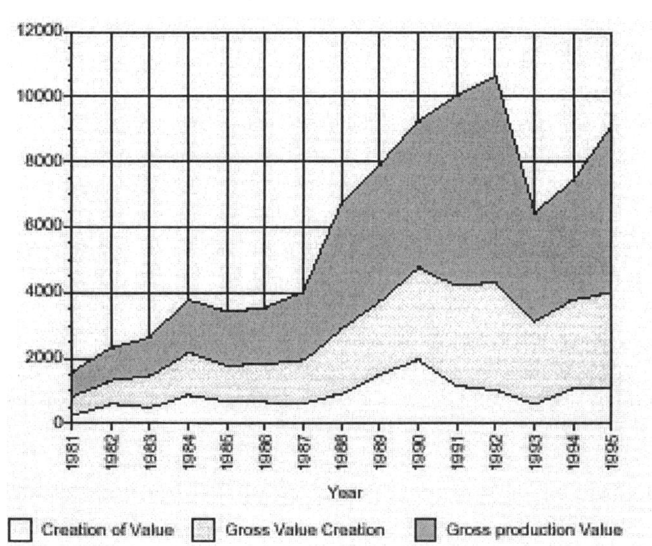

Source: Confederación de Asociaciones Empresariales de Baleares 1998.

Fig. 22.7 Gross production value, gross value creation and creation of value in Minorca, in million pesetas

The Search for Responses to Problems of Global Competition

Besides the quantitative changes, one can observe far-reaching changes in the sales organisation and distribution in each region. While historically the regions' production systems were internally integrated and relatively autonomous, the problem during the 1990s has become how the firms can participate in a global system of production and consumption. These changes are explained in this section.

a) Kaufbeuren-Ostallgäu and Enns/Oberösterreich

The situation in Oberösterreich and Ostallgäu is fairly similar, although there are some structural differences concerning the numbers of firms and their distribution. Neither regions has developed new innovative strategies. An important point is the undermining of the myth mentioned above. The manufacturers and decision-makers, who lived through the re-foundation of the industry after the war, have now stepped down and handed over their firms and responsibilities to the next generation. However, this new generation has a more distant position to the 'Neugablonz' myth. This means, among other things, that the traditional division of labour between manufacturers and exporters is accepted less and less. Exporters tend to buy cheaper Asian or Czech goods, and manufacturers want to sell directly to retailers. The gateways between the regional world of production and the world market have become more open.

The key problem in such a situation of radical change is that there have been no serious attempts to establish a new path of distribution which could preserve the districts in working order or preserve their specific advantages. Therefore most of the manufacturers act without certainty. The result is an 'every man for himself' mentality. Yet there are a few firms which develop some innovative ideas mostly by diversifying products and applying process technologies to other products. Many of the firms in Ostallgäu operate as suppliers for the car industry. This is one explanation why the turnover of regional industry is relatively constant, while the number of costume jewellery firms has dropped so dramatically (see Fig. 22.8). Although the regional production system in Kaufbeuren-Ostallgäu is still known as a costume jewellery production system, in fact only 34 percent of the turnover came from jewellery goods in 1997. For a further 27 percent of firms, less than 20 percent of their turnover came from jewellery goods. However, this small group of manufacturers had a 41 percent share of the turnover for the whole district.

Another element of change within the organisational structure has been the introduction of computer-controlled machines which provide increasing flexibility within the firms. This results in an integration of many steps of production in one firm. But because the number of firms is decreasing, a manufacturer does not have as much selection of suppliers as in the past. The main problem in Ostallgäu and Oberösterreich is that this vertical integration remains at the firm level and does not include the district as a whole.

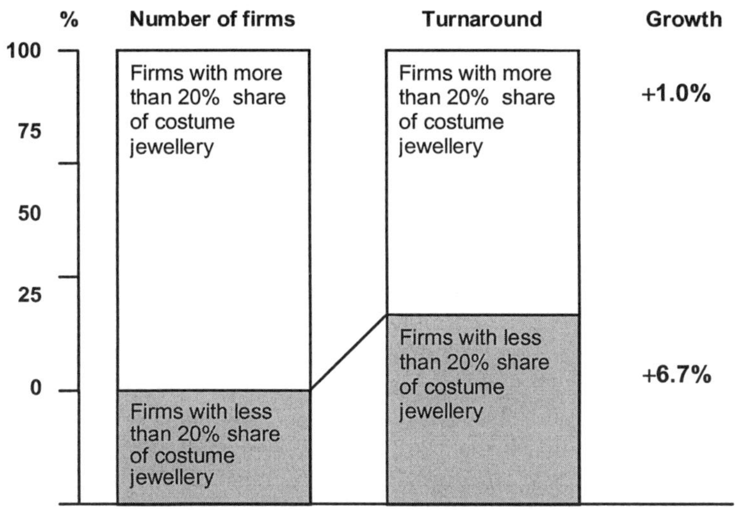

Source: Bundesverband der Gablonzer Industrie e.V. 1998.

Fig. 22.8 Share of the costume jewellery production in Ostallgäu of the turnaround in 1997

In Section 22.4, the important role of the exporters was mentioned. In the past, the distribution was always organised as shown in Fig. 22.9 (a) and organised by an exporter. This exporter belonged to the regional network and was responsible for distributing the goods to importers, wholesalers or retailers in other countries or regions. Besides tradition and geographical reasons, the lack of knowledge of foreign languages and intercultural competence of the manufacturers strengthened the position of the exporters. But over the years these traditions have lost their binding force, and new technologies have made communication possible over long distances. In general, people today are more highly educated. The result is a pluralism in the distribution paths. The main goal in the past was to achieve as much as possible of the profit margin of approximately 90%. Nowadays, all conceivable combinations of distribution exist in all four regions, adding to the uncertainty and a lack of trust within the regional network.

b) Minorca

Compared to costume jewellery production in Germany and Austria, the changes in Minorca have been quite small. The absolute number of firms is constant, apart from some years in the early 1980s (see Fig. 22.4). As explained in Section 22.4, organisational changes have however been far more radical. After getting rid of the 'viajantes' as key element within the regional system, the manufacturers could organise their distribution directly as shown in Fig. 22.9 (b) and (c).

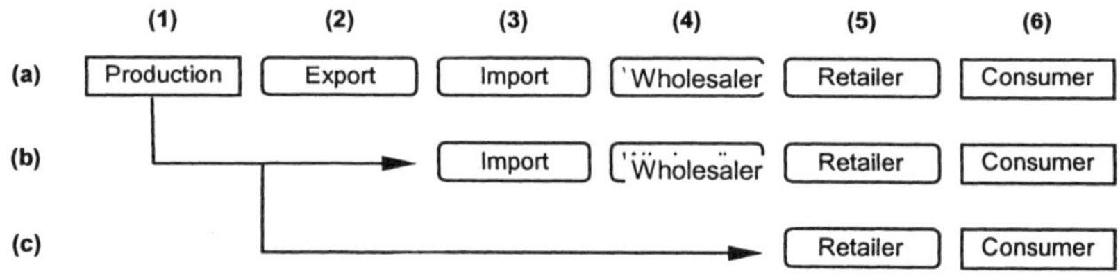

Fig. 22.9 Distribution of costume jewellery goods

Another important element of the organisational change is the integration of production within a single firm. In the past, the regional production system in Minorca, as in the other regions, consisted of a large number of subcontracters and firms which produced semi-finished goods and were specialised in specific techniques. Today, the majority of firms produce a good from the first step to the final product. Therefore the size of firms has increased, but the absolute number of firms has decreased. This however has another important implication.

While in the past, the diversity and redundancy of the regional network guaranteed meeting the demand for ever-changing styles and fashions, a lot of firms now have serious problems in assimilating market information and producing appropriate collections. Furthermore, the exporters who were once key-elements in the flow of information from the consumer to the manufacturer, no longer exist (Garí 1997). In the past, the great variety of offers and the information provided by exporters, meant that real market or trend research was not necessary. For the moment, only in Minorca has the local association 'Sebime' established, in co-operation with the government, a design institute 'Institut Balear de Disseny', which promotes workshops and attempts to provides the firms with information in order to adapt the collections of local producers to broader fashion trends.

c) Jablonec

The transformation which occurred after 1989 had radical effects on the production of costume jewellery in the region of Jablonec. The elimination of the Eastern European market and world market integration resulted in a crisis in the local production system. Privatisation set certain parameters for the new economic environment. But rather than creating new conditions, people referred back to the structures which existed before nationalisation in 1948. Firms attempted to re-establish the pre-war organisational structure and system of distribution, and tried to revive the old myth of Gablonz. The problem was that this identity is no longer embedded in the local culture and cannot function as source of innovative action. Most of the exporters who emerged since 1989 have already vanished. In the last two years, production has been relatively constant because of low labour costs (nearly 10% less than in Germany). This is also a reason why manufacturers from

Spain, Germany and Austria buy goods or semi-finished products in Jablonec and use them to create their own collections or sell them directly as a special label.

22.6 Conclusions

As we have shown, the regions of costume jewellery production – as low-tech industries – are subject to strong pressures from the world market. They neither have specific know-how that enables them to produce a special product, nor can they protect their position through the creation of well-known labels, like for example the textile products of Benetton. Furthermore, they lack the support of large capital resources which would allow the creation of innovative products, established through heavy expenditure on marketing.

The small size of most of the enterprises means that far-reaching innovative reactions are not possible. The specific structure of production and distribution, the rules of conduct and regional identity lead to inflexibility in the regions concerned. Although in the past, the embeddedness of firms was a guarantee of their success, today it seems to hinder innovative action. Firms which act flexibly destroy the specific advantages of the district. The innovations of some progressive entrepreneurs have sometimes had worse consequences than traditional behaviour. The advantage and added value of the region as an industrial district has been the reduction of transaction costs, because the economy, institutions and culture established symbiotic interrelations and underlay a governance which improved the specific market position.

Moreover, it has become clear that innovators are occasionally leaving the milieu which produced them and in which they were embedded. The consequence is an additional weakening of the regional milieu. We found that some kinds of blockage have arisen which do not fit the general story of success of industrial districts. In Section 22.3, the interrelations within the industrial districts which constitute institutions were defined as 'heterarchical'. Heterarchy is the condition in which relationships take place and by which the commercial community is constituted. Marshall described this phenomena in his original notion of the industrial district: "[...] good work is rightly appreciated, inventions and improvements in machinery, in processes and the general organization of the business have their merits promptly discussed; if one person starts a new idea, it is taken up by others and combined with suggestions of their own; and thus it becomes the source of further new ideas." (Cooke 1998, p. 9)

Regarding innovative action, two key system weaknesses have been identified in the classical form of the industrial district (see Cooke *et al.* 1998). The first concerns the form of development of the district. Because of strategic co-operation between the firms, a common set of strategic expectations about behaviour arises. This is what we have described as the establishment of institutional memory, rules, routines and ways in which mutual expectations are regulated (see also Hülsmann *et al.* 2000). All this converges, so that dissonance within the district becomes muted. Thus, the specific district culture is reproduced through the absence of dissenting voices and may hinder strategic creativity. The second point is that this is not a problem until the regional system of production encounters a critical point. In our case, such a critical point was triggered by the contraction in demand and the emergence of new competitors in Asian countries with low labour-costs. These factors affected the responses and led to radical changes in the world of costume jewellery production. It is in times of fast-changing circumstances, when rapid responses are necessary, that strategic creativity is of great importance.

The development of these idiosyncratic production systems has occurred within specific territories. Consequently, the nature of the knowledge acquired tends to be contained within the boundaries of the system. Spatial proximity and the social mechanisms of sharing knowledge facilitate its local transmission. But contextual knowledge cannot be completely transformed into more general knowledge able to satisfy the requirements of current circumstances. In contrast with the majority of the Italian industrial districts, the regional production systems of costume jewellery production in Europe have not yet become truly 'global'. As processes of globalisation are likely to have far-reaching effects over the next decade, they will be responsible for radical changes in the landscape of European costume jewellery production. The problem will be that of finding suitable strategies and paths of development which will lead towards a sustainable competitive future.

References

Bathelt, H. (1998) Regionales Wachstum in vernetzten Strukturen: Konzeptioneller Überblick und kritische Bewertung des Phänomens 'Drittes Italien'. Die Erde 129(3), 247-271

Becattini, G. (1990) The Marshallian Industrial District as a Socio-Economic Notion. In: Pyke, F., Becattini, G., Sengenberger, W. (eds.) Industrial Districts and Inter-firm Cooperation in Italy. International Institute for Labour Studies, Genf, 37-52

Becattini, G. (1991) 'Industrielle Distrikte' und ihre Bedeutung in der sozio-ökonomischen Entwicklung Italiens. In: Manz, T. (ed.) Klein- und Mittelbetriebe im Prozeß der industriellen Modernisierung. Dietz, Bonn, 30-50

Carlsson, B., Stankiewicz, R. (1995) On the Nature, Function and Composition of Technological Systems. In: Carlsson, B. (ed.) Technological Systems and Economic Performance: The Case of Factory Automation. Kluwer Academic Publishers, Dordrecht

Cooke, P. (1998) Introduction: Origins of the Concept. In: Braczyk, H.-J., Cooke, P., Heidenreich, M. (eds.) Regional Innovation Systems. UCL Press, London, 2-27

Cooke, P., Uranga, M.G., Etxebarria, G. (1998) Regional Systems of Innovation: An Evolutionary Perspective. Environment and Planning 30, 1563-1584

Edquist, C., Johnson, B. (1997) Institutions and Organizations in Systems of Innovation. In: Edquist, C. (ed.) Systems of Innovation. Technologies, Institutions and Organizations. Pinter Publishers, London, Washington

Garí, F. (1997) Meandering Through the History of Sebime. Asociación Española de Fabricantes Exportadores de Bistuerìa, Mahón

Glasmeier, A. (1994) Flexible Districts, Flexible Regions? The Institutional and Cultural Limits to Districts in an Era of Globalization and Technological Paradigm Shifts. In: Amin, A., Thrift, N. (eds.) Globalization, Institutions, and Regional Development in Europe. Oxford University Press, Oxford, New York, 118-146

Grabher, G. (1994) Lob der Verschwendung. Redundanz in der Regionalentwicklung: ein sozioökonomisches Plädoyer. Edition Sigma, Berlin

Granovetter, M. (1985) Economic Action and Social Structures. The Problem of Embeddedness. American Journal of Sociology 91(3), 481-510

Hülsmann, T., Pohl, J., Rehle, N. (2000): Kulturelle Determinanten des regionalen Strukturwandels. Das Beispiel der europäischen Modeschmuckherstellung. Zeitschrift für Wirtschaftsgeographie 44, 217-227

Lazerson, M. H. (1990) Subcontracting in the Modena Knitwear Industry. In: Pyke, F., Becattini, G., Sengenberger, W. (eds.) Industrial Districts and Inter-Firm Cooperation in Italy. International Institute for Labour Studies, Genf, 108-133

Lundvall, B. (1992) National Systems of Innovation: Towards a Theory of Innovation and Interactive Learning. Pinter Publishers, London

Maillat, D., Lecoq, F., Nemeti, F., Pfister, M. (1995) Technology District and Innovation: The case of the Swiss Jura Arc. Regional Studies 29, 251-263

Miegel, M. (1991) Wirtschafts- und arbeitskulturelle Unterschiede in Deutschland. Zur Wirkung außerökonomischer Faktoren auf die Beschäftigung. Bertelsmann Verlag Stiftung, Gütersloh

Nelson, R.R., Rosenberg, N. (1993) Technical Innovation and National Systems. In: Nelson, R.R. (ed.) National Systems of Innovation: A Comparative Analysis. Oxford University Press, Oxford, 3-22

Storper, M. (1997) The Regional World. Territorial Order in a Global Economy. Guildford Press, New York, London

List of Figures

List of Tables

Subject Index

List of Contributors

Franz-Josef Bade
University of Dortmund
Faculty of Spatial Planning
Department of Economics
August-Schmidt-Strasse 6
D-44227 Dortmund
E-Mail: Bade@rp.uni-dortmund.de

Eckhard Bode
The Kiel Institute of World Economics
Düsternbrooker Weg 120
D-24105 Kiel
E-Mail: ebode@ifw.uni-kiel.de

Martina Brandt
Institut für Regionale Innovationsforschung (IRI)
Prenzlauer Promenade 149-152
D-13189 Berlin
E-Mail: iriinstitut@aol.com

Boris Braun
University of Bonn
Department of Geography
Meckenheimer Allee 166
D-53115 Bonn
E-Mail: une413@uni-bonn.de

Oliver Bürgel
Foundation of Entrepreneurial Management
Regent's Park
Sussex Place
London NW1 4SA
United Kingdom
E-Mail: oburgel@lbs.ac.uk

Andreas Fier
Center for European Economic Research (ZEW)
Department for Industrial Economics and International Management
L7,1
D-68161 Mannheim
E-Mail: fier@zew.de

Michael Fritsch
Technical University Bergakademie Freiberg
Faculty of Economics and Business Administration
Lessingstrasse 45
D-09596 Freiberg
E-Mail: fritschm@vwl.tu-freiberg.de

Ernst Giese
Justus-Liebig-University of Giessen
Department of Geography
Senckenbergstrasse 1
D-35390 Gießen
E-Mail: ernst.giese@geogr.uni-giessen.de

Ulla Große
Institut für Regionale Innovationsforschung (IRI)
Prenzlauer Promenade 149-152
D-13189 Berlin
E-Mail: iriinstitut@aol.com

Reinhold Grotz
University of Bonn
Department of Geography
Meckenheimer Allee 166
D-53115 Bonn
E-Mail: r.grotz@uni-bonn.de

Hans-Dieter Haas
Ludwig-Maximilians-University of Munich
Institut of Economic Geography
Ludwigstrasse 28
D-80539 München
E-Mail: haas@bwl.uni-muenchen.de

Johannes Hampe
Ludwig-Maximilians-University of Munich
Department of Economics
Ludwigstrasse 28
D-80539 Munich
E-Mail:
Johannes.hampe@lrz.uni-muenchen.de

Frank Hartmann
Institut für Regionale Innovationsforschung
Prenzlauer Promenade 149-152
D-13189 Berlin
E-Mail: iriinstitut@aol.com

Sven Henschel
Humboldt-University Berlin
Institute of Geography
Unter den Linden 6
D-10099 Berlin
E-Mail: sven.henschel@rz.hu-berlin.de

Thorsten Hülsmann
Reinhold Grotz
University of Bonn
Department of Geography
Meckenheimer Allee 166
D-53115 Bonn
E-Mail: huelsmannn@giub.uni-bonn.de

Knut Koschatzky
Fraunhofer-Institut für Systemtechnik und Innovationsforschung
Breslauer Strasse 48
D-76139 Karlsruhe
E-Mail: ko@isi.fhg.de

Barbara Lenz
University of Stuttgart
Institute of Geography
Azenbergstrasse 12
D-70174 Stuttgart
E-Mail: blenz@zvw.de

Georg Licht
Center for European Economic Research
Department for Industrial Economics and International Management
L7, 1
D-68161 Mannheim
E-Mail: licht@zew.de

Jörg Maier
Universität Bayreuth
Lehrstuhl Wirtschaftsgeographie und Regionalplanung
Universitätsstrasse 30
D-95440 Bayreuth
E-Mail:
LS.WiGeo-RegPlg@uni-bayreuth.de

Jörn Mallok
Mechanik Center Erlangen GmbH
Günther-Scharowsky-Strasse 21
D-91508 Erlangen
E-Mail: joern.mallok@erl8.siemens.de

Gordon Murray
Foundation of Entrepreneurial Management
Regent's Park, Sussex Place
London NW 1 4SA, United Kingdom
E-Mail: gmurray@lbs.ac.uk

Annekatrin Niebuhr
HWWA Hamburg Institute of International Economics
Neuer Jungfernstieg 21
D-20347 Hamburg
E-Mail: niebuhr@hwwa.de

Frank Obermaier
Universität Bayreuth
Lehrstuhl Wirtschaftsgeographie und Regionalplanung
Universitätsstrasse 30
D-95440 Bayreuth
E-Mail:
LS.WiGeo-RegPlg@uni-bayreuth.de

Jürgen Oßenbrügge
Universität Hamburg
Institut für Geographie
AB Wirtschaftsgeographie
Bundesstrasse 55
D-20146 Hamburg
E-Mail:
ossenbruegge@geowiss.uni-hamburg.de

Michael Plattner
Philipps-Universität Marburg
Fachbereich Geographie
Deutschhausstrasse 10
D-35037 Marburg
E-Mail:
plattner@mailer.uni-marburg.de

Jürgen Pohl
University of Bonn
Department of Geography
Meckenheimer Allee 166
D-53115 Bonn
E-Mail: jpohl@slide.giub.uni-bonn.de

Norbert Rehle
Bundesverband der Gablonzer Industrie
Neue Zeile 11
D-87600 Kaufbeuren
E-Mail: nre@fast.de

Javier Revilla Diez
University of Hannover
Department of Economic Geography
Schneiderberg 50
D-30167 Hannover
E-Mail: diez@wigeo.uni-hannover.de

Ludwig Schätzl
University of Hannover
Department of Economic Geography
Schneiderberg 50
D-30167 Hannover
E-Mail: schaetzl@wigeo.uni-hannover.de

Matthias Schönert
BAW Bremen Institute for Economic Research
Wilhelm-Herbst-Strasse 5
D-28359 Bremen
E-Mail: mschoene@uni-bremen.de

Christian Schwirten
Bundesverband deutscher Banken
Geschäftsbereich Wettbewerbs-politik, Bankenaufsicht, Mittelstandspolitik
Burgstrasse 28
D-10178 Berlin
E-Mail: christian.schwirten@bdb.de

Sven Siebert
Konzept-grün
Büro für umweltbezogene Konzeption und Kommunikation GmbH
Fasanenweg 44 a
D-82194 Gröbenzell
E-Mail: dialog@konzept-gruen.de

Martin Steininger
Technische Universität München
Lehrstuhl für Volkwirtschaftslehre
Arcistrasse 21
D-80333 Munich
E-Mail: Martin.Steininger@vwl.wiso.tu-muenchen.de

Rolf Sternberg
University of Cologne
Department of Economic and Social Geography
Albertus-Magnus-Platz
D-50923 Köln
E-Mail: sternberg@wiso.uni-koeln.de

Simone Strambach
University of Stuttgart
Institute of Geography
Azenbergstrasse 12
D-70174 Stuttgart
E-Mail:
simone.strambach@po.uni-stuttgart.de

Christine Tamàsy
University of Cologne
Department of Economic and Social Geography
Albertus-Magnus-Platz
D-50923 Köln
E-Mail: Tamasy@wiso.uni-koeln.de

Rainer Voß
Technische Fachhochschule Wildau
Friedrich-Engels-Strasse 63
D-15742 Wildau
E-Mail: r.voss@igw.fhg-wildau.de

Christian Zeller
Universität Hamburg
Institut für Geographie
AB Wirtschaftsgeographie
Bundesstrasse 55
D-20146 Hamburg
E-Mail: zeller@geowiss.uni-hamburg.de

Andrea Zenker
Fraunhofer-Institut für Systemtechnik und Innovationsforschung
Breslauer Strasse 48
D-76139 Karlsruhe
E-Mail: az@isi.fhg.de

Contributions to Economics

Stefan Traub
Framing Effects in Taxation
1999. ISBN 3-7908-1240-4

Pablo Coto-Millán
Utility and Production
1999. ISBN 3-7908-1153-X

Frank Riedel
Imperfect Information and Investor Heterogeneity in the Bond Market
2000. ISBN 3-7908-1247-1

Kirsten Ralf
Business Cycles
2000. ISBN 3-7908-1245-5

Michele Bagella/
Leonardo Becchetti (Eds.)
The Competitive Advantage of Industrial Districts
2000. ISBN 3-7908-1254-4

Frank Bohn
Monetary Union and Fiscal Stability
2000. ISBN 3-7908-1266-8

Jaime Behar
Cooperation and Competition in a Common Market
2000. ISBN 3-7908-1280-3

Michael Malakellis
Integrated Macro-Micro-Modelling Under Rational Expectations
2000. ISBN 3-7908-1274-9

Stefan Baumgärtner
Ambivalent Joint Production and the Natural Environment
2000. ISBN 3-7908-1290-0

Henri Capron, Wim Meeusen (Eds.)
The National Innovation System of Belgium
2000. ISBN 3-7908-1308-7

Tobias Miarka
Financial Intermediation and Deregulation
2000. ISBN 3-7908-1307-9

Chisato Yoshida
Illegal Immigration and Economic Welfare
2000. ISBN 3-7908-1315-X

Nikolaus Thumm
Intellectual Property Rights
2000. ISBN 3-7908-1329-X

Max Keilbach
Spatial Knowledge Spillovers and the Dynamics of Agglomeration and Regional Growth
2000. ISBN 3-7908-1321-4

Alexander Karmann (Ed.)
Financial Structure and Stability
2000. ISBN 3-7908-1332-X

Joos P. A. van Vugt/Jan M. Peet (Eds.)
Social Security and Solidarity in the European Union
2000. ISBN 3-7908-1334-6

Johannes Bröcker/Hayo Herrmann (Eds.)
Spatial Change and Interregional Flows in the Integrating Europe
2001. ISBN 3-7908-1344-3

Kirstin Hubrich
Cointegration Analysis in a German Monetary System
2001. ISBN 3-7908-1352-4

Nico Heerink et al. (Eds.)
Economic Policy and Sustainable Land Use
2001. ISBN 3-7908-1351-6

Friedel Bolle/Michael Carlberg (Eds.)
Advances in Behavioral Economics
2001. ISBN 3-7908-1358-3

Volker Grossmann
Inequality, Economic Growth, and Technological Change
2001. ISBN 3-7908-1364-8

Thomas Riechmann
Learning in Economics
2001. ISBN 3-7908-1384-2

Miriam Beblo
Bargaining over Time Allocation
2001. ISBN 3-7908-1391-5

Peter Meusburger/Heike Jöns (Eds.)
Transformations in Hungary
2001. ISBN 3-7908-1412-1

Pablo Coto-Millán (Ed.)
Essays on Microeconomics and Industrial Organisation
2002. ISBN 3-7908-1390-7